FROM SPLENDOR TO REVOLUTION

ALSO BY JULIA P. GELARDI

In Triumph's Wake

Born to Rule

Julia P. Gelardi

FROM SPLENDOR
TO REVOLUTION

The Romanov Women,

1847–1928

ST. MARTIN'S GRIFFIN ✒ NEW YORK

FROM SPLENDOR TO REVOLUTION. Copyright © 2011 by Julia P. Gelardi.
All rights reserved. Printed in the United States of America. For information,
address St. Martin's Press, 175 Fifth Avenue, New York, N.Y. 10010.

www.stmartins.com

The Library of Congress has cataloged the hardcover edition as follows:

Gelardi, Julia P.
  From splendor to revolution : the Romanov women, 1847–1928 / Julia P. Gelardi.
—1st ed.
    p. cm.
  ISBN 978-0-312-37115-9
  1. Romanov, House of—History—19th century. 2. Romanov, House of—History—
20th century. 3. Maria Feodorovna, Empress, consort of Alexander III, Emperor of
Russia, 1847–1928. 4. Saxe-Coburg and Gotha, Marie Alexandrovna, Duchess of,
1853–1920. 5. Ol'ga Aleksandrovna, Grand Duchess of Russia, 1882–1960. 6. Marie,
Grand Duchess of Russia, b. 1890. 7. Nobility—Russia—Biography. 8. Russia—
History—19th century. 9. Russia—History—20th century. I. Title.
  DK37.8.R6G45 2011
  947.08092'2—dc22

                                                                      2010039444

ISBN 978-1-250-00161-0 (trade paperback)

First St. Martin's Griffin Edition: April 2012

10   9   8   7   6   5   4   3   2   1

To Alec

Simplified Genealogy

TABLE I

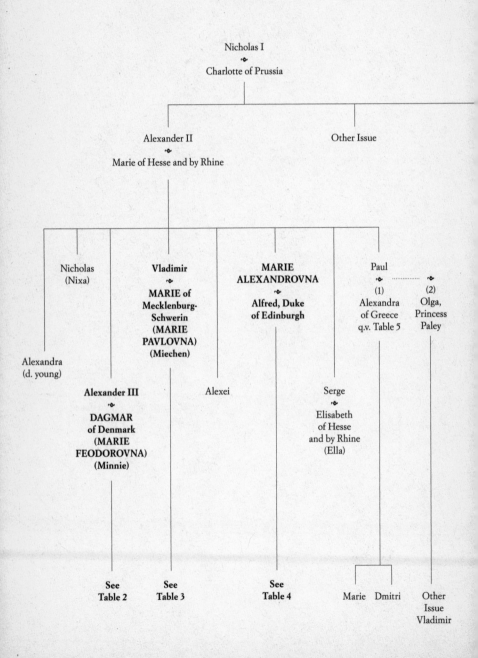

Nicholas I
&
Charlotte of Prussia

Alexander II
&
Marie of Hesse and by Rhine

Other Issue

Nicholas
(Nixa)

Vladimir
&
**MARIE of
Mecklenburg-
Schwerin
(MARIE
PAVLOVNA)
(Miechen)**

**MARIE
ALEXANDROVNA**
&
**Alfred, Duke
of Edinburgh**

Paul
&   ⋯⋯⋯   &
(1)   (2)
Alexandra   Olga,
of Greece   Princess
q.v. Table 5   Paley

Alexandra
(d. young)

Alexander III
&
**DAGMAR
of Denmark
(MARIE
FEODOROVNA)
(Minnie)**

Alexei

Serge
&
Elisabeth
of Hesse
and by Rhine
(Ella)

**See
Table 2**

**See
Table 3**

**See
Table 4**

Marie   Dmitri

Other
Issue
Vladimir

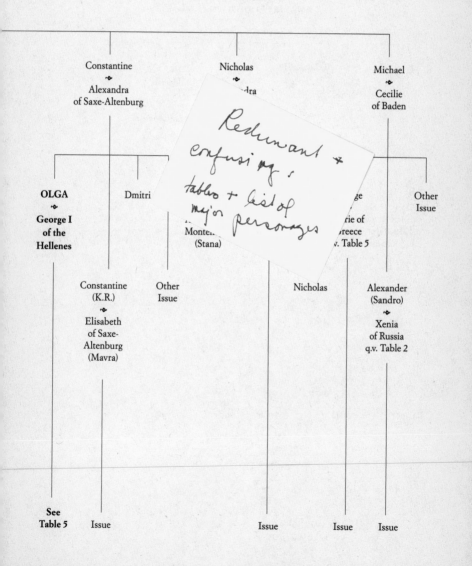

Constantine
⚭
Alexandra
of Saxe-Altenburg

Nicholas
⚭
...dra

Michael
⚭
Cecilie
of Baden

OLGA
⚭
George I
of the
Hellenes

Dmitri

...ge

Other
Issue

Constantine
(K.R.)
⚭
Elisabeth
of Saxe-
Altenburg
(Mavra)

Other
Issue

Monte...
(Stana)

...rie of
...reece
...v. Table 5

Nicholas

Alexander
(Sandro)
⚭
Xenia
of Russia
q.v. Table 2

See
Table 5

Issue

Issue

Issue

Issue

[handwritten note:] Redundant + confusing - tables + list of major personages

TABLE 2

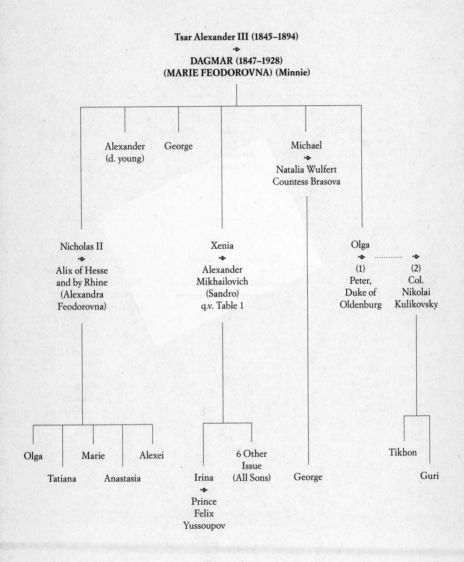

Tsar Alexander III (1845–1894)
⚭
DAGMAR (1847–1928)
(MARIE FEODOROVNA) (Minnie)

Alexander (d. young) — George — Michael ⚭ Natalia Wulfert Countess Brasova

Nicholas II ⚭ Alix of Hesse and by Rhine (Alexandra Feodorovna)

Xenia ⚭ Alexander Mikhailovich (Sandro) q.v. Table 1

Olga ⚭ (1) Peter, Duke of Oldenburg ⚭ (2) Col. Nikolai Kulikovsky

Olga — Tatiana — Marie — Anastasia — Alexei

Irina ⚭ Prince Felix Yussoupov

6 Other Issue (All Sons)

George

Tikhon — Guri

TABLE 3

Grand Duke Vladimir (1847–1909)
⚭
MARIE of Mecklenburg-Schwerin (1854–1920)
(MARIE PAVLOVNA) (Miechen)

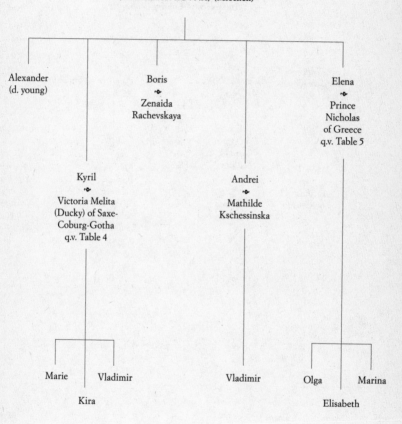

Alexander
(d. young)

Boris
⚭
Zenaida
Rachevskaya

Elena
⚭
Prince
Nicholas
of Greece
q.v. Table 5

Kyril
⚭
Victoria Melita
(Ducky) of Saxe-
Coburg-Gotha
q.v. Table 4

Andrei
⚭
Mathilde
Kschessinska

Marie   Vladimir

Kira

Vladimir

Olga   Marina

Elisabeth

TABLE 4

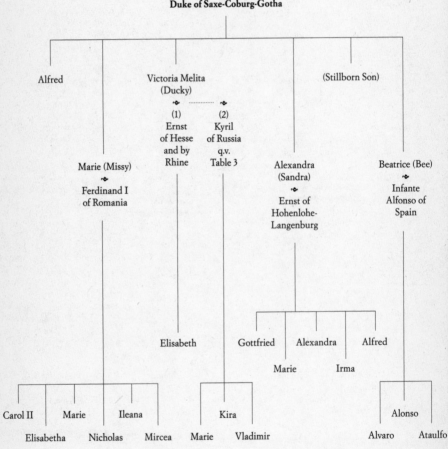

MARIE ALEXANDROVNA (1853–1920)
⚭
Alfred, (1844–1900)
Duke of Edinburgh
Duke of Saxe-Coburg-Gotha

Alfred

Victoria Melita
(Ducky)
⚭ ·············· ⚭
(1)   (2)
Ernst Kyril
of Hesse of Russia
and by q.v.
Rhine Table 3

(Stillborn Son)

Marie (Missy)
⚭
Ferdinand I
of Romania

Alexandra
(Sandra)
⚭
Ernst of
Hohenlohe-
Langenburg

Beatrice (Bee)
⚭
Infante
Alfonso of
Spain

Elisabeth

Gottfried Alexandra Alfred
Marie Irma

Carol II Marie Ileana
Elisabetha Nicholas Mircea

Kira
Marie Vladimir

Alonso
Alvaro Ataulfo

TABLE 5

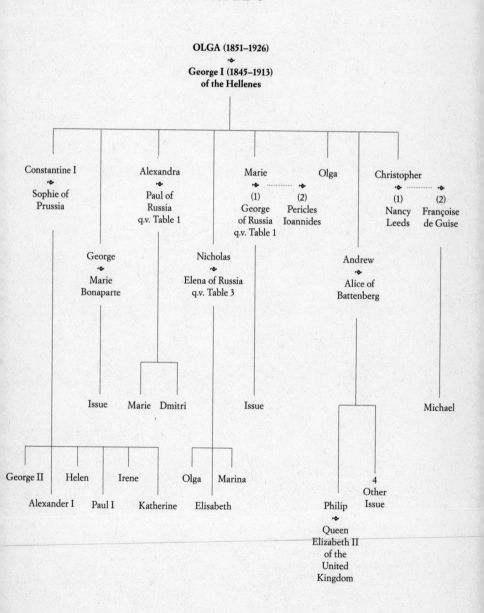

OLGA (1851–1926)
❧
**George I (1845–1913)
of the Hellenes**

Constantine I	Alexandra	Marie	Olga	Christopher
❧	❧	....		❧ ....
Sophie of Prussia	Paul of Russia q.v. Table 1	(1) George of Russia q.v. Table 1	(2) Pericles Ioannides	(1) Nancy Leeds	(2) Françoise de Guise

George
❧
Marie Bonaparte

Nicholas
❧
Elena of Russia
q.v. Table 3

Andrew
❧
Alice of Battenberg

Issue   Marie Dmitri   Issue   Michael

George II   Helen   Irene   Olga   Marina

Alexander I   Paul I   Katherine   Elisabeth

Philip
❧
Queen Elizabeth II of the United Kingdom

4 Other Issue

Contents

CONTENTS

PART II
Revolution (1905–1928)

Dramatis Personae

MAIN PROTAGONISTS

Empress Marie Feodorovna of Russia ("Dagmar," "Minnie") (1847–1928)
= Emperor Alexander III of Russia (1845–1894)
Children:

1. Tsar Nicholas II (1868–1918) = Princess Alix of Hesse and by Rhine ("Alexandra Feodorovna")
2. Grand Duke Alexander Alexandrovich (1869–1870)
3. Grand Duke George Alexandrovich (1871–1899)
4. Grand Duchess Xenia Alexandrovna (1875–1960) = Grand Duke Alexander of Russia ("Sandro")
5. Grand Duke Michael Alexandrovich (1878–1918) = Natalia Wulfert, Countess, Brasova
6. Grand Duchess Olga Alexandrovna (1882–1960) = 1) Peter, Duke of Oldenburg
   = 2) Colonel Nikolai Kulikovsky

Queen Olga of Greece (1851–1926) = King George I of the Hellenes (1845–1913)
Children:

1. King Constantine I (1868–1923) = Princess Sophie of Prussia
2. Prince George (1869–1957) = Princess Marie Bonaparte
3. Princess Alexandra (1870–1891) = Grand Duke Paul of Russia

4. Prince Nicholas (1872–1938) = Grand Duchess Elena of Russia
5. Princess Marie (1876–1940) = 1) Grand Duke George of Russia
                                = 2) Pericles Ioannides
6. Princess Olga (1881)
7. Prince Andrew (1882–1944) = Princess Alice of Battenberg
8. Prince Christopher (1888–1940) = 1) Nancy Leeds
                                   = 2) Princess Françoise de Guise

Marie Alexandrovna, Duchess of Edinburgh and Duchess of Saxe-Coburg-Gotha (1853–1920) = Alfred, Duke of Edinburgh and Duke of Saxe-Coburg-Gotha (1844–1900)
   Children:
1. Prince Alfred (1874–1899)
2. Queen Marie of Romania (1875–1938) = King Ferdinand I of Romania
3. Princess Victoria Melita (1876–1936) ("Ducky") = 1) Ernst Louis, Grand Duke
                                                       of Hesse and by Rhine
                                                    = 2) Grand Duke Kyril of
                                                       Russia
4. Princess Alexandra ("Sandra") (1878–1942) = Ernst, Prince of Hohenlohe-Langenburg
5. Stillborn son (1879)
6. Princess Beatrice ("Bee") (1884–1966) = Infante Alfonso of Spain ("Ali")

Marie Pavlovna, Grand Duchess of Russia ("Miechen") (1854–1920)
= Grand Duke Vladimir of Russia (1847–1909)
   Children:
1. Grand Duke Alexander Vladimirovich (1875–1877)
2. Grand Duke Kyril Vladimirovich (1876–1938) = Princess Victoria Melita of Saxe-Coburg-Gotha ("Ducky")
3. Grand Duke Boris Vladimirovich (1877–1943) = Zenaida Rachevskaya
4. Grand Duke Andrei Vladimirovich (1879–1956) = Mathilde Kschessinska
5. Grand Duchess Elena Vladimirovna (1882–1957) = Prince Nicholas of Greece

OTHER ROYALTY

RUSSIA

Emperors of Russia:
Alexander II (1818–1881) (reigned 1855–1881)
Alexander III (1845–1894) (reigned 1881–1894)
Nicholas II (1868–1918) (reigned 1894–1918)

Empresses of Russia (consorts):
Marie Alexandrovna (1824–1880), née Princess Marie of Hesse and by Rhine - consort of Alexander II
MARIE FEODOROVNA (1847–1928), née Princess Dagmar of Denmark, see above - consort of Alexander III
Alexandra Feodorovna (1872–1918), née Princess Alix of Hesse and by Rhine - consort of Nicholas II

Grand Dukes of Russia (brothers of Alexander III and of Marie Alexandrovna):
Nicholas Alexandrovich ("Nixa") (1843–1865), affianced to Princess Dagmar of Denmark
Vladimir Alexandrovich (1847–1909) = Duchess Marie of Mecklenburg-Schwerin ("Miechen")
Alexei Alexandrovich (1850–1908)
Serge Alexandrovich (1857–1905) = Princess Elisabeth of Hesse and by Rhine ("Ella")
Paul Alexandrovich (1860–1919) = 1) Princess Alexandra of Greece
                                       = 2) Olga, Princess Paley

Grand Dukes of Russia:
Constantine Nikolaevich (1827–1892), father of Queen Olga of Greece
Constantine Constantinovich ("K.R.") (1858–1915), brother of Queen Olga of Greece
Nicholas Constantinovich ("Nikola") (1850–1918), brother of Queen Olga of Greece
Nicholas Mikhailovich (1859–1919), brother of "Sandro"
Michael Mikhailovich ("Miche-Miche") (1861–1929), married morganatically, Countess Sophie of Merenberg, brother of "Sandro"

Alexander Mikhailovich ("Sandro") (1866–1933), husband of Grand Duchess Xenia of Russia, son-in-law of Empress Marie Feodorovna

George Mikhailovich (1863–1919), husband of Princess Marie of Greece, son-in-law of Queen Olga and brother of "Sandro"

Nicholas Nikolaevich ("Nikolasha") (1856–1929), general in World War I and husband of Anastasia of Montenegro

Peter Nikolaevich (1864–1931), husband of Militza of Montenegro

Dmitri Pavlovich (1891–1942), son of Grand Duke Paul of Russia and Princess Alexandra of Greece, grandson of Queen Olga of Greece; involved in Rasputin's murder

Grand Duchesses of Russia:

Alexandra Iosifovna (1830–1911), wife of Grand Duke Constantine Nikolaevich and mother of Queen Olga of Greece

Elisabeth Feodorovna ("Ella") (1864–1918), wife of Grand Duke Serge and sister of Empress Alexandra

Alexandra Georgievna (1870–1891), daughter of Queen Olga, wife of Grand Duke Paul, mother of Grand Duke Dmitri Pavlovich

Marie Georgievna (1876–1940), daughter of Queen Olga, wife of Grand Duke George Mikhailovich

Anastasia Nikolaevna ("Stana") (1868–1935), wife of Grand Duke Nicholas Nikolaevich ("Nikolasha")

Militza Nikolaevna (1866–1951), wife of Grand Duke Peter Nikolaevich

Elisabeth Mavrikievna ("Mavra") (1865–1927), wife of Grand Duke Constantin Constantinovich ("K.R."), and sister-in-law of Queen Olga

Grandchildren of Empress Marie Feodorovna of Russia:

From Tsar Nicholas II:
Grand Duchess Olga Nikolaevna (1895–1918)
Grand Duchess Tatiana Nikolaevna (1897–1918)
Grand Duchess Marie Nikolaevna (1899–1918)
Grand Duchess Anastasia Nikolaevna (1901–1918)
Tsarevich Alexei Nikolaevich (1904–1918)

From Grand Duchess Xenia:
Princess Irina Alexandrovna (1895–1970) = Prince Felix Yussoupov, involved in Rasputin's murder

Prince Andrei Alexandrovich (1897–1981)
Prince Feodor Alexandrovich (1898–1968)
Prince Nikita Alexandrovich (1900–1974)
Prince Dmitri Alexandrovich (1901–1980)
Prince Rostislav Alexandrovich (1902–1978)
Prince Vasili Alexandrovich (1907–1989)

From Grand Duke Michael:
George Mikhailovich, Count Brassov (1910–1931)

From Grand Duchess Olga:
Tikhon Nikolaevich Kulikovsky (1917–1993)
Guri Nikolaevich Kulikovsky (1919–1984)

GREECE

Kings of Greece (of the Hellenes):
George I (1845–1913), born Prince William of Denmark, husband of Queen Olga of Greece
Constantine I (1868–1923), son of Queen Olga of Greece
Alexander I (1893–1920), grandson of Queen Olga of Greece
George II (1890–1947), grandson of Queen Olga of Greece
Paul I (1901–1964), grandson of Queen Olga of Greece

Queens of Greece (Consorts):
OLGA *(1851–1926)*, née Grand Duchess Olga Constantinovna of Russia = King George I of Greece; for children, see above
Sophie (1870–1932), née Princess Sophie of Prussia = King Constantine I of Greece
Elisabetha (1894–1956), née Princess Elisabetha of Romania, granddaughter of Marie Alexandrovna, Duchess of Edinburgh = King George II of Greece

Grandchildren of Queen Olga of Greece:

From King Constantine I:
George II of Greece (1890–1947) = Elisabetha of Romania
Alexander I of Greece (1893–1920) = Aspasia Manos
Helen (1896–1982) = King Carol II of Romania

Paul I (1901–1964) = Princess Frederike of Hanover
Irene (1904–1974) = Prince Aimone of Savoy
Katherine (1913–2007) = Richard Brandram

From Prince George:
Prince Peter of Greece (1908–1980)
Princess Eugenie of Greece (1910–1989)

From Princess Alexandra:
Grand Duchess Marie Pavlovna of Russia ("the younger") (1890–1958)
Grand Duke Dmitri Pavlovich of Russia (1891–1942); see above

From Prince Nicholas:
Princess Olga of Greece and Denmark (1903–1997)
Princess Elisabeth of Greece and Denmark (1904–1955)
Princess Marina of Greece and Denmark, Duchess of Kent (1906–1968)

From Princess Marie:
Princess Nina of Russia (1901–1974)
Princess Xenia of Russia (1903–1965)

From Prince Andrew:
Princess Margarita of Greece and Denmark (1905–1981)
Princess Theodora of Greece and Denmark (1906–1969)
Princess Cecilie of Greece and Denmark (1911–1937)
Princess Sophie of Greece and Denmark (1914–2001)
Prince Philip of Greece and Denmark (1921–) = Queen Elizabeth II of the United Kingdom

From Prince Christopher:
Prince Michael of Greece and Denmark (1939–)

DENMARK

King Christian IX (1818–1906) = Princess Louise of Hesse-Cassel (1817–1898)
Children:
1. King Frederick VIII of Denmark (1843–1912)
2. Queen Alexandra (1844–1925) = King Edward VII of the United Kingdom
3. King George I of Greece (1845–1913) = Grand Duchess Olga of Russia
4. ***EMPRESS MARIE FEODOROVNA OF RUSSIA ("Dagmar," "Minnie") (1847–1928)*** = Emperor Alexander III of Russia

5. Princess Thyra (1853–1933) = Ernst August of Hanover, Duke of Cumberland
6. Prince Waldemar (1858–1939) = Princess Marie of Orléans

UNITED KINGDOM

Queen Victoria (1819–1901) = Prince Albert of Saxe-Coburg-Gotha (1819–1861)
Children:
1. Princess Victoria (1840–1901) = Frederick III, German Emperor and King of Prussia
2. King Edward VII (1841–1910) = Princess Alexandra of Denmark, sister of ***EMPRESS MARIE FEODOROVNA OF RUSSIA***
3. Princess Alice (1843–1878) = Louis IV, Grand Duke of Hesse and by Rhine
4. Prince Alfred (1844–1900), Duke of Edinburgh and Duke of Saxe-Coburg-Gotha = ***GRAND DUCHESS MARIE ALEXANDROVNA OF RUSSIA***
5. Princess Helena (1846–1923) = Prince Christian of Schleswig-Holstein-Sonderburg-Augustenburg
6. Princess Louise (1848–1939) = John Campbell, Duke of Argyll
7. Prince Arthur (1850–1942) = Princess Louise Margaret of Prussia
8. Prince Leopold (1853–1884) = Princess Helen of Waldeck-Pyrmont
9. Princess Beatrice (1857–1944) = Prince Henry of Battenberg

$\mathcal{I}$ntroduction

On September 22, 2006, the final chapter at last unfolded, in the long, drawn-out saga that was the life story of Empress Marie Feodorovna, mother of Russia's ill-fated Tsar Nicholas II. On that day, ceremonies began at the Cathedral at Roskile that saw the repatriation of the empress's remains from her native Denmark to her adopted country. Symbolically, the return took place 140 years after Marie Feodorovna, as Princess Dagmar, left Denmark for Russia to marry the future Emperor Alexander III. This final journey from Denmark back to Russia, so long overdue, was carried out on a Danish frigate. As the ship arrived in Russian waters, the Russians honored the late empress by firing off a thirty-one-gun salute from the Baltic port of Kronstadt, the gateway to St. Petersburg. During the funeral service held in the city's splendid St. Isaac's Cathedral, a multitude of gorgeously robed clergy of the Russian Orthodox Church intoned prayers before the late empress's coffin, which was covered in the gold and black imperial standard of the double-headed eagle. The event, so suffused in imperial and Orthodox symbolism, could never have taken place in the atheistic Soviet Union. Thus was the repatriation truly remarkable. For the reburial had to wait until Russia, like a phoenix, arose from the ashes of what had once been the Soviet Union. With the full approval of Denmark's Queen Margrethe II and Russia's President Vladimir Putin, the six-day-long repatriation finally took place, nearly eighty years after Marie Feodorovna's death. Her remains were laid to rest at last next to those of her husband, Emperor Alexander III, at the Romanovs' imperial crypt in the Cathedral of Sts. Peter and Paul in St. Petersburg.

What must have it been like for this Danish princess who, as an eighteen-year-old, left her family and journeyed to Russia in 1866 as the Tsarevich

Alexander's bride? No doubt, Princess Dagmar, who took the name Marie Feodorovna upon embracing Russia's Orthodox faith, was full of excitement and trepidation at what the future held. In the ensuing years, Marie Feodorovna, as a member of the Romanov dynasty, would come to experience the full panoply of what life had to offer. Great happiness and heart-wrenching tragedies would come her way. As I pondered the empress's life, I could not help but also reflect on a less famous historical figure whose life story was just as steeped in drama. This individual, another Romanov, was Queen Olga of Greece, who also happened to be Marie Feodorovna's sister-in-law. On further reflection, I came to the conclusion that two other women—contemporaries of Marie Feodorovna and Olga Constantinovna—had equally compelling life stories that were worth telling in tandem with those of the Russian empress and Greek queen. And so, I embarked on my latest literary endeavor, the end result of which I wish to share with you, the reader. It is a journey to imperial Russia—a journey that will take us from the splendors of the Russian imperial court of the nineteenth century to the tragic days of World War I, the Russian Revolution and the decade that followed. We will also delve into the tumultuous history of nineteenth and early twentieth century Greece, but this work will largely focus on imperial Russia and the Romanovs.

Despite the massive body of literature on the Romanovs—a reflection of the intense interest in and profound impact on history of this famous family—missing still in the dynasty's tales of triumph and tragedy is the collective story, as witnessed by four Romanov matriarchs, of imperial Russia's inexorable march toward catastrophe and the destruction of this old world.

In order to redress this gap, I present in the following pages, the stories of this special group of Romanov women in one volume, focusing on the years 1847 to 1928. I chose that interval because it is the life span of the longest living of the four, Empress Marie Feodorovna (1847–1928), consort of Emperor Alexander III. Her story is accompanied by that of another consort, Queen Olga (1851–1926), wife of King George I of the Hellenes, a brother of Marie Feodorovna. My third protagonist is the Grand Duchess Marie Alexandrovna (1853–1920), Emperor Alexander III's sister and a daughter-in-law of Queen Victoria through her son, Alfred, Duke of Edinburgh, who later reigned over not an empire or a kingdom, but a duchy within Germany, that of Saxe-Coburg-Gotha. The fourth protagonist, the Grand Duchess Marie Pavlovna (1854–1920), the wife of Alexander III's brother, the Grand Duke Vladimir, did not grace a throne. Instead, she dominated St. Petersburg society, appropriating this important position, a role that normally belonged to the empress or tsarina.

Of course, other Romanov women were contemporaries of my four protagonists. Why then focus on these four and not the others? One reason is that my four subjects were among the most senior female members of the Romanov dynasty of their generation. Another is that Marie Feodorovna, Olga Constantinovna, Marie Alexandrovna, and Marie Pavlovna can rightly be termed "matriarchs," as all four have descendants to this day. Because Grand Duchess Elisabeth ("Ella"), by marriage a contemporary of her sisters-in-law, Marie Feodorovna and Marie Pavlovna, did not have children, I omitted her from the group. I excluded Ella's sister Tsarina Alexandra as well, because her children were massacred in 1918 at Ekaterinburg, and so Alexandra has no direct descendants. Moreover, Tsarina Alexandra does not technically belong to the same generation as her mother-in-law, Marie Feodorovna, and aunts Marie Alexandrovna, Marie Pavlovna, and Olga Constantinovna.

Two of the four women were born Romanovs: Marie Alexandrovna (Duchess of Edinburgh) was the daughter of Tsar Alexander II while Queen Olga was the daughter of Grand Duke Constantine Nikolaevich. Two of the women, on the other hand, married into the Romanov dynasty: Empress Marie Feodorovna, born Princess Dagmar, daughter of King Christian IX of Denmark; and the Grand Duchess Marie Pavlovna, born Duchess Marie of Mecklenburg-Schwerin, daughter of Grand Duke Frederick Franz II of Mecklenburg-Schwerin.

The women's early lives unfolded during a time when the Romanov tsars, as autocrats of all the Russias, wielded unlimited power and the grandeur of the Russian court was at its apogee. But because these women witnessed the Russian Revolution of 1917, they were uniquely positioned as well, to experience the destruction of imperial Russia and the devastation the revolution left in its wake in the lives of countless Russians. In Queen Olga's case, the turbulent politics that consumed Greece in the early part of the twentieth century meant that this Russian grand duchess was even more uniquely positioned in comparison to her three counterparts in that she had the dubious distinction of living through the tempestuous histories of these two countries.

A proliferation of Maries, Alexanders, Nicholases, Alexandras, and Olgas characterized several generations of Romanovs. To minimize the confusion, I use nicknames and second names. As second names, Russian males have "vich" added to their fathers' name, and females have "-ovna" or "-evna" added to their fathers' name. Thus, Queen Olga was "Olga Constantinovna" meaning "daughter of Constantine," while her niece Grand Duchess Olga had as her second name, "Alexandrovna," meaning "daughter of Alexander" (Emperor Alexander III). To distinguish the Duchess of Edinburgh and the Empress of Russia from each other and from other Maries, second names are included (Marie Alexandrovna and Marie Feodorovna). Marie Feodorovna, who was also called "Dagmar," and "Minnie," is initially referred to by these names early in the book. Later on, after she becomes empress, she will be known primarily as "Marie Feodorovna." Marie Pavlovna was also known as the "Grand Duchess Vladimir." Though occasionally called by these two names, she will largely be referred to as "Miechen," her nickname among family members.

Throughout, the titles "empress" and "tsarina" are used interchangeably, as are "emperor" and "tsar." Moreover, dates are given in both the Julian and Gregorian calendars when appropriate because Russia and Greece followed the Julian calendar, which was twelve days (in the nineteenth century) and thirteen days (in the twentieth) behind the Gregorian calendar in use in most parts of the world. Not until 1918 did Russia adopt the Gregorian calendar, while Greece did not do so until 1923.

Like my previous books, *Born to Rule* and *In Triumph's Wake*, *From Splendor to Revolution* is in no way a definitive biography of my protagonists. Such a venture is impossible to achieve in one volume. Instead, I chose to present an overview of the lives of an empress, a queen, a duchess, and a grand duchess, all of whom belonged to the Romanov dynasty. What emerges, is a unique portrait of imperial Russia and Greece in the mid-nineteenth to early twentieth centuries, as rendered through the lives of this special group of women.

In immersing themselves in the vivid stories of Marie Feodorovna, Olga Constantinovna, Marie Alexandrovna, and Marie Pavlovna, readers will delve into a long lost world that is unlikely ever to be replicated. Of that lost world, which these women had been so much a part of, Countess Marguerite Cassini, a Russian aristocrat, had once written: "Some say it was a wicked world, an anachronism that deserved to be swept away, as it was, by the tides of history. So be it. Yet it is too often forgotten that there was much that was good and beautiful in it too, which was also swept away, and is fast becoming legend."[1]

I invite readers to journey with me to discover something of that lost world as the moving stories of Marie Feodorovna, Olga Constantinovna, Marie Alexandrovna, and Marie Pavlovna come to life. We will revisit and savor the dazzling days of late imperial Russia and relive the troubled times that came to consume the lives of this special group of Romanovs. In so doing, it is my hope that readers will come to empathize with these protagonists, as they read of the women's struggles to come to grips with the tragedies that fate had so cruelly placed in their paths.

PART I

SPLENDOR

(1847–1905)

4 too many —
confusing

A work of popular list
my of a 50 pages of endnotes +
a 16-page bibliography of
both primary & secondary sources
either in English or tr&s.
for the author.

I

A SPLENDID IMPERIAL COURT

*N*othing as meaningful and sacred as the coronation of a Romanov tsar could take place anywhere but in the very heart of the Russian Empire. Even resplendent St. Petersburg, Peter the Great's creation and the most western city in the empire, was unworthy. Only historic Moscow, the most Russian of cities, would do. Since the days of old Muscovy hundreds of years before, sentiment about rulers had changed little in the heart and soul of the average Russian. "Russians had been taught" from their cradle "to regard their ruler as an almost god-like creature. Their proverbs embodied this view: 'Only God and the tsar know,' 'One sun shines in heaven and the Russian tsar on earth,' 'Through God and the tsar, Russia is strong,' 'It is very high up to God; it is a very long way to the tsar.'"[1] Coronations in Moscow were "intended to bring home to the minds" of the emperor's "subjects in the most vivid manner the Heaven-appointed nature of his functions and inheritance."[2] Thus, in accordance with tradition and mindful of the sacredness of the occasion, the Empress Marie Feodorovna traveled to Moscow for the coronation of her husband, Emperor Alexander III. It was May 1883, two years after he had ascended the Russian throne.

Widespread excitement surrounded the emperor and empress's coronation. Hundreds of thousands of their subjects descended upon Moscow to celebrate the momentous event that spring day. Festivities officially began when Russia's "little Father and little Mother"—the thirty-eight-year-old emperor and his thirty-five-year-old empress—made their majestic state entry into the city. A journalist who witnessed the scene from the Kremlin ramparts observed the royal retinue in their carriages to have been of "interminable length."[3] Not just long, the procession was of incomparable majesty, a dazzling and awe-inspiring sight. An impressive array of royalty, nobility, dignitaries, and soldiers processed before packed crowds, producing a rarely seen panorama of splendor. Crowds continually gasped with admiration over such sights as the imposing *chevalier-gardes* with their silver cuirasses and white tunics, along with the Cossacks with their long red lances, looking "perfectly wild and uncivilized." Especially arresting in appearance were the Asiatic deputations from the Russian Empire's far-flung provinces. These exotic representatives with their lyrical titles included the Khan of Khiva and the Emir of Bokhara who wore "high fur caps" and jewels flashing on their belts and headpieces.[4] Even prancing horses made an indelible impression, thanks to their eye-catching harnesses embedded with glistening semiprecious stones.

Most spectacular of all was the imperial family. The colossal frame of the bearded Emperor Alexander III was impossible to miss. His subjects were awed to see him astride a white charger and dressed as a Russian general, his head topped by an Astrakhan cap. Following the emperor were his sons, the fifteen-year-old heir, the Tsarevich Nicholas, and twelve-year-old Grand Duke George. Riding next to Alexander III and enjoying a special place of honor was his brother-in-law, the Duke of Edinburgh, in the scarlet uniform of a British general. Grand Duchess Marie Alexandrovna, the emperor's only sister, accompanied her husband the duke, second son of England's venerable Queen Victoria.

When the Empress Marie Feodorovna appeared amidst the pealing of bells and the booming of cannons, the crowds reverently crossed themselves and greeted their empress with a thundering ovation. The emperor's petite, dark-haired consort made her way in a gold carriage, "a veritable mass of glass and gilding . . . drawn by eight perfectly white horses in gold harness, each horse led by a groom in blue velvet and white plumed casques."[5] With the empress sat her sister-in-law, thirty-one-year-old Queen Olga of Greece, and Marie Feodorovna's elder daughter, eight-year-old Grand Duchess Xenia, who, according to an eyewitness, looked "astonished at the homage that was being paid to them."[6] Following Marie Feodorovna's carriage were those of the Romanov grand duchesses, including Marie Feodorovna and Marie Alexandrovna's sister-in-law, twenty-nine-year-old Marie Pavlovna ("Miechen"), wife of the emperor's brother Grand Duke Vladimir. Like her imperial counterparts, Miechen dazzled the crowds in her white gown and glittering diamonds and pearls.

Spectacular as the procession was, there was a palpable, underlying tension, for the imperial family was under threat from Russian terrorists, known as the Nihilists. A number of the distinguished guests noted this anxious atmosphere, including Mrs. Frederic Chenevix Trench, wife of the military attaché to the British embassy in St. Petersburg. Mrs. Trench was impressed by the gorgeous pageantry of the coronation entry, but she was even more struck by Marie Feodorovna's brave face before her adoring subjects. "On the very morning of the entry," recalled Trench, "several anonymous letters had been received by both the Emperor and Empress telling them to prepare for the worst if they persisted in their intention of going in state to the Kremlin . . . Yet, there sat the Empress with a smile on her face, not knowing at what moment there might be a desperate attempt upon her own or upon the Emperor's life. Not only did the imperial couple receive such letters of warnings, but many of the attendants who were to form part of the pageant, and the little pages and postilions who accompanied the Empress's chariot, each received separate letters telling them that they would not reach the Kremlin alive."[7] Mary King Waddington, wife of a French diplomat and guest of the emperor and empress, also noticed the "highly charged atmosphere" and surmised why the Empress Marie Feodorovna, behind the smiles and bows looked "grave and very pale." Waddington concluded that "it must have been an awful day for her, for she was so far behind the Emperor [in the procession], and such masses of troops in between, that he might have been assassinated easily, she knowing nothing of it."[8]

Despite these sinister threats, Alexander III and Marie Feodorovna, their entourage and the imperial family, including Marie Alexandrovna, the Duchess of Edinburgh; Queen Olga; and Miechen, survived their state entry and made their way unscathed to the Kremlin, the medieval walled citadel dominating the banks of the Moscow River. Mrs. Waddington thought the Kremlin with its "great crenulated wall . . . quantities of squares, courts, churches, palaces, barracks, [and] terraces," along with its "gilt domes, pink and green roofs, and steeples," presented a unique and splendid vision. The color "pink predominated," she observed, most likely because of the "rose flush of the sunset which gave a beautiful color to everything."[9] For the following three days the emperor and empress remained secluded in the Kremlin on a religious retreat. In the meantime, "more and more stringent measures," noted Mrs. Trench, were "taken to prevent any un-authorised person from entering the walls of the Kremlin, for, as the all-important day of the coronation draws near, no amount of precaution seems too minute to counteract and prevent any possible machinations of the Nihilists."[10]

On the day of their coronation, the emperor and empress emerged. They "walked under a splendid canopy held aloft on long golden staffs by sixteen generals, whilst sixteen other officers held the silken cords which steadied it. The Metropolitans of Novgorod, Moscow, and Kieff, who had prayed all night . . . came forth with their clergy to meet the imperial pair." Inside the Cathedral of the Assumption, "the deacons swung their censers to and fro. Clouds of incense rose in the air and the censers danced in them like balls of molten gold. All around was a sea of eager and excited faces."[11] Inside the cathedral, the brilliant gold and precious stones that adorned much of the interior dazzled observers. Vying for attention were exquisite frescoes and sparkling icons along with the gorgeously vested clergy. The coronation ceremony began with Queen Olga of Greece and the Tsarevich Nicholas leading the imperial procession into the cathedral. As Alexander III and Marie Feodorovna entered the cathedral, nearly all eyes were firmly fixed on them. "I could see," recalled Mrs. Trench, "that the poor Empress was very much agitated; her chest was heaving with emotion, and she was nearly as white as her silver dress."[12] Mary Grace Thornton, daughter of the British ambassador to Russia, thought the Empress Marie Feodorovna had possessed "a certain stateliness" on her coronation day. "She was very pale," recounted Thornton, "but I thought that I had never seen her look more sympathetic."[13]

Emperor Alexander III first crowned himself. Marie Feodorovna then knelt humbly before her husband, whereupon Alexander lifted his crown from his head and placed it on hers momentarily. Afterward, he took Marie Feodorovna's own crown and held it in place on her head. Once the emperor crowned his wife empress, Marie Feodorovna unexpectedly embraced Alexander in a touching moment. Grand Duke Constantine ("K.R."), Queen Olga's brother, was moved by the sight, confiding in his diary: "I cannot describe, cannot express how touching and tender it was to see these embraces of husband and wife and kisses under the imperial crown—this ordinary human love in the glitter and radiance of imperial majesty."[14] The emperor and empress then took Holy Communion, signaling the end of the ceremony. The imperial couple walked from the cathedral to receive their subjects' wild acclamation. Church bells rang to signal great rejoicing.

In a letter to her mother, Queen Louise of Denmark, Empress Marie Feodorovna described the coronation experience: "I felt myself literally as a sacrificial lamb. I wore a silver train and was bare-headed having only a small pearl necklace on my neck . . . We had a truly blissful feeling on return to our rooms when everything ended! I had the same feeling as right after I had given birth to a baby."[15]

The Duchess of Edinburgh's eldest daughter and the empress's niece Missy recalled the splendors of the coronation years later. Three relatives made a vivid impression on her—Marie Feodorovna ("Minnie"), Marie Pavlovna ("Miechen"), and her own mother, Marie Alexandrovna. "Aunt Minnie," wrote Missy, "is crowned with a tiara of sapphires so large that they resemble enormous eyes; cascades of pearls and diamonds hang round her throat down to her waist . . . Close behind the Empress stands Aunt Miechen. More gorgeous than the sunset is her gold-embroidered orange gown. Each time she moves the pear-shaped pearls of her diadem sway gently backwards and forwards. She is not thin enough for classical lines but she wears her clothes better than any other woman present; her shoulders are superb and as white as cream; there is a smartness about her that no one else can attain. And there beside her stands my mother curiously at home in that radiant assembly, much more at home than she is in London or Windsor. Her gown is deep gentian blue, trimmed with sable, and the rubies she wears are like enormous drops of blood."[16] The young Missy was unaccustomed to standing for so long in church; and as if to encourage her young daughter, the Duchess of Edinburgh, looking at Missy, put "a finger to her lips: 'Patience,' she seems to say. Little Protestant that I am, I must not disgrace her."[17]

Such was the splendor and success of the festivities that it lulled the four grand dukes—the Tsarevich Nicholas and his brother George, their uncle Serge, and cousin Alexander Mikhailovich ("Sandro"), into believing that Russia had entered a new, more peaceful phase. Complacency prompted Grand Duke Serge to say with confidence: "Just think, what a great country Russia will have become by the time we will have to escort Nicky to the Cathedral of the Assumption!"[18]

Whatever one thought of the present or future in connection with the spectacular events in Moscow, there was no doubt that Alexander III and Marie Feodorovna's coronation underscored "the popular spiritual bond between the masses and the tsar at the same time as it presented the church as the institution expressing the nation's spirit."[19] Indeed, the emperor and empress's crowning emphasized the truly Russian character of the occasion, for Moscow, with its numerous distinctive church onion domes, stood out for its ties to Orthodoxy, the Christian faith professed by Russians.

Orthodoxy was promoted even further under Alexander III's reign. This energetic promotion of Orthodoxy was hardly surprising, considering both the emperor and his empress held deeply religious views. Sandro concluded that the empress's "blind faith in the truth of every word of the Holy Scripture gave something more than just courage."[20] Alexander III and Marie Feodorovna were not the only Romanovs who were sincere adherents to the Orthodox faith, for many in the family were of like mind. For the Romanovs, Orthodoxy bound church with state, as the Duchess of Edinburgh's governess Anna Tiutcheva noted at the Grand Duchess Marie Alexandrovna's christening in 1853: "There is some strange mixture of the divine and worldly in these half secular, half religious court celebrations. The most sacred church sacraments are carried out, and it is necessary to point out that the members of the Imperial family always attend them with a sort of deepest devotion."[21]

Thirty years later at the solemn coronation, young Missy caught this feeling of deep faith as she watched her mother. Having calmed her young daughter during the long ceremony, Marie Alexandrovna then turned "again towards the priests, as one enraptured by some great revelation, fervently she makes the sign of the Cross." Of the occasion, Missy wrote: "Mamma is at home here; Mamma belongs to them; her soul is theirs, Mamma is part of Russia."[22] And so it was as well, with the other matriarchs: Empress Marie Feodorovna, Queen Olga, and Grand Duchess Marie Pavlovna.

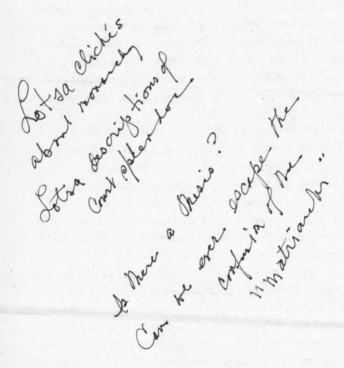

THE EARLY YEARS

The Grand Duchess Marie Alexandrovna was born into the world's wealthiest and most illustrious family. The Romanov dynasty had reigned supreme over Russia since 1613, leaving a profound mark upon their empire. Autocrats with unlimited power, Romanov tsars ruled over a "vast and complex domain" that "at its height in the mid-nineteenth century . . . would stretch almost halfway around the globe, from Prussia's eastern frontier to Canada's northwestern boundary and, even, to California." The story of the Romanovs "is a tale of glory and pathos, of heroism and cowardice, of victory and defeat,"[1] and included giants of history such as Peter the Great, Catherine the Great, and Alexander I.

The grand duchess's father, Tsarevich Alexander, was poised to join this exclusive pantheon, but the burden of having to rule Russia was evident early in his life. The future tsar's tutor wrote to him that: "There is, alas, no doubt, that the crown of Russia is the hardest to wear . . . As an autocrat, the Tsar can do everything, but he remains answerable for all he does to God . . . Far from being an unlimited privilege, autocracy is a fearful responsibility."[2] Despite the heavy burden that lay before the young man, Alexander exhibited a genial personality. Intelligent, good-looking, and affable, twenty-one-year-old Tsarevich Alexander had impressed the twenty-year-old Queen Victoria during a visit to London. The queen found Alexander "frank . . . and merry" exhibiting an "open countenance with a sweet smile." When it came to dancing with the future tsar, Victoria confessed: "I never enjoyed myself more."[3] One contemporary British journalist on a visit to Russia concluded that "Alexander's face" was nothing short of "kindly."[4] The Comte de Morny, the French envoy to Russia, noted Alexander's amiability commenting that: "He is worshipped by his people . . . I have no doubt that he will confer great benefits to his people in every respect."[5]

With Princess Marie of Hesse, Tsarevich Alexander found a love match. He married her despite strong rumors that his bride was fathered not by Louis II, Grand Duke of Hesse, but by his master of the stables, Baron August de Grancy. Once ensconced in St. Petersburg, Marie embraced her Russian life, becoming a loving wife and mother and a fervent convert to the Orthodox religion.

Tsarevich Alexander and his wife, Marie, welcomed their daughter, the Grand Duchess Marie Alexandrovna, into the world at her birth, on October 5/17, 1853, at Tsarskoe Selo, the sprawling imperial estate some sixteen miles south of St. Petersburg. "The little girl is a great delight to the Imperial family. She was eagerly expected and wanted," recalled the grand duchess's governess, Anna Tiutcheva.[6] The family was composed of eight children, six boys and two girls. The sons were Grand Dukes Nicholas (b. 1843) ("Nixa"), Alexander (b. 1845) ("Sasha"), Vladimir (b. 1847), Alexei (b. 1850), Serge (b. 1857), and Paul (b. 1860). Another daughter, Alexandra, had died young; hence, Marie Alexandrovna was the only girl among six boys. Through the years, the grand duchess became her younger brothers' closest friend. She was their champion, and her governess noted that Marie Alexandrovna "cannot stand when someone reprimands any of her brothers. This brings her to the state of real despair."[7]

When the little grand duchess was not yet two years old, her grandfather, Tsar Nicholas I, died, ushering in the reign of her father, Tsar Alexander II. To his thirty-seven-year-old successor, Nicholas I had bequeathed a battered Russia that had suffered defeat at the hands of the British, the French, and their allies during the Crimean War of 1853–1856. Nicholas I's death in 1855 left his son to conclude the peace talks and deal with increasing domestic turmoil.

Beyond defeat in the Crimean War, imperial Russia struggled with a myriad of other problems. The country's industrial backwardness hampered its ability to compete with Britain and France, the other "Great Powers," as they were then called. Revolutionary fervor was brewing. Increasing pressure on the tsarist regime from certain disgruntled segments of the population spelled trouble for Russia's tsar. Just fourteen years before, the Marquis de Custine vividly recorded the turbulent state of the tsarist empire when he noted that: "The Russian government is an absolute monarchy moderated by assassination; and when the prince is not under the influence of lassitude, he is under that of terror. He lives, therefore, between fear and disgust. If the pride of the despot must have slaves, the feelings of the man must yearn for equals; but a czar has no equals: etiquette and jealousy maintain invidious guard around his solitary heart. He is more to be pitied than even his people, especially if he possesses any amiable qualities."[8] Though de Custine wrote this before Alexander II's accession, much of the foreigner's message pertained to Nicholas I's successor.

This, then, was the tsar who was Marie Alexandrovna's father, Olga of Greece's uncle, and Miechen and Marie Feodorovna's father-in-law. As Tsar of All the Russias, Alexander was sovereign of 90 million subjects, consisting of some 56 million Russians, 5 million Poles, 3 million Jews, and 1 million ethnic Germans. The rest of the far-flung empire included Finns, Tartars, Tajiks, Circassians, Georgians, and many other races. The overwhelming majority of the tsar's subjects adhered to the Russian Orthodox faith, while some 20 million were of the Roman Catholic, Protestant, and Jewish faiths. Alexander II's rule extended west to the Baltic in present-day Poland and east to the Pacific, with Russian influence encroaching into far-away California. The empire covered roughly one-sixth of the world's surface, totaling some 8.5 million square miles. Like his progenitors, Alexander II ruled his vast empire from the capital, St. Petersburg, in or near which the imperial family lived.

Peter the Great's dream of a spectacular imperial capital forced from the swampy marshes near the Baltic Sea was in full fruition. After Peter, who founded St. Petersburg in 1703, successive monarchs had built upon his vision, producing a capital that glorified both the mighty span of Russia's presence on the globe as well as the tsars themselves. By the time of Marie Alexandrovna's birth, St. Petersburg was the undisputed center of imperial Russia, a major capital that rivaled Europe's more historic cities—London, Paris, Vienna, and Berlin. Visitors to St. Petersburg have often rhapsodized over the imperial city. "The capital itself is like no other European city," wrote one visitor. "It is on such a colossal scale, with its immensely wide streets and magnificent churches, the richness and gorgeousness of which are well-nigh impossible to describe. The buildings in the streets are all of different-coloured stone, and they stand out to perfection against the superb Northern sky."[9] Another described St. Petersburg as "a city of sumptuous distances . . . The streets are broad, the open squares vast in size, the avenues interminable, the river wide and rapid, and the lines of architecture seemingly endless . . . It is a city of churches and palaces" where "everything that meets the eye is colossal." The city's churches alone, of which there were over two hundred, were impressive, "most of which are crowned with four or five fantastic cupolas each, and whose interiors are opulent in gold, silver, and precious stones."[10] Thanks to the "physical fabric of the place," with its "legacy of grand design and Imperial munificence," "St. Petersburg impresses the visitor as the creation of a truly imperial mind. Massive palaces, royal monuments, stately cathedrals, immense public buildings—all betoken unbounded wealth lavished almost recklessly upon it by its munificent rulers during the two centuries of its development."[11] St. Petersburg was built to impress and impress it did.

The Grand Duchess Marie Alexandrovna spent her early childhood in this resplendent city, with summers at Hapsal on the Gulf of Finland. There, the imperial children enjoyed walks, bathing in the sea, and riding. Her parents remained devoted to each other and to their children, of whom Marie Alexandrovna was the center of attention. "The whole family adores this child," observed Anna Tiutcheva. Her parents "shower her with kisses and affection, as well as her aunts and uncles."[12] This fondness for the little grand duchess went well beyond her family. In St. Petersburg, "the whole court idolised the child." Marie Alexandrovna's popularity also extended to the "sailors on guard outside the Peterhof Palace [who] would prepare little surprises for her—a bunch of strawberries, a stick half-peeled as though a white ribbon had been wound around it, or a small wooden flute."[13] As the only girl in a family of six boys, Marie Alexandrovna became somewhat tomboyish and straightforward in her manner. Allowed free rein, she was extremely close to both her parents. The tsarina liked to keep her children near. When at work at her desk or welcoming visitors to her study, it was not unusual to find the toddler near her mother playing unceremoniously with her toys. The Tsarina Marie felt nothing short of "boundless adoration" for her only surviving daughter, an adoration the little grand duchess felt "instinctively."[14]

Close as Marie Alexandrovna was to her mother, the grand duchess enjoyed an even closer relationship with her father, even after he assumed the burdens of his empire. "Almost every evening I come to feed soup to this little cherub," the tsar confided to Anna Tiutcheva. "This is the only enjoyable minute of my whole day, the only time when I forget the troubles that weigh upon me."[15] Early in Marie Alexandrovna's life, Tiutcheva noticed that, "she is only one year and eight months old, but she is being turned into a toy of her father, who dotes on her."[16] The tsar never lost this special affection for his daughter, whom he allowed to burst into his study and interrupt his meetings with ministers. Marie Alexandrovna could often be found during such important work sessions being bounced by the tsar on his knees. This practice was eventually curtailed by the grand duchess's other governess, Countess Alexandra Tolstoy.

Countess Tolstoy was a cousin once removed of the famous author, Count Leo Tolstoy. As a "vivacious, witty, sensitive" and "moral" being, she "brought out the best" in Leo Tolstoy.[17] She was regarded as the person "who probably came to know Tolstoy better than anyone else in the world, including his wife."[18] Countess Tolstoy's charms also became a mainstay in the imperial family. "Kind in the extreme, just, and absolutely unselfish," the countess "knew how to appeal to the best instincts of her pupil, and inspired her with a strict feeling of duty, compassion for the miseries of the world, truth, soundness of judgment, and love of occupation."[19]

As she grew, Marie Alexandrovna retained her straightforward personality. "She is absolutely genuine and never changes in front of strangers," observed Anna Tiutcheva. "She does not possess extreme courage or timidity, but kindness and natural delicacy would make a very sweet princess."[20] Such at least, was Tiutcheva's hope concerning her charge, for Marie Alexandrovna was not all sweetness and laughter. Too much commotion and noise made her nervous. Tiutcheva noted that the grand duchess, once confronted by a curious crowd that pressed against her carriage window, "expressed a not-so-liberal wish to pluck a twig from a tree and chase the people away."[21]

As Tsar Alexander II's only surviving daughter, it came as no surprise that Grand Duchess Marie Alexandrovna, doted on by the court and her adoring parents, came to possess a stubborn streak and strong awareness of her standing in life. Closely observing her charge, Tiutcheva became concerned that the imperial family and court were spoiling Marie Alexandrovna. She "is accustomed to being the center of the world and that everyone yields to her," confided Tiutcheva in her diary.[22] Tiutcheva continued to worry about the grand duchess's "uncompromising" character, so much so that the governess was compelled to be "stricter with her than I would be with any other child when she does not want to share her toys or candy with others." Tiutcheva concluded that "she needs to be handled carefully, but steadily, one cannot treat her roughly or reason with her a lot."[23] "Her persistence is gentle, but unrelenting," wrote an exasperated Tiutcheva. "She never forgets what she decided, and with her, time does not help like it does with other children because she always returns to her own ideas."[24] Both Countess Tolstoy and Tiutcheva had their hands full in caring for and trying to develop Marie Alexandrovna's character.

In the summer of 1864, the imperial family visited Tsarina Marie's brother, Prince Alexander of Hesse and by Rhine, at his home, Schloss Heiligenberg, in Jugenheim in Hesse. A comfortable, sprawling villa, Heiligenberg became a favorite gathering place for the Tsarina Marie and her children. Prince Alexander's daughter, Princess Marie of Battenberg, recalled her cousin, eleven-year-old Marie Alexandrovna, during an 1864 visit as possessing "a sweet round face and fair hair, which she wore in pig-tails."[25] The impression the Russian imperial family gave during the mid-1860s was of a united and contented unit. Princess Marie of Battenberg noticed this during their family visits and so too did individuals such as Lothar von Schweinitz, the Prussian military attaché attached to St. Petersburg. Watching the imperial family during a procession in the Russian capital in 1865, von Schweinitz recalled: "As their majesties came out of the chapel, followed by five sturdy sons and a daughter just developing into a young lady, I felt the comforting impression produced by a combination of power, beauty, and family happiness."[26]

The passage of time in no way diminished the grand duchess's standing within the imperial family. She continued to be a clear favorite with her father. In 1867, a visitor in audience with the tsar described the teenaged Marie Alexandrovna as "a pretty little girl of fourteen summers, simply dressed and with a winning and gentle face." So close was she to her father that the visitor speculated as to "the power of that child over the Autocratic Ruler."[27]

Besides his only daughter, the tsar was especially close to his brother, the Grand Duke Constantine Nikolaevich (b. 1827). His brother's loyal and indispensable adviser and a noted liberal, Constantine, who was bent on urging Alexander II to implement reforms, seemed nothing short of a dangerous radical to the old guard. Liberals extolled Constantine as a courageous crusader for change. Little wonder then that the grand duke "was the most praised and the most hated man in the whole of the Empire."[28]

The Grand Duke Constantine headed a junior branch of the imperial family, the "Constantinovichi." Unlike many of the Romanov males, Constantine was physically unprepossessing, being somewhat short and lacking the handsomeness that distinguished his father and brothers. Like Tsar Alexander II, Grand Duke Constantine chose his young bride out of genuine affection. In 1848, he married the tall, dark-haired Princess Alexandra of Saxe-Altenburg (b. 1830) who, upon her conversion to Orthodoxy, had taken the name of Alexandra Iosifovna. The grand duchess was said to possess a "marvellous grace" and pictures gave "but a faint idea of her extreme beauty."[29] The early married years for Alexandra Iosifovna, nicknamed "Sanny," were happy ones, though she disliked the strain of court life. The grand duchess's contemporary, Countess Marie Kleinmichel, admired Alexandra Iosifovna as "a fearless rider, a first-rate whip, and drove either four-in-hand or tandem in a masterly fashion."[30]

Miechen's niece, the German Crown Princess Cecilie, described Olga's mother as being "very lovable and yet naturally reserved."[31]

Through the years, the grand ducal couple had six children: Nicholas (b. 1850), Olga (b. 1851), Vera (b. 1854), Constantine (b. 1858), Dmitri (b. 1860), and Viacheslav (1862). The couple's eldest daughter, Grand Duchess Olga Constantinovna, was born at Pavlovsk, an imperial estate seventeen miles from St. Petersburg. Pavlovsk, which traced its history to Catherine the Great, was noted for its elegant neoclassical palace and vast parkland of hundreds of acres. Olga's first cousin, Marie Alexandrovna, grew up in grander palaces such as the Winter Palace; Peterhof, Russia's version of Versailles on the Gulf of Finland; and the imperial estate at Tsarskoe Selo, but Olga's childhood home of Pavlovsk was equally impressive and enchanting. With the Slavyanka River meandering through the estate, Pavlovsk was celebrated for its English-style landscaped garden and rolling countryside dotted with thousands of silver birch trees and firs. Then there was the palace itself: "Rising like a dream at the end of an *allée* of burnished golden linden trees, the yellow and white Palladian colonnaded palace and its graceful neoclassical temples and statues appear to their greatest advantage, blending the beauty of nature and art, of East and West, in a harmony which only the measure and refinement of the eighteenth century could conceive."[32]

In a letter to Olga's teacher, Madame Rossiet, the Grand Duchess Alexandra Iosifovna boasted that "My Olga is a cute child; she is my joy and pride. She is so tender, joyful, simple, and obedient."[33] Indeed, Grand Duchess Olga inherited her mother's endearing personality. Countess Kleinmichel found Olga to have been "a delightful child, gifted with incomparable grace and kindness; her big blue eyes reflected the innocence of her angelic soul."[34]

Yet during these happy years, the grand duchess also witnessed the rumblings of discontent that were soon to plague the Russian and Greek dynasties with frightening regularity. When Olga was twelve years old, her father was appointed Viceroy of Poland. This meant that home for part of the year became the lovely neoclassical-style Lazienki Palace in Warsaw, surrounded by lakes and a splendid park. Life in Poland, however, was not without problems. Polish discontent with Russia was strong. Two assassination attempts aimed at Grand Duke Constantine failed, leaving Olga and her family in fear for his life.

Another royal contemporary was the Duchess Marie Alexandrine Elisabeth Eleonore of Mecklenburg-Schwerin, who was familiarly known as "Miechen."

The only daughter of Grand Duke Friedrich Franz II of Mecklenburg-Schwerin and his first wife, Princess Augusta of Reuss, Miechen was born on May 14, 1854, at the family's summer home, the neoclassical palace of Ludwigslust. When Miechen was still young her mother died. Miechen's father then married Princess Anna of Hesse and by Rhine. After Duchess Anna died, Miechen's father married Princess Marie of Schwarzburg-Rudolstadt, who was only four years older than Miechen.

The grand duchy of Mecklenburg-Schwerin, with an area of just over five thousand square miles, was located in what is today northern Germany. Bordering the Baltic Sea, Mecklenburg-Schwerin was a relatively minor state, raised to grand ducal status at the Congress of Vienna in 1815. The grand duchy tended to be among the poorest of the German territories, largely due to a mediocre agricultural environment. The duchy's capital, Schwerin, looked somewhat like Denmark with its flat topography. The British diplomat, Lord Augustus Loftus, who visited Schwerin in the 1860s, thought Schwerin "resembled England in many respects, and specially in the hedgerows, which gave a picturesque appearance to the landscape."[35] As a "clean, cheerful, pretty town, well paved, well lit, and prettily situated,"[36] Schwerin seemed almost fairy tale–like. Lakes surround this picturesque Mecklenburg city, which is dominated by the grand ducal home, a delightful French Renaissance–style castle built in the mid-nineteenth century. Lord Augustus described the castle as a "diminutive Versailles—the whole interior richly decorated and magnificently furnished. It is beautifully situated close to an extensive lake and near the town."[37] Miechen's niece, Crown Princess Cecilie, echoed this impression: "Its position on the lake is incomparable . . . and its immediate surroundings on the island are wonderful. Trees of great antiquity rustle in the wind, and green lawns spread down to the shore of the lake, where weeping willows dip their graceful branches into the waters . . . In the spring and autumn wild swans fly across overhead, and the sharp cries of ducks and waterfowl can be heard. On all sides is Nature, vast and unconfined."[38] Such then was the tranquil setting of Schwerin, Miechen's childhood home.

Miechen's father was a respected Prussian general who had commanded forces during the Austro-Prussian War of 1866 and later defended forces of the German army in the Franco-Prussian War of 1870. By the mid-1870s, Mecklenburg-Schwerin had a population of 550,000, the overwhelming majority belonging to the Lutheran faith. The grand ducal court of Miechen's father, though modeled on the militaristic court of the Hohenzollern dynasty that ruled from Berlin, was nevertheless cultured. It cultivated the sciences and arts, in particular opera and theater. A form of absolute rule also existed in Mecklenburg-Schwerin during Miechen's childhood where permission was needed from the grand duke for such things as emigrating. Yet the grand dukes of Mecklenburg-Schwerin also enjoyed a close relationship with their subjects and customarily held frequent "open houses" for people "who wanted to consult him [a grand duke] in any way or put forward any proposal." Crown Princess Cecilie, fondly recalled that the court "created the most beautiful patriarchal relations that can be imagined" between "the ruler and his people."[39]

Back in Russia, Marie Alexandrovna's father became increasingly occupied with troubles at home. Inherently, he was "not a reformer by nature, inclination or vocation."[40] In order to uphold Russia's position as a Great Power on the world stage, the tsar was compelled to implement much needed reforms. Russia needed to modernize and central to this drive for modernization was the issue of serfdom, but emancipation was a long time coming. The tsar had alluded to this momentous move in 1856, saying that "it is much better that this [emancipation] come from above, than from below."[41] At the same time Tsar Alexander II also hinted of the reforms he was contemplating: "Let [Russia's] internal well-being be confirmed and perfected; let justice and mercy reign in her courts . . . and let everyone, under the protection of laws that give equal justice and protection to all, enjoy peace in the fruits of his honest labor."[42]

Alexander II proclaimed the Emancipation Manifesto of 1861, freeing tens of millions of serfs who had been chattels of a select elite. Emancipation signaled a new era for Russia. On returning from St. Petersburg's Kazan Cathedral where a Te Deum was held in thanksgiving for the issuance of the manifesto, Alexander II admitted to his daughter that "this is the happiest day of my life."[43] But confusion and misunderstanding over what the manifesto involved also reigned and sporadic violence broke out. Shouts of: "Stands to reason we must have land" or "we starve"[44] filled the air.

Pressured by circumstances to become Russia's reformist tsar, Alexander II earned the moniker "Tsar-Liberator" for his bold action. Other bold reforms followed. "Between 1857 and 1864, reform legislation [not only] freed Russia's serfs . . . [they also] established institutions of representative government in key parts of the Empire, introduced trial by jury, and placed justice in Russia for the first time in the hands of a judicial profession that could exercise authority over the law independently of the autocracy. Russia thus began her evolution from a nation of servitors into a nation of free men and women obliged to assume increasing responsibility for their destinies and those of their neighbors.[45]"

In an unanticipated twist, Alexander II's Great Reforms created mounting pressure to dispense completely with the autocratic principles that had been so carefully cultivated in previous reigns. The reforms of the 1860s, therefore, had major repercussions, for they amounted to no less than "the end of the *ancien regime* in Russia."[46] During the Grand Duchess Marie Alexandrovna's early years, these burdens on the tsarist regime were still held in check. A certain tranquility persisted and a sense of serenity still pervaded the imperial family's lives.

This was especially evident when the family was in the Crimea, the balmy paradise that was Russia's version of the Riviera. Craggy hills enveloped in lush landscaping afforded commanding views of the Black Sea. A temperate climate made for a calming and pleasurable stay for the elite who came to the fashionable resort. The imperial family's wooden villa there was called Livadia. There the famed American author Mark Twain met the tsar, tsarina, and their teenaged daughter, Marie Alexandrovna, in the 1860s. The author described "the modest little Grand Duchess Marie" as being "blue-eyed, unassuming, and pretty."[47] Twain noticed that Marie Alexandrovna and her mother were dressed simply in blue foulard silk adorned with matching blue sashes, finished off with flesh-colored gloves and straw hats. The grand duchess made quite an impression on Twain, who wrote that "I was glad to observe that she wore her own hair, plaited in thick braids against the back of her head, instead of the uncomely thing they call a waterfall, which is about as much like a waterfall as a canvas-covered ham is like a cataract." But even more telling than Twain's observation about Marie Alexandrovna's coiffure was his reflection on the impact that this cherished child had on her father. "Taking the kind expression that is in the Emperor's face and the gentleness that is in his young daughter's into consideration, I wondered if it would not tax the Czar's firmness to the utmost to condemn a supplicating wretch to misery in the wastes of Siberia if she pleaded for him. Every time their eyes met, I saw more and more what a tremendous power that weak, diffident schoolgirl could wield if she chose to do it. Many and many a time she might rule the Autocrat of Russia, whose lightest word is law to seventy millions of human beings! She was only a girl, and she looked like a thousand others I have seen, but never a girl provoked such a novel and peculiar interest in me before."[48] Twain's impression of the teenaged grand duchess's effect on her father was reinforced by Alexander II's significance on the world stage. Twain noted that here "was a man who could open his lips and ships would fly through the waves, locomotives would speed over plains, couriers would hurry from village to village, a hundred telegraphs would flash the word to the four corners of an empire that stretches its vast proportions over a seventh part of the habitable globe, and a countless multitude of men would do his bidding . . . If this man sprained his ankle, a million miles of telegraph would carry the news over mountains—valleys—uninhabited deserts—under the trackless sea—and ten thousand newspapers would prate of it; if he were grievously ill, all nations would know it before the sun rose again; if he dropped lifeless where he stood, his fall might shake the thrones of half a world!"[49]

Hundreds of miles to the west in Copenhagen, another royal family with young children flourished. The Danish capital, which in the 1830s had been described as having a "beauty and elegance" that was due to "the uniformity of its architecture,"[50] was home to an unpretentious family destined for an illustrious future. This family was headed by the future King Christian IX and his wife, Louise of Hesse-Cassel. Their children included Frederick (b. 1843), Alexandra (b. 1844) ("Alix"), William (b. 1845) ("Willie"), Dagmar (b. 1847), Thyra (b. 1853), and Waldemar (b. 1858). The second daughter, Marie Sophie Frederica Dagmar, was born on November 26, 1847, and came to be known as "Dagmar." Among family members, Dagmar's nickname was "Minnie." The trio of Alexandra, William, and Dagmar remained close their entire lives.

The Danish royal family lived modestly in the heart of Copenhagen at the unprepossessing Yellow Palace, more a town house than a palace. In the summers, the family decamped to Bernstorff, a stuccoed villa surrounded by verdant parkland not far from the capital. The Danish royals put on no airs. "There was a delightful charm of simplicity and kindness about Prince Christian which won all hearts," recalled the wife of a British diplomat posted to Denmark, "and the patriarchal and unostentatious setting of the family life of this Royal couple was most attractive."[51]

So frugal was the family that the Princesses Dagmar and Alexandra shared a bedroom as well as sewed and mended their own clothes. Vacations were never extravagant, consisting largely of visits to Rumpenheim near Frankfurt. These Rumpenheim gatherings were unsophisticated meetings full of mirth, gossip, and practical jokes. Well into adulthood, Dagmar and her siblings continued to exhibit elements of this Rumpenheim joviality whenever they met. At Rumpenheim, Dagmar would occasionally meet her contemporaries from Russia. The Tsarina Marie, who suffered from poor health aggravated by the bitter Russian winters, liked to escape regularly to Germany's milder climate. She frequently brought her children to Rumpenheim, including her daughter, Grand Duchess Marie Alexandrovna. Of the five eldest who usually accompanied their mother, it was the heir, the Tsarevich Nicholas ("Nixa"), who was the gentlest of the brood, while his brothers, Sasha, Vladimir, and Alexei, were the "barbarous bandits, scornful of petticoats, who headed a lusty gang as boorish as themselves."[52]

As the 1860s unfolded, the Danish royals' once rather nondescript life changed dramatically because their fortunes quickly rose. The first major change to affect Princess Dagmar's family occurred in the spring of 1863 and was directly related to events in Greece. After the Greeks won independence from the Ottoman Empire at the end of the Greek War of Independence (1821–1829), the Great Powers established an independent kingdom of Greece through the Treaty of London of 1832. In 1833, a prince of Bavaria became King Otto of Greece. But after a turbulent reign of thirty years, Otto was compelled to leave Greece and abandon his throne. In their search for a new king, the Greeks originally offered the throne in 1863 to eighteen-year-old Prince Alfred, the second son of Britain's venerable Queen Victoria, though as a member of a royal family of one of the three Great Powers, he was ineligible. Alfred's destiny was not tied to the volatile Greek throne, but to the German duchy of Saxe-Coburg-Gotha, for he was already heir to his uncle Ernst, the reigning Duke of Saxe-Coburg-Gotha. Lord Palmerston, the British prime minister, reminded Queen Victoria of the conflict that this might cause, saying that: "the Duke should make up his mind either to accept the throne of Greece singly and permanently . . . or at once to say that he prefers to remain Duke of Coburg."[53] Alfred himself was not enthusiastic about becoming king of Greece, for not only was he already heir to his uncle, he had already established himself as an officer in Britain's Royal Navy, a career that was very much to his liking. The question of Prince Alfred becoming king of Greece invigorated the queen somewhat, for she had been deeply depressed since the death of her husband, Prince Albert, in December 1861. Still, there was little doubt of the outcome. "The diplomatic engagements of her Majesty's Crown, together with other weighty considerations, have prevented her Majesty from yielding to this general wish of the Greek nation,"[54] concluded a contemporary publication in an editorial that discussed Prince Alfred's candidature.

Having failed to secure Prince Alfred as their king, the Greeks next set their sights on Denmark for a candidate who was acceptable to the Great Powers. In March 1863, Prince William of Denmark—Princess Dagmar's seventeen-year-old brother Willie—was accordingly elected king of Greece. A contemporary publication declared that "Upon the decree being made known, a *Te Deum* was celebrated, and was followed by public festivities, illuminations, and general rejoicings."[55] Queen Victoria had her own opinion about the matter, writing to her eldest daughter, Vicky, the Crown Princess of Prussia: "Our foolish government is bent on making poor Willie King of Greece."[56]

Willie's father, Prince Christian, was also against his son accepting the Greek offer. "All my family and my friends are against his going there. From all sides I am told to be prudent," remarked the prince. Moreover, if Willie stayed in Denmark, his father noted that his son would "not [be] exposed to the vicissitudes and dangers he will have to encounter in Greece."[57] According to Adolphe Dotézac, the French minister in Copenhagen, "the Prince and Princess of Denmark see in the Greek crown nothing but a crown of thorns."[58]

In the end, Prince Christian acquiesced to the inevitable. "The young Prince's eagerness for his kingdom is one of the strongest arguments with Prince Christian," noted Dotézac.[59] The story goes that young Willie learned of the news that he had been chosen king of Greece in the most casual manner. He took his lunch with him to the naval academy, and there in the newspaper that wrapped his sardine sandwich was the announcement. Willie accepted the offer of the Greek crown, took the name of King George I, arriving in Athens in October 1863. The young man faced an unenviable task, summed up in an editorial that discussed Prince Alfred's candidature. This editorial noted that a king of Greece "must be aware of the embarrassments and mortifications he must inevitably undergo . . . and of the . . . perpetual turmoil, that he must be liable to within his little kingdom."[60] In the years to come, the new King George of Greece would find this assessment not far off the mark.

Next to become king within the Danish royal family after Willie was his father. In November 1863, the prince ascended the throne as King Christian IX. Earlier that year, in March, his eldest daughter, Alexandra, joined Queen Victoria's family when she married Albert ("Bertie"), the Prince of Wales. Queen Victoria and Vicky had chosen the beautiful and well-mannered Alix for Bertie after careful deliberation. The Danish royals accompanied Princess Alexandra to England for the nuptials. It was a trip full of excitement for Dagmar, dampened by sadness because their happy family unit had been broken up by Alix's marriage. Dagmar returned to her native Denmark after the wedding, but it would not be long before the pretty princess became the object of attention from a young man whose illustrious connections surpassed even those of Alix's new husband, the Prince of Wales. Imperial Russia beckoned.

BRIDAL TRAVAILS

*P*rincesses Dagmar and her sister Alexandra were ideal choices as future consorts not only for England but for Russia as well. Dagmar was not yet four years old in 1851 when the Empress Alexandra, wife of Emperor Nicholas I, exclaimed, "this one is reserved for us" when she met Princess Louise of Denmark and the little Danish princess.[1]

Queen Victoria too considered Princess Dagmar as a possible wife for her son Alfred. Writing to Vicky in 1862, the queen admitted: "I hear that the Emperor of Russia has not given up his intention of asking for Alix or Dagmar for his son . . . I should be very sorry if any thing [*sic*] were decided for Dagmar before you had seen her, as it would be one chance less for Affie [Prince Alfred]."[2] Only days later, the queen changed her mind, telling Vicky: "Respecting Dagmar, I do not wish her to be kept for Affie; let the Emperor have her."[3] Victoria anticipated German objections to two Danish princesses marrying into the British royal family, especially since Prince Alfred was also destined to reign one day as Duke of Saxe-Coburg-Gotha. That German feelings against Denmark over the disputed territories of Schleswig-Holstein ran high also scuttled Queen Victoria's enthusiasm for a marriage between Dagmar and Alfred. Procuring Alix as a bride for Bertie had been the greater priority. And so, concluded Queen Victoria to Vicky: "Dagmar should be entirely dropped and the mother encouraged to give her to the future Czar if that will secure Alix."[4]

In comparing the two sisters, Queen Victoria noted that Alix was "calm and sweet and gentle and lovely . . . Dagmar is cleverer, and would I am sure be very fit for the position in Russia; she is a very nice girl."[5] Queen Victoria's cousin, Princess Mary Adelaide of Cambridge, also compared the two Danish sisters, finding Princess Alexandra to be "strikingly handsome" while Princess Dagmar was "sweetly pretty."[6] Even as a child, Dagmar's best feature—her "splendid dark eyes"—already made an impression.[7]

The Danish princess remained a prime candidate for a bride of Russia's imperial family. In 1864, the Tsarevich Nicholas ("Nixa") accordingly paid a visit to Denmark. Nixa promptly became infatuated with the comely princess. In reporting his impressions, Nixa wrote to his mother excitedly: "How can I describe her? She is so pretty, direct, intelligent, lively yet at the same time shy. She is even prettier in real life than in the portraits that we had seen so far. Her eyes speak for her: they are so kind, intelligent, animated."[8] Dagmar greatly appreciated the twenty-one-year-old tsarevich, a slightly built, intelligent young man who was popular with all who knew him. His teachers referred to the heir as "Russia's hope" as well as "a brilliant young man." Grand Duke Constantine was no less enthusiastic about his nephew, this future tsar, referring to Nixa as "the crown of perfection."[9]

The tsarevich and the Danish princess became engaged in 1864; and soon enough Princess Dagmar was showered with expensive betrothal gifts from the Romanovs. From her future mother-in-law, Dagmar received an exquisite pearl necklace. Nixa gave her spectacular diamonds. Not long after the engagement became official, Nixa visited his mother in the Riviera where she was staying with his brother Serge and his eleven-year-old sister, Marie Alexandrovna. From there, the young grand duchess wrote a letter to her father, the tsar, saying that she hoped Nixa "will stay for a long time." She added her regret that "the Winter Palace is very empty, and will be terribly dull for Christmas and Easter." The part that must have most touched the tsar was Marie Alexandrovna's message, "I'm also very upset that I won't be with you on Sunday, walking and driving in a stately carriage."[10]

The year that sixteen-year-old Dagmar became engaged, the princess solicited support from her future father-in-law on behalf of Denmark, as it embarked on war against Prussia over the disputed territory of Schleswig-Holstein. In a letter, Dagmar beseeched Tsar Alexander II: "Use your power to mitigate the terrible conditions which the Germans have brutally forced Papa to accept . . . the sad plight of my fatherland, which makes my heart heavy, has inspired me to turn to you." Dagmar ended the letter asking the tsar to kiss on her behalf the empress, "the dear brothers and [Grand Duchess] Marie."[11] Help was not forthcoming, and so a humiliated Denmark lost the coveted territories. Dagmar and her sister, Alexandra, never forgot the defeat nor forgave the Germans.

Princess Dagmar's great destiny in Russia nearly came to naught. Nixa was taken seriously ill with cerebrospinal meningitis, confessing to Prince Vladimir Meschersky: "Sometimes it seems I'm on the verge of death."[12] By April 1865 the tsarevich was in Nice, with the hope of recuperating. "I fear he is so reduced he can't get through it," wrote Princess Alice to her mother, Queen Victoria.[13] Receiving the shocking news of Nixa's condition, Dagmar and her mother hurriedly made their way to the dying man. The imperial family, including eleven-year-old Marie Alexandrovna, also hastened to say their last goodbyes to their beloved Nixa. N. P. Litvinov, who was a mentor to Nixa's brothers, the Grand Dukes Vladimir and Alexander ("Sasha") accompanied them. He noted how "many Russians were there to meet the Tsar. All had eyes red from crying or very sad faces."[14]

When Nixa saw Dagmar at his bedside, he told his father, "She is so sweet, isn't she?"[15] The fatally ill tsarevich commended his brother Sasha to the tsar, saying: "Papa, take care of Sasha; he is such an honest and good person."[16] The tsarevich then made a symbolic gesture that had great repercussions. Taking the hands of his brother, the twenty-year-old Sasha, and his fiancée, Dagmar, Nixa joined them together in a silent hope that their futures would be linked. The symbolic gesture did not go unnoticed. Another witness to the event, D. S. Arsenyev, wrote that "it seemed like the Tsarevich was handing his fiancée over to his beloved brother, to whom he was also leaving his place on earth."[17] Twenty-one-year-old Nixa died on April 12/24, 1865. Sasha was now Tsar Alexander II's heir. Litvinov, who witnessed the sad scene, recalled how Nixa's other brother, "Vladimir Alexandrovitch was crying the most, the Empress—the least, she was very firm. They could hardly pull Princess Dagmar away from the corpse and carry her out."[18] News of Nixa's death and Dagmar's plight touched a chord with many, including Princess Mary Adelaide of Cambridge who wrote of "poor dear Minny's [sic] sorrow and the blight which has fallen upon her young life."[19] No less moved was Queen Victoria, who wrote: "how terrible for poor Dagmar . . . the poor parents and bride are most deeply to be pitied."[20]

In writing of Nixa's death, the grieving Dagmar told her father: "The poor Emperor and Empress! They are so kind to me in their sorrow; and his poor brothers, especially the oldest, Sacha [sic], whom he loved so much, not only as his brother, but also as his only and best friend; it is hard for him, poor fellow, and it is terrible for him that now he must become what his beloved brother was!"[21] Sasha, the new heir, was the very antithesis of his late lamented brother. Unlike the refined and slightly built Nixa, hardheaded Sasha was tall, heavy-set and possessed of Herculean strength. His impressive muscle, "massive build, the slow *tempo* . . . the upward scowl . . . the side gait, awkward bearing, and bovine butting of the head suggested 'bullock' as a term of endearment which his father first conferred upon him."[22] The tsarevich was strong enough to bend horseshoes with his bare hands. Despite his physical gifts, Sasha was not intellectual, a slow counterpoint to his intelligent brother. Their tutor, Constantine Pobedonostsev, had reputedly enthused about "the marvellous talents of the elder brother," but regretted that the Grand Duke Alexander "had been so badly misused by Nature, who sent him into the world with the shabbiest of intellectual gifts."[23] Pobedonostsev was so taken aback by Nixa's death that he described the event as "a decisive hour for the destinies of Russia."[24]

Since Sasha's shortcomings made him seem ill prepared to take on the eventual mantle of tsar, there were rumors that Alexander II would bypass Sasha and name his son Vladimir heir instead. This did not happen, so plans to get Sasha and Dagmar engaged continued. Tsarina Marie was eager to get Dagmar to visit Russia right away, but the grieving princess's mother, Queen Louise, wrote that she wanted her daughter first to "strengthen her nerves . . . [and] avoid emotional upsets."[25]

Nixa's death devastated Dagmar and Sasha, but the expectation that they were to marry created an additional emotional hurdle. Both had to will themselves to transfer their affections—Dagmar's from Nixa to Sasha, and Sasha to his dead brother's fiancée. Sasha was in love not with Dagmar, but with one of his mother's maids of honor, Princess Marie Mescherskaya. Countess Marie Kleinmichel, who knew Mescherskaya, described her as "a great beauty," noting that "there was something Oriental about her whole person, and especially about her great dark velvety eyes, which fascinated everyone."[26] Sasha acknowledged that marrying Mescherskaya was completely unacceptable, but in May 1865 wrote in his diary: "I want to refuse to marry Dagmar, whom I cannot love and don't want . . . Perhaps it would be better if I relinquished my right to the throne. I feel incapable of ruling. I have too little respect for people and get fed up with everything that concerns my position."[27]

As the new heir, Tsarevich Alexander's stress mounted. He had to reorient himself and prepare for the frightening task of becoming tsar, a fate he did not welcome. Overwhelmed by the prospect before him, the new tsarevich could not hide his apprehensions. Soon after Nixa's death Sasha and his siblings went to Jugenheim, where his cousin Princess Marie of Battenberg found him alone one day feeling "so unhappy." She wrote that he had thrown "himself despairingly on a sofa, then "wailed, *'Je ne suis pas elevé pour être Empereur.'* ['I was not raised to be Emperor.'] He is twenty years old, and hitherto has been free from care; now poor Sacha [*sic*] sees himself suddenly faced with a future of great difficulty."[28]

Eventually, the heir began to accept his duty and turn his attention to Dagmar. "I have thought more about Dagmar and pray to God every day to arrange this matter, which will mean my happiness for the rest of my life," wrote Sasha. "I increasingly feel the need to have a wife, love her, and be loved by her. I wish to arrange this business quickly without losing heart, fearlessly putting my faith in God."[29] By the end of 1865, however, Sasha was still under Mescherskaya's spell.

Disgusted by Sasha's threats to renounce his rights, the tsar finally confronted his son, in May 1866, about his reluctance to let go of Mescherskaya. Alexander II could not understand his son's willingness to renounce his obligations. The tsar exploded in anger at Sasha, telling him that he was ordering Mescherskaya away. When the tsarevich asked his father to "leave her in peace," Alexander II then told his son bluntly: "Get out of here. I don't want to talk to you or know you."[30] Shortly after his confrontation with Alexander II, Sasha finally relented and bowed to the inevitable. Determined to make the best of what seemed to be an impossible situation, he went to see Dagmar in Copenhagen in June 1866, accompanied by his brothers, Vladimir and Alexei. When the tsarevich saw Dagmar again, he was pleasantly surprised to find himself attracted to her. Sasha, who possessed "a heart so profoundly and loyally loving" along with "a nature so upright," finally found the courage to propose, asking Dagmar if she could love him after having loved Nixa, to whom they were both devoted. She answered by kissing Sasha and telling him that she could love no other except him, who had been so close to his brother. "We both burst into tears," recalled the tsarevich, "then I told her that my dear Nixa helped us much in this situation and that now of course he prays about our happiness. We talked much about my brother, his death and his last days in Nice."[31] In the end, the tragedy that had so profoundly saddened Dagmar and Sasha—Nixa's death— brought the couple together.

Once Princess Dagmar became engaged to the Tsarevich Alexander, the imperial family again inundated her with opulent gifts that ranged from her wedding trousseau of the finest material in furs and silks, to the most spectacular jewels any bride could have dreamed of receiving. The presents Dagmar received as Nixa's fiancée reputedly cost a million and a half rubles. Betrothal to the Tsarevich Alexander precipitated a similar avalanche of gifts from her groom and his immensely wealthy family.

When eighteen-year-old Princess Dagmar set off for Russia, the famed Danish author Hans Christian Andersen witnessed her departure, writing of "the king's noble and amiable daughter." "As she left," recounted Andersen, "I stood in the crowd of men on the wharf where she, with her royal parents, went on board. She saw me, stepped up to me and shook my hand warmly. Tears started from my eyes: they were in my heart for our young princess. Everything promises for her happiness; an excellent family like that she has left, is that she has entered. A fortunate pair are [*sic*] she and her noble husband."[32]

The princess from Denmark received an enthusiastic welcome from her future countrymen. At St. Petersburg, where the official welcome took place, cheering spectators crowded platforms decorated with flags and flowers. So numerous were the onlookers that nearly every rooftop, window and balcony on the parade route was crammed. A witness to Princess Dagmar's arrival in Russia, S. D. Sheremetyev, who had known the tsarevich since his childhood, recalled that the princess "charmed everybody." The festivities included fireworks, illuminations, and balls, though the events seemed to be "a burden on the Tsarevich," recalled Sheremetyev. "But Dagmar's popularity was growing She was seen as a key to prosperity, all the hopes were laid on her and she would light the hearts with her eyes, her simplicity and charm promised happiness and peace."[33]

Prior to marrying the Tsarevich Alexander, Dagmar was received into the Russian Orthodox faith in a very public ceremony and took the name of Marie Feodorovna. Looking "most charming in a simple dress of white satin, trimmed with swan's down, without any ornament on her head, and no jewels save a cross," the future empress of Russia underwent a conversion ceremony that was not easy.[34] It demanded that Marie Feodorovna abjure her previous faith. Facing west and then east when asked to repudiate her old religion, Marie Feodorovna answered, "I renounce and reject them."[35] The convert prostrated herself, then recited at length the Orthodox Church's ten Articles of Religion in the Slavonic language. At one point Marie Feodorovna publicly professed that she sincerely believed in the Orthodox faith "undefiled to my last breath."[36] As she underwent absolution for her sins, Marie Feodorovna again lay prostrate on the floor. Then upon rising, she was anointed with holy oil. "The exquisite clearness and perfection with which she pronounced the Confession of Faith . . . as well as the answers and professions in the office of Conversion, struck all present with delight and astonishment."[37]

The wedding, held at the chapel of the Winter Palace on October 28/November 9, 1866, was magnificent. Prior to the ceremony, Marie Feodorovna stood in the Malachite Room for three interminable hours before a gold-edged mirror that belonged to the Empress Anna and was dressed in the tradition of Russian imperial brides. The regal attire was difficult to carry, for "her body [was] imprisoned in the stiff, immensely heavy antique gown of genuine silver tissue, her shoulders torn by the sweltering ermine train, dropping in endless folds behind her."[38] The wedding was an ordeal for the eighteen-year-old. "Entangled in a web of incomprehensible Romanoff ritual and tradition, she was the harassed slave of a relentless master of ancestral ceremonies."[39] At the ceremony, the Tsarevich Alexander's younger brother, Grand Duke Vladimir, held a crown over Sasha's head while Crown Prince Frederick, Marie Feodorovna's brother, held another over her head. The one sadness for Dagmar during this time was her parents' absence from her wedding. Owing to the high expense required of them to entertain in St. Petersburg, King Christian and Queen Louise opted to stay at home.

After the wedding celebrations, the newlyweds left for Ropsha in the countryside for a brief honeymoon. Even there, Marie Feodorovna—Minnie—could not escape the rituals imposed by the Romanovs. Protocol demanded that on his wedding night, Sasha wear a ridiculous outfit composed of a hulking silver gown and matching slippers that curled at the toes. On his head, Sasha wore a silver turban topped by cupids. The effect was nothing short of hilarious and sent the bride into hysterical fits of laughter.

In recording his marriage to Marie Feodorovna, the Tsarevich Alexander wrote in his diary: "I am married at last and the most important step in my life has been made . . . My darling Minnie was especially smart on this day."[40] Sasha reported the imperial marriage's success a few weeks after the wedding when he wrote: "God grant that . . . I may love my darling wife more and more, she who loves me with all her heart, a love for which I am so grateful, and for the sacrifice that she made by leaving her parents and her fatherland for my sake. I often feel that I am not worthy of her, but even if this were true, I will do my best to be."[41]

Marie Feodorovna—now tsarevna—was a positive influence on Sasha and on nearly everyone she met. She impressed many with her joie de vivre and sociability. Not long after her wedding, she appeared at a ball in a nobleman's home where, according to a witness, the tsarevna was "indefatigable" and "was also the prettiest woman there."[42] Dressed in a white tulle dress, with "a triple diamond necklace of great size and weight," noted the witness, Marie Feodorovna "was in high spirits, and, with her cheeks flushed by dancing, she had a freshness of look very rare in Russia."[43]

A busy schedule of festivities honored the newlyweds, and special guests including Marie Feodorovna's brother-in-law, the Prince of Wales. One such event was a reception at the famed Marble Palace, the St. Petersburg home of Grand Duchess Olga's father, Grand Duke Constantine. Entering through the opulent marble façade, guests discovered the interior to be even "more complete and perfect in its appointments."[44] Every room, including the private ones, was open that evening to hundreds of uniformed and bejeweled guests. One such guest, the Englishman, Edward Dicey, described traversing the rooms: "Out of halls blazing with light and colour you passed into low galleries; then into bed-chambers hung with rich tapestries; then into alcoves surrounded with gorgeous flowers; then into corridors where fountains sparkled brightly; and then again into new ranges of halls, each more splendid than the last which you had traversed."[45] Dicey admitted to being unable to catalog the "treasures and riches displayed in that long labyrinth of chambers, to which there seemed—when you once entered it—to be neither end nor beginning; even if I could, I doubt whether I should convey by doing so any idea of what it was like."[46] Strelna, not far from Peterhof, was another of Constantine's magnificent homes. Surrounded by large parklands, on the shores of the Gulf of Finland, Strelna was large and grand enough to rival any reigning European monarch's residence.

Olga Constantinovna was very close to her immediate family. As the little girl, whom her father liked to call "Muguet," French for "lily of the valley," grew into her teens, she captured attention with her good looks and "radiant expression."[47] Beyond that, Olga already had qualities that endeared her to those who met her in coming years, for she was "the girl with an iron character and kind heart."[48]

Tsarevna Marie Feodorovna thought that Olga would make an ideal wife for her brother Willie, now George I of Greece. Minnie seized her chance in getting the two acquainted when the twenty-one-year-old king visited St. Petersburg in 1867. Upon George I's arrival, the Russian court wasted no time in dazzling him. Three thousand guests, bedecked in finery, attended a banquet in his honor, providing "a scene of medieval pageantry lit by 10,000 candles in the blue and silver hall running the length of the Winter Palace." In comparison to the Romanovs, King George might think himself "a *poor relation*, indeed, if it should really happen that he entered the family circle,"[49] undisputedly, the grandest dynasty in the world.

During a visit to Pavlovsk, George was intrigued to find a fair-haired, oval-faced teenager peering discreetly at him from behind some curtains. It was the Grand Duchess Olga Constantinovna. Before long, George took a fancy to the young girl, agreeing with his sister that he had found his future wife. Marie Feodorovna convinced Olga's parents of her brother's suitability as a husband. In a letter to Minnie, King Christian IX asked his daughter outright: "Where in the world have you, little rogue, ever learned to intrigue so well, since you have worked hard on your uncle and aunt, who were previously decidedly against a match of this kind."[50]

Olga's age was the biggest obstacle to her marrying King George. Only in her mid-teens, Olga was still much the little girl—so much so that during their engagement King George found his future wife playing with her toys in a specially built playhouse. More than one person hinted that Olga might be too young to marry, to which the Grand Duchess Alexandra Iosifovna replied, "Olga would not stay sixteen all her life."[51]

As for the prospective bride's thoughts about her groom, Olga always contended that, "I fell in love with the man and not the King."[52] From a political and dynastic point of view, King George's choice of a Romanov wife might improve Russia's benevolence toward Greece. Moreover, a wife from an established and illustrious dynasty would increase the Greek royal family's prestige. Most importantly, that the queen was born and raised Orthodox was bound to endear her and the Greek royal family to the Greek people.

King George and Grand Duchess Olga's wedding took place on October 27, 1867, at the Winter Palace in St. Petersburg. The imperial bride was attired in a silver gown and an ermine-lined train, diamonds flashing brilliantly in her hair.

On her way to Athens from St. Petersburg, the new queen stopped in Vienna with her husband. Olga struck the Court Chamberlain in Vienna, Count Wilczek, with her charm and youthful air. Count Wilczek was also impressed that the diligent teenaged queen tried to give a good first impression to the ladies of the city's Greek community. Olga had ten chairs arranged in a room and on each chair she placed the name of the invited Greek lady who was to sit there. Then standing in front of each chair, Olga wrote in a notebook the greeting she was to give to each lady and what she intended to say. When the audience took place, Count Wilczek thought that young Queen Olga acquitted herself well.

When Queen Olga and King George arrived in Greece, enthusiastic crowds greeted the young couple, but all did not go smoothly. Her new life suddenly overwhelmed the sixteen-year-old Olga. During an official reception, the young queen went missing. Not until later did someone find her hiding under a staircase, weeping copious tears while clutching a favorite stuffed bear.

More radical changes were in store. Just before she turned seventeen, Olga fulfilled her obligatory role as consort by giving birth to a male heir in July 1868. The baby boy's name was a foregone conclusion. The chant of "Constantine" rose in crescendo from crowds gathered outside the palace, because there was a long-standing belief that when a Constantine ruled Greece, a new Byzantium—a greater Greece—would rise. In the coming years, Queen Olga gave birth to: George (b. 1869), Alexandra (b. 1870), Nicholas (b. 1872), Marie (b. 1876), Olga (b. and d. 1880), Andrew (b. 1882), and Christopher (b. 1888). The Greek dynasty had been firmly established.

Another wedding between a Romanov grand duchess and a foreign-born prince was in the works. The prince was Alfred, or Affie as he was known, Queen Victoria's second son whose refusal to become king of the Greeks paved the way for George I's accession. Alfred had embarked on a naval career that took him on voyages abroad to distant places such as South Africa and Australasia. He eventually commanded his own ship, the H.M.S. *Galatea*, and had also been created Duke of Edinburgh by Queen Victoria. Lord Charles Beresford, who served with the duke on the *Galatea*, described Prince Alfred as having "a great natural ability for handling a fleet," and noted that he "would have made a first-class fighting admiral."[53]

Of all Queen Victoria's sons, Alfred was the most prickly. She once complained to Vicky that "Affie makes me very unhappy; he hardly ever comes near me, is reserved, touchy, vague and wilful and I distrust him completely . . . He is quite a stranger to me."[54] Queen Victoria believed that like her eldest son, Bertie, whose behavior had also caused the queen much distress, the best remedy for Affie was a good wife. There was even talk from Vicky about having Grand Duchess Olga as Alfred's bride, telling Queen Victoria: "It is a great pity that Sanny's [Grand Duchess Alexandra Iosiforna] charming daughter is a Greek [meaning of the Orthodox faith]—she would do so well."[55] By 1867, Queen Victoria was getting anxious about marrying off Prince Alfred, so much so that she told Vicky, "the choice is becoming so narrow that I think we must get over the difficulties concerning religion—that is to say as regards the Greek religion—and I believe it could be got over easily if there was a person likely to suit. I had thought and hoped at one time for dear little Olga who is now to marry

King George."[56] In the end, Affie chose none other than Olga's cousin, the Grand Duchess Marie Alexandrovna. The couple met at Jugenheim in 1868 where Marie Alexandrovna made a favorable impression on the prince. By 1869, Alfred made clear his intention of marrying the grand duchess. Some thought that the prince's interest in Marie Alexandrovna stemmed mainly from the fact that she was immensely wealthy. Alfred's secretary "maintained that his concern with money 'amounted to a disease.'"[57] Queen Sophie of the Netherlands touched upon this in a letter to an English friend, stating bluntly that Marie Alexandrovna's "superior attraction is her fortune."[58]

Fortune aside, whoever courted the grand duchess had to compete with her affection for her father. At around the same time, Sir Horace Rumbold, who served at the British embassy in St. Petersburg during 1868–1869, recalled seeing the tsar and his daughter walking near the Winter Palace, accompanied by police guards. Rumbold noted a "bright-looking girl of about sixteen, with very pretty hair escaping behind from her fur cap," who was nothing less than Alexander II's "inseparable companion." Rumbold added "so great a favourite was she with her father that, at the first reception held by the young princess of foreign *diplomates* to be presented to her, it was said the Emperor stood listening the whole time behind the half-open door."[59]

The American consul to Moscow, Eugene Schuyler, also met Marie Alexandrovna. "Marie," noted Schuyler, "is rather pretty, though her nose and mouth are not good." At her presentation, Schuyler observed that "she was a little embarrassed, though on the whole she did very well, and everybody was charmed with her. The ladies were taken to her one by one, and then the men of the *Corps Diplomatique*, about sixty, were put in a circle and she went the rounds, having quite a conversation with each one in French, English, or German, as the case might be." The grand duchess prepared herself well for the ordeal. Schuyler noted how "she was apparently crammed up beforehand, for she seemed to know something about each man's private history." This was no small feat for a sixteen-year-old. "It was," concluded Schuyler, "a trying ordeal for a young girl," though Schuyler thought "she looks fully nineteen. She was dressed in rose-pink silk, much flounced, with white trimming, low-necked, with a pearl necklace, one pearl bracelet and one diamond one, and a rose in her hair."[60]

Queen Victoria's son, Alfred, was determined to make the grand duchess his wife and serious negotiations began. However, by then only seventeen years old, the grand duchess was not enthused about leaving Russia. Nor were her parents keen on seeing their daughter leave the family nest. When Prince Alfred met Tsar Alexander II in 1871 in Germany, the suitor found his prospective father-in-law hesitant. In a letter to Queen Victoria, Alexander II wrote: "Your praises for our daughter flattered us a great deal, but [Alfred] has surely told you, Madam, that while not in any way opposing a union between our two families, we have made it a principle never to impose our will upon our children as regards their marriages. Although speaking to him of a term of one year before taking any definitive decision, we expressly declared that neither he nor we would consider ourselves bound in any way, neither before nor after, and he seemed to understand this perfectly."[61] Queen Victoria was also against the idea that the couple live in Russia. This was simply out of the question and something Victoria declared she could "never consent to."[62]

Hence, the projected marriage between the Grand Duchess Marie Alexandrovna of Russia and Prince Alfred was delayed. Even Queen Victoria was convinced that nothing would happen, telling her daughter Vicky: "You know the Russian project is over—The young lady won't hear of marrying as she is very happy at home and I believe her parents don't wish to part with her at all and wish her to marry in Russia."[63] Besides, the queen heard that Marie Alexandrovna was too "indulged and spoilt,"[64] characteristics which Victoria did not hold in high esteem. Even Tsarina Marie sent Alfred a disheartening note, saying: "How should we venture to form hastily a resolution which will bind her for all her lifetime and must naturally separate her from us! . . . This is the plain truth, as I am bound to tell you, my dear Alfred; you may believe me, when I say, that I am very sorry to be obliged to send you this reply."[65]

However, by the time Marie Alexandrovna was twenty, family life in Russia was no longer blissful. Her father's acknowledged mistress bore him a son, which created a rift between Alexander II, his wife, and their children, with the sons "barely on speaking terms with their father."[66] With such a fractious family life in Russia, Marie Alexandrovna began warming to the thought of making a future with Prince Alfred abroad. In 1872, the Tsarina Marie wrote to her brother, Prince Alexander of Hesse, admitting as much: "Marie inclines much more to him [Alfred]—and especially his position—than to Stuttgart, Strelitz, or Schwerin; but if you could find me a *charming Prince* who would be prepared to stay in Russia, I should prefer him to any of them."[67] But no such prince charming ever came the Romanovs' way.

And so by the beginning of 1873, negotiations were again underway for the marriage. When Queen Victoria heard that the Tsarina Marie agreed to meet Alfred in Italy, the queen told Vicky: "Two things I have made a *sine qua non*— viz that there must be mutual attachment and if there is—then they must be married within this year or else it must finally be put an end to."[68]

MARIE ALEXANDROVNA

AND MIECHEN

*I*n April 1873, Alfred visited the tsarina and Marie Alexandrovna in Sorrento, Italy, to renew his appeal. This meeting was not the great success Alfred had hoped for, as his intended bride fell ill with fever. Even more disappointing, his official engagement did not materialize. Alfred's sister Alice, who accompanied him, reported to Queen Victoria about "poor Alfred. He is very patient and hopeful."[1] Princess Alice added a good word about the young woman who might become her sister-in-law, reassuring the queen that the grand duchess "was very dear and kind."[2] Nevertheless, in June, the on-again-off-again courtship was on again, owing to Alexander II's decision to abide by his daughter's wish to marry Alfred. He invited the prince to visit them in Hesse.

Meanwhile, "as a prelude to closer relations with the Romanovs, Bertie invited"[3] his brother-in-law the tsarevich, his wife, and his young son Nicky to visit the Princess of Wales and him. In London, Alexandra and Marie Feodorovna sparkled in society, delighting everyone by dressing alike. "The sisters set each other off," recorded Lady Antrim, "and became the centre of a glittering crowd wherever they went."[4] During their stay in London, Alfred visited Sasha and Minnie frequently, cultivating them as allies in his pursuit of Marie Alexandrovna. They warmed to Affie's cause and hoped for a positive outcome in the long-standing drama. Sasha and Minnie had by then been blessed with a family. Nicholas, named after Nixa, but called "Nicky," was born in 1868 at Tsarskoe Selo to great excitement, followed by Alexander (b. 1869 d. 1870) and George (b. 1871). Tsarevich Alexander described his first son's birth, recording that "God has sent us a son . . . What a joy it was—it is impossible to imagine. I rushed to embrace my darling wife, who at once grew merry and was awfully happy."[5] As his father's direct heir, Nicky's appearance in the world was a special event. Yet, Nicky's birth on the feast of Job would later give him cause to associate himself with the suffering biblical figure.

Nicky's parents, the petite, vivacious Minnie and the bearlike Sasha, were a compatible pair. Of Minnie, Vicky wrote to Queen Victoria: "She seems quite happy and contented with her fat, good-natured husband who seems far more attentive and kind to her than one would have thought. I was pleased to see that she has not become grand—and does not give herself airs as all the Russian Grand-Duchesses do. She has remained simple and unaffected; she has only been a short while in Russia since her marriage—but it does not seem as if the splendours of the Russian Court would dazzle her, and turn her head nor the servile flattery, which is the tone there, could spoil her. She seems so little occupied with herself."[6] As for Sasha, Vicky wrote, "I like him very much . . . He is awkward, shy and uncouth, from being so very big, but he is simple and unpretending not proud and capricious as most Russians are, and has something straightforward and good-natured about him which I like and I think you would also . . . I think they are very domestic and happy and attached to each other; he makes a very good husband."[7]

Tsarevich Alexander's love for his wife is reflected in his letters, which always began with the words, "My dear love Minny." When the couple had been married for nearly a dozen years, their love was still strong, with the tsarevich writing his wife: "I would to embrace you in my thoughts and with my whole heart wish us both our old, sweet, dear happiness; we do not need a new one, and preserve, O Lord, that happiness which we, thanks to his grace, have enjoyed for more than 11 years!"[8]

By this time, Marie Feodorovna's life had undergone tremendous changes. Unlike her early days in Copenhagen when she mended and made her own clothes, Minnie was now fabulously wealthy, with an army of servants at her disposal. Her main home in St. Petersburg, the Anichkov Palace, dominated one end of the capital's most fashionable thoroughfare, the Nevsky Prospekt. Built in the mid-eighteenth century, the Anichkov Palace was originally designed in the Baroque style, but in the nineteenth century it underwent changes. By the time Minnie made it her home, the palace façade had taken on its neoclassical style. Its huge rooms, exquisite parquet floors, marble rooms, profusion of decorative gilt, and lavish appointments made an impressive home. There, the imperial couple raised their children and entertained, with the sparkling Minnie charming her way into people's hearts.

Many recognized Minnie's gift of relating to people. Baroness Rahden wrote to a friend that "Pobedonostsev [the tsarevich's tutor] tells me that . . . the Czarevna is forming a real, warm sympathy for that country which is receiving her with so much enthusiasm."[9] Seven years later, Marie Feodorovna still had the magic touch. During an 1876 visit to Helsinki made by Sasha and Minnie, enthusiastic shouts of "Hurray!" were, above all, "directed to the wife of the heir apparent." The local papers reported the people's exuberance, noting that, "Dagmar's name is on everyone's lips."[10]

More than an asset and adornment, Minnie had become Sasha's soul mate and support, upon whom he relied for happiness, particularly because relations within the imperial family were increasingly strained. Tsar Alexander II continued his liaison with the Russian aristocrat Princess Ekaterina (Katya) Dolgorukaya, who was nearly thirty years his junior. The tsar did little to hide his infatuation with his mistress, who bore him four children in the 1870s.

Alexander II's infidelity destroyed his marriage, a failure made more tragic by the couple's devotion to one another early in their marriage. Tsarina Marie retreated even further from court life. Already far from robust, she developed tuberculosis and before long was an invalid. Only the Orthodox faith seemed to sustain Marie Alexandrovna's mother, by now reduced physically and emotionally. Though Alexander II continued to pay courtesy visits to his wife, the marriage had broken down irretrievably. Never really popular in Russia, the ill and wronged tsarina earned the pity of some, such as the British diplomat, Sir Horace Rumbold, who described her as a *sainte femme* [holy woman]."[11] Others referred to her as "the sad Tzarina."[12]

Tsar Alexander II's long-standing affair was not the only scandal. In 1874, Queen Olga's brother, Grand Duke Nicholas Constantinovich ("Nikola"), mortified the family when it was discovered that he stole diamonds from his mother's icon to cover debts related to his affair with an American courtesan, Fanny Lear. The infuriated tsar and his brother Constantine declared Nikola mad and banished him to the Urals. Nikola then married a commoner, which prompted Alexander II to strip him of his title and banish him farther, to Tashkent, in present-day Uzbekistan. There, Nikola continued to pursue affairs with various women.

Nikola's sordid life was not the end of the scandals plaguing the imperial family. Olga and Nikola's father, Grand Duke Constantine, had an illegitimate daughter, later sent to Greece to become a lady-in-waiting to her half-sister, Queen Olga. Constantine embroiled himself more when he embarked on an affair with a young ballerina, Anna Kuznetsova, who bore him five children. With very little in common other than their children and an appreciation for the arts, Constantine and Alexandra Iosofivona grew apart. Like Tsarina Marie, the grand duchess kept a dignified silence about her husband's affair. Thus, Queen Olga and Grand Duchess Marie Alexandrovna both witnessed the tragic breakdown of their respective parents' marriages.

With her parents' marriage in tatters, Grand Duchess Marie Alexandrovna's thoughts clung to a happy future as Prince Alfred's wife. In June 1873, her dearest wish occurred with the announcement of the official engagement. The joyful prospective bride wrote to an aunt: "I know that you will be glad to know how much I love Alfred, and how happy I am to belong to him. I feel that my love for him is growing daily; I have a feeling of peace and of inexpressible happiness, and a boundless impatience to be altogether his own."[13]

In October, the bride-to-be turned twenty, prompting her brother Serge to record his impressions: "It is sad to think that dear Marie will spend this day with us for the last time, while she is still unmarried! She is so cheerful, so happy that it is a pleasure to look at her. *She is so carefree!*"[14] And of their final Christmas gathering before the family unit was broken, Grand Duke Serge noted that "Marie received such lovely jewelry! It was so, so pleasant! . . . We were all so happy!"[15]

Back in England, Queen Victoria still harbored misgivings about the match, admitting that she was "greatly astonished at the great rapidity with which the matter has been settled and announced."[16] Victoria confided that she "felt quite bewildered" and had "thoughts and feelings [that] are rather mixed."[17] Disappointed by his mother's tepid response to news of his engagement, the Duke of Edinburgh wrote to Lord Granville: "I am deeply grieved that the Queen's telegram to me only expressed surprise so that the only person I cannot show the congratulations from, to the Grand Duchess & her parents, is my own mother. I feel it most painfully."[18]

In telling Vicky about the engagement, the queen wrote caustically: "The murder is out!"—meaning that her fears were realized. But the queen then added:

> I say nothing but that I pray God to bless both and grant that it may
> be the cause of harmony and peace in the family! It is, you know,
> not what I wished or like—religion—politics—views of Court—and
> nation, are all contrary to ours and I own I foresee many difficul-
> ties, but I shall receive Marie with all love and affection and if she
> can alter his hard, selfish, uncertain character she will be a blessing
> to us all, and I shall be the first to acknowledge it—but I personally

cannot rejoice yet . . . What I fear is the moral impropriety and the coarseness which exists [*sic*] in Russia. Her brother Alexis has got into a scrape with a maid of honour which if it happened here I think would upset the Throne . . . Then Vladimir is very bad and so is Sanny's son . . . All this is not what I like or can like. However I must make the best of it now.[19]

Four days later, the queen continued in her letters to Vicky, saying: "Affie and Marie seem very happy and I pray she may continue so, for she really seems a very sweet girl, who marries him entirely for his sake (!!)—I wonder—but never mind that."[20] This correspondence underscored Queen Victoria's high hopes that Marie Alexandrovna might temper Prince Alfred's mercurial moods.

Writing to her friend, the German Empress Augusta, Queen Victoria added words of hope concerning her future daughter-in-law, whom she still had not met: "On all sides I hear the highest praise of Marie, who knows all the difficulties and sacrifices of her future position, and yet does not shrink from them." The queen was also full of sympathy for the bride-to-be's mother and father, commenting that "her parents are very much upset over it, as well as at the idea of giving up their only daughter, which I admit would be impossible for me."[21]

Resigned as she was to the marriage, Queen Victoria nevertheless could not forego her imperious ways when it came to the wedding preparations—to the point of exasperating the Tsarevich Alexander and his brother-in-law, the Prince of Wales. Sasha wrote of his impressions to his mother weeks after the engagement became official: "How I am tired of the Queen . . . horror of horrors! Bertie was in despair and did not know what to do . . . Every day there is a new telegram from the Queen, and there are new suggestions in regards to the meeting with Marie . . . I am just afraid to come in her [the queen's] sight, she will bite my head off after everything!!!"[22] Queen Victoria was equally overbearing toward her own family. When Princess Alice agreed with Tsarina Marie's invitation that the queen travel to Cologne to meet the prospective bride, Queen Victoria fired off an angry tirade to her daughter: "You have *entirely* taken the Russian side, and I do *not* think, dear Child, that you should tell *me* who have been nearly 20 *years longer* on the throne than the Emperor of Russia and am the Doyenne of Sovereigns & who am a *Reigning* Sovereign which the Empress is *not,—what I ought to do*. I think I know *that*." Queen Victoria did not end there but added: "The proposal received . . . for me to be at *Cologne* . . . was one of the *coolest* things I ever heard . . . How could I who am not like any little Princess ready to run to the slightest call of the *mighty Russians*—have been *able* in 24 *hours* to be *ready* to travel! I *Own, every one* was shocked."[23]

If Queen Victoria had her qualms about the marriage, so too did Queen Sophie of the Netherlands. "With her habits and religion," wrote Sophie about Marie Alexandrovna to her English friend, the Countess of Derby, "it will be difficult to adapt entirely to the English ways."[24] Queen Sophie expressed this months before the betrothal became official. A month before the marriage took place, Queen Sophie was even more explicit in her concerns about the future Duchess of Edinburgh, stating outright: "I wonder how the only and spoilt daughter of the Czar will accept her secondary position."[25]

In the end, Queen Victoria did not attend the wedding in St. Petersburg and admitted that "I felt it very trying to be absent!"[26] For the British public, the event was too glamorous and too significant to ignore. Contemporary periodicals eagerly reported the wedding festivities and related stories. *The Graphic* described that some of the bride's extravagant trousseau was "laid out in the Salle Blanche of the Winter Palace," where admirers could marvel at silk, satin, velvets, Indian shawls, bonnets and gloves, along with the "50 magnificent dresses, not including ball-dresses, to say nothing of splendid furs and lace at 1,000 roubles a yard."[27] All in all, the trousseau cost roughly £40,000, amounting to an immense £2.7 million in today's currency.

The bride's dowry of £100,000 was truly staggering. It was one of the two most significant points of the twenty-nine articles covered in Marie Alexandrovna's marriage treaty, the other one being Article III, which declared that the future Duchess of Edinburgh was "not to be in any way hindered in the full, free, and unrestrained exercise of the religious profession of the Orthodox Church [though any children born to her would be raised as Protestants]." Article V dealt with money, and stipulated the following mind-boggling amounts be given to the bride:

> The Emperor assigns to his daughter the usual marriage portion
> granted to Emperors' daughters of 1,000,000 roubles (about 150,000*l.*),
> which is to remain in Russia, and bear interest at the rate of 5 per
> cent. per annum, which will be paid half-yearly to her Imperial High-
> ness, who is to have the separate and exclusive enjoyment of it, and
> is to be at liberty to dispose of it at will. The Emperor also, "as a mark
> of his peculiar affection, and which is not to be considered as a pre-
> cedent for the future," grants the Duchess an annual sum of 75,000

roubles (11,250*l.*), for life, which her Royal Highness is also at liberty to dispose of according to her own free will and pleasure. The Emperor also assigns to his daughter a special marriage portion of 1,000,000 roubles (150,000*l.*), to be dealt with in the same manner as the ordinary marriage portion. Her Royal Highness retains possession of her private capital, amounting when the Treaty was signed to 600,000 roubles (90,000*l.*).[28,29]

A month before Marie and Alfred's wedding Queen Victoria had already expressed her hope that her son would take the institution of marriage seriously, telling his eldest sister, Vicky: "Oh! May he really enter on this most eventful moment in his life with true earnestness and with the firm resolution to make that sweet young creature, who all praise and who really is so attached to him, happy!" Then the queen also added, "I feel so much for her and will be so ready and anxious to be a mother to her if only she shows me confidence."[30] Queen Victoria's anxiety over Alfred continued; days later she confessed to Vicky that she wrote to him saying that, "I hoped and prayed he felt the very solemn and serious step he was going to take, how I prayed he would make the dear, amiable, young girl—who is leaving all for him—happy and that she alone must have his heart and love—and old habits must be given up."[31]

Queen Victoria dispatched Arthur Stanley, the dean of Westminster, to Russia, to conduct the English service part of the wedding. His wife, Lady Augusta Stanley, accompanied him and recorded her impressions of the bridal couple, imperial family, and the wedding festivities. She was especially struck by the close relationship the grand duchess and her parents enjoyed. The Tsarina Marie, Lady Augusta noted sympathetically, was "comforted . . . by the sight of Her Daughter's happiness, but it [the wedding and her departure] is simply *agony* to Her—to them both." Alexander II "constantly has tears in his eyes." As for the bride, her "truth, frankness, simplicity, [and] straightforwardness" were "quite unusual." Moreover, Marie Alexandrovna was "practical, sensible and without caprice." In contrast to Queen Sophie, Lady Augusta saw signs that boded well for the future. "She thinks herself quite determined to be a thorough Englishwoman," wrote Lady Augusta of Marie Alexandrovna, "and her Mother's example in Russia has taught her how to adopt her Husband's country."[32]

The wedding between the twenty-year-old Grand Duchess Marie Alexandrovna and the twenty-nine-year-old Prince Alfred, Duke of Edinburgh, took place at St. Petersburg on January 11/23, 1874, and consisted of two religious ceremonies—Orthodox and Anglican. Outside, the weather was raw with cold, damp winds, but this did little to mute the festivities inside the palace. On her wedding day, the grand duchess looked "very pale but sweet, and earnest and calmly happy."[33] Marie Alexandrovna was dressed as was customary, in the regal finery of a Russian imperial bride, in a gown that trailed off in a silver train with an ermine-trimmed purple mantle. On her head she wore a glimmering crown as well as a fabulous tiara embedded with a magnificent pink diamond. Watching the bride's parents, Lady Augusta was struck by their emotional faces. Alexander II had, after all, confided that throughout these days "the only sufferers are the parents," for Marie "has been the joy in our lives, but it must be."[34] Another wedding guest, Lord Augustus Loftus, the British ambassador to Russia, came to the same conclusion as Lady Augusta Stanley regarding Alexander II. Loftus thought the emperor "looked pale and appeared deeply moved, no doubt feeling acutely his separation from his only daughter, to whom he was devotedly attached." The empress too "showed symptoms of suffering, both physical and mental."[35] Meanwhile, the Tsarevna Marie Feodorovna and her sister, the princess of Wales, offered a contrasting picture. The two were "beaming with beauty and delight at being together, and on [them] the eyes of all rested with admiration and pride."[36]

Recording his impressions of the day, Grand Duke Serge noted "all this time Marie was <u>very sweet</u> and surprisingly calm, she is such a sweetheart." That evening, Marie Alexandrovna devoted some time to her mother and Serge, discussing the special day. "It was very, very pleasant," recalled Serge, "I will never forget these hours!!!"[37] Alexander II was so overcome with emotion that at the end of the wedding ceremonies, the bride's father commented resignedly: "It is for her happiness, but the light of my life is gone."[38]

After a prolonged stay in Russia lasting several weeks, the newlyweds finally bid farewell to Russia and journeyed to England. The first meeting between Marie Alexandrovna and Queen Victoria took place on a bright, springlike day at Windsor. Queen Victoria met the pair on the platform at the train station and warmly embraced the Duchess of Edinburgh. In recording their first meeting, Queen Victoria confided to feeling "quite nervous and trembling, so long have I been in expectation." Nevertheless, the queen was pleased with this first encounter, noting how "dear Marie has a very friendly manner, a pleasant face, beautiful skin and fine bright eyes, and there is something very fresh and attractive about her. She speaks English wonderfully well."[39]

To commemorate her arrival in England, the Poet Laureate, Alfred, Lord Tennyson, composed a poem entitled "A Welcome to Her Royal Highness

Marie Alexandrovna, Duchess of Edinburgh" in which one of the lines stated: "Marie, shall thy name be blest."[40] Marie Alexandrovna's arrival in England captured the public's imagination. In honor of Queen Victoria's Romanov daughter-in-law, the British confectioners, Peek Freans, created the Marie biscuit in 1874. Still sold widely today, the Marie biscuit continues to be a favorite around the world.

The Duchess of Edinburgh's welcome to England reached its highlight days later on a bitterly cold and snowy day described as "almost Siberian,"[41] when enormous crowds cheered as she, Prince Alfred, and Queen Victoria rode in a carriage in London and made their way to Buckingham Palace. Some thirteen thousand police and soldiers lined the route, which was decorated with masses of colorful flowers, bunting, drapery, and greetings. So huge were the crowds that welcomed the Duchess of Edinburgh that according to a contemporary publication, the famed Trafalgar Square "was literally crammed with spectators—roads, pavements, housetops, windows, stands, and balconies, the stone balustrade around the quadrangle, the base of the Nelson column, and the celebrated lions, were alike crowded with men, women, and children, all gazing in eager expectation as the vanguard of the procession came in view, and sending up a tremendous shout of welcome when the Royal carriage itself appeared."[42]

The same year that Grand Duchess Marie Alexandrovna married Prince Alfred, the Russian imperial family received another addition when Grand Duke Vladimir married. As young men, Vladimir, Sasha, and their brother, Alexei, "developed into young ruffians, the stories of their exploits keeping St. Petersburg on its ear."[43] All three brothers, who were built like battleships, had a tendency to plumpness. These three had booming personalities to match their expanding girth.

Intelligent, artistic, and attuned to current political events, Grand Duke Vladimir, with his immense wealth, was as fine a catch as his own sister. In the 1870s, the question arose as to who would be Vladimir's wife. With her royal background as the Duchess Marie of Mecklenburg-Schwerin, the seventeen-year-old Miechen could see no reason why it could not be she. When the couple became acquainted in Berlin, Vladimir was immediately smitten with Miechen, whom he described as having "wonderfully expressive eyes; and what is important, she is extremely smart, talkative, and amiable."[44] At the time, however, Miechen was recently engaged to her stepmother's cousin, Prince George Schwarzburg. Queen Victoria's daughter Vicky, who was at Schwerin at the time that negotiations over Miechen and George's future were being held, was unimpressed with Schwarzburg, whom she acerbically described as "stupid" to her mother.[45] Regardless of what Vicky thought, it was Miechen's opinion that counted, and it did not take long for her to decide to terminate her engagement with Schwarzburg.

With Schwarzburg out of the way, the Duchess Marie of Mecklenburg-Schwerin became eligible again. At one point, Queen Victoria became anxious that her son Prince Arthur might fancy Miechen while visiting Germany in search of a bride. The queen accordingly wrote to the prince's governor to watch over Arthur. Miechen, warned the queen, was "said to be vy pretty but a gt. coquette—who has thrown over one Pce. she was engaged to—for one of the Russian Gd. Dukes, and who might vy possibly try to catch Pce. Arthur. She must not be thought of."[46] To Queen Victoria's relief, nothing came of this potential match.

Eventually, negotiations between the Schwerin and Russian courts over a possible marriage between Miechen and Vladimir began. When Vladimir first heard that Miechen was interested in marrying him, he supposedly exclaimed to his father: "poor girl!" When Alexander II asked Vladimir to elaborate on this odd reaction, the son dutifully obliged by stating: "What sort of a husband shall I make, Sire? I am drunk every night, and cure the headache of the next morning by getting drunk again!"[47] But by 1872, Vladimir was determined to change his life and had told his brother Alexei that "it was time to bid adieu to my single life . . . and to seriously think about marriage. It has always been my favorite dream to marry well, following my heart."[48]

Vladimir's reputation for carousing did not keep Miechen from wanting to marry him, so the negotiations proceeded. All was not smooth sailing, however. Miechen herself knew that there was one major stumbling block. She acknowledged it to Vladimir who told his brother, Alexei, "she was worried about one problem: the problem of religion."[49] Having been confirmed as a Lutheran, Miechen could not bring herself to change religions. The prospective bride's stubborn refusal to convert to the Orthodox faith, "a step that had been demanded of every Romanov bride for generations,"[50] was the one step Miechen could not take. So intransigent was the young duchess that she risked losing her chance at marrying into the Romanov dynasty. Vladimir's mother, Tsarina Marie, herself a Lutheran convert to Orthodoxy, was disappointed about Miechen's stance. The tsarina thought that [the Russian Orthodox] church was "quite good enough for any daughter-in-law of hers."[51] In writing about her hopes for Miechen to Vladimir, the tsarina told her son: "May she become Russian in body and in soul."[52] This contest over whether or not Miechen should retain her Lutheran religion as a Romanov bride was the first major challenge of her life. After three years of wrangling, the young duchess achieved a decisive victory when Tsar Alexander II acquiesced. Though he disagreed in principle with Miechen's refusal to become Orthodox, he nevertheless thought well of her resolute stand. The tsar's decision to let Vladimir's future wife keep her faith established a new precedent and did not go unnoticed. Princess Alice reported as much to Queen Victoria, writing to her: "My mother-in-law tells me that since Miechen has been allowed to retain her religion, this right will of course be conceded to all Princesses in the future."[53]

When Miechen arrived at the Russian frontier for her wedding, Grand Duke Vladimir met her and took her to Tsarskoe Selo where the imperial family awaited her. She stayed at Tsarskoe Selo for two weeks before she made her triumphant entry into the capital. The welcoming ceremonies in St. Petersburg for the Duchess Marie of Mecklenburg-Schwerin were planned to impress, and impress they did. An army maneuver, a naval review, and illuminations were but a few of the festivities. The procession in the streets of St. Petersburg to welcome Miechen proved to be the most brilliant of welcoming spectacles. Bright colored bunting decorated the buildings that lined the Nevsky Prospekt. Unending lines of cavalry wearing gleaming helmets topped by the imperial symbol of the double-headed eagle lined the famed street. The bride was preceded in an impressive procession by the tsar's personal guards: Georgians and Circassians from the Caucasus resplendent in their colorful uniforms and lances. Next the imperial carriages, gilded in gold and drawn by fine gold-colored horses rolled by. Loud cheers broke out when the carriage carrying Miechen and the Tsarina Marie came into view. The smiling bride graciously waved to her future countrymen, emanating a youthful spontaneity that was lacking in the austere-looking empress. Next to Miechen and the tsarina rode Vladimir and Alexander II on horseback. Behind them were other members of the imperial family and court, escorted by Cossacks and other troops. The imperial family made their way to the Kazan Cathedral, with its impressive double row of colonnades. Here, in the church that celebrated Russia's defeat of Napoleon, the fiercely Lutheran Miechen joined her new family to pay homage to the revered icon of Our Lady of Kazan and receive the blessing of the Orthodox Church. All in all, it was a spectacular welcome for the imperial family's latest foreign bride.

At the time, the bride was twenty, the groom twenty-seven. Miechen, with her regal bearing and piercing stare, was the latest in a long line of Germans who married into the Romanov dynasty. Princess Dagmar of Denmark had been the recent exception to this rule. Miechen nevertheless had her share of Russian blood since she was the great-great-granddaughter of the Emperor Paul I. Miechen made it a point to highlight her descent from Russia's Paul I by taking the patronymic "Pavlovna."

On her wedding day, Marie Pavlovna donned the same spectacular Romanov tiara with the pink diamond that Grand Duchess Marie Alexandrovna wore when she married the Duke of Edinburgh just seven months before. Like other Romanov weddings, Vladimir and Miechen's was a lavish affair, held at the chapel of the Winter Palace. In some respects, this latest imperial wedding lacked the grandeur that marked Marie Alexandrovna's wedding. For one thing, Miechen's wedding took place during what was deemed "the empty season" at St. Petersburg. Consequently, although numerous Russian officials hurried back to the capital for the wedding from their summer journeys, a number could not. This meant, according to the reporter for the *New York Times* who was at St. Petersburg, that "the throng of guests was not so brilliant" as it had been at Marie Alexandrovna's wedding.[54] Lord Augustus Loftus concurred, noting how:

> Every thing went off very well; although the marriage was not so resplendent as that of the Duke of Edinburgh. At this season of the year this town is a desert and therefore only those came who were obliged to come.
>
> The Protestant part of the ceremonial was nothing like as imposing as our Dean Stanley: and fell very dull after the magnificent Russian Service. Fortunately it was *short*.
>
> The young Grand Duchess is a superior person, not actually pretty but very intellectual and with a graceful and dignified deportment.
>
> At the Te Deum on the Emperor's Birthday she stood erect when the others were genuflecting and crossing themselves. It is a matter of surprise here for a Foreign Princess married to a Grand Duke to retain her own religion but it is a process to which they will have to accustom themselves or they will find no wives for the Russian Grand Dukes. I think it is a healthy practice and it will do them good.[55]

The significance of Miechen's victory in refusing to convert was not confined to British diplomatic circles. In an official dispatch to Hamilton Fish, the U.S. Secretary of State, Eugene Schuyler penned off the following regarding the imperial wedding: "The Grand Duchess will retain the Lutheran religion.

This is worthy of note, as hitherto the Russian laws have required the wives of all grand dukes to adopt the orthodox Russian faith."[56]

Nuptial festivities in the capital lasted for days. An American visitor, Thomas W. Knox, attended some of the events and described his time in St. Petersburg as a "memorable week." Days after the wedding huge crowds congregated on the streets of the capital to see the illuminated buildings and homes. "The principal avenues were so crowded with the rejoicing populace," noted Knox. At the Nevsky Prospekt, Knox added that, "I never saw a denser crowd."[57] On the outlying islands of the capital, "the opulent inhabitants had vied with one another to make their houses as bright as possible." At one nobleman's villa, the gardens were lit so brightly that it appeared as if "half the stars in the sky had fallen and found lodgment there."[58]

Among the nuptial festivities Miechen attended was a gala at the St. Petersburg Opera House. Knox thought Miechen looked "rather flushed and not altogether at ease" while Vladimir appeared "just a shade uneasier than the lady he has sworn to protect." The Tsarevna Marie Feodorovna, on the other hand, was "perfectly collected and evidently happy,"[59] The Romanovs seated in the imperial box in their bejeweled finery and uniforms were so impressive to behold that Knox was moved to admit: "I do not think I ever saw a more gorgeous picture than was presented in that box after the party was seated." As to Miechen, Knox concluded:

> Vladimir's bride is good-looking, solid, well-formed, with plump and finely rounded shoulders; a neck neither long nor short; regularly formed features, with the exception of the nose, which has a slight tendency to pugginess . . . With her evening toilet, a coronet of diamonds, and a string of diamonds around her neck in which each stone appears as large as a walnut, she is prettier than when I saw her two weeks before at the frontier, where she arrived in a plain traveling dress of brown hollands. Say what you will, a princess appears more like a princess when dressed like one than when attired like an English governess or a New York shop-girl. As I saw Vladimir's bride at the frontier I don't think many men would propose to her, but as she looks to-night at the opera she would not want for offers. Many a man would be willing to encumber himself with the princess just for the sake of the diamonds on her neck and head. The loot of that young woman, who probably never earned a six-

pence in her life, would set up a first-class hotel, including all the furniture and table-ware.

Nor was Knox impressed with Vladimir's looks, finding him in possession of a "fat and rather meaningless face." To Knox, Marie Feodorovna seemed resplendent with "no lack of diamonds . . . but sparkle as bright as they may, they can not surpass the beauty of her keen, clear, and flashing eyes. Less inclined to stoutness than the bride, she does not display such a plumpness of shoulder, and her neck rises more swan-like, and gives fuller play to her finely formed head, with its curly hair and Grecian outline of face. No wonder the emperor likes her, and no wonder the Russians like her. I like her, and I am neither emperor nor any other Russian, and never exchanged a thousand words with her in my life."[60]

5

ROSSIISKAIA IMPERIIA

er secrets . . . remain unconquerable and unsolved. Radiant beauty and stark, hideous ugliness, gladness and sorrow, greatness and tragedy and brutal, savage cruelty—over them all she draws a veil of impenetrable mystery, smiling with soft, inscrutable eyes," so wrote Meriel Buchanan, the daughter of Britain's ambassador to Russia from 1910 to 1924, in her book, *Recollections of Imperial Russia*.[1] The English journalist, Edward Dicey, who visited Russia in the mid-nineteenth century, described the country in a similar vein: "Russia is a country about which it is very hard to avoid exaggeration. You may dwell upon its splendour, you may dilate upon its squalor; and each description will be literally true. But yet neither the colours of the rainbow on the one hand, nor all the shades of sepia on the other, will suffice to paint Russia faithfully. You have to use both in turn, and avoid all neutral tints, if you wish to produce anything like an accurate portraiture of this extraordinary land."[2] These were lyrical yet accurate observations. It was almost as if to come to some appreciation, let alone understanding, of the vast mysterious empire, one needed to visit, even live in Russia among the Russians.

Acquiring an understanding of this vast domain as it was in the mid- to late nineteenth century involves delving into the political and cultural life of this contradictory, enigmatic land, which, since Peter the Great's reign, had taken on the appellation of *Rossiikaia Imperiia*—the Russian Empire. On the one hand, there was ostentatious, fantastic wealth and splendor as epitomized by the Romanovs, a grandeur unmatched by any court in Europe. In fact, under Tsar Alexander II, "the Russian imperial court had reached the apex of its splendor."[3] The nobility also delighted in fabulous displays of grandeur, as the Tsarevna

Marie Feodorovna had discovered at the Beloselsky Palace in St. Petersburg, an occasion that marked her first visit to a future subject's home. Edward Dicey described the Beloselsky Palace as a "grandiose" place; and "everywhere," he added, there was a "profusion of wealth and splendour . . . Silks and velvets, marble and ormolu, gilding and tapestry, plate and pictures, inlaid floorings and mosaic tables, were all literally scattered everywhere."[4]

But amidst all this splendor, there also existed widespread ignorance and wrenching poverty on the other end of the spectrum, in startling, disturbing contrast to the riches of a notable few. Miechen's niece, Crown Princess Cecilie, found this disparity the "sharpest" in St. Petersburg where "nowhere else could one see luxurious splendour so close to the most bitter poverty: men and women in rags among the carriages of the rich, and miserable wretches among elegant officers and uniformed officials. Here was the visible clash of Western civilisation with the primitive life of Asia."[5] St. Petersburg, as one account had it, "is a place at once grave and gay . . . where one passes from the lively to the severe . . . Here a life of the wildest dissipation or of the most sober seriousness may be led, according to inclination. Contrasts abound. You will behold the most refined luxury side by side with the blackest misery."[6]

This mixture of incredible wealth and grinding poverty was echoed in Russia's political and military spheres. The renowned nineteenth-century French diplomat Talleyrand alluded to this when he described the tsarist empire in a famous sentence: "Russia is never as strong as it looks, Russia is never as weak as it looks." Russia had emerged, after her astonishing defeat of Napoleon in the early nineteenth century, a much respected power. Russians were justifiably proud of becoming "the saviors of Europe and the conquerors of Napoleon in 1814."[7] And though Russia was defeated in the Crimean War four decades later, as the years passed, the lure of pursuing an expansionist policy became irresistible. Thus, as Alexander II's reign unfolded, Russia embarked on such a path, acquiring territory in Central Asia during its Turkmenistan campaigns. By 1860, Russia had wrestled from China the port of Vladivostok, which eventually grew into Russia's major city in the Far East.

Despite's Russia's successful forays into Asia, the Romanovs never took their eye off Europe, for there was a strong need to be recognized "as the rulers of a European great power and empire." This, in fact, was "central to the Romanovs' self-esteem and identity, not to mention the *raison d'être* and legitimacy of their regime."[8] A new united Germany, created after Prussia defeated the French in the Franco-Prussian War of 1870–1871, along with a powerful Great Britain, ensured that Russia's focus did not stray from Europe. But other forces were at play, among the most influential being the Pan-Slavism move-ment that dominated Russian thought in the nineteenth century. This move-ment, whose proponents advocated unity among Slavic peoples, was linked to the Slavophile movement that arose in Russia in the 1840s. The Slavophiles extolled the uniqueness and superiority of all things Russian and Slavic. An idealized view of Russia prior to Peter the Great's time was a central theme, as was a vigorous Orthodox faith. Not St. Petersburg, with its Western orienta-tion, but Moscow should rightly be Russia's capital, for as one chronicler de-scribed it: "St. Petersburg is Russian, but not Russia."[9] Moscow, on the other hand, was thoroughly Russian in character. Here throbbed the heart of the empire where the fortress complex of the tsars, the Kremlin, loomed large. To the Slavophiles, Moscow was unique in that the city was the "third Rome" af-ter the original Rome and the second Rome (Constantinople). The poet and art critic Sir Sacheverell Sitwell captured the essence of the Slavophiles' attach-ment to Moscow in comparison to St. Petersburg in his work *Valse des Fleurs*: "To the devout Russian, Moscow was the Third Rome, to which the Church and the true religion transferred after the fall of Byzantium. St. Petersburg, the artificial creation of one man, could never compete in this. Moscow was Russia: St. Petersburg, the bastard child of Russian adultery with the manners and fashions of the West."[10]

Opponents of the Slavophiles were found in the form of the Westernizers who expounded the virtues of the West. An early proponent and one who ig-nited the intellectual battle between the two opposing schools of thought was Peter Chaadaev. Chaadaev saw little in Russia's past to help propel herself to a greater future; nor did Chaadaev extol Russian Orthodoxy, but instead saw much to admire in Roman Catholicism. As a force that united Western Europe, Chaadaev viewed Catholicism as having enabled "the West to outstrip Russia in the eighteenth and early nineteenth centuries."[11] Chaadaev's provocative writ-ings earned him the enmity of Tsar Nicholas I, who ordered Chaadaev declared insane. To Chaadaev and others of his intellectual persuasion, Peter the Great showed the way toward modernizing and developing Russia, which meant an orientation that was pro–Western European. This admiration for Western Eu-ropean values such as constitutional government, along with a diminution or rejection of Slavic and Russian culture, inevitably meant a clash between the two intellectual movements. A gulf thus divided certain elements of Russia's educated class during the ensuing decades, pitting the Westerners against the Slavophiles.

The Duchess of Edinburgh's mother was among the Slavophile supporters found in the upper echelons of Russian society. A fervent adherent to Orthodoxy and all things Russian, she surrounded herself with avid Slavophiles, such as the poet Feodor Tiutchev, finding a favorite work in his poem "Rossia." The Tsarevich Alexander also came under the influence of Slavophile ideas and individuals, such as the journalist Ivan Aksakov. Another individual impacted by Slavophile views was Constantine Pobedonostsev. An archconservative, Pobedonostsev was clear in his views concerning numerous topics. A fierce critic of many things, he was especially harsh on the press, of whom he declared: "The Press is one of the falsest institutions of our time."[12] Pobedonostsev also wrote how "corruption and disintegration have destroyed the simple, organic relations of public and family life," which were replaced by "abstract principles" that were "false in themselves."[13] The intellectually intimidating Pobedonostsev appealed to Marie Feodorovna; and in him, she saw just the right person to guide her obstinate and sometimes crude giant of a husband. It did not take long for the tsarevna to welcome the ascetic Pobedonostsev into her circle. It mattered little to Marie Feodorovna that Pobedonostsev was "a forbidding figure, who puzzled and frightened many of her friends by his cool assumption of authority."[14] The steely-eyed, bespectacled, and balding professor of civil law with the intimidating stare and gaunt physique proved to be one of the most influential individuals in the lives of Marie Feodorovna's husband the tsarevich and their son Nicholas. Soon after Minnie's marriage, Pobedonostsev met several times a week with the Tsarevich Alexander and Tsarevna Marie Feodorovna. This close contact with the heir and his wife allowed Pobedonostsev to observe the future emperor and empress together. Initial impressions were not promising. In the late 1860s Pobedonostsev concluded that the couple lived "like children in a wilderness, like sheep."[15] At first Sasha was frustratingly slow in taking in what his tutor was teaching, but in the early days, Pobedonostsev despaired of Minnie too. In his eyes the tsarevna seemed unenthusiastic when it came to learning the language and Russian history, appearing at times to be "empty-headed and dull."[16] However, as time passed, the couple's tutor saw a marked improvement in his students. Of Minnie, Pobedonostsev concluded that "the future empress made considerable progress in understanding her new country and its history."[17]

By the late 1870s, Pobedonostsev had emerged as the future emperor's éminence grise. As befitting to men who were firm adherents to the Orthodox faith that had characterized Russia for a millennium, Pobedonostsev was also "immensely active in strengthening that faith [in the tsarevich] and in emphasizing the ties between Orthodoxy and Russian national history."[18] Orthodoxy and Russia were inseparable; in fact, so inseparable had both become that religion ended up playing "a far more central role in defining what was 'foreign' than language or 'ethnicity' . . . [and thus] the role of the Orthodox religion (*Pravoslavie*) for Russian identity cannot be overstated."[19] With the tsar and his people adhering strongly to one faith, "the term 'Holy Russia'—uniting land, people, church and ruler" came to be used in such a manner that it "express[ed] a deeply-felt national spirit."[20] A visitor to Russia captured the pervasive influence of Orthodoxy in the country: "Almost immediately one is struck by the deeply religious feeling of the Russians, and on all sides—whether in the streets of a town, or out in a little hamlet in the country—one sees the *ikon*, which is a sacred representation, generally of the Virgin and the Holy Child, whose garments are often adorned with precious stones and jewels, and before which a little lamp is hung." This was why "no one, rich or poor, passes the *ikon* without making either the sign of the cross, or a salutation, whether it is a man, woman, or child, and one quickly learns why the term 'Holy Russia,' is applied to that surprising land."[21]

The concept of Holy Russia greatly appealed to Tsarevich Alexander and his tutor. As a champion of Orthodoxy, Pobedonostsev perceived atheism—and by its extension secularism in the political sphere—as nothing short of a harbinger of chaos and devastation. Pobedonostsev had no sympathy for the rise in secular philosophy that was infecting Russia's intellectual elites. In his work, *Reflections of a Russian Statesman*, Pobedonostsev expounded on this: "Does it not follow then that the atheist State is no more than an impossible Utopia, infidelity being negation of the State? Religion and, above all, Christianity is the source of every right in political and civil life, and of all true culture. It is for this reason, then, that those political parties the most inimical to social order, parties radically denying the State, are the first to declare that religion is a personal thing in which private and individual interests alone are concerned."[22] For Pobedonostsev, Russia meant autocracy under the tsars. Not surprisingly, the future emperor's tutor was also sympathetic to Slavophile doctrines and counted among his Slavophilic friends and acquaintances Anna Tiutcheva, Grand Duchess Marie Alexandrovna's governess. Hence, the key Romanovs Tsarina Marie, Sasha, and Minnie, as well as the Slavophile Pobedonostsev, promoted a policy closely aligned with Russia's Slavic neighbors.

Since Russia was the largest and most powerful of the Slavic nations, Slavophiles naturally espoused the notion that striving for political and cultural unity under Russia's leadership and under the banner of Pan-Slavism was essential. After the mid-nineteenth century, Pan-Slavism took on a more belligerent turn, because a military element infused its spiritual and cultural dimensions. When Slavs in the Ottoman regions of Bulgaria and Bosnia and Herzegovina revolted against their Turkish masters, Russia and Serbia came to their aid, thus embarking on a conflict known as the Russo-Turkish War of 1877–1878. The war was part of the ongoing Eastern Crisis in opposition to the Ottoman Empire, that animated Great Power politics throughout the nineteenth century. Pan-Slavic sentiment forced Tsar Alexander II to go to war and in the process "began the final act of his often frustrated, increasingly tragic reign."[23]

Foreign affairs impinged upon the life of the imperial family. For one thing, the war had compelled the future Alexander III and Vladimir to fight at the front. Marie Feodorovna also grappled with foreign policy matters directly. Minnie was on the receiving end of requests for help from her father, King Christian IX of Denmark, who had hoped through her to gain some leverage in getting Russia to help return the contested territories of Schleswig-Holstein to the Danish fold. With this in mind, King Christian wrote to his daughter after Prussia decisively defeated France in the Franco-Prussian War: "My Own dear Minny . . . It is truly a blessing from God that we were able to keep out of it [the war]; and for this I must partly thank Tsar Alexander . . . If he would only strive with equal zeal to induce his uncle [King Frederick Wilhelm IV of Prussia] at last to give Danish Schleswig back to us . . . I don't want to burden the Emperor by writing to him about all this, but I beg my dear Minny with her warm Danish heart to speak to him on the subject and try to induce him to influence his uncle in favour of this restitution . . . Please talk to him as soon and as pressingly as possible on the subject." However much she dearly wanted to please her father and help resolve the festering Schleswig-Holstein issue, Minnie was not successful in persuading the tsar. She wrote, "that in reply to her pleading, her father-in-law said that . . . for the moment he could give no advice."[24]

Even the marriage of Prince Alfred and the Grand Duchess Marie Alexandrovna had been tinged with foreign policy implications. Queen Victoria contemplated what impact Marie Alexandrovna might have on Britain. When the Eastern Crisis of 1875–1878 erupted, which exposed Britain and Russia's competing interests, she told her son, Bertie: "I can't say <u>how</u> very unfortunate I think it that Affie shd have married <u>a Russian</u>." Then, in a knowing tone, Victoria added: "<u>I always said so</u>."[25] Marie Feodorovna had her own particular and not so charitable views about the queen and Victoria's behavior toward the Duke of Edinburgh, whom the queen viewed with some suspicion, owing to his marriage to a Russian. Writing to her father, King Christian IX, Minnie noted of Queen Victoria: "she is <u>completely mad, the poor woman;</u> in her last letter to Alfred . . . she called him a traitor because he received young Battenberg [Alexander of Hesse's son] aboard who was visiting his oldest brother, whom she probably considers a <u>Russian spy</u>. This is why she recalls her son, considers him unworthy any longer to command a frigate, and adds that he should not imagine that he will be appointed Admiral—that is out of the question now that he is <u>married</u> to a <u>Russian</u> wife!"[26] In the end, Marie Alexandrovna's marriage had no bearing on relations between Britain and Russia, just as Marie Feodorovna's Danish connection made no impact on Russian foreign policy when it came to Schleswig-Holstein. No longer did alliances between royal houses exert the impact they had previously, especially when it came to Great Power politics.

Besides wrestling with other powers over spheres of influence, Russia had to contend with domestic concerns. Within Russia, repression and censorship competed with a flowering of artistic talent to create a country that was a mass of contradictions. Russian literature was a combination of panegyric as well as critical works on the state and tsarist officialdom. Alexander Pushkin, who was a descendant of an Abyssinian prince in the service of Peter the Great, was one such artist. The flamboyant poet, who died fighting in a duel, is well known for one of the greatest works in Russian literature, *The Bronze Horseman*, a tribute to Peter the Great. Although Pushkin produced this paean to the famed tsar, Tsar Alexander I exiled the poet to the Caucasus for daring to mock autocracy in his 1817 poem, "Ode to Liberty." This tension that saw works daring to question authority juxtaposed against those celebrating the tsars was not confined to Pushkin. To a lesser extent, the composer Michael Glinka, who pioneered the Russian nationalist school, was also confronted with the power of autocracy, though in a more subtle manner than Pushkin. Nicholas I, concluding that the title of Glinka's 1836 opera should emphasize sacrifice in defense of the tsar, demanded that the artist change the title from *Ivan Susanin* to *A Life for the Tsar*. But it was in literature more than anywhere else in the arts, that the conflict raged between the need to extol the tsar and Russian values, and the increasing desire to criticize them. Nikolai Gogol, in his satirical 1842 play, *The Inspector General*, ridiculed the tsarist bureaucracy. Yet Nicholas I encouraged the play to be staged, viewing the play "as both amusing and salutary."[27] Gogol's *Dead Souls*, however, with its critique of serfdom, found far less official support.

As the nineteenth century progressed, more literary greats made an impact on the Russian Empire, including Ivan Turgenev. In his *Fathers and Sons*, published in 1862, Turgenev popularized the term "Nihilism," which, in its total rejection of authority as well as religious and moral values, advocates the destruction of social and political institutions. Nowhere was the Nihilist view more chilling than in Turgenev's *Fathers and Sons*, where the character Evgeny Bazarov proclaims that "a nihilist is a man who bows before no authority."[28] Besides popularizing the term Nihilism, Turgenev also cast doubt upon central aspects of Russian society, such as the sacrosanct trinity of principles that had been embraced by Russian tsars since the time of Nicholas I: Orthodoxy, Autocracy, and Nationality. Turgenev questioned serfdom as well, earning the author the opprobrium of officialdom.

As Nihilism took root in Russia in the mid-nineteenth century among the country's educated class, it took on the tone of a radical, destructive force, virulently shunning the optimistic tone that had characterized previous generations of the educated elite, the intelligentsia. Since many of the intelligentsia increasingly embraced Nihilism by the close of the 1800s, "one use of the term was beginning to crowd out all others: the view of the intelligentsia as the bearers of a radical or socialist outlook."[29] Animated by German idealism and French socialism, "put together, they generated the distinctive Russian variety of socialism."[30] Theorists such as Alexander Herzen and Michael Bakunin brought the debate over socialism into the fore. Herzen extolled what he saw as the virtues of the village commune, but he also feared violent revolution. The impassioned Bakunin, a founder of anarchism, on the other hand, best summed up his beliefs when he said, "the urge to destroy is a creative urge!"[31] As time passed, Bakunin's fiery tenets took increasing hold in Russia so that the disorder and violence advocated by the Nihilists permeated the very fabric of society, especially in St. Petersburg.

This challenge to authority invited repression, as evidenced in the experiences of Turgenev and another of Russia's literary greats, Feodor Dostoyevsky: "Exile as in the case of the young Turgenev," and "near death on the scaffold" in the case of Dostoyevsky.[32] Dostoyevsky was sentenced to death in 1849 for being a member of a progressively minded literary circle whose intellectual views tilted toward pro-liberal, pro-Western ideals. After enduring a mock execution, his sentence was commuted to hard labor and four years of exile in Siberia. Dostoyevsky's years of exile changed him. He became much more religious and, spurning his previous Western sympathies, turned to extolling Russian values, in particular Orthodoxy. His most well-known works include *The Brothers Karamazov* (1880) and *Crime and Punishment* (1866), the famed novel that was Dostoyevsky's "first major testing of nihilist ideas."[33] Rodion Raskolnikov, the protagonist in *Crime and Punishment*, felt that his Nihilistic philosophy excused him for murdering an elderly woman, so as to rid the world of what Raskolnikov deemed to be a parasitic creature. In the end, reflecting Dostoyevsky's belief in man's salvation through Christianity, Raskolnikov seeks the higher good in his quest for "repentance, redemption, and resurrection through suffering in Siberia."[34] But it would not be an easy journey, for "his new life had not been given him gratis, that he would have to purchase it dearly, pay for it by a great heroic deed that still lay in the future."[35]

The other great Russian author of the time, Count Leo Tolstoy, produced his masterpieces, *War and Peace* (1865–1869) and *Anna Karenina* (1873–1877), to critical acclaim. In *War and Peace*, the themes of rebirth, freedom to choose, and the laws of history intertwine in a sweeping, massive, and complex novel of Russia set during the Napoleonic war, while *Anna Karenina* grapples with the issues of morality and hypocrisy. Like Dostoyevsky, Tolstoy, whose life was no less tumultuous than his literary colleague's, came to embrace Christianity. But whereas Dostoyevsky's faith stayed within the bounds of conventional Orthodoxy, Tolstoy's strayed into "a kind of Christian Socialism which was based on nothing less than a sweeping condemnation of the whole social system."[36]

Dostoyevsky's belief in "the true Orthodox [faith] and popular Russia" along with his view that "this true Russia" was a "beacon to other nations"[37] squared nicely with Pobedonostsev's thinking as well as that of the empress, the tsarevich, and the tsarevna. The appeal of Dostoeyvsky's message—a strand that was also shared to some degree by Tolstoy—was centered on the "instinctive desire to seek after a better moral life and to find a right path in accordance with God's laws."[38] As such, in his capacity as tutor to the future emperor and empress, Pobedonostsev promoted Dostoyevsky and his works to the imperial family. Shortly before the author's death, Marie Feodorovna listened to a reading of *The Brothers Karamazov* and, along with her husband, had an audience with Dostoyevsky.

In the last decades of his life, Tolstoy scorned the autocracy that marked the Romanov dynasty and in the process became "Pobedonostsev's arch intellectual rival and moral nemesis."[39] At Dostoyevsky's death in 1881, Pobedonostsev "arranged a state funeral to honor his remains." But at Tolstoy's death in 1910, Pobedonostsev (who had been Procurator of the Holy Synod or lay head of the Orthodox Church) had the last word, although he had died three years earlier. The excommunication imposed by the procurator on the author still held sway. And so, "from beyond the grave, Pobedonostsev thus denied one of Russia's greatest writers the comfort of all Church rites."[40] Here, strains between publicly expressed tenets of the permissible and unacceptable clashed—this

time played out in the lives of two contemporary giants of literature who dominated the Russian landscape in the late nineteenth century.

Thanks to the celebrated works by the empire's literary greats, "literature as
the bearer of Russian national identity"[41] came into being. And what was more,
Russian literature, as embodied by the "classic Russian novel, whose great age
was amazingly brief—a mere quarter century," took hold "all within the reign
of Alexander II."[42] The artistic life that blossomed in the Russian Empire during the turbulent nineteenth century was of such caliber that Russia's cultural
impact on the world continues to be felt today, for "in the nineteenth century,
this empire's ruling elites spawned a musical and literary high culture which
made an immense contribution to global civilisation."[43]

As Russia's competing intellectual movements—both artistic and political—
took stronger root, they began wreaking havoc on the empire's fragile stability.
This meant that Alexander II's reign, which had in its first decade offered much
hope through his Great Reforms, moved into a more reactionary phase by the
1870s. No longer did the emperor have the appetite for pursuing vigorous reforms in the name of progress. Above all, he consistently refused to "crown his
reforms with a constitution"[44] and so Russia "remained in essence as before
an autocratic monarchy with no place for either a constitution or parliament."[45]
In part, this put the tsarist regime on a collision course with its opponents, the
"disenchanted intelligentsia, socialists, populists and others all aiming to rid
Russia of the Tsar."[46] And as time passed, some opponents became increasingly radicalized, particularly after restrictions were imposed on universities
where student radicals were agitating and promoting their socialist agendas.

By the 1860s and 1870s, the revolutionary movement that arose in Russia had
become thoroughly socialist. It was also "during these decades that Russian
socialism acquired both a definite doctrine and a fighting organization." In the
revolutionaries' eyes, the Russian peasant living in a village commune was "a
socialist by instinct and tradition, whose mission it was to save Russia from
capitalism and to bring her directly into the communist era." Moreover, there was,
for "the majority of Russian socialists of the period," an obvious "complete distrust of parliamentary democracy, which in their eyes had no value whatsoever
even as an intermediary stage of development." Their goal for Russia was "immediate social revolution and not a gradual approach to socialism by the long
way of evolution."[47] Many of these revolutionaries fanned out into the countryside, convinced that the peasants would embrace their doctrines immediately
and unquestioningly.

However, the peasants were dismissive of the revolutionaries' "over-bearing manners and city ways." They "did not understand their literature and were bored to death by their mysterious talk of Karl Marx."[48] Many peasants turned in these agitators to the authorities, resulting in several thousand being arrested. Having failed to convert the masses through propaganda, the revolutionaries sought new methods to bring drastic change to Russia and embraced terror as their new weapon. Those who had clamored for a peasant revolution in order to create a socialist utopia now became radical extremists. Their message was encapsulated in the following tract:

> Too long and with too little success we have worked for the goal of social revolution from below, for a people's uprising to achieve peasant commune socialism . . . Let us change our goal to political revolution, to the overthrow of the tsarist regime. Concentrate revolutionary activity in St. Petersburg . . . use organized terror against tsarist officials, including the Tsar himself. Terror will weaken the government by eliminating key figures . . . demonstrate to "the people" that the autocracy is vulnerable.[49]

The most militant of these emerging radicals created an organization called *Narodnaya Volya*, meaning "the People's Will." "The emergence of the People's Will marked a watershed in the history of the Russian Revolution. For one, it established violence as a legitimate instrument of politics: enlightenment and persuasion were rejected as futile and even counterproductive. But even more important was the arrogation by the revolutionary intelligentsia of the right to decide what was good for the people: the name People's Will was a deceptive misnomer, since the 'people' not only did not authorize an organization of thirty intellectuals to act on their behalf but had made it unmistakably clear that they would have no truck with anti-tsarist ideology. When the terrorists defined as one of the tasks 'lifting the revolutionary spirit of the people,' they were well aware that the real people, those tilling the fields and working in the factories, had no revolutionary spirit to lift. This attitude had decisive implications for the future. Henceforth all Russian revolutionaries, whether favoring terrorism or opposed to it, whether belonging to the Socialist-Revolutionary or Social-Democratic Party, assumed the authority to speak in the name of the 'people'—an abstraction without equivalent in the real world."[50]

Having embraced political terror through violence, assassination became the tool of the People's Will; and their main target was none other than Tsar Alexander II. Little wonder then that when Elizabeth Narishkin-Kurakin, a lady-in-waiting, observed the tsar at this time, she noticed a drastic change in Alexander II, noting how: "He seemed restless and irritated, his eyes had lost their customary kind expression and he looked sullen and suspicious."[51]

With each passing year, opposition to the tsar increased and was manifested in attempts on his life. The first assassination attempt on Alexander II occurred in 1866 when Dmitri Karakozov tried to gun down the tsar. Thanks to a bystander, Karakozov's revolver was deflected and the tsar was saved. When the news came out that Alexander II survived the attempt on his life, excitement swept the imperial capital. The tsarevich wrote that "all of St. Petersburg came spilling out onto the street. Traffic, agitation was unimaginable . . . Groups of people, singing 'God Save the Tsar' . . . and thunderous 'Hurrahs.' " Another contemporary wrote that "the capital is mad with joy."[52] As the 1870s unfolded, the dangers to Alexander II's life increased in intensity.

Life for the imperial family had obviously taken on an anxious hue with constant worries about the tsar's safety. For Minnie and Miechen, their consolation amidst the turmoil lay in their immediate families. Both women enjoyed happy marriages. Sasha and Vladimir, having gone through their share of amorous escapades in their youth, had finally settled down and, unlike their father who was blatantly unfaithful, both brothers reveled in their marital bliss. The birth of children had also brought Minnie and Miechen much joy. Marie Feodorovna's family was augmented by the arrival of more children, Grand Duchess Xenia (b. 1875) and Grand Duke Michael (b. 1878), while Miechen became the mother of Grand Dukes Alexander (1875–1877), Kyril (b. 1876), Boris (b. 1877), Andrei (b. 1879), and Grand Duchess Elena (b. 1882).

Life for the Russian imperial family continued to revolve around official events, a number of which took place at the massive Winter Palace. In size alone, few buildings in the world could compete with the place. The famed "headquarters" as it were, of the Romanovs, the Winter Palace was "built to reflect autocracy," with its "walls and pillars of malachite, multi-veined marble, porphyry and rare granite . . . ambassadors and foreign visitor described the palace functions and confessed themselves beggared of words to do full justice to their magnificence."[53] Entertainments continued to be lavish affairs. The *Bal des Palmiers* offered a glimpse of the extent to which court entertainments could dazzle. While the temperature outside dipped to a frigid five degrees below zero Fahrenheit, inside the palace, a winter garden was created with tables to sit fifteen built around large palm trees that had been especially grown and trucked in from the imperial conservatories at Tsarskoe Selo. The palm trees reputedly underwent such a shock from all the decorating done on them that one chronicler of the court was told that the trees required "three years to recover from the exposure they undergo in one night's decoration."[54] "The effect of the immense room as one enters it," one observer wrote, "is that of a tropical grove in some gorgeous fairy scene."[55] These "splendid fêtes" were so sumptuous that one observer described the court's magnificence as nothing short of "barbaric."[56] Yet for all the lavishness that marked court life, by 1879 the entertainments had also been clouded by the heavy atmosphere of gloom that pervaded St. Petersburg. "Social life continued to move in its well-worn grooves. But there was no zest in it" recalled Elizabeth Narishkin-Kurakin.[57]

Something sinister was clearly brewing in Russia. Nihilists and other such radicals were set to unleash a new wave of terror. By the late 1870s, "the Czarist government was bewildered as to how to control the tidal wave. When the sluice-gates were open the water poured through; when they were shut it flooded over the top."[58] The empire was nothing less than a "vast, schizophrenic country"[59] that was slowly descending into lawlessness. In recording her impressions of Russia, Vicky, the crown princess of Prussia, captured the country's prevailing sentiment: "Altogether I am very glad I went to Russia, though profoundly thankful I am not a Russian and need not spend my days there" wrote Vicky to her mother, Queen Victoria, "for there is much much that is very sad—and over the whole of Russia there seems to me to hang a dull, heavy, silent melancholy very depressing to the spirits!"[60]

6

A RUSSIAN IN QUEEN VICTORIA'S COURT

As Russia continued its quest to be a dominant power and grappled with its internal problems, across the Baltic and North seas lay Marie Alexandrovna's new home, Great Britain, another colossus on the world stage. Throughout the nineteenth century these two giants wielded their commanding presence. Fundamental differences distinguished these competing entities. The Russian Empire by the 1890s had reached impressive proportions, consisting of 8.6 million contiguous square miles with a population of over 130 million. Britain's empire, however, was much more extensive; its impact upon the world much more pervasive. Today, Britain's former influence is evident throughout the world where the English language is still widely spoken in its former colonies. Even though Russia ruled millions, its language did not extend past its own borders. Moreover, Britain had advantages over Russia on many fronts. Freedom prevailed in Britain thanks to a parliamentary democracy; Russia stagnated under an autocracy. Britain's Industrial Revolution propelled the nation to great wealth, whereas Russia still had plenty of catching up to do. Much of Britain's population was literate, not so in Russia.

Presiding over Great Britain and the British Empire was the indomitable Queen Victoria. Victoria—*regina et imperatrix*—queen and empress[1]—ascended the throne in 1837 as an eighteen-year-old. As her reign unfolded, her kingdom and empire flourished. Queen Victoria rightly described herself as the doyenne of sovereigns; her long reign through the nineteenth century established an impressive reputation, unmatched by any monarch or statesman. She could justifiably take pride in a successful reign that saw the British Empire unfold in all its glory. By the time the Grand Duchess Marie Alexandrovna joined the British royal family in 1874, the queen was a potent symbol of power, embodying all that was grand and good about empire. Respect for Victoria was so great that a glorified aura seemed to surround her. It was once said of her: "Whenever the Queen withdrew, the effect was 'like an ascension to heaven,' those left behind stared after her, transfigured."[2]

Commanding as she was, Queen Victoria's majesty was tempered by warmth and compassion. "What a wonderful woman she was!" extolled the Earl of Warwick and Brooke. "From her," recalled the earl, "I never had aught but kindness and sympathy, and yet it was impossible to carry on a conversation with her and remain quite at ease, for her calm, clear gaze seemed to read your innermost thoughts. History has yet to do full justice to her varied gifts and strange, commanding nature."[3] The British diplomat Lord Howard of Penrith wrote of the impact Queen Victoria made on him upon being presented to her. "She made an ineffaceable impression on my mind," recalled Howard. "There was an extraordinary dignity and even grace" to the queen.[4] William Boyd Carpenter, Bishop of Ripon, who knew the queen well, had similar observations. Boyd Carpenter was struck by Victoria's "queenly bearing" and noted that "she knew how to sustain, with fitting reserve, the character of Empress-Queen."[5] This was all the more impressive considering that the gray-haired queen was diminutive, standing less than five feet tall, with a wide girth that grew ever wider as she aged.

Even among her august family, Queen Victoria elicited much respect and even fear both as monarch and family matriarch. The German chancellor and architect of a unified Germany, Otto von Bismarck, commented on this: "In family matters she is not used to contradiction."[6] One of Queen Victoria's granddaughters wrote that the queen's children were "in great awe" of their mother and "her veto made them tremble."[7] Hermann Eckardstein, the German ambassador to London in the late Victorian and early Edwardian eras, recalled that "her children had the highest veneration for her."[8]

One observer, Lord Frederic Hamilton, who had been impressed by the unmistakable aura that marked Tsar Alexander II of Russia as a sovereign found the same quality in Queen Victoria. Of the queen, Hamilton wrote that she "had the most inimitable dignity, and no one could have mistaken her for anything but a Queen."[9] Much of this admiration for the queen stemmed not so much from her innate dignity and ability to project an air of majesty, but from her standing as a much admired monarch and arbiter of values, for the queen greatly extolled morality and integrity. By carefully promoting moral probity through her own example and through "an iron will, unshakable in-

tegrity, and a character so strong," the queen managed to "change the sensibil-
ity and moral consciousness" not only of Great Britain but "of the entire
world."[10] By the late nineteenth century, Queen Victoria had become legendary, lending her name to an era.

As the mother of nine children, Queen Victoria took a keen interest in her
family. Her eldest daughter, Vicky, the most intelligent and precocious of the
siblings, had married, at the age of seventeen, Prince Frederick Wilhelm of
Prussia. Their eldest son was destined to rule Germany as the infamous Kaiser
Wilhelm II. The queen's next child and heir, Albert Edward, or "Bertie," the
Prince of Wales, who was married to Marie Feodorovna's sister Alexandra,
continued to exasperate the queen with his sybaritic lifestyle. But as time passed,
the relationship between mother and son gradually improved. Alice came next
in order, followed by Alfred, Helena, Louise, Arthur, Leopold, and Beatrice.
Queen Victoria had been fortunate in that all her children lived into adulthood during an era when infant mortality still plagued many families, including royalty. Nevertheless, all was not perfect with her children. Prince Leopold,
the son who resembled his father in intelligence, was plagued by the bleeding
disease, hemophilia. Queen Victoria was a carrier of the hemophilia gene and
her descendants would introduce the dreaded disease into some of Europe's
royal houses with devastating consequences. In time, Marie Feodorovna would
find that this deadly gene of the queen would directly affect her family and have
a terrible impact on Russian history.

As Queen Victoria's reign unfolded, imperial rivalries held sway over governments and monarchs alike. This was certainly the case when it came to relations between Britain and Russia. As rivals for power and influence, particularly
in Central Asia, the two empires inevitably clashed. With keen interest, Queen
Victoria monitored her realm's fortunes relative to relations with Russia. The
Crimean War in the mid-nineteenth century was one major clash between the
two nations that preoccupied her. The Russo-Turkish War of 1877–1878 was
another conflict that riled the queen because a Russian defeat of the Turks
would likely have led to Russian domination of the Bosporus Straits. Control
of the straits and possibly the Suez Canal represented a direct threat to Britain's interests in India. To Vicky, the queen wrote, "we should take care to
prevent Constantinople becoming their [Russia's] prey." Tsarina Marie wrote
to her brother complaining that England was "certainly hostile to us. That
makes the Tsar very anxious, on Marie's account too."[11] Word got around to
the Romanovs that Queen Victoria was furious with Russia, eliciting indignation in turn from the tsarina, who complained caustically: "The insulting things

that the Queen says in her letters to Alfred about the Tsar and the Russian people are worthy of a fish-wife. Added to this is her grief that 'our dear Marie' should belong to a nation from whose vocabulary the words truth, justice, and humanity are lacking. Silly old fool."[12] Queen Victoria never took imperial rivalry between Britain and Russia lightly. A defiant statement made by the queen in 1877 said it all: "England will *never* stand (not to speak of her Sovereign) to become *subservient* to Russia, for she would then *fall down* from her high position and become a *second-rate* Power!!"[13]

Within Queen Victoria's family, friction inevitably arose during this time when it came to the Edinburghs. The queen complained to Vicky that, "Affie is I am afraid quite Russian and I have had to warn him strongly."[14] Months later, Queen Victoria again vented her frustration: "Affie, I am grieved to say, has become most imprudent in his language and I only hope he does not make mischief. It is very awkward with this Russian relationship just now. This is what I always feared and dreaded."[15] As for Alfred's wife, the queen reported to Vicky that: "Poor Marie A. is totally deceived . . . she hears no news but a great victory in Asia—which happens to be a great defeat."[16] A few weeks later, Queen Victoria complained about her Russian daughter-in-law to Vicky, saying: "That Marie A. should be so happy and blooming with thousands and thousands of her poor countrymen sacrificed and cruelly neglected (only she don't [*sic*] know that) is too, too extraordinary." The queen added of the Romanovs: "I think they are brought up with a notion of human beings very different to ours so that in her (much as I love her) there is not much depth of feeling though great good feeling and sense of duty . . . I can't understand it and it grieves me. She has never drunk the cup of sorrow or been mixed up with it as we have been."[17]

When she first met her new daughter-in-law, Queen Victoria had very little idea of how Russian in outlook Marie Alexandrovna would remain. That could only be ascertained with the passage of time. Instead, the queen had naturally taken a careful look at the young woman's physical appearance and relayed her impressions in detail to Vicky. There had been some positive comments but also blunt ones: "The chin is so short and runs into the throat and the neck and waist are too long for the dear little child's face though the bust is very pretty and then she holds herself badly and walks badly." Then hinting that the new Duchess of Edinburgh seemed unafraid of her, Queen Victoria added that she was "quite at ease with me and we get on very well—and she is very sensible . . . Marie is very civil which is a great thing. She is not a bit afraid of Affie and I hope will have the very best influence upon him."[18] When Queen

Victoria had first taken stock of her Russian daughter-in-law, the queen penned her observation to Vicky: "People do not think Marie pretty, but frank and pleasant. Her little short, abrupt way gives a little appearance of haughtiness—but I don't think it is really that. Only the Russian family do look upon themselves as greatly above others, and therefore they have a little that manner. Still she speaks very kindly to all high or low if one names people to her. She is very anxious to devote herself to some charitable and other establishments and fond of serious books."[19]

Marie Alexandrovna had initially made a good impression on people. The British diplomat Lord Augustus Loftus commented that "the Duchess of Edinburgh is charming—simple in her manner—amiable—and with a serious and inquisitive mind. I am glad that H.I.H. is appreciated."[20] The "H.I.H." here refers to "Her Imperial Highness," which was higher in rank than "Royal Highness," the Duchess of Edinburgh's new ranking upon marrying Prince Alfred. As it turned out, Marie Alexandrovna was finding it difficult to forget that she was first and foremost a Romanov. The Duchess of Edinburgh's standing within the British royal family proved to be an area where her pride in being a Romanov became glaringly evident. Not long after her arrival in England the question of Marie Alexandrovna's rank and precedence came up for discussion. Her father wrote to Queen Victoria broaching the subject, insisting that his daughter's title of "imperial highness" should be used before the "royal highness." It made sense to Alexander II that this use of the titles stand in England "as in all civilized countries."[21] The queen, however, sharply commented that "royal" had to come first before "imperial" if Marie Alexandrovna wanted to use "imperial" as well. This admonition harked back to Queen Victoria's distaste for the Russians and their *Asiatic ideas of their Rank,* as reflected during Alfred and Marie Alexandrovna's courtship when the tsarina wanted the queen to meet her with very little advance notice.[22] Queen Sophie of the Netherlands wondered about this tussle over titles, opining that, "I cannot well understand why the Queen does not allow her daughter-in-law to be Imperial Highness."[23]

When it came to rankings and precedence within the royal family, the Duchess of Edinburgh was of the same mind as her father. Though Tsar Alexander conceded that the Princess of Wales, as wife of the heir, should be senior in rank to Marie Alexandrovna, his daughter should, as an emperor's child, outrank Queen Victoria's daughters and daughters-in-law. The queen thought otherwise and refused to concede. Showing her irritation at what she considered an affront, the Duchess of Edinburgh "exacted her own subtle revenge"[24] by appearing among her new family in a blaze of spectacular jewelry as befitting a Romanov grand duchess. The Duchess of Edinburgh made her point, eliciting from the queen, her mother-in-law, no less, a shrug of the shoulders, appearing "like a bird whose plumage has been ruffled, her mouth drawn down at the corners in an expression which those who knew her had learned to dread."[25]

The tussle over Marie Alexandrovna's precedence at court did not prevent Queen Victoria from ensuring that Tsar Alexander II's visit to England in May 1874 was a success. Queen Victoria was content to see father and child reunited. "They seem to be so happy to be together,"[26] wrote a satisfied Victoria. During one dinner, Queen Victoria admired the Duchess of Edinburgh's "beautiful"[27] sapphires, a gift from the Romanovs. The dinner was held in Windsor Castle's St. George's Hall with the band of the Coldstream Guards playing music for the guests. One of the most moving moments came when Tsar Alexander II told the queen, speaking, as she noted, "with tears in his eyes, so as to be almost unable to speak, of Marie, saying: *'Je vous remercie encore une fois pour toutes vos bontés pour ma fille; je vous la recommande.'* [I thank you once again for all your kindness towards my daughter. I commend her to you]." Of the touching moment, Queen Victoria recorded in her journal that, "I put my hand out across the Emperor and took Marie's, she herself being nearly upset."[28]

At London's Guildhall, where Alexander II was a guest of honor at a lavish banquet given by the mayor, more evidence of the father's attachment to his daughter again surfaced. The "tall, handsome, commanding" tsar was not merely the great "potentate of the North"[29] that day for the "love of father and child, is patent to all," according to Anne Beale, who witnessed the scene. Because of the obviously strong father-daughter bond, Beale noted that "we English can appreciate the tenderness that has brought a Czar of Russia to our country, to see the daughter he so lately gave, in pledge and friendship and peace, to our care and affection."[30] In his speech at the Guildhall, Alexander II moved his audience further when his voice faltered on the words, "my beloved daughter." "Those three tender words," concluded Beale, "reach[ed] every heart in the vast assembly."[31]

In the early months of her marriage, Marie Alexandrovna made every effort to adapt to her new country. In May 1874, one English periodical reported that a reputable Russian newspaper, the *Grashdanin*, "noted for its good Court intelligence," told readers that the Duchess of Edinburgh had written to her friends and relations, describing "her life in England as one of perfect happiness." The paper noted how "she speaks with great gratitude of the cordial and friendly reception she has met with from all with whom she has come into contact—the Queen, the Royal family, the Court, and the people at large."[32] The Duchess of Edinburgh's life in England centered mainly upon being a working member of the British royal family, which entailed attending various ceremonial functions and gracing events with her presence. As Marie Alexandrovna settled into a regular routine in England, these gatherings allowed some of her new countrymen to appraise her. One such individual was Benjamin Disraeli, the British prime minister. During a banquet at Marlborough House, the Prince of Wales's home, Disraeli found the Duchess of Edinburgh to have been "lively as a bird." Disraeli noted that "she does not like our habit in England of all standing after dinner . . . In Russia the Court all sit. She asked me who a certain person was, talking to a lady. I replied, 'That is my rival.' 'What a strange state society is in here,' she said. 'Wherever I go there is a *double*. Two Prime Ministers, two Secretaries of State, two Lord Chamberlains, and two Lord Chancellors.' "[33] In another instance, Disraeli described Marie Alexandrovna as breaking through "all the etiquette of courtly conversation. Even the Queen joined in her vivacity, and evidently is much influenced by her."[34]

When the newly married Duchess of Edinburgh moved to London, she took up residence at Clarence House, not far from Buckingham Palace. Originally built for the Duke of Clarence who became King William IV, Clarence House was also at one time the home of Queen Victoria's mother. A few years after her death, her grandson, the Duke of Edinburgh, took possession of the house. Feeling that the place was "unworthy"[35] of his Romanov bride, Prince Alfred made various improvements and enlarged the house. An ornate Orthodox chapel proved to be the most spectacular addition, created in deference to the Duchess of Edinburgh's desire to practice her faith. Marie Alexandrovna cherished the Orthodox faith that was "so fundamentally part of her inner being"[36] and "she clung to her Church with all her soul."[37] During Orthodox services in her chapel, the Duchess of Edinburgh's face would exhibit an "ardent expression of belief" that was so moving it was sometimes "difficult to describe."[38] Decorated with beautiful icons and intricate carvings, the Orthodox chapel in Clarence House was one of the clearest manifestations that Marie Alexandrovna was determined not to shed her Russian heritage. The British diplomat Sir Horace Rumbold's description of the Duchess of Edinburgh as the "daughter of Russia,"[39] characterized Tsar Alexander II's daughter precisely. In no time the young duchess began to find life in England not to her tastes.

As Marie Alexandrovna's impressions of England began to sour, so too did some people's views of the Duchess of Edinburgh. This stemmed largely from perceptions that Marie Alexandrovna was unable to adapt to England and to English ways. Queen Sophie of the Netherlands anticipated this. In a letter to a friend, the queen noted how she could see parallels between her own sister-in-law Queen Olga of Württemberg, who was a Russian grand duchess, and the Duchess of Edinburgh. Queen Sophie wrote how Olga of Württemberg "could <u>not</u> understand everyone and everything <u>not</u> submitting to her sway. It was not assumed, it was a feeling perfectly serious and genuine, her <u>birthright</u>. Should the Duchess of Edinburgh have the same feeling, how will she be able to exist in England near the Queen and near the Princess of Wales, sur-rounded by people who are no slaves!"[40] Before the end of 1874, Queen Sophie heard stories about the duchess, remarking that "in that family [Queen Victoria's] it is whispered the Duchess of Edinburgh has nostalgia of home, which does not quite coincide with the bright spirits and gayety [*sic*] others observe in her. Her fate is one that interests me, I wonder how her caracter [*sic*] and her intelligence are to develop themselves."[41]

Like most members of the upper echelons of society, Marie Alexandrovna became the chatelaine of a country home. In the Duchess of Edinburgh's case this home was the picturesque Eastwell Park situated near Ashford in Kent, the county known as the "garden of England." The property sat on over two thou-sand acres in one of the loveliest parts of the country. Here, amidst the verdant countryside with its undulating terrain, deer and wide-horned cattle leisurely grazed beneath impressively large mature trees. The Edinburghs entertained friends and family at Eastwell Park, usually in the fall when the scent of dead leaves heralded the arrival of cooler weather. Marie Alexandrovna made no secret of the fact that she preferred life at Eastwell to London. In a letter to her old governess, Countess Tolstoy, written in 1879, the duchess described the countryside around Eastwell as being "very pretty, everything is so green, so fresh." This, confessed the duchess, "reconciles me a little to the English coun-tryside."[42]

One visitor to Eastwell, the Earl of Warwick and Brooke, thought "the Duke and Duchess were the kindliest people, and unaffectedly simple in their lives."[43] "It was not only for the shooting that I remember Eastwell Park," re-called the earl. As it turned out, the wealthy aristocrat was struck by the fact that it was at Eastwell Park that "I saw the finest jewels I have ever seen in my life." Ever attentive to the likes and dislikes of her guests, Marie Alexandrovna tried to ensure that guests would find interesting things to see and do in her home. When she heard that the Earl and Countess of Warwick and Brooke were discussing jewelry, the duchess said to the countess: "If you would like to see my jewels, I will tell my maid to put them all out in my room to-morrow evening, after tea, and if your husband is interested, bring him too." At the appointed hour, the earl and countess went to Marie Alexandrovna's room, where she received them. The couple were astonished to find that the room was ablaze with "precious stones; the bed, the tables, the chairs were covered with cases containing tiaras, dog-collars, ropes of pearls, necklaces, bracelets, brooches of rarest lustre and beauty and of inestimable value. One would have thought that the world had been ransacked to lay these treasures at the Duchess's feet, and there seemed to be enough for an entire royal family rather than for one member of it."[44]

Much as she tried to see good in her guests, the Duchess of Edinburgh found a number of them lacking for scintillating conversation. Marie Alexandrovna, after all, was a cultured woman, fluent in several languages. She craved intelligent company and preferred politicians to sportsmen and soldiers. Queen Victoria approved of the Duchess of Edinburgh's intelligence and moral leanings and admitted this to Vicky, telling her: "I have formed a high opinion of her; her wonderfully even, cheerful satisfied temper—her kind and indulgent disposition, free from bigotry and intolerance, and her serious, intelligent mind—so entirely free from everything fast—and so full of occupation and interest in everything makes a most agreeable companion. Everyone must like her." However when it came to the Duke of Edinburgh, Queen Victoria had harsher words: "But alas! not one likes him! I fear that will never get better."[45]

On October 15, 1874, Alfred and Marie Alexandrovna became parents when the duchess gave birth at Buckingham Palace to Prince Alfred of Edinburgh. Queen Victoria was pleased to see that Marie Alexandrovna recovered quickly from the birth. She "shows a very healthy constitution which is a great thing is it not?" wrote the queen to Vicky. However, there was one thing Victoria disapproved of and it was the new mother's desire to nurse the baby herself. Of the situation, Queen Victoria told Vicky: "As long as she remains at home—and does not publish the fact to the world—by taking the baby everywhere . . . I have nothing to say (beyond my unfortunately—from my very earliest childhood—totally insurmountable disgust for the process)."[46] The baby Alfred was christened in London in the presence of Queen Victoria and the ailing Tsarina Marie. In writing to the baby's godmother, the German Empress Augusta, Queen Victoria noted how "little Alfred is a very strong, beautiful child, who will some day, I think, be like his very big Russian uncles."[47]

As for the senior Alfred, the new baby's father, Queen Victoria continued to despair of him. She hoped that Marie Alexandrovna could be a steadying influence on the duke, but this was a tall order, for "Affie was simply beyond saving."[48] The Duchess of Edinburgh blamed her husband's "thoroughly English education"[49] for his tiresome attitude. Gruff, obstinate, and boorish, Queen Victoria's second son had not mellowed after settling down. The queen had expressed to Vicky her anxiety over Affie. "He can be so hard," lamented his exasperated mother, "and so sharp and unkind in speaking of and to others when he disagrees and he always knows best. This makes him not a pleasant inmate in a house and I am always on thorns . . . when he is at dinner."[50] Others agreed. One courtier put it bluntly: "No officer knows his duty better or is more devoted to it" but nevertheless "no-one likes him—why?" As it turned out, the Duke of Edinburgh's negative traits included a propensity to drink. This was difficult enough for Marie Alexandrovna to deal with, but the fact that Alfred also "treated his wife like a stowaway found in the hold of his ship"[51] did nothing to endear him to her. Nevertheless, despite the difficulties in the marriage, the Duchess of Edinburgh gave birth to a succession of children. Young Alfred was followed by the firstborn daughter, Marie, in 1875. Affectionately known as "Missy," she would become one of the most well known of Queen Victoria's grandchildren. In a letter to the Countess Tolstoy, the Duke of Edinburgh described the confinement as being "of the shortest possible duration barely over an hour in all . . . The baby was born in the most natural and easy manner without any sort of assistance and nobody was with Marie but Mrs. Johnson and myself; we had not even time to call the Doctor from the other room . . . The recovery continues to be as satisfactory as possible and Marie is sure to be about again very soon. The baby is as fine a child as her brother and gives every evidence of finely developed lungs and did so before she was fairly in the world."[52]

Three years after Missy was born, the Duchess of Edinburgh gave birth to the Princesses Victoria Melita ("Ducky") in 1876, Alexandra ("Sandra") in 1878, and Beatrice ("Baby Bee") in 1884. Ducky was named Melita in honor of Malta, her birthplace. The Duke of Edinburgh had been assigned to serve with the Royal Navy's Mediterranean fleet and was based for a while in Malta before returning to England. The Duchess of Edinburgh relished her stay in Malta, which proved a much needed respite from England.

No matter how she tried to accommodate herself to England, Marie Alexandrovna found little to like in her adopted country. England's perpetual dampness paled in comparison to the frigidity and pristine snows of Russian winters as well as the endless northern summers. The Duchess of Edinburgh was especially critical of the English capital's smutty air, along with its depressing fogs. "Marie thinks London hideous," wrote the duchess's mother, adding that Marie Alexandrovna found "the air there appalling, the English food abominable, the late hours very tiring, the visits to [the queen's homes] Windsor and Osborne boring beyond belief."[53] Nor did the young Duchess of Edinburgh find sympathy among some members of the English court. One court intimate, Mary Ponsonby, wrote to her husband about Marie Alexandrovna's skills at the piano, a year after the bride's arrival in England. Though the duchess had reputedly been a competent pianist, Ponsonby scathingly recorded, "After dinner the Duchess of Edinburgh played on the pianoforte with Mr. Butler, but it was bad, so very bad that nobody pretended to listen. I must say I think people are less sycophants than they used to be, for the whole society turned their backs and talked."[54]

Hardly anything seemed to agree with Marie Alexandrovna in her adopted country—not the society, nor her husband Alfred, not the damp winters, nor the dreadful food, and most certainly not her humble position at court. Then there was her formidable mother-in-law. Sadly for Marie Alexandrovna and Queen Victoria, the initial goodwill that existed between them when Alfred's bride first arrived in England quickly dissipated. Both imperious, the queen and the duchess found themselves at loggerheads over even some seemingly trivial matters, such as the indoor temperature. The duchess, long accustomed to the hothouse atmosphere of the Romanov palaces, found it difficult to believe her maid when she told her that Queen Victoria did not allow fires to be lit in the bedrooms. When the queen, who could never abide warm temperatures indoors, found a roaring fire in Marie Alexandrovna's room at Balmoral, she ordered the fire smothered and the windows flung open. In another instance, as related by the duchess's mother, "Marie has discovered that the Queen drinks whisky, sometimes with water but generally without . . . when Marie was given some of this whisky to taste, she made such a face that she is never offered anything but water now."[55] Seeing what her daughter had to put up with, the Tsarina Marie had some unsympathetic words about the queen: "To be quite frank, it is difficult to take such a mother-in-law seriously, and I am sorry on Marie's account."[56] Missy best described the Duchess of Edinburgh's situation, saying simply: "I do not think my mother always found it easy being Queen Victoria's daughter-in-law, though they had a great respect for each other."[57]

All the difficulties and disillusionments she encountered amounted to a discontented life for Marie Alexandrovna in her adopted country. Tsarina

Marie witnessed this firsthand when she visited her daughter for Prince Alfred's birth. Once the tsarina departed from England, she wasted no time in writing to her brother of her daughter's misery. "The parting," wrote the tsarina, "was terrible. Marie felt it nearly as much as she did the first time, and she had great difficulty in growing accustomed to England again, with its dreary, monotonous life and its sleepy climate. She hated the English as soon as she got on to the steamer."[58] Missy too recalled this abhorrence, noting how, "my mother dearly loved her native country, and she never really felt completely happy in England."[59]

The Duchess of Edinburgh expressed her homesickness for Russia in a letter to the poet Prince Vladimir Meschersky, recalling "times past and the happy carefree days of my youth. What has happened to them? . . . since then everything has changed . . . and we are all pulled in different directions . . ." Marie Alexandrovna also spoke of her "Russian heart" and that "every sympathetic voice from the Fatherland is sacred and dear to me."[60]

HELLAS

*U*nder a clear blue Adriatic sky, a prince from a northern kingdom arrived to claim his throne. The Athens that greeted eighteen-year-old King George I of the Hellenes upon his arrival in October 1863 was a city *en fête.*[1] Long known for its association with the great philosophers, Aristotle, Plato, and Socrates, Athens was transformed into a place of celebration. On the famed Acropolis overlooking the city, guns thundered a booming welcome. To commemorate the event, hundreds of large clay pots filled with fire dotted the Acropolis, creating memorable illuminations, and fireworks exploded in celebration.

On the day of the king's arrival, the chaos that had so recently plagued the ancient city was distinctly absent. The city of Athens, though revered as the cradle of Western civilization, appeared to be on the verge of pandemonium during the 1860s. When the British diplomat, Horace Rumbold visited in 1862, his "first impressions of Athens were disappointing."[2] The place was steeped in lawlessness and swarmed with soldiers "in a state of complete insubordination." *Hellas,* or Greece, as it was (and is) called, was then "prey to anarchy."[3] Athens, with its venerable ruins of the Parthenon, was so chaotic during the early 1860s that one needed to roam the streets with a revolver for protection. Rumbold wrote of bands of "the most picturesque cut-throats imaginable, armed to the teeth"[4] wandering the streets, imposing their own rules on those they encountered. Even during recognized holidays such as saints' days, innocent bystanders were easily killed by exuberant revelers who fired real bullets from their guns into the air. Little wonder then that Rumbold was moved to describe Athens as "perhaps the most tiresome, and certainly the most troublesome, of minor capitals."[5]

The Greeks placed much hope on the shoulders of the young man who had come from Denmark to become their monarch. From the beginning of his reign, King George's lot was not an easy one. When Sir Horace Rumbold witnessed the eighteen-year-old king's arrival at Athens, he noted that "it was impossible not to feel compassion for the boy-king whose lot was cast among so turbulent and fickle a race as the Greeks. He was, and looked, so young and artless the experiment seemed to all of us questionable and indeed highly hazardous."[6] When King George took his oath to the constitution in the National Assembly, the "slight, delicate, stripling, standing alone amidst a crowd of callous, unscrupulous politicians, many of whom had been steeped to the lips in treason,"[7] seemed woefully insufficient to the daunting task ahead of him. Nevertheless, Maria Feodorovna's brother proved up to the task and worked tirelessly to bring antagonistic rivals together to work for the good of Greece. He also endeavored to embrace the Greek culture and learn its language. Much as he tried to immerse himself in the culture of his adopted land, though, George could not relinquish some aspects of his Danish upbringing. For one thing, though he scrupulously respected all that was attached to Orthodoxy in public, the king remained a Lutheran, eschewing the Orthodox religion that was so integral to the lives of his subjects and his Russian wife, Olga Constantinova.

As in Russia, political turmoil plagued Greece. In 1866, when the inhabitants of the island of Crete wanted to be free from Turkish rule and unite with Greece, an international crisis involving Britain erupted. War between the Ottoman Empire and Greece loomed over Crete. King George's brother-in-law, the Prince of Wales, as well as Queen Victoria, followed the crisis keenly, with Bertie siding strongly with Greece. The situation eventually cooled.

Law and order eventually resulted in a more stable and vibrant Athens during the 1870s. By 1877, the Greek capital was rightly described as being a "bright and almost busy city"[8] with a population hovering around sixty thousand. The population of Greece (the total area of which was roughly twenty thousand square miles) according to the 1870 census, amounted to about 1.5 million inhabitants.

Through the years, King George succeeded in garnering his subjects' respect through "his truthfulness and straightforwardness" that was "united to a considerable firmness of character and high personal courage."[9] Despite earning his people's respect, George I was nevertheless a realist and was well aware of how fickle his subjects could be. The king let it be known that he "kept a portmanteau ready packed" and should the need come, "he was prepared to leave them at any moment" if they wanted to be rid of him.[10] Such was the life that Queen Olga's husband faced in Greece, the land to which he and his wife came as teenagers. But despite the fact that they were foreigners, Olga and George did not deviate from their goal of serving their adopted land.

Though King George "never forgot he was a foreigner . . . [and] did his best to help his people forget," Olga "did not do the same."[11] She never hid her pride in being a Russian and visited the land of her birth as often as she could. In fact, Olga's youngest child, Prince Christopher, was born at Pavlovsk, her childhood home, in August 1888. Marie Feodorovna, who was a godparent, attended the baby's christening at Pavlovsk. All who attended, including Marie Feodorovna and Miechen, were attired in full court dress. According to an eyewitness, Miechen looked "radiant in rose-pink faille embroidered in silver," while Marie Feodorovna stood out in her dress of "white satin, richly embroidered in gold. A diamond *kokoshnik* [Russian headdress], veil of priceless lace, and magnificent jewels gleaming from her bare arms and shoulders, completed her ensemble."[12]

In Greece tangible proof of Queen Olga's abiding attachment to Russia was reflected in the chapel installed in the Royal Palace, which, like the Duchess of Edinburgh's, was Russian Orthodox. According to Olga's son Prince Nicholas, the queen possessed a "deep and sincere faith," so that at times of great difficulties she accepted what came her way, knowing in her heart that "we cannot question the will of God."[13] Queen Olga ensured that her children not only understood, but also came to love their faith. Prince Nicholas admitted that, "we were very religiously brought up by our mother."[14]

Despite her passionate desire to remain Russian, Queen Olga, was determined to raise her children as Greeks. "We were born and educated to serve Greece alone,"[15] noted Prince Nicholas. In addition to this, the prince recalled that their parents ensured that they were to "forget we were princes; we were to become true gentlemen, capable and disciplined, well informed, with a high sense of duty and humble about our attainments."[16]

The royal family's favorite home was Tatoi, their country residence outside Athens. Located on hilly terrain on the slopes of Mount Parnes, with its groves of pine forests and cedars, Tatoi was a sprawling fifty-thousand-acre estate, complete with a Danish-style dairy farm. Not far from the estate's main villa, Queen Olga had a small chapel built where the family worshiped on Sundays and feast days. Queen Olga's youngest daughter, Princess Marie, described

Tatoi as the place they loved "more than anything else in the world."[17] While the royal family spent summers at Tatoi, in spring they moved to the lovely Ionian island of Corfu and stayed at the family's villa, Mon Repos, surrounded by a seasonal profusion of flowers.

The family's home in Athens was the Royal Palace. Designed by a German architect and erected during King Otto's time, the stuccoed Royal Palace was constructed of limestone and marble. The queen had a modest suite of seven rooms, which included a library and a narrow gallery containing busts of members of the Romanov dynasty. Queen Olga's Athenian home never came close to vying in splendor with any of her homes in Russia. Even the Russian imperial train that awaited Queen Olga at Sebastopol for her Russian visits had more luxurious appointments than the Royal Palace at Athens. Poor heating in winter made palace occupants shiver; and lighting was still fairly primitive for the most part, so oil lamps were used. All these discomforts did not diminish the royal children's memories of their palace home. Queen Olga's youngest son, Prince Christopher, happily recalled his "delight of bicycling on wet afternoons through the enormous ball-rooms that ran the whole length of the Palace!"[18] Though a strict father, King George occasionally joined his children in these cycling forays, often leading them in a procession around the palace ballrooms. These indoor cycling forays were far from circumspect. "We smashed into one another," recalled Prince Christopher of these games "and came to earth in a tangled heap, some of us shrieking with laughter, others with the pain of bruises."[19] The princes' and princesses' other wild pranks included baiting Tatoi's wild stags to the point that the children had to run for their lives from the incensed animals. Thanks to the rambunctious and dauntless creatures her children became, Queen Olga found that their "playtime was her daily terror."[20]

Charles K. Tuckerman, who was the First Minister Resident of the U.S. to Greece in the 1860s, gave a glimpse of the contented family life enjoyed by Queen Olga. "The Queen's chief happiness was in the society of her husband and children," recorded Tuckerman. " 'Would you like to see a picture?' she one day asked, and conducted me to the bedroom adjoining the nursery. There, on the silken coverlet of an immense bed, lay the three royal babies taking their mid-day nap. In their previous frolic they had tumbled themselves nearly naked, and now lay in profound slumber, a confused group of plump little rosy limbs and faces, commingling with a grace of posture which only Nature can bestow. It was indeed a 'picture,' and one that would have delighted the eyes of an artist of *genre*."[21]

Queen Olga's family was a close-knit one. Though the queen's children received their share of admonishments from their father and had to endure elements of a strict upbringing, their childhood was full of merriment and cheer and was largely devoid of the heavy formality and rigid etiquette that plagued other royal families. Like the Russian imperial family, members of the Greek royal family were great linguists. Languages most spoken were English, Greek, and German, while the children also learned Danish, French, and Russian. The children spoke English and Greek amongst themselves, while King George and Queen Olga spoke German to each other. Olga mastered Greek within a year of her arrival in Athens, but communicated to her children in English. This facility with languages came in handy whenever the Greek royals gathered for their holidays in Denmark. There, in the most unpretentious manner, King Christian IX and Queen Louise were delighted to welcome an ever burgeoning number of grandchildren. Thanks to the marriages of their daughters, Alexandra, Marie Feodorovna, and Thyra, these grandchildren represented the royal houses of England, Russia, and Hanover and included future kings of England and Greece as well as a future emperor of Russia.

Prince Nicholas of Greece remembered his father's sisters, his aunts Alix, Minnie, and Thyra, as "the sweetest women one could meet anywhere."[22] It was always a joy for Queen Olga's children to receive Christmas gifts from these Danish aunts, two of whom were destined to be queen of England and tsarina of Russia. Aunts Alix and Minnie were favorites with Prince Christopher, who found the former "beautiful" and "very witty" while the latter, though "a smaller and less beautiful edition of her sister," was full of the "same charm, the same tact" with the added advantage of having had "more strength of character." Christopher also related an amusing incident involving his aunt, the future Russian empress. Minnie, who was a regular smoker and liked to try and hide it, resorted one day to hiding her lit cigarette behind her back. This resulted in a comical scene, for she was "oblivious of the clouds of smoke arising like incense"[23] behind her.

Another favorite relative of the royal children who frequented these Danish family gatherings was Minnie's husband, the Tsarevich Alexander, fondly known by the youngsters as Uncle Sasha. The six-foot-five-inch giant liked to dazzle his nephews and nieces with his brute strength by tearing packs of cards with his bare hands. Unlike his more sophisticated brother-in-law, Bertie, the Prince of Wales, who endured these Danish holidays with boredom, the Tsarevich Alexander reveled in the children's fun and games. At one point Uncle Sasha drenched a distinguished visitor, King Oscar of Sweden, with a garden hose supplied by the children. The Russian imperial family thoroughly enjoyed these Danish sojourns because Denmark was the only place where they truly felt at ease. Life in Russia was heavily laden with anxiety over the Nihilists' increasing boldness as well as tensions within the family over the infidelities of the tsar and Queen Olga's father, Grand Duke Constantine.

Queen Olga could not have been anything but saddened by the deterioration in her parents' once happy marriage. Grand Duke Constantine's illegitimate family caused what he called his "government-issue"[24] wife, the Grand Duchess Alexandra Iosifovna, pain and embarrassment. The couple's interaction in their later years afforded a glimpse of their fractious relationship. During this time, Olga's father had suffered a stroke that rendered him speechless, but his mental faculties were still fairly intact. Once he became an invalid, Alexandra Iosifovna watched over Grand Duke Constantine devotedly. Nevertheless, the maligned wife could not resist putting her husband in his place. She forbade Grand Duke Constantine's retainers from taking her husband to visit his former mistress, who lived near the Pavlovsk estate. These retainers took their orders seriously. During a drive, the grand duke assumed he would be visiting his one-time paramour. When the carriage did not go in the direction he desired, an incensed Constantine "hammered with his stick on the carriage door," pointing his retainers in the direction of the lady's house. Under strict orders from Olga's mother, the retainers innocently replied: "Yes, indeed, Your Imperial Highness, the leaves are turning brown very early this year." After more loud gesticulating, the grand duke gave up and stayed silent. Prince Christopher of Greece recounted the encounter between husband and wife when the drive ended. "Grandmother was waiting for them, triumph in her eyes," wrote Olga's son. The triumph was short-lived, however. "Grandfather answered it with one equally honeyed. But the moment she came close to him he seized her by the hair and brandished his stick. Before anyone could stop him he gave her a sound beating!"[25] Such was the volatile relationship between Queen Olga's parents during their twilight years.

Queen Olga's family was deeply affected when her youngest brother, Viacheslav, died suddenly from a brain hemorrhage in 1879. The loss of this youngest son greatly aged Olga's father, who took Viacheslav's death hard. Another of Olga's siblings, her sister Vera, had been a problem child whose violent temper prompted her parents to send her off to her aunt and uncle Queen Olga and King Karl of Württemberg in Stuttgart. They eventually adopted Vera, who in time outgrew her difficult personality. After her sister Olga married and settled in Greece, Vera periodically visited her there.

With her brother occupying the Greek throne, Greece's fate was never far from the Tsarevna Marie Feodorovna's mind. When the Russo-Turkish War of 1877–1878 took place, Minnie had hoped that Greece could benefit from the conflict in terms of territorial aggrandizement. Both Greece and Russia coveted the Ottoman Empire's capital, Constantinople, and eagerly sought to bring it into the Orthodox fold. However, the Great Powers—Britain and France—forced Greece to stay neutral in the conflict even though Russia wished to have Greece on her side. In the end, Greece obtained some territory, though minor in scope.

Nevertheless, Greece's appetite for territory was not tempered. Throughout the nineteenth century, all Greece was dominated by the *Megali* ("*Great*") *Idea,* an irredentist aspiration that drove Greek nationalist ideals. This nationalist vision was a Greek state that would resurrect the Byzantine Empire by liberating lands held then under the Ottoman Empire's rule. Constantinople, "the dream and hope of all Greeks," was to be the capital of this Greater Greece.[26] This messianic concept was both alluring and enduring because so many Greeks were scattered around the Near East. Part of the attraction in finding a Romanov bride for King George of the Hellenes lay in the Russian connection, for "in the first decades after [Greek] independence had been achieved, Russia was seen as the power most likely to assist Greece in achieving her irredentist ambitions."[27] The *Megali Idea* became so deeply rooted that it animated Greek policy for decades to come.

Back in Russia, Marie Feodorovna was settling into her role as the empire's future empress. She had finally mastered her adopted country's difficult language. Once ignorant of Russian, Minnie became so proficient that when Sasha was away, he wrote to her not just in French as he had done years before, but mostly in Russian. Minnie's husband was intensely Russian in outlook and conviction, far more so than his father had been. When he was tsarevich, Alexander II preferred speaking French to Russian, but his son Sasha preferred Russian above all other languages—so at his insistence, he and Minnie spoke to their children in Russian. The future empress came to appreciate the subtleties of her adopted country's language, once telling the American minister to Russia that "the Russian language is full of power and beauty, it equals the Italian in music, the English in vigorous power and copiousness." She also claimed that "for compactness of expression" Russian rivaled "Latin, and for the making of new words is equal to the Greek."[28]

During the 1860s and 1870s Minnie and Sasha made annual visits to their various homes, which of course included indispensable sojourns to Denmark. Spring usually saw Minnie and her family at the sprawling palace of Gatchina outside St. Petersburg. In summers, they moved to Peterhof. While there, they stayed at the Cottage Palace, a delightful small villa where the couple and their children savored their time together as a family, reveling in the calm that was such an increasingly rare occurrence in St. Petersburg.

Winters for Marie Feodorovna and her family meant St. Petersburg. Their home was the Anichkov Palace on the Nevsky Prospekt. Vast and lavish as befitting an abode for an heir to the throne, the Anichkov Palace was nevertheless a home and Minnie's favorite home too. Despite its sumptuous surroundings, there were still elements of restraint, evidence of Sasha and Minnie's determination to raise their children with some semblance of normalcy. A visitor to the Anichkov thought the children's schoolroom "was severity itself, a parish schoolroom, indeed, more than an Imperial one. The walls, I remember, where not hung with maps, were pasted over with pictures of the chief battles in the Russo-Turkish War, taken from the *Illustrated London News* and other illustrated English papers."[29] Living at the Anichkov Palace also signaled a busy season for Minnie. Winters in St. Petersburg meant being at the center of official court entertainments where Marie Feodorovna always sparkled with vivacity, the perfect foil to her crusty husband. Minnie, however, was not the only senior-ranking female member of the Romanov dynasty for whom the winter season was a whirl of balls and parties. Miechen likewise occupied herself with hosting numerous guests in her impressive St. Petersburg home, the Vladimir Palace.

The Grand Duke and Grand Duchess Vladimir established themselves among the most fashionable hosts in all of St. Petersburg. Home was the newly built and aptly named Vladimir Palace. Located on the fashionable Palace Embankment, a major street fronting the Neva River, the Vladimir Palace faced the imposing Peter and Paul Fortress, home to the Peter and Paul Cathedral, burial place of the Romanovs. Designed in a Florentine manner, the Vladimir Palace's sober façade belied the grandeur that marked the building's interior. Inside Miechen and Vladimir's vast and sumptuous home, splendidly decorated rooms and marvelous objets d'art dazzled visitors. The main staircase alone, made of marble, was a garishly gilded confection that assaulted the senses. Not content with keeping to one or two particular styles, Vladimir and Miechen's craftsmen and artisans embellished their home in a myriad of styles that included Russian Revival, Renaissance, Byzantine, Rococo, Gothic Revival, Venetian, and even Moorish. Miechen imported silk from Germany to line the walls of her main drawing room. She selected furniture made from exotic woods: "Light oak—for the front drawing room . . . red polished oak—for the main hall . . . polished brazil nut—for the study" and "karelian birch, wavy poplar" and more brazil nut for the nursery.[30]

In no time, the Vladimir Palace became a center of princely entertainments, with Miechen regarded as one of St. Petersburg's most accomplished hostesses. One courtier who attended a party at the palace described it as having been "conducted in the most luxurious style."[31] It was during one such reception that the maternal grandparents of the famed fashion designer, Oleg Cassini, met. Oleg's mother, Countess Marguerite Cassini, related her mother's description of the evening at Miechen's "baroque palace on the ice-covered Moika Canal . . . the great hall lit with hundreds and hundreds of candles where late guests were being helped out of their ermine and sable wraps and fur-lined boots; the magnificent wide marble stairway lined with white-wigged footmen in black satin and gold-embroidered velvet; the imposing major-domo at the top announcing in stentorious tones the names of the illustrious guests; the sweeping expanse of foyers, galleries, ballrooms and music rooms; the soft warm blur of candlelight, crystal and flashing jewels . . . of gowns brilliantly gleaming satin and velvet and lace, and colorful uniforms bright with medals and gold braid and ribands."[32]

That evening Miechen was especially gracious to Oleg Cassini's maternal grandmother, the actress Stefanie Van Betz, because Stefanie was nervous about singing for the distinguished audience. Miechen, whom Marguerite Cassini described as being "especially partial to actors," gave Stefanie "a most unroyal and almost imperceptible wink and nod of encouragement."[33] The grand duchess's encouragement must have worked because before the night was over, Stefanie Van Betz had so entranced Arthur Paul Nicholas, Marquis de Capizzucchi de Bologna, Count de Cassini, that he fell in love with her. Years later, their daughter, Countess Marguerite Cassini acted as official hostess for her father, who was imperial Russia's first ambassador to the United States during the McKinley administration. While in Washington, D.C., Marguerite befriended Alice Roosevelt, daughter of Theodore Roosevelt. Together, the lively duo of Alice and Marguerite became fodder for a gossip-hungry media. Decades later, Marguerite's sons, Igor and Oleg, gained great fame in America— Igor as the society columnist "Cholly Knickerbocker" and Oleg as the designer whose elegant outfits for Jacqueline Kennedy helped make her famous as the most glamorous woman in the world. It is tempting to ruminate that had it not been for Miechen's lavish evening reception and her encouragement of Stefanie Van Betz, Oleg Cassini's impact on the fashion world, and by extension, Jacqueline Kennedy's, might not have had such effect generations later.

But beyond the lavish Romanov parties, the specter of danger continued to lurk—for the Nihilists' menacing threat still shadowed the Romanovs. Besides the Nihilists, the imperial family was divided due to Tsar Alexander II's continuing affair with the Russian aristocrat, Princess Katya Dolgorukaya. Katya with the "sensuous mouth and light chestnut tresses" was "an exquisite creature,"[34] while the tragic tsarina was an invalid whose "life as a woman and a wife . . . was finished." One witness described her as "a skeleton with a white face covered with powder and rouge to hide her skin disease—she looked like a cadaver."[35] Alexander II continued to pay his wife polite visits in her apartments and was scrupulously civilized toward her publicly. When the tsarina's "health permitted her to appear at public functions, anyone unacquainted with the background would never have imagined that he saw two strangers bound by a vow kept by one and irrevocably broken by the other."[36]

In 1878, the tsar took a drastic and highly unusual step. He ordered Katya to move into the Winter Palace with their children, and insult was added to the tsarina's injury. However painful it was, the tsar felt compelled to protect Katya and their children, for rumors were rife about a possible assassination attempt on the princess. For her part, Katya agreed to this move as a way of keeping the tsar from traveling out to see her, thus diminishing the chance of his becoming a target for assassins. With this momentous step, the brewing rift within the family finally ruptured.

Preexisting battle lines erupted. None of the grand dukes who had embarked on adulterous affairs ever established their mistresses under the very same roof as their wives, but the tsar's brothers nevertheless sided with Alexander II. This was not surprising considering that Nicholas Nikolaevich and Constantine Nikolaevich were both carrying on affairs of their own at the time. However, all the emperor's sons, except Grand Duke Alexei, and their wives sided with their wronged mother. Marie Alexandrovna disapproved but was more tolerant than her brothers, excluding Alexei. She loved both her parents, and "could not find it in her heart to blame him [her father] for anything, believing that as their father and Sovereign he should be beyond criticism."[37] Nevertheless, this unusual family arrangement had its uncomfortable moments and prompted the tsar's daughter to complain that: "I find it most unbearable that Papa prohibited us from coming in unannounced."[38]

The affair was so painful that the tsar's children found it difficult to discuss the matter even among themselves. In one incident, Marie Alexandrovna and Serge were happily riding with their father in the park at Pavlovsk when suddenly a carriage passed them by. The tsar ordered his driver to stop. Alexander II then bid Marie Alexandrovna and Serge goodbye, left and went to the other carriage, which contained Katya and their illegitimate children. The spectacle flabbergasted Serge and Marie Alexandrovna. Of the incident, Grand Duke Serge said: "Can you believe, during this drive from Pavlovsk to Tsarskoe [Selo] Marie and I not only did not exchange a single word about what had happened but also did not exchange a single glance."[39]

It was not an easy time for Alexander II either, whom one lady-in-waiting at court described as having "changed noticeably during these months." The emperor was "restless and irritated, his eyes had lost their customary kind expression and he looked sullen and suspicious."[40] As the liaison became more blatant, life for the tsar's daughters-in-law also became more strained. Relief from the hothouse atmosphere that pervaded life at court became nearly impossible. But tense as this domestic situation was, it was invariably the increasing danger posed by the Nihilists that made the greatest impact on the Romanovs. Autocracy had failed to eliminate the opposition, but had driven "it underground, where, like other matter that has been forced into a subterranean channel, it assumes a molten form, and becomes explosive."[41]

8

HOUNDED TO DEATH

espite Tsar Alexander II's Great Reforms and efforts at political emancipation, frustration over social inequality and continued government repression of dissidents inflamed tsarist opponents. The peasants' continuing apathy further exasperated the revolutionaries who itched for rapid and radical changes to Russian society. In their quest to impose immediately a socialist utopia, they turned to terror. To bring down the autocracy, the revolutionaries' chosen means was murder. It mattered not to them that murder was not only immoral, but that their killings were also "much more likely to lead to less liberty, not more." This fact "did not seem to interest them, for they were drunk with egotism, dramatising themselves as the saviours of humanity."[1] Hence, one of the most frightening aspects of the volatile 1870s was the widespread killings of tsarist officials perpetrated by the extremists.

Emboldened, brazen, and successful in terrorizing tsarist officialdom, the Nihilists were not content to kill tsarist officials only, but set their sights on the mightiest prize of all, the Romanovs. Wherever senior members of the imperial family could be found, the security apparatus was on the alert for possible attacks, particularly in St. Petersburg, which turned into a hotbed of intrigue and attacks. A senior official of the Third Section admitted that, "the Emperor is the most watched person in all St. Petersburg."[2] Even the Third Section of His Majesty's Own Chancery (and forerunner of the infamous *Okhrana,* or "secret police"), which was tasked with overseeing security, was itself a victim of the growing wave of assassinations. In 1876, an assassin stabbed to death General Nicholas Mezentsov, the Third Section's head. This political killing was significant because "this was the first instance of a new rule in Russian terror—claiming responsibility publicly for murder."[3] The high-profile political murder was followed by more. All in all, some fifteen hundred Nihilists in a country of fifty million became so effective in terrorizing the empire that "Russia resembled a country in a state of siege."[4]

The year 1878 also saw another significant development in the battle between the extremists and autocracy. Vera Zasulich, a young woman from the gentry, shot and seriously wounded the St. Petersburg chief of police, General Trepov, in order to avenge the flogging of one of her comrades. The shooting of Trepov was designed to gain maximum exposure and sympathy for the cause. It succeeded. At Zasulich's trial, her lawyer gave an effective plea on her behalf, portraying her as an idealistic young woman intent on seeking sympathy for a wronged comrade. This swayed the verdict in Zasulich's favor, thus gaining her freedom in a blaze of publicity. Not only was the jury swayed, so were the spectators and countless others. Vera embodied the "*nigilistka* or girl 'nihilist'"[5] with her plain, unfashionable look, and her example catalyzed extremist views propounded by the revolutionaries.

Count Leo Tolstoy questioned those who admired Zasulich's obvious contempt for law and order, prompting the famous author to declare: "It is open war . . . The Zasulich business is no joking matter. This madness, this capriciousness that has suddenly seized hold of people is significant. These are the first signs of something not yet clear to us. But it is serious . . . and I am inclined to think that this madness is the precursor of revolution."[6]

By the spring of 1879 all-out war between the terrorists and tsarist officials broke out. The chief of the Third Section, General Drenteln, ordered the arrest of hundreds of suspected subversives. They retaliated by murdering Drenteln. The dark cloud hanging over St. Petersburg darkened more as Cossacks escorted officials as they drove in the streets. So oppressive did the capital become for fear of terrorist attacks that "few ventured out-of-doors for exercise."[7] Tsar Alexander II, however, still continued his daily constitutional walks along the palace quay, much to the anxiety of the police who watched him. In April 1879, he was nearly killed by an assassin during one of these walks. Throughout the following months, as the peril grew, measures to protect Alexander II visibly increased and took on extraordinary form. Bulletproof wadding lined his uniform; his clothes and linen were carefully inspected and cared for; police watched the imperial cooks prepare dishes that were kept simple and sauceless, then tasted the food before the tsar was served. Sheets of steel lined Alexander II's carriage; secret police and soldiers escorted him everywhere. These bodyguards learned of their assignment to guard the tsar only a half hour before starting off and were often sworn to secrecy as well.

Sandro, Alexander II's nephew, was dumbfounded by the extent of the protection surrounding his uncle. Sandro described the four hundred miles that linked St. Petersburg to Moscow as "closely guarded by soldiers. All along the route," he recounted, "we saw bayonets and uniforms; at night thousands of camp-fires were lighting the way . . . extraordinary measures had been taken to protect his [Alexander II's] train against the attempts of the revolutionaries. This revelation struck us all most painfully."[8] The besieged capital, St. Petersburg, Sandro wrote, "reeked of imminent tragedy and continuous sorrow."[9]

The highly charged atmosphere produced such anxieties on the beleaguered Alexander II that one contemporary, Peter Valuev, bluntly portrayed the Duchess of Edinburgh's father as "a crowned semi-ruin."[10] A visitor to Russia during the mid-1870s commented on the emperor being "so dreadfully afraid of being shot at, that nobody ever knows exactly when he is going anywhere."[11] In 1879, the executive committee of the People's Will formally condemned the emperor to death. From then on "every effort of the movement was directed to his assassination."[12] The two most dedicated members of the executive committee, Nicholas Kibaltchitch and Sophia Perovskaya were the brains and spirit behind this intense new commitment to perpetrate regicide. Kibaltchitch was a gifted engineer. Instead of devoting his talents to benign causes, he used his knowledge of foreign languages to pore over scientific material and soon became the best explosives expert in the country. Like Kibaltchitch, Perovskaya too had everything going for her. Granddaughter of a minister of the interior, daughter of the governor of St. Petersburg, Perovskaya had the advantage of belonging to a family long associated with serving the emperor, but she turned her back on her privileged background and became a fanatical revolutionary. As the People's Will systematically planned attacks that "took their toll of innocent victims," Perovskaya's sympathies came to the fore. Evidence points to Perovskaya's indifference toward "the victims of the tsarist police state." "There is no evidence she wept over the victims of the terrorists' dynamite."[13]

Three more attempts on Alexander II's life took place when he was returning from the Crimea to the capital in the fall of 1879. The would-be assassins missed killing the tsar at Odessa. After this mishap, another lost opportunity occurred when mines laid under the railroad tracks did not explode as planned. Then in Moscow, part of the imperial train was blown to bits but the tsar, who had been on board, was miraculously unharmed. Hunted mercilessly, Alexander

II muttered in exasperation: "Am I such a wild beast that they should hound me to death?"[14] Thus continued "a deadly game of cat and mouse, in which the People's Will pursued Alexander relentlessly across the face of Russia, even through the halls of the Winter Palace itself."[15] The most spectacular attempt on the tsar's life took place in February 1880. In a daring move, Stepan Khalturin, a terrorist who had insinuated himself into the Winter Palace in the guise of a carpenter, slowly smuggled in over a hundred pounds of dynamite for the sole purpose of killing Alexander II. The explosion was set to go off at the moment the imperial family was to sit down to dinner. On the appointed day, Khalturin detonated the charge and escaped. But because the tsarina's brother and nephew arrived late, none of the imperial family was injured or killed by the powerful blast. The damage created was devastating. Grand Duke Vladimir rushed to the dining room, which was enveloped in smoke. Broken china and glass were strewn all over, windows blown out, and a large gaping hole in the wall attested to the explosion's force. The area below the dining room, which housed Finnish sentries, bore the brunt of the blast. Over 125 pounds of dynamite destroyed two-foot-thick walls and extensively damaged the large guard room, which measured sixty feet by twenty feet. There, the powerful explosion killed eleven guards and wounded forty-four. Sasha and Vladimir hurried to help the sentries picking their way through blood and debris. "It was a heartbreaking picture," recalled the tsarevich, "and I will never forget that horror in my life!"[16] Queen Olga's father recorded the impact of the audacious attack: "We are reliving the Terror [of the French Revolution], but with this difference: the Parisians during the revolution saw their enemies face to face. We neither see them nor do we know them."[17]

Alexander II declared to Lord Dufferin, Britain's ambassador to Russia: "Providence has again mercifully saved me." Lord Dufferin sent a report of the horrifying incident to Queen Victoria, partly to explain what had happened and partly to reassure the queen that Marie Alexandrovna, who was staying with her father, was safe. Lord Dufferin noted that the "Duchess of Edinburgh exhibited great coolness and presence of mind,"[18] especially considering that her apartments were "in very close proximity to the scene of the catastrophe."[19] The damage was extensive. An eyewitness noted that in order to get to the duchess's rooms, "one had to work one's way through mountains of rubbish."[20] Thus did the Duchess of Edinburgh come very close to being killed along with her father in what could have been one of the most spectacular acts of regicide since the beheading of King Louis XVI and Queen Marie Antoinette of France.

Miechen was among the family members nearly killed during the Winter Palace explosion. Her recollections of the event, as told to the painter Henry Jones Thaddeus, provide one of the most vivid accounts of what it was like to have lived through the frightening event. Thaddeus noted that Miechen's nerves were still rattled as she recounted her experience, since "her emotion at times obliged her to pause and recover her composure." The grand duchess began her story by telling Thaddeus that "the Czar attached great importance to punctuality, and all members of the family were expected to assemble for dinner before he made his appearance, which happened, invariably, as the dinner-hour was striking."

"To be late was to incur his displeasure—a thing we all dreaded, none so more than myself."[21] Miechen once admitted to a friend that though Tsar Alexander II "was devoted to her" and "was kindness itself," he could also be "a martinet."[22] And so this comment about tardiness was not off the mark.

Miechen explained that "the anarchists evidently timed the explosion to occur during . . . dinner." During the day prior, the grand duchess had wavered about going to the Winter Palace that evening. "On the afternoon of this dreadful day one of my children was taken ill; I was very much upset and distressed in consequence. When reminded that it was time to dress for dinner I was loth [sic] to leave the bedside of the little sufferer, who supplicated me to stay, and I lingered on.

"At last I was obliged to tear myself away, and before my toilette was quite completed heard with dismay the clock striking the dinner-hour. I finished as rapidly as possible, and hurried to the Czar's apartment, where I found everybody assembled." Miechen added, "You cannot imagine the feeling of relief I experienced when I remarked that the Czar was not in the room." Apparently, "he had not yet arrived, and such an unusual occurrence was the subject of general comment." So odd was this that Miechen remarked: "It was the first time I had known him to be late, and most fortunately for me, it was also the only occasion I had been unpunctual myself." Upon reaching the palace, Alexander II asked Miechen about her ill child and then the family proceeded to the dining room. "At this moment the most awful explosion rent the air," recounted Miechen, "the dining-room vanished from our view, and we plunged into impenetrable darkness." When Miechen reached this point of her recollections, Thaddeus reported that "the Grand Duchess was overcome with emotion as she recalled this tragic moment, and it was some little time before she resumed." "A poisonous gas filled the room, suffocating us, as well as adding to our horror," continued Miechen. "How can I possibly describe the agony of mind we suffered, expecting, as we did, at any moment another explosion beneath us! It is impossible—impossible for me to tell or for you to conceive.

"The impending fear almost made our hearts stop beating as, silent and motionless, we awaited our doom," Miechen recounted. "When the echoes of the explosion died away, a dead silence succeeded, which, united with the darkness prevailing, so dense as almost to be felt, conduced to render our helpless position still more painful and unendurable.

"We dared not move. There was no escape from the peril which surrounded us." Then, added Miechen: "Out of the darkness came the clear, calm voice of the Czar," who said, "my children, let us pray!" Hearing his voice also "relieved the awful strain on our nerves, and brought comfort to our hearts." The family then sank to their knees sobbing. "How long we remained so, I really do not know," noted Miechen. "It seemed an eternity of anguish before the guards appeared with candles, little expecting to find us alive.

"Some of us were nearly demented when the welcome relief arrived, and our feelings were not calmed as we then contemplated the awful nature of the destruction we had escaped. A few feet in front of the Czar was a black chasm, where so short a time before had been the brilliantly lit dining-room filled with servants. Not a trace of it or of them remained! It really seemed as if the hand of Providence had delayed the Czar's arrival; otherwise we should have shared the same fate. The dim lights of the candles intensified the terrifying aspect of the scene before us, and we hastened to leave it for the comparative safety of our own apartments.

"The dread of further explosions haunted us like a hideous nightmare during that long and dreary night, whilst the fear of danger to the children nearly distracted me. Never, I pray," concluded Miechen, "may I have to undergo such agony again!"[23]

The Tsarevna Marie Feodorovna was not with Miechen or Marie Alexandrovna when the terrorists nearly killed them. Minnie arrived at the Winter Palace not long after the explosion went off. The tsar greeted his daughter-in-law upon her arrival and told Minnie: "We just had a powerful gas explosion." Marie Feodorovna thought the statement was odd, prompting her to answer that, "it doesn't smell like gas—rather like gunpowder."[24] In recording the event, Marie Feodorovna wrote: "Awful. God has once again saved the Emperor and us all for it was . . . the dining room that was to be blown up!"[25]

Back in Britain, Queen Victoria reacted with shock. She wrote to Vicky of "the awful monstrous new attempt on the poor Emperor of Russia's life. In his own house! It is too, too awful. What a merciful escape—and poor dear Marie, what a state she must be in about both parents." The queen finished with a flamboyant suggestion: "They ought all to go away at once and he abdicate."[26] Minnie's sister, Alexandra, was equally stunned. A perturbed Alix wrote to her sister: "How can I find words to thank Our Lord, who has <u>saved</u> you <u>all</u> . . . No my Minny! Imagine that <u>such things</u> can take place <u>in our day</u> . . . it is all too <u>horrifying</u>! . . . What will come <u>next</u>? Poor Marie [Alexandrovna], how desperate and yet how courageous . . . My Minny, Minny, I wish I were with you . . . Alfred is leaving this evening; I am glad for Marie's sake . . . your ever-loving Alix."[27]

The imperial family escaped the explosion unharmed, but "the psychological impact of the attack was immense." Terrorists had missed the mark, but achieved another objective—the attack "proclaimed to the world that, even within the walls of his own palace, Alexander was not safe from the revolutionaries' vengeance."[28]

After the Winter Palace explosion, St. Petersburgers felt more besieged than ever. Near panic reigned. The government declared a curfew, and many individuals were watched with great suspicion. Numerous residents fled the capital for fear that the violence would intensify. Even operagoers became victims of the terrorized mentality that gripped the capital; "people would no longer buy tickets for the opera until they had ascertained that" Alexander II was unlikely to be attending.[29] Lord Dufferin's wife recounted that the Nihilists warned everyone that "all persons valuing their lives" should "keep as far as possible from the Emperor!"[30] A contemporary publication described the prevalent atmosphere as near bedlam when it told its readers: "Russia is almost as much a jungle as ever."[31]

In order to "root out sedition" and "consider ways of improving the government's relationship with the people," a committee of nine men was created and granted unrestricted power.[32] This Supreme Executive Commission had dictatorial powers, though Alexander II was still the autocrat, as he "would be delegating authority, not relinquishing it, and the head of the commission would be responsible directly to him."[33] Alexander II appointed Count Michael Loris-Melikov, a hero of the Russo-Turkish War, to serve as chairman of the committee. Loris-Melikov sought order by aggressively pursuing the Nihilists while simultaneously encouraging Alexander II to offer a significant gesture of conciliation to the people by granting more representation to them. Clearly, the Winter Palace explosion had more than rattled the nerves of the tsar and his high-ranking officials.

When the explosion took place at the Winter Palace, Alexander II rushed to the apartments of Katya and the Tsarina Marie to check on them. Both were unharmed. The tsarina, a bedridden invalid, was heavily sedated because of her terminal illness. Consequently she slept through the explosion, unaware of the chaos.

By May 1880, the tsarina's health had been despaired of and the Duchess of Edinburgh hurried to be at her mother's side. Emotions ran high; and the duchess finally lost patience with Alexander II over his affair with Katya, precipitating an argument between father and daughter. It could not have been easy for the tsar to find that his daughter, to whom he was so close in the past, had clearly sided with her mother, who was at death's door. Marie Alexandrovna, aghast that Katya lived under the same roof as her dying mother, talked her father into moving Katya to Tsarskoe Selo.

The long-suffering tsarina's earthly trials finally came to an end when she died in her sleep a month later. The tsarina's death was a blow to Marie Alexandrovna, which Minnie described to her mother, Queen Louise of Denmark: "I . . . had a long letter from Marie, the first in which she speaks of what has happened, and gives me some insight into her profoundly grief-stricken heart! Poor little thing; I cannot tell you how sad she makes me! With the death of her beloved mother, she <u>lost</u> everything . . . how disconsolate she . . . must be!"[34] Marie Alexandrovna had "loved and venerated her mother with all the strength of her soul."[35]

When the imperial family bid their final farewell to the late empress, "the Emperor was much overcome." He and his sons carried the coffin to the vault. Later, when Queen Victoria's representative, Lord Torrington conferred the queen's deepest sympathy to the emperor, Alexander II replied, "I thank you. I quite understand." The Duke and Duchess of Edinburgh and their children were also in attendance. Lord Torrington was touched by Alexander II's "most charming and tender" manner toward the Edinburghs, kissing these particular grandchildren, and telling Lord Torrington, "these are my joy."[36]

After the minimum forty days mourning period as prescribed by the Church ended, the widowed tsar wasted no time in regularizing his relationship with Katya. He married her in haste, without fanfare and in great secrecy at Tsarskoe Selo. Alexander II later granted his new wife the title Princess Yurievskaya and legitimized their children. The marriage was a morganatic one, meaning that Katya was not empress and her children were not in line for the throne. Nevertheless, the tsar had the right to have his new wife later crowned empress.

Tsar Alexander II's second marriage mortified Sasha and Minnie, who were now compelled to meet Katya. The meeting took place by means of a ruse, prompting Minnie to declare "we were—trapped!"[37] Minnie daringly refused to allow her children to stay with Alexander II and his second family, thus incurring the tsar's anger. "I cried incessantly, even by night," confided Minnie to Countess Tolstoy. "As for my children . . . They used to steal them from me . . . There were grave scenes between me and the Sovereign, caused by my refusal to let my children to him."[38]

Minnie and Sasha were not the only family members scandalized by the tsar's hasty marriage. The Duchess of Edinburgh was just as appalled. Marie Alexandrovna, like so many of the Romanovs, was incredulous. She wrote to her father, telling him: "I pray that myself and my junior brothers, who were particularly close to Mama, would one day be able to forgive you."[39]

Miechen too thought the tsar's morganatic marriage a disgrace. She vented her frustration in a letter to Prince Alexander of Hesse, the late tsarina's brother. Miechen, though, waited for the right opportunity to send her thoughts in writing. She mistrusted the Russian couriers and instead waited until she could send the letter via German hands. Miechen did not mince words: "This marriage of the Tsar's six weeks after the death of our dear Tsarina, is hard enough to bear in itself. But that this woman, who for fourteen years has occupied such a very invidious position, should be introduced to us as a member of the family surrounded by her three children is more painful than I can find words to express."[40] Miechen effectively echoed Minnie's sentiments, as both women were very much imbued with Victorian ideals of fidelity in marriage. Like Minnie, Miechen enjoyed a stable marriage with the Grand Duke Vladimir. Thus the tsar's situation seemed all the more disgraceful in the eyes of these two upright daughters-in-law of Alexander II.

Miechen went on to add in her letter about Katya: "She appears at the family dinners large or small, and also in the private chapel before the whole court. We are forced to receive her and to visit her." Miechen added more details, explaining that "the Tsar goes on visits with her in a closed carriage, though not yet in a sleigh. Since her influence is very great, things go a step farther every day, so that one cannot see where it will all end." Miechen had not much good to say about Katya, adding: "Since the Princess is very uneducated, and has neither tact nor intellect, you can imagine the kind of life she leads us." As she continued to confide about the difficult domestic situation, the tone Miechen took increased in severity, betraying an obvious sympathy for the much maligned tsarina. "Every feeling, every sacred memory, is trodden under foot," continued the grand duchess; "we are spared nothing." Then, indignant and helpless, Miechen wrote: "The Tsar has commanded us as his subjects to be friendly with this wife; if not he would force us to it. You can imagine the internal conflict that agitates us all, and the perpetual struggle between feelings, duty, and external pressure."[41]

Miechen was repelled and wanted to rebel, but defying the tsar was impossible. The grand duchess could only express her anger and frustration on paper. "The new wife," she added, "is nearly always ill-humoured, treats her husband very badly and without the least consideration, and he takes it all smiling. I have hardly ever heard her speak a kind word; she has something unpleasant to say of everybody, and since he believes everything she says, she is doing incalculable harm." But much as she had already confided by letter, Miechen still exercised some caution. She was mindful of the hurt that could come to Tsarina Marie's brother if Miechen confided too much. "Things occur which I cannot bring my pen to set down. They would pain your fraternal feelings too greatly. My heart is so full that I cannot find the right words to give you an idea of the complete overthrow of everything that one had hitherto thought to know as rules of conduct." Then, betraying a sense of exasperation, Miechen added: "I often feel that things *cannot* go on for long in *this* way, that the Tsar's eyes must at length be opened to the worthlessness of the creature who seems to have him bound as in a spell, to make him deaf and blind. Up to the present he is utterly and blissfully happy, looks very well, and years younger."[42]

Amidst the terror that surrounded the imperial family, the domestic turmoil involving the tsar and his morganatic wife continued to fester. Both Minnie and Miechen's hostility toward Katya did not abate. Things finally came to a dramatic head at the start of Lent in February 1881 in the Malachite Hall at the Winter Palace. The seasonal custom demanded that the imperial family gather together to ask forgiveness of each other. When Katya greeted Marie Feodorovna, Minnie gave her hand, but did not kiss her husband's stepmother. This omission caught Alexander II's attention, who then "broke into a torrent of impassioned language" and reproached his daughter-in-law for what he perceived to have been a very public snub. "Sasha is a good son," decried the emperor, "but you—you have no heart!"[43] By now no one but the tsarevich was immune from a sharp remark from Alexander II. The tsar's acute reprimand upset Marie Feodorovna greatly, leaving her in tears. The next day Minnie did not justify her behavior and instead begged her father-in-law to pardon her for grieving him. He did so, and the two were thus reconciled. A relieved

Alexander II was touched by Marie Feodorovna's gesture, moving him to confide to his confessor: "I am so happy today—my children have forgiven me!"[44]

Alexander II's happiness was short-lived. Sophia Perovskaya and the executive committee of the People's Will declared that the time had come to act. On March 1/13, 1881, all was set. The terrorists were ready. Alexander II had committed to Loris-Melikov's plan to convene the elected representatives to join the State Council, which had, up to that point, consisted purely of unelected members. This significant move was a first step toward some kind of constitution and diminution of autocracy. The manifesto was prepared and ready to be signed by the tsar. Perovskaya and the People's Will wanted to prevent this type of bold initiative, designed to bring liberal reforms to the people, from materializing. For a group that purported to perpetrate terrorist acts in the name of the people, such bizarre thinking was completely in contradiction with their supposed aims.

Early in the afternoon, Tsar Alexander II attended a military review then drove to pay a visit to his cousin, Grand Duchess Catherine. The routes taken by the tsar were periodically changed for security reasons, but Perovskaya and her accomplices were ready. As Alexander II made his way back to the Winter Palace, Sophia Perovskaya stationed herself at a vantage point for orchestrating the movements of four selected bomb throwers. One of them changed his mind and did not show up, but the other three did. These three fanatics knew that they would likely die should they throw the bomb, for the bombs "were so constructed that they had to be thrown at close range, and the user's body therefore became virtually a part of the infernal apparatus."[45] In the end, two of the three, Nicholas Rysakov and Ignatius Grinevitsky, carried out the dreaded deed. When Alexander II's carriage, escorted by six Cossacks, neared Rysakov, Sophia Petrovskaya gave the signal to throw the bomb. The explosion damaged the tsar's carriage, killing and maiming several innocent bystanders in the process. Rysakov survived the bombing and was apprehended. Intent on helping the injured, Alexander II got out of his carriage. He was urged to return immediately to the palace for his own safety. "Yes, yes," the tsar replied, "but these poor people must be seen to." Then a policeman approached Alexander and said, "Thank God, your Majesty is safe." "I am, thank God," answered the tsar. "But look at these—" pointing out to the dead and injured.[46] The captured Rysakov then exclaimed: "Still thanking God?"[47] Just then, Grinevitsky approached the tsar and threw his bomb at Alexander II's feet. The powerful explosion injured twenty others. Glass and other debris as well as blood and human flesh splattered the pristine snow. The terrorist was fatally wounded and died later that day. The tsar too was fatally wounded, his legs shattered by the second blast. Just before lapsing into unconsciousness, Alexander II murmured: "So cold . . . Help . . . Take me home to die."[48] The tsar's escort rushed their dying sovereign back to the Winter Palace.

At the Vladimir Palace, Miechen was sitting with her husband in his study. Suddenly, they were astonished by the unexpected entry of a doorman's wife. Tearfully, the sobbing woman cried out to Miechen and Vladimir: "He's dead! He's dead!" Then a servant rushed in, muttering, "the Emperor has just been driven by—dead in his brougham."[49] Vladimir rushed off in his carriage immediately. Miechen followed soon afterward. When she arrived at the Winter Palace, Miechen followed the trail of blood left by Alexander II as he was carried into the study.

At the Anichkov Palace, Minnie and Sasha heard the two explosions and met an officer who hurriedly told them that the emperor was gravely wounded. Minnie was set to take her eldest son, Nicky, to go ice-skating with his cousin Sandro and Sandro's brothers. Instead, she, her husband, and Nicky rushed to the Winter Palace. Sandro and his family also hastened to the palace. Once they entered Alexander II's study, they found the dying tsar, lying underneath a portrait of his beloved daughter, Marie Alexandrovna.

"He presented a terrific sight," recalled Sandro, "his right leg torn off, his left leg shattered, innumerable wounds all over his head and face. One eye was shut, the other expressionless." Clinging to Nicky, who at thirteen was old enough to have the sight of his mutilated grandfather seared in his mind, Sandro also noticed Marie Feodorovna. She was still holding the skates she was set to use that day in "her trembling hands." Now, faced with the sight of Alexander II's mangled body, Minnie was completely "stunned by the catastrophe."[50] Minnie later described the horror of the moment in a letter to her mother, Queen Louise: "Oh, what sorrow and despair, that our beloved Emperor should be torn away from us and even in this <u>dreadful</u> way! No, anyone who has not seen the appalling sight himself can never imagine anything like it! The poor, innocent Emperor—to see him in that terrible condition was truly heartrending! His face and head and upper body were untouched but his legs were completely crushed and torn up to the knees, so that at first I did not understand what I was actually looking at, a bleeding mass with half a boot on the right foot; all that was left of the left was the sole of his foot! Never in my life have I seen anything like it; no, it was horrible."[51]

The tsar's study was crammed with people, all dazed by the cruelty of what had just taken place. They were met with another pitiable sight when the

Princess Yurievskaya burst into the room screaming, "Sasha, Sasha!"[52] Katya begged Alexander II's surgeon: "Do everything possible to save him!"[53] The doctors tried to save the tsar, but it was hopeless. He was given the Last Rites of the Orthodox Church; and less than an hour after he was taken into the Winter Palace, Alexander II—the "Tsar-Liberator"—died from his wounds, a victim of the terrorist threat that had plagued him for years. Upon hearing the fateful words, "the Emperor is dead," Princess Yurievskaya "gave one shriek and dropped on the floor like a felled tree. Her pink-and-white negligee was soaked in blood."[54]

Miechen, like the rest of the family, witnessed the final agonizing moments as her father-in-law's life drew to a close. After the emperor was declared dead, Miechen watched her husband, "his face drawn and ravaged by grief, cross the room and fling open the windows looking out on the great square, packed now with a throng of people kneeling in the snow." In keeping with tradition that required that the word "death" not be mentioned, Vladimir instead announced in a booming voice: "His Majesty the Emperor orders you to live long."[55] Upon hearing those fateful words, the crowds, which had been silent, broke down sobbing.

The murdered tsar's eldest son, Alexander Alexandrovich was now Emperor Alexander III, and his wife had just become the Empress Marie Feodorovna. Alexander III, his huge lumbering frame dominating those around him, hastened with Minnie to an awaiting carriage. Together, the new tsar and tsarina—"Sasha the Bull and Dagmar the adored"[56]—made their way past the large crowds that had gathered outside the Winter Palace. Bundled against the cold winter, the couple, surrounded by armed guards with their lances drawn, made their way back to the Anichkov Palace in an open sleigh drawn by two horses.

Thus the new reign began with tragedy, with Russia entering a more menacing era—for "never again would a Russian Czar be able to think of his subjects in terms of boundless confidence." There was no denying that "the future of the empire, possibly of the entire world, depended upon the issue of the coming contest between the new Czar of Russia and the fast increasing forces of destruction."[57] The new Empress Marie Feodorovna was well aware of this, telling her mother: "my poor, beloved Sacha . . . I am disconsolate . . . My peace and calm are gone, for now I can never again rest assured about Sacha."[58]

9

THE IDOL OF HER PEOPLE

$\mathcal{W}$ ord of Alexander II's murder quickly reached England. The Duchess of Edinburgh received the anguishing news at Clarence House. "I remember quite well our being brought down to her room," wrote Missy, "and the terrible shock it was to find Mamma in tears."[1] In inconsolable sorrow, Marie Alexandrovna set off for Russia immediately.

Queen Victoria too was "quite shaken and stunned by this awful news . . . Poor, poor Emperor, in spite of his failings, he was a kind and amiable man, and had been a good ruler, wishing to do the best for his country."[2] The queen also admitted to feeling "overwhelmed . . . My poor dear Marie, what a terrible grief and ordeal for her!"[3] Vicky hastened to send Queen Victoria her thoughts: "Poor darling Marie!! How will she stand so terrible a shock? To lose both parents within a year and her Father, whom she doted on, in such a manner!! . . . I am so sorry for Sacha and Minny, to take up a murdered father's Crown is *too* dreadful."[4] "Poor darling Marie on whom her father doted, it is too much almost to bear," wrote Queen Victoria to Vicky. "But she is very courageous."[5]

On arriving in St. Petersburg, Marie Alexandrovna went to the very spot where her father was murdered and knelt in prayer. A shrine had been erected in Alexander II's memory, decorated with flowers and sacred pictures. Also rushing to St. Petersburg was Alexandra, the Princess of Wales, who found her sister Minnie looking tired and troubled. As a precaution against terrorist attacks, workers dug trenches around the Anichkov Palace; while Alexander III could hardly venture outside his home, even for some fresh air. The government eventually took over all the houses of an entire street behind the Anichkov

Palace in order to prevent tunnels from being built from there into the imperial residence.

There was the ordeal of the funeral itself, which was held under the tightest security. The public was "kept at a considerable distance . . . while the inhabitants of the surrounding houses were ordered to keep their double windows closed, and to admit no strangers to witness the procession."[6] Black prevailed everywhere—from the windows of residences hung with black crepe to the borders that lined the edges of the capital's newspapers. For a fortnight, St. Petersburg "was nothing but a solemn, sorrow-stricken mortuary chamber."[7]

Funeral ceremonials and services lasted over two weeks and were, according to the U.S. Ambassador John W. Foster, "of the most imposing character. Probably no mortal ever received a more regal internment."[8] Foster's wife was equally impressed by the service at the Cathedral of Sts. Peter and Paul where the late tsar's body was taken before internment. According to Mrs. Foster, "the cathedral was most elaborately and beautifully decorated, and one might easily have imagined it the *coronation* instead of the *burial* of a monarch."[9] At this service, standing next to Empress Marie Feodorovna were the Duchess of Edinburgh and the Grand Duchess Marie Pavlovna. The imperial ladies were in deepest mourning. Dressed entirely in black and swathed in long black crepe veils, the ladies had four-yard long trains trailing behind them.

The imperial family's emotional farewell to the late tsar marked the debut of Marie Feodorovna as empress, but the burden of inheriting the throne under such tragic circumstances had taken its toll. The Marchioness of Dufferin and Ava saw Marie Feodorovna during these tense days, noting that the empress "seemed to have cried away all beauty from her face."[10] On the day of internment at the cathedral, Mrs. Foster remarked that Marie Feodorovna was "oppressed with anxiety for her son,"[11] the Tsarevich Nicholas. Ambassador Foster noticed the difference too: "I found her much changed in spirit . . . Before, she was quite gay and cheerful. Now she looked sad, weary, and careworn. In the course of our conversation of less than seven minutes, she referred four times to the 'terrible affair,' the assassination and its results. Her womanly and tender nature evidently feels it more than the phlegmatic Emperor."[12]

Just as the Romanovs' lives were altered abruptly and profoundly so too was Katya's, who found herself not only a widow but also at the mercy of the new emperor and empress. However, Marie Feodorovna, long mortified by the presence of Katya by Alexander II's side, was now overcome with pity for the newly widowed Princess Yurievskaya, who in time might have been crowned empress. The circumstances of Alexander II's death moved Marie Feodorovna to show Katya sincere compassion during the funeral rites, where she embraced the grieving widow. In relating her feelings about what happened, Marie Feodorovna told her mother that "to see the unfortunate widow's despair was more than heartrending, so that in an instant, everything that we previously felt against her was gone and only the greatest, most sincere sympathy for her boundless pain remained. I cannot tell you how much I pity her; in such moments, one <u>forgets</u> and <u>forgives</u> everything."[13] The murder transformed the Romanovs' treatment of the widowed Katya to understanding and kindness. After the late tsar was buried the widowed Princess Yurievskaya decided to move to France with her children.

As empress of Russia, Marie Feodorovna held one of the most prestigious positions of her time. One contemporary publication described it as such: "Her position is the most splendid in the world—this girl who used to make her own dresses and trim her own bonnets."[14] Far from shying away from what was expected of her as empress, Marie Feodorovna embraced her role. Her legendary vivacity and elegance continued as a foil to her husband's ill humor and distaste for formal court entertainments.

Much as he disliked presiding over court functions, Alexander III bowed to the inevitable and grudgingly attended obligatory events. Most of the grand court entertainments were held at the Winter Palace. Its polished marquetry floors, crystal chandeliers, marble and granite pillars and staircases, gold-inlaid ebony door, huge vases of spectacular green malachite, and lapis lazuli decorated furnishings were a magnificent backdrop for Marie Feodorovna as she graced these occasions. At one court ball, the empress presided over a table that was decorated in pure gold. Attired in pale yellow silk, Marie Feodorovna glistened in diamonds "so large" that had they been "worn by any other person," the jewels would have been thought not to have been real. The adornment included "four rows of diamonds around her neck, with pendants in front and at the back, a beautiful tiara, in which the splendid stones were set open with just enough silver to hold them together; brooches all around the neck of her dress, two of them at least, consisting of single stones of incredible size, and diamond ornaments on her skirt." In sum, Empress Marie Feodorovna was "a blaze of splendor."[15]

Far from treating her position as a burden, Marie Feodorovna savored the role, which demanded that she entertain and look at ease doing so. Moreover, she possessed a "childlike capacity for enjoyment"[16] and it showed. Marie Feodorovna struck the perfect balance of being imperial and approachable. Miechen's niece, Crown Princess Cecilie, touched upon this: "She was very short," recalled Cecilie of the empress, "but her bearing, her distinguished and forceful personality, and the intelligence which shone in her face, made her the perfect figure of a queen. Wherever she went, her winning smile conquered the hearts of the people. The way in which she bowed when passing in her carriage was charming in its gracefulness. She was extraordinarily well loved in Russia, and everyone had confidence in her . . . and [was] a real mother to her people."[17]

Marie Feodorovna's sister-in-law, the Grand Duchess Marie Pavlovna, continued to preside over lavish entertainments too. The Vladimirs' 1883 costumed ball at their St. Petersburg home stood out for its brilliance. For weeks, St. Petersburg's elite feverishly prepared costumes from Russia's old days. The cloth manufacturer Saposhnikov was so inundated with orders for costumes that it struggled to keep up with the demand. The end result was a magnificent array of authentic costumes woven from expensive brocades, created in the old Russian boyar style. Altogether, 250 invited guests attended the much anticipated event. The guests of honor at Miechen's party were of course Alexander III and Marie Feodorovna. Dressed as a boyar and boyar's wife, Miechen and Vladimir greeted the imperial couple with the traditional sign of welcome, bread and salt. Dressed as a Russian tsarina of old, Marie Feodorovna was covered in jewels, though the heavy costume did not overwhelm her. Instead, she "wore it with such grace that it only added new attractions to her slight figure, and that evening can be reckoned as one of her greatest triumphs."[18] The ball was a tremendous success. "That evening," recalled one guest, "transported all the participants in the festival back to the days of their ancestors, and everyone regretted the advent of morning."[19]

Miechen and Vladimir's marriage continued to thrive. They shared ideals and ambitions, as well as a love of culture and beautiful things; and as the years passed, the couple's bond deepened. Vicky, the Crown Princess of Prussia, had once expressed her misgivings about them: "I don't think this marriage of Marie of Schwerin and Wladimir [sic] of Russia promises to be a happy one."[20] Yet despite Vicky's reservations, Miechen thrived in Russia and led a contented life with Vladimir and their children, Kyril, Boris, Andrei, and Elena.

Unlike Marie Feodorovna, who was consistently praised, Miechen had both admirers and detractors. Some found her to be "lovely"[21]—"a handsome and charming woman."[22] There was, also, talk that one could find a bit of Catherine the Great in the grand duchess. Could it be that Miechen, like the former princess from a small German principality, aspired to power and influence? There was, after all, the same "proud carriage of the head, the enigmatic smile, the fire in the deep-set eyes." Moreover, Miechen was a "forceful" character possessed of "keen judgement" with the ability to make "quick, unfaltering decisions."[23]

Alexander III's accession heralded a new era in Russia. Hopes of drastic reforms and lessened repression were soon dashed, however. Those responsible for Alexander II's murder received no clemency. Five, including Perovskaya and Kibaltchitch, were hanged for their crimes. Other revolutionaries, when apprehended, were imprisoned or exiled. What emerged in the aftermath of the late emperor's grisly murder was the level of retaliation that the autocracy's opponents had feared. "The long-drawn-out campaign of murder against Alexander II had created in his family an atmosphere of nervous tension which warranted the fierce reactionary feelings of most of them. Even Marie Feodorovna herself with her democratic upbringing fell prey to the general spirit."[24] For instance, a university threatened with closure by the government because so many of its women students belonged to revolutionary organizations appealed to the new tsarina. Marie Feodorovna rejected the chance to intervene, because "they breed revolutionaries there."[25]

Alexander III's political opponents wasted no time before threatening him. Just after his father's assassination, the new emperor received a Nihilist ultimatum, warning him of "the inevitable revolution" if he did not "comply with the will of the people." The Nihilists made no secret of their wish to inflict harm on the imperial family. St. Petersburg was described by a visiting Englishman as "reeking of dynamite—a nest of invisible assassins."[26] To protect the imperial family and maintain public order, the government introduced emergency rule. This meant that officials could curb civil liberties anytime. This emergency rule was imposed upon St. Petersburg, Moscow, and ten provinces. It stayed in effect until 1917. Thus, "certain areas of Russia . . . could at any time have judicial guarantees suspended and be placed under police rule."[27]

Alexander III, out of deference to his dead father, had contemplated going through with Loris-Melikov's program. But his adviser, Constantine Pobedonostsev, hastened to reshape Alexander III's thoughts. During a critical meeting that included Pobedonostsev, Grand Duke Vladimir, and Count Loris-Melikov, the emperor's former tutor dramatically argued his points, stating emphatically at one point: "If siren songs are sung to you about the necessity of pacification, of continuation of a liberal regime, and yielding to so-called public opinion, oh, please God, do not . . . hearken to them. This will mean ruin, the ruin of Russia and of you."[28] Pobedonostsev clearly struck a chord with the emperor when he "sharply reminded" Alexander III "that the obligations of an autocratic monarch had precedence over those to a dead father."[29]

Pobedonostsev's influence translated into official policy when the emperor promulgated the *Manifesto on Unshakable Autocracy*, which stated that Alexander III would "take up vigorously the task of governing . . . with faith in the strength and truth of the autocratic power that we have been called upon to affirm and safeguard for the popular good from any infringement."[30] Loris-Melikov had no alternative but to resign.

Observers also wondered if Empress Marie Feodorovna would exercise political influence on her husband. A newspaper article alluded to this: "Greece has now unquestionably a zealous champion in the Empress of Russia. Her first effort will be directed toward a policy more favorable to Greece." It was a prospect potentially "disquieting to Europe."[31] Marie Feodorovna was influential with her husband to some extent, but did not pursue political agendas the way she could have.

As sovereign, Alexander III emerged as the *moujik* tsar,[32] thanks to his deep-seated Russianness. Earlier in the century, Tsar Nicholas I had stated that an autocrat, "above all . . . must remember that he was Russian. 'That,' Nicholas I remarked, 'means everything.' "[33] Alexander III embraced this concept wholeheartedly. By inclination and temperament, Marie Feodorovna's husband was Russian to the core, taking as his motto for his reign: "All for Russia." Alexander III replaced French with Russian as the official language of elite society. He pursued the Russification of his multiethnic empire. The policy was enforced, not voluntary, and had serious negative consequences for a number of ethnic groups. The Jews, in particular, suffered curtailed rights during this time. They were forbidden to live outside the twenty-five provinces in Poland and Russia that constituted the "Pale of Settlement," on Russia's western border. Anti-Jewish pogroms (attacks) persisted, and discrimination against Jews became widespread and codified. The emperor dispatched his brother, Grand Duke Vladimir, to the Baltic regions to convey orders that Russian was to be the dominant language, not German. Learning Russian became obligatory in schools, while German was prohibited. It was the same for the Polish language in Polish schools. The policy of Russification even extended to military uniforms, which took on a much more distinctly Slavic look, by contrast to the German look that had long been in vogue. The busby of black Astrakhan wool was the new headgear, replacing the previously ubiquitous German helmet. At home, the emperor took to wearing a Russian costume of baggy trousers, a colored shirt, and high boots.

With the exception of their 1883 coronation in Moscow, life for Empress Marie Feodorovna and her husband took on a predictable pattern, though pervasive domestic terrorism remained the regime's central concern. The constant danger further compromised the imperial family's lifestyle. While Emperor Alexander III and Empress Marie Feodorovna were in St. Petersburg, they lived at the Anichkov Palace, which was deemed easier to secure than the Winter Palace. However, they spent most of their time at a new location, Gatchina, thirty miles from the capital. Unlike other Romanov palaces with their Baroque splendors, Gatchina stood out for its austere, fortresslike look. Massive in size with nine hundred rooms, and devoid of color and flamboyant decorations on its façade, Gatchina was surrounded by formal gardens and extensive parkland that was dotted with several lakes. In no time, Gatchina became Alexander III and Marie Feodorovna's principal residence, thanks largely to the fact that it was easier to guard the imperial family there. A huge security detail provided a complicated chain of protection that included detectives, police, palace guards, infantry, and cavalry patrols. The government created a new unit of the police called the *Okhrana*, whose members went undercover in all strata of society. The division was entrusted to battle subversive elements of the state, sometimes using controversial means. In no time, control, secrecy, and repression became bywords linked to the *Okhrana*.

Gatchina—the "citadel of autocracy"—was a gilded cage for Marie Feodorovna and her family. No one from the imperial entourage was allowed to lock their rooms at Gatchina so that the *Okhrana* could come and go as they pleased to inspect them at all hours of the day. Despite the prisonlike existence, Marie Feodorovna tried her best to provide a happy family atmosphere for her husband and children. She also acquiesced to her husband's wish for a simpler private life at Gatchina without complaint, bearing the "ensuing discomfort and *ennui* with invariable good humour."[34]

Instead of inhabiting the splendid rooms found throughout Gatchina, Alexander III insisted that the family live modestly. The imperial family's spartan personal quarters contrasted starkly with Gatchina's other rooms, including the guest rooms, which were impressive and luxurious. Lord Frederic Hamilton noted this contrast, observing that "nothing could be plainer than the large study in which" the tsar received him.[35] The bedroom assigned to Lord Frederic, on the other hand, had "light blue silk walls embroidered with large silver wreaths. The mirrors were silvered, and the bed stood in a species of chancel, up four steps, and surrounded by a balustrade of silvered carved wood."[36] Priceless objets d'art, tapestries, and paintings adorned numerous rooms. Elaborately garbed servants lent the place an air of barbaric splendor. The most exotic were the two Nubians, sporting scimitars and turbans, who stood on guard outside the empress's audience chamber.

The couple's private apartments were on the ground floor, where the ceilings were low and the furniture was comfortable as opposed to luxurious. Except when entertaining guests, the family ate most of their meals in a room that had formerly been the bathroom of the Tsarina Alexandra, wife of Tsar Nicholas I. To make the room more attractive and comfortable, Empress Marie Feodorovna had the huge white marble tub filled with flowers. Even though Alexander III had hundreds of servants at his disposal, he made his own coffee in the mornings and shared a plain breakfast of rye bread, butter, and boiled eggs with his empress. Oftentimes, they were joined by their youngest daughter, the Grand Duchess Olga Alexandrovna, who had been born at Peterhof in June 1882. Olga was the only one of Marie Feodorovna's children born while she was empress.

During the mid-1880s, the Romanovs welcomed two new members into the family fold. In 1884, Princess Elisabeth of Saxe-Altenburg (who became the Grand Duchess Elisabeth Mavrikievna, nicknamed "Mavra") married Grand Duke Constantine Constantinovich ("K.R."), thus becoming Queen Olga's sister-in-law. As predicted, Miechen's refusal to convert from Lutheranism to Orthodoxy had set a precedent that would prompt future foreign brides to do the same when marrying into the imperial family. Mavra was one such bride. Mavra and Miechen were glaring exceptions to the roster of devoted Orthodox adherents among the Romanovs. Mavra adamantly refused to forsake Lutheranism, much to her husband's chagrin. K.R. also worried that his sister, Queen Olga, would not accept Mavra. "I am afraid," wrote K.R., "that our Olya will not like her much."[37] K.R. craved his sister's approval, since he held her in esteem, as the following 1882 poem he wrote to Olga attests:

> Do you remember those scarlet flowers,
> That captivated us so much . . .
> But that time is buried forever . . .
> Now that we are in the distance from each other,
> When you are under luxurious southern sky,
> And I am where a north snow-storm cries,
> By chance if your look falls down
> On those flowers, Oh, remember me
> And think that

Loving soul of poet is sending you his greetings,
That this soul is warmed by reminiscing you.[38]

On the heels of K.R. and Mavra's wedding, another took place in 1884 involving yet another German royal. This latest German princess to enter the imperial family also followed Miechen and Mavra's example by remaining Lutheran. This time the Duchess of Edinburgh's brother, the Grand Duke Serge, married Queen Victoria's granddaughter, Princess Elisabeth ("Ella") of Hesse, whose late mother, Princess Alice, had so strongly supported the marriage between Prince Alfred and the Grand Duchess Marie Alexandrovna. The tall and svelte Ella with the gray-blue eyes had grown into one of the most beautiful princesses in Europe and suitors besides Serge included the future German Kaiser Wilhelm II, son of Queen Victoria's daughter Vicky.

Queen Victoria was extremely unhappy that Ella married into the Romanov dynasty. She bluntly told Ella's sister, Princess Victoria: "Russia, I cd. not wish for any of you." The concerned grandmother added: "Ella's health will *never* stand the climate . . . besides the dreadful state Russia is in, & the very depressed bad state of Society."[39] The queen tried her best to dissuade Ella from marrying Serge. This infuriated the Duchess of Edinburgh, who was close to Serge, and naturally wished him to marry Ella, as this was his wish. In August 1883, an agitated Marie Alexandrovna wrote to a friend: "That happy and so entirely satisfactory . . . prospect of marriage of my brother Serge is going I think to fall through, under the deplorable influence of the Queen. The young lady having just returned from her long visit to England and told by her father that after her own wish and consent, I was coming over to Darmstadt with my brother, boldly declared that she would have nothing to do with him . . . I am not angry with the poor girl because I know she was well disposed towards my brother, but I have no words strong enough to blame the Queen. I knew that from the very first she sett [*sic*] her heart against it saying that she had only heard his praise, but he had the greatest of all misfortunes, he was Russian and she had enough of <u>one Russian</u> in the family (meaning me of course)." Marie Alexandrovna went on to add that Serge had been "fully encouraged in every way." Moreover, he was "an exceptionally nice young man . . . and can be recommended in every possible way, not because he is my brother, but because he is an exception among princes."[40]

The Romanovs welcomed Ella as a family member. The Duchess of Edinburgh referred to Ella in one of her letters as "my lovely *belle-soeur*."[41] The emperor and empress also welcomed their new sister-in-law into the family.

Ella, in turn, felt grateful for their friendship. She visited Gatchina and reported to Queen Victoria that, "Sasha and Minny are both so very kind, and I spend the whole afternoon with her . . . the time passes very pleasantly."[42]

Nevertheless, these pleasant and peaceful days were to become few and far between. Living under constant surveillance was beginning to take its toll, which was why Alexander III and Marie Feodorovna cherished their carefree holidays in Denmark so much. The Danish sojourns allowed the emperor to unwind and play the jovial uncle. Prince Nicholas of Greece remembered his uncle Sasha as "an unending delight . . . when with us he was just a schoolboy up to all kinds of pranks."[43] Marie Feodorovna was elated to see her children pay their regular visits to their grandparents, King Christian IX and Queen Louise (known affectionately by their grandchildren as "Apapa" and "Amamma"). During these Danish visits, the imperial children came to know their numerous royal cousins, among them the Greek and British royal families. The British cousins were the Princess of Wales's children: the Princes Albert Victor ("Eddy") and George and the Princesses Louise, Victoria, and Maud. The tsar and tsarina's youngest daughter, Olga, wistfully recalled how the imperial family relished their freedom there: "No member of the *Okhrana* was there to guard us from dangers which did not exist."[44] During one visit, the Princess of Wales wrote about the family parting to her son, Prince George, of "that *awful* moment of tearing ourselves away from one another, not knowing *where* and *how* our next meeting may be. Poor little [Minnie], I can see her now, standing on top of the steps in utter despair, her eyes streaming over with tears, and trying to hold me as long as she could. Poor Sacha too felt the parting very much and cried dreadfully."[45]

In 1888, catastrophe struck as Marie Feodorovna, Alexander III, and their children were traveling from the Caucasus back to the north. As the imperial train neared the town of Borki in the Ukraine, and the family awaited dessert to be served in the dining car, the train suddenly derailed. Everyone was thrown violently onto the floor; then the roof collapsed. Alexander III crawled out of the debris and, with superhuman effort, held up the mangled roof in order to allow his family to escape. Ten of the fifteen cars were destroyed, dozens of people were injured, and twenty-one killed. Upon ascertaining that her family was accounted for, Marie Feodorovna wasted no time in assisting the doctor, despite the fact that she had been injured by broken glass, sustaining cuts and bruises all over her body. When the relief train arrived, Alexander III and Marie Feodorovna refused to board it, ensuring first that the wounded and the dead bodies were taken on board. The cause of the accident was debated. It was thought that two bombs were placed on the track. Another version had it that a bomb was smuggled aboard the imperial train. The wreck might have been due to the rotten state of the sleepers and excessive speed of the train. It was also believed that the train was traveling too fast and jumped the track. This judgment was echoed by an investigation into the accident.

The impact of the Borki disaster had made its mark on the empress and emperor. It had left the empress in shock. A fortnight after the accident, Marie Feodorovna wrote to her father: "The more I think about it, the more our salvation seems incomprehensible, and the miracle becomes more and more obvious."[46] When Elizabeth Narishkin-Kurakin visited Marie Feodorovna at Gatchina not long after the tragedy, she found the empress "still noticeably nervous." It was not a surprising reaction, considering that Marie Feodorovna "had seen the wreckage of the train hanging over her head threatening to drop down and crush her any minute." Shaken as she was by the experience, the empress told Narishkin-Kurakin "with pardonable pride about the unselfish help her sons had given" the rescue party.[47] As for Alexander III, his nerves were never quite the same after that day; and even more ominously, his Herculean effort to save his family would have a grievous effect on his health.

10

THE MATERNAL INSTINCT

*L*ong before, Marie Feodorovna had become "the idol of the Russian people"[1] and as empress, her popularity did not abate. She was widely recognized as "the only person on the face of the earth in whom the Autocrat of all the Russias puts any real trust. In his gentle consort he has unlimited confidence."[2] Alexander III was proud of his wife's accomplishments and willingness to assume the responsibilities of being empress, calling Marie Feodorovna "the Guardian Angel of Russia."[3] It was an appropriate moniker, for the empress was not content to be a mere adornment to her husband, presiding over court entertainments. She also embraced philanthropic work. As tsarevna, she had assumed patronage of the Marie Institutions from her mother-in-law. Encompassing over 450 charitable and educational establishments, the Marie Institutions were originally founded to "succor the homeless, helpless, and forlorn, and to bring up the young in the principles of true religion and love to their neighbor."[4] Far from being a mere figurehead, the empress's interest in the success of these institutions was active and sincere. In 1882, she founded a number of establishments called Marie schools, to give young girls a solid elementary education. The empress frequently visited institutions of which she was patron, schools of the Marie Institutions among them. These establishments aided tens of thousands of the empress's subjects. The empress received innumerable petitions, begging her for help of all kinds. After reviewing the petitions, the empress gave aid where she deemed appropriate and donated money to causes she deemed worthwhile. As patroness of the Russian Red Cross, Marie Feodorovna oversaw that philanthropic organization's numerous important projects, assuring that they ran well or came to fruition. Her charity included donations to the coffers, medical supplies, medical training, and the smooth running of hospital trains. It was not unusual for the empress to visit charitable institutions unexpectedly.

During a cholera epidemic in the late 1870s in St. Petersburg, an intimate of the imperial family reported that Marie Feodorovna and her husband "visited the sick and dying in hospitals in the districts isolated by the troops to prevent contact with the outside world." It was also said that Marie Feodorovna visited mental institutions "in order to satisfy herself that they were properly managed, and from her private funds she educated and brought up a number of orphans."[5] Thus did Marie Feodorovna strike a perfect balance as empress, combining philanthropic work with her role as the dazzling hostess par excellence in the imperial capital.

Marie Feodorovna, a lenient mother, had an exceptionally close relationship with her children and delighted in being called "Mother dear." Nicky continued to be her favorite, while Olga and Michael gravitated more toward their father. Marie Feodorovna's middle son, George, an inveterate prankster, often got away with his antics, largely because the empress could never bring herself to reprimand him. As Grand Duchess Olga explained, "mother had a great weakness for him."[6] Marie Feodorovna also supervised her children's religious upbringing. A Protestant convert to Orthodoxy, the empress "strove to inculcate [a] strong faith and encourage ritual practices in her children."[7]

Marie Alexandrovna did not have the same close relationship with her only son, Prince Alfred, but felt nearer to her daughters. The Duchess of Edinburgh was an exacting mother who tried to instill Victorian concepts of duty in her children. She counseled her children not to succumb to illness and to eat everything set before them. "Children," the duchess would say to them, "don't let English people persuade you that certain foods are indigestible . . . English people spoil their digestion from earliest childhood by imagining that they cannot eat this or that. I always ate everything; in Russia no one ever spoke about their digestions [sic], it's a most unpleasant subject and not drawing-room conversation." Never, insisted Marie Alexandrovna, must her children, refuse a dish set before them. "But if they are not good, Mamma?" came the searching question. "Then you must just behave as though they were good," came the pragmatic and dutiful answer. "But if they make you feel sick!" came the retort. "Then be sick, my dear, but wait till you get home. It would be most offensive to be sick then and there!"[8] The Duchess of Edinburgh also trained her children to be good conversationalists, as she herself was—in a half dozen languages. Missy recalled that "no one could tell a story better than Mamma . . . [who]

could keep a whole table amused." Marie Alexandrovna encouraged her off-spring to follow suit. A princess who kept silent was a near anathema to the duchess. "Besides," she declared, "it is very rude and please remember that, my dear children."[9]

Much as she loved her children, Marie Alexandrovna was also somewhat disappointed in them, for none fulfilled her great ambition of giving birth to a wunderkind. The Duchess of Edinburgh nursed hopes that at least one of her offspring would be exceptional in some talent. When it became obvious to her that this would not materialize, Marie Alexandrovna felt let down and did not push to have her children especially educated. Missy later regretted this. "She adored us," wrote Missy years later of her mother, "gave up her life to us, but for all that she had little faith in us; that was the strange, strange thing."[10] More-over, "she never took us seriously, we were of a younger generation, nor had we been educated as perfectly as she had been; and above all we were Protestants, and therefore some parts of our souls were shut off from hers."[11] Marie Alex-androvna's unambitious agenda for educating her children was a curious omis-sion, since as one contemporary put it, the duchess was "a very remarkable person, clever without being brilliant, extremely well read, and gifted with a strong amount of common sense."[12]

Marie Alexandrovna dominated her children's lives, since her husband was so often absent due to his naval duties. From 1886 to 1889, the Edinburgh fam-ily lived in Malta when the Duke of Edinburgh took command of the Royal Navy's Mediterranean fleet. Marie Alexandrovna excelled as the wife of the commander of the Mediterranean Fleet. A senior officer in the Royal Navy, Sir Seymour Fortescue, recalled how the duchess, "certainly succeeded, in her position as wife to the Commander-in-Chief, in making herself extremely pop-ular with the Naval Officers at Malta." Fortescue also concluded that Duchess of Edinburgh was "a very remarkable woman."[13]

While in Malta, the duchess never faced the ever painful issue of prece-dence that rankled her at Queen Victoria's court. By this time, the duchess and the queen had arrived at a truce in their battle of wills. Marie Alexandrovna was the only one of Queen Victoria's immediate relations whom Victoria did not "attempt to domineer." The "exceedingly imperious" queen failed to elicit the same "unswerving obedience" from Maria Alexandrovna that she de-manded from her own children.[14] The Duchess of Edinburgh's defiant attitude annoyed her mother-in-law. During the search for a bride for the queen's son, Prince Arthur, the queen made it clear: "God knows we *don't* want a *second Russian* Element" in the family.[15] But Queen Victoria also felt a grudging admiration for Marie Alexandrovna's steadfast independence, and as a sign of her respect, the Duchess of Edinburgh's portrait was the only one of her family the queen allowed to be hung in her private breakfast room at Windsor Castle.

There was more to the Duchess of Edinburgh than her stubborn, independent streak and obsession with status. Missy summed up her mother's character, noting how: "Outwardly she may have appeared haughty, a stickler for form and proud of her rank, but inwardly she was humble, always tormenting herself, tortured with the idea that she had never lived up to the ideal set for her by her parents and those who had educated her." Marie Alexandrovna was also extremely generous. She may have been wealthy, but "she gave even beyond what it was reasonable to give, gave and gave, to big and small, to rich and poor; her very reason of existence was to be able to give."[16] A publication recounted the Duchess of Edinburgh's generosity, telling readers that her "goodness to the poor in an absolutely unobtrusive manner has always been remarkable. She is generous to a fault, and most considerate to her dependants."[17]

Marie Alexandrovna was equally considerate to her children. When she was compelled to leave them behind to accompany her husband on trips, Marie Alexandrovna wrote letters to her children, describing the people she met and the places she visited. In one letter, written in 1887, the duchess described her visit to Montenegro, a "curious country [that] is so unlike anything else that I think myself in a dream." Marie Alexandrovna spoke of the Prince of Montenegro, saying how "he is very strict and everybody obeys him in a wonderful way and is devoted to him. Only imagine that they all walk about with loaded revolvers, even all the servants when they wait at dinner." Keeping in mind that her children would find such stories interesting, the duchess added: "the Prince killed a very poisonous snake that was going to get up on its tail." The duchess ended her letter: "I was so pleased to get news twice from you here . . . I send you all many kisses. Your old Mamma."[18]

One of the individuals Marie Alexandrovna mentioned in her letter was a certain "George." This George was none other than the second son of the Prince and Princess of Wales, who was destined to become King George V. The young prince, in his early twenties, was serving in the Royal Navy under his uncle, the Duke of Edinburgh. Though George's mother and sisters looked at the Edinburgh princesses condescendingly, Prince George found his Edinburgh cousins to be great company. He was especially attracted to the golden-haired and vivacious Missy, who was ten years his junior and whom he referred to as his "darling Missy."

During his time in the Royal Navy, Prince George had several opportunities to meet with other royals, among them Miechen. In 1887, Prince George went to Greece where he stayed with his "dear Uncle Willy" and "darling Aunt Olga"[19] at Tatoi, the grounds of which, George wrote, were "so pretty and remind me so much of Scotland."[20] At Tatoi, George became reacquainted with his Greek cousins: Alexandra, Marie, and Andrew. George confessed at being "delighted to see them again" after five years, and finding that they had "not changed a bit."[21]

A special bond had already grown through the years between the twenty-two-year-old Prince George of Wales and his thirty-five-year-old aunt Olga, evidence of the queen's kindness and strong maternal streak. Queen Olga became like a mother to Prince George during his transitional years that took him from boyhood to manhood. The tone of Queen Olga's letters to the man who was one day to become King George V was always affectionate. Even when George was a young adult, the queen could not resist writing to him as if he were still much younger: "I kiss your tootsum head. Ever your loving devoted A[unt] Olga xxx my little adopted sunbeam child!"[22] During his visits to Greece, Prince George spent many hours talking to his aunt Olga, whom he liked to refer to touchingly in his diary as being "such a Tootsum dear."[23] Queen Olga once gave her nephew a card inscribed: "To darling Tootsum Georgie in remembrance of our walks in Tatoi," signing it, "loving old A. Olga."[24]

Prince George was not Queen Olga's only admirer within the British royal family. Queen Victoria also found the Queen of the Hellenes to be an extraordinary person. "How charming Olga of Greece is!" exclaimed Queen Victoria to her daughter Vicky, "so handsome & so dear & charming. She has *none* of the *bourgeoiserie* of the rest of the Russian family even including our dear excellent Marie [Duchess of Edinburgh]."[25] Whenever possible, the Duchess of Edinburgh, as well as Queen Olga visited Emperor Alexander III and Empress Marie Feodorovna during the summer months at their residence at Peterhof. Empress Marie Feodorovna's daughter, Grand Duchess Olga Alexandrovna, formed impressions of both her aunts, Olga and Marie Alexandrovna, during their summer visits. Grand Duchess Olga recognized an "enthusiasm that was infectious" in the Queen of Greece. She also "looked a saint and her serenity did us all much good. She brought masses of exquisite Greek embroideries to Russia so as to raise money for one or another of her many philanthropic activities in Greece." As for the grand duchess's other aunt, Olga confessed that, "I liked my aunt Marie, but I don't think she was very happy. She relaxed at Peterhof, though."[26]

Marie Alexandrovna eagerly set off on her visits to her native land. She would rhapsodize over the weather, saying "nowhere does one enjoy the summer more than in Russia,"[27] which was in stark contrast to damp England. Marie Alexandrovna referred to the dull weather there as that "hideous climate" that tended to "spoil, as usual, all the enjoyments."[28] The duchess's description of these visits also pointed to a close family bond. "Nearly all of my relatives live in the neighbourhood," went one letter, "you never saw such a family party. The Queen of Greece is here with nearly all her children, grown-up young men and babies, she herself looking younger than me, and dancing away merrily whilst I look on." Then in a wistful but also humble vein, the Duchess of Edinburgh added: "I cannot make up my mind to dance in the same place which witnessed my début some sixteen years ago, a slim young lady then, a fat matron now. So I walk about, renew old acquaintances, have people presented, and try to make myself agreeable. All welcome me with joy and such cordiality that the task is an easy one."[29]

"After my London life," admitted Marie Alexandrovna, "I feel perfectly confused at this very animated existence [in Russia]; but it does me a great deal of good." Having reveled in her Russian sojourn, Marie Alexandrovna ended this letter to Lady Randolph Churchill characteristically complaining about England: "London must be detestable now. I quite pity you, and wish you were here."[30] Lady Randolph Churchill was one of Marie Alexandrovna's closest friends. Both were of the same age and born of privilege, though the former was certainly not in the same league as the latter in terms of wealth and an illustrious parentage. Lady Randolph was the former Jennie Jerome, the Brooklyn-born daughter of a wealthy American. Jennie made a big impression in England; and such was her fame that by 1901 it was said that "in England there is no woman below the royal family whose name and personality are so generally known as Lady Randolph Churchill's" and that she held "a place second to that of no other American woman in Europe."[31] Jennie was the mother of one of the great historical figures of the twentieth century, Sir Winston Churchill. When he was a young child, the red-haired Winston visited the Edinburgh children and took a fancy to the eldest daughter, Missy, declaring that he would one day marry her.

In many ways, the friendship that developed between Jennie and Marie seemed inconceivable. For one thing, Jennie was one of the great beauties of the day, while the duchess had never had extraordinary looks, and by her own admission had become heavy and matronly. Jennie, lively and approachable, was raised in the democratic and freedom-loving United States, while Marie Alexandrovna, notorious for her hauteur, was the favored child of Russia's autocrat. The married Jennie was courted by men of society and politics, acquiring numerous prominent lovers, while the morally upright Marie Alexandrovna did not stray from her marital vows. Yet despite their differences, the two women became close friends. They were drawn together by their mutual interest in politics, love of intelligent conversation, and music. Lady Randolph and the Duchess of Edinburgh especially delighted in playing duets on the piano. "I greatly enjoy our music performances at Lady Randolph's and only hope, that it does not tire her! I always had and still have the feeling, that royalty must spoil every entertainment," wrote the Duchess of Edinburgh.[32] Jennie recorded her high esteem for the Duchess of Edinburgh for posterity:

> I cannot leave the subject of Russia and the Russians without speaking of the one it has been my privilege to know best; namely, the . . . Duchess of Edinburgh . . . A warm-hearted woman of rare intelligence and exceptional education, her early life . . . was a most interesting one, as, quite apart from the exalted position she held, it was her duty for two hours daily to read her father's correspondence and the secret news of the world, in itself a liberal education. An excellent musician, [Anton] Rubinstein [the famed Russian pianist and composer] once said of her, so she told me, *'Vous ne jouez pas si mal pour une Princesse.'*[33] A fine linguist, speaking fluently several languages, the Duchess wrote them equally well."[34]

Marie Alexandrovna also found Jennie's husband, Lord Randolph, who became chancellor of the Exchequer and leader of the House of Commons, fascinating company. Lord Randolph, who "had a way of speaking with great rapidity and vehemence and a compelling intensity,"[35] was exactly the type of individual who appealed to her. The Duchess of Edinburgh once confessed to Jennie, that "I have a *faible* [weakness] for him."[36] When Jennie made Marie Alexandrovna laugh with her stories about Lord Randolph's resignation as chancellor and Queen Victoria's indignation, the duchess wrote to Jennie: "I am dying to hear some more of Lord Randolph's Windsor stories . . . Fancy if it was all reported to her [Queen Victoria] . . . And that I was encouraging a minister 'in disgrace'. But the ex-minister is really too amusing and makes me die with laughter."[37] And in another letter, Marie Alexandrovna told Jennie: "How I should enjoy another good talk with him."[38]

In January 1886, the Duchess of Edinburgh wrote Lord Randolph an intriguing letter, in which Marie Alexandrovna not only speaks of her enthusiasm for the man but also gives a tantalizing hint of her own political beliefs:

Dear Lord Randolph

I am very sorry indeed that you could not come this afternoon, but understand perfectly well the great amount of work you have to do just now. I only thought that a quiet Sunday in the country and some cheerful company might do you good in the middle of all your political and government troubles! I pity you with all my heart, when I think of all the boredom that awaits you now, but still I was always of [the] opinion, that a clever man must always feel some satisfaction in working hard for his country or even, for himself alone. And then, may I add, that a man ought to be ambitious if he wants really to do good in this world! Please excuse all this unnecessary talk, but since I have learnt to know you well I feel real interest in you, though I am a liberal at heart and . . . but I will not finish my sentence, as my ideas would carry me too far. I wish you only not to think me anymore the proud Russian Princess you thought me at first and to realise that my country and people have also many good qualities, one of the first one being their true appreciation of clever men! . . . If you still think it possible to come, we shall be delighted to see you. If not, please forget my rank that frightens you and come to see me at Clarence House like any ordinary mortal . . . Au revoir,

Marie[39]

The Duchess of Edinburgh was especially pleased when the Churchills visited Russia, telling Jennie: "I am sincerely glad that you have both gone to Russia and have such pleasant impressions." Marie Alexandrovna added her own observations of her fellow Russians to Jennie, telling her that, "my countrymen and women are very lively and demonstrative: they have kind, warm hearts, and are really fond of one. I feel that more and more when I go back to Russia."[40]

By this time, the Duchess of Edinburgh was unhappy with her marriage. Apart from music and their children, she and her husband had few things in common. Moreover, Alfred's irascible nature did not mellow with time. His drinking problem made him ever more difficult and rancorous. Courtiers, family, and friends close to the couple were aware of Affie's tendencies to drown his sorrows in drink. Henry Ponsonby knew that the duke had been ill with "incipient *delirium tremens*," becoming in turn "chastened" by it.[41] Alfred's friend Sir Arthur Sullivan, famed for the Gilbert and Sullivan operas, tried to help him out of his drinking problem. Sullivan confided as much to Affie's favorite sister, Louise. "All my life I have tried to influence him . . . in the right way," wrote Sullivan. "Years ago even, before he was married, I have tried to check the evil tendency which was manifesting itself . . . I never allowed timidity to prevent me from saying what I thought was right . . . But after his marriage I naturally saw less of him, and dared not attempt to resume the relative position I occupied before." Sullivan thought that Alfred might have benefited from better support from Marie Alexandrovna, but found little sympathy from her, as he related to Princess Louise: "I saw there was a distinctly *hostile element* risen against me, which made me feel very uncomfortable, and always embarrassed. I saw that in any effort I made even to hint or indicate what I thought was judicious or discreet, I *got not help* whatever from one to whom I desired to be a faithful servant and ally [Marie] . . . He *never had any support or help in his home life* . . . I have seen things—witnessed little scenes—heard words which have pained me dreadfully. And yet withal he was so sweet and gentle—so patient and forebearing that I could not help admiring and respecting him more than ever, and could hardly blame him if he sought a little 'soulagement' [relief] in a resource which was neither right nor healthy."[42]

In spite of her unhappiness in her marriage and with life in England, it was to Marie Alexandrovna's great credit that she hid her sadness from her children. "My mother kept all worry and conflict from us," recalled Missy, "we lived in a real fool's paradise . . . I thank her for it all . . . because with that life which she helped us to lead, she sowed a seed of idealism in my soul which nothing, nay, neither conflict, disappointment, disillusion nor stern reality, was ever quite able to uproot."[43]

Queen Olga's son, Prince Nicholas, found the Duchess of Edinburgh severe. He recalled his "Aunt Marie" as being "rather austere" and disapproving of Queen Olga's rambunctious children.[44] As the years passed, these rambunctious children grew into young adults who took their responsibilities as princes and princesses of the royal house of Greece very seriously. Their mother set a fine example before them, for as Queen of Greece, Olga assumed her responsibilities seriously, busying herself above all with philanthropic work. The diplomat Sir Horace Rumbold, who served in Greece in the 1880s, was impressed by this. "Although brought up in the most splendid and luxurious of Courts," Rumbold wrote, "no princess of a great reigning house ever led a saintlier life of perfect self-denial and charity than Queen Olga. Her days were almost entirely given up to good works."[45] A sense of personal responsibility animated Olga, who was motivated by Christian love and obligation. Olga believed that it was her Christian duty to help her people, particularly those who were the least fortunate. From her earliest days as queen, Olga took a special interest in the social welfare of her subjects, truly acting as the mother of her country. She founded a number of institutions with the goal of dispensing charitable assistance. Olga spearheaded prisons reforms, which up to then had been run inefficiently, barely functioning under the most dreadful conditions. Helping the destitute and women was central to Olga's philanthropic goals. She aided poor women by the hundreds of thousands through the creation of a workshop. After founding a school to train nurses, Olga established the first Greek hospital, the Evangelismos. Among her philanthropic endeavors, the Evangelismos became Queen Olga's favorite project, prompting her to encourage those she knew to donate funds toward it. Opened in 1884, the hospital eventually developed into a respected institution. Under Queen Olga's patronage and supervision, the Evangelismos became what Sir Horace Rumbold called "a hospital worthy of any great Western capital."[46] Queen Olga frequently visited the Evangelismos, ministering to the sick and dying. One mortally ill soldier comforted by the queen died looking at her, whispering, "My Mother!" Upon his death, it was Olga who closed his eyes. On another occasion, a worker was brought to the Evangelismos with a severe back injury. When Olga tried to comfort the patient, he replied: "Your words are good, my queen, but I have five mouths to feed back home, and God doesn't drop loaves of bread from the sky."[47] When she heard this, Olga sent orders that his family be fed anonymously until the man could recover fully from his injury and return to work. From the Royal Palace, an exhausted Olga made regular inquiries about the hospital's most serious patients, whose condition greatly concerned her. Such was the generous nature of Greece's Russian queen. In time, she had rightly earned the title and been proclaimed publicly "Queen of the poor."[48] By her own example, Olga followed the precept: "Love one another," a saying that she ordered posted at the Evangelismos.[49]

Far from ministering solely to her Greek subjects, Queen Olga also gave her attention to Russian sailors who came to Athens. The queen had built a hospital for sick and dying Russian sailors, whom she frequently visited to comfort. Crown Princess Cecilie recalled that "the Russian sailors on the ships which visited Athens literally worshipped the queen like a saint."[50] Queen Olga especially liked to show her Navy Room in the Royal Palace to Russian sailors. This room housed gifts sailors and officers had presented to her over the years. The room was filled with models of Russian ships and photographs of crews and ships, as well as commemorative plaques and books of naval interest. "After such visits my soul is so warm and peaceful!" the queen once wrote. "All the rooms are filled with the smell of Russianness; it smells like boots and Russian cloth."[51]

On a personal level, Queen Olga's ties to Russia were reinforced when her eldest daughter, nineteen-year-old Princess Alexandra, married the Duchess of Edinburgh's youngest brother, Grand Duke Paul, in 1890. Queen Olga greatly approved of the Duchess of Edinburgh's youngest brother as a son-in-law, telling Prince George of Wales: "Paul is a lovely character, he is so noble, so clever and so full of feeling—he adores her [Alexandra] . . . they will be exceedingly happy together."[52] The charming Princess Alexandra was a favorite with her family. Her brother Nicholas described Alexandra as having the "sweetest possible nature, and everyone loved her for her perfect naturalness, her generous heart."[53] Alexandra soon became a favorite with the Romanovs as well. Her arrival at the Russian court added a luster to the roster of sisters-in-law of the Empress Marie Feodorovna. Princess Catherine Radziwill recalled in her memoirs that "among all the remembrances" of her youth, "one of the liveliest that has remained engraved upon my mind is a quadrille danced at one of the balls at the Winter Palace. In it Marie Feodorovna was surrounded by her three sisters-in-law, the Grand Duchesses Marie Pavlovna, Elisabeth Feodorovna [Ella], and Alexandra Georgievna . . . These four lovely women, in the splendour of their festive attire and of their sparkling jewels, made one of those sights that one likes to evoke in after life."[54]

Another of Queen Olga's children had married soon after Grand Duke Paul and Princess Alexandra's nuptials. In 1889 the heir to the Greek throne, twenty-one-year-old Crown Prince Constantine ("Tino") married nineteen-year-old Princess Sophie of Prussia, Vicky's daughter. Vicky, by then, had become Germany's widowed Empress Frederick. Queen Olga was at first hesitant about her son's wish to marry a non-Orthodox, but ultimately accepted the marriage. The Greeks welcomed Crown Prince Constantine's marriage to Princess Sophie, for the union of this young couple presaged a long-awaited prophesy that said when a Constantine and a Sophia reigned, the city of Constantinople, which fell to the Ottomans in 1453, would return to the Greek fold. This cherished dream would place a heavy burden on Queen Olga's eldest son during years to come. The year after Constantine and Sophie married, a son, George, was born to them, three months after Grand Duchess Alexandra had given birth to a daughter, Marie Pavlovna, thus making Queen Olga a grandmother at the young age of thirty-eight. Not long after the birth of her grandson, Prince George of Greece, Queen Olga was happy to learn that her daughter-in-law, Sophie, had decided to convert to the Orthodox faith. The move infuriated Sophie's brother, Kaiser Wilhelm II, who made a public row out of the matter. Queen Victoria wanted to intercede in the quarrel, telling Olga: "How gladly I would help to restore peace in the family. I need hardly tell you. As soon as I heard of the matter I sent word to William that I could not blame Sophie."[55]

Life was much less fractious for Queen Olga's daughter Alexandra as she settled in Russia. During a visit to Alexandra in 1890, her mother was pleased to report that her daughter and Grand Duke Paul "are indescribably happy [and] so love their sweet little baby."[56] More good news followed the next year when Alexandra became pregnant with their second child. All seemed well, but while visiting Paul's brother Serge and his wife, Ella, at their country home, Ilinskoe, outside of Moscow, Alexandra, who was seven months pregnant, jumped into a boat, and fell. She collapsed the next day and went into a coma. Six days later, Alexandra gave birth prematurely to a son, Dmitri. After receiving word from Ella of the alarming state of their daughter's health, King George and Queen Olga hurried to Russia from Denmark to be at her side. They arrived just in time to see their beloved daughter die. Alexandra was just twenty-one years old. Upon hearing the dreadful news, Emperor Alexander III and Empress Marie Feodorovna also left Denmark for Russia, taking with them the rest of Queen Olga's children.

The Duchess of Edinburgh was at Coburg in Germany when she received news of the death of her young sister-in-law. Missy recalled how the tragic news came to them "like a thunderbolt." To hear that the "happy young creature . . . was no more" was "unbelievable." Marie Alexandrovna took her daughters, Missy and Ducky, with her to St. Petersburg for the funeral because as Missy noted of her mother: "above all she wanted to be with the brother she so dearly loved."[57] The death of Queen Olga's daughter Alexandra profoundly affected both the Greek and Russian royals. Emperor Alexander III summed up tearfully what all had felt when he exclaimed: "Why should this angel be taken from us, and we old ones remain?"[58] Years later, Alexandra's daughter, Grand Duchess Marie, wrote how her mother's untimely death "prostrated the family."[59]

Prince Nicholas of Greece recalled that "sorrow overpowered us all, particularly my father, who never got over it."[60] No less affected was Alexandra's mother. In answering a letter of sympathy sent by Prince George of Wales, Queen Olga replied:

> Sympathy does one so much good when one suffers, and I know how you feel for us, you sweet darling! If you knew, tootsums what we went through, it is impossible to describe. I only wonder how it did not kill us— . . . I can't realize it yet that I will never see the sweet child again in this world!! It all seems like an awful dream w[hi]ch can't be reality!!! Yes, we did arrive 48 hours before the end and . . . she was unconscious and did not know us, but still I was full of hope, I could not believe that I would have to give her up—I don't say to lose her because we don't lose our dead—they only go before to wait for us till the beautiful day comes, when we shall see them again . . . The agony began at 4½ in the afternoon and she died at 5 minutes to 3 in the night! Oh, tootsums, I thought it would kill me when I said with a crushed heart: "Thy will be done."[61]

Queen Olga added "and poor U[ncle] Willy whose treasure she was since she was born . . . The thought of U[ncle] Willy & Paul nearly breaks my heart . . . The poor little boy, 'Dmitry' is doing well now & the oldest baby is too lovely & sweet . . . never to know their sweet mother"[62] The death of Queen Olga's daughter Alexandra was the latest in a series of tragedies to beset the Romanov dynasty.

11

LOVE IN THE AIR

The American writer, Maturin M. Ballou, traveled to Russia during the reign of Alexander III. Ballou produced a book detailing his observations of the people and country. Of the Nihilists and tsarist Russia, he concluded that: "Discontent among the mass of the people does not exist to any material extent . . . It is the few scheming . . . members of society who ferment revolution and turmoil in Russia,—people who have everything to gain by public agitation and panic. Nine tenths and more of the people of Russia are loyal to 'father the Tzar,'—loyal to his family and dynasty . . . To hold up the Russian government as being immaculate would be gross folly," wrote Ballou, "but for foreigners to represent it to be so abhorrent as has long been the fashion to do, is equally incorrect and unjust. Nihilism means *nothingness*; and never was the purpose of a mad revolutionary combination more appropriately named. This murderous crew has been well defined by an English writer who says, 'The Nihilists are simply striving to force upon an unwilling people the fantastic freedom of anarchy.' The very name which these restless spirits have assumed is an argument against them. Some have grown sensitive as to having the title Nihilists applied to them, and prefer that of Communists or Socialists." And yet, concluded Ballou: "Socialism is the very embodiment of selfishness; its aim is that of legalized plunder. Communists, Socialists, Nihilists, are one and all disciples of destruction . . . National freedom is not what these anarchists desire, they seek wholesale destruction."[1]

Despite the fact that they were far outnumbered by the general populace, many of whom did not understand or subscribe to their destructive doctrines, the Nihilists were effective in inflicting fear and destruction on tsarist officialdom. Danger from Nihilists continually plagued the imperial family and the government in a spectacular way. Nihilists assassinated the chief of the secret police and also infiltrated the upper echelons of the army. In Warsaw, two hundred people were arrested for conspiring against the emperor; four of their leaders were hanged. By the mid-1880s, a veritable army protected Alexander III and his family when they traveled within Russia. It was not an exaggeration to say that "a lane of troops [were used] to protect him from the bombs, and mines, and other machinations of his own subjects. Every bridge, every culvert, every level-crossing of the railway lines by which he journeyed was guarded by well-tried sentries, and the whole route patrolled by soldiers . . . and his Majesty's destination was never known until he reached it."[2] In 1887 in St. Petersburg, the emperor escaped an assassination attempt after the police arrested several young revolutionaries who were carrying bombs concealed in books. They intended to kill Alexander III on the anniversary of his father's murder. The emperor did not tell Marie Feodorovna of the arrests until they returned from St. Petersburg to Gatchina. Upon hearing the news, the empress "broke down utterly and wept" and "shuddered with horror."[3]

One of the revolutionaries arrested was a young man by the name of Alexander Ulyanov from the town of Simbirsk on the banks of the Middle Volga. Intelligent and idealistic, Ulyanov was a star student at university in St. Petersburg. He had immersed himself in the revolutionary world, becoming a member of the People's Will. Arrested for his part in plotting to kill the emperor and found guilty, Ulyanov was hanged. Ulyanov's equally gifted younger brother, Vladimir, never forgot what the tsarist government did to his brother. Years later, the world would come to know the younger Ulyanov as the infamous Vladimir Lenin.

Behind the charming façade Marie Feodorovna presented to all was constant anxiety for her husband's life. Her fears were sometimes evident when functions placed the emperor in a vulnerable position. The journalist Theodore Child noticed this during the ninth centenary celebrations of Christianity's introduction into Russia, in which the emperor and empress participated in a procession along with the grand dukes and senior Church dignitaries. Thousands of spectators watched as the procession made its way from the Winter Palace to the foot of the Alexander Column, a magnificent memorial of red granite standing 154 feet high, erected in the memory of Napoleon's conqueror, Tsar Alexander I. The crowd was far from menacing, for when the holy icons appeared, signaling the arrival of the priests and imperial family, "the spectators incessantly crossed themselves and bowed, swaying their whole bodies from the waist, and not contenting themselves with merely bending the neck."

Theodore Child recorded that "the spectacle was impressive, and so was the stentorian greeting that rose from the crowd as the Czar drove away in an open carriage, with the Empress by his side, holding herself always a little in front of her husband, as if to shield him with her body." It was, admitted Child, a "curious attitude" on Marie Feodorovna's part, but it "made us realize the dark side of autocratic splendor, and the existence of unceasing anxiety in which the imperial couple live."[4]

Miechen and her husband, Vladimir, also lived under the Nihilists' shadow of violence, though because the couple did not rule, they were obviously a less spectacular target for the revolutionaries than Alexander III and Marie Feodorovna. Alexander III valued his brother to a degree and kept Vladimir at his post as president of the Imperial Academy of Art. It was an appropriate posting, considering that Miechen's husband was a connoisseur of art and an aesthete. Vladimir became known as *"le Grand-Duc Bon vivant."*[5] Vladimir had acquired this nomenclature thanks to stories such as the one that had him carousing with actors who were enjoying a supper party at St. Petersburg's Restaurant Ernest. What initially began as an innocent attempt to inject excitement into a staid dinner quickly degenerated into a scandal that involved Miechen too. A bored Vladimir and his entourage were intrigued by laughter and noise emanating from a neighboring room and decided to join the party. The astonished actors of the *Troupe française* welcomed their imperial guests. After Vladimir had too much to drink, however, a ruckus ensued. The inebriated grand duke placed his arm around the leading lady, who was also the wife of the principal actor, and kissed her. The husband, irritated by Vladimir's actions then retaliated by placing his arm around Miechen and daringly kissed her. Upon seeing this, an infuriated Vladimir slapped the actor's face. A battle then broke out, with chairs, tables, and broken china flying through the room. The police arrived, stopped the fight, and closed down the restaurant. The manager was punished for "his short-sightedness in having permitted a 'mixed' party with those 'French plebeians.'"[6] The next day, an indignant Alexander III summoned Vladimir for a talk. The emperor ordered that Miechen "should live for a while in the cooler social atmosphere outside Russia."[7]

Such escapades did little to endear Vladimir or Miechen to the empress. Of all her Romanov brothers-in-law, Marie Feodorovna's favorite remained Grand Duke Alexei, who reputedly liked slow ships and fast women. Alexander III retained Alexei's post as chief admiral of the Fleet, but placed his greatest confidence in Grand Duke Serge who shared his deep devotion to the Orthodox Church. It came as no surprise to find that in 1891 the tsar named Serge as governor-general of Moscow.

Serge's wife, Ella, further endeared herself to the Romanovs when she announced that she wished to convert to the Orthodox faith. Ella wrote of her decision to her father, the Grand Duke of Hesse, begging him, *"please* do not yet tell *anybody* at Darmstadt until I write again when Miechen knows."[8] Predictably, Miechen, who was still staunchly Lutheran, took the news of Ella's conversion badly. Kaiser Wilhelm, who once loved Ella and wanted desperately to marry her, agreed with Miechen's view on the matter, saying that it was "a disgrace for a German Protestant princess to go over to the Orthodox faith." Moreover, the kaiser totally agreed with Miechen's remark that "the great, powerful German Reich and its Kaiser" were "the stronghold and the refuge" of the Lutheran Church. Thus would Ella, upon her conversion, become "an apostate and a traitor to her faith and her Fatherland." Miechen and Wilhelm believed that Ella was motivated by "an inordinate pursuit of popularity, a desire to improve her position at court, a great lack of intelligence and also a want of true religiousness and patriotic feeling."[9] Angered by Ella's religious conversion Miechen felt "isolated and betrayed by her sister-in-law's action."[10]

The cordial relationship once shared by Serge, Ella, Vladimir, and Miechen was almost nonexistent between Vladimir, Miechen, Alexander III, and Marie Feodorovna. In fact, the two sisters-in-law were never close. Miechen's German origins already prejudiced Marie Feodorovna against her. Rumors about the grand duchess's friendship with the German chancellor Otto von Bismarck did not help matters, with stories circulating that Miechen was spying for the wily old Iron Chancellor. There was also talk that Miechen tried to influence Russian policy, when she could, to incline toward Berlin. St. Petersburg gossip had it that the chagrined grand duchess was cast aside and lost whatever influence she had in the corridors of power when Alexander III assumed the throne. This meant that she could no longer be a conduit of information to Berlin. This "inevitable change" left Miechen with "a keen feeling of disappointment and of anger." She supposedly complained in a letter to Prince Bismarck about being pushed aside. Added to this were "bitter criticisms directed against the Emperor, his views, opinions, and future plans, such as she imagined them to be." Miechen's letter fell into the hands of her husband's aide-de-camp, who promptly reported it to the authorities, and from there inevitably made its way to Alexander III. The grand duchess accused the aide of having stolen the letter. Grand Duke Vladimir dismissed the aide, who was then promptly appointed an aide to the emperor, "which set tongues wagging with more energy than ever." The scandal only died down because Miechen fell ill and was sent abroad to recover. When Miechen returned, the scandal had "blown over," according to the gossipy chronicler, Princess Catherine Radziwill, "but its effects were not so easily forgotten."[11]

Regardless of the Grand Duchess Vladimir's attempts to bring Russia and Germany closer, it was Miechen's abrasive personality and refusal to keep her opinions to herself, above all, that alienated her from Marie Feodorovna. For one thing, Miechen did not hide her disappointment when it came to Alexander III. In the grand duchess's opinion, her husband was far more suited to the role of emperor than Alexander. Miechen also hinted that her brother-in-law Grand Duke Paul was being too familiar with Ella. Such gossip and innuendo did not endear Miechen and Vladimir to the tsar and tsarina. Though a "perceptible crack" was already in evidence in Alexander and Vladimir's relationship years before, when Miechen joined the family "the crack became a chasm."[12] Little wonder that years later, Marie Alexandrovna's daughter, Missy, recalled that: "There was, I believe, a certain rivalry between Aunt Miechen and Aunt Minnie, and less friendship and good understanding than was politely played up to during those big family gatherings I so vividly remember."[13]

Competition between the two couples erupted into outright indignation. In 1884, Emperor Alexander III reprimanded Grand Duke Vladimir for his propensity to travel abroad, especially to Paris, where Vladimir and Miechen liked to spend part of the year. Relations between the imperial couple and Vladimir and Miechen continued to deteriorate, due in part to Miechen's growing pride and ambitions for her own family. The grand duchess publicly demonstrated her independence from Alexander III. She avoided, when she could, paying court to the emperor and empress. The uneasy relationship between the two sisters-in-law was not a family secret. Princess Antoine Radziwill was blunt in a letter she wrote to General Robilant in 1891: *La Tsarine a une véritable aversion pour sa belle-soeur la grand-duchesse Vladimir* [The Tsarina has a veritable aversion to her sister-in-law, the grand-duchess Vladimir]."[14]

The animosity grew between the two sisters-in-law until there was virtually no informal contact between the two couples and their families. The empress especially disapproved of Miechen's passion for gambling. Roulette was such a special favorite with the grand duchess that she even kept a roulette table at her palace and encouraged others to play. Soon enough, a disapproving Marie Feodorovna refrained from acknowledging Miechen at formal functions. Marie Feodorovna even dispensed with giving the grand duchess aloof nods. An infuriated Miechen found it difficult to stomach these public humiliations. During one particular ball, Empress Marie Feodorovna could not help make a highly disparaging remark that was soon whispered about. Seeing Miechen, the empress remarked caustically: "God knows what she looks like, she is so red that it makes one think that she has been drinking."[15] The cutting remark stung Miechen. It was to Miechen's eternal annoyance that Marie Feodorovna remained popular. Had the empress's charm and vivacity diminished, Miechen might have reigned as St. Petersburg's supreme hostess and become the most influential lady in all Russia. Evidence that Marie Feodorovna and Alexander III saw Vladimir and Miechen as ambitious near rivals for the crown surfaced with the Borki disaster in 1888. "I can imagine how disappointed Vladimir is going to be," remarked the emperor gloomily, "when he learns that we all stayed alive!"[16] And even more telling was Miechen's alleged remark: "We shall never have such a chance again."[17]

Marie Feodorovna's husband sought to rein in the rest of his family too. Gone were the days when grand dukes could drop in on the emperor unannounced. Alexander III had to grant them permission first. As head of the dynasty, the emperor found the wayward lives of a number of the grand dukes intolerable. He was already disgusted with the infidelities of Queen Olga's father, Grand Duke Constantine, and Grand Duke Nicholas Nikolaevich. When another Romanov relation, their nephew Grand Duke Michael Mikhailovich—Sandro's brother, known in the family as "Miche-Miche"—attempted to marry a commoner, the emperor forbade it. When, in 1891, Miche-Miche eventually eloped with another commoner, Countess Sophie of Merenberg, he did so without asking permission from the emperor. Miche-Miche's elopement enraged the Empress Marie Feodorovna, who was a stickler for keeping up imperial standards. The empress called the grand duke a "swine,"[18] and Alexander III shared her opprobrium. He was so incensed by Miche-Miche's action that he "deprived him of his right to wear his adjutant's tunic, and took the captaincy of his regiment away from him."[19] The emperor gave his orders not only to punish Miche-Miche but also to set an example to other Romanovs who might dare to transgress imperial laws. Sergei Witte, who became Alexander III's minister of finance in 1892, noted that "the entire Imperial family respected and feared Alexander III, who wielded the influence of a veritable patriarch."[20] Witte, one of the ablest tsarist ministers, had an insider's view of his master, the emperor. Witte found Marie Feodorovna's husband especially prudent with money, recording that: "Neither in the Imperial family nor among the nobility was there anyone who better appreciated the value of a ruble or a kopeck than Emperor Alexander III."[21]

The Romanovs' wealth during Marie Feodorovna's tenure as empress was astounding. "Every son of a tsar drew an annual allowance of 150,000 rubles, a birthday present of 1 million rubles on his coming of age, and 235,000 after marriage. His wife got 40,000 rubles a year, and children between 50,000 and 150,000 rubles (until they came of age). By comparison, a factory worker's annual wage was, on average, 246 rubles a year (in 1910); the average incomes of peasants were even lower."[22] In today's currency, 100,000 rubles from the 1880s equals approximately $1 million.[23] The grand dukes' monetary entitlements were huge, but the emperor's annual income was truly staggering, amounting to "an estimated nine million roubles ($4.4 million then/$94 million now)."[24] Despite this wealth, Alexander III remained personally frugal and did not begrudge the expenses Marie Feodorovna incurred when it came to clothes, and these expenses were not trivial. The empress rarely wore the same ball gown twice; and these gowns were masterpieces, often made in Paris. John Logan, a visitor who chronicled late nineteenth century Russia, described Marie Feodorovna as having been "conceded to be the best dressed woman in Europe." Though the Empress Elisabeth of Austria may have "excelled her in beauty," noted Logan, "no one touched" Maria Feodorovna "in frocks."[25] The famed Parisian couturier Charles Frederick Worth, from whom the empress often purchased her gowns, greatly admired Marie Feodorovna's ability to carry off his creations. A high-ranking aristocratic lady once asked Monsieur Worth why he could not dress her in " 'the sublime triumphs that you make every week for the Empress of Russia?' 'Madame, it is impossible,' answered Worth. 'It is not enough that you pay me when your robe is accomplished . . . it is necessary first that you inspire me before your robe is begun here,' tapping his brow and then his heart. 'Her Majesty the Empress of the Russias, she gives me the inspiration sublime, divine. And when she carries my work she so improves it, I do with difficulty recognise it. Bring to me any woman in Europe—queen, *artiste*, or *bourgeoise*—who can inspire me as does Madame Her Majesty, and I will make her confections while I live and charge her nothing."[26]

Marie Feodorovna's exquisite gowns by Worth were not her only costly accouterments. During a function at the Winter Palace, Lady Randolph Churchill had seen a sentry guarding "a magnificent sable cape" nearly all in black. The cape, which belonged to the empress, had apparently "taken years to collect the skins at a cost of £12,000 [$1.25 million]."[27] Then there are the most famous of Marie Feodorovna's possessions—the Fabergé eggs, which have come to symbolize imperial Russian extravagance and exquisite craftsmanship. Beginning in 1885 and each Easter thereafter Emperor Alexander III gave his wife a valuable token of affection and symbol of life to commemorate this most important event for Christians. The first imperial Easter egg Fabergé crafted for Marie Feodorovna was the 1885 Imperial Hen Egg. It was a simple but finely crafted confection in white enamel. Future Easter eggs were even more elaborate and epitomized the finest of Fabergé's creations.

When the time came for Marie Feodorovna and Alexander III to celebrate their silver wedding anniversary in 1891, they had much to be thankful for. One courtier described their marriage as being "solely happy" and crowned by a "perfect" family life.[28] Marie Feodorovna had much to look forward to. Her beloved husband, after all, was not yet fifty and appeared the picture of health. She continued to be popular. Moreover, they were blessed with offspring, including sons who were in line to the throne. The two youngest children, thirteen-year-old Grand Duke Michael and nine-year-old Grand Duchess Olga, were still in the schoolroom. Their twenty-year-old brother, Grand Duke George, was the greatest cause of concern, having developed tuberculosis when he was touring Egypt, India, and the Far East with his brother the Tsarevich Nicholas. The absence of her two sons for a prolonged period deeply saddened Marie Feodorovna. Her letter to her "dearest darling Nicky" shows the close bond they shared. "My thoughts follow you everywhere—every minute I seem to hear your steps and see you enter the room and every time it is a fresh disappointment and sadness and I do not believe I can get used to the idea of living so without you two, my dear boys, whom I miss so horribly!"[29]

By the early 1890s, Marie Feodorovna's elder daughter Grand Duchess Xenia had grown into an attractive brunette with the same velvety eyes for which her mother was famed. Xenia and Sandro had formed an attachment to each other and wished to marry. Sandro, however, had to contend with Xenia's parents. When he spoke to the emperor, Alexander III told the suitor to wait a year because "Xenia's mother does not want her to marry too soon."[30] After a year had passed, the empress finally gave in and the wedding took place at Peterhof in July 1894. Marie Feodorovna confided to Nicky about her mixed feelings over Xenia's marriage. "It may be easier to lose her like this— little by little: still—my heart *cannot yet* get used to it, though *all* my *reason* bids me do so."[31] In writing of the wedding to Queen Olga's mother, the empress was relieved to admit: "Praise God, that we will at least have them here, that is my comfort."[32]

Empress Marie Feodorovna was not the only one having to contend with a daughter's romance. The Duchess of Edinburgh was keeping her eye on Missy. Very close in age to Xenia, Missy of Edinburgh had grown into one of the loveliest princesses in Europe. Her blond hair and blue eyes, her expansive personality and her illustrious pedigree combined to make Missy one of the most eligible princesses available. "Few princesses her age could better hold their own in society"[33] and Marie Alexandrovna knew it. The Duchess of Edinburgh was far more successful in influencing the outcome of her daughter's marriage than the empress had been with hers.

By the time Missy was being seriously considered as a royal bride, the Edinburgh family had changed homes yet again. No longer were they in Malta or England, but in the small German duchy of Coburg. A new chapter in Marie Alexandrovna's life began as she bid farewell to her home, Eastwell, and England. The family accompanied Alfred, who settled in Coburg in preparation for taking over as reigning duke, since his uncle, the aging and childless Duke Ernst, was in the waning years of his life. Coburg, with its quaint houses and picturesque buildings from centuries before, also appealed to Marie Alexandrovna's autocratic character since the "social climate of feudalism" clearly "still clung to these little duchies."[34] Missy best summed up what Coburg meant to Marie Alexandrovna: "There she was sole arbiter of her own fate, no tribunal sat over her, weighing all she did or left undone. There she was her own mistress; it was a small kingdom perhaps, but her will was undiscussed, she took her orders from no one, and could live as she wished."[35]

Now that there was serious talk of Missy marrying, the Duchess of Edinburgh worked furiously to find the right suitor. Her nephew Prince George of Wales still pined for Missy, but he was not acceptable to Marie Alexandrovna. George's mother, Princess Alexandra, also opposed George's desire to marry Missy, because she felt that Missy was "too German." "The girl," complained the Princess of Wales to her son in 1891, was "a perfect baby yet—altho [sic] Aunt Marie begging her pardon does *all* she can to make her *old before her time* . . . and what do you say to Aunt Marie having *hurried* on the *two girls* [sic] *confirmation*—& in Germany too so that now they won't *even know* that they have ever been English—particularly as they have been confirmed in the German church . . . Even Aunt Vicky was furious about it."[36]

Tragedy struck the British royal family in January 1892 when Eddy, George's elder brother and second in line to the throne, died from influenza at the age of twenty-eight. Empress Marie Feodorovna felt great sympathy for her sister Alexandra but this unexpected tragic event precipitated other concerns. It now became imperative for Prince George to marry and secure the succession to the throne. Well aware that Queen Victoria backed her sons the Duke of Edinburgh and the Prince of Wales when it came to securing a marriage between George and Missy, Marie Alexandrovna knew she had to act and act quickly. The duchess was determined that her mother-in-law would not get her way when it came to Missy's future.

Another George had already asked for the sixteen-year-old princess's hand in marriage. While visiting Russia during the funeral of Queen Olga's daughter Alexandra, Missy had caught the attention of Grand Duke George Mikhailovich, Sandro's brother. Much as the duchess loved her Romanov relations and Russia, Marie Alexandrovna could not countenance a marriage for her daughters with any Russian at that time and refused the offer. Marie Alexandrovna did not want Missy to endure a marriage with yet another potentially adulterous Romanov. Having dismissed Grand Duke George Mikhailovich, Marie Alexandrovna now had to contend with Prince George of Wales.

When a formal proposal came for Missy's hand, the duchess refused it. Missy's mother instructed her daughter on what to say, in effect, dictating what Prince George read. In answer to Prince George's letter to Missy that he thought they would marry as soon as Missy was old enough, Missy wrote back, saying that "he must not think that there was anything definite in the friendship that had sprung up between them at Malta."[37]

The Duchess of Edinburgh soon settled on her ideal suitor for Missy—Crown Prince Ferdinand of Romania. A Hohenzollern prince by birth and cousin to German Kaiser Wilhelm, Prince Ferdinand ("Nando") was a nephew of and heir to Romania's King Carol I. Ten years Missy's senior, Nando was intelligent but not especially handsome. With a hawk nose and protruding ears, the crown prince was also hampered by a sense of timidity. But these drawbacks mattered not to the Duchess of Edinburgh. Instead of having Missy become queen of England, Marie Alexandrovna was now positioning her daughter ultimately to become queen of Romania. To this end, she whisked Missy off to Germany and placed her squarely in Crown Prince Ferdinand's path. In no time, Ferdinand summoned up enough courage to propose to Missy, who accepted him. It was easy to see why he was attracted to Missy, but aside from Ferdinand's position as a future king, it was more difficult to see what could have drawn Missy to Nando. It would appear that she found something appealing and sympathetic in the young man's intense shyness. In reality, the romance and betrothal had been so carefully planned that Missy had very little time to think; and like the obedient child that she was, she acquiesced to the inevitable.

The Duke of Edinburgh too had no choice other than to accept the fait accompli. His wife, who had the last say in family matters, got her way. The Duke, who could not override his wife when it came to Missy's engagement to Ferdinand, confessed his feelings to Missy. When he told her about her dowry of one million French francs, the distraught duke embraced his daughter, broke down crying, confessing that he had wanted another future for Missy than the one her mother planned.

The engagement, which took place in 1892, was officially celebrated at a family dinner in the presence of Kaiser Wilhelm II and a triumphant Duchess of Edinburgh. News of the sixteen-year-old Missy's engagement caught many off guard, including the princess's paternal grandmother. Queen Victoria admitted as much to Missy's cousin, Victoria of Hesse. "We have been much startled lately to hear of *Missy's Engagement* to *Ferdinand of Rumania*," wrote the queen. "He is nice I believe & the Parents are charming—but the Country is very insecure & the immorality of the Society at Bucharest *quite awful*."[38] Queen Victoria wrote similarly to her daughter Vicky. Missy's engagement, acknowledged her grandmother, has taken "us all by surprise . . . it seems to have come very rapidly to a climax. The Country is vy insecure & the Society—dreadful—& she is a mere Child, & quite inexperienced!—Of course the marriage cannot take place till next year; Missy herself wld *not* have Georgie . . . It was the dream of Affie's life." The queen also added, "I fear Bertie is very angry . . . Poor Georgie . . . is not bitter."[39] Princess Mary ("May") of Teck lunched with the Duchess of Edinburgh not long after Missy's engagement became official. The duchess exuded a jubilant and contented tone, prompting May to confide in her diary: "Aunt M. was looking flourishing and seems delighted at Missy's engagement."[40]

One royal watcher, Lady Geraldine Somerset, had stronger words. "Disgusted," confided Lady Geraldine in her diary, "to see the announcement of the marriage of poor pretty nice P. Marie of Edinburgh to the P. *of Roumania*!!! It does seem too cruel a shame to cart that nice pretty girl off to semi-barbaric Roumania . . ."[41]

"Carted off" or not, in January 1893 Missy married Crown Prince Ferdinand in Sigmaringen, Germany. When the bearded and austere King Carol I of Romania descended on Sigmaringen for the wedding, the seventeen-year-old bride was naturally anxious about meeting *"der Onkel."* Even the Duchess of Edinburgh was "a little excited and nervous" about meeting the man who ruled Romania. "But," recalled Missy, her mother "tried to cheer us up and give us courage with brave words."[42] Another royal guest was none other than Kaiser Wilhelm II. Bombastic and theatrical, surrounded by a fawning entourage, Wilhelm II was roundly disliked by his British uncles, Queen Victoria's sons, who saw him as something of a loud bully. Curiously, the Duchess of Edinburgh "was one of the few who really got on" with the kaiser, Missy noted. As it turned out, "he interested her and her own masterfulness kept him at bay."[43]

The night before the newly married Missy left Coburg for her new country, a touching scene took place. The Duchess of Edinburgh had insisted Missy go to bed early, so as to give Marie Alexandrovna time to give some well-meaning advice to her new son-in-law. When they had finished talking, Missy heard her mother turn to Nando and say, "I must just have a last look at her."[44] Missy then saw her mother peer into her room, with tears streaming down her face. Missy held herself in check. Much as she wanted to fling her arms around her mother, she dared not. She had been trained too well not to make a scene. And so mother and daughter simply nodded and smiled at each other. For months on end, the scene would haunt the homesick bride in Romania where Missy's early days were interminably lonely.

At the same time that Missy and Xenia married their respective husbands, the Tsarevich Nicholas nursed his own affairs of the heart. He was carrying on an affair with one of the stars of the Imperial Ballet, the petite, dark-haired, dark-eyed Mathilde Kschessinska. The tsarevich had also met Princess Alix of Hesse years before, when the twelve-year-old girl arrived in Russia to witness her sister Ella's marriage to Nicky's uncle, Grand Duke Serge. Nicky, sixteen at the time, took a fancy to the pretty princess. The couple met again in 1889 when Alix visited Ella. By this time, the princess from Hesse had blossomed into a beauty, but was handicapped by intense shyness that impeded her ability to charm many, including the Empress Marie Feodorovna, who thought her gauche. Nicky, however, found little in Alix to fault. By 1891, he confessed in his diary: "My dream—one day to marry Alix H[esse]."[45] With Nicky's romance with Alix progressing, Kschessinska increasingly faded into the background. Nicholas knew he could never marry her; and so the liaison between the tsarevich and the ballerina eventually ended.

Marie Feodorovna was distressed that the romance between Nicky and Alix was moving into a more passionate phase. The empress tried to steer her son in another direction. In her eyes, the statuesque Princess Hélène, daughter of the Comte de Paris, pretender to the French throne, would make a far better match. A union between the tsarevich and the French princess would cement the Franco-Russian alliance that had recently been concluded. But above all, Hélène, unlike Alix, was not German. Nicky felt pressured to choose as his mother advised, confiding in his diary that he was "in an awkward position. I am at the crossing of two paths; I myself want to go in the other direction, while Mama obviously wants me to take this one! What will happen?"[46]

12

THE BEGINNING OF THE END

efore the Duke of Edinburgh settled permanently into his inheritance at Coburg, Affie had become an Admiral of the Fleet. He was also made commander-in-chief at Devonport, which required his having to spend some time in southwestern England in the early 1890s. The Duchess of Edinburgh, who much preferred Coburg, occasionally visited Devonport, but kept these stays to a minimum. When at Devonport, the Edinburghs stayed at Admiralty House, but as there were no grounds attached, Marie Alexandrovna liked to go to nearby Government House, home of Sir Richard Harrison, the general-in-command. Harrison recalled how the duchess would visit Government House where "she was glad to take her morning walks undisturbed" in the garden.[1] Many years later, Hilda Picken, a resident of the area, remembered Marie Alexandrovna's stays at Devonport. The duchess, noted Picken: "obviously felt she had come down in the social scale, having married a mere Duke, and being obliged to come into contact with the likes of us. All their pretty daughters . . . apparently found life in a Service town a very cheerful affair. The contrast between their gay young faces and Mama's glowering looks was quite remarkable."[2]

Rarely did Marie Alexandrovna display those glowering looks back in her beloved Coburg. The one person who could most likely elicit a disapproving look in Coburg, however, was the reigning Duke Ernst, Queen Victoria's brother-in-law. The lecherous and ogreish duke was exactly the type of character the upright duchess disliked. When Duke Ernst died in August 1893, the Duke and Duchess of Edinburgh finally became the reigning Duke and Duchess of Saxe-Coburg-Gotha.[3] The duchy was small, totaling just over 750 square miles with a population of under a quarter of a million. But despite its modest size, Coburg suited the new reigning duchess well, for Marie Alexandrovna could now feel superior to her British sisters-in-law.

Marie Alexandrovna was mistress of all she surveyed, and Coburg with its simple life and uncomplicated society was very much to the duchess's liking. Moreover, she loved Germany, "and all things German, a feeling that had been nurtured by her own German mother and her happy childhood sojourns in Darmstadt." Marie Alexandrovna felt an affinity for the fairy tale–like duchy of Coburg situated near the Thuringian Forest, having "completely fallen under its spell. Everything about the place suited this difficult woman perfectly— the simplicity, the proud and ancient culture, the beauty of the countryside, the quaintness, the unhurried way of life, and most of all, the total independence and freedom it gave her."[4]

Vicky, now the Empress Frederick, understood what becoming the reigning Duke and Duchess of Saxe-Coburg-Gotha meant for her brother and sister-in-law. In a letter to her daughter Crown Princess Sophie, Vicky wrote: "For Uncle Alfred, this is a difficult time, he will have to give up dear old London for good, and devote himself to his German home and his new duties. But he will do it all so well, and Aunt Marie will love being No. 1 and reigning Duchess, I am sure."[5]

Being a reigning duchess also likely helped to keep Marie Alexandrovna's mind off her bad marriage. Unlike Marie Feodorovna and Miechen, whose marriages remained strong, Marie Alexandrovna's marriage continued to be unhappy. It was not until Missy had been married for several years that she discovered the sad truth about the state of her mother's marriage. Only then did the duchess confide to her that she felt she was nothing more than her husband's "legitimate mistress." It was a painful revelation, for Marie Alexandrovna found the role "simply degrading," especially for one who had been the daughter of the tsar of Russia.[6] Moreover, Affie's difficult personality, which did not improve, made him a hard man to live with. Taking up his duties as the reigning Duke of Saxe-Coburg-Gotha did nothing to make Affie any less rancorous. Though he had known for many years that his destiny lay in the small German duchy, when he did become the reigning duke, Alfred could not muster the same amount of enthusiasm for Coburg as his wife did. A committed naval man, he missed serving in the Royal Navy and found the provincial Coburg uninteresting. Affie once confessed to finding Coburg "deadly dull."[7] This boredom with his role and life at Coburg aggravated Affie and Marie Alexandrovna's relations. The breakdown in the Edinburghs' marriage was not unknown. A contemporary publication revealed that though the duke may not have "given rise by his conduct to any matrimonial scandal," his disposition made Affie a difficult man to live with. "He is blest at best, with an abominable temper, the most glaring want of tact, and has lost much of that comeliness which caused the Grand Duchess Marie to fall in love with him, and to persist in marrying him."[8] Thus did Missy come to appreciate the extent to which her mother hid her misery from her children, an act of selflessness that garnered Missy's admiration.

Missy, in the meantime, found herself friendless in an alien court and felt as if she lived in a gilded prison. This feeling of imprisonment was largely caused by King Carol's suspicious nature, which prompted him to keep her isolated from others. King Carol I became even more involved in Missy's life as he tightened his protective grip over her once it was confirmed that the crown princess was expecting a baby. As her confinement grew closer, Missy was relieved to find her mother at her side to assist her. Marie Alexandrovna's presence in Romania inevitably led to a showdown with King Carol over the impending birth. Both stubborn, the duchess and the king argued over everything, especially when it came to nurses and doctors. Despite wielding her autocratic ways at King Carol, Marie Alexandrovna could not get him to budge on many issues. In the end, Queen Victoria saved the day. She ordered an English doctor to preside over Missy's confinement, thereby agreeing that Marie Alexandrovna's personal physician should go to Romania. But even in this delicate matter of Missy's confinement and care of her baby, Queen Victoria and Marie Alexandrovna too came to loggerheads. "I had terrible fights with Granny dear about an English . . . nurse for you," wrote the Duchess of Coburg to Missy before arriving in Romania, "but will not give up the admirable one I have already engaged and will bring her with me, instead of the old gossip Granny wants you to have."[9]

In October 1893, Crown Princess Marie of Romania gave birth to a boy, named Carol after his great-uncle. Missy had done her duty and provided the Romanians with a native-born heir. The Duchess of Coburg emphasized this to her exhausted and bewildered daughter. "Listen to the cannon," said the new grandmother, encouraging Missy to savor the moment. "Think of how delighted the people will be when they hear the hundred and one salutes."[10] Grateful for her mother's presence at this first birth, Missy acknowledged that her mother "was a precious necessity." "I could hardly bear her to leave the room," admitted Missy, "she was so safe, so capable, and she was home; the home I had lost."[11]

Donning her splendid pearls, the Duchess of Coburg proudly watched as her grandson, Prince Carol of Romania, was christened in an Orthodox ceremony on the day Missy turned eighteen.

While the Duchess of Coburg reveled in being a grandmother for the first time, and a grandmother of a future king at that, her nephew Nicky was experiencing his own emotional upheavals. The growing bond of affection that tied the Tsarevich Nicholas and Princess Alix of Hesse did not abate through the years. Nevertheless, objections were raised from many corners over Alix as a potential bride for Nicky. St. Petersburg society was unimpressed with the Hessian princess. They, as well as the Empress Marie Feodorovna, found Alix too awkward, tongue-tied, and shy. Alix simply showed too little potential as a future tsarina. Obstacles also arose within the family. Not only were Nicky's parents averse to seeing Alix become their son's wife, Queen Victoria was also adamant that this favorite granddaughter not be sacrificed to Russia. The queen already had to contend with Alix's sister Ella's marriage to Nicky's uncle, the Grand Duke Serge. But to have Alix join Ella in Russia as Nicky's bride was too much for the queen. She expressed her misgivings to Ella and Alix's sister, Victoria, telling her that "I regretted Alicky's again going to Russia as it led to every sort of report . . . moreover Minnie does not *wish* it [the marriage]. In short *that* cld *not* be . . . tell Ella that no marriage for *Alicky in Russia* wld be *allowed*, then there will be an end of it."[12]

As the emperor and empress of Russia tried to dissuade Nicky from marrying Alix, Queen Victoria was busy trying to get Alix to marry someone else. The queen insisted that Alix marry Marie Feodorovna's nephew, Eddy of Wales. Alix refused him. He eventually proposed to Princess May of Teck and was accepted. Eddy, though, died in 1892, before he could marry May.

Despite opposition from Queen Victoria and Nicky's parents, as time passed the greatest obstacle to the union proved to be none other than Alix herself. Deeply religious, she could not bring herself to forsake her Lutheran faith and embrace the Orthodox religion, a requirement for any wife of the heir to Russia's throne. Ella, Miechen, and Mavra may have been able to retain their Lutheran faith as grand duchesses, but Alix could not if she wished to marry the future tsar. And so a battle of wills ensued. By 1893, Alix decided to end the romance, despite her strong feelings for Nicholas. To his sister Xenia, Alix wrote: "I cannot become untrue to my own confession . . . I don't want him [Nicky] to go on hoping, as I can *never* change my Religion."[13] Alix's obstinacy left Nicky despondent, prompting him to admit to feeling "shattered by this implacable obstacle."[14]

As Nicky and Alix's courtship continued its torturous path, Nicky's cousin Prince George of Wales, his hopes of marrying Missy dashed, finally settled on a bride. Prince George's aunt, Queen Olga, nudged him toward Princess May of Teck, who had once been Eddy's fiancée. Eddy's death cleared the way for George. Impressed by her intelligence and calm dignity, Queen Olga urged George to propose to the princess. After all, his aunt Minnie married Alexander III after his elder brother died, establishing a precedent—and that marriage proved to be very strong. "I'm sure, tootsums, that she will make you happy," wrote Queen Olga encouragingly to George (to whom Queen Victoria granted the title of Duke of York). "They say she has such a sweet disposition & is so *equal* and *that* in itself is a great blessing, because nothing can be more disagreeable in everyday-life, than a person which is in high spirits today & low tomorrow." And as a word of advice, Queen Olga also added that George should heed his wife-to-be's interests: "There are many little things wch. are *dear* to a woman's heart, wch. men would think *trifles*, forgetting that our lives consist mostly of trifles, & that great events are rare."[15] Fortified by Queen Olga's blessing and encouragement, Prince George proposed to Princess May. In July 1893, the couple married in London in the presence of numerous family members, including the Tsarevich Nicholas. Nicky, with his full beard, so resembled his cousin George that the tsarevich was sometimes mistaken for the groom and congratulated on "his" wedding.

At the next major royal wedding the Edinburghs' other daughter, Ducky, married Princess Alix's brother Ernie, the Grand Duke of Hesse and by Rhine. Queen Victoria and the Duke of Edinburgh had been determined not to let Marie Alexandrovna outmaneuver them when it came to Ducky's matrimonial prospects. In a letter to Ernie and Alix's sister Victoria, the queen wrote: "I had it out with Aunt Marie having written kindly but strongly to her. She is most anxious abt. Ernie & Ducky & I have written *twice* to Ernie abt. the *necessity* of his showing some attention & interest . . . Aunt Marie fears *he* no longer wishes it, wh. I am sure is not the case. Georgie lost Missy by waiting & waiting."[16] In the end, Queen Victoria won, to her great satisfaction. The prospective bride and groom were less overjoyed. Ernie was not really attracted to women and only saw his cousin as a friend. Moreover, Ducky's affections lay with Grand Duke Kyril, Miechen's eldest son. The Duchess of Coburg dreaded the possibility that Ducky might be drawn even closer to Queen Victoria after her marriage to the Grand Duke of Hesse and admitted as much to Missy, saying that "I had a long talk with Ernie . . . about the English family, about Granny and explained to him why we could not really like them and how often they had been nasty and spiteful to me . . . he must not always be dragging Ducky to England in perpetual adoration of Granny and . . . [he must] understand the reasons why *we* can *never* adore her."[17]

Like the great potentate that she was, the bride and groom's grandmother, Queen Victoria, majestically descended upon Coburg to attend the couple's wedding in April 1894. The grand social event of the year drew a bevy of royal relations to the small German town. Among the guests was a contingent of Romanovs including the Grand Duke and Grand Duchess Vladimir, the Grand Duke and Grand Duchess Serge, and the Tsarevich Nicholas. Nicky almost did not go, but just days before his relatives were scheduled to leave, the tsarevich secured permission from his parents to go and propose to Princess Alix. By this stage, Emperor Alexander III and Empress Marie Feodorovna were resigned to Nicky's choice of a wife. It was an uncharacteristic retreat on their part. Nicky, who had never caused his parents much trouble, startled the emperor and empress with his intractable stance, refusing to listen to objections raised over Alix. Even his uncle, Grand Duke Vladimir, objected to Alix joining the family. Vladimir, like Miechen, was an ardent Francophile. He raised the specter of political complications besetting Russia should the Anglophile Alix join the family. In Vladimir's eyes, Nicky's marriage to "that English ramrod" would only bring international trouble to Russia.[18]

The emperor's ill health precipitated the permission for Nicholas to propose to Alix. For months, Alexander III had been feeling unwell, which redoubled the necessity of securing the succession to the throne. Marie Feodorovna convinced Nicky to go to Coburg to try his luck with Alix, urging her son to ask for Queen Victoria's help while he was there. Thus was Nicky given the chance he was seeking. Everything now appeared to be falling into place. Yet the most difficult objection to the marriage persisted—Alix's refusal to convert.

Arriving at Coburg, Nicky was in great turmoil. Eager to see Alix, but also fearful that she might reject him yet again, the tsarevich was gambling his whole future on a final attempt to get her to say "yes." During their first meeting, Nicky pleaded with Alix for two interminable hours, but still she refused him. Then, the day after Ducky and Ernie's wedding, Miechen and Kaiser Wilhelm prodded Alix, at which point she finally relented. "A wonderful, unforgettable day in my life—the day of my betrothal to my beloved Alix," recorded Nicky in his diary, of the fateful event.[19] After telling Queen Victoria, Nicky and several family members went to Marie Alexandrovna's private chapel for a service of thanksgiving.

Alix finally capitulated for a number of reasons. Nicky's steadfast devotion to her was certainly the great determining factor, but so too was the impending presence of the high-spirited and self-assured Ducky as first lady of Hesse. Nor did Alix savor the thought that her aunt, the Duchess of Coburg, could well be "playing the dictator around Darmstadt" once Ducky was ensconced there.[20] Alix finally accepted Nicky because she felt she could be a great help to the tsarevich, whose timorous character was evident to his intimates. "To love and to serve" Nicky was "her true vocation," and "therein lay God's will for her," concluded Alix.[21] In finally reconciling herself to converting, "Alix welded this irrevocable decision to a greater calling. She was to be an instrument of God, sent to transform the future Nicholas II and the Russian Empire. In tandem, she and Nicky would work for the greater good of Russia."[22]

Nicky and Alix's drama completely overshadowed Ducky and Ernie's wedding festivities. Queen Victoria, who had so vehemently opposed a marriage between Alix and Nicky, accepted the news magnanimously and congratulated the betrothed couple.

Upon hearing the news of her son's engagement, Empress Marie Feodorovna wrote to him from Gatchina: "I can't say how delighted I am, and what great joy it gave me to hear the happy news!"[23] Upon her return to Russia, Miechen gave the empress a letter from Nicky that moved Marie Feodorovna to tears. "Thank you a thousand times for every word of affection," wrote the empress to Nicky, "they go straight to my heart, so full of love for you and open to receive your dear Alix, who already is quite like a daughter to me, and whom I am awaiting impatiently to see . . . Do tell Alix that hers [her letter] has touched me so deeply—only—I don't want her to call me 'Aunty-Mama;' 'Mother dear', that's what I am to her now."[24]

The happy tone of Marie Feodorovna's letter belied the anxiety she felt about Alexander III, who was suffering from insomnia and extreme fatigue. At the same time, the empress was deeply worried about her son George too. His tuberculosis necessitated that he reside in an area with an ideal climate. His parents chose Abbas Touman in the Caucasus, where they hoped the grand duke's health would improve. After seeing her son settled in a comfortable villa with picturesque views of the surrounding valleys, the empress left and returned to St. Petersburg. "Poor Georgie!" she wrote to Nicky in June 1894:

> Life is really *too sad* for him: it is wonderful with what fortitude he bears it, without a murmur of complaint. I am so deeply grieved by this that the tears come to my eyes when I think of it and of the incessant suffering and sorrow our poor little Georgie has had to bear all through these last four years. Yes, indeed, it is a terrible ordeal and for me and Papa *doubly so* because we are suffering not only for him but also because it is so terribly hard to *see* one's child suffer and not be able to relieve it! But God alone knows why He imposes this heavy cross upon us, and we have to carry its burden with patience and resignation, crying to ourselves: 'Thy will be done'—even if the heart breaks.[25]

Less than three months after she wrote these words, Marie Feodorovna was plunged into even greater anxiety over her husband's health. Insomnia, lethargy, coughs, lack of appetite, and weight loss had turned the once mighty tsar into a weak man. The emperor was finally diagnosed with nephritis, an inflammation of the kidney. Damage to the kidney from the Borki train disaster, chronic overwork, and mental fatigue, plus Alexander III's habit of occupying very cool, damp rooms, contributed to this life-threatening illness. The imperial family journeyed to Livadia, their home in the Crimea, in September 1894 so the emperor could try to recuperate in a more temperate climate. Queen Olga hurried to Livadia and invited her cousin to convalesce at the royal villa, Mon Repos, on Corfu, which he eagerly accepted. But as Alexander III's condition worsened, the family decided to stay put in the Crimea, where the death watch soon began. Prince Nicholas of Greece, who had accompanied his mother, was shocked to find his Uncle Sasha so ill. "To see that great man, always so respected, so dignified and yet so full of fun, tormented morally and physically by his cruel disease, was sad indeed," recalled Queen Olga's son. "It was like seeing a magnificent building crumbling."[26] Other members of the family made their way to Livadia, including the Prince and Princess of Wales as well as the Duchess of Coburg, who, upon her arrival, blurted out to her critically ill brother: "Thank God I've arrived in time to see you once more."[27] Also rushing to Livadia was the emperor and empress's sickly son, George. The sight of her dying husband and desperately ill son was not easy on Marie Feodorovna. Her nerves gave way that October, helpless as she was to stop the progress of the nephritis and tuberculosis that slowly robbed her husband and son of their lives.

Alarmed at the grave state of his father's health, the Tsarevich Nicholas summoned Princess Alix to the Crimea. Upon hearing the news, Queen Victoria panicked. "All my fears abt. her future marriage now show themselves so strongly," wrote the queen to Alix's sister, Princess Victoria, "& my blood runs cold when I think of her *so* young most likely placed on that vy. unsafe Throne, her dear life & above all her Husband's constantly threatened . . . It is a great additional anxiety in my declining years!"[28]

On arriving at Livadia, the tsarevich's fiancée found a family immersed in grief. In honor of Princess Alix's arrival, a very weak Alexander III struggled into his uniform in order to give his future daughter-in-law a proper welcome. Alix's stay at Livadia proved an eye-opener. All around her, Alix saw Nicky being ignored, with all attention being given to the dying emperor and his empress. It was during these last ten days of Alexander III's life "that the foundations of the future unfortunate relationship" between the Empress Marie Feodorovna and Alix "were laid." As the emperor lay dying, Alix discovered to her consternation, that "everyone consulted her [future mother-in-law], everyone deferred to her, everyone sympathized with her." And though Marie Feodorovna "might be sick with grief and worry," she nevertheless "remained mistress of the situation" while no one deferred to Alix and Nicky.[29]

Seeing the heir ignored, Alix urged her future husband to assert himself. "Be firm," she exhorted Nicky, "and make the Drs. . . . come alone to you every day and tell you how they find him . . . Don't let others be put first and you left out . . . Show your own mind and don't let others forget who you are."[30] It was almost as if Alix had echoed what was expressed in the *New York Times* at the time concerning what was needed in Russia's emperor: "Strength and force of character are absolutely necessary in her ruler if the empire is to be kept together. To a weakling, or even to man of medium vigor, the Czarship is impossible." The newspaper went on to speculate that Princess Alix might possibly represent "in her own person the plans of Berlin and London Courts for the controlling of Nicholas II. She will find none but enemies at Livadia, for they are concentrated there two or three other schemes for running the young man, all agreeing in hostility to her. Of these rival interests that of the Grand Duke Vladimir continues to be one of those most worth watching."[31]

According to an article published a decade after the death of Marie Feodorovna's husband, Alexander III called the Prince of Wales to his deathbed because it "would serve as a protection to the latter against the designs of the

Grand Duke Vladimir." If "Vladimir attempted to seize the throne, the presence of the English prince would have proved a serious obstacle. It would have been impossible to carry out a *coup d'état* without subjecting the British heir apparent to indignities that might have had serious consequences."[32] Reputedly, so great was Alexander III's fear that Miechen's husband might attempt a coup, that he also summoned General Count Moussine-Pouchkine, who was commander of the Seventh and Eight Army Corps, headquartered at nearby Odessa. At Livadia, it was said that the emperor and the general "perfected military arrangements to prevent Vladimir from making any attempt to secure possession of the throne, on Alexander's death, by means of a *coup de main*."[33]

As the end neared, Father John of Kronstadt, a much loved religious cleric, was summoned to Livadia. In writing of her husband's time with the priest, Marie Feodorovna told her mother that "it was an <u>exceedingly gripping</u> moment in which my angelic Sacha's whole wonderful, devout soul was revealed."[34] On October 20/November 1, 1894, as the fog outside thickened, Alexander III sat in his armchair with Marie Feodorovna by his side, awaiting that final call from God. On that day, the emperor called for his cousin, the Queen of Greece. Taking her hand as she knelt by him, the dying man said, "Olga Constantinovna!" as he pressed his hand into hers.[35] In the afternoon, the emperor was wheeled near a window. "I feel the end approaching. Be calm. I am calm," muttered the emperor to his wife.[36] Father John had administered the Last Sacraments. The emperor bid his family farewell. Kneeling by her husband's side, Marie Feodorovna wrapped her arm around Alexander III's shoulder. He then closed his eyes, rested his head on his wife's shoulder, and died. Alexander III was just forty-nine years old.

"The sun of the Russian Land has set down!" wrote Queen Olga to her brother, K.R. "He has died just exactly as He lived in simplicity and piety; that's the way my sweet sailors die and the ordinary Russians as well."[37] Of the momentous and tragic event, Nicky confided in his diary: "Lord, help us in these terrible days! Poor, dear Mama!"[38] The thought that he had ascended the throne petrified the twenty-six-year-old monarch. Turning to his brother-in-law, Grand Duke Alexander, Nicholas II broke down, "Sandro, what am I going to do. What is going to happen to me, to you, to Xenia, to Alix, to mother, to all of Russia? I am not prepared to be a Czar. I never wanted to become one. I know nothing of the business of ruling."[39]

The Prince and Princess of Wales arrived at Livadia just after the emperor died. Seeing how timid his nephew, the new tsar, was and how much in shock Marie Feodorovna was, the Prince of Wales oversaw much of the preparations and details at Livadia concerning the funeral. Meanwhile, the Princess of Wales was indispensable in consoling her distraught sister, whose sorrow moved Queen Olga. "One can only be amazed at how a human heart can bear such turmoil!" wrote Olga to K.R. "The Empress is heartbroken; and every day this grief becomes more and more unbearable; the loss is felt even more; there is such a terrible void! Of course, only God can give solace by healing such heartache."[40] In Queen Olga's eyes, Alexander III's death was not merely a personal tragedy that befell the imperial family, but the entire empire. "There is no single soul in Russia," she noted, "which has not experienced that deep grief; it is personal for everyone."[41]

In recounting Alexander III's final hours, Marie Feodorovna told her mother, "how heartrending it all was! Incomprehensible that one can survive such sorrow and despair and now the eternal longing and emptiness everywhere I go! How shall I bear it! And the poor children, who are in despair as well, and poor, sweet Nicky, especially who is to begin this difficult life at such an early age."[42] Marie Feodorovna went on to add: "Now my happiness is gone, and I must live on without him, he who was everything to me!! I simply do not know how I can stand the pain and awful sadness! Our Lord alone can help me bear this heavy, heavy cross that he has placed upon me!"[43]

Marie Feodorovna's twenty-eighth wedding anniversary fell within days of Alexander III's death. The anniversary was all the more poignant when she discovered that her late husband had ordered a bracelet for her which his valet presented to Alix, who in turn, gave it to her future mother-in-law. Overcome by the dramatic events, both Alix and Marie Feodorovna were full of tender sympathies for each other. "Alicky," wrote the empress to her mother, "was so sweet and has truly shared everything with us as if she had always belonged to us."[44]

Amidst the grieving for the dead emperor, one ray of happiness touched Nicholas II and the imperial family, the reception of Princess Alix into the Orthodox Church in a simple ceremony at Livadia. Along with her new faith, she took the name of Alexandra Feodorovna. All that was left for the couple was the all important step of marriage. But that had to wait until after the late emperor's funeral.

Funeral ceremonies for Alexander III lasted for seventeen days. The first lying-in-state took place in a humble church amidst the cypresses at Livadia. The new tsar and widowed Marie Feodorovna, in heavy mourning, shared the funeral obsequies with Queen Olga, the Duchess of Coburg, the Prince and Princess of Wales, and Princess Alix. Alexander III's body then was somberly brought to St. Petersburg. The manner in which her late husband was mourned deeply moved the newly widowed Marie Feodorovna: "The enormous crowd of people who all look <u>disconsolate</u>," wrote the widowed empress to her mother, "show me much sympathy!"[45]

At the end of the final funeral rites at the Sts. Peter and Paul Cathedral, Marie Feodorovna said her last goodbye. Accompanied by Nicholas II and "her aged father, the King of Denmark, the Empress ascended the bier and kissed her dead husband for the last time amid bitter sobs and tears."[46] The Duke of York, one of the pallbearers, was full of admiration for the widowed empress. "It was most impressive and sad," wrote George of the funeral, "& I shall never forget it. Darling Aunt Minny was so brave."[47] Toward the end of the ceremony, the widow broke down and cried out, "Enough! Enough! Enough!"[48]

On the funeral's heels came Nicholas II's wedding. Marie Feodorovna did not look forward to Nicky's wedding. Charlotte Knollys, who accompanied the Wales family to Russia, perceived the tsar's mother's torment: "The poor Empress is so dreading the wedding tomorrow fancy having to take off her [widow's] weeds & facing the 8000 people who will be invited, in a State dress to say nothing of the Ordeal of seeing herself superseded by a young girl of whom she knows but little & of having to step down into the 2nd place when she has so long held the 1st . . . One thing is that she is certainly blessed with the best & most devoted son in the world."[49]

The wedding took place on the Empress Marie Feodorovna's forty-seventh birthday (November 14/26, 1894) at the chapel of the Winter Palace. The ordeal for the groom's mother was clearly evident. If it had not been for the solicitous presence of her father, King Christian IX, Marie Feodorovna might easily have found it impossible to watch the whole ceremony. Still, mourning was put aside for the day, and the wedding proceeded with all the pomp for which the Russian court was renowned. In writing of her wedding to Queen Victoria, Alix spoke of "poor Aunt Minnie all alone. She is an angel of kindness and is more touching and brave than I can say."[50]

Of Alix, Marie Feodorovna reassured her mother "how *sweet* and *affectionately sympathetic* she has been to me the entire time, and how close she has come to my heart in all this sadness and despair, which she has shared with us so beautifully."[51] A week later, the empress wrote again to her mother: "Naturally the children are my first concern now. May God just give me understanding, and *what* I beg of him is to help my beloved Nicky a bit in his difficult lot."[52]

K.R. spoke with Marie Feodorovna during these tumultuous days and was moved by her predicament. She told him that "she did not want to go anywhere, as there was no escape from her grief. She bears it," K.R. noted, "with such resignation."[53] Queen Victoria also felt for Marie Feodorovna, telling the new tsar: "How your poor dear Mama could go through it all is a marvel! All speak and write of your devotion to her."[54] Nicky's devotion to his mother was indeed of great help to Marie Feodorovna, and one that would not abate anytime soon. A measure of this devotion was evident in the living arrangements agreed to by the new tsar. Instead of living separately from Marie Feodorovna, the newly married Nicky opted to start his new life with Alix at his mother's home, the Anichkov Palace where his married quarters consisted of the same small set of rooms Nicholas II had occupied as a boy. From the Anichkov, Tsarina Alexandra wrote a letter to her sister, telling her how Nicky's "affection for his mother is touching, and how he looks after her, so quietly and tenderly."[55]

Before the year ended, most of Marie Feodorovna's relatives from abroad, including Queen Olga and the Duchess of Coburg, had left. "The poor dear Empress is so brave and touching in her great sorrow," confided the Tsarina Alexandra to the Bishop of Ripon. The tsarina added that Marie Feodorovna was "always thinking of others and trying to do good. It was a great comfort to her, having her sister, the Pss of Wales on such a long visit."[56]

Out of respect for Alexander III's wishes in summoning the Prince of Wales to his "death-bed and afterwards by the side of his son and successor," Marie Feodorovna's brother-in-law extended his visit and was among the last to leave. Bertie acted as the new tsar's "supporter and mentor—indeed, one might say as a second father." The Prince of Wales did not leave Russia and Nicky's side until the tsar was "safely married and firmly established on the throne."[57] It was an open secret that the Vladimirs had coveted the crown; and it came as no surprise there was some real concern over the ambitions of Miechen's husband at the time of Alexander III's death. Luckily for Marie Feodorovna, no such coup materialized. Moreover, "neither Nicholas nor his mother . . . have ever forgotten their debt of gratitude to [the uncle and brother-in-law who became] King Edward [VII]."[58]

Amidst her intense grief, Marie Feodorovna was attentive to her son and new daughter-in-law, upon whose shoulders rested Russia's future. The dowager empress wrote to her mother, Queen Louise, of the hopes she placed upon Alix and Nicky: "Oh, may the present dear boy be well advised, *bien inspiré* [well inspired]. What a benefactor to his country, what a saviour to his poor oppressed nation, what a godsend to Europe he might be! . . . no one ever had a finer mission than dear Nicky has."[59] What Marie Feodorovna did not then realize, was that her husband's death hastened the end for imperial Russia.

A FAILURE TO UNDERSTAND

Marie Feodorovna's eldest son aspired to honor Alexander III's memory by ruling according to the same ideals, namely Autocracy, Orthodoxy, and Nationality. Nicholas II made his strategy clear when he received representatives from the Tver *zemstvo*;[1] the tsar announced that he would "safeguard the principles of autocracy as firmly and unswervingly as did my late, unforgettable father."[2]

Nicky's personal priorities lay with his mother and new wife. But if he thought that these two women who meant so much to him would continue to feel sympathetic toward each other, those hopes were soon dashed. To begin with, there was no privacy for the newlyweds at the Anichkov Palace. Though luxurious, the place felt overcrowded because it housed the dowager empress, her daughter Olga, Nicholas and Alexandra, and even Xenia and Sandro. In Russia, dowager empresses took precedence over reigning empresses. Hence Alexandra had to concede to her mother-in-law, and as mother and mistress of the house, Marie Feodorovna continued to exercise authority over everyone at the Anichkov, right down to choosing Tsarina Alexandra's ladies-in-waiting. At official functions, the tsar escorted his mother, while Alexandra followed behind, accompanied by the senior-ranking grand duke, Grand Duke Vladimir. The prevailing gossip was that Tsarina Alexandra resented having to take a backseat to her mother-in-law. "Poor Alicky could not have been happy" with this arrangement recalled Grand Duchess Olga, because Vladimir's Anglophobia "was a by-word." Moreover, Olga noted that Alexandra knew Vladimir "had opposed Nicky's marriage to the last."[3]

In no time, Alexandra confided of her sadness to a friend: "I feel myself completely alone . . . I weep and worry all day long."[4] The new tsarina's frustrations grew, because the dowager empress also usurped the mantle of political adviser, regularly dispensing political advice to the novice tsar. Unlike Tsarina Alexandra, who knew so little of Russia, Marie Feodorovna had been empress for thirteen years and lived in Russia for nearly thirty. In her eyes, she was more than well qualified to act as a mentor to her son. Her shy, tongue-tied daughter-in-law would do well to sit on the sidelines to watch and learn the art of being the empress. This inevitably further eroded the tsarina's confidence.

The two empresses, so strikingly dissimilar, provided a study in contrasts for many, including Maria von Bock, daughter of Peter Stolypin (who was to become one of the most important political figures in Nicholas II's reign). She marveled at the aura exuded by the dowager empress. "How could anyone of such small stature exude such imperial stateliness?" wondered von Bock. "Kind, amiable, simple in her discourse, Maria Fedorovna was an Empress from head to toe, combining an inborn majesty with such goodness that she was idolized by all who knew her." The Tsarina Alexandra, on the other hand, though "young" and "very beautiful," was "nervous" and possessed "weary movements." She also "dressed not only simply but in outdated style." "I will always remember Aleksandra Fedorovna's sad eyes and anxious speech," wrote Maria von Bock, "she was not born to be Empress of one of the largest countries on the face of the earth."[5] Meriel Buchanan made similar observations. Marie Feodorovna, "small and slender in her deep black dress," was "possessed of an incredible dignity" and carried on an "easy, effortless conversation." "How much easier it was to talk to this little lady in black, with her flashing diamond rings, than to talk to the tall beautiful woman in the violet velvet dress," Tsarina Alexandra. All in all, Marie Feodorovna possessed a "gracious and delightful charm of manner."[6] It did not take long for many to realize that the Tsarina Alexandra could never compete with the Dowager Empress Marie Feodorovna for people's affections. In a letter to a friend, Grand Duke Nicholas Mikhailovich summed up what many felt about Marie Feodorovna, "my Empress mother [the dowager empress] is always our guardian angel."[7]

Tensions increased between these two highly divergent women. "They tried to understand each other and failed," recalled the dowager empress's daughter Olga, but because "they were utterly different in character, habits, and outlook,"[8] the chasm that separated the two women became increasingly impossible to bridge. Baroness Sophie Buxhoeveden, Tsarina Alexandra's close friend, concurred, noting that "the temperaments and tastes of mother and daughter-in-law were so dissimilar that, without actually clashing, they seemed each fundamentally unable thoroughly to understand the other."[9] F. S. Olferev, one of the imperial pages who served both empresses, touched upon the marked differences. Olferev was impressed that Marie Feodorovna not only spoke Russian but that she also "understood Russians and knew how to talk with them comprehensively and clearly. With that attribute she was able to charm Russians and her smile immediately brought them into her aura." On the other hand, Tsarina Alexandra, in those early days, "spoke quite often in French, which was not her native language . . . Often a theme for conversation would be whispered to her and she would make awkward remarks, making one feel that her comments were forced and insincere."[10]

Instead of retreating behind her widowhood, the Dowager Empress Marie Feodorovna sought out company, entertained, and continued to be as vivacious and gracious as ever. In an audience with the empress, Andrew Dickson White, who had been the U.S. minister to Russia from 1892 to 1894, found Marie Feodorovna "graceful, with a most kindly face and manner." "She put me at ease immediately," recalled White, "addressing me in English, and detaining me much longer than I expected." She was "in every way cordial and kindly."[11] In contrast to Marie Feodorovna's gift of rapport, Tsarina Alexandra's inability to relate to people not only hampered her self-confidence; with the passage of time, it created an impenetrable barrier between her and others. Nowhere was this handicap more in evidence than in the mandatory court entertainments over which Alexandra was expected to shine. Far from relishing the court balls where up to two thousand guests cast their gaze on her, Tsarina Alexandra "felt absolutely lost" and yearned "to disappear under the ground," recalled Baroness Buxhoeveden."[12] A seasoned court observer and grand dame of St. Petersburg society, Countess Kleinmichel surmised that the tsarina's "austere nature joined to an absolute inexperience of life,"[13] combined to make Alexandra a poor candidate for the role of tsarina. Sadly for Alix, instead of eliciting sympathy for her predicament, society began turning against her.

The elite gave the new tsarina very little time to acclimatize herself to her new position, her new country, and her new language. Tsarina Alexandra's introversion made a profound impression. "Ah yes," came the whispers, "she is beautiful but so cold!"[14] Baroness Buxhoeveden summed up what unfolded between Marie Feodorovna's daughter-in-law and the elite of the capital: "Society did not know her, and her timidity was ascribed to haughtiness, and her reserve to pride."[15] Perhaps if St. Petersburg society had been more forgiving, Alexandra might also have tried harder at being an effective tsarina. However, gossip and unrelenting criticisms of her missteps only served to alienate Alexandra from them.

The immorality of her new Romanov relatives and other Russian elite appalled her. A product of her proper Victorian upbringing, supervised no less by Queen Victoria herself with her own exacting standards of behavior, Tsarina Alexandra was highly critical of St. Petersburg society, including the Romanov grand dukes, whose romantic escapades invited much gossip. The dowager empress subscribed to the same high ideals of moral probity espoused by Alix and Queen Victoria. Nevertheless, Marie Feodorovna held firm to these ideals while simultaneously avoiding alienating St. Petersburg society. Contemptuous as she was of the lax morality she encountered around her, Marie Feodorovna cleverly managed to balance this with an amazing ability to elicit empathy from this segment of her subjects. Throughout her years in Russia, the dowager empress succeeded with St. Petersburg's elite in a way her daughter-in-law could only envy.

Tsarina Alexandra might have felt less estranged had she and the dowager empress managed to cultivate a friendship, but because they were so fundamentally different in character and tastes, whatever goodwill Marie Feodorovna initially felt toward Alexandra evaporated. Friction between the women increased as both failed to understand each other. They vied to exercise their influence over Nicholas II. In the first years of Nicky's reign, Marie Feodorovna held the upper hand. She had, after all, a head start as his adoring mother, and it was a position she relished and exercised without restraint. But in so doing, she alienated Alexandra, a mistake Marie Feodorovna's own mother had warned her about. Shortly after Nicky and Alix had become engaged, Queen Louise of Denmark gave Marie Feodorovna motherly advice: "For yours and Nicky's sake start treating her like your own child, without fear, right away . . . Pull her [Alix] towards you, then you will keep him and pull her towards you with love!"[16]

Relations between Marie Feodorovna and Miechen were still frosty too. In the summer of 1895, Marie Feodorovna complained of Vladimir and Miechen's seeming lack of respect toward the late emperor and Nicholas II, telling her son: "The Wladimirs [sic] seem to have *forgotten everything already*; nothing prevents them from celebrating the 22nd January with a gypsy party . . . It is so unseemly and I cannot understand that Uncle W. [sic] is unable to restrain her. I can hear Papa saying: 'I am not surprised at all.' With her, pleasure goes before everything."[17]

Nicholas II agreed wholeheartedly with his mother. The tsar even daringly asserted himself as head of the family, in an attempt to put his uncle Vladimir and aunt Miechen in their place. When Nicholas discovered that Miechen took over the imperial box at the Mariinsky Theatre in St. Petersburg during a masked ball to entertain her friends there, he was furious. He wrote to Grand Duke Vladimir, admonishing him and advising him that outsiders were not allowed in the imperial box. In response, Vladimir, according to K.R., sent "a curt letter that he had never been subjected to such a sharp reprimand by either his father or his brother." K.R. wondered how Vladimir could "permit himself to write to the Emperor in such terms!" adding that "Minnie saw his letter and was appalled."[18]

Therefore, one might suppose that the Grand Duchess Marie Pavlovna and Alix might have become allies. Considering Miechen's senior position within the Romanov clan and her reputation as St. Petersburg's preeminent hostess, the awkward tsarina might have benefited tremendously if she had warmed to her aunt by marriage. And the ambitious Miechen "was certainly not averse to the idea of getting her [Alix] under her own influence, rather than that of the Empress Marie."[19] But it was not to be.

Like her husband, Miechen was leery of Nicholas II's choice for a wife. According to Countess Kleinmichel, Alix and Miechen had a regrettable meeting years before. When Alix first visited St. Petersburg as a child for Ella's wedding, the Grand Duchess Vladimir treated her "very cavalierly, like a little princess of no importance." Countess Kleinmichel surmised that Alexandra never forgot how the grand duchess "spoke of her" in such a way that it "aroused anger and resentment in her heart." Nonetheless, Miechen had tried to reach out to her new niece when Alix first arrived as Nicholas II's bride. Even so, Marie Pavlovna went about the first meetings with the young and inexperienced tsarina in an unsubtle way, taking "the attitude of a governess eager to guide all her movements." Miechen's haughtiness prompted Alexandra to counter as if to make "her aunt feel that she [Alix] in her turn had the upper hand." The grand duchess "never forgave her, and consistently used her [i.e., Miechen's] powerful influence in Petersburg society to promote anything that could harm the Empress. She incited ladies holding high positions to give advice to the Tsarina, applauded their courage when they criticised her adversely, and made public the contents of their letters or the gist of their conversations."[20] A. A. Mossolov, who headed the Court Chancellery and had close access to the imperial family, concurred with this view. "When she found herself cold-shouldered," wrote Mossolov, "Marie Pavlovna, over-bearing and irascible by nature, gave full vent to her spleen in acid comment on everything that her niece did or did not do. The Court—*her* Court—followed the example set to it. It was from the immediate entourage of Marie Pavlovna that the most wounding stories about the Empress emanated."[21]

If one is to believe a courtier intimate's anecdote regarding a Winter Palace reception soon after Tsarina Alexandra's wedding, either Miechen was not averse to giving bad advice or the tsarina was prone to misunderstanding. When Alexandra asked Miechen whether a certain elderly lady, a "Madame A.," was of importance, the grand duchess replied: "Oh she is an old frump. Give her your hand to kiss, and she will be satisfied." This, however, was the last thing that Madame A. would have liked. She expected more than a perfunctory greeting from the tsarina; and when Alexandra did just that and then "coolly turned her back upon her and passed on without having said a single word," Madame A. was scandalized. The infuriated Tsarina Alexandra blamed the Grand Duchess Vladimir for "having led her into a snare, and, boiling with rage," went to Madame A. and said loudly: "I am sorry, Madame, not to have treated you with the respect to which you are entitled, but it was the Grand-Duchess Marie Pawlowna [*sic*] my aunt, who had advised me to do it." This backfired and Madame A. told those around her: "It is not with the help of a treachery, Madame, that one can excuse a rudeness." Madame A. then immediately left the palace, leaving the Tsarina Alexandra well aware "that in the space of five short minutes she had contrived to make for herself two mortal enemies."

The tension did not end there, for the imperial family sided with Miechen in all this. Grand Duke Vladimir went to Nicholas II and "complained bitterly" of the tsarina's conduct, while most of the grand duchesses vowed to avoid, when possible, dealing with Alix. Miechen, meanwhile, "swore that she had never meant to advise her niece to show herself rude to such a respectable personage as Madame A.; that her words had been a mere joke, to which she had never imagined that any importance could be attached, and that it had been a cruel thing to denounce her in such a ruthless way to the worst gossip and most malicious tongue in St. Petersburg."

Marie Feodorovna joined in the fray. The dowager empress "expressed herself as shocked beyond words at her daughter-in-law's behavior," but when she tried to talk to Alix about it, the tsarina "recognized the right of no one to criticize her actions." Supposedly, Alexandra then produced a caricature in which she had drawn Nicky in "swaddling-clothes, seated at a dinner-table in a high-backed chair, with his uncles and aunts standing around him, and threatening him with their fingers, adding that she was not going to follow the example of her spouse, and that if he chose to forget before his relatives that he was Emperor of All the Russias, she would never not do so for one single minute."[22]

As time passed, the tense relationship between Marie Feodorovna, Miechen, and Alexandra grew even more tetchy. Marie Feodorovna and Alexandra remained leery of each other. Miechen, an accomplished hostess, viewed Alexandra and her lack of social graces with contempt. The ambitious grand duchess viewed Nicholas and Alexandra as inept reminders that her family had been denied their place on the Russian throne. "Torn between two mutually antipathetic sisters-in-law, the shy Alix withdrew even more into herself. In doing so, she inadvertently made a lifelong enemy of Grand Duchess Vladimir." Inadvertent or not, it was not a good move, for Miechen was "a useful person to have as a friend, but the last woman of whom to make an enemy."[23] Marie Feodorovna and Miechen, it seems, had finally found common ground in their mutual antipathy toward Alix.

The tension that simmered between the dowager empress and tsarina eased slightly when Nicholas and Alexandra finally moved into a home of their own, the Alexander Palace, on the grounds of Tsarskoe Selo. It was here, in November 1895, that Alexandra gave birth to her first child, Olga Nikolaevna. This made Marie Feodorovna a grandmother for the second time, for earlier that year, Grand Duchess Xenia gave birth to her first child, Princess Irina.

In May 1896, the dowager empress traveled to Moscow for Nicholas and Alexandra's coronation. The sacred event was set to be another magnificent demonstration of imperial grandeur. The help needed for the coronation to run smoothly was impressive, requiring no less than "1300 full time servants and 1200 part time. The livery division required 600 horses and 800 coachmen with horses and carriages. Guards came from 83 battalions, 47 squadrons and hundreds of batteries."[24] Marie Feodorovna was greatly moved by the event, which took place thirteen years after her own coronation. Yet, those who had attended both coronation festivities noted a palpable difference. Though the "same amount of pomp and splendour" was visible, Nicholas II's coronation "lacked the enthusiasm which had been so remarkable" in Alexander III's. The cheers for Tsar Nicholas II came not from the crowds watching, but largely from the troops who lined the processional route, while Tsarina Alexandra met with "dead silence." Moreover, the "silent and undemonstrative" manner in which the crowds received Nicholas and Alexandra were in startling contrast to the reception for the dowager empress. "The shouts" that greeted Marie Feodorovna when she came in sight in her golden carriage were "almost deafening."[25] The American journalist, Richard Harding Davis, who was in Moscow, was similarly struck. "It was she," wrote Davis of the dowager empress, "who was more loudly greeted than either the Emperor or the Czarina."[26] Kate Koon, another American visitor to Moscow, concurred. Koon noted that Marie Feodorovna "provoked more cheering from the people than did her son. The people have had thirteen years in which to know this woman and they have learned to love her very much." But far from looking thrilled, the dowager empress, Koon observed, had a "sad face, poor woman, with one son at death's door [the tubercular Grand Duke George], she had not much heart for the joys of the other."[27] Another American, John Logan, made similar observations about the dowager empress. Marie Feodorovna, "throughout all the ceremonies," recalled Logan, was the "widowed mother whose chastened grief seemed to sanctify and ennoble every scene upon which she gazed."[28]

On coronation day as the dowager empress entered the cathedral, Logan noticed that "she bore herself with regal dignity" and "looked well, but sad."[29] At the end of the coronation, amidst the pealing of bells, the thunderous booms of cannons and the shouts of congratulations, Marie Feodorovna gave homage to her newly crowned son. "It was pathetic to see the wistful look in the face of the Dowager Empress," wrote a witness, "as she tenderly embraced her son, and both were overcome by deep emotion."[30] "As difficult as it was for me," wrote Marie Feodorovna to her mother, Queen Louise, of the coronation, "I would always have reproached myself if I had not been there . . . it was my duty, . . . But how gripping and solemn it all was! My heart truly bled to see my Nicky at this, so young, in his beloved father's place."[31]

Numerous royal guests came for Tsar Nicholas II's coronation, including the Duchess of Coburg and Queen Olga of Greece. During one procession, Kate Koon noticed that Queen Olga of Greece, who suffered from poor eyesight, "used her lorgnettes continually and seemed to enjoy gazing at the crowd." "All the women," added Koon, "had on diamond diadems and wore magnificent jewels. . . . The gowns," she gushed, "were perfect wonders."[32] Like the other imperial ladies, Miechen was a dazzling sight with her magnificent gown and impressive pearls that hung in rows around her neck.

Though the Grand Duchess Marie Pavlovna and Dowager Empress Marie Feodorovna were absorbed in the coronation rituals and festivities, they did not ignore those who served them, especially the imperial pages. During one sumptuous lunch at the Kremlin, Miechen remembered that the pages needed to eat and ordered that refreshments be given to them. Thanks to Miechen's consideration and quick-thinking, the pages managed to eat quickly before the hall filled with guests. One imperial page later recorded that "it was a treat to be named the Kamer-page of Grand Duchess Maria Pavlovna who always showed her pages respect."[33] Marie Feodorovna was just as thoughtful. Unable to be at all the coronation events, Marie Feodorovna nevertheless tried to ensure that her pages attended some of the celebrations. One way she managed this was by asking a favor of her brother-in-law, Grand Duke Serge, who gave a ball in his capacity as governor-general of Moscow. Marie Feodorovna's pages were informed that they should be at the ball, all of them assuming that the dowager empress would be there and that they would be in attendance. But upon their arrival, the Grand Duke Serge announced that: "The Empress Maria Feodorovna asked that I invite you Kamer-pages to the ball. She is sorry that because of her absence you have been deprived of seeing many triumphal ceremonies. I am happy to fulfill the wishes of the Empress and I would like for you to feel that while you are here you are not Kamer-pages of Her Majesty, but my guests." The astonished page who recalled this extraordinary act of kindness noted that "we, of course, were proud of the Empress's consideration and taking advantage of being a guest we wandered through all the halls of the palace."[34]

Sadly, a tragedy of tremendous proportions overshadowed the coronation festivities. A stampede of people at Khodynka Field killed thousands of peasants who had gathered there to celebrate. The Dowager Empress Marie Feodorovna had just started to make her way in her carriage toward Khodynka Field when she encountered shocking scenes of corpses covered in blood. "The dreadful accident . . . was appalling beyond all description," wrote Marie Feodorovna to her mother, "and has . . . draped a black veil over all the splendor and glory! Just imagine how many poor unfortunate people were crushed and fatally injured!"[35] The tragedy stunned many, including the imperial family. In a show of sympathy, the tsar, tsarina, and dowager empress visited the numerous wounded victims.

The Duchess of Coburg accompanied by her daughters Missy and Ducky, was also in Moscow for the coronation. Marie Alexandrovna had been a pillar of support for Missy, who led a frustrated life in Bucharest. Stifled in Romania, with a husband who could not contradict his domineering uncle, an exasperated Missy sought to escape to her mother in Coburg when she could. King Carol, however, did not make it easy for Missy to leave the country, prompting the Duchess of Coburg to tell her daughter to be firm with *der Onkel*. The duchess urged Missy to be cold toward the king until he gave way. "I know best how to deal with this sort of self-willed obstinate people," wrote Marie Alexandrovna emphatically. "If you give way you *are lost* and they regularly trample upon you and stamp out every bit of life and pleasure out of you."[36]

Missy was not the only one of Marie Alexandrovna's daughters enduring personal problems. Ducky's marriage was already floundering. She and Ernie had a daughter, Elisabeth, in 1895, but the couple could not stay together, even for the daughter's sake. Temperamentally unsuited to each other, Ducky and Ernie's marriage continued to deteriorate, particularly when Ernie's homosexual tendencies became undeniable. Frustrated, Ducky increasingly longed to be free of Ernie and the provincial atmosphere of Darmstadt. Her attentions became increasingly focused on Russia and her other cousin, Grand Duke Kyril, her aunt Miechen's son.

By the late 1890s, Grand Duke Kyril and his brothers Boris and Andrei had grown into handsome young men. They, along with their sister, Grand Duchess Elena, stood out for their dark good looks. The Vladimir children had been raised in a loving environment, though they were also spoilt. As the only girl in the family, Elena was especially pampered. As a child, Elena Vladimirovna was a handful, eliciting a scathing remark from her aunt, the dowager empress: "Poor little thing, I feel sorry for her, for she is really quite sweet, but vain and pretty grandiose."[37] Grand Duchess Elena, who bore the brunt of her brothers' teasing, was turning into her mother's daughter: independent, willful, and assured. Henry Jones Thaddeus, who painted the grand duchess when she was a young child, recalled Elena as a "bright-eyed, fascinating child, but rebellious and hot-tempered." As he painted the little grand duchess, Thaddeus noticed how much she pouted the entire time. Elena was "evidently nurturing some grievance against the nurse," recalled Thaddeus, for as he tried to pacify Elena, she "suddenly seized a large paper-knife from a table near and made a lunge at the nurse." But that was not the end of the escapade. "The little lady then transferred her attention to me," added Thaddeus, "her black eyes ablaze with fury. Before I realized her intention, over went the picture and easel, and, quite unprepared for the impetuous charge, I nearly went over myself as well. I caught her up, she still furiously stabbing, took the paper-knife from her chubby little fist, and eventually restored peace." It was, concluded Thaddeus, "a revelation of passion in one so young."[38]

The unsavory incident took place in Cannes where the Grand Duchess Vladimir rented a villa in the mid-1880s. Miechen, like numerous royals and aristocrats of the time, liked to decamp to the French Riviera with its picturesque scenery and temperate weather. The villa she rented on this particular occasion was palatial, "replete with every luxury." Nevertheless, it was still too small to house Miechen's entire entourage, consisting of a veritable "small army of cooks, servants, and *valets de pied*, all Russian."[39] In Cannes, like in St. Petersburg, Miechen played the consummate hostess. Thaddeus admired the grand duchess's social skills, describing her as being the "ideal hostess. With a winning smile and most gracious, sympathetic manner she greeted her guests, reserving for each, some cordial, pleasant remark, which delighted the recipient." But Miechen's graciousness went beyond greeting visitors. "During dinner," Thaddeus recalled, "Her Imperial Highness was the life and soul of the company, the most brilliant contributor to the general conversation." Besides jovial conversation, gambling was de rigueur. The grand duchess insisted that her guests play roulette "for trifling harmless stakes." With her brother, Frederick Francís III, the Grand Duke of Mecklenburg-Schwerin, the croupier, Miechen the banker "reigned supreme, enlivening the game with her wit and merry badinage," and would pronounce pleasantly: "*Messieurs et madames, faites vos jeux* [Ladies and gentlemen, play your game]." To those who hesitated, Miechen would add: "*Mais jouez d'avantage, mes petits moutons, vous allez tous gagner* [But play to advantage, my little lambs, you will all win]." "Such irresistible pleading could not be denied," recalled Thaddeus, "the stakes were increased, to the imperial banker's satisfaction, and the wheel sent whirling around."[40] The grand duchess was in her element, a sight of which the Dowager Empress Marie Feodorovna and the Tsarina Alexandra would have heartily disapproved.

In 1899, Miechen and Vladimir celebrated their silver wedding anniversary. The couple received spectacular presents to mark the occasion. Nicholas and Alexandra gave Miechen "an aigrette and diadem composed of magnificent diamonds. The three stones of the aigrette alone," it was reported, "are worth a fortune." Each grand duke and grand duchess gave one of thirty-six golden plates, which formed "the most magnificent service that can be imagined."[41] Life was good no doubt; and fate, it would seem, did indeed smile upon Miechen.

IN MOURNING

iechen was not the only one celebrating her twenty-fifth wedding anniversary in 1899. Marie Alexandrovna also reached that milestone.
Though she and the Duke of Coburg stayed married, their uneasy marriage
made the duchess happy to live apart from her husband as often as she could.
"If you only knew how easy and comfortable life is without him," wrote a relieved duchess to Missy when Affie stayed for a time with their eldest daughter.[1]

By the late 1890s, most of the Duchess of Coburg's children, with the exception of Alfred and Bee, had married. Sandra, whom her mother thought to
be the least interesting of her offspring, married Prince Ernst of Hohenlohe-
Langenburg in 1896. Sandra caused her mother few worries, unlike Alfred. At
a young age, the sensitive Alfred was sent away from his family to be educated
in Germany, where he suffered under the charge of a cruel tutor in Coburg.
Once out of his tutor's influence, Alfred pursued a fast life of drinking and
women. In 1896, the Duchess of Coburg sent her wayward son to his sister in
Romania in the hope that Missy could knock some sense into the twenty-one-
year-old prince. The crown princess told her mother that she would do her
best: "I certainly will talk to him as you wish it . . . because I find the whole
thing so loathsome."[2] But it was to no avail.

Alfred's Russian cousin, Grand Duke Boris, accompanied him to Romania.
Miechen's son was hardly a model companion, being a lothario of the greatest
magnitude. Few womanizers could outcompete the debonair Boris Vladimirovich. Even Crown Princess Marie of Romania was not immune to the
grand duke's charm. He made no secret of his admiration for the beautiful

Missy, which soon sent tongues wagging. The Duchess of Coburg warned her daughter of the flirtation, but Missy succumbed to Boris's amusing company. It would appear that Boris was "the first of [Missy's] numerous lovers." When Marie Alexandrovna learned of her daughter's transgression, she warned her about her "disorderly life" as well as her "vulgar ideas."[3] Missy did not heed her mother's admonishment and became pregnant, in 1897, not by Crown Prince Ferdinand or Boris, but the princess's aide-de-camp, a Lieutenant Zizi Cantacuzène. The scandal compelled Missy to flee to her mother in Coburg. Nothing is known about the child who may have been "stillborn or put in an orphanage." The fate of the illegitimate child was "one secret" Missy "apparently took with her to her grave."[4] Meanwhile, Alfred's dissipation continued.

Frustrated by the machinations of Queen Elisabeth of Romania, who installed a dictatorial governess to watch over Prince Carol, Missy resumed her friendship with Cantacuzène in the late 1890s. The gossip about her daughter's waywardness spread outside the family, infuriating Marie Alexandrovna, who was aghast with Missy. The determined duchess took matters into her own hands by writing to King Carol I and to Missy. To the Romanian king, the Duchess of Coburg admitted that Missy was guilty of a "serious and unpardonable fault," but she also chastised Ferdinand's infidelity. The duchess also could not understand why the king "did not try to keep the deplorable story within the family." Because this was so, wrote Marie Alexandrovna, all her relations heard of the gossip, hinting that the news came "directly from Roumania and evidently spread to blacken the reputation of my daughter!" The duchess added that she could not understand why spies were planted in Missy's household and her children taken away from her. "As culpable as she is," Marie Alexandrovna wrote, "*nothing* will excuse the indignity of such procedures."[5] To Missy, the concerned mother wrote: "Your old Mama grieves but will never abandon you." The Duchess of Coburg went on to admonish and encourage, saying how, "you have greatly sinned, but it is time still to become a good steady woman."[6]

Missy became pregnant again during this scandal. This time, the father was Grand Duke Boris. During a fiery audience with King Carol I, Missy claimed outright that "she loved her cousin Boris, that she wanted a divorce, and that the child she was carrying was Boris's." The Duchess of Coburg again took matters into her own hands. She acted quickly and pressed Missy to come to her. "My plan," wrote the anxious mother, "is to take you immediately to Coburg, where we can wait until you give birth . . . The most important problem is to restore your reputation and to save you from this terrible situation . . .

I will take care of the rest." Missy did as her mother urged. She gave birth in January 1900 to a daughter, named Marie after herself, her mother, and her Russian grandmother, though this grandchild of Marie Alexandrovna's would always be known in the family as "Mignon." In order to avoid a scandal, Ferdinand "reluctantly agreed to accept the child as his own."[7]

While Missy's scandalous troubles plagued Marie Alexandrovna, young Alfred continued to spiral out of control. Joining the First Prussian Corps, "the fastest of all the [German] Regiments," greatly aggravated the prince's fragile physical and mental state, wrote Marie Mallet, one of Queen Victoria's maids of honor. Mallet added that he "simply had no chance whatever and humanely speaking his life has just been drained away."[8] Some sources reported that the prince married a certain Mabel Fitzgerald in Potsdam and that his indignant mother ordered immediate annulment. But according to an authority on Queen Victoria's descendants, the marriage is "a legend that has been fostered" but "no evidence of this exists."[9]

Prince Alfred's drinking and womanizing took a heavy toll. When Alfred joined his mother at Ilinskoe, the duchess was shocked at her son's appearance. "He seems completely done up morally and physically and looks like an old man," recounted the distraught Marie Alexandrovna. "I never saw him in such a state before, but he hardly utters, feels weak and depressed." Prince Alfred was suffering from syphilis, news that sent his shamed mother into despair. The Russian imperial family soon heard of the true nature of the prince's illness. It turned out that the Russian doctor treating the prince could not resist telling Miechen, "who, though she felt ill and nervous on hearing the news, did not hesitate long in relaying it."[10]

When Missy arrived in Coburg to celebrate her parents' silver wedding anniversary, she was taken aback to find her brother so debilitated. "He hardly recognises anyone and often does not know what he says, poor boy," wrote Missy despairingly to their sister, Sandra.[11] In the middle of Marie Alexandrovna's silver wedding celebrations, twenty-three-year-old Alfred shot himself. His mother, bewildered and furious at what her son had done, sent the severely injured young man to Merano, Switzerland. He died there shortly afterward without his family, attended only by a doctor and a servant. The doctor who had accompanied Alfred to Merano had warned his parents not to move him, but according to Marie Mallet, "they truly refused to believe him." Having died as the doctor prophesied, the Duke and Duchess of Coburg "lament and weep at his having died quite alone," reported Mallet. She also added that "the end" was caused by "paralysis of the larynx caused by the state of the brain, which in its turn was the result of the terrible fast life he had led in Berlin from the time he was 17."[12]

Prince Alfred's funeral took place at Gotha. In writing of his son's death to his sister Princess Louise, Affie spoke of his "terrible grief" and "what a fearful blow his loss is to me."[13] Marie Alexandrovna was equally distraught. As the church bells tolled, the Duchess of Coburg, who was normally undemonstrative, was overcome by grief. She fell to her knees, crossed herself numerous times, and burst into tears. Missy was stunned by the scene, recalling it to have been "an overwhelming sight; Mamma weeping for her first-born."[14]

The circumstances surrounding Alfred's tragic death had been kept fairly quiet. Even the Duke of Cambridge, a member of the British royal family, admitted to have been taken "entirely by surprise, as I was not aware he had been ill."[15] Queen Victoria wrote to the duke of the tragedy, describing "my poor dear grandson Alfred's" death as a "most sad event." "It is indeed," Queen Victoria added sadly, "a most grievous calamity, and poor dear Alfred and Marie are quite broken hearted and crushed by the loss of their *only* son. It makes my heart bleed to think of their grief."[16] Young Alfred's death brought the succession to the duchy of Coburg into question. The dispute about the succession "involved almost all" of Queen Victoria's immediate family, "stretching her powers of mediation to the full."[17] In the end, Prince Charles of Albany was chosen—the son of Prince Leopold, Marie Alexandrovna's favorite brother-in-law.

The Duchess of Coburg was not alone in grieving for a son that tragic year of 1899. Dowager Empress Marie Feodorovna fretted deeply over the tubercular Grand Duke George. A member of her security team said, "more than once I detected the anguish of the mother stealthily trying to read the secret of her son's hectic eyes, peering at his pale face, watching for his hoarse, hard cough, as he walked beside her, or dined opposite her."[18] Marie Feodorovna was right to worry about her sickly child. In August 1899, twenty-eight-year-old George collapsed at the roadside, while riding his motorcycle in the Caucasus. A peasant woman discovered him and stayed with him until he died. The news devastated George's mother. "My poor dearest son passed away quite alone," went the telegraph message the dowager empress sent to Queen Victoria. "Am heartbroken."[19] In replying to Queen Victoria's letter of sympathy, Nicholas II wrote that, "not having been with our dear Georgy at the last makes it all the harder for her [Marie Feodorovna] to bear."[20] The funeral was an ordeal for the bereaved mother. The dowager empress held Xenia's hand tightly, then staggered and collapsed, loudly muttering: "Home, let's go home, I can't stand any more." Marie Feodorovna had snatched her dead son's hat from atop the coffin, pressed it to her breast, and cried piteously for the second child she had buried. "It was such a nightmare," recalled Xenia, "it will remain with me for ever!"[21] Three months later, Marie Feodorovna was still distraught. "My heart is bleeding from the fresh cruel wound of no longer having my beloved Georgie," wrote Marie Feodorovna to Tsar Nicholas II in October 1899.[22] A grieving Marie Feodorovna summoned the peasant woman who had found George dying on the roadside, so that she could recount what had taken place. As soon as the two women met, they were closeted together in deep conversation for hours.

An earlier bereavement had already saddened the dowager empress. Marie Feodorovna's mother, Queen Louise, had passed away shortly before George's death. The dowager empress was very close to her mother and took her death hard. Much as her mother's passing grieved the dowager empress, it paled in comparison to George's death. A little over a year after George died, death almost snatched Marie Feodorovna's eldest son when Tsar Nicholas II nearly succumbed to typhoid fever and pneumonia. By this time, Vladimir and Miechen's ambitions for the throne were so evident that Tsarina Alexandra hastened to keep her uncle and aunt from usurping power while her husband lay at death's door. She, reportedly, sent a telegram in the tsar's name to the Vladimirs in Paris, where they were staying, asking them to remain there until notified. She made the request under the pretext of easing any public alarm that might ensue by an abrupt reentry to Russia. "The real purpose of the order, however," it was reported years later, "was to prevent Vladimir from taking advantage of his position as governor-general of the military district of St. Petersburg and commander-in-chief of the division of guards—the *corps d'élite* of the Muscovy army—to proclaim himself regent on account of the Czar's illness, and of the Grand Duke Michael's absence from the country, as well as the latter's youth and inexperience." Miechen and Vladimir "strongly . . . resented this treatment" and showed it "by the extraordinary indifference which they displayed with regard to the emperor's sufferings, and to the anxieties of the empress, taking part in all sorts of gaieties at the very time when Nicholas's life was reported to be in most serious danger." Despite the seriousness of the illness, "imperial orders were issued as usual—through the empress—while all papers submitted for consideration and approval were returned in the ordinary course indorsed with the wishes of the sovereign. In this way all necessity for a regency, which Vladimir would have been quick to claim, or even to seize forcibly, was averted."[23]

LEFT: Princess Dagmar of Denmark with her fiancé, Tsarevich Nicholas ("Nixa"), eldest son and heir of Tsar Alexander II of Russia. Nixa's death in 1865 deeply saddened seventeen-year-old Dagmar.

RIGHT: Following Nixa's dying wish, Princess Dagmar (who took the name Marie Feodorovna upon her conversion to Orthodoxy), married his younger brother, Alexander. The marriage proved to be a happy one. In 1881, Alexander succeeded his assassinated father as emperor, becoming Alexander III. Emperor Alexander III and Empress Marie Feodorovna were the parents of the ill-fated Tsar Nicholas II.

Marie Feodorovna with her son, the future Tsar Nicholas II, who was to have a tragic reign.

Emperor Alexander III and Empress Marie Feodorovna with their children: the Tsarevich Nicholas, Grand Duke George, Grand Duchess Xenia, Grand Duke Michael, and Grand Duchess Olga.

A portrait of a superbly bejeweled Empress Marie
Feodorovna in Russian court dress.

Three sisters-in-law dressed similarly. *From left to right*: England's Queen Alexandra, Queen Olga of Greece, and the Empress Marie Feodorovna. Olga, born a grand duchess of Russia, married Alexandra and Marie Feodorovna's brother, King
George I of Greece, in 1867.

A close sisterly bond united Queen Alexandra and the Empress Marie Feodorovna. In later years, the sisters bought a villa, Hvidovre, in their native Denmark. It was at Hvidovre that Marie Feodorovna died in 1928.

The Dowager Empress Marie Feodorovna with her son, Tsar Nicholas II, and her granddaughters, the Grand Duchesses Olga, Tatiana, Marie, and Anastasia. In July 1917, Nicholas, his wife, Alexandra, their daughters, and their son, Alexei, were murdered by the Bolsheviks. (*Romanov Collection. General Collection. Beinecke Rare Book and Manuscript Library, Yale University*)

Tsar Nicholas II, his wife, Tsarina Alexandra, and their children: Olga, Tatiana, Marie, Anastasia, and the longed-for heir, the Tsarevich Alexei, whose hemophilia had such a devastating impact on his mother.

Empress Marie Feodorovna's elder daughter, Grand Duchess Xenia, and her husband, Grand Duke Alexander ("Sandro"). Their only daughter, Princess Irina, married Prince Felix Yussopov, who was involved in the plot to assassinate Gregory Rasputin.

Grand Duke Michael, Empress Marie Feodorovna's youngest son, and his wife, Natalia. Once in love with Grand Duchess Marie Alexandrovna's daughter, Princess Beatrice, Grand Duke Michael scandalized his mother by marrying the twice-divorced commoner Natalia Wulfert, in 1912. Michael was killed by the Bolsheviks in 1918. (*School of Slavonic and East European Studies Library, University College, London*)

The younger daughter of Empress Marie Feodorovna,
Grand Duchess Olga, with her husband, Colonel Nikolai Kulikovsky.
The couple survived the Russian Revolution of 1917
and died in exile in Canada.

LEFT: Prince Felix Yussopov and his wife, Princess Irina, Empresss Marie Feodorovna's granddaughter. Prince Felix and his accomplices were behind the murder of Gregory Rasputin in the Yussopov Palace in St. Petersburg in 1916.

RIGHT: Grand Duchess Marie Alexandrovna in Russian court dress. *(Royal Russia Collection)*

Marie Alexandrovna, the newly married Duchess of Edinburgh, is officially welcomed to London in March 1874. Sitting beside her in the carriage is her formidable mother-in-law, Queen Victoria.

Marie Alexandrovna, now Duchess of Edinburgh, in May 1874, with her brother, Grand Duke Alexei; her father, Tsar Alexander II; and her husband, Alfred, Duke of Edinburgh, Queen Victoria's second son. (*National Portrait Gallery, London*)

The issue of the succession worried Grand Duke Nicholas Mikhailovich, a liberal and respected historian, and first cousin of Alexander III. The grand duke, who was no fan of the Vladimir clan, was concerned that only Nicholas II's brother Michael, the heir, stood in the way of Miechen's family becoming the next reigning family. "If some misfortune should befall him [Nicholas II's brother, Michael]," wrote Nicholas Mikhailovich to the French historian Frédéric Masson, "[it would put] the Vladimir branch, finally on the throne. It's this last eventuality . . . which must be avoided at all cost . . . it must be hoped that the ardent prayers of all the Russians will conserve for us the life of the young monarch."[24]

Nicholas II survived his brush with death. But his near fatal illness underscored the need to secure the dynasty. Thoughts centered again on the lack of a son for Nicholas and Alexandra, especially after two more daughters, Marie Nikolaevna and Anastasia Nikolaevna, were born to the couple in 1899 and 1901. When Anastasia was born, K.R. recorded in his diary: "Forgive us Lord, if we all felt disappointment instead of joy; we were so hoping for a boy, and it's a fourth daughter."[25] The Dowager Empress Marie Feodorovna was of a similar mind, sending Xenia a telegram stating: "Alix has again given birth to a daughter!"[26]

No such succession worries plagued the Greek royal family. Succession was secure in the male line through the heir, Crown Prince Constantine, and his wife, Sophie, who were the parents of three boys: George, Alexander, and Paul, as well as two daughters, Helen and Irene. Yet all was not smooth sailing at Athens. The Empress Frederick explained to her youngest daughter, Mossy, that "the state of things in the family—at Athens are very sad." King George I's inability to concede that his sons were adults strained relations between the father and his sons. Like his sisters, Alexandra and Marie Feodorovna, King George I looked upon his sons as if they were still boys, imposing an artificial sense of adolescence that was hard to break. "Poor Aunt Olga is miserable about it," recounted the Empress Frederick. Vicky added that the Princess of Wales "is so afraid that if things go on like this there will be 2 parties in the Kingdom—one for the King & the other for his sons!"[27]

By the time Queen Olga's sons had reached maturity, Greece was well on the way to becoming a modern nation. The Corinth Canal, completed in 1893, was an engineering feat that shortened the sea route between Greece and Italy by half. By 1896, nearly a thousand kilometers of railways had been constructed. Also that year, a symbolic event showcased Greece's ancient history and touted Greece as a modern state—the country hosted the games of the first modern

Olympics. Before a crowd of tens of thousands in Athens, King George and Queen Olga appeared at the opening of the games. Fourteen nations competed in over two hundred events. The euphoria, however, was short-lived.

Flush from its triumphant staging of the modern Olympics, Greece soon became embroiled in a disastrous war. Lying just south of mainland Greece, under the rule of the Ottoman Empire, was the island of Crete. Many mainlanders saw Crete, with its largely Greek population, as part of their unredeemed land. In pursuit of the *Megali Idea*, clamourous calls demanded that Crete be freed from its Turkish yoke. King George, though cautious and reluctant, found himself with little choice but to go to war against the Ottoman Empire. The Duke of York understood his uncle's predicament, noting that had George I "not declared war—and he did so much against his will,—he would have been assassinated."[28] In April 1897, war broke out, pitting Greece against the Ottoman Empire. The Greeks were ecstatic. When the royal family appeared in public in Athens, the populace heartily cheered them with shouts of "Hurray for War" and "Long Live the King."[29]

The American writer Stephen Crane, who was in the Greek capital during these heady times, wrote of crowds "in the streets, in the square before the king's palace, and in every place of public congregation." He saw that "practically every man in Athens is arming to go and fight the Turks. Every train into the city is loaded with other troops. Yesterday crowds broke into the gun shops and took the practicable weapons. It was unanimous throughout all classes. To-day Greece is armed to fight for her life."[30]

Crown Princess Sophie's brother, Kaiser Wilhelm II, sided vehemently against the Greeks. He also resented the supposed influence wielded by the Dowager Empress Marie Feodorovna, the Princess of Wales, and their female Danish relations when it came to the Greek crisis, prompting Wilhelm to thunder scornfully: "These petticoats should keep their fingers out of things."[31]

The kaiser's grandmother, Queen Victoria was dismayed by the crisis. The Empress Frederick wrote to Crown Princess Sophie, telling her that, "Grandmama wishes me to tell you how awfully sorry she is for you and Tino and Papa and Mama. She is so anxious and troubled, and as far as she *may*, and as she *dare*, she tries at ways to make peace and to soften asperities."[32] The aged queen followed events in Greece closely. She was especially impressed by the nursing efforts of Queen Olga and Sophie, noting that they also cared for Turks in their Greek hospitals. Because of these actions, Queen Victoria recognized Olga and Sophie for their work by giving them the Royal Order of the Red Cross.

Queen Olga's concerns extended well beyond just nursing and rehabilitation. She took a personal interest in as many of the wounded soldiers as she could. In one instance, when the queen ordered that the infected leg of a Greek soldier be amputated in order to save his life, she patiently calmed him down when the young man reacted badly to the discovery that his leg had been amputated. The queen then took the young soldier under her wing by building a house for him at Tatoi and appointing him to be the bell-ringer of Tatoi's church. Olga also bought the young man a knitting machine so that he could support himself.

The outcome of the Greco-Turkish War of 1897, decided within a month of hostilities breaking out, was a disaster for the Greeks. Their military had been unprepared for war; and Crown Prince Constantine, who had led Greek troops in battle, bore the brunt of the blame for the humiliating outcome of the war. The Queen of the Hellenes played a role in ending hostilities. On May 17, "at the request of his aunt, Queen Olga, the Russian tsar sent an urgent message to the sultan [of Turkey] requesting an immediate suspension of hostilities. The sultan ordered a cease-fire in deference to the wishes of the Ambassadors and those of the Tsar of Russia. Thus ended the short Greco-Turkish War."[33]

The disastrous war "sent Greece's fortunes (and the royal family's) plummeting."[34] Calls for Tino to be court-martialed resonated. So low had the family's popularity fallen that Edward Egerton, the British minister in Athens, reported: "Today in Church the prayer for the Royal Family could not be said by the Metropolitan owing to the cries and hisses of the congregation."[35] The Empress Frederick summed up what she and many felt about the situation to the Bishop of Ripon, by telling him that "the anxiety and sorrows about poor Greece were terrible." Aside from the joyous event of Queen Victoria's Diamond Jubilee, wrote the Empress Frederick, "this has been, a most trying and harassing year."[36] It was a sentiment echoed by Queen Olga, who admitted to the American archaeologist and nurse, Harriet Boyd-Hawes, that 1897 was "the never to be forgotten year."[37]

Not long after Queen Olga's admission, the Greek royal family's precarious fortunes suddenly took a turn for the better in an astonishing twist. While King George I and his daughter, Princess Marie, rode in an open carriage, a gunman fired bullets at them, but failed to kill his targets. When news of the assassination attempt spread, the Greeks were overcome with relief and sympathy for the royal family. No longer were the royals disliked; they were now back in favor. This ominous portent tied the royal family's fortunes to the fickleness of their Greek subjects.

After the attempt on the life of King George I and his daughter Marie, the royal family's soaring popularity did not last long. Soon enough, an unexpected controversy erupted over Queen Olga's innocuous desire to have the Gospels translated into vernacular Greek. Queen Olga came up with the idea after visiting a village woman and her son. During her visit, Olga read an excerpt from the Gospel to the invalid son. After finishing the reading, the queen asked the woman: "Did you hear, my lady, what beautiful words Jesus says? Have your hope in him, and your child will become well, only believe in the power of Jesus." "I hear, my Queen," replied the woman, "but I didn't understand them, because they are in Frankish, show me Jesus' writing for me to believe them." This need for a popular Greek translation was buttressed whenever the queen read the Gospels to maimed soldiers. She always asked them "if they had understood what she had read to them." The reply was "no, my queen, because these [words] are for the educated ones." It turned out that the text Olga read them was in a form of Greek alien to the common man.

In 1898, as she exited a church with her private secretary, Ioulia N. Karolou, the queen told her: "How I am saddened, because none of the soldiers and country folk here understand what is read during the Sundays and Feast Days at church."[38] Karolou eagerly embraced the queen's plan for a translation and undertook the task of translating the Gospels into colloquial Greek. The queen then invited the Metropolitan of Athens to check Karolou's translations and approve them if he was satisfied. He did and a delighted queen proceeded to get the translation printed. She wrote to the Holy Synod for approval in December 1898. In her letter, the queen admitted that some argued that translating the Gospel into colloquial language might lead to losing its "prestige." Nevertheless, Olga responded, "the prestige and level of the Gospel is not only dependent on the words, and the dead letter, but in the level and the power of the ideas and substance" and that it was important for "the masses to understand it [i.e., the Gospel]."[39] In no time a firestorm of protest ignited over the translation, which was opposed by prelates of the Orthodox Church and university professors. The Holy Synod eventually ruled against the queen, praising her intentions, but they were adamant that the Gospels could not be translated into a lowly language for fear of distorting the meanings. Queen Olga answered their concerns, writing that their reply "saddens me deeply." She went on to say that "I deem the measure of this translation necessary, so that it can temporarily heal the urgent needs of the souls of the people, who [are] . . . unable to comprehend the language of the Holy Gospel." She then pleaded her case again. Again, the Holy Synod refused Queen Olga's request.

The queen decided to print a limited number of texts of the translation and had one thousand copies distributed in early 1901. Another translation into the vernacular Greek appeared from Alexander Pallis and was serialized in a leftist Athenian newspaper. Pallis's translation, considered sacrilegious, met fierce opposition from many quarters. Queen Olga's and Pallis's translations were not novel; previous attempts at translating the Gospels into vernacular Greek had been undertaken. Nevertheless, controversy and vociferous opposition greeted these latest undertakings. The ferocity connected to the queen's translation in particularly was surprising. It appears that disapproval for her translation "centered around the strong belief that since Olga was Russian, it naturally followed that her translation was motivated by Pan-Slavism and therefore it was anti-Orthodox and anti-national." Stoked by fears of Pan-Slavism, laymen perceived "a sinister plan: to deprive Greece of her rightful claims in Macedonia."[40] Pallis's serialized translation moved events to a flashpoint. In November 1901, riots broke out in Athens, resulting in the deaths of eight people. Revolution was soon in the air. The Russian diplomat, Baron Roman Rosen, who was in Athens, recalled that "the streets resounded with shouts of 'Down with Olga!' 'Down with Russia!'"[41] During these turbulent times, Queen Olga, accompanied only by one lady-in-waiting, never hesitated to drive daily in an open carriage toward the Piraeus to visit her charitable institution, the Russian hospital. Olga did this, even though she knew she risked being jeered at or even attacked. Baron Rosen noted that though the queen was unpopular at the time, "to the credit of the populace of Athens let it be said, the hostile crowds would always let her pass in respectful silence."[42]

Eventually, calm prevailed, and the controversy died down. The crisis, though, was serious enough that Charles S. Francis, the U.S. ambassador to Greece, filed official reports to his superiors at the State Department. On November 22, 1901, Francis reported that "Athens has been the scene of [a] mob demonstration which yesterday almost assumed the proportions of a revolution."[43]

The whole Gospels translation episode was a confusing and painful chapter in Olga's life as Queen of the Hellenes, especially as there had been calls for excommunicating all involved, including the queen and her secretary. What began as a well-intentioned exercise in helping the Greeks had turned into a nightmare. Nevertheless, Olga did not let it keep her from trying to help her subjects become enlightened when it came to their faith. She founded a magazine called the *Helping Hand*, which contained stories of a moral and religious character. The magazine's message and writing were meant to be accessible to rich and poor alike. Queen Olga also published children's books that promoted sanctification in everyday life and booklets with sayings from the Old and New Testaments. The queen translated most of the booklets' texts from German and Russian into Greek. Thus was Olga untiring in her quest to improve her subjects' spiritual and material well-being, never ceasing to do as much good as she could.

Unlike Queen Olga, Marie Alexandrovna did not have to navigate treacherous political waters. Such troubles were nonexistent in Coburg where she continued to savor her role as the reigning duke's consort. Though pleased to be living permanently in the small, placid German duchy, Marie Alexandrovna did not cut her ties completely with England. She visited the country as Queen Victoria's guest when the queen celebrated sixty years on the throne with her Diamond Jubilee in 1897. Through all the impressive celebrations, the Duchess of Coburg tried to make light of the impact of the milestone. When Missy told her mother how frightfully disappointed she was not to able to visit London for the historic occasion, the duchess merely replied with a torrent of complaints about the weather and the royal family.

In the meantime, back in Russia, Marie Alexandrovna's niece Alexandra still struggled at being tsarina. K.R. concluded that Alexandra "is terribly shy . . . It's noticeable that she does not have her mother-in-law's charm, and still does not, therefore, inspire general adulation."[44] Nadine Wonar-Larsky, who was a maid of honor to both empresses, recalled that Alexandra was "extremely shy even at such an informal affair as receiving" Wonlar-Larsky and her mother to tea. Marie Feodorovna, on the other hand, observed Wonar-Larsky, "was adored by everyone. She [Marie Feodorovna] absorbed Russian ways, thoughts and traditions and became completely Russian at heart . . . Her smile cheered everyone and her gracious manner always suggested a touch of personal feeling which went straight to the hearts of her subjects. She also possessed that priceless royal gift of never forgetting a face or a name."[45]

The tsarina never warmed to the dowager empress and remained closer to Queen Victoria, her surrogate mother, than to Marie Feodorovna. In 1896, Nicholas and Alexandra paid a visit to the rapidly aging queen in Balmoral. It was the last time grandmother and granddaughter were to see each other. Signs that the queen was slowing down were evident to the Duchess of Coburg, who wrote to Countess Tolstoy: "She feels old . . . and also sees badly."[46] Nevertheless, Marie Alexandrovna conceded that the queen still possessed a lucidity that was a wonder to behold.

In 1900, the Duchess of Coburg and Queen Victoria faced the disturbing news that Affie was dreadfully ill from cancer of the throat. Marie Alexandrovna kept the news of his terminal cancer from her husband, believing it to have been the best course for Affie. The Duke of Coburg's last months were spent in near agony as his breathing became more labored; and nourishment had to be given through a tube. By the end of July 1900, Affie was "a brave but pathetic figure gasping for breath." He spent his last days at the Rosenau, near Coburg, where he sat in the garden "gazing fondly at—but unable to smell—the roses which Marie had planted and tended so lovingly."[47] On July 30, 1900, Affie died in his sleep, surrounded by his daughters, Ducky, Sandra, and Bee, as well as Marie Alexandrovna. The duke died just shy of his fifty-sixth birthday, leaving Marie Alexandrovna a widow at forty-six.

"We cannot bear to think of the desolation in that house at Coburg, my poor sister-in-law still mourning the death of her only son but a year and ½ ago," wrote Affie's youngest sister, Princess Beatrice. "But she is so good and brave, I know she will bear with resignation, this further crushing blow."[48]

In London, signs of mourning were everywhere as flags flew at half-mast. In response to a message of sympathy sent by the mayor of London, the widowed Duchess of Coburg replied: "I am deeply touched by the kind expressions of sympathy which you convey to me in the name of the citizens of London, and I beg you to express my heartfelt thanks to all who have shown so faithful an attachment to the late Duke and myself. Marie."[49]

Queen Victoria was understandably distraught by her son's death. "My third grown-up child [dead] . . . it is hard at eighty-one! . . . Poor darling Marie," lamented the queen.[50] The Empress Frederick, who was also seriously ill with cancer, wrote to her grieving mother: "To think of our darling beloved Alfred being taken at this time—at his age—is too dreadful . . . Unhappy Marie, how I feel for her and the poor girls."[51] Queen Victoria admitted to Vicky about how her daughter-in-law was in sad spirits with all that was going on: "Poor Marie talked very openly to me about her sorrow."[52] But whatever rapprochement the two women may have enjoyed was short-lived.

In January 22, 1901, Queen Victoria died at Osborne at the age of eighty-one, signaling the end of an era. Victoria's reign had been the longest in English history. The British Empire at her death amounted to some 12.1 million square miles, an increase over her lifetime of 4 million square miles, while the empire's population doubled to 240 million people. Moreover, the queen had earned and commanded the esteem of millions the world over. She entered the annals of history, a much respected figure. Yet in recounting the death of the venerable queen to Crown Princess Marie of Romania, the Duchess of Coburg narrated events purely from a family perspective, devoid of any musings or analyses of the impact Queen Victoria had on the monarchy and the world. To Missy, Marie Alexandrovna referred to the late queen simply as "Granny."

The duchess wrote to Missy of the "dreadful" and "very sad" time at Osborne "as Granny sank much more rapidly than anybody expected." Marie Alexandrovna was moved by her mother-in-law's final hours. "It was almost too much for our nerves. They thought she was conscious and understood that we were all about her. She tried to speak even, but I could understand nothing. It seems that her terror was always to die alone and not surrounded by all her family, so if she still felt anything, she must have been pleased in her dying hour . . . We all still kissed her hand and then she passed away quietly. She looked quite fine and very peaceful not one feature was distorted or changed. In fact she died of no illness, but simple old age and gradual sinking." The duchess added that Kaiser Wilhelm—"William Imperator" as Marie Alexandrovna called him—"was quite admirable. Never left her bed side, helped to prop her up and made himself most useful with advice and practical help."

But in relating Queen Victoria's last moments to Missy, the Duchess of Coburg could not avoid criticizing the English, whether they be her sisters-in-law or the Royal Household. Marie Alexandrovna described "those foolish childish aunts" (Queen Victoria's daughters who were present at Osborne) as "having lost their heads and did not know what to do." "Poor Aunts are either much upset and crying, or occupied in quarelling with Aunt Louise or terrible busy-bodies and absorbed by small things," noted Marie Alexandrovna bitingly. "Aunt Louise is terribly *méchante* [malicious] and at times looks absolutely poisonous that Helen [Duchess of Albany, another sister-in-law] arrived too with the children."

As for the Royal Household, the Duchess of Coburg had scathing words. "The English people are one must say, a 'rum lot.' Nobody knew at all what to do on such an occasion nobody had even ordered the coffin! . . . They didn't even understand in the royal household, that [Uncle] Bertie had to be called King at once and went on saying the Prince of Wales." So indignant were Marie Alexandrovna and her sister-in-law Princess Louise, at this breach, that they went to the Master of the Royal Household and told him that "it was highly improper and that he was to give orders to the household to call their new Majesties by their proper and due names. He seemed rather astonished, but we were so energetic about it that he gave the orders." Still unable to repress more criticisms, Marie Alexandrovna added her thoughts on her sister-in-law, Queen Alexandra: "Naturally good Aunt Alix was of false sentimentality but she did not wish to be called queen so long as she was at Osborne. Too naïf for words! But so they are here! One would really think one was living amongst a pack of babies. And I who had gone twice through such changes in my family, could not cease wondering at this naïf and foolish sentimentality."[53] Even on this sad and momentous day, Marie Alexandrovna found fault with the English and her relations, including the Dowager Empress Marie Feodorovna's sister, the new queen.

15

LOVE AND WAR

After Queen Victoria's funeral, the Duchess of Coburg proceeded to her home on the French Riviera, the Château Fabron, with her daughters, Missy, Bee, and Ducky. Ducky announced that she was not returning to Ernie and committed to a divorce. Queen Victoria's death removed the one obstacle that prevented this. When Ducky returned to Coburg, she told her mother that she was not going back to Ernie. Marie Alexandrovna was aghast at first, refusing to listen to her daughter. But "after Ducky flooded her with a litany of suffering and sorrow, plus a description of her son-in-law's true sexual nature, she put her arms around Ducky and pledged her support."[1]

The social mores of the time meant that society viewed divorce as a scandal. News of the breakup shocked Tsar Nicholas II and the Dowager Empress Marie Feodorovna. "Can you imagine," wrote Nicky to his mother of Ernie and Ducky, "getting divorced, *yes*, actually *divorced*! . . . Divorce was the only possible way out. Such is Aunt Marie's opinion and Ducky's too . . . In a case like this even the loss of a dear person is better than the general disgrace of a divorce." Nicholas added how sad it was for Ducky, Ernie, and their countrymen but also for "their poor little daughter." According to Nicholas II, the Duchess of Coburg "feels responsible for having arranged their marriage rather hurriedly; what a huge mistake it has proved to be!"[2]

The dowager empress's reply was equally infused with surprise and sadness: "All you tell me about Erni[e] and Ducky has been *such a shock* to me that I could not *sleep* the whole night. It is simply awful: how dreadful to think of their future and that of the poor little child! I am also *extremely* sorry for poor Alix . . . Aunt Marie . . . is in despair, of course . . . I myself entirely agree with you when you say that even the loss of a dear person is better than the general disgrace of a divorce!"[3]

News of the divorce spread throughout Europe. From Berlin, Princess Antoine Radziwill, wrote how "the Hesse-Darmstadt divorce [pre-]occupies everyone . . . here [it is] unanimous to blame the mother even more than the girl who acts by passion and inexperience."[4] [The] empress of Russia and the grand duchess Serge are furious towards their ex-sister-in-law."[5] She added that the German empress, Augusta, wife of Kaiser Wilhelm, was outraged about the Hesse divorce. "The last time I saw her," wrote the princess to a friend, "she spoke to me with great severity about the duchess of Coburg, who, according to her, must have raised her daughters very badly."[6] There were strong suspicions, noted the princess, that Ducky pushed for a divorce so she could marry Kyril. "You can understand how this will be received by the Tsarina."[7]

The romantic escapades of Marie Alexandrovna's two eldest daughters clearly upset her. Even as she charged them with being "only too ready to get rid of your husbands," she went on to add advice laced with her own scathing opinion of men, most likely inspired by her own male Romanov relations: "Flirt, amuse yourselves, but don't lose your heart, men are not worth it and if you could, really could see their lives, you would turn away in disgust, for you would find there nothing but dirt, even in the lives of those who seem good and noble."[8]

Many Romanov males thought nothing of being unfaithful to their wives, but Tsar Nicholas II was an exception. The tsar remained content in his marriage to Alexandra; and together the couple preferred to have as little to do with St. Petersburg as possible. They isolated themselves at the Alexander Palace at Tsarskoe Selo, leaving imperial entertaining to the "two brilliant rivals" who "offered a striking contrast to the dullness of the Grand Court" of Nicholas and Alexandra. At the Anichkov Palace reigned Marie Feodorovna with her well-received parties "distinguished by the best French food and wine," while at the Vladimir Palace Marie Pavlovna dominated, impressing one and all with her "glittering balls studded with celebrities from every part of Europe."[9] Miechen's court "entirely eclipsed" Tsarina Alexandra's, concluded A. A. Mossolov. So brilliant was the grand duchess's court that it became almost more of an honor to serve her than Tsarina Alexandra. "An appointment as maid of honour to Marie Pavlovna," wrote Mossolov, "would have carried with it the best of opportunities for becoming a Beauty Queen if beauty competitions had been organized in Russia in those days."[10]

As an intimate of the imperial family, Mossolov came to know Miechen's daughter, Grand Duchess Elena. The one-time tomboy and rebel had grown into an attractive young woman with dark hair and dark eyes, whom Mossolov described as being "lovely and gracious . . . [and] a passionate waltzer." She was so fond of waltzing that "officers were permitted to invite her to dance instead of waiting for her to send for some particular one. I am sure," concluded Mossolov, "they were all desperately in love with this princess."[11] Elena Vladimirovna's illustrious pedigree made her a highly desirable candidate on the royal marriage market. Ambitious Miechen had hoped to marry Elena off to Prince Max of Baden, who duly proposed to the young grand duchess. But Prince Max later broke off the engagement, to Miechen's consternation. K.R. recorded that Miechen and Elena were "desperate to find another husband" after this incident.[12] Miechen set her eyes on marrying her daughter to a bigger catch, Prince Albert of Belgium, who was likely to succeed as king of the Belgians one day. Miechen first planned to invite the Belgian prince and his father to visit Russia, but when she learned of Albert's engagement to Elisabeth of Bavaria, Miechen told Tsar Nicholas II that it was no longer necessary to invite the Belgians to Russia. Another rumor circulated that Miechen was plotting to marry off her daughter to King Ferdinand of Bulgaria. Empress Frederick wrote to her brother, the Prince of Wales, asking if there was any truth to the story. After he spoke with his sister-in-law, Marie Feodorovna, the prince wrote back, saying "she [Marie Feodorovna] knew nothing about it & hoped that there was no foundation. But the Mother of the young lady has become so strange that she would not be surprised at anything—especially as she wants to marry the girl 'a tout prix' as she is in her way!" It was "a spiteful comment" from the dowager empress, which "says more about the way she and Marie Pavlovna felt towards one another than it does of Elena."[13]

Elena eventually fell for Prince Nicholas of Greece. Miechen had hoped for a more illustrious marriage and tried to discourage Elena from setting her heart on Queen Olga's son. In Miechen's eyes, Nicky of Greece had neither a crown in his future nor a great fortune and consequently was not good enough for her only daughter. When Miechen once discovered that the couple went riding, she chastised Elena for doing so, in the vain hope that Elena would desist from encouraging Nicholas. But the prince persisted in his courtship. He found Elena "lovely and fascinating" as well as possessing a "sweet nature" tinged with "unselfishness."[14] Prince Nicholas and Elena became engaged in June 1902. In recording the event, K.R. described the engagement as "unexpected and joyous." He also noted that Miechen "has had to change her mind, as her search for other suitors for her daughter has been in vain."[15]

The wedding took place at Tsarskoe Selo in August 1902, with Queen Olga and Grand Duke and Grand Duchess Vladimir in attendance. This wedding uniting Miechen's twenty-year-old daughter to Olga's thirty-year-old son was resplendent, like all Russian imperial court events. Also in attendance was Queen Olga's only surviving daughter, Princess Marie. Two years before, she had married into the Russian imperial family, just as her late sister Alexandra had done a decade earlier. Princess Marie's husband was Grand Duke George Mikhailovich, Sandro's brother and a one-time suitor for Missy of Edinburgh's hand. Grand Duke and Grand Duchess George gave Queen Olga two more Russian grandchildren when Princesses Nina and Xenia were born in 1901 and 1903. The Queen of the Hellenes welcomed the arrival of more grandchildren when Elena and Nicholas became the parents of Olga (1903) and Elisabeth (1904).

Miechen's Greek granddaughters were untainted by scandal, but her grandson Vladimir's paternity was in question. Miechen's son Andrei had been carrying on a liaison with none other than the ballerina Mathilde Kschessinska, who had been Nicholas II's paramour when he was tsarevich. Mathilde had gone from Nicholas to Grand Duke Serge Mikhailovich (George and Sandro's brother). Mathilde, though, was never fully enamored of Serge Mikhailovich but lost her heart to Andrei instead. When Mathilde gave birth to a son, Vladimir, in 1902, there were questions as to whether Serge Mikhailovich or Andrei Vladimirovich was the father. Andrei later recognized Vladimir as his son.

It was precisely this sort of scandal that the Dowager Empress Marie Feodorovna deplored and hoped would not taint her immediate family. In the early 1900s, her son Grand Duke Michael came close to precipitating a scandal when he became romantically involved with his cousin Baby Bee, the Duchess of Coburg's daughter. Bee was a pretty young woman, who was physically a cross between her blond, vivacious sister Missy, and the dark, mercurial Ducky. Michael, meanwhile, had grown into the handsomest of Marie Feodorovna's sons. Unlike Nicholas II who was slight in stature like his mother, Michael stood at over six feet tall like his father. With his dark hair and blue eyes, as well as the famed charm of his mother, Michael presented a fine catch for any young woman. When he and Bee attended Elena and Nicholas's wedding in 1902, their feelings for each other transformed into romance. Michael then was twenty-three years old and Bee, eighteen. Soon separated by distance, their romance blossomed through letters.

The romance was doomed from the start. Michael and Bee could not marry because the Russian Orthodox Church frowned upon marriages between first cousins. Michael's brother, Tsar Nicholas II, was in complete agreement with the Church's view. Pressured to end the romance, Michael eventually did so by letter. Bee hesitated to accept the inevitable and became ill and thin, prompting her mother to send her to Egypt where it was hoped Bee could recover from her broken heart. Of the doomed romance, Xenia confided in her diary: "It seems Aunt Marie is dreadfully cross with Mama over this, all in all God knows what happened."[16] Bee continued to pine for her lost love, but in 1905 Grand Duke Michael wrote his last letter to her: "You don't know how it worries me that on account of me you should be worried or unhappy. Please darling girl don't be sad . . . I will remain your friend forever."[17]

Marie Feodorovna's youngest child, Olga, meanwhile, gave no hint that she would be embroiled in any such trouble of the heart like Michael. Of all of Marie Feodorovna's children, Olga was the one who most took after Alexander III. Less pretty than her sister Xenia, Olga had, like her father, eschewed luxurious living, preferring the down-to-earth life that so appealed to the late emperor. Olga had none of her mother's enthusiasm for dressing up and entertaining, though both mother and daughter shared an affinity and talent for painting. Olga's cousin, Marie Pavlovna,[18] Grand Duke Paul's daughter, liked visiting Gatchina and seeing Olga, whom she found to have a "child-like and disarming simplicity." Marie also, noted that Olga had a "generous heart. She loved to surround herself with simple people . . . Peasants in particular, fascinated her; and she knew how to talk with such people and win their confidence."[19]

In 1901, Marie Feodorovna insisted on imposing a husband on her nineteen-year-old daughter. Olga was accordingly married to thirty-three-year-old Prince Peter of Oldenburg. The news was received with incredulity in certain quarters of the capital, as Prince Peter was believed to be a homosexual. Olga believed that Prince Peter's mother, who was one of the dowager empress's close friends, had convinced her mother to press for the match. By marrying off Olga to Peter, who lived in St. Petersburg, Marie Feodorovna ensured that her daughter stayed in Russia. Like her sister Alexandra, the dowager empress was a possessive mother who could not contemplate having her children, especially her youngest daughter, far from her side.

For a while, it appeared as if Grand Duke Paul, who had been so crushed when his wife, Alexandra of Greece, had died tragically, might not find love again. But such was not the case. The Duchess of Coburg's youngest brother became romantically involved with a commoner, the elegant Olga von Pistolkors, wife of an aide-de-camp to his brother, Grand Duke Vladimir. In 1897, Olga, the mother of four children from her husband, bore a son, Vladimir, whose father was Grand Duke Paul. After Olga and her husband were divorced, Grand Duke Paul married Olga morganatically in Italy in 1902, without obtaining Nicholas II's permission. This infuriated the tsar, who told his mother: "The nearer the relative who refuses to submit to our family statutes the graver must be his punishment. Don't you agree with me, dear Mama? Uncle Serge has earnestly requested me to appoint him guardian of the poor children and their estate; this will be put through at once . . . Uncle Wladimir [*sic*], I hear, is quite undone by the whole affair . . . How painful and distressing it all is and how ashamed one feels for the sake of our family before the world! What guarantee is there now that Cyril [Miechen's son] won't start the same sort of thing tomorrow and Boris, or Sergei Mikhailovich the day after? And, in the end, I fear, a whole colony of members of the Russian Imperial Family will be established in Paris with their semi-legitimate and illegitimate wives! God alone knows what times we are living in, when undisguised selfishness stifles all feelings of conscience, duty or even ordinary decency!"[20] The dowager empress's reaction to her brother-in-law's morganatic marriage was equally indignant. "This marriage of Uncle Paul's is really too distressing!" wrote Marie Feodorovna to Nicholas II, "alas, he seems to have forgotten everything—his duty to his children, to his country, service honour, all, *all*, have been sacrificed . . . How could he go through with it after all he had been told by his brothers and by us all? . . . The thought of the misery of his poor little children for whom he had been everything and whom he has abandoned distresses me more than I can say . . . And then there is the *scandal*! I am simply *ashamed* of it . . . So he is even slinging mud at our family! Awful, awful! And into what an awkward and disagreeable *position* it puts *you*, my poor Nicky, you who will have to punish him, because such an act cannot remain unpunished, and, into the bargain, marrying a divorced woman!"[21]

When Queen Olga's twelve-year-old granddaughter, Grand Duchess Marie Pavlovna, and her eleven-year-old brother, Dmitri, received a letter from their father explaining his situation, they were shocked. Since their father was banished from returning to Russia and stripped of custody of his children, Grand Duke Serge and his wife, Ella, became Marie and Dmitri's guardians. This seemed to please the childless Serge, who kept telling these grandchildren of Queen Olga: "It is I who am now your father, and you are *my* children!"[22]

Fortunately for Queen Olga, her children did not indulge in marital scandals. Thus far, they had contracted satisfactory marriages. Her latest child to marry, Prince Andrew, chose Princess Alice of Battenberg, niece of the Tsarina Alexandra and Grand Duchess Serge, as his wife. Within weeks of the wedding, tragedy struck when the Duchess of Coburg's granddaughter, Princess Elisabeth of Hesse, fell ill with typhoid. She and her father had been staying with the tsar and tsarina at their shooting lodge in Poland. The illness progressed rapidly, killing the eight-year-old. A shocked Ducky attended her child's funeral in Hesse. Afterward, she became more determined than ever to start a new life, hoping that Grand Duke Kyril and she could marry in the not too distant future.

The tsar agreed to let Grand Duke Paul see his children, Marie and Dmitri, a year after Paul's banishment from Russia. The reunion took place at Sengerschloss, the Duchess of Coburg's villa by the beautiful lake of Tegernsee in Upper Bavaria. The Duchess of Coburg's niece, Marie, once reunited with her father there, thought Tegernsee to have been "a fascinating place."[23]

In the meantime, Marie Alexandrovna's niece, Tsarina Alexandra, was as anxious as ever to present Russia with a male heir. She fell under the influence of the King of Montenegro's daughters, the Grand Duchess Militza (married to Grand Duke Peter Nikolaevich) and her sister, Anastasia ("Stana"), married to the Duke of Leuchtenberg. The Montenegrin sisters convinced the tsarina they could help her conceive a male child. Militza introduced Alexandra to a dubious Frenchman, "Dr. Philippe"—who claimed to be a mystic faith healer. Soon enough, Alexandra thought she was pregnant with the hoped for son, but it turned out to be a false pregnancy. After visiting the recuperating but embarrassed Alexandra, the dowager empress warned Nicholas II about Philippe. Peter Rachkovsky, the chief of the Russian secret police in France, had submitted evidence to Marie Feodorovna proving Philippe to be a charlatan. For his role in exposing Philippe to the dowager empress, Rachkovsky was dismissed from his position. Marie Feodorovna was shocked by Rachkovsky's dismissal, prompting her to declare: "*C'est un crime!* [It's a crime!]"[24] The controversial Philippe was finally sent away in 1903. But a more sinister replacement would soon enter Tsarina Alexandra's world and send the memory of "Dr. Philippe" into near oblivion.

The tsarina's susceptibility to Militza and Stana, and by extension to such characters as Philippe, began to preoccupy many. The Grand Duchess Vladimir voiced concerns to her uncle, Prince Henry VII of Reuss. The prince then passed on Miechen's observations to Prince Bernhard von Bülow, chancellor of the German Empire, telling him that:

> All that I have managed to gather has left a very disturbing impression . . . certain influences, which can only be described as perni-

cious, are beginning to make themselves felt. These influences . . . with a very dubious admixture of mysticism, emanate from the Montenegrin princesses . . . wielded so decisive a power over the reigning Tsarina that even the Dowager Empress cannot combat it . . . The Grand Duchess Vladimir is convinced that the mystic preoccupation of this clique form a grave danger to the dynasty. The Russian people sense corruption and the Little Father's [Nicholas II] prestige suffers accordingly. All this is being carefully used by the Nihilists to undermine Imperial prestige still further. Revolution, to-day, has changed its tactics. The *mot d'ordre* is no longer to assassinate a sovereign, but to discredit dynastic infallibility with the people. At the top there is utter ignorance of this danger . . . Everybody else is ignored. No one who tells the truth can get a hearing, but is jealously watched and pushed aside.[25]

The popular American periodical *Munsey's Magazine* published an article that touched upon the fractious relationship between the Grand Duke and Grand Duchess Vladimir and the Tsarina Alexandra. The grand duke and grand duchess, it was asserted, were the main culprits behind Alexandra's unpopularity, spreading as they did, gossip about the tsarina's supposed real reason for marrying Nicholas II (which they claimed was ambition). Alexandra was also supposed to have been an insincere convert, a political intriguer, and prone to such extreme melancholia that she was at risk of going mad. These "baseless" and "malicious" reports, the article pointed out, "has [sic] undoubtedly had its [sic] origin among the entourage of the Grand Duke and Grand Duchess Vladimir." Moreover, "the latter in particular is specially active in circulating malicious reports. Passionately fond of high play, and regarding the roulette wheel as an indispensable article of furniture in every well ordered house, she bitterly resents the young empress's attempts to check gambling and smoking among the ladies of the court and of the *beau monde* of St. Petersburg." The author of the article asserted that when an expedient time came, "I assume as a matter of course that the grand duchess would abjure Lutheranism rather than forfeit the crown of Russia. Consequently there are many who are disposed to turn their faces toward the Czar's uncle as toward the rising sun."[26]

Personal problems between Tsarina Alexandra and Miechen paled in comparison to the troubles that lay ahead for Russia, not just from the Nihilists, but also from the Far East. Russia's expansionist policy in Asia at the end of the nineteenth century disquieted other nations, especially Japan, fearing that

Russia was poised to move more forcefully beyond Manchuria, which fell under Russia's sphere of influence. Negotiations between Russia and Japan went nowhere due to Russian intransigence. Confident that they could easily defeat the Japanese in an armed conflict, Russia risked war by its refusal to budge in these negotiations. In February 1904, an exasperated Japan broke off diplomatic relations with Russia and attacked Port Arthur, Russia's only Pacific warm-water port, precipitating the Russo-Japanese War. The French military attaché in Russia reported that the Russian people's enthusiasm for the war was fever pitch: "All the Russians, apart from a handful of fanatics, are prepared to make any sacrifice to bring it to a victorious conclusion and avenge the insult to the Russian flag. We are witnessing a great outburst of national vigour and the grim determination which animates even the lowest classes—particularly the lowest classes—is most impressive."[27] One of the few exceptions to the general enthusiasm for war was the dowager empress. According to Elizabeth Narishkin-Kurakin, Marie Feodorovna "disapproved with all her heart of the conflict" and that "several times during that talk with me, tears came to her eyes."[28]

In waging war against Japan, Russia took a dangerous gamble. If the Russians won, victory would bring the nation untold glory. If Russia lost, humiliation along with the people's wrath could bring about revolution. Russia thus treaded in perilous waters. It did not take long to see what direction Russia was headed. From the onset of hostilities, the war went badly for the Russians. Unpreparedness, incompetence, poor leadership, and difficulties with resupplying troops five thousand miles away over the Trans-Siberian Railway all resulted in setback after setback. In the first two months alone, Russia lost an astonishing five warships, while another three were seriously damaged. The Japanese army soon overtook Korea and the Liaotung Peninsula. Forced back to Mukden by the Japanese, the Russians then went on the offensive but failed to gain a decisive victory.

Miechen's sons, Grand Dukes Kyril and Boris, went off to the Far East and saw action during the Russo-Japanese War. Kyril was an officer aboard the *Petropavlovsk*, the flagship of the First Pacific Squadron, when it exploded after hitting a mine and sank in Port Arthur. Boris witnessed the sinking of the *Petropavlovsk* from Dacha Hill in Port Arthur. Mortified at what he saw and knowing his brother was on board, Boris's mind raced. The explosion was ferocious, blowing off "the bridge, the foremast, the funnels and the bow turret . . . in less than two minutes the sea seemed to open and it [the ship] sank bow downwards."[29] Kyril was thrown into the water and sustained burns as well as

a back injury, but by a miracle he survived. Upon hearing the news, Boris telegraphed their parents. In thanksgiving, Miechen and Vladimir attended church.
The dowager empress paid the Vladimirs a visit, offering her support during
this time of great anxiety. The sinking of the *Petropavlovsk* was a bitter blow.
Of the more than seven hundred serving on board, only eighty were saved,
with Kyril being one of the lucky few. A tearful and grateful Miechen greeted
her son upon his return to St. Petersburg.

Amidst the terrible losses sustained during the war, one happy event took
place in 1904. In August at Peterhof, the tsarina delivered a healthy eleven-
pound baby boy, to great rejoicing. Upon arriving at Peterhof, the dowager
empress was overcome with joy and spent some time with Nicholas II before
meeting her grandson, Alexei Nikolaevich, for the first time. The ecstatic father, recorded in his diary of the "great and unforgettable day . . . during
which we were clearly visited by the grace of God."[30] At St. Petersburg, a three-
hundred-gun salute announced the birth of a male heir to the reigning tsar, the
first such salute in three centuries. Marie Feodorovna's infant grandson, on
whom so much hope lay, was christened in great pomp at the chapel of Peterhof in the presence of his godmother, the Dowager Empress Marie Feodorovna, and Queen Olga. Marie Feodorovna entered the chapel escorted by her
favorite brother-in-law, Grand Duke Alexei. Immediately behind Marie Feodorovna came Queen Olga, escorted by the baby's uncle, Grand Duke Michael. Both women wore impressive trains that were nine feet long. Two pages
carried the dowager empress's train, but Olga had only one page and a novice
at that, F. S. Olferev. Olferev, who carried Olga's ermine wrap too, could not
cope. As he recounted, "I was attempting to keep the train from catching on
something and to keep it out of the path of Grand Duke Vladimir Aleksandro-
vitch when suddenly the wrap I was carrying caught on the handle of a door
we were passing and the lace inside it split a little. I quickly freed the wrap and
went on farther. However, to my horror and shame, the blasted lace inside the
ermine wrap attached itself to the next door and split further." The mishap
caught the attention of Miechen's husband, who boomed: "Olga, your page
is splitting you apart!" The queen ignored Vladimir. According to Olferev, "I
was saved evidently by the fact that she was used to the grand duke's teasing
and did not believe him. Olferev expected a severe reprimand for the mishap.
His anxiety grew after the christening ceremony, when an official announced:
"Queen Olga of Greece would like to see her page."

"Queen Olga's page!" came the resounding call through the ranks of pages.
Olferev stepped out, believing himself a "condemned man." When the nervous

page entered the room where the imperial family had congregated, he was surprised to find the imperial crib with the baby tsarevich in it. Among the ladies who congregated around the crib was Queen Olga. She approached Olferev and brought him to the crib, saying, "I would like you to see our heir." The astonished page had his chance to look closely at the baby Alexei, then Queen Olga led Olferev out of the imperial rooms herself and in her kindly way said, "I hope to see you again soon."[31] It was a gracious act from a gracious queen.

For the first six weeks after Alexei's birth, the dowager empress, tsar, and tsarina were content, even jubilant, knowing that this infant secured the succession to the throne. But then, an ominous sign appeared that struck fear in the hearts of his doting parents. "Alix and I were very worried," recorded the tsar, "because little Alexei started bleeding from the navel, and it continued on and off until the evening!"[32] The bleeding continued intermittently for three days. In time, came the news of the tsarevich's affliction. The verdict was devastating: Alexei was a hemophiliac.

PART II

REVOLUTION

(1905–1928)

16

THE YEAR OF NIGHTMARES

As the Russo-Japanese War continued to go badly, many Russians began questioning the expansionist venture. At the end of 1904 on a visit to Paris, Countess Kleinmichel apprised the exiled Grand Duke Paul, his wife, and the French diplomat Maurice Paléologue of the turbulent atmosphere permeating Russia. "You have no idea," declared Countess Kleinmichel, "of the intensity of the feeling aroused in Russia during the last few months. Our *mujiks* are now objecting to being killed for what they call *a bit of territory we've never heard of* . . . Not a week passes without a mutiny in the barracks, or riots along the line when reservists leave for the front . . . In the universities it's even worse; revolutionary demonstrations, provoked by the slightest incident, are everyday occurrences. You can be sure that the peasants will come on the scene before long. That will mean the end of Tsarism and Russia!"[1]

The new year brought more disturbing news, as Maurice Paléologue recorded in January: "Port Arthur, the Gibraltar of the Far East, the great fortress which, symbolizing Russian domination in the China Seas . . . surrendered this morning."[2] Thus did Port Arthur's fall have the effect of "piling national humiliation on national anger."[3] Then came the Battle of Mukden in February 1905. For two weeks, 330,000 Russian soldiers desperately fought 270,000 Japanese in one of the largest land battles in history. The Russian army was forced to withdraw forty miles to the north, losing 90,000 men in acknowledged defeat.

In Russia itself, signs were ominous. During the annual Blessing of the Waters on the river Neva, live shells fell near the tsar. Maurice Paléologue concluded that "there can be no doubt that it was an attempt on the Tsar's life; a plot was the only possible explanation of the fact that the guns were loaded with shrapnel; the possibility of mistake was excluded."[4] Nicholas II escaped serious injury. Many, though, were rattled. "It seemed like an attack on the lives of the Tsar and the high officials who were present in such large numbers," wrote the tsar's uncle K.R., who was standing next to Nicholas II when the firing began.[5] As frightening as the incident was, another event of greater magnitude increased the mood of fear and foreboding.

In early January, striking workers, urged on by a fiery young priest, Father Gregory Gapon, marched in St. Petersburg to demand a constituent assembly as well as better working conditions, such as an eight-hour workday. Father Gapon and the workers hoped that Tsar Nicholas would receive them and agree to their requests. The tsar, however, was not in St. Petersburg at the time, but at Tsarskoe Selo. The crowd of some two hundred thousand workers converged peacefully on the Winter Palace, singing religious hymns. Many carried icons and portraits of the tsar. When the crowd was told to stop their march, they ignored the order. The government's reaction was disastrous. Following orders from Grand Duke Vladimir, who commanded the St. Petersburg garrison, the police and soldiers fired upon the crowd, killing hundreds and wounding thousands. The tragic event went down in history as "Bloody Sunday."

Reaction to Bloody Sunday was electrifying. The Russian Social Democratic Party issued a highly inflammatory announcement, designed to frighten the tsarist authorities and incite the people: "Yesterday you saw the savagery of the monarchy. You saw the blood running in the streets . . . Who directed the soldiers' rifles and shot against the breasts of the workers? It was the Tsar! the Grand Dukes, the ministers, the generals, the scum of the Court! . . . may they meet death. To arms, comrades! Seize the arsenals, depots and magazines of arms . . . destroy the police and gendarme stations and all the Governmental buildings. Down with the monarchic government!"[6] Bloody Sunday was the first in a series of events to shake the tsarist empire in 1905. After Bloody Sunday, the Marxist revolutionary Leon Trotsky declared: "The Revolution has come."[7]

In a report to London, the British ambassador to Russia, Sir Charles Hardinge, described Bloody Sunday's serious impact: "The incident will have created a deep gulf, which will not be easily bridged, between the Emperor and the working classes who have hitherto been the most loyal subjects of the throne, and a blow will have been struck at the autocracy from which it will be difficult to recover."[8]

The tsar reacted to news of the tragedy with dismay, confessing that it was "a terrible day!"[9] In Paris, Grand Duke Paul and his wife, Olga, were horrified by the news of Bloody Sunday. Olga declared to Maurice Paléologue: "What a horrible day! Now we shall have revolution—it's the end! . . . To-day's disaster is irreparable!" Grand Duke Paul expressed similar sentiments, saying through the tears he shed: "We're lost, aren't we? . . . within and without, everything's crumbling!"[10] In Paléologue's view, Grand Duke Vladimir as military governor of St. Petersburg "was solely responsible, morally and politically" for Bloody Sunday. "The Tsar had at first announced his intention of receiving the workmen's deputation," noted Paléologue, "but his uncle Vladimir, who has always advocated the strong hand, was so violently opposed to the idea that the weak Tsar soon gave in."[11]

Following right on the heels of Bloody Sunday, Marie Alexandrovna's brother, Grand Duke Serge, became a target for assassination. A member of the Social Revolutionary Party, Ivan Kaliaev, spotted Serge in February as he rode through Moscow by carriage with Ella and their wards, Dmitri and Marie, Queen Olga's grandchildren. Seeing the children, Kaliaev did not hurl the bomb he was carrying as he intended. Two days later, though, Kaliaev acted, throwing a bomb at the grand duke who again traveled in a carriage near the law courts. Ella heard the powerful explosion and ran to find a horrific sight. Her husband had been blown to bits.

In recounting the ghastly event to Sir Charles Hardinge in an official report, the British consul in Moscow noted that "the force of the explosion was enormous." The bombing was so powerful that "nearly all the windows of the Law Courts and Arsenal . . . were shattered or blown in." Grand Duke Serge's body "was terribly mutilated, the head being torn off, as also an arm and a leg." Despite the ghastly scene, a witness was struck by "the stolidity, one might almost say apathy, of the crowd."[12]

Grand Duke Nicholas Mikhailovich also recounted the event, describing the gruesome aftermath of the murder of his cousin to the French historian, Frédéric Masson: "The unfortunate grand duke was reduced to pieces and we literally found nothing of his head which must have been shattered into tiny pieces. Parts of his body, such as two fingers were found on the roof of the palace of Justice, and those which were laying on the snow, were fragments full of blood and frightful limbs etc."[13]

Grand Duke Serge's savage murder stunned the imperial family. Nicholas II, Alexandra, Marie Feodorovna, and Serge's brothers wanted to attend the funeral, but the authorities deemed it too dangerous for them to do so.

Nevertheless, four prominent members of the Romanov dynasty attended, Ella naturally being one of them. Ella bore her grief with resignation and great dignity, visiting her husband's killer and forgiving him. "I admire this act," recounted Grand Duke Nicholas Mikhailovich of Ella, "but I cannot grasp this incredible piety."[14] Ella's niece and ward, Grand Duchess Marie, recalled that during these sad days, the new widow "gave proof of an almost incomprehensible heroism; no one could understand whence came the strength so to bear her misfortune."[15]

Other imperial mourners who defied the possibility of a terrorist attack by attending the funeral included Serge's sister, the Duchess of Coburg, and Queen Olga's brother, K.R. Nicholas II also granted Grand Duke Paul permission to return Russia to attend the funeral. Before leaving France, Paul expressed his fears about Russia and his nephew: "Where will the effrontery of these anarchists end? Heaven protect the Emperor! Pray God he may be spared my father's fate."[16] When Paul returned from Russia after the funeral, he confided his anxieties about the situation and the tsar's position relative to the upheaval to Maurice Paléologue. The grand duke recounted that Nicholas II "discussed the war with *alarming complacency* ... The revolutionary outbreaks hardly worry him at all; he claims that the masses are not in the least interested in them; he believes he is one with the people."[17] Paul, however, did not find the tsar's mother complacent. Grand Duke Paul thought that the dowager empress was "extremely pessimistic about the future." "Oh, Marie-Feodorovna!" exclaimed the grand duke, "she has several times said to me: 'We've lost our last chance of winning in the Far East; we're beaten already; we ought to make peace at once; otherwise there'll be a revolution.' "

When Paul asked Marie Feodorovna if she had spoken to the tsar in such terms, she answered: "I tell him so every day, but he won't listen to me; he doesn't realize our military situation any better than the position at home. He can't see that he's leading Russia into disaster." Her final words to Paul were: "I know only one man who can open Nicholas's eyes and that's M. Delcassé.[18] He's the best friend we have in Europe; he has immense influence in every country. So tell him from me that he will be doing us a signal service if he will offer to mediate for us."[19] Paul passed on the dowager empress's request. Delcassé was willing to help, but the French ambassador to Russia, Maurice Bompard, urged caution, for he considered "that intervention on the lines desired by the Empress Marie-Feodorovna would be premature, to say the least of it."[20] In the end, Delcassé hesitated to mediate because there was the risk that "Russia would blame France for any unfavorable peace that resulted."[21]

Since the birth of the Tsarevich Alexei, Marie Feodorovna's influence with Nicholas II waned—her place being overtaken by the tsarina. It was an unfortunate, even ruinous, turn of events, because the dowager empress, being more levelheaded than her son and daughter-in-law, was better equipped to gauge Russia's troubles. Regrettably, troubles brought on by the Russo-Japanese War intensified the frosty relations between Alexandra and Marie Feodorovna. When Alexandra expressed a wish to become active with the Red Cross, which was under the dowager empress's supervision, Alexandra was told that as an outsider, she could not work independently within the organization. Saddened and shocked by this, which she viewed as an affront, a tearful tsarina asked Elizabeth Narishkin-Kurakin to intervene on her behalf, saying, "I don't dare ask this of my mother-in-law."[22] When Narishkin-Kurakin discussed the situation with the dowager empress, Marie Feodorovna consented to help. She believed that an independent branch of the Red Cross could be organized for Alexandra.

"She has splendid ideas," said Marie Feodorovna to Narishkin-Kurakin about Alexandra. "But she never tells me what she does or expects to do. When we two are together, she always converses about everything but herself. I shall be very glad if she will only drop her reserve." Narishkin-Kurakin then replied, "Pardon me, Madame, but these are the very words the Empress used. She regrets no less speaking with you only on indifferent topics, and would be happy if you would let her help you with the work." "I should wish nothing better," answered Marie Feodorovna, "but it is very difficult to understand her."[23]

The dowager empress's exasperation was the result of repeated incidents that tended to underscore Alexandra's shortcomings. In one example, Alexandra and Nicholas II made their way to the Crimea on the imperial train, but the tsarina refused to appear to a crowd that strained to catch a glimpse of her and the tsar. The minister of the court, Count Vladimir Fredericksz, advised Nicholas II to greet the crowds in some way. The tsar agreed and went to one of the windows, leaving an unhappy Alexandra in the background. When Marie Feodorovna heard the story, she remarked: "If *she* was not there Nicky would be twice as popular. She is a regular German. She thinks the Imperial family should be 'above that sort of thing.' What does she mean? Above winning the people's affection? There's no need to go in for what I should call vulgar ways of seeking popularity. Nicky himself has all that is required for popular adoration; all he needs to do is to show himself to those who want to see him. How many times I have tried to make it plain to her. She won't understand; perhaps she hasn't it in her to understand. And yet, how often she complains of the public indifference towards her."[24]

On May 27, 1905, catastrophe hit imperial Russia. The Russian Baltic Fleet, after traveling tens of thousands of miles in seven months, was making its way to the Russian Pacific port city of Vladivostok via the Tsushima Strait, which separates Korea and Japan. Awaiting them was the Japanese navy. The Japanese fired upon the Russians in the largest naval engagement since the Battle of Trafalgar, one hundred years before. On the first day of the Battle of Tsushima, the Japanese hit the Russian flagship, *Osliabia*, which sank in just half an hour. Before night fell on the first day, the Russian battleships *"Aleksandr III, Borodino*, and the *Kniaz Suvorov* all joined the *Osliabia* at the bottom of the sea, as did several Russian cruisers and destroyers."[25] The Japanese navy's onslaught proved calamitous for Russia. At the end of the brief battle, the Russians had lost an astounding twenty warships and over four thousand men, with nearly six thousand captured. Another five ships were captured; only four Russian ships managed to reach safety at Vladivostok. In contrast, the Japanese lost only slightly more than one hundred men and three torpedo boats. On day two, the Russians surrendered to the Japanese. According to the Grand Duchess Olga, who was with her brother at Tsarskoe Selo when he received news of the astonishing defeat at Tsushima, Nicholas II "turned ashen pale, he trembled, and clutched at a chair for support. Alicky broke down and sobbed. The whole palace was plunged into mourning that day."[26]

In St. Petersburg and the rest of Russia, the devastating news stunned nearly everyone. Sir Charles Hardinge reported to his superiors in London that "a shadow of gloom and consternation spread over the land."[27] Russia's defeat at the hands of the Japanese dealt a grave blow to Russian prestige. Russia's ambassador to France, Alexander Nelidov, reported as much from Paris: "I don't even have the strength to describe the destructive impression which the destruction of our fleet produced here."[28]

The humiliating specter of Tsushima cast a long shadow on the Romanovs. The British-born aristocrat Princess Daisy of Pless encountered Miechen a month after the Russian defeat at the Battle of Tsushima, at the wedding of the latter's niece Duchess Cecilie of Mecklenburg-Schwerin to German Crown Prince Wilhelm of Germany. Daisy found Miechen "so gentle and nice but her face was very sad." As for the Grand Duke Vladimir, Daisy surmised that he was not present, "not daring, I expect, to appear in public after the terrible naval defeat of Russia—their second Fleet annihilated."[29]

Defeated and humiliated, the Russians had no choice but to end the war.

Nicholas II sent the most able man in Russia, Sergei Witte, to Portsmouth, New Hampshire, to negotiate peace. Witte negotiated brilliantly at Portsmouth, such that Russia retained her Far Eastern possessions with the exception of the Liaotung Peninsula, which included Port Arthur, but "even Witte could not shield Nicholas from the stigma of being the first ruler in Europe to admit defeat at the hands of Asians."[30] The troubles did not end with Tsushima and the Treaty of Portsmouth. On the contrary, troubles multiplied. In Odessa harbor, on the Black Sea, the eight hundred-man crew of one of the most modern ships in the Russian Black Sea Fleet, the battleship *Potemkin*, killed their officers in a mutiny in June. In a highly symbolic gesture, "the red banner of revolt waved from the mast of an Imperial ship of war," for the very first time in Russian history, while "Odessa suffered what may have been bloodiest fighting of the entire year," resulting in the deaths of two thousand people.[31]

As the year unfolded, unrest continued to grow. Throughout the summer months, the workers, numbering three quarters of a million people, kept striking and peasants went on the rampage. It became increasingly evident that Bloody Sunday had been but "the first bloodletting of the year." By late fall, the tsar and his military advisers had "assigned 15,297 companies of infantry and 3,665 squadrons of cavalry, with 224 cannon and 124 machine guns, to suppress strikes and peasant riots."[32]

Meanwhile, in Switzerland, Vladimir Lenin was positioning himself to lead a socialist revolution in Russia. Infighting racked the revolutionaries, but Lenin was single-minded in his determination. In fact, many socialists "were shocked by the spectacle of the man who proclaimed himself the true leader of all Russian Marxists wasting so much of his own (and other people's) energy on endless introverted quarelling, while Russia herself seemed to be poised on the very brink of a titanic upheaval."[33] This was no exaggeration. K.R. confided in his diary in June: "What is happening to Russia? What disorganization, what disintegration, just like a piece of clothing that is beginning to rip and tear along the seams, and fall open."[34] Grand Duchess Xenia was equally aghast. "I feel so depressed," she wrote in her diary, "it's impossible. It's terrible what's happening—strikes, murders, discontent, a general lack of authority!"[35] As shocking as the troubles were up to this point, more unrest was in store.

Two months after Xenia expressed her fears, Nicholas II approved the creation of a consultative body of representatives, the Duma. Though its power was very limited, it was hoped that approving the Duma's establishment would quell the widespread violence. Nicholas believed that enough calmness had returned to warrant a family cruise on the Baltic. Among those joining them was Anna Tanaeva, a chubby, friendly twenty-year-old who was the Tsarina Alexandra's new lady-in-waiting. Another friend who entered the life of Marie Feodorovna's daughter-in-law was a peasant by the name of Gregory Rasputin. The reputed "holy" man had left his home and family in Siberia. He eventually made his way to St. Petersburg, where he came to the attention of numerous important personages, including Grand Duchess Militza who introduced Rasputin to Nicholas and Alexandra at the end of 1905. Of the fateful first meeting with Rasputin, the tsar recorded: "We made the acquaintance of a man of God—Grigory, from the Tobolsk region."[36]

Rasputin's introduction to Nicholas and Alexandra occurred as a destabilized Russia grappled with escalating upheaval. In October, near anarchy engulfed the country. For ten days that month, a spontaneous strike afflicted the entire empire. A major railway strike broke out, bringing Russia to a near standstill. In St. Petersburg, nearly everyone ceased working, including the corps de ballet of the imperial Mariinsky Theatre. University students were especially infected with revolutionary fever. Nothing functioned in the capital, sending people into a panic, especially when electricity was cut off and provisions became scarce. The strikes spread all over Russia, their tentacles reaching as far as Siberia and the Caucasus. Far from being peaceful demonstrations, workers brandished weapons and unfurled red flags, symbols of revolution. Strikers sang the revolutionary song, the "Marseillaise," and shouted their grievances: "Down with Autocracy!" And "Long Live the Revolution." Prominent in the October strikes and demonstrations were calls "for the right to determine their fate and that of their fellows."[37] Demands to the tsar from all corners of Russia were loud and clear—grant political concessions. All the troubles amounted to "a storm unlike any Russia had ever seen."[38]

The tsarist government panicked. Fearful that the workers were set to overthrow the tsar, soldiers were placed on standby, prepared to carry out orders to fire real bullets on striking agitators. Leon Trotsky became a prominent leader, as a new body, the Soviet ("Council") of Workers' Deputies, emerged to coordinate strikers and provide platforms for their political grievances. In Moscow, open insurrection was the rule with the local Soviet being the de facto authority. So serious were the outbreaks of violence and so feverish were calls for the revolution that fear over the fate of the imperial family prompted preparations for their evacuation. Two destroyers received orders to move them to safety from their residence at Peterhof if necessary.

The Dowager Empress Marie Feodorovna was in Denmark while Russia teetered on the brink of the abyss in October 1905. Consumed with anxiety, she wrote to the tsar, offering her support and advice. "I am so worried and tormented sitting here reading the papers, and knowing *nothing* of what is happening," went one desperate letter. "My poor Nicky! May God give you the *strength and the wisdom* in these terribly difficult times to take the right measures and so overcome this evil . . . May God help you, that is my constant prayer." Marie Feodorovna urged her son to call for Sergei Witte's help. "I am sure that the only man who can help you now and be useful is Witte . . . he certainly is a man of genius, *energetic* and clear-sighted."[39] In urging her son to go to Witte, the dowager empress showed a clear-sightedness that her son lacked. Though Witte was "arrogant, cunning, and given to backstage intrigues," even his most acerbic critics conceded that he was a "rare Russian talent." Besides his success at Portsmouth, Witte had, as minister of finance between 1892 and 1903, brought Russia into the industrial age and modernized the country in order "to assure the political power and greatness of the state." In "those eleven years Witte's achievements were, by virtually every standard, remarkable."[40] Little wonder, then, that the dowager empress recommended Witte as a man who could help her son during Russia's critical hour.

Witte (who had been made a count) was then chairman of the Committee of Ministers. He presented the tsar with two alternatives: grant a constitution to his subjects, paving the way for the creation of a Duma, or install a military dictatorship. Witte, though not sympathetic to constitutional government, was nevertheless inclined to follow the former course. Tsar Nicholas consulted a number of individuals for advice. Among those the tsar summoned was his father's cousin, the towering and imposing soldier, Grand Duke Nikolai Nikolaevich ("Nikolasha"), who favored Witte's proposal of a constitution. When the tsar asked the chief of police of St. Petersburg, General Dmitri Trepov, how long he could hold the capital and at what cost, Trepov replied that much blood would be spilled. This finally prompted Nicholas II to concede to agreeing to Witte's plan for a constitution; but in a last-ditch effort to rally Nikolasha to oppose Witte, the tsar summoned the grand duke again. Upon his arrival at Peterhof, the minister of the court, Count Fredericksz, pleaded with Nikolasha to abandon his support for Witte's plan. The plea backfired. A furious Nikolasha took out a revolver and brandished it at Fredericksz, saying excitedly: "You see this revolver? I'm going now to the czar and I will beg him to sign the manifesto and the Witte program. Either he signs or in his presence I will put a bullet through my head with this revolver."[41] That same day, Nicholas II signed what became known as the October Manifesto. The manifesto signaled the formal end of autocratic rule for the Romanovs. Besides allowing the formation of the Duma, or parliament, it also granted Russians freedom of speech and assembly as well as freedom of the press. Sergei Witte became head of what amounted to the first constitutional government for Russia, though "it did not go as far as the constitutional monarchy in England." In Russia, Nicholas still "retained his prerogative over defense and foreign affairs and the sole power to appoint and dismiss ministers. But the Manifesto did propel Russia with great rapidity over difficult political terrain which it had taken Western Europe several centuries to travel."[42]

The imperial family was aghast at the tsar's actions. The tsarina never forgave Nikolasha for bullying her husband. Among those Romanovs deeply concerned about unfolding events was Miechen's husband, Vladimir, whose harsh response in January had resulted in Bloody Sunday. Prince Gavril Constantinovich, K.R.'s son, noted that Grand Duke Vladimir suffered because of the "misfortunes that befell Russia. He was deeply Russian," recalled Gavril, "and very intelligent, so he clearly saw what the events were leading to."[43] The tsar's approval of the October Manifesto infuriated Sandro. "That was the end," recalled the tsar's brother-in-law. "The end of the dynasty and the end of the empire. A brave jump from the precipice would have spared us the agony of the remaining twelve years."[44] The tsar confided his anguished feelings to Prince Vladimir Orlov. Nicholas felt guilt, tinged with shame at what he had done, which amounted to reneging on the oath taken at his coronation where he swore to uphold autocracy. With tears flowing, Nicholas muttered: "I am too depressed. I feel that in signing this act I have lost the crown. Now all is finished."[45]

The tsar did not have his mother at his side at this critical juncture. She was still in Denmark. Having agreed to the creation of a Duma and ending autocracy with the stroke of a pen, Nicholas II wrote to Marie Feodorovna, confiding the difficulties he faced and felt in these momentous days.

> *My dearest Mama,*
> *We have been through such grave and unprecedented events . . . You remember, no doubt, those January days when we were together at Tsarskoe—they were miserable, weren't they? But they are* nothing *in comparison with what has happened now! . . . in the end, invoking God's help, I signed [the manifesto]. My dear Mama, you can't imagine what I went through before that moment; in my telegram I could not explain all the circumstances which brought me to this terrible decision, which nevertheless I took quite consciously. From all over*

Russia they cried for it, they begged for it, and around me many— very many—held the same views . . . There was no other way out than to cross oneself and give what everyone was asking for. My only consolation is that such is the will of God, and this grave decision will lead my dear Russia out of the intolerable chaos she has been in for nearly a year. The situation is very serious . . . We are in the midst of a revolution with an administrative apparatus entirely disorganised, and in this lies the main danger . . . I assure you we have lived years in these days, such torments, doubts, and indecisions . . . I know you are praying for your poor Nicky. Our Saviour be with you! May God save and give peace to Russia. Yours with all my heart,

Nicky[46]

In early November, Marie Feodorovna replied. In her letter, Nicholas's mother was full of sympathy:

I was overjoyed to get your letter, knowing how difficult it would be for you to find time to write. I have suffered so much and so intensely that I feel at least ten years older in this short time. Thank God that in the last few days things are a little quieter in St. Petersburg, and that you have recovered at least some of your peace of mind, my poor Nicky. How terrible it must have been for you and how you must have suffered when confronted with such tremendous decisions—I felt all this in my heart and suffered with you . . . It is still hard for me to believe that all this has been happening in Russia, but, in the end, I am sure you could not act otherwise than you have done. Our Lord has helped you to solve this terrible problem . . . He reads in the hearts of men, and knows with what patience and resignation you carry the heavy cross put on you. I am sorry for Witte, too. He has his measure of terrible difficulties, the more so as he did not expect them to be so great—it is essential for you to show him all your confidence now, and to let him act according to his programme.[47]

If Marie Feodorovna and her son had hoped that the issuing of the October Manifesto might calm Russia straightaway, they were mistaken. Civil unrest continued. In mid-November, the tsar was compelled to tell his mother: "For the most part the peasant disturbances are still going on . . . They are difficult to put down because there are not enough troops or Cossacks to go round. But the worst thing is another mutiny of the naval establishments in Sebastopol and part of the garrison there. How it hurts, and how ashamed one is of it all."[48] The tsar was not the only one in despair. Witte too saw that his plan did not tame the masses. Instead, "the situation grew steadily worse. The Right hated him for degrading the autocracy, the Liberals did not trust him, the Left feared that the revolution which it was anticipating would slip from its grasp."[49]

By December, lawlessness had spread throughout Russia. "St. Petersburg is swarming with Cossacks," reported the *New York Times*. "It is understood that the whole Cossack forces of the empire, some 450,000 men, will be mobilized." There was no doubt, that "the Russian people are being led uncomprehendingly into civil war and self-destruction."[50] In another report, the *New York Times*'s St. Petersburg correspondent reported that "we are drifting rapidly into complete anarchy. Count Witte is powerless to stem the tide. The people are hoping for a miracle to avert a cataclysm."[51] Poland became one of the most violent parts of the Russian Empire. Workers in Lodz shouted, "Down with the autocracy! Down with the war!" as they struck in solidarity with their Russian counterparts in the early part of 1905.[52] The *Times* of London reported that a massive crowd of at least one hundred thousand persons marched through Warsaw "shouting and carrying red flags and singing revolutionary songs."[53] During 1905–06, the tsarist government dispatched three hundred thousand soldiers in order to keep Poland in its place.

Witnessing the awful ferment that gripped the empire Miechen wrote to her uncle, Prince Henry Reuss, of her thoughts:

> *The saddest thing of all is the absolute lack of a* ligne de conduit *from above. One oscillates from one system to another, often from one day to another and you can imagine the effect of this. There is therefore neither hope nor safety, and the apparent reforms achieve nothing because they are given no time. They are scarcely proclaimed before they are supplanted by others. Either those in command can't or they won't see, and warning voices such as Vladimir's are unheard. I am afraid we shall soon have the added terror of outrages to increase the general confusion. If only a fairly decent peace would come soon, things might be staved off. A firm and energetic lead could still save everything. Well, that lies in God's hand!*
>
> *With fond love,*
> *Maria*[54]

Plainly, this letter criticized Nicholas II's leadership. Miechen had much more confidence in her husband's abilities and lamented that he was ignored in the corridors of power. During the first year of the Russo-Japanese War, the Vladimirs had wielded some influence in the capital and were a force to be reckoned with, especially since the tsar and his unpopular tsarina continued to isolate themselves from St. Petersburg society. According to one published report, Miechen and Vladimir were "now more than ever a source of trouble, and even of danger, to the Czar and his consort."[55]

As the year 1905 drew to a close, the armed struggle that had so radically changed the Russian political landscape increased to ferocious levels. Fighting in Moscow was especially savage. The city was under siege for ten days when the local Soviet directed thousands of students and workers to revolt. Soldiers loyal to the tsar quelled the uprising, but many civilians were killed. Reports from Moscow described harrowing events. "The guns have been bombarding one barricade after another . . . the cannonades being followed by charges by the dragoons, who set fire to the débris . . . In many cases dragoons fired into private houses in which they suspected that Revolutionaries had taken refuge . . . With Moscow's baptism of blood the Revolutionaries made good their threat to transform the strike into an armed rebellion."[56] A day after this account was printed, five thousand people were killed and fourteen thousand wounded in Moscow, "with fighting still proceeding . . . It is impossible to move about the city in consequence of the frequency of stray bullets. Many innocent persons have been accidentally killed." The ferocity of the fighting was captured in the following report: "The driving force behind both the troops and the rebels is no longer that of enthusiasm or of any human impulse. It is the force of super-human hate, and hence the deeds reported are not the acts of patriots, soldiers, or otherwise, but the enormities of madmen."[57]

Serge's widow, Ella, who lived in Moscow, and who quietly worked to care for the city's sick, wrote to her brother Ernie what it was like in Russia's second city: "All is going from worse to worse; one must not make oneself any illusions of better times coming for months. We are in the revolution—What turn all will take, nobody knows, as the government is so weak as, sooner to say, does not seem to exist."[58]

The tsar urged his mother not to come home until stability returned. "It is so sad to be without you, dear Mama, and it is so sad for you too, but all of us [the family] and all our trusted friends implore you not to come for yet a while! The risk is too great."[59] In reply, the dowager empress wrote: "one's heart has not a moment's peace and I suffer intolerably for *you* and with you for *Russia and everybody* . . . What a disgrace all these strikes are—what a ruin for one and all! No patriotism on one side, no *authority* on the other—it is simply frightful! God Almighty alone can lead us out of this chaos and save our country . . . All this is unbearable and terribly worrying. My *anguish* is so great that I can hardly bear it any longer! One really and truly does not know sometimes *what* to expect, what to *hope* for even—everything is so incredible, yet it actually is happening *in Russia*!!"[60] The year 1905, declared Marie Feodorovna, was without doubt, the "year of nightmares."[61]

SCANDAL

The years had not diminished the Dowager Empress Marie Feodorovna's desire to escape to her native Denmark whenever she could. As the twentieth century unfolded, there was an added urgency to these trips, as her father, the widowed King Christian IX, was aging rapidly. Still in Demark in 1906, Marie Feodorovna asked her father if he was tired after conducting a long audience. "Not at all," answered King Christian, "no more than an old man is allowed to be. Come, you shall see!" As proof, he danced a few steps with his fifty-nine-year-old daughter, to whom he jokingly commented, "you are an old woman too," but added, "I only mean, of course, that you are not as young as you were!"[1] Later that same day, as he rested, Marie Feodorovna's eighty-seven-year-old father died peacefully.

After their father's death, the Dowager Empress Marie Feodorovna and Queen Alexandra purchased Hvidovre, a comfortable villa outside of Copenhagen that became their home whenever both sisters returned to Denmark. Located near the sea, the white Italianate villa offered the sisters a respite during the autumn months from their hectic lives in England and Russia. When the Spanish Infanta Eulalia visited the sisters at Hvidovre, she marveled at their closeness and the casual manner in which they lived. "They adore each other, are absolutely happy in each other's society, and in the simplicity of the life they lead," wrote Eulalia. The dowager empress and the queen were eager to show their guest around Hvidovre. "Come and see my writing-table," enthused Marie Feodorovna, pulling Eulalia to her end of the room. "No," exclaimed an equally eager Alexandra, "come see my writing-table." "This is my chair," Marie Feodorovna proudly chimed. "And this is my chair," echoed

Alexandra. The sisters then showed Eulalia their garden and a small kitchen. "This is where I make my tea," said Queen Alexandra. "And this is where I cut the bread-and-butter," added the dowager empress. When the three royal ladies were walking on the beach, the repartee continued. In comparing each other's collection of beach amber, Marie Feodorovna was luckier than her sister, touching off another round of bantering. "It is most unfair," said Alexandra in a happy and animated manner. "I always pick up more than you do," Marie Feodorovna piped triumphantly. Eulalia found the sisters "as happy as two schoolgirls . . . untrammelled by Court etiquette and without even a single lady-in-waiting to attend them."[2]

Another visitor to Hvidovre, Lady Constance Battersea, was impressed by the "note of simplicity throughout, and the atmosphere of sisterly affection which seemed to pervade the place." Portraits of the dowager empress greeted visitors near the stairs that led up to the "prettily furnished living-room." Two small bedrooms were situated near each other—"that of the Empress hung with an icon and pictures of saints and angels, that of the Queen with photographs of the members of her family." Each sister had insisted on taking the smaller of the two bedrooms, so that in the end, they had to draw lots. Queen Alexandra drew the larger lot, "much to the delight of the Empress." With its "garden with its sweet-smelling flowers on one side, and on the other the open sea," Lady Constance was struck by Hvidovre's "peace and seclusion."[3] Little wonder then that Marie Feodorovna enjoyed staying at Hvidovre, for such tranquility was a rarity in Russia.

After the ferocious violence of 1905, the first months of 1906 in Russia had some semblance of calm. But peace came at a price. According to a report in the *New York Times*, "repression is more stringent than ever" in Russia in defiance of the spirit of the October Manifesto. The prefect of St. Petersburg gave the police "full powers to search all persons and dwellings without distinction and to confiscate arms." Moreover, "at the first shot fired by the Revolutionaries the city will be placed under martial law."[4]

In April, Nicholas II, never as great a believer in the abilities of Count Witte as his mother had been, dismissed the chairman of the Council of Ministers. That same month, the much anticipated Duma was inaugurated in the Winter Palace. The British chargé at St. Petersburg, Cecil Spring Rice, reported that "the most elaborate precautions" had been taken "for the safety of the Emperor on the occasion of his journey to St. Petersburg to open the Duma."[5] Queen Olga's granddaughter, Grand Duchess Marie, echoed this, noting that "the Winter Palace looked more like a fortress, so greatly did they fear an attack or hostile demonstrations."[6] The Duma opening took place at St. George's Hall, the throne room in the Winter Palace. In the vast 150-foot-long room "resplendent with its Corinthian pillars and superb chandeliers" were Russians from all walks of life.[7] Never before had such an assemblage gathered at the Winter Palace. Members of the imperial family were there in force. The event was a glittering one, with the dowager empress and the tsarina, along with the other ladies of the court, dressed in imperial court dress, as was customary for formal occasions. Vladimir Kokovtsov, the Russian minister of finance, left a record of his impressions. In contrast to the dazzling, bejeweled ladies of the court were Duma members who, in their simple frocks, looked out of place. Kokovtsov observed that "the overwhelming majority" of Duma members "occupying the first places near the throne, were dressed as if intentionally in workers' blouses and cotton shirts, and behind them was a crowd of peasants in the most varied costumes. Some in national dress, and a multitude of representatives of the clergy."[8]

Vladimir Gurko, a government official, echoed Kokovtsov's observation, adding that the contrast between the imperial family and the peasants was startling. Gurko concluded, "Naively believing that the people's representatives, many of whom were peasants, would be awed by the splendor of the Imperial court, the ladies of the Imperial family had worn nearly all their jewels; they were literally covered with pearls and diamonds. But the effect was altogether different . . . What it did achieve was to set in juxtaposition the boundless Imperial luxury and the poverty of the people." And so, "far from promoting goodwill and harmony," wrote one historian, "such an encounter between the privileged and the elected representatives could only deepen the distrust with which the two sides eyed each other."[9] Grand Duchess Marie noted that the majority of the Duma members "wore a lugubrious aspect; and it was easy to believe yourself at a funeral. Even the Emperor, ordinarily able to hide his feelings, was sad and nervous."[10]

Tsar Nicholas, controlling his emotions, gave a brief speech in a firm voice from the throne. His mother and wife, both looking stately but perturbed, stood to his right. Further to the right were the grand dukes and grand duchesses, including Vladimir and Miechen. Those who attended could not help but notice the air of animosity that permeated the proceedings. The elected delegates were especially unsympathetic to the tsarist government. Cecil Spring Rice reported to his London superior, Sir Edward Grey, that "out of the nearly 493 members [of the Duma], 380 have been elected. Of these, the Government can count on the support of 20."[11] In describing the opening session to his superiors in Washington, D.C., George L. Meyer, admitted that "in watching the deputies I was surprised to note that many of them did not even return the bows of His Majesty, some giving an awkward nod, others staring him coldly in the face, showing no enthusiasm, and even almost sullen indifference."[12] Cecil Spring Rice reported that "there can be no doubt that the reception accorded to it [Nicholas II's speech] by the members of the Duma was a cold one."[13]

For members of the imperial family, one look at the menacing faces from numerous Duma members said it all. Grand Duchess Xenia described the Duma as "such filth, such a nest of revolutionaries, that it's disgusting."[14] Tsarina Alexandra and Dowager Empress Marie Feodorovna were equally distraught. Kokovtsov watched Marie Feodorovna as she listened to her son read his speech. Kokovtsov noted that the dowager empress "could hardly fight back the tears." A few days later, Marie Feodorovna granted Kokovtsov an audience during which she described the "terrible reception" given to the tsar. Kokovtsov was struck by the fact that the dowager empress "was still unable to calm herself." "They looked at us," she said, "as upon their enemies and I could not make myself stop looking at certain faces, so much did they seem to reflect an incomprehensible hatred for all of us." She expressed her worry that such a Duma would be unable and unwilling to work with the government. "All this frightens me greatly," Marie Feodorovna added, "and I ask myself if we would be able to protect ourselves from new revolutionary outbursts, if we have enough strength to suppress another revolt as we did the Moscow one." She closed her audience with Kokovtsov by telling him that she saw that "my poor son has very few people he can trust, while you have always told him the truth."[15]

In the midst of the political turmoil that beset Russia during the "year of nightmares," romantic scandals continued to erupt amidst the imperial family. The first romance involved the dowager empress's son, Grand Duke Michael, with a lady-in-waiting, Alexandra ("Dina") Kossikovskaya. Unlike Michael's earlier liaison with Baby Bee (Marie Alexandrovna's youngest daughter), Dina was older than Michael by three years and was no beauty. But what Dina lacked in looks, she made up for in charm and intelligence. Michael enjoyed having long talks with this woman who was "a wonderfully bright conversationalist" and who was "exceedingly popular among the younger generation of St. Petersburg society."[16]

Yet, Michael's latest romance was doomed too because Dina was a commoner. This did not deter the ambitious thirty-year-old Dina from wishing to marry the grand duke. Michael, though urged by a number of friends to take Dina on as his mistress, did not wish to do so. Michael, who "had inherited his father's inflexible honesty," coupled with "his mother's high moral principles," had thus "never for a moment thought of doing otherwise than marrying" Dina Kossikovskaya.[17] Michael's insistence on marrying her met with consternation among his family. His sister, Xenia, described the situation as causing "so many complications" and being "extremely tiresome."[18]

As vexing as Michael's romance with Dina was, an even greater scandal was set to break. The Duchess of Coburg, "an untiring and unstoppable force of nature,"[19] took Ducky under her wing after her divorce from Ernie. The newly disgraced Ducky was an additional problem for Marie Alexandrovna, on top of Missy in Romania, with her unhappy marriage and her continuous difficulties with King Carol and Queen Elisabeth. The Duchess of Coburg had much in common with this unhappy daughter Ducky, for both shared "passionate Slavic temperaments" combined with "uncompromising honesty." Moreover, both mother and daughter "placed integrity, sincerity, and simplicity above all else and despised affectation and duplicity."[20] Marie Alexandrovna decided to take Ducky and Bee away from Coburg and ride out the opprobrium that was being heaped on Ducky. They fled to the Château Fabron. Grand Duke Kyril's ship conveniently docked at nearby Toulon, giving Ducky and him the opportunity to see each other again. Much as they wished to marry, however, there were two seemingly impossible obstacles to overcome. One was the Russian Orthodox Church, which frowned on first cousins marrying; the other was Ducky's status as a divorcée.

By this time, Grand Duke Kyril had acquired a reputation for "being the bright dashing young leader of the imperial 'smart set' at St. Petersburg, 'the idol of all women and the friend of most of the men.'" This did not make Ducky's sister, Missy, feel any easier about Kyril as a husband for Ducky. On the contrary, Miechen's son seemed to Missy, to be the "marble man" who was especially "cold and selfish."[21] Kyril's parents were not at first keen on seeing their son marry Ducky, but acquiesced when they saw how insistent Kyril was in having her as his wife. Ducky's mother gave her tacit approval to the romance.

After the end of the Russo-Japanese War, Kyril and Ducky decided to make their move. Before leaving Russia, Kyril sought the opinion of the Tsarina

Alexandra's confessor, Father Yanishev. The priest gave Kyril the answer he wanted to hear. Assured by Yanishev that there was no impediment to a marriage, Kyril left for Coburg to proceed with the wedding.

Originally, the wedding was to take place at the Duchess of Coburg's home on the Tegernsee, but at the last minute, the venue changed. The simple, quiet wedding took place on October 8, 1905, at the Tegernsee home of the duchess's friend Count Adlerberg. The religious ceremony was conducted by Father Smirov, the Duchess of Coburg's personal confessor, as no Russian priest would have risked incurring the tsar's wrath for performing the wedding. Besides the bride's mother and sister Bee, only Count Adlerberg, his housekeeper, and three other servants were in attendance. Marie Alexandrovna's brother Grand Duke Alexei was invited, though he was not privy to what was in store. Alexei arrived after the ceremony. Faced with a fait accompli, the grand duke took the news in stride and congratulated Ducky and Kyril. After a few days' honeymoon, Kyril returned to Russia to tell his parents, who took the news well. Not so the tsar.

In his letter to his mother about Kyril's marriage, Nicholas II described Kyril's return to Russia after the wedding as an act of insolence. "I have to say that such impudence made me very cross," wrote Nicholas, "impudence because he knew very well that he had no right to come *after the wedding*."[22] The tsar sent Count Fredericksz, the minister of the court, to inform Kyril and his parents of the punishment he was meting out.

Count Fredericksz arrived at the Vladimir Palace just as Kyril was set to play a game of bridge. The unsuspecting Kyril and his parents listened to Count Fredericksz's message, conveyed on behalf of the tsar, with incredulity. Nicholas II ordered Kyril dismissed from the navy and deprived him of his military rank, orders, and honors and stripped him of his title. The Vladimirs were struck dumb. They knew that Nicholas might have been angered by what Kyril had done, but they were stunned by the tsar's severity. When the issue of Kyril's proposed marriage to Ducky had been broached to Nicholas in the past, the tsar did not seem overly perturbed. But when it took place, his reaction clearly showed his fury. It was an unfair and overly harsh punishment. Evidently, the blessing Kyril extracted from the tsarina's confessor prior to the deed shows that Father Yanishev "may have been the confused victim of the persuasive young grand duke's enthusiasm."[23]

Kyril's father, Grand Duke Vladimir, was so enraged that he stormed the next day into Tsar Nicholas's study at Tsarskoe Selo and "shouted so violently at his nephew that the court chamberlain, waiting outside the door, feared for his master's safety and almost ran off to summon the imperial guards."[24] The grand duke would not accept Kyril's harsh punishment, even though Kyril was far from innocent. Though Grand Duke Vladimir conceded that Kyril's marrying a divorcée was not quite right, the severity of the punishment was simply uncalled for. Nicholas's calm demeanor and refusal to be cowed into submission infuriated the loud and temperamental Vladimir even more. In a final act of vehement objection, Vladimir smashed his fist on the tsar's desk in front of Nicholas, tore the decorations from his uniform, threw them on the floor, and slammed the door on his way out of the room.

Reports of the stormy interview made it all the way to America, with the *New York Times* telling its readers: "Recent reports" had it that "a violent scene" took place at Tsarskoe Selo. "The trouble was between Emperor Nicholas and the Grand Duke Vladimir and was relative to the Grand Duke Cyril [*sic*]."[25] Miechen's furious husband reputedly told his nephew, Nicholas II: "I have served your father, your grandfather and you. But now as you have degraded my son I no longer wish to serve you."[26]

The Vladimir clan attributed the retribution to Tsarina Alexandra's influence on her husband. Though Alexandra was highly displeased with the marriage, she was not vindictive. In the end, it was the tsar, not the tsarina, "who felt obliged to punish his cousin, following a precedent set by his father, and many other members of the family supported the action he took."[27]

Nevertheless, the Vladimirs' perception concerning Alexandra's supposed role deepened the chasm between the two families. Incensed by what they interpreted as Alexandra's meddling, the fury of Kyril's parents knew no bounds. Miechen would forever view the tsarina in the harshest light. "Indifference and veiled contempt" that had characterized the grand duchess's opinions of Alexandra turned into "abiding hatred."[28] Miechen never forgave Alexandra. "This did not mean," however, that Miechen "cut herself off from the Imperial Court, merely that her sharp tongue was more indefatigable than ever in tearing the Empress to shreds."[29] The tsar knew the incendiary impact his actions would elicit from his aunt and how he and Alexandra would look in her eyes. Nicholas II told his mother as much: "It would be interesting to know what Aunt Michen [*sic*] thinks? How she must have hated us!"[30]

In a lengthy letter to her uncle, Prince Henry Reuss, the Grand Duchess Vladimir tried to explain their side of the story in the whole sordid affair:

> *My dear Uncle,*
> *On Sunday 8th October (new style) Cyril [sic] got married to Victoria Melitta of Coburg. The wedding took place at Tegernsee and was*

celebrated by my sister-in-law's priest. The situation had become impossible and, since peace has come at last, Cyril [sic] was keeping his promise to wait till then. We have done all we could these last four years to hinder this marriage; but their love refused to be separated and so finally we considered it better for both Cyril's [sic] name and honour that the business should end with a wedding. We knew that the matter would not pass off very smoothly here, and were ready for some passing unpleasantness. But the blind vindictiveness and rage of the young Tsarina has, for sheer malice, exceeded everything the wildest imagination could conceive. She stormed and raged like a lunatic, dragging her weak husband along with her until he lent her his power and so made it possible for her to revenge herself on her ex-sister-in-law for marrying the man of her choice. The matter has been dealt with as though some terrible crime has been committed and judgment has been passed in this sense. Yet all these storms are directed against a Grand Duke, a war victim, a man who made a name for himself at Port Arthur, who has chosen an equal for his wife, and who, instead of deserting like the others, came here at once to take his punishment from the Tsar. It is too much that the son of the eldest uncle of the man who for the last twenty-five years has been the true and indefatigable head of the Army, who has saved the Tsar a hundred times, should be treated in this way at such a moment. One unanimous cry of indignation has been raised by all classes of the people. Vladimir has resigned as a protest at the indignity of the treatment meted out to his son. Even he, the truest of the true, says that he can no longer serve the Tsar with such anger against him in his heart. The troops are in a state of ferment at the loss of their beloved Chief, and I know the Tsar is being warned on all sides how dangerous it is to let his uncle go. That is why his answer has been delayed six days. But I do not think that Vladimir will consent to stay, even at the Tsar's request, unless our son is rehabilitated. What puts the last straw upon our patience is that Cyril [sic] came here with the Tsar's sanction to announce his marriage, and yet this very appearance here has now been made his chief offence. You, my dear uncle, will find this hard to believe; but, alas, here everything is possible; and when I add that this permission was given without the knowledge of the Empress, you will be able perhaps to form a just idea of the position here. This is how it was done: scarcely had Cyril [sic] arrived when the House Minister came with an order that he must leave Russia at once. The Tsarina wanted him to go that very night but that would only have been possible in a balloon. Then he was dismissed from the Fleet and the Army, he was to lose all uniforms and rank, to lose his regiment which was conferred on him at birth by his grandfather, to lose his appanage, his name, his title. He was to go in perpetual banishment. As far as his name was concerned the Tsar had to retract a few days later, since all the Ministers declared to him that this could simply not be done. And why all this? Because the Tsarina does not want her hated ex-sister-in-law in the family. All the other reasons given are mere formalities which could easily all have been arranged, since even if we did not desire this marriage there is nothing dishonourable about it. We have suffered much and still suffer, and in addition to it all I am worried about Vladimir's health. The Tsar knows that strong emotions are a danger to him. What does he care about that? Think of us.

Your Maria[31]

According to Prince von Bülow, who was privy to Miechen's confidences via Prince Henry Reuss, the whole affair that scandalized St. Petersburg "contributed in singular fashion towards making the Tsar appear a weakling, a man under his wife's thumb."[32]

In the end, the tsar decided to exercise some magnanimity. "I was having doubts about punishing a man publicly several times over, and at the present time; when people are generally ill-disposed towards the family," wrote Nicholas II to his mother. "After much reflection . . . I decided to use the occasion of your little grandson's nameday, and telegraphed Uncle Vladimir, saying that I was restoring Kyril's title. The other forms of punishment will, of course, remain in force."[33]

Kyril may have had his title restored by the tsar, but he was still banished from Russia in disgrace. He retreated to Ducky at Coburg where his mother-in-law, Marie Alexandrovna, also "flew into a rage against the injustice and stupidity of her imperial nephew."[34] The Duchess of Coburg supported Kyril and Ducky financially and emotionally. The couple went to live in Paris, but often visited the Duchess of Coburg. In the beginning of 1907, she was gratified to learn of Ducky's conversion to the Russian Orthodox faith. In relating the news to Missy, Marie Alexandrovna did not hesitate to bring a disappointing tone to her letter. "I had so hoped that you would also one day turn Orthodox," said the duchess, "especially on account of the children! But no, it is better so, as one must take it seriously and your life is not like that."[35] In January 1907, Ducky gave birth to a girl, Marie ("Masha"), to the Duchess of Coburg's delight.

In Russia, attempts at addressing the political tensions led to the replacement of the ineffective prime minister Ivan Goremykin by the more dynamic Peter Stolypin in July 1906. A visionary, the burly and energetic Stolypin set himself the task of trying to make Russia a great nation. In an attempt to defeat the terrorists, Stolypin sought to bring them to heel through special courts. Those found guilty were hanged. In no time, hundreds were executed. Nevertheless, terrorist killings of government officials still far outnumbered government executions. Stolypin also attempted to transform the country's agricultural system by promoting private ownership of land by the peasants. The tsar sanctioned Stolypin's plan and "proposed that four million acres of the crown lands be sold to the government, which in turn would sell them on easy terms to the peasants." Though Nicholas's mother and uncle Vladimir opposed the plan, the tsar went ahead and sold the land in the hope that the aristocracy would "follow his example. But none did so."[36]

Like other high government officials, Stolypin had his share of enemies. Scarcely a month after becoming prime minister, Stolypin was nearly killed when a powerful bomb exploded in his home while he was hosting a reception. The explosion was so huge that it tore off the façade of the house. It injured thirty-three people, including Stolypin's three-year-old son and killed twenty-eight, among them Stolypin's fifteen-year-old daughter. The scene at Stolypin's home was horrific. According to one report, "persons were literally blown to pieces. Those who were not killed instantly were horribly maimed or lacerated, and all the others present were prostrated by the shock."[37] The terrorist attack appalled the dowager empress, who wrote to Nicholas II, "When will these horrible crimes and revolting murders stop? There can be no peace or safety in Russia before these monsters are exterminated! . . . How awful it is for the poor parents to see the sufferings of their own innocent children! It is the mass of these innocent victims that revolts me so. I cannot find words strong enough to express my feelings!"[38]

The numerous assassination attempts never ceased to horrify Marie Feodorovna. The Duchess of Coburg, on the other hand, seemed almost inured to such incidents. This was in evidence in May 1906, when Marie Alexandrovna was on a visit to Madrid, a guest at the wedding of her niece Princess Victoria Eugenie of Battenberg to Spain's King Alfonso XIII. Wedding festivities were marred when a bomb exploded near the bridal carriage, killing numerous innocent victims. The bride and groom barely escaped with their lives. Victoria Eugenie was understandably unnerved by the horrendous act. She arrived at the Royal Palace with blood splattered on her bridal gown. The blood was not hers, but that of a guardsman who had been decapitated by the explosion. The newly married queen was composed but in obvious shock as she repeatedly muttered, "I saw a man without any legs." The guests were equally perturbed by what had happened. The Duchess of Coburg, on the other hand, took the news in stride, displaying a sangfroid that distinguished her from the rest. Her cousin, Princess Marie zu Erbach-Schönberg, recalled that Marie Alexandrovna "kept saying heavily," almost as a badge of honor, *"Je suis tellement accoutumée à ces choses* (I am so accustomed to these things)."[39]

Of all Miechen's sons, her favorite was Grand Duke Boris, despite his being "the least conscientious and the least regal, his behavior more resembling that of a newly rich merchant than a grand duke, determined only to have a good time."[40] Boris was an unapologetic "world class womanizer, absolutely unscrupulous . . . the terror of jealous husbands as well as of watchful mothers."[41] In fact, "of all the Romanovs, Boris was the one more likely to be shot by a husband than by an assassin."[42] Broad-shouldered, and sporting a "close-cut black moustache, turned up at the ends in the style affected by Emperor William of Germany," Boris cut a dashing figure, which he used to his advantage with women. After his romantic escapade with the Duchess of Coburg's daughter, Crown Princess Marie of Romania, Boris also fell for Missy's cousin, Victoria Eugenie of Battenberg—the same princess who married King Alfonso XIII of Spain. Boris's notoriety with women crossed the Atlantic during a visit to the United States where he left a "trail of chorus-girl slippers out of which he had quaffed his champagne."[43] Boris perpetuated his reputation as a carouser in New York City, where the grand duke said he liked the smell of the city air, saying that, "it's like champagne." True to form, it was the women of America Boris extolled. "What strikes me of greatest interest," chimed the grand duke, "is the beauty of the American women. They are a distinct type, and whenever I see a lovely woman anywhere in my tour around the globe, I will be sure that she was born in America."

While in New York, Boris and his entourage stayed in a suite of twelve rooms at the famed Waldorf-Astoria Hotel. Miechen's wayward son impressed Americans with his nearly impeccable English, spoken only with a slight accent. When he attended a play at the Knickerbocker Theatre, word spread among the cast that the Russian grand duke was watching from a balcony box. With that, the chorus girls "kicked higher than usual, and it was noticeable that all of their smiles were to the broad shoulders in the balcony box," unmistakably Boris's.[44] Miechen's son's reputation as a rake was so well known that it was the deciding factor in Mrs. Theodore Roosevelt's refusal to meet with him during his sojourn in the United States.

When Theodore Roosevelt visited Sweden, Crown Princess Margaretha (a niece of the Duchess of Coburg) asked whether there was any truth to the story about his wife's refusal to meet Boris. Roosevelt replied that "the Grand Duke in question had led a scandalous life in America, quite openly taking women whose character was not even questionable to public places, and behaving in restaurants and elsewhere so that the police would have been warranted in interfering." The Roosevelts were not at the White House when Boris requested his visit, but at their home Sagamore Hill in Oyster Bay, New York. Roosevelt felt obliged to receive Boris, but only very formally, to avoid giving the impression that he approved of the grand duke's dissolute life. In relating the story of Boris to the crown princess, Theodore Roosevelt explained that his wife, "who more than shared my feelings, and regarded his presence in our private house as both a scandal and an insult, said she intended to go out, as she saw no necessity why she should meet him, and her absence would emphasise the entirely formal character of the reception. Accordingly out she went." Boris and the Russian ambassador to the United States, who accompanied the grand duke to Sagamore Hill, keenly felt Mrs. Roosevelt's absence.

Upon hearing the story from Theodore Roosevelt himself, Crown Princess Margaretha could not resist telling her husband, who was in the same room at the time: "There! I was right. I told you that Mrs. Roosevelt would not meet him because of his [Boris's] conduct." Then turning to Roosevelt, Margaretha said: "I was so pleased that Mrs. Roosevelt would not meet him because my father and mother would never allow him to be presented to me, his conduct had been so disgraceful."[45]

Another scandal involving Boris took place when he struck a lady openly with his hand after she rebuffed his advances. Her brother, a young officer, in defense of his sister's honor, challenged Boris to a duel, which he accepted. They met the next day in the gardens of the island of Wassily Ostroff. According to one of the seconds, Boris and the young officer, who was clearly "nervous and unsteady," stood opposite each other. That Boris's challenger was unnerved is understandable, considering that the mere act of aiming at a grand duke with a pistol was a treasonable offense. The flamboyant Boris, in the meantime, "stood smiling, cool and unperturbed." The gentleman whose role it was to give the word to fire, "purposely fussed and delayed, to give the younger man time to break down and withdraw; he had himself in hand, however, and when at last the word was given he fired quickly."

The bullet missed. Then, in dramatic fashion, Boris "deliberately discharged his bullet into the ground before him. The challenger was not equal to a second shot, and there the matter ended, and before night St. Petersburg knew that the choicest rake in Russia, the most remorseless and unsoftened pirate of society, had played a small part as a gentleman." According to the chronicler of the story, so audacious and uncharacteristically selfless did Boris appear in the duel that "St. Petersburg was not willing to believe it." Nevertheless, as "the most notorious of the cousins of the Czar," Boris's action that day on the Wassily Ostroff was, as of 1905, "the only chivalrous action recorded of him."[46]

Miechen's sons, Boris, Andrei, and Kyril, contributed to the impression that Russia's grand dukes were bent on flouting strict dynastic rules and leading a hedonistic life. Marie Feodorovna's daughter Olga touched upon their impact on the monarchy's prestige, confessing that "too many of us Romanovs had, as it were, gone to live in a world of self-interest where little mattered except the unending gratification of personal desire and ambition. Nothing proved it better than the appalling marital mess in which the last generation of my family involved themselves. That chain of domestic scandals could not but shock the nation—but did any of them care for the impression they created? Never."[47]

The romantic escapades of the Romanovs continued to provide fodder for gossip. After the scandal of Ducky and Kyril's marriage, another Romanov marriage rocked senior family members. Princess Anastasia of Montenegro, known as "Stana," divorced her husband of fifteen years, Duke George von Leuchtenberg. Six months later Stana abruptly married Grand Duke Nicholas Nikolaevich in 1907. The appearance of another divorcée in the family did not sit well with the dowager empress. Her daughter Xenia confided in her diary that "Mama is beside herself—and so upset that she had to take tranquillizing drops."[48]

Appalled as she was over Stana and Nikolasha's marriage, Marie Feodorovna's anger redoubled with the fury she felt over her own son Michael's continuing romance with the lady-in-waiting Dina Kossikovskaya. Nicholas II refused to give his consent to a marriage between the two. Writing to the dowager empress about the situation, the tsar told Marie Feodorovna: "I share your sorrow with all my heart, my dear Mama, and am myself deeply grieved and anxious about what may follow! . . . Do help me, dear Mama, to restrain him!"[49]

Marie Feodorovna was just as anxious as Nicholas and told him that Michael's letter to her explaining his wish to marry Dina "made me *quite miserable* . . . I try appealing to his sense of duty, his duty to his country, his obligations, etc. etc. . . . You must realise and understand what this new tormenting sorrow means to me—day and night I worry over it! And to think this should be added to all our other miseries!"[50]

18

A DELUSORY WORLD

In the summer and fall of 1906, Russia again descended into near chaos. Reports from British officials attest to this. Viscount Crawley recorded that "letters from the Caucasus describe a deplorable condition of affairs" with kidnappings for ransom, murders and strikes rampant. Crawley added that "unrest and anarchy are almost universal" in Russia.[1] Another report noted that famine was "raging" in the Volga region where "half of the province is starving" as a result of over 800,000 acres of crops perishing. People were "dying in the streets of starvation" and the government authorities "are apparently without funds, and powerless to deal with the situations." Moreover, "the financial condition of the country is deplorable. Everybody who is able to realize is sending their money out of the country."[2] Cecil Spring Rice, secretary at the British embassy, wrote to the foreign secretary, Sir Edward Grey, in London that "the temper of the workmen both here [St. Petersburg] and in Moscow is reported to be menacing. There is undoubtedly a general feeling of alarm."[3]

The British consul in Riga discussed the lawlessness in the Baltic provinces: "The state of affairs in these provinces is decidedly growing from bad to worse . . . The Baltic provinces are paralyzed. The revolutionists, or rather the bands of scoundrels which infest the forests, are keeping the whole country in such a state of terrorism that nobody seems to know what to expect next. The farmers & peasants who, under ordinary circumstances, would now be hard at it with the autumn ploughings & sowings, hardly dare move from their homes."[4]

In order to counter disturbances, the tsarist government continued to crack down, to the point that more than two thousand civilians were executed "by sentence of ordinary courts-martial during 1905–08. In the year following the October Manifesto, 7,000 persons (according to official figures) were fined, 2,000 expelled from regions under exceptional law, and 21,000 banished to distant provinces—all by administrative fiat. Such violations of due process seemed justified as a matter of self-preservation to a government which reckoned that more than 4,000 of its servants, from policemen to governors, had been killed or wounded in 1906 and 1907.[5] The British ambassador to Russia, Sir Arthur Nicolson, told Sir Edward Grey that "the peasants were animated with hostility against the upper classes, Governmental or others." Relaying the impressions of a source who had visited the provinces, Nicolson noted that "this informant told me that the peasants in his district openly said that they were convinced that the Czar now was aware of their desires, and if he did not satisfy them they would dispense with the Romanoffs and elect others in their place."[6] In a similar vein, Cecil Spring Rice reported that "the Emperor, shut up in his palace, is unapproachable except on rare occasions . . . But now, it is said, the country has spoken, and the Emperor can hear its voice through its chosen representatives. If he now neglects their advice and refuses their petition, then it can no longer be said that his actions are due to ignorance and want of proper counsellors. And when such statements are spread abroad through the country the effect cannot fail to be disastrous to the Imperial prestige, and possibly to the continuance of the autocratic régime."[7]

With the empire in such fierce ferment, there was no denying that "in few countries was belief in the possibility of revolution as widely held, in fear or hope, as in Russia" in the beginning of the twentieth century.[8] Though peaceful spells sometimes descended upon the turbulent landscape of the tsarist empire, a revolutionary spirit had clearly taken hold of the masses like never before.

While Russia continued to shift precariously between bouts of violence, the Romanov dynasty showed little sign of shedding the splendors for which it had been renowned. The family resided and entertained as always amidst the grandeur of some of the world's most beautiful palaces: the Winter Palace, Peterhof, the Anichkov Palace, Pavlovsk, the Vladimir Palace, and the Alexander palace at Tsarskoe Selo. Both the Anichkov and Vladimir Palaces continued to impress visitors with their exquisite décor. Queen Olga's daughter Marie recalled that the dowager empress's rooms at the Anichkov "were filled with beautiful pictures and wonderful objets d'art."[9] To observers and visitors alike, there was no doubt that the Russian imperial court was still the most opulent in all Europe; for "even in the rarefied world of contemporary European royalty few, if any, could surpass the gilt-encrusted fairy-tale kingdom of imperial Russia where luxury and opulence were the bywords of the Romanov dynasty."[10]

The heart of the Russian Empire was now at Tsarskoe Selo, where Nicholas and Alexandra had retreated from St. Petersburg. No longer were the Winter, Gatchina, or Anichkov Palaces the nerve centers of imperial Russia, as during Marie Feodorovna's heyday decades ago. Amidst the beautiful enclave of Tsarskoe Selo, with its lakes and lush lawns dotted with statuary, Nicholas and Alexandra decided to make the multi-colonnaded neoclassical Alexander Palace their permanent home. As befitting a granddaughter of Queen Victoria, Tsarina Alexandra decorated her private quarters in English chintzes. Her favorite room was the Mauve Boudoir, decorated in shades of her favorite color. From there, Alexandra rested, wrote letters, played with her children, sewed, entertained intimate friends, and isolated herself from nearly all the Romanovs, especially her mother-in-law, Marie Feodorovna, and her aunt, Marie Pavlovna.

After years in Russia, Alexandra still felt uncomfortable in her role and could not relax her rigid façade. Queen Olga of Greece's daughter Marie noticed this when she married into the imperial family and came to know Alexandra. The tsarina, Marie concluded, "was rather silent" and also "extremely shy and self-conscious." Moreover, "she was over sensitive, and in a way haunted by the notion that she was unpopular and unloved," persisting in "this fixed idea even with members of the family."[11] Even so, Alexandra was a loving wife and mother, completely devoted to her immediate family. She could be amusing among her intimates, but she could never shake off her reserve outside this intimate circle. The dowager empress, on the other hand, continued to stand in stark contrast to the tsarina. Marie, who discovered a second mother in Marie Feodorovna, extolled the dowager empress's virtues. "Aunt Minny was not very tall," recalled Queen Olga's daughter, "but she held herself in such a way that she could never have been taken for anything but a[n] Empress." She had "a personal charm that captivated every one she met." Marie concluded that "Aunt Minny was really human, like all the Danish family, and consequently was most popular and beloved in her adopted country."[12]

Much to Marie Feodorovna's chagrin, Alexandra continued to care nothing for St. Petersburg society, refusing to try to understand, let alone accommodate, its members. Tsarskoe Selo was an escape from the gossip of the capital. As the years passed, Alexandra's increasingly frail health gave her even more excuses to stay away from St Petersburg. Above all, the specter of hemophilia consumed Alexandra, who wished to keep her precious son, Alexei, away from prying eyes. And so, the secret of the tsarevich's disease "was hidden and carefully guarded within the inner world of Tsarskoe Selo,"[13] the Russian people kept in ignorance of the heir's fragile health.

Tsarina Alexandra's pride and joy was Alexei Nikolaevich, whom she referred to as "my sunbeam."[14] This frail child represented the future of imperial Russia. As it happened, Marie Feodorovna's hemophiliac grandson was an especially delightful child. The imperial children's Swiss-born French language tutor, Pierre Gilliard, recalled meeting Alexei for the first time when the boy was eighteen months old, noting that the tsarevich was "certainly one of the handsomest babies one could imagine, with his lovely fair curls and his great blue-grey eyes under their fringe of long curling lashes. He had the fresh pink colour of a healthy child, and when he smiled there were two little dimples in his chubby cheeks." Gilliard also noticed that the tsarina pressed "the little boy to her with the convulsive movement of a mother who always seems in fear of her child's life." The look on Alexandra's face "revealed a secret apprehension so marked and poignant that I was struck at once," recalled Gilliard.[15]

Simultaneously adored and pitied by those who knew him well, Alexei led a difficult life from the start due to his hemophilia. As a lively child he was bound to get into scrapes and falls. When this happened, the fretful watch began. Even the smallest bump could precipitate an agonizing hemophilia attack that might lead to death. As a hemophiliac, Alexei's blood did not clot as does a normal person's. Instead, his blood flowed "unchecked for hours, making a swelling or hematoma as big as a grapefruit." Sometimes, when the bleeding occurred in the joints, excruciating pain ensued. Moreover, the blood had the effect of destroying tissue, cartilage, and bones. Thus, "as the bone formation changed, the limbs locked in a rigid, bent position." What made all this all the more tormenting was the fact that because morphine had a "habit-forming quality, the Tsarevich was never given the drug. His only release from pain was fainting."[16] Whenever these hemophilia attacks occurred, all distraught onlookers, and most poignantly his mother, could only watch helplessly.

To the tsarina, only God could offer solace. Having committed herself to Orthodoxy, Alexandra was now a fervent adherent. The faith, rich in its external practices and infused with pervasive mysticism, appealed to the tsarina's sensitive soul. The impressions of a visitor to Russia at the time provide a window into Alexandra's devotion. Orthodox services were "extremely beautiful," with "that peculiar Russian chant" having an ability "to carry one away into another world—a dream world full of mystic ideals."[17] Bitter acknowledgment of Alexei's hemophilia reinforced Tsarina Alexandra reliance on her faith.

Despite being burdened with his debilitating disease, the tsarevich grew into a charming boy, who was caring, considerate, and "endowed with a naturally happy disposition." Alexei, the center of his close-knit family, remained the "focus of all its hopes and affections . . . his parents' pride and joy. When he was well the palace was, as it were, transformed. Everyone and everything seemed bathed in sunshine."[18]

In constant jeopardy, Alexei was raised in a constricted manner. Two burly sailors from the imperial navy acted as his bodyguards, constantly on watch to keep the tsarevich from getting hurt. Understandably, Alexei longed to get away from his sailor nurses, eventually attempting to escape "and running into his sisters' schoolroom, from which he was soon fetched."[19] Alexei's sisters were very fond of their only brother, the baby of the family, on whom they lavished much attention. Olga, Tatiana, Marie, and Anastasia—"OTMA" as the girls collectively referred to themselves—may have been raised as a unified group, but their individuality also easily shown through to family intimates such as Pierre Gilliard. The eldest girl, Olga Nikolaevna, blue-eyed with chestnut-brown hair, a wide forehead, and a small nose, was the most intellectual of the siblings. Olga loved to read and was very musical, being a fine singer and instrumentalist. Gilliard found that Grand Duchess Olga "possessed a remarkably quick brain" that "picked up everything extremely quickly."[20] Tatiana Nikolaevna, eighteen months younger than Olga, was the most reserved of the sisters. With her dark hair, pale skin, and brown eyes, Tatiana, according to Baroness Buxhoeveden, had "a poetic far-away look" and "fine" features that recalled "pictures of ancestresses who had been famous beauties."[21] The next shared her grandmother's name, Marie. Grand Duchess Marie Nikolaevna had a talent for drawing like her grandmother. Pretty, with brown hair and gold highlights, Marie Nikolaevna's greatest features were her large, expressive blue-gray eyes. "Her tastes," recalled Pierre Gilliard, "were very simple, and with her warm heart she was kindness itself." Marie's sisters took advantage of this good nature and called her "fat little bow-wow."[22] Anastasia Nikolaevna, destined to be the most famous of Marie Feodorovna's grandchildren, was the least attractive of the four sisters. What Anastasia lacked in looks, however, she made up for in personality. Impish, with a wicked sense of humor, Grand Duchess Anastasia was "the originator of all mischief, and was as witty and amusing as she was lazy at her lessons."[23] Often the "source of much despair" to her tutors, Anastasia was "hopelessly stubborn, delightfully impertinent, and in general a perfect *enfant terrible*"—so thought Gleb Botkin, the children's playmate and son of the imperial physician, Dr. Eugene Botkin.[24]

Marie Feodorovna's granddaughters often dressed alike, sometimes in simple frocks with matching hats, at other times in more delicately executed confections of white. Though they lived privileged lives, Olga, Tatiana, Marie, and Anastasia had unassuming tastes and were raised simply. They slept on uncomfortable camp beds, often shared belongings, and received very modest allowances. From this meager pocket change, the girls purchased small gifts for their family and retainers. Intensely Russian to the core and sequestered at Tsarskoe Selo, the grand duchesses were rarely exposed to outside influences, including other children. Sometimes they saw Marie Feodorovna's other grandchildren, Xenia's seven children. Overall, Nicholas and Alexandra, in their insular fashion, thought it sufficient that the four girls grow up together and be content in each other's company.

Frosty relations between the dowager empress and their mother kept the children from becoming truly close to their paternal grandmother. Nevertheless, in time the grand duchesses visited Marie Feodorovna on almost a weekly basis, when their mother allowed her growing daughters the chance to escape for the day from the Alexander Palace. In the charge of their aunt, Grand Duchess Olga, whom they saw as a kind of elder sister, the girls left Tsarskoe Selo by train each Sunday and arrived at the imperial capital for an early lunch with their grandmother at the Anichkov Palace. These lunches were formal; consequently, the girls and their aunt Olga (who, like the tsar and her father Alexander III, preferred simplicity) were always relieved when they were over. From the Anichkov, the five then proceeded to the Grand Duchess Olga's home where they enjoyed tea, dancing, and lighthearted games. Olga ensured that some young people were invited as well, so that her sheltered nieces could revel in the company of others their own age. These delightful Sunday gatherings at Olga Alexandrovna's home ended promptly at ten in the evening when the grand duchesses were fetched by a lady-in-waiting and returned to the Alexander Palace at Tsarskoe Selo.

Marie Feodorovna had not been to London for three decades, but in 1907 she paid a visit to her sister Queen Alexandra. The dowager empress delighted in visiting her sister and spent the forty-forth wedding anniversary of Queen Alexandra and King Edward VII with them at Windsor Castle. The visit had raised the dowager empress's spirits. She wrote to the tsar of her stay in England, telling him, "in thoughts I am always with you, my dear Nicky, I do wish you too could come over here a little to breathe another air and live for a while in different surroundings—*how good* for you that would be! I myself already feel as if I were a different person, and *twenty years* younger!"[25]

Marie Feodorovna journeyed to the fashionable French resort of Biarritz on the Atlantic coast too, where she was reunited with her daughters Xenia and Olga. Grand Duchess Olga prided herself in being able to travel in simpler style and was amused to find her sister arrive with her entire family and a huge entourage, which necessitated the renting of an enormous villa. Olga's entourage consisted of a "mere" thirty people. The Dowager Empress Marie Feodorovna traveled in true imperial style, with an impressive retinue of two hundred retainers. She journeyed in a luxurious train that "roused a sensation when it arrived at Biarritz, and the crowds watched fascinated as an army of colorful Russian servants and body-guards poured out of it."[26]

With so many family members and King Edward VII at Biarritz, Marie Feodorovna could not resist injecting her brand of gaiety when she met with society. Her son-in-law Sandro deferred to her because of her position and age, but he also considered Marie Feodorovna as his "pal and associate when it came to going out to a party or arranging a party."[27] She was great company, as those who had the good fortune to spend time with her always attested.

Not far from Biarritz was France's other famed resort, the French Riviera. In the early twentieth century, the French Riviera was still "the favorite playground of the Romanovs."[28] Russia's revolutionary fever was not sufficient to convince the Romanovs to retreat and embrace moderation, as Miechen and her husband's lifestyle demonstrated. While grand style at the Vladimir Palace continued, they still traveled regularly to France, with the Riviera an especially favorite destination. Miechen also liked to frequent the casinos of Monte Carlo. When the Romanovs vacationed abroad, accompanied by their retinues, they were welcomed by eager hoteliers, restauranteurs, and shopkeepers. The imperial guests would descend upon the finest hotels, pay for a large number of rooms and suites, rent villas, shop for bibelots, carouse at the most expensive restaurants, and tip lavishly. Grand Duke Vladimir, the "grand seigneur of Russia," as Sandro called him, simultaneously terrified and pleased the chefs and waiters of the Ville Lumière, where in his loud, censorious way, Vladimir complained about the menu.[29] When it came time to leave, the grand duke then lavished those who worked at the establishment with generous tips.

As Grand Duke Vladimir aged, he looked more and more like his late father, Alexander II. Still a great patron of the arts, the grand duke was president of the Imperial Academy of Art. Vladimir made many purchases at the St. Petersburg World of Art exhibitions (1899–1906). The World of Art founders included the painter and stage and costume designer Léon Bakst, from whom the Vladimir children had taken art lessons, and the impresario Serge Diaghilev, famous as the founder and director of the Ballets Russes. Diaghilev, whose original financial patron was Vladimir, had the highest praise for Miechen's husband, whom he described as "a highly cultivated man who thought no sacrifice too great in the cause of art, and he played a very important part in the development of Russian culture. All the artistic institutions of the country were placed under his control and he directed, inspired, and encouraged art in a great variety of forms."[30]

Tsar Nicholas too encouraged the flourishing of art. Thanks to his patronage (and that of other Romanovs), the most unusual, well-known artistic objects associated with imperial Russia and the Romanovs are undoubtedly the Fabergé eggs, which still dazzle the eye and command outstanding prices at auctions. Tsar Nicholas perpetuated his father's tradition of presenting bejeweled Fabergé eggs to his wife and mother. Father and son gave a total of fifty of these Fabergé eggs during the span of both reigns, during which the imperial Easter eggs became increasingly exquisite and elaborate, a far cry from the simple yet ingenious first egg that Alexander III had presented to his wife in 1885. Among the most exquisite was the Gatchina Palace Egg that Nicholas presented to his mother. Created to commemorate Gatchina, Alexander III's favorite home, the egg was crafted from diamonds, gold, and enamel. Inside was a gold replica of Gatchina. Another beautiful gift from the tsar to his mother was the Peacock Egg. The bejeweled creation made from rock crystal contained an enamel peacock studded with precious stones.

That Tsar Nicholas II continued to order Fabergé eggs for his wife and mother as the twentieth century progressed was another sign that the Romanovs were living in a delusory world. The chaos and revolutionary fever that inflamed Russia in 1905 did nothing to prevent the Romanovs' extravagance. Nor did events extinguish their hopes for the future as evidenced by the building of a new palace at Livadia. Enamored of the buildings they had seen in Italy during an official visit to King Victor Emmanuel III, Nicholas and Alexandra embarked on the creation of an Italianate-style home in the Crimea. Begun in 1909, the new Livadia Palace was an impressive edifice built of white granite. The imperial family envisioned it as a home for successive generations of Romanovs for many years to come, whenever they might journey to this favored part of the empire.

Nonetheless, despite the privilege, the palaces and opulent objets d'art that surrounded them, there was no denying the fear and sorrow that permeated the lives of the Romanovs—and the Dowager Empress Marie Feodorovna was no exception to this. Constant threat from the Nihilists meant that Marie Feodorovna was always fearful that her son Nicholas II might suffer the same fate as his grandfather. Marie Feodorovna could never forget the sight of her father-in-law, Alexander II, horribly and mortally wounded, dying at the hands of terrorists, right before her eyes. Sorrow for her dead husband and children also cast a long shadow in the dowager empress's life. She deeply regretted Nicholas and Alexandra's unpopularity, which she attributed to her daughter-in-law's reserve. Then there was the never-ending anxiety over Tsarevich Alexei's health. Added to this were the disintegrating marriages of her daughters Xenia and Olga. Olga continued to live unhappily with Prince Peter, who still would not allow for a divorce; he seemed almost to relish Olga's frustrated relationship with the devoted commoner Nikolai Kulikovsky, while all three lived under the same roof. Xenia, meanwhile, saw her marriage failing as she and Sandro fell out of love. Xenia and Sandro found themselves drifting into the arms of others, even though they maintained a façade of a united family for the sake of their children. Of Marie Feodorovna's married children, only Nicholas II's marriage remained intact. Even the tragedy of hemophilia did not destroy Nicholas and Alexandra's enduring love for each other. Theirs was a marriage that was rare in royal circles, like that of Marie Feodorovna and Alexander III—a happy union.

The dowager empress's younger son, Michael, was the only one of Marie Feodorovna's children to remain single, a status he tried to change by attempting to marry Dina Kossikovskaya abroad. The imperial family, however, were on Michael's trail and sent the *Okhrana* to foil the union. They apprehended Dina in Odessa before she could leave Russia. Michael finally capitulated to pressure from his mother and brother and gave up Dina, who eventually left Russia for a life in exile. But if the dowager empress thought that her son's romantic escapades had finally ended, she was mistaken. For before the year ended, a new, more glamorous woman entered Grand Duke Michael's life. To Marie Feodorovna's consternation, Michael soon fell for the beautiful divorcée Natalia Wulfert.

19

DISCORD

*G*rand Duke Michael first met Natalia Wulfert at the end of 1907, around the time that Dina Kossikovskaya left Russia for good. Natalia, or Natasha, as she was more commonly known, was the daughter of a Moscow lawyer. With her first husband, Sergei Mamontov, who worked for the Bolshoi Theatre, she had a daughter, Natalia ("Tata"), but even having Tata was not enough to keep the restless Madame Mamontov from staying married. After Natasha and Mamontov divorced, she married Captain Vladimir Wulfert, an officer with the elite Blue Cuirassiers.

The Wulferts settled in the city of Gatchina, where Natasha's husband was stationed. Though Gatchina's hostesses were reluctant to invite a divorcée to their homes, plenty of eager young officers flocked to the Wulfert home—the main attraction being the willowy Natasha. Though "Wulfert might be said to have stolen her from her first husband," these young officers who "sipped their wine in the candlelight" of the Wulfert home, "looked across the polished table, [and] the thought occurred that many men would have done exactly that, had they had the same opportunity."[1]

At the time Grand Duke Michael met Natasha, she was twenty-seven years old, a year and a half younger than he. She stood five feet six inches tall, "slender, fair-haired and possessed of deep-set velvety blue eyes which once seen would be rarely forgotten."[2] Dmitri Abrikossov, an early suitor, had been so captivated by her most distinguishing feature that he admitted: "I must confess I have never forgotten Nathalie with her sad eyes."[3] Grand Duke Michael too was struck by Natasha Wulfert's "sad eyes." For him, it had been love at first sight. Michael would later tell Natasha: "I so tenderly remember . . . that afternoon in the riding school when for the first time I saw and asked 'who's that lady?' and then finally had the courage to come up and be introduced to that unknown lady."[4] Tata soon became accustomed to seeing Grand Duke Michael, who became part of her mother's life. Years later, Tata recalled that as a very young child, she found that Michael assumed "the proportions of a legendary figure, rather like St. George with his dragon."[5] She also met Marie Feodorovna's daughter Olga, whom Tata found to be "a very charming, simple woman." Always accompanying Olga was Captain Nikolai Kulikovsky, whom Tata grew fond of because "he used to be a marvel at mending toys."[6]

As his feelings for Natasha Wulfert grew stronger, Michael knew that he would face his brother's objections and most assuredly his mother's wrath. The dowager empress vehemently opposed Grand Duke Michael's latest infatuation. Having successfully averted a scandal by keeping Michael from marrying Dina, Marie Feodorovna hoped that she could effect the same result with the once divorced and currently married Madame Wulfert.

The dowager empress would discover that Michael was much more intransigent this time. By 1909, the couple was deeply in love. In a letter to Natasha, Michael wrote of his happiness: "Your love for me is such joy and I trust you so—it is great happiness. Believe me that I love you infinitely . . . I am so happy, despite all the hard experiences one has to suffer now."[7]

In the meantime, Grand Duke Michael's former love, Bee, tried to put her romance with Michael behind her. The Duchess of Coburg took Bee with her to Madrid in 1906 to attend the wedding of the duchess's niece Princess Victoria Eugenie of Battenberg to Spain's King Alfonso XIII. At a celebratory ball, Bee's uncle, Grand Duke Vladimir, introduced her to the Infante Alfonso ("Ali") of Orleans, the king of Spain's cousin. Part Spanish and part French, Ali was the son of the Infanta Eulalia who so enjoyed visiting Marie Feodorovna at Hvidovre. Known as the black sheep of the Spanish royal family, progressive-thinking Eulalia was something of a radical. In her 1911 book, *The Thread of Life*, Eulalia railed against "very nearly every convention that royalty is brought up to respect," including the right for women to divorce. "Could a Spanish Princess," asked the *New York Times*, in its review of the book, "wave the red flag of revolution more vigorously?"[8] Such was the colorful character of Ali's mother.

At the wedding ball, the tall, blond Ali, who was two years Bee's junior, was smitten with the attractive dark-haired princess. He asked Bee to dance and while they were on the dance floor Ali stunned her when he proposed: "Princess, will you marry me?"[9] A romance did not immediately blossom, but the couple met again. Marie Alexandrovna liked Bee's new suitor, who besides his illustrious pedigree, was also well educated and cultured. Writing to Missy, the Duchess of Coburg told her that "Ali is very cosmopolitan and really I cannot determine which nationality he really belongs [to] . . . The father [Ali's] spent his money in a scandalous manner and Eulalia . . . well, everyone knows how she is. I believe that she will not oppose [a match] and will be very content to see her son established." Marie Alexandrovna added that Ali implied a money problem with his father, making her fear that Ali was not rich. "It is a serious question," wrote the duchess, "because I cannot give to Baby [Bee] more than you [girls]" received in terms of money.[10] Bee's only real concern about a potential marriage was the religious issue, since she was determined not to convert to Roman Catholicism. She was allowed to stay a Protestant with the agreement to raise any future children as Catholics. The couple became engaged in 1907, to Marie Alexandrovna's satisfaction, for here was a young man able to counter her daughter's volatile character. Of her future son-in-law, the Duchess of Coburg wrote: "He is the type of man who will know how to tame and dominate her . . . she has accepted him freely, of her own free will."[11]

To the Duchess of Coburg's consternation, the Spanish court sent no official announcements regarding the engagement. The Spanish government raised objections to the fact that Bee refused to convert to Catholicism. Her cousin Queen Victoria Eugenie had converted, and the Spaniards expected nothing less from a princess who was to marry an infante of Spain. In May 1908, the Duchess of Coburg wrote from the Château Fabron to Missy, expressing her "great preoccupation" with Bee's situation, since "nothing has advanced." Marie Alexandrovna also railed against "so much dishonesty and false games," and complained that she and Bee did not know where to go "to ask for help and advice."[12]

When in January 1909 the Duchess of Coburg learned that Bee's future mother-in-law planned to visit Coburg, a stupefied Marie Alexandrovna wrote to Missy: "Who would have thought that Eulalia would be staying under my roof?" The normally staid and upright Duchess of Coburg found the colorful Infanta Eulalia "very funny narrating about her past and present friendships . . . She tries to love Bee and always speaks of the future grandchildren" in front of Bee and Ali. The duchess also told Missy that Eulalia "eats a lot" and the infanta's active digestion interrupts her bridge game and other pastimes. After getting to know Eulalia, the Duchess of Coburg concluded: "What an original creature!"[13]

The prolonged engagement continued with no wedding in sight. Ali, serving as an officer, was sent to Morocco in 1909 to fight in a war in which Spain had become embroiled. The Duchess of Coburg was furious. She fired off a telegram to Eulalia: "Letter received, how can there be a question of a marriage when Alfonso [XIII] sends Ali to die in Morocco. My indignation knows no bounds."[14] The Duchess of Coburg sent similar missives to King Alfonso. In a message that Queen Maria Cristina of Spain passed on to her son the king, the Duchess of Coburg fulminated about "how cruel" it was to send Ali off "to Morocco!" Marie Alexandrovna claimed that "Alfonso wants" to "get rid of Ali so as to avoid the wedding [taking place]." "I have suffered enough in silence these two years," added the duchess, but she could remain silent no longer with her daughter's happiness hanging in the balance. An exasperated King Alfonso finally replied to the duchess: "I believe that it is better, dear aunt, that you not telegraph me. When I make a decision I do not allow discussion and I am not accustomed to giving explanations. I deplore the circumstances that have forced me to take this decision."[15]

To Marie Alexandrovna's satisfaction, Bee and Ali finally married in July 1909 after waiting twenty long months, but without Alfonso XIII's permission. The king was compelled to strip Ali of the dignity and honors accorded to an infante of Spain. The couple was barred from living in Spain. In August 1909, the Grand Duchess Vladimir paid a visit to King Alfonso and Queen Victoria Eugenie at their summer palace of Miramar in San Sebastián. Miechen was accompanied by her son Boris who had courted Victoria Eugenie years before. In the course of the visit, Miechen broached the subject of her niece Bee. The grand duchess blamed her sister-in-law Marie Alexandrovna for forcing the wedding. Miechen, who was also Eulalia's friend, went on to defend the groom's desire to marry, saying that Ali could not "be blamed, a youngster of twenty-two very much in love with his girl . . . they offer him to marry her that same day, he could not refuse!"[16]

Back in Russia, Miechen continued to play the rival to the Tsarina Alexandra. It was a role Alexandra ceded, since she much preferred living quietly at Tsarskoe Selo. There, the tsarina contented herself with her family and a few close friends such as Anna Tanaeva, who married Alexander Viroubov and became Anna Viroubova in 1907. Yet, the marriage was unhappy and dissolved after a year. From then onward, Anna was even closer to Alexandra and her family, becoming almost like another daughter to the tsarina. Unassuming, unsophisticated and sentimental, Anna Viroubova was precisely the type of person who appealed to Marie Feodorovna's daughter-in-law. Both Alexandra and Anna shared a keen interest in mysticism and a belief in Gregory Rasputin as a "holy man." Rasputin continued to represent himself as a *staretz*, an ascetic religious guide to help others in their struggles in life. His knowledge of sacred scriptures and other such demonstrations of his role as a conduit to God convinced many that he was a genuine man of faith. To his supporters, he could do no wrong. Even his acceptance of the name "Rasputin," meaning "dissolute," was a "touching symbol of his humility."[17] However, Rasputin was not a genuine *staretz*, not an ascetic who eschewed sin, because he continually indulged himself in temptations of the flesh.

Rasputin's debauched escapades brought him notoriety. Hostility against the dissolute *staretz* grew among some Russian Orthodox Church members. Alarm also mounted among Duma members, government officials, police, and the press as people worried about Rasputin's familiarity with the tsar and tsarina. Many could not fathom why the tsarina was so enthralled with the unkempt, infamous peasant from Siberia.

Rasputin possessed one physical characteristic that many spoke of as a source of the man's "power" and fascination—his mesmerizing eyes. Count Bohdan de Castellane, who knew Rasputin, found the peasant to have "rather an ugly face on account of his large, red, and somewhat bulbous nose, but his eyes were most remarkable. They were small and of a vivid emerald green, sunk so deeply that the whites did not show at all, producing a most extraordinary effect."[18] Rasputin frequently tried to overwhelm people with his piercing gaze, which seemed to be accompanied by spellbinding powers.

Even Peter Stolypin nearly succumbed to Rasputin's attempt to overpower him. "He ran his pale eyes over," recalled Stolypin, and "mumbled mysterious and inarticulate words from the Scriptures, made strange movements with his hands, and I began to feel an indescribable loathing for this vermin sitting opposite me." Though repulsed by Rasputin, Stolypin still felt a kind of hypnotic power emanating from the *staretz*. Stolypin finally fought off Rasputin: "I pulled myself together and addressing him roughly . . . ordered him to leave St. Petersburg immediately of his own free will for his native village and never show his face here again."[19] After this encounter with Stolypin, Rasputin left the capital for a while, although he eventually resurfaced.

Beyond Rasputin's penetrating gaze and hypnotic powers, there were other unexplained "gifts." "I have seen myself," recalled Count de Castellane of Rasputin, "how he could reduce fever by simply laying his hand on the sufferer's head." And besides this, "he could also read one's thought." De Castellane added that he felt prejudiced against Rasputin when he first knew him and "often, with a smile" Rasputin would say to de Castellane "absolutely in answer" to the count's "unspoken thought": "I am not such a bad man as you think."[20] Lili Dehn, a close friend of Tsarina Alexandra, had the same impressions of Rasputin as de Castellane did. Dehn did not wish to meet Rasputin, but when she eventually did, Lili admitted that "his eyes held mine, those shining steel-like eyes which seemed to read one's inmost thoughts." Lili also echoed de Castellane's observation about Rasputin's "curing" abilities. When Lili's young son was seriously ill, she reluctantly took Anna Viroubova's advice to have Rasputin pray over the boy. He did so, telling Lili emphatically: "Tomorrow thy child will be well."[21] True to Rasputin's word, the child's symptoms and fever disappeared the next day. Soon enough, the boy was well, leaving his doctor baffled.

Count Bohdan de Castellane and Lili Dehn were not the only ones struck by Rasputin's singular ability to "cure." Tsarina Alexandra became a convinced adherent, thus ensuring Rasputin's indispensability. Her dependency was, of course, tied to his astounding ability to help her ill son, Alexei. When the director of the imperial theaters, V. A. Telyakovksy, asked a friend about the mysterious peasant, the friend replied with an anecdote about Rasputin and his ability to help Alexei: "He's a strange one. He was taken to the bedside of the tsarevich . . . The child looked at him and began to bubble with laughter. Rasputin laughed too. He laid his hand on the boy's leg and the bleeding stopped at once. 'There's a good boy,' said Rasputin. 'You'll be alright. But only God can tell what will happen tomorrow.'" Even the imperial surgeon, Professor S. P. Fedorov, was at a loss for words in explaining Rasputin and his "healing" abilities with Alexei. "And look, Rasputin would come in," noted the doctor, "walk up to the patient, look at him and spit. The bleeding would stop in no time . . . How could the empress not trust Rasputin after that?"[22]

Rasputin's unexplained ability to heal the hemophiliac Alexei even played itself out from afar. In 1908, the five-year-old Alexei slipped on the floor, hitting his ankle. Swelling set in under his knee, accompanied by a high fever. The doctors could do nothing. Helpless, his terrified mother sat by her son's bedside, watching Alexei's agony. In desperation, Tsarina Alexandra sent Rasputin a telegram, asking for his help. From his village in Siberia, he replied reassuringly that the tsarevich would not die of his hemophilia attack. When the tsarina returned to Alexei's bedside, she found that his temperature had dropped. The worst appeared to have passed. The relieved mother attributed Alexei's startling improvement to Rasputin's intervention.

One of the most unexpected events to take place among the Romanovs during the early twentieth century was the Grand Duchess Marie Pavlovna's religious conversion. For thirty-five years, Miechen had clung steadfastly to her Lutheran faith. But in 1908, she took the bold and unexpected step of embracing Orthodoxy. Some surmised that the ambitious Miechen acted in an attempt to improve the chances of her sons ascending the throne. After all, only the sickly Tsarevich Alexei and Grand Duke Michael stood in the way of the Vladimirs. Others gave Miechen the benefit of a doubt. Meriel Buchanan, daughter of a British ambassador to Russia, found a note of sincerity in Miechen's conversion, writing that: "For some time past the Grand Duchess had turned more and more to the colour and ceremonial of the Russian Church; she had prayed to the Virgin for the safety of her son [Kyril when he was injured during the Russo-Japanese War], and seeing in his escape from death an answer to these prayers, she finally adopted the Orthodox religion."[23]

A tsarist loyalist shared this view, saying that "no one knew of her intention, which had been maturing for years, except her husband and her children." On the morning of the grand duchess's conversion, she had sent her friend, Madame de Peters, a letter to deliver personally to Miechen's German pastor. "The letter was a long one, and contained all the reasons which had strengthened her irrevocable decision to be converted to the Orthodox Church." One of the strongest reasons for Miechen's conversion was the appeal of the Blessed Virgin Mary. Even when she was a Lutheran, Miechen had an icon of the Blessed Mother in her sanctuary. Kyril's miraculous escape cemented Miechen's decision to convert, for she had attributed the saving of his life when the *Petropavlovsk* sank to the Virgin Mary's protection. And so, "out of the gladness of her heart she promised to become a member of the Church . . . still it took several years to break entirely with her religious past." Even on the very day that Miechen converted many were taken completely by surprise. During a luncheon then held at the Vladimir Palace a certain Count Fersen heard Madame de Peters say that the grand duchess had converted. He could not believe it and whispered to one of the guests that, "Poor Madame de Peters had suddenly gone mad."[24]

In connection with this momentous event Tsar Nicholas II published a pronouncement: "Our Dearest Aunt, the Grand Duchess Maria Pavlovna, having learned and tried in union with His Spouse the truth of Orthodoxy, started wishing, on the movement of Her own soul, to be united with Us in faith and in belonging to the Church ceremonies and sacraments. Today, to Our greatest joy, She was received into Our Orthodox faith and accepted the Holy Confirmation. Announcing this long wished for occasion to Our loyal subjects, we command to call Her Imperial Highness the Blessed Grand Duchess."[25]

Miechen's sister-in-law Ella, meanwhile, took her Orthodox convictions further. She had undergone a transformation since Grand Duke Serge's assassination. Increasingly devoted to the poor, Ella dedicated her life to serving others by founding a convent and becoming an Orthodox nun. It was an unconventional move, but one that Ella wholeheartedly embraced.

Other dramatic changes took place within the Romanov family. In November 1908, Marie Feodorovna's favorite brother-in-law and Nicholas II's favorite uncle, Grand Duke Alexei, died at the age of fifty-eight. Among the intimates who had enjoyed Alexis's joviality, Marie Feodorovna, in particular, never forgot the friendship he extended to her when she first arrived in Russia in the 1860s. Grand Duke Alexei's death reduced the number of Marie Feodorovna's brothers-in-law to just Grand Dukes Paul and Vladimir. By January 1909, there were worries about Vladimir's rapidly deteriorating health. This compelled his nephew Nicholas II to rehabilitate the disgraced Kyril and Ducky. The rehabilitation was prompted by the Tsarevich Alexei's fragile health and Grand Duke Michael's situation with Natalia Wulfert, which meant that the throne could easily pass on to the Vladimirs. Restoring Kyril's position within the imperial family became imperative. In Nicholas's eyes, Kyril's marriage to Ducky was reduced to a "breach of etiquette rather than a criminal act."[26] The way was therefore paved for welcoming Kyril and his wife back to Russia. In a time of great anxiety over her husband's health, Kyril's rehabilitation was a great joy for Miechen, who proudly cabled Kyril with the words: "*Ta femme est grande duchesse* [your wife is a grand duchess]."[27] Ducky was now officially recognized as the Grand Duchess Victoria Feodorovna.

Happiness and excitement were short-lived, for within days of receiving the good news, Miechen's husband, Grand Duke Vladimir, died at the age of sixty-one. The grand duke was taking his tea when he was suddenly seized with an asthma attack and died of heart failure. Miechen was with Vladimir when he died. Boris and Andrei arrived soon afterward. The tsar and dowager empress rushed to the Vladimir Palace, where they paid their respects to the newly widowed Miechen.

Vladimir's death in February 1909 profoundly saddened Miechen. Their thirty-five-year marriage had been solid, based on compatibility and mutual interests. Miechen never stopped mourning Vladimir and chose to honor his memory by wearing mourning clothes for the rest of her life.

A little over a year after Grand Duke Vladimir died, the Dowager Empress Marie Feodorovna went into mourning again for another brother-in-law, King Edward VII. Queen Alexandra had been staying at Corfu with Queen Olga when the news arrived that the king had fallen ill. The queen arrived back in London just before King Edward died. Marie Feodorovna rushed to England to comfort her sister and attend the funeral. The impressive funeral attracted nine crowned heads of Europe, including the king's successor, King George V. The dowager empress described the funeral of her brother-in-law to Nicholas II as being "very touching and solemn."[28]

Accompanying the dowager empress to London was her son Grand Duke Michael. His liaison with Natasha Wulfert continued to worry Marie Feodorovna—and there was much to be anxious about, for Michael's attachment to Natasha was as strong as ever. They were bound even closer by the birth of a son, George, in July 1910. The infant, named after Michael's dead brother, was illegitimate, since his parents were unmarried. In fact, Natasha was still not divorced from her second husband, a situation she and Michael hoped the issuance of another divorce would clarify. Illegitimate or not, George's birth greatly touched Michael, as he later wrote to Natasha: "Let God give Baby a happy life and let our boy always bring us joy."[29] Nicholas II granted his nephew George the surname "Brasov," which derived from Grand Duke Michael's estate at Brasovo. Later, Nicholas also allowed Natasha to use the surname Brasova.

Meanwhile, scandalous tales about Gregory Rasputin continued to circulate widely in St. Petersburg. He had captured the attention of nearly everyone in the Russian capital. Such was the conclusion of Russia's minister to Bulgaria, Anatoli Neklyudov. "In the salons of St. Petersburg, which I frequented fairly regularly," wrote Neklyudov, "Rasputin was the sole topic of conversation."[30]

It became imperative to address this festering problem. Concerned about Rasputin and his impact on the monarchy, Peter Stolypin ordered that he be placed under surveillance. Stolypin wanted the tsar to read the "secret agents' reports and to convince him, finally, of the profligacy of the 'holy peasant.' "[31]

Rasputin's hold on the imperial family was directly linked to the tsarina's growing dependency on him, but, because very few knew of Alexei's hemophilia, Rasputin's indispensability garnered gossip, not sympathy. As the stories about Rasputin's debauchery multiplied, newspapers in many parts of Russia carried these tales. Even the censors could not keep a lid on the growing scandals. In no time, disturbing rumors about Rasputin's closeness to the imperial family included even a supposed debauched relationship with the tsarina and the grand duchesses. Alexandra dismissed these sordid stories about Rasputin, believing them to be calumnies hurled at a holy man.

In addition to Michael's liaison and Rasputin, Marie Feodorovna was disconcerted by the ongoing political troubles besetting Russia. The country's exercise in semi-democracy was proving tenuous. Russia's first two Dumas were soon dissolved; hope was pinned on the Third Duma, which convened in the fall of 1907. This Duma strengthened Prime Minister Peter Stolypin's hand.

Stolypin, with the "dead-white face and a dead-black beard," who spoke "in a cold and even voice, as cold as the clasp of his white hand," impressed a number of individuals. The British ambassador to Russia between 1906 and 1910, Sir Arthur Nicolson, described Stolypin as "a great man" who was "the most notable figure in Europe. His task as Minister of the Interior, and subsequently as Prime Minister was a gigantic one," noted Nicolson. In the ambassador's view, Stolypin possessed "courage, great determination, an ardent love for his country, and a most earnest desire to steer her safely through the troubles and difficulties by which she was surrounded. He was anxious to develop her great resources and lead her progressively to a higher level."[32] Nicolson's successor, Sir George Buchanan, echoed those sentiments, finding Stolypin, "a true patriot, and despite his faults, a great Minister."[33] Stolypin aimed to create a working government by trying to gain allies from the center and the right in order to weaken the left. "What you want are great upheavals," he disdainfully told the left. "But what *we* want is a GREAT RUSSIA!" His agrarian reforms gave numerous peasants titles to land. By destroying the peasant commune, Stolypin allowed "a class of small farmers, each with a solid stake in the existing order" to rise, thereby resulting in "a rapid and very dramatic increase in Russia's agricultural production."[34]

In 1911, Stolypin proposed that elected *zemstvo* institutions be established in Russia's western provinces. When the Council of State (the Duma's upper house), rejected the formation of these local governing entities, Stolypin resigned. The resignation greatly agitated Marie Feodorovna, who summoned Stolypin for an audience. Four days after he resigned, Stolypin traveled to Gatchina for the interview. When Stolypin arrived at the dowager empress's study, he encountered Nicholas II, whose face was "red from weeping." The tsar did not say anything to Stolypin as he left his mother's study. The dowager empress greeted Stolypin "with exceptional warmth," and "began at once, kindly and persuasively, to question his decision to resign." She told him of the conversation she just had with the tsar.

"I have informed my son," said Marie Feodorovna, "of my deep conviction that you alone possess the strength and ability to save Russia and bring her back to the true way." The dowager empress admitted that Nicholas II was under Tsarina Alexandra's influence and was hesitant to heed his mother's words. However, Marie Feodorovna reassured Stolypin, adding: "I believe that I have convinced him." In recounting the event, Stolypin's daughter, Maria von Bock, noted that "in very touching and impetuous terms, the Empress [Marie Feodorovna] implored my father to give his consent without wavering when the ruler should ask him to withdraw his request to resign. Her words breathed deep love for Russia and such firm assurance." The meeting "made a deep impression" on Stolypin.[35] Marie Feodorovna's support of Stolypin "quickly became the talk of the political class and a source of embarrassment to the tsar."[36] In the end, however, Nicholas II heeded his mother's advice and wrote to Stolypin asking him to reconsider his resignation. Stolypin, moved by the tsar's letter and Marie Feodorovna's plea, returned to power, though only after the tsar agreed to Stolypin's conditions. One of these conditions amounted to adjourning the Duma for several days so that Nicholas II could enact the *zemstvo* bill.

Ultimately, Stolypin did not have a chance to rescue his teetering country. In September 1911, he was in Kiev with Tsar Nicholas and his daughters the Grand Duchesses Olga and Tatiana for the dedication of a memorial to Tsar Alexander II. Security was tight when the tsar, his daughters, and Stolypin watched a performance of Nikolai Rimsky-Korsakov's *Tale of Tsar Saltan* at the Kiev Opera House. But despite the extraordinary security precautions, a double-agent succeeded in shooting Stolypin at point-blank range during the second intermission. Wondering what the commotion was about, Nicholas turned to find the stricken Stolypin slowly make the sign of the cross in the tsar's direction. Fatally wounded, Stolypin died days later.

The dowager empress wrote to her son from Hvidovre: "I cannot say how distressed and indignant I am about the murder of Stolypin. Is it true that you and my granddaughters saw the horror? How disgusting and revolting it is and just at a moment, too, when all was going well and the country was recovering its spirits. I am so sad about it and regret so much that this scoundrel was not torn to pieces on the spot! It is horrible and scandalous and one can say nothing good of the police whose choice fell upon such a swine as that revolutionary to act as informer and as guard to Stolypin. It exceeds all bounds and shows the stupidity of the people at the top."[37]

Stolypin's death eliminated the leading force upon whom Russia's political fortunes had rested, and who had also been poised to try to sort out the Rasputin debacle. Marie Feodorovna was mortified by the newspaper reports and gossip surrounding Rasputin. One of Marie Feodorovna's friends told her that Michael Rodzianko "is the only man, thoroughly informed, on whom you may rely to tell you nothing but the absolute truth." The burly six-foot-four Rodzianko, the speaker of the Duma, referred to himself as the fattest and biggest man in Russia. He was also known for his courage. The dowager empress accordingly commanded Rodzianko to come and speak to her. "You are of course aware of the object of our interview?" began the dowager empress, who added: "I only learnt all these details [of the whole Rasputin story] a few days ago from a person of my acquaintance, and I was absolutely aghast. It is terrible, terrible," Marie Feodorovna kept repeating. She then wanted to see a letter Tsarina Alexandra wrote "to that dreadful man," as the dowager empress described Rasputin. "Show it to me," she commanded Rodzianko. He replied he could not do so. Marie Feodorovna then laid her hand on Rodzianko and said, "You will destroy it, will you not?"

"Yes, your Majesty, I will destroy it."

"That is good."

The empress then cautioned him: "I hear that you intend to speak to the Emperor about Rasputin. Do not do so. Unfortunately he will not believe you, and it will cause him much pain. He is so pure of heart that he does not believe in evil."

Rodzianko responded that he was compelled to speak to Nicholas II as "the affair was too serious, and the consequences might be too dangerous."

"Have matters gone so far then?" inquired the dowager empress.

"Madam, it is a question of the dynasty . . . You see me now profoundly perturbed by the thought of the responsibility which rests upon me. I most humbly ask you to give me your blessing."

Marie Feodorovna looked at Rodzianko with those sympathetic eyes that had captivated so many, laid her hand on his, and said in a trembling voice:

"God bless you."

Then as Rodzianko left, Marie Feodorovna added, softly: "Do not hurt him too much."[38] K.R. confided in his diary that Marie Feodorovna "is in despair that they [Nicholas and Alexandra] continue to receive the holy fool Grisha [Rasputin]."[39] Soon after Rodzianko's audience with Marie Feodorovna, the dowager empress deemed it necessary to intervene personally with Nicholas and Alexandra. She did so in February 1912 and spoke to them about her deep-seated anxieties regarding Rasputin. The tsarina resisted, explaining to

Marie Feodorovna that Rasputin was an exceptional person and that the dowager empress needed to acquaint herself with him. Marie Feodorovna listened, but advised her daughter-in-law to be rid of him right away.

The Bulgarian minister Anatoli Nekludov recalled that reliable sources described Marie Feodorovna's "heart-to-heart talk with her son and daughter-in-law." The dowager empress was blunt in her talk, telling Alexandra: "It is no question of you, of your affections, your convictions or rather your religious manias," insisted Marie Feodorovna to Alexandra, "it is a question of the Emperor, of the Dynasty, of Russia! If you go on in this way, you will be the undoing of us all!"[40] Rodzianko also heard that the dowager empress had declared before Nicholas II that, "either I am here or Rasputin."[41] The tsar and tsarina appreciated Marie Feodorovna's candidness but told her that they could not send Rasputin away, with the tsarina effectively declaring that he was indispensible.

In February 1912, Marie Feodorovna invited Vladimir Kokovtsov, Stolypin's successor, to speak to her about Rasputin. Kokovtsov recalled that Marie Feodorovna "wept bitterly and promised to speak to the tsar, but added: 'My poor daughter-in-law does not perceive that she is ruining both the dynasty and herself. She sincerely believes in the holiness of an adventurer, and we are powerless to ward off the misfortune which is sure to come.'"[42]

20

GRANDEUR AND PAIN

*U*nlike the Grand Duchess Vladimir and Dowager Empress Marie Fe-odorovna, Queen Olga dealt with no rash of romantic scandals among family members. Olga did however have to contend with her husband's occasional infidelity. Though their marriage was solid and happy enough, King George occasionally strayed from his marital vows. An avid traveler, George had an eye for actresses in Paris and delighted in speaking to the laundry-women of Aix-les-Bains, France, who greeted him heartily and with familiarity by shouting "Good-morning, M.[onsieur] Georges! Three cheers for M. Georges!" According to Xavier Paoli, who guarded the king during his visits to France, George I was popular with these laundresses "not only because of his good-nature and good-humour, but because the girls had more than once experienced the benefits of his un-obtrusive generosity."[1] Queen Olga did not let her husband's occasional lapses destroy her marriage. She forgave George, stayed faithful to him, and remained the dutiful wife.

By 1910, nearly all of Queen Olga's sons had married. The latest princess to join the family was Marie Bonaparte, who married Olga's son George in 1907. According to the British ambassador to Greece, Sir Francis Elliot, a certain amount of discord existed among the queen's daughters-in-law. When Marie Bonaparte arrived, Elliot reported that: "Rumour has it that some of the King's daughters-in-law of longer standing are not particularly pleased at [the princess's] intrusion into their midst, and my daughter tells me of an incident she noticed last night, which seems to forebode some want of harmony. The Royal Family were retiring, and Princess Nicholas [Elena] was approaching the door, when Princess George came hurriedly up from behind and passed through first without a smile or word to her sister-in-law, who drew back her skirts as if not to be touched by her."[2] Elena, whose priorities were said to be "God first, then the Russian Grand Dukes, then the rest,"[3] could be just as elitist as her mother, Miechen. Since Elena looked askance at her sister-in-law, Alice of Greece (married to Prince Andrew) because of her morganatic blood, it was not surprising that Miechen's daughter snubbed Marie Bonaparte, whose wealthy grandfather, François Blanc, operated the Monte Carlo Casino.

Elena presented Miechen and Olga with another granddaughter when she gave birth in 1906 to Princess Marina. At least once a year, Miechen's Greek granddaughters visited her in Russia. When in St. Petersburg, Miechen's granddaughters stayed with her at the Vladimir Palace, where "everything," according to the children's English nurse, Kate Fox, was "exquisite." Kate wrote home of her impressions of the grandeur of the Vladimir Palace. "My nurseries consist of eight beautifully furnished rooms; dining-room, two saloon ante-rooms, night nursery, dressing-room, bathroom and so on . . . There must be a regular army of servants here; it is a huge place. The King's Palace in Athens is supposed to be big, but it is nothing like this. We are such a distance from the Grand Duchess's rooms that when I take the children along to their mother I have to wait for them. It is too far to go again to fetch them."[4]

Sir George Buchanan's daughter, Meriel Buchanan, recalled the sight of Marie Pavlovna's pretty Greek granddaughters during their visits to Russia. During the winter months the princesses would often be found "driving in an open sledge, their faces, rosy with the cold, framed in fur-trimmed velvet bonnets." Their grandmother doted on the girls, although Marina's name "came most often to her [Miechen's] lips." Meriel Buchanan heard Marie Pavlovna say "Marina is the cleverest one" or "Marina is the most un-selfish. She has the sweetest nature. Marina is the most affectionate."[5] Miechen fussed over her granddaughters, showering them with beautiful gifts. She bought their layette in Paris; and when the princesses visited Russia, she gave them "dresses, dolls, prams, bicycles, a pony and carriage and jewellery suitable for their ages, such as silver muff-chains, watches, strings of pearls and diamonds and turquoise pendants."[6]

If Miechen's Greek granddaughters had been old enough to notice, they would have observed that the ladies who waited on their maternal grandmother were infinitely more attractive and youthful than those who attended their paternal grandmother. Whereas Queen Olga's ladies-in-waiting were mostly elderly, the Grand Duchess Vladimir demanded that her court ladies be young and good-looking, largely because Miechen enjoyed being surrounded by young people. But much was demanded of these young ladies. The grand duchess, a stickler for decorum and duty, ordered no deviation from prescribed norms of behavior. Should her attendants break the rules, Miechen mercilessly meted out punishment. Such was the case when it came to the seventeen-year-old grand-daughter of a former American minister to Russia, whom the Grand Duchess Vladimir had honored by appointing as one of her ladies. The young lady, named Halla, had asked to go to Estonia, using the excuse that her grand-mother had died. In reality Halla stayed in St. Petersburg and accompanied a young man, with whom she was in love, to the Aquarium (a restaurant, garden, and theater complex). To ensure anonymity, Halla veiled herself heavily. But someone noticed and reported Halla's transgression to Miechen. When Halla returned to duty, the Grand Duchess Vladimir gave her a frosty reception, ask-ing her pointedly: "Do you consider the Aquarium a suitable place for the cel-ebration of your grandmother's funeral?" At that Miechen dismissed "the love-lorn truant" from her court.[7]

Miechen was happiest when Elena, Nicholas, and their girls stayed with her, since their presence alleviated the loneliness she felt since Grand Duke Vladimir's death. When the Nicholas family returned to Greece, Miechen faced her cavernous home, again devoid of Vladimir's presence. In order to fill her days and nights, Miechen entertained frequently, often having people over to play bridge, a game the grand duchess much enjoyed.

Meriel Buchanan, a guest at the Vladimir Palace for dinner parties, recalled "the huge white and gold rooms full of a shifting mass of colour, the bright dresses of the women, the varying uniforms of the men, the dazzle of jewels and decorations. Here one always met only the prettiest and smartest women, the most distinguished men, the most entertaining members of the diplomatic body. And the Grand Duchess herself, invariably dressed in black, always wearing wonderful jewels, entering when all the other guests had assembled, knowing exactly what to say to each individual person, an inimitable gift which royalties do not always possess, but which she herself had at her com-mand in the fullest sense."[8] Her "extreme amiability," noted another observer of Marie Pavlovna, "and her use of language bordered on perfection, since she could always find the precise word for the occasion."[9]

Miechen never forgot that the tsarina lacked her knack for conversation, nor did she let others forget. During a visit to Sofia, the capital of Bulgaria, Miechen impressed A. A. Mossolov with her mastery of the craft of being a royal. Mossolov, head of the court Chancellery, apprised Miechen, in the space of only "a few minutes . . . about the outstanding personalities in Bulgar society" who were to attend a banquet and reception. Mossolov was astonished at what followed. It was Miechen at her finest: a superb performer in command of herself and of the facts that had just been given to her about the guests. "For three hours," wrote the admiring Mossolov, "the Grand Duchess was the centre of animated and brilliant conversation. She was talking to persons whom she had never before met; and she did not make a single mistake." When Mossolov congratulated Marie Pavlovna on her "adroitness," the grand duchess replied: "One ought to know one's job. You may pass that on to the Grand Court." It was one of the most caustic public remarks Miechen ever made about Tsarina Alexandra's clumsy attempts at entertaining. "It must be admitted," noted Mossolov of Marie Pavlovna, "that she knew her job to perfection."[10]

Like the dowager empress, who had a "natural buoyancy,"[11] Miechen did not withdraw fully from society after Grand Duke Vladimir's death, but continued to seek out some of the most interesting and glamorous individuals of the era and encourage their pursuits. One such person was the famed British romantic novelist Elinor Glyn. Her most famous work, the risqué *Three Weeks*, centers upon a mysterious Balkan queen who was trapped in a cruel marriage and has a brief affair with a young British aristocrat. Though tame by today's standards, the novel created a sensation when it was published and made Elinor Glyn one of the most famous women of her time. For all its "infamy," *Three Weeks* was infused with a strong underlying theme of romance. Glyn admitted that "I made the 'Lady' pay for her failure to observe her matrimonial vows with her life, and I believed it quite just that she should do so, and that the tragic ending of the story restored the moral balance of the whole book."[12] Glyn herself acknowledged in her autobiography that she adhered to more traditional concepts of matrimony, stating that: "The idea that a woman could share herself between two men has always appeared to me wholly repulsive. As long as marriage is a reality, physical faithfulness is a *sine qua non*, for the husband has the right to be sure that children bearing his name are his own."[13] Such was the intriguing personality whom Grand Duchess Vladimir decided to invite to Russia.

Both Miechen and her daughter-in-law Ducky read *Three Weeks*. They agreed that Elinor Glyn's appreciation of the Russian character might translate into an admirable book with Russian court and society as the background. Glyn eagerly took up Miechen's invitation to visit Russia and gather material. When she first met her host in 1910, Glyn found the Grand Duchess Vladimir "a most stately, magnificent looking princess."[14] Glyn observed that the Grand

Duchess Vladimir, being the "kind lady . . . spoke always to her sons and son-in-law in English whenever I was present."[15] "She had a very highly cultivated and far-seeing mind, with a delightful sense of humour, and was adored by everyone. She was looked upon as the real Empress of Russia from a social point of view," concluded Glyn, who affectionately called Miechen "my" grand duchess.

Marie Pavlovna was a consummate host and saw to it that Glyn gained entrée into many fine houses of the capital. Because the grand duchess was still in mourning for her husband, she somewhat limited her court gaieties and did not always accompany her guest. "After every party," however, recalled Glyn, Miechen would ask to hear all that had taken place—to which Miechen responded "chuckling with pleasure, or commenting with deep insight upon every detail."[16]

As encouraged, the author used material she gathered on Russia and its society and produced a work of fiction, where one of the characters, a Princess Ardacheff, was modeled after Glyn's patroness. She dedicated the work to Miechen in the most glowing terms, saying that "her kind appreciation of the finished work is a source of the deepest gratification to me."[17] Elinor Glyn's book *His Hour* is a portrait of imperial Russia on the brink. Thanks to Miechen's intervention, Glyn gave readers a glimpse of a world that, at the time of *His Hour*'s publication in 1910, was fast disappearing.

Unlike Miechen's niece, the tsarina, who led a simple life at Tsarskoe Selo, the grand duchess reveled in the high life and conspicuous consumption, especially when it came to jewelry. As a major client of the famed House of Cartier, the grand duchess delighted in flaunting their works. Her appetite for magnificent jewelry was legendary, and Cartier was a main source for these pieces. One of them was an aigrette tiara—"its three curving aigrette bundles, set with Indian-cut briolettes like cascades of blossom, evoked the illusion of dewdrops shaken from a stem" whenever they moved.[18] Miechen's buying sprees took on a life of their own after Grand Duke Vladimir died. As his widow, Miechen was left with plenty of discretionary income, part of which she used to spend at Cartier's. In addition to the aigrette tiara, the grand duchess purchased a ruby tiara and a *kokoshnik* tiara with a 137-carat sapphire in the center as well as a large stomacher dominated by a 162-carat sapphire.

Miechen was also instrumental in allowing Louis Cartier to participate in a Christmas charity bazaar organized by the Society of Nobles, of which she was the president. The annual grand charity bazaar lasted for four days and took place the week before Christmas in the Hall of Nobles. Miechen obsessed over every detail at her stall. She "welcomed everybody who approached [her] with the same gracious smile, never pressing them to buy, but always managing to sell more than anybody else, never showing any signs of the weariness she must have felt in the incessant noise and heat, and the long hours of standing surrounded by pressing crowds."[19] The cause, after all, was an excellent one. And Miechen did her best to raise money during these hectic days for Russia's poor.

At the bazaar, Cartier recalled that "I gazed down into the cathedral-like interior and at the vast horseshoe-shaped sales counter over which presided the Grand Duchess together with the flower of St. Petersburg's aristocracy." Knowing Cartier's eye, Marie Pavlovna, to whose right sat the Duchess of Leuchtenberg, asked him, "Guess whose necklace she's wearing?" As it turned out, the duchess was wearing a necklace Napoleon had given to Josephine. Cartier recorded that "at the end we were able to present the Grand Duchess with a sum of between 23,000 and 26,000 roubles, which was distributed among the poor people of St. Petersburg."[20]

After over four decades as Queen of the Hellenes, Queen Olga had earned her reputation for being deeply concerned with the welfare of her subjects. Strong as her charity work was, Olga's reputation as queen was mixed. The British chargé d'affaires in Athens in the late nineteenth century, Sir Vincent Corbett, appreciated the queen as "a kindly, charitable and pious woman," who "was revered by those who knew her best as little less than a saint." Yet Corbett believed that Olga, who "spoke Greek admirably and was profoundly anxious to do her duty," did not inspire much sympathy from her subjects. Corbett attributed this to Queen Olga's overt pride in being Russian. As an admiral in the Russian navy, an honor she was proud of, Olga continued to visit Russian ships at Athens's port, the Piraeus, oftentimes remaining to dine. The queen's cherished nephew, the English King George V, had teased his aunt "mercilessly" about her "nautical entertainments" when he was still a sublieutenant. According to Prince Nicholas of Greece, Queen Olga "scolded" George, assuring him that "Russian sailors were all angels."[21]

Sir Vincent Corbett, noted that Olga's "visits to the Russian ships were warmly resented by the Greeks and gave rise to incredibly offensive comments in the Press, which I hope and believe she never read."[22] The Russian diplomat Baron Rosen came to the same conclusion as Sir Vincent about Queen Olga: "Although most loyally attached to the country of her adoption, [she] was nevertheless a great Russian patriot, and on that account rather unpopular in

Greece."[23] One contemporary publication of 1897 reported to its readers that "the Queen of Greece is intensely Russian."[24]

Queen Olga always took a keen interest in the Russian sailors who came to Greece. When one fell seriously ill with consumption and was transferred to a local hospital, the queen visited him. Having "attracted her special attention," Olga ordered "many delicacies to be supplied to him from the Royal kitchen."[25] When the queen heard that his last wish was to see his mother, who was living in Estonia, Olga promptly had the mother fetched and sent hurriedly to Athens just in time to see the son before he died. The mother was later escorted back to Estonia by a royal aide-de-camp. One of the best examples of Olga's thoughtfulness toward her compatriots is evident in a detail she extended to those who died in Greece. The queen, who kept a supply of earth from Russia, invariably offered the soil to be sprinkled on the coffins of Russians who died in Greece.

Even within her own family, Queen Olga was well known for her strong pro-Russian sentiments, making them "all heartily sick of it." One relative admitted that the queen "rammed Russia down her family's throat" to such an extent "and turned them so much against it that they all became violently pro-Greek."[26] Of all her children, only Prince Christopher showed a strong interest in Russia—the rest were much more Greek in outlook, especially Princess Marie and Prince Andrew.

As well as criticizing Queen Olga's very public attachment to Russia, Sir Vincent Corbett also found fault in her public demeanor. He believed she "lacked personal grace of manner, probably because she was naturally shy and because she suffered from extremely short sight." Corbett, who spent a week as the royal family's guest at Tatoi, recorded that Queen Olga showed "real kindness" to him and "hers was a saint-like character, but the rôle of Queen of the Hellenes was one for which she was not fitted."[27]

The British writer E. F. Benson had a different view. Benson described the queen as "a wonderfully beautiful woman" with "an engaging habit when she came round the room at balls or after dinner in order to talk to the guests, of putting her hands on the shoulders of the women she was conversing with, and shoving them back into their seats, so that they should sit down without ceremony. Sometimes she would want to talk to two or three people together, and down they went like ninepins, while she stood."[28] Constance Battersea was another who had good firsthand memories of Queen Olga, whom she visited in Athens. Battersea, like Benson, thought Olga was adept as a queen when it came to granting audiences. Constance Battersea found the queen to have "had a charming face, intelligent and sympathetic, and very simple manner; when I was going to kiss her hand, she drew it away rapidly and said, 'Oh, we do not do such things here.' "[29]

In 1909, trouble brewed for the Greek royals. British diplomats in Athens reported that "bad trade, scarcity of money, unemployment . . . a deplorable lack of public security" and the unresolved Cretan question all contributed to "a general feeling that something may happen, no one knows exactly what."[30] Cretans, including a talented lawyer from the island by the name of Eleuthe-rios Venizelos, called for union with mainland Greece. Since the Great Powers "would not rescind their agreement . . . that the island should remain under the sovereignty" of the Ottoman Empire, the desired for political union failed, "much to the chagrin of the Greeks and most of the Cretans."[31] This "disaf-fection played into the hands of a number of embittered military officers, pav-ing the way for a takeover of power by the country's military."[32] In the summer of 1909, this gave rise to what became known as the Military League. Consist-ing of junior officers intent on pushing military and political reforms, the Military League flexed its muscle to the detriment of the Greek royal family; for "without having to fire a single shot, the military reaped an unexpected triumph as, one after another, the institutions of the state surrendered to their demands."[33]

Among the casualties of the military dictatorship were Queen Olga's sons. The Military League demanded that "the Crown Prince and all the royal princes . . . should be relieved of their army commissions."[34] In order to spare their father further humiliation, the princes relinquished their military com-mands. "It is not difficult to imagine how my father and mother felt during all this unhappy period," recalled Prince Nicholas. "In ordinary families any in-justice towards the sons would have brought forth violent protests from the parents; in our case, our father and mother admitting the injustice, had tacitly to side with the nation against us."[35]

Greece was so volatile and the danger to the dynasty very real, that the British ordered ships of the Royal Navy near Athens to be on standby in case they were needed to evacuate the Greek royal family. Sir Francis Elliot, Brit-ain's ambassador to Greece, concluded that the situation in Greece looked dire for the royal family. The ambassador reported to London that King George "is between the devil and the deep sea,"[36] seeing that George I had admitted to Elliot that "he would take his departure the next time he came into conflict with them [the Military League]; he had made all his prepara-tions and was ready to leave at a moment's notice."[37] When a serious fire broke out at the Royal Palace in January 1910, it prompted all types of speculation. Sir Francis Elliot reported as much to London: "I was not surprised to hear, before I had been half an hour on the spot, that it was being said that the King had had the Palace set alight in order to attract sympathy. Today the legend is circulating in various forms that it was known before hand that the Palace would be burnt down on Christmas Eve—the actual date according to the Orthodox Calendar."[38]

Fortunately for the Greek royals, by the fall of 1910, political passions in Greece subsided; and the Military League eventually disbanded. In the midst of the crisis, Eleutherios Venizelos's rise to power began in earnest after he became the country's prime minister. From this time onward, Venizelos would come to play a highly significant role in the country's capricious politics and in the process affect the royal family's fortunes.

During these difficult years, Olga was saddened by the deaths, in rapid succession, of her mother, Grand Duchess Alexandra Iosifovna (d. 1911); her brother-in-law, King Frederick VIII of Denmark (d. 1912); and her sister, Vera (d. 1912). The Queen of the Hellenes took solace in the Christian belief in the resurrection. On her mother's death, Queen Olga wrote, "I simply wish to think of my mother in her present state of joy, in her heavenly homeland, near our Savior." When Olga's only sister Vera died too, the queen, with tears in her eyes, told a friend: "I am at peace, because my sister is going directly to Jesus . . . and she died during this Easter Week, when as it is said, the doors of heaven are open, though they would always be open for my sister because her only concern, and the purpose of her life was to do the will of Jesus."[39]

In Russia, the fate of the dowager empress's grandson, the Tsarevich Alexei, took a dramatic turn in the autumn of 1912 when Nicholas and Alexandra took their family to stay at the imperial hunting lodge in the forest of Bialowieza in Poland. After eight-year-old Alexei hurt his thigh and knee, the imperial family, alarmed by the tsarevich's condition, left immediately for their residence at Spala, not far from Warsaw.

Alexei's latest hemophilia attack was unlike any other. In no time, internal bleeding set in; a large swelling was discovered in the boy's groin and left thigh that should have been operated on, but this could not be done because of the risk of bleeding to death. Alexei was also struck down with a very high fever and suffered excruciating pain. The tsarina's loyal confidante Anna Viroubova recalled the anguish felt by a helpless Nicholas and Alexandra as they watched Alexei hover between life and death. When it seemed that the tsarevich's condition was nothing short of "desperate," a look of "despair" was "written on the parents' faces."[40] Pierre Gilliard, who was also privy to the agony at Spala, remembered the "distracted and terror-stricken look" on the tsarina's face.[41] A. A. Mossolov recorded that "the unfortunate boy suffered dreadfully" and that "the anxiety of his father and mother was beyond description."[42]

Baroness Buxhoeveden, an intimate of the family, described how "at first the poor child cried loudly, but as his strength gave out, this was followed by a constant wailing, which grew hoarser and hoarser. He could not take food and could find no restful position in bed."[43] Alexei was so overcome with pain that he pathetically asked his anxious mother: "When I am dead, it will not hurt any more, will it?"[44] So grave was Alexei's condition that bulletins were issued preparing Russians for the news that the tsarevich had died.

In desperation, Alexei's distraught mother sought Rasputin's help, hoping for a miracle. Anna Viroubova sent Rasputin, who was in Siberia, a telegram on the tsarina's behalf. Rasputin replied with reassuring words, telling Tsarina Alexandra: "The little one will not die."[45] Miraculously, within an hour, Alexei, who had been so near death's door, showed remarkable signs that he was on the road to recovery. Even the doctors present at Spala were perplexed by the tsarevich's mysterious sudden improvement. Only a week later, Alexei was fit enough to travel to St. Petersburg. When A. A. Mossolov saw him, he was astonished to find the tsarevich playing "peacefully in his bed, and did not seem to be feeling the slightest pain." Tsarina Alexandra then told Mossolov: "It is not the first time that the Staretz has saved his life."[46]

Nicholas II recounted the tragic episode of Tsarevich Alexei's near fatal hemophilia attack to the dowager empress:

I am writing to you with my heart filled with gratitude to the Lord for His mercy in granting us the beginning of dear Alexei's recovery . . . The poor darling suffered intensely, the pains came in spasms and recurred every quarter of an hour. His high temperature made him delirious day and night; and he would sit up in bed and every movement brought the pain on again. He hardly slept at all, had not even the strength to cry, just moaned and kept repeating: "O Lord, have mercy upon me." I was hardly able to stay in the room, but had of course to take turns with Alix, for she was exhausted by spending whole nights by his bed. She bore the ordeal better than I did while Alexei was very ill; but now that, thank God, the danger is over she is beginning to feel the after effects, and her poor heart has weakened under the strain. She is being more careful now, however, and spends her day on the couch in Alexei's room.[47]

The grave illness of Marie Feodorovna's grandson at Spala in 1912, followed by his astounding recovery following Rasputin's telegram, spelt serious trouble for the monarchy, for this event cemented Tsarina Alexandra's unwavering faith in Rasputin.

21

A TERRIBLE BLOW!

*N*atasha Wulfert's earliest admirer, Dmitri Abrikossov, described her as a woman "not easy to forget."[1] Grand Duke Michael came to the same conclusion. His romance with Natasha remained as strong as ever, especially now that he had fathered her child. Though Michael had promised Nicholas II that he would not marry Natasha, the tsar still worried that his brother might do something precipitous. Nicholas ordered that the couple be subjected to close surveillance. The *Okhrana*, instructed to avert a marriage, kept an eye on Michael and Nastasha. Even so, Nicholas II's apprehensions mounted once Natasha was finally divorced from her second husband, because he feared that the couple might flee Russia to marry. And indeed they did. In October 1912, Michael and Natasha outwitted the *Okhrana*, fleeing to Vienna where they were married by a Serbian priest in October 1912. The wedding ceremony was held in secret, with only two witnesses, who were provided by the priest. Two weeks after the ceremony, Michael confessed to his mother what had taken place:

> *My Dear Mama,*
> *If only you knew how painful and distressing it is for me to upset you,*
> *yet I know my letter will bring you great sorrow and I ask you in ad-*
> *vance to hear me out and forgive me . . . I am obliged to inform you*
> *that on the 16/29 October, that is two weeks ago, I was married to*
> *Nathalie Sergeyevna Brasova . . .*
> *   It is now five years since I met Nathalie S. and I love and respect*
> *her more each year. But, morally it was always very hard on me and in*

particular the last year in St. Petersburg convinced me that the only way out of this painful and false situation was marriage. But I never wanted to distress you and might never have had decided on this step, were it not for little Alexis's illness and the thought that as Heir I could be separated from Nathalie, but now that can no longer happen.

Let me say again, that more than anything I am tortured by the fact of distressing you and Nicky so terribly, but to go on living as before was simply not bearable. And so I beg you, my dear Mama, to forgive and understand me as a mother, whom I love deeply with all my heart.

Your Misha[2]

To Nicholas II, Michael wrote in a similar vein, but also added: "I know that punishment awaits me for this act and I am ready to bear it."[3] As expected, the dowager empress took the news badly. She had always wished that Michael would marry well. And when she heard that Michael married the twice-divorced Natasha, Marie Feodorovna was furious. Her letter to Nicholas II bears this, describing the event as a *"terrible cruel new blow!"*[3]

I have just got a letter from Misha in which he announces his marriage! It is unbelievable—I can hardly understand *what* I am writing—it is so appalling in every way that it *nearly kills* me! I beg only this one thing of you: that it be kept *absolutely secret* to avoid *another scandal*! There have been secret marriages in the past which one *pretended to know nothing about.* I think this is the only way out—otherwise I won't be able to show my face *anywhere* for the *shame and disgrace of it all*! May God forgive him—I can only pity him. But what sorrow it brings, and how difficult it is to bear up under such blows! Thank God dear Xenia is here with me. She consoles me and is such a comfort to talk to![4]

Three days later, Nicholas II replied to the dowager empress's letter, describing Michael's marriage—"the appalling news," as a "new disaster to our family." "Yes, dear Mama, I will say with you, may God forgive him! Between him and me everything is now, alas, at an end; because he has broken his pledged word . . . What revolts me more than anything else is his reference to poor Alexei's illness which, he says, made him speed things up . . . I am ashamed and deeply grieved . . . I see clearly that *now* he must not return to

Russia."[5] Michael, who "seemed more concerned about his mother's reaction than his brother's," again wrote to the dowager empress:

> *My dear Mama,*
> *I await stern punishment for my act, which was dictated to me solely by my conscience. I am ready to bear all the punishments and depriva-tions. I do not fear them, the only thing which is very painful is the distress, which I have unintentionally caused you. Dear Mama, surely I have only acted as befits any honourable man—in that my con-science is clear. With all my heart I beg you not to judge me harshly, but to give me your blessing, as a mother whom I love deeply. May the Lord keep you, my dear Mama. I embrace you warmly. I love you with all my heart, Misha.*[6]

Grand Duke Michael's manifestations of affection did nothing to dampen the severity of the tsar's punishment. Nicholas II banished his brother from Russia, froze his assets, "and most astonishingly making him [Michael] person-ally subject to guardianship, a measure normally reserved for minors or mad-men."[7] Nicholas also relieved Michael of his command as colonel and commandant of the Chevalier Gardes Regiment of the dowager empress and removed Michael from the regency. The punishment was severe, but eventu-ally attempts at a reconciliation took place. Michael's cousin Grand Duke An-drei was the first to visit Michael and Natasha in exile. Grand Duchess Xenia also met with her brother. She recorded their meeting: "As I told him about Mama . . . the terrible winter and her health and state of mind, I was unable to hold back my tears—nor was he. We cried on each other's shoulders . . . He says . . . he suffers for Mama and regrets having to break his word to Nicky, but that he was obliged to act in this way."[8]

Then, in 1913 came the eventful meeting between Michael, Natasha, and the dowager empress in London. Xenia noted that their mother had been "very agitated at the prospect of seeing him" and had been "completely unable to sleep—she was so excited and upset." Xenia was reassured to hear that the initial meeting between Michael and his mother went well, admitting with re-lief: "thank God it went all right." That same evening, Michael met his mother again, this time with Natasha. Xenia confided in her diary about the meeting, writing that Marie Feodorovna "saw his wife and told her a few home truths in front of Misha, which she also repeated to me in front of him. She is so sad and upset. In general it's terribly *penible* [unpleasant] on all sides."[9]

Marie Feodorovna recounted the meeting to Nicholas II in a letter: "Although our first meeting was rather disturbing and we *both* were rather shy at first, which, after all, was only too natural, I was happy to see that he has remained the same: just as nice and good and even kinder than ever. We talked everything over *quite* frankly and all was said so nicely and quietly without a bitter word, that for *the first time* after all those dreadful worries *my heart felt relieved* and so, I think, did his. He even mentioned it in his letters and thanked me for my kindness . . . Loving you with all her heart, your old Mama."[10]

The Duchess of Coburg continued to be the anchor of her family, a reliable source of support for her daughters, especially for Bee, who in 1910, gave birth in Coburg to a son, Alvaro, the first of the Duchess of Coburg's Spanish grandchildren. Despite being banished, the duchess's son-in-law, Ali, tried to serve Spain, going into active military service. At the end of 1911, Marie Alexandrovna wrote Ducky telling her that "we are returning to a life full of anxiety because Ali leaves today for Morocco [which was at war with Spain]."[11]

In 1912, Marie Alexandrovna was pleased to hear that at long last, Bee and Ali were finally allowed to return to Spain. The Duchess of Coburg wrote that Bee "is very satisfied with the reception" that she and Ali received upon their return. The duchess also noted that Bee was "content with her new house. Only she is not accustomed to so many visits, audiences and courtesies as one has to endure there. *Very good for her.* This sad episode [of the exile] has arrived at its conclusion, now the creation of a good position in Spain will depend on her tact and her *savoir faire.*"[12] While living in Spain, Bee gave birth to two more sons, Alonso (b. 1912) and Ataulfo (b. 1913). That year also marked the last time that all Marie Alexandrovna's daughters would spend a holiday together with their mother. It was a summer the sisters would always remember with nostalgia.

Despite the fragile peace that reigned over Europe during the summer of 1913, political conflicts on the continent boded ill for the future. In the Balkans, the powder keg of Europe, violence loomed large. The political vacuum created by a weakening Ottoman Empire emboldened a number of rapacious Balkan countries. They were also driven by ambitions to liberate their brothers from the Turkish yoke and avenge Ottoman oppression. In October 1912, the Balkan League, consisting of Bulgaria, Greece, Montenegro, and Serbia, attacked the disintegrating Ottoman Empire in a conflict that came to be known as the First Balkan War.

Greece, in particular, was anxious to avenge its defeat at the hands of the Turks in 1897. Moreover, Greek politicians were still inflamed by the *Megali Idea*, with Eleutherios Venizelos pushing Greece to strike and strive for the coveted goal. With this in mind, Venizelos appointed Crown Prince Constantine as commander-in-chief of the army. This time, the Greek army was disciplined and prepared for war. Constantine acquitted himself well, gaining a major victory in November 1912 when the city of Salonika fell into Greek hands after some five centuries under Turkish rule. The humiliating debacle of 1897 was finally avenged. Greece was victorious. Queen Olga's eldest son entered Salonika a conquering hero. The newly liberated city's Greeks were ecstatic. Weeping for joy, a number of them flung themselves at Constantine's feet in gratitude; others clamored to kiss his coat or boots. The fall of Salonika was of great significance and made such an impression that the Greeks living in New York City collected $3,000 in order to have a special commemorative sword crafted for Constantine. Made of fine Toledo steel, the sword had a "jeweled Byzantine hilt of gold" and was inscribed, "To Constantine the Liberator, from the Greeks in America, 1913."[13]

A proud King George I hurried to Salonika. He made his official entry into the city with Crown Prince Constantine, amidst widespread rejoicing from the Greek populace. In the meantime, Queen Olga continued her philanthropic works unceasingly. Despite having to undergo treatments for her bad eyesight, Olga never stopped planning and acting upon her charitable endeavors. The queen busied herself with plans for women prisoners and the Greek army simultaneously, by having female inmates make blankets for the soldiers. Added to this was Olga's determination to establish a new maternity hospital. Often, the queen dipped into her own savings to fund her charitable works during this time. As war raged, Olga made endless rounds to visit injured soldiers, comforting the dying and aiding their families. Yet for all she did, Olga was never satisfied that she was doing enough for others. "How much I wish I could be more useful to the people," she once confessed to her close friend Ioulia Karolou. When Karolou tried to assure the queen that she was being very useful to her people, Olga humbly replied: "I am a big nothing, and don't try to dispute it."[14]

In December 1912, while Queen Olga was in Salonika, Tsar Ferdinand of Bulgaria arrived, intending to give the impression that Bulgaria had a right to the city as well. At a meeting between King Ferdinand and King George, Queen Olga did not hesitate to press Greece's point, endeavoring "to persuade Ferdinand firmly that Salonika would have to form an integral part of the

Greek dominions. Tactfully, Ferdinand remarked that it would be a matter for future discussions between their respective governments."[15]

In the realm of foreign policy, Ferdinand of Bulgaria also harbored dreams of acquiring "the greatest prize of all—Constantinople."[16] But increasingly, it was the Greeks who laid claim to that elusive dream. They could not be blamed for feeling that this fervent wish they had harbored for so long might just come tantalizingly close to fruition. In early March 1913, the Greeks' jubilation mounted as they became masters of the Epirus. After "a long and stubborn re-sistance," the city of Janina surrendered to them. Crown Prince Constantine ordered the attack, the result of which ended in "immense losses to the enemy" and an operation that was "completely successful" for the Greeks. King George of the Hellenes issued a telegram to the prime minister, telling Venizelos: "God be praised for this fresh triumph of our brave army . . . I am proud of this fresh national glory."[17] The fall of Janina into Greek hands was significant and prompted the *Times*'s Athens correspondent to tell its readers that: "The whole of Greece is celebrating the victory. Congratulatory telegrams from all quarters have been sent to the Crown Prince . . . As a result of this fresh feat on the part of the Crown Prince, which adds another important province to Greece, and the bravery shown by the other Princes during the war and the assistance rendered by the Princesses, the dynasty may now be considered to be naturalized and definitely linked to Greece."[18]

During the Balkan conflict, Queen Olga's daughters-in-law emulated her philanthropic endeavors by organizing hospitals and nursing work. Miechen's daughter, Elena, was no less active than her sisters-in-law and Queen Olga in helping the sick and wounded. With Elena busy with her nursing work and her husband, Prince Nicholas, preoccupied with overseeing the governance of Salonika, the couple acquiesced to Grand Duchess Vladimir's suggestion that she take care of her Greek granddaughters. However, the manner in which Marie Pavlovna went about this illustrates how domineering the grand duch-ess could be.

Long accustomed to wielding influence and getting her way, the grand duch-ess was no less tyrannical when it came to her relationship with her only daugh-ter, Elena. The bone of contention centered on Elena's closeness to her daughters' English nurse, Kate Fox, whom Miechen never took to. Kate had much of the know-it-all attitude, a characteristic the grand duchess thoroughly disliked. Miechen was also indignant that Kate Fox did not hesitate to spank her royal charges when disciplining them, prompting Miechen to complain to her friends that "that dreadful woman knocks them about."[19] By 1913 things had come to a head. The catalyst that set the grand duchess vehemently against Kate was a letter from Elena to Kate, in which she dared to warn her children's nurse about the grand duchess. And so, "everything that happened afterwards happened because of this letter."[20]

When the First Balkan War broke out, Princess Marina was being treated at a clinic in France for a twisted foot, a problem she was born with. The Grand Duchess Vladimir was in Paris at the time. Kate was with Marina. Elena joined them in France. Elena, believing that her children would be safer with their Russian grandmother than back in Greece, let her girls stay with her mother in Paris. Miechen indulged her granddaughters, taking them for drives in the Bois de Boulogne, showing them off to her French friends, "showered them with toys, presents and chic new dresses and sent them off in blue reefer coats and patterned bonnets to look at Punch and Judy shows—which they seemed to like best of all."

Soon, a full-blown family war erupted, pitting Miechen against Kate Fox and Elena. The grand duchess had had enough of "that dreadful woman" nurse Fox and was determined to get rid of her.[21] Miechen appealed by letter to Queen Olga's son, Nicholas, telling him that Princesses Olga and Elisabeth "are now old enough to be without a real nurse under the care of their mother who nursed the poor soldiers and will have <u>learnt to take care of her own children</u>." Then came Miechen's painful accusation that Kate and Elena were neglectful about raising the girls. But Prince Nicholas was unable to do anything; his position at Salonika kept him too busy to intervene. In a letter to Kate, Nicholas was sympathetic, telling her that the Grand Duchess Vladimir "has been cruel to you, cruel to the children, and cruel to us parents." Moreover, the prince also said that Marie Pavlovna had threatened to "withdraw her protection" from Princess Marina, "meaning of course that she will force us to pay for everything!"[22]

The discord caused by Grand Duchess Vladimir's meddling in Prince and Princess Nicholas's domestic situation did not ease until Miechen forced Elena's hand. "The Gd Dchss wants me <u>absolutely</u> to send you away," confided Elena to Kate.[23] Prince Nicholas tried to soften the blow by writing to Kate and telling her: "Letting you go Foxie is one of the hardest things we have ever done."[24] It was inevitable that when it came to two stubborn creatures like Kate Fox and the Grand Duchess Vladimir, both could not dominate the family and the nursery simultaneously; and in the end, Miechen was the victor. Nonetheless, even after Kate's dismissal, the Grand Duchess Vladimir did not relent. Still protesting the nurse's close connection to Elena and her family,

Miechen withdrew "all financial support from her daughter's family for a full year to show her disapproval" and even "refused to meet the Prince and Princess and their older children" for a time.[25]

Miechen's "jealous guard of her children's affections" was not unusual for a woman of her class and time. The Dowager Empress Marie Feodorovna and her sister Queen Alexandra had similar priorities. As time went on, the aging sisters expected one of their daughters to be constantly at their side, a practice exercised by Queen Victoria when it came to her youngest daughter, Princess Beatrice. Victoria allowed Beatrice to marry, only with the stipulation that she, her husband, and their children live with the elderly queen year round. The Grand Duchess Vladimir was therefore not alone in being a demanding mother and grandmother. "Particularly in royal and aristocratic circles, where the elder generation held the power and the purse strings and where there was a public dimension to the upbringing of children, the grandparents' word could be hard to oppose"; and this was the case with the Grand Duchess Vladimir and Prince and Princess Nicholas of Greece.[26]

In March 1913, tensions had eased enough for Miechen's two eldest granddaughters to return to Greece. Elena set off for Vienna to meet her mother, then escort the princesses back to their homeland. On March 17, King George I accompanied Elena to the train station to bid her goodbye. Only the week before, the king had also bid farewell to his wife, Olga, who had returned to the Greek capital to work at the military hospital there. Elena only made it as far as Belgrade before she had to return suddenly to Greece.

On March 18, George I lunched with his sons, telling them that he would most likely abdicate after his golden jubilee in October that year. George thought that after fifty years on the volatile Greek throne, he was entitled to a little rest in his old age and was ready to hand the reins of power to his eldest son, Constantine. After wresting Salonika from the Turks in a victorious war, it seemed a fitting time to abdicate. And so, that afternoon, King George went off on his postprandial stroll, a contented man.

Only an equerry and two guards accompanied the sixty-eight-year-old king, walking behind him. Moving leisurely through the crowded streets of Salonika, they passed a café where a man watched them in earnest. The king and his small party continued their stroll until they reached the White Tower, marking the end of their customary walk. The group turned around and as they walked next to the café they had passed earlier, the man who had been watching them shot King George in the back with a revolver. Shot through the heart and lungs, the mortally wounded king was dead by the time he arrived at the hospital. The assassin turned out to be a mentally unbalanced Macedonian by the name of Alexander Schinas. Later, while awaiting trial, Schinas threw himself from a window and died. Had the assassin been a Bulgarian, widespread violence would have likely broken out at Salonika, pitting Greeks against Bulgarians. But because the assassin was a Greek, shocked as the Salonikans were, calmness prevailed.

Prince Nicholas was the first member of the Greek royal family to learn that something was tragically amiss. A soldier rushed to him, shouting excitedly: "They have struck the King."[27] Nicholas's eldest brother, forty-four-year-old Constantine, was commanding Greek troops at Janina when his father was murdered. As the new king, Constantine I went immediately to Athens to be with his mother and wife. Constantine's wife, Sophie, who was seven months pregnant with her sixth child, was resting in her palace with her sixteen-year-old daughter, Princess Helen. Sophie's tranquil rest was suddenly shattered when the marshal of the Court came to her and gravely announced: "Your Royal Highness, I bring very bad news." At first Sophie thought something had happened to Constantine, but then the marshal spoke hesitatingly and gravely: "His Majesty has met with a serious injury." Fearing the worst, Sophie asked, "You mean . . . he is dead?"

"An hour ago, he was shot by an assassin in the streets of Salonika, and died immediately" came the answer. Straightaway, Sophie, now Queen of the Hellenes, accompanied by Princess Helen, rushed to the Royal Palace to be with Queen Olga. Olga was already aware of the dreadful news through her sons Andrew and George, who had broken the dreadful tragedy to her gradually. They had at first informed their mother that King George was seriously injured. The queen's close friend, Ioulia Karolou, was with her at that fateful time and recounted how Olga cried bitterly and knelt praying for the king to live. Through her sobs, the queen told Karolou: "Throughout my whole life I have been so happy with my King." When Queen Olga finally learned the truth, she cried out in anguish. Upon meeting, the two queens—Olga and Sophie—embraced. Then with her head bowed, the newly widowed sixty-one-year-old Queen Olga muttered, with tears falling down her cheeks: "It is the will of God."[28]

That evening, the new widow confided to Ioulia Karolou that she felt very ill. The shock had shaken the queen to the core. The next morning, however, Queen Olga, dressed in black, greeted Karolou calmly. "Her expression was that of deep sorrow, and, at the same time, of angelic tranquility," recalled Karolou. "She was the personification of Christian hope and unmoving faith, with touching obedience to the Holy Will of God!"[29]

Queen Olga traveled to Salonika to be with her son Prince Nicholas and to escort King George's body back to the capital for the funeral. When Olga went to see her husband's body for the first time, she stayed and prayed for an hour. She also insisted on helping place her husband's body in the casket.

King George's body was taken to Athens for the funeral. Thousands of Greeks lined the capital's streets to pay their respects. A service was held at the city's cathedral in the presence of the royal family and other dignitaries. On the evening after the funeral service ended, Queen Olga told Karolou, "It is all finished! . . . It is so terrible, but yet so true!"

On March 22, Queen Olga wrote a letter to the Greek people that was published in the newspapers: "The expression of the heartfelt participation of the Greek People in my sorrow have [*sic*] touched me deeply . . . I thank the Greek People from the bottom of my heart for their expression of their sincere compassion towards me . . . and may the Almighty God, in whose Holy Will we all obey uncomplainingly, send us the Heavenly dew of the Divine comfort from above."[30]

In assessing King George I's life and death, Sir Francis Elliot, wrote:

> Tragic as was the manner of the King's death, he was at least happy in the moment of it. He had seen the edifice he had laboured to construct for fifty years crowned by the victories of his army under the leadership of his Son and Successor. He had the assurance that his dynasty was at last firmly seated upon the throne which he had often during his long reign been tempted to abandon in despair. He had seen his aspirations realized beyond his most ambitious dreams. He will live on in the memories of his people as a martyr to the national cause.[31]

The assassination of King George I of the Hellenes was a great tragedy not only for Queen Olga, but also for her sister-in-law Marie Feodorovna. Always close to her brother, the news that he had been killed was yet another bitter pill in the life of the dowager empress. Queen Olga's daughter Marie, upon hearing the news of her father's murder, immediately started off for Greece from her home, Harax, in the Crimea. Once in St. Petersburg, she hurried to the Anichkov Palace where she found her aunt, the Dowager Empress Marie Feodorovna "in a terrible state of mind."[32]

Queen Olga buried her husband at Tatoi, where, for a long time, she visited the graveside almost every day. Olga, who wished to be referred to as Queen

Mother of the Greeks, left Greece in the summer of 1913 for Germany for eye treatments, then went on to England to visit her sister-in-law Queen Alexandra. Afterward, Olga went to Russia and stayed for a while in her beloved Pavlovsk. Writing to Ioulia Karolou from Russia, Queen Olga told her friend: "If you only knew how I fear the return and life in the deserted and orphaned [Royal] palace [of Athens]! . . . I must start again with all that terrible pain! . . . I try though to not be faint-hearted—baby Jesus will help me."[33]

Queen Olga's pain and loneliness at the beginning of her widowhood was understandable, particularly as her husband of forty-five years had died under the most tragic circumstances. Though her eldest son, Constantine, ascended the throne because his father had been murdered, Queen Olga could take comfort in one thing: Constantine became king at a time when his popularity was at its zenith. The *Times* was full of admiration for the new king, confidently telling its readers that "King Constantine will live in history as a soldier monarch and as the first military leader of rejuvenated Greece."[34]

22

ON THE EVE

Queen Olga's son did not have long to wait before commanding his army in battle again. Only three months after King George I's assassination, Greece went to war again. Having successfully collaborated to defeat the Ottoman Empire during the First Balkan War, Greece and her erstwhile allies—Bulgaria, Serbia, and Montenegro—fought amongst themselves over the spoils. A dissatisfied Bulgaria, rapacious for more territory, attacked Greece and Serbia. Greece fought back, and forces under King Constantine's command defeated the Bulgarians at the Battle of Kilkis. In July 1913, Romania joined Greece in attacking Bulgaria. Facing defeat, Bulgaria surrendered. In less than six weeks, the Second Balkan War ended with Bulgaria forfeiting all the lands gained from the First Balkan War.

Thanks to its victory in both Balkan wars, Greece gained significant amounts of territory, increasing its territorial holdings from some 25,000 square miles to nearly 42,000 square miles, while her population grew from 2.6 million to 4.3 million people. Salonika, Kavala, Janina, Epirus, and southern Macedonia became Greek, while Crete formally came into union with Greece in December 1913. It seemed as if the *Megali Idea* was finally coming into fruition.

So successful was Greece under the leadership of Queen Olga's eldest son in the Second Balkan War that Sir Francis Elliot reported to London that King Constantine, already "a popular idol" when he ascended the throne, completed "his apotheosis" with "the successful Bulgarian campaign." The future looked bright for the Greek royals, prompting the British embassy in Athens to report that "the rest of the Royal Family have [*sic*] entirely recovered the respect and affection of the people."[1] Queen Olga could take great comfort in this. Moreover, the queen could not have asked for better relations between the Greek prime minister, Eleutherios Venizelos, and her son, King Constantine. At the conclusion of the negotiations that culminated in the Treaty of Bucharest, Constantine I thanked Venizelos and told him that "a new and glorious era is opening for us . . . The Nation is grateful to you."[2]

The Greeks, in turn, expressed their gratitude for Constantine I's outstanding leadership by honoring him with a triumphant welcome to Athens in August 1913. Into Phaleron Bay, the whole Greek fleet accompanied the king, who was aboard the battle cruiser *Averoff.* Disembarking at Athens, King Constantine was met by Queen Sophie and together they rode in a procession through streets lined with wildly cheering crowds. Many were so moved by the occasion that they shed tears of joy. The bond between the king, his soldiers, and his subjects on that day seemed strong and indissoluble. Prince Christopher recalled King Constantine's "stupendous" welcome where "crowds besieged the Palace, [and] waited for hours to get even a glimpse of him."[3] When King Constantine arrived at the Royal Palace, his proud mother awaited her victorious son.

Though grateful that her eldest son's reign was starting out so well, the queen was still very much immersed in mourning for her late husband. Throughout the following months, Olga remained preoccupied by her husband's tragic death—so much so that it took nine long months after her husband's assassination before the queen took pen to hand and wrote a letter to her favorite nephew, Britain's King George V. She asked him to forgive her for having taken so long to acknowledge his sympathy on his uncle's murder. "I don't want to excuse myself," wrote the queen, of her "unpardonable long silence . . . but I must say, that I was . . . stunned and could not write—til now heaps of letters remain unanswered and their sight tortures me! And it is certainly not ungratefulness, no, I feel so deeply grateful for every sign of sympathy, but something I can't explain. As time passes the pain and heartache does not pass—it is dreadful and this big empty house, all the rooms, so full of remembrances and now X-mas eve without him—it is all too painful for words . . . , of course . . . I don't want to complain and God knows best. I have had long years & a very large part of happiness in my life and God be thanked and praised for it!"[4]

Months later, Queen Olga went to England where her sister-in-law Marie Feodorovna, who was also visiting, welcomed her. In her diary, the dowager empress recorded that she went to the station "to meet dear Olga . . . This was our first meeting with her since God took our angel Willy [King George I] away."[5] Olga and Marie Feodorovna, finally reunited after the murder, consoled each other. During their stay with Queen Alexandra, the three grieving women gradually raised each other's spirits, deriving much needed peace and solace from each other's company. Marie Feodorovna's diary entry affords a glimpse into their tranquil time together: "along with Alix [Queen Alexandra] and Olga we went to Windsor; where we walked down numerous halls of the castle and then drank tea with the gardener in the garden with wonderful blooming roses and other pretty flowers."[6]

For Marie Alexandrovna these years were largely quiet. The Duchess of Coburg rightly felt proud of how her daughter Crown Princess Marie of Romania acquitted herself during the Second Balkan War. During the deprivations brought on by the war, Missy unflinchingly helped the Romanian soldiers who were stricken with cholera. As she visited hospital wards and aided the sick amidst squalor and hardship, Missy gained not only the gratitude and admiration of her countrymen; she also found herself being drawn closer to Romania. Moreover, Missy began to understand and take a keen interest in the Byzantine intricacies of Romanian and Balkan politics. King Carol grudgingly appreciated the princess and acknowledged what an asset she was to Romania. With her intelligence, vibrant personality, and eagerness to espouse Romania's cause, Marie Alexandrovna's eldest daughter was poised to serve Romania well in the difficult years to come.

While war had raged in the Balkans, in nearby Russia the three hundredth anniversary of the reign of the Romanov dynasty—the Romanov Tercentenary— was under way. The official Tercentenary celebration began in St. Petersburg in February (n.s. March) 1913 with a twenty-one-gun salute from the Fortress of Sts. Peter and Paul. A lavish procession then made its way from the Winter Palace to the Cathedral of Our Lady of Kazan for a service of thanksgiving. Crowds watched a retinue of Cossacks escort the imperial family to the cathedral. Tsar Nicholas II and his heir, Alexei, led the family procession in an open carriage. Behind them rode the Tsarina Alexandra and the Dowager Empress Marie Feodorovna in a carriage drawn by four white horses. A special guest turned up at the Kazan Cathedral. Dressed in a "magnificent Russian tunic of crimson silk, patent-leather top boots, black cloth full trouser's and peasant's overcoat," Rasputin demanded to be allowed inside. Michael Rodzianko, the Duma's president, confronted Rasputin, who then tried to hypnotize Rodzianko by staring intently into his eyes. Rodzianko fought off Rasputin and angrily denounced him with the words: "Clear out at once, you vile heretic, there is no place for you in this sacred house!"[7] Eventually realizing that he would be denied entrance into Kazan Cathedral, Rasputin left.

The Tercentenary celebrations continued through the following weeks. Anna Viroubova recalled that the imperial visit to Kostrama "was a magnificent success, the people actually wading waist deep in the river in order get nearer the Imperial boat."[8] Princess Nicholas Galitzine recorded a similar reception, as she recalled how excited the people were at Yaroslavl, in anticipation that Nicholas, Alexandra, and their children would celebrate the Tercentenary there. "Immense crowds" awaited the imperial family's arrival at Yaroslavl, some two hundred and fifty kilometers from Moscow. When the crowds saw the small ship bringing the tsar, tsarina, and their children nearing them, "loud exclamations" and "exultant" outbursts were heard."[9]

Others, though, had different views of the Tercentenary celebrations. Count Kokovtsov, who was with Nicholas II on his trip down the Volga, thought that "there was nothing in the feeling of the crowd but shallow curiosity."[10] Even Anna Viroubova detected an underlying sadness to the celebrations. During a performance in St. Petersburg at the opera of Glinka's *Life for the Tsar*, Viroubova felt "that there was in the brilliant audience little real enthusiasm, little real loyalty."[11]

The tsar and tsarina's daughters took part in a number of the Tercentenary celebrations. Those who caught a glimpse of the two eldest grand duchesses could see that Olga and Tatiana had grown into lovely young ladies. With her two sheltered granddaughters rapidly maturing, Marie Feodorovna felt the time had come to give a special ball in their honor. In the early days of 1914, eighteen-year-old Olga Nikolaevna and sixteen-year-old Tatiana Nikolaevna eagerly went to their grandmother's home, the Anichkov Palace, for their first real formal ball.

Guests marveled at the dowager empress's appearance. Despite her sixty-six years, Marie Feodorovna surprised many at how youthful she looked. Tsarina Alexandra could not avoid the big event held in honor of her two eldest daughters and came out of her sequestration to lend her presence to the ball. Though Alexandra left the Anichkov at midnight, Nicholas II stayed until four thirty in the morning. His daughters had so thoroughly enjoyed themselves that they could not leave any earlier. Now that they had officially made their debut, talk of marriage would soon surround these two granddaughters of Marie Feodorovna.

Their cousin Princess Irina, Xenia's only daughter, was also of a marriageable age. With her blue eyes, pretty features, and illustrious background, Irina was one of the most desirable catches. A favorite grandchild of the Dowager Empress Marie Feodorovna, Princess Irina was a shy, intelligent young woman who soon caught the fancy of Russia's most eligible bachelors.

Among them was Prince Felix Yussoupov.[12] Eight years Irina's senior, he had become heir to one of the greatest fortunes in all Russia after his elder brother was killed in a duel. The family's wealth came from Felix's mother, Zenaida Yussoupova, who had been one of the great beauties of her day. The immensely wealthy Zenaida followed her heart and had married Count Felix Sumarakov-Elston, a guards officer. The Yussoupovs, of Tartar origin, served Russia's tsars in successive generations, gaining enormous influence and wealth. In order to perpetuate his wife's illustrious family name, Felix requested permission to use her surname—a request Emperor Alexander III had granted.

The Yussoupovs' estates and palaces counted in the dozens. So plentiful were their residences that "they occasionally sold them off to the imperial government for use as official buildings"; and in the Caucasus, one estate "skirted the Caspian Sea for 125 miles." In fact, the Yussoupov holdings were so numerous and vast that "many of their houses, rarely occupied and in distant corners of European Russia, were simply forgotten."[13] Besides their extensive estates, the Yussoupovs were also great patrons of the arts, possessing numerous works by the great masters such as Gainsborough, Rubens, and Rembrandt. Felix Yussoupov had grown up amidst this rarefied world of luxury and privilege. It was not much different from the world in which his friend Grand Duke Dmitri Pavlovich was raised.

Dmitri, the only son of Queen Olga's deceased daughter, Alexandra, had been raised by the tsarina's sister, the Grand Duchess Elisabeth. However, after Ella became an Orthodox nun, Dmitri spent much time in the company of Nicholas and Alexandra at Tsarskoe Selo. Grand Duke Dmitri enlivened the monotonous lives of the imperial family at the Alexander Palace, making the tsar "rock with laughter, and all the children besides, with his jokes and anecdotes."[14] So popular was Dmitri with the family that he even became a great favorite with the reticent tsarina. Dmitri also became one of Felix Yussoupov's closest friends.

Felix described Dmitri as being "tall, elegant, well-bred, with deep, thoughtful eyes" whose "charm won the hearts of all but the weakness of his character made him dangerously easy to influence."[15] Of delicate health, with a propensity to depression, Dmitri was, concluded Albert ("Bertie") Stopford of the British embassy in St. Petersburg, "always helpless and desolate," whereas Felix was "so clever he will get all he wants."[16]

Like a number of the grand dukes, Felix and Dmitri fell into a dissipated lifestyle dominated by carousing and the pursuit of pleasure. Rumors swirled that the two were more than close friends. Felix was already known to have indulged in affairs with women and men. Whatever the nature of Dmitri and Felix's friendship, Felix's decision to wed the dowager empress's granddaughter, Irina, put it to the test.

Felix at one time wanted to emulate Ella and dispose of his riches to help the poor, but was dissuaded by his mother. Princess Zenaida urged him in another direction. As Felix was the sole heir to the honors and wealth of the Yussoupov family, Zenaida convinced him that he needed to marry and produce the next heir. Since a marriage with any of the four grand duchesses would have been impossible (because a marriage with Felix would have been considered morganatic), the next best catch was undoubtedly Marie Feodorovna's other granddaughter, Princess Irina. There was, however, the question of another suitor for Irina's hand, and that suitor was none other than Queen Olga's grandson Grand Duke Dmitri, Felix's best friend.

When Felix told Dmitri that he intended to make Irina his wife, Dmitri objected; he too wanted Irina for his wife. In a letter to Felix, Princess Zenaida tried to reassure her son: "My dear boy. [Irina's] parents have explained their position . . . Her mother [Xenia] does not deny that the grandmother [the dowager empress Maria Fyodorovna] is for Dmitry. But she [Xenia] says that she herself would have nothing against [you] if Irina will hear of no one else."[17]

Even when Felix confessed his sordid past, Irina freely agreed to marry him, so Dmitri eventually capitulated. Irina's parents, however, became hesitant about allowing Irina to marry Felix, with his homosexual tendencies, even though he was the heir to the Yussoupov fortune. Xenia and Sandro decided to put an end to the engagement. Felix, though, was persistent. He barged in on Xenia and Sandro, who were in Copenhagen with Irina and staying with the dowager empress. Felix admitted to his past, but also somehow managed to be persuasive enough about his current state and his love for Irina that Xenia and Sandro believed him.

Felix's next task was to overcome the dowager empress's reservations. Marie Feodorovna had a special affection for Xenia and Irina. With the Grand Duchess Olga being "too independent to be thoroughly approved of by her mother," the Grand Duke Michael being married morganatically, and Tsar Nicholas II dominated by the Tsarina Alexandra, Grand Duchess Xenia easily became the dowager empress's favorite child. Since Xenia was "her mother's consolation," Xenia's children too were "a constant source of interest and loving care to their grandmother."[18] It was therefore natural that the gossip surrounding her granddaughter's future husband motivated the dowager empress to learn what she could about Felix. If rumors about his past were true and Felix was unrepentant, then Marie Feodorovna was certain to obstruct the marriage. Determined to discover what she could, the Dowager Empress Marie Feodorovna summoned Felix to an audience with her.

During their exchange, the dowager empress listened at length to Irina's suitor. "Little by little," recalled Felix, "I was winning her over to my side," so that at the end of their talk, the dowager empress rose and said kindly: "Do not worry; I will do what I can for your happiness."[19] Felix was again victorious. With approval from the dowager empress and Irina's parents, the wedding finally took place in February 1914 at the Anichkov Palace. Unlike other imperial brides, Irina was dressed in a modern confection made of white satin, her veil held in place by Felix's gift to her, a diamond and crystal tiara created by Cartier.

Though Princess Irina was not pressured into marriage, pressure came to bear on Marie Feodorovna's granddaughter Grand Duchess Olga. In the interests of cementing a Russian-Romanian alliance, attempts were made to try to marry off the Duchess of Coburg's grandson, Prince Carol, with the dowager empress of Russia's granddaughter. Carol and his parents visited the imperial family at Tsarskoe Selo in the hopes that a spark of attraction might take place between the two young people. But nothing of the sort happened.

In mid-June 1914, another attempt at matchmaking took place. The tsar, tsarina, and their children sailed on the imperial yacht, the *Standart*, from Yalta to the Black Sea port of Constanza in Romania. They were ostensibly on an official visit to King Carol I and Queen Elisabeth, but the main object of the visit was to get Carol and Olga interested in each other. Again, not a spark of attraction occurred. The eighteen-year-old grand duchess was especially adamant that she remain in her native land and not make a new life for herself abroad. She stated so emphatically to her tutor, Pierre Gilliard, telling him that, "I don't want to leave Russia . . . I'm a Russian and mean to remain a Russian!"[20]

The Constanza visit underscored the glaring disparity between the two prospective mothers-in-law—Marie Feodorovna's daughter-in-law Tsarina Alexandra and Marie Alexandrovna's daughter Crown Princess Marie. For Alix the visit was an ordeal, and she remained withdrawn, almost morose. Not having cultivated or practiced skills for public appearances, Alix was at a loss, and in fact the brief visit took its toll, sending her into a near collapse. Missy, on the other hand, was the perfect hostess: ebullient and at ease. Moreover, her popularity with the Romanians was in abundant show. Had the Duchess of Coburg been present at the visit, she would have been proud to see that her eldest daughter had captured the hearts of her future subjects, an advantage that the tsarina could only have envied. Marie Alexandrovna's periodic lectures to her daughter Missy had borne fruit. The crown princess had by this time matured and had come to understand her responsibilities as a future queen. She admitted to having "learnt something of patience and abnegation and had understood the necessity of constant effort towards a central goal, had understood also that 'serving' was the real object of life."[21]

A kind of peace had finally descended upon the turbulent personal life of the Duchess of Coburg's eldest daughter. To Marie Alexandrovna's pleasure, Missy ensured that her children would come to know their grandmother well through annual visits to Tegernsee. Once Missy and her children arrived, the entrance hall bustled with the Duchess of Coburg's welcoming embraces. Marie Alexandrovna would fuss over each grandchild, marveling at how much they had grown since she saw them last. Missy and her children then repaired to rooms that had been "lovingly prepared, everywhere flowers and the odour of a certain scent special to Mamma's house, also the smell of Russian cigarettes."

Reunions at Tegernsee were eagerly anticipated events for Missy. The familiar routine of drives around the verdant countryside, eating wonderful meals, seeing old servants, getting mild scoldings from her mother, and seeing the lovely gardens with their numerous roses—all were a kind of tonic for Marie Alexandrovna's daughter. These visits were sometimes marred by rain, which elicited complaints from the Duchess of Coburg. Nevertheless, Missy's mother remained an intriguing combination of endearing eccentric and formidable matriarch. As Missy put it: "Mamma" would "also excuse herself just a little as though it [the rains] were her fault, as though she were responsible for the behaviour of the skies."

Marie Alexandrovna had tried to raise her daughters with an iron hand, but had less control over her grandchildren. When the Duchess of Coburg tried to rein in Nicky, Missy's younger son, the duchess found him unreceptive. "Accustomed to giving orders, to being obeyed," as Missy put it, her mother could not get her little fair-haired grandson to listen to her. "Girls are really much nicer than boys," concluded the Duchess of Coburg. "He deserves a whipping," she would declare, but in the end, like many an indulgent grandmother, Marie Alexandrovna could not bring herself to discipline Nicky. The tranquility Missy found at Tegernsee was invaluable. "I am far from politics, far from intrigue, strife. There is rest under Mamma's roof,"[22] wrote Missy affectionately years later when those idyllic days had long gone.

In the summer of 1914, Crown Princess Marie of Romania was planning another of her Tegernsee visits. But the summer of 1914 was unlike any other, for on June 28, a shocking event took place that would change the course of history.

On that day, the heir to the Austro-Hungarian Empire, Archduke Franz Ferdinand, and his morganatic wife, Sophie, made an official visit to Sarajevo, which was then part of the empire. The Habsburg dynasty that ruled Austria-Hungary had wielded power over central Europe and parts of the Balkans for hundreds of years, but by 1914, their hold over their Slavic subjects was tenuous. Serbia, a hotbed of intrigue, was proving a political minefield for its rulers back in Vienna. It was hoped that Archduke Franz Ferdinand's goodwill visit might mitigate tensions that had been building within the Habsburg empire.

As Franz Ferdinand and Sophie made their way through a narrow street in Sarajevo, a young Bosnian student, Gavrilo Princip, neared the couple's car and fired his pistol at them. The archduke was shot in the neck, his wife in the abdomen. Before collapsing, Franz Ferdinand begged his wife to live, exclaiming: "Stay alive for the children!"[23] Such were the fatally wounded archduke's last words. Both husband and wife died soon afterward. When the eighty-three-year-old Emperor Franz Joseph, who had already endured the agony of his son's death and his wife's murder, heard the dreadful news of the murder of his heir and his wife, the old emperor muttered: "Horrible, horrible! No sorrow is spared me."[24]

In Greece, King Constantine was at the Olympic Stadium in Athens when he was handed a telegram informing him of the double murder at Sarajevo. When it came to interpreting what the murders might precipitate, few were as prescient as Queen Olga's son. Horrified, he turned to his daughter, Helen, and said with a sense of foreboding: "Now, we can expect trouble."[25]

In the Finnish fjords where the tsar, tsarina, and their children were cruising on board the *Standart*, news of Archduke Franz Ferdinand's murder "greatly impressed and horrified the Imperial Family," noted Baroness Buxhoeveden, "but at first it was never supposed that this tragic event would be followed by such terrible consequences."[26] As was often the case, attention centered on the Tsarevich Alexei, who had this time twisted his ankle. The boy was in pain yet again as the ankle swelled. Moreover, news arrived that an attempt on Rasputin's life took place in his village in Siberia. He was seriously wounded but lived.

One of the few imperial family members who seemed to take the news of the Sarajevo killings with greater gravity was Miechen. The Grand Duchess Vladimir was residing at her home at Tsarskoe Selo that summer. Staying with Miechen was her niece Grand Duchess Marie. Marie's father, the disgraced Grand Duke Paul, and his wife, Olga, were finally pardoned by Tsar Nicholas II and had returned to Russia after a ten-year exile in Paris (Nicholas II in 1915 granted Olga the title "Princess Paley"). They were "completely happy—especially my father—to be at home in Russia," recalled Paul's daughter, Marie. Grand Duke Paul and Olga lived not far from Miechen's home at Tsarskoe Selo. Marie recalled that her Aunt Miechen "gave dinners and entertained a great deal" at the time.[27] These entertainments abruptly ceased after news filtered through of the assassinations at Sarajevo. Marie and Miechen were watching military maneuvers at Krasno Selo when they heard the report of the killings. They hurried back to Tsarskoe Selo, feeling "disquieted." The Grand Duchess Vladimir's house, noted Marie, "until then always filled with guests, had suddenly emptied. Now Aunt Miechen and I often seemed alone, interminably discussing the turn of political events, anxiously awaiting the outcome."[28]

Besides Miechen, another Romanov was anxious about the implications of the Sarajevo murders—the dowager empress. In a message to Xenia, Marie Feodorovna wrote of her fears about the future: "It seems that all are mad . . . I am absolutely depressed. All that happened is so terrible . . . My God, what awaits us and what will that end with?"[29]

Despite the shock of the Sarajevo killings, "most Europeans refused to consider the Archduke's assassination a final act of doom."[30] Hence, most went about their business as if nothing of major consequence was expected. In Russia, preparations continued for the visit of President Raymond Poincaré of France to St. Petersburg. He duly arrived in early July and was impressively entertained by the imperial family.

After Poincaré's visit, Marie Feodorovna traveled to England to stay with her sister, Queen Alexandra. The dowager empress had hoped that this latest visit would be another placid one. As the weeks passed, however, it became increasingly apparent that the murders in Sarajevo had ignited a crisis of great magnitude. Nearly one month after Archduke Franz Ferdinand and his wife were murdered, Austria-Hungary sent Serbia an ultimatum, designed to pressure Serbia into war. Austria-Hungary hoped to defeat Serbia quickly before Russia, Serbia's ally, could respond. Unsatisfied with Serbia's answer to the ultimatum, Austria-Hungary, as planned, declared war on Serbia on July 28, 1914. A series of alliances were quickly called upon that would lead to widespread war. Russia mobilized its troops in defense of Serbia. This Russian mobilization was interpreted by Germany as an act of war against its ally, Austria-Hungary. Germany thus declared war on Russia on August 1 and on Russia's ally France on August 3. Germany went on to invade Belgium in an attempt to get to Paris and occupy the French capital. Great Britain, as a guarantor of Belgian neutrality, defended Belgium, signaling Britain's entry into the war. World War I—the Great War—had begun.

Queen Olga's youngest son, Christopher, was visiting his aunt Queen Alexandra in England, when Britain entered the war. Queen Sophie was also in England at the time, accompanied by her youngest children. Sophie knew that she had to make her way to Athens as quickly as possible; so, leaving her children in England, the queen rushed off to Greece.

Like Prince Christopher and Queen Sophie, Marie Feodorovna was also in England. When Queen Olga's daughter, Marie, visited her aunts—the dowager empress and Queen Alexandra—at the latter's London home, Marlborough House, she found both of them "in a terrible state of anxiety."[31] The dowager empress told her niece that she was going to return to Russia shortly and proposed to take the grand duchess and her daughters back with her, but Marie declined.

The Russian ambassador to Germany cabled the dowager empress, warning her not to travel to Germany due to strong anti-Russian sentiments there, but Marie Feodorovna never received the warning. Even in the best of times, Marie Feodorovna was accustomed to avoiding German soil if she could help it. The Russian diplomat Alexander Izvolsky recalled that whenever Marie Feodorovna visited Copenhagen "she arrived always on her yacht, in order not to have to cross Germany; when bad weather or the season of the year obliged her to return by land through Germany, she refused to cross the narrow straits between the Danish isles and the German coast in a steamer flying the German colours, and, instead, took a Danish boat to Warnemünde, where a special train of Russian railway carriages awaited her and transported her to the Russian frontier with as few stops as possible."[32] In the summer of 1914, however, the dowager empress could not afford to be so fastidious.

The fact that Marie Feodorovna was willing to pass through Germany to get to Russia as quickly as possible was indicative of the sense of urgency that gripped her. Accompanied by her daughter Grand Duchess Xenia the dowager empress journeyed from London and arrived at the Berlin train station in the imperial train. Also in Berlin were Felix and Irina Yussoupov and their entourage. Upon hearing that the couple was also trying to make their way back to

Russia, Marie Feodorovna ordered them to join her in the imperial train to make the journey with her. The dowager empress, though, did not realize that Kaiser Wilhelm II had ordered Felix and Irina detained.

Berlin was in a state of feverish excitement. With German troops preparing to leave for the front, its train station was nothing short of "an armed camp, and the platforms were packed with departing troops, accompanied by their wives and relations." Anti-Russian feelings were running high in the city and in the train station. When the crowds noticed the imperial train in their midst, near chaos broke out. The howling mob jeered and cursed at the train carrying Marie Feodorovna. The dowager empress had no choice but to pull "down the blinds near her and ordered all the windows to be covered." In their fury, the crowd began to smash the train, sending shards of glass flying. The irate mob came close to harming the dowager empress, as they tore down the blinds of the car where she was sitting. Thanks to the police, who rushed in to protect Marie Feodorovna, the dowager empress escaped serious harm. Kaiser Wilhelm II, who was informed about the incident could not detain the dowager empress in Germany, fearing the political repercussions that might ensue. But he did refuse "to give passage to the Imperial train, ordering it to leave German soil by the shortest route—to be diverted to the Danish frontier." In the end of the sorry spectacle, Marie Feodorovna's train "slid away from the platforms in its battered splendor with guards and policemen running beside it, fierce execrations and a shower of stones sped its passage."[33]

23

POOR, DOOMED RUSSIA!

Rasputin made a devastating prophecy. In a telegram sent to Nicholas II, Rasputin warned the tsar about his premonition for the empire: "Let Papa (Nicholas II) not plan war; it will be the end of Russia and of all of us; we shall lose to the last man."[1] The tsar ignored the telegram. As a sign of his displeasure with Rasputin's impertinence, Nicholas tore up the telegram in front of Anna Viroubova who had delivered it to him.

As the threat of armed conflict escalated during summer 1914, Germany's ambassador to Russia, Count Friedrich von Pourtalès, calculated that Russia would ultimately refuse the risks of war. However, his British counterpart, Sir George Buchanan, told Pourtalès, "Russia means it." The incredulous Pourtalès still refused to believe that Russia would fight Germany. But Buchanan was insistent. He put both his hands on the German ambassador's shoulders, looked him in the eyes, and repeated emphatically: "Count Pourtalès, Russia means it."[2]

Lines were drawn in two rival groups. On one side were the Central Powers, consisting of Austria-Hungary, the German Empire, Bulgaria, and the Ottoman Empire. Their enemies were the Allied or Entente Powers, consisting of Great Britain, France, and Russia. Although other countries subsequently joined either side, these countries bore the brunt of the fighting.

On August 2, a sweltering summer's day, Tsar Nicholas II, Tsarina Alexandra, and their daughters made their way from the relative peace and tranquility of Peterhof to the imperial capital of St. Petersburg to mark the formal declaration of hostilities. When the imperial family arrived by boat at St. Petersburg, they received a thunderous ovation. Excited masses shouted, "*Batiushka, Batiushka*, lead us to victory!"[3] More crowds greeted Nicholas and Alexandra upon their arrival at the Winter Palace to attend a Te Deum service. "Old men in court uniforms, young ones in fighters' khaki, women in light gowns and pretty summer hats"—all had filled the cavernous reception halls of the palace awaiting the sovereigns. Princess Julia Cantacuzène, U.S. President Ulysses S. Grant's granddaughter who married into the Russian nobility, was present at the Winter Palace on that momentous day. She described the crowds inside the palace as looking "tremendously tense and alive, as if gathering up their strength to offer it collectively to their Ruler." The religious service took place in the majestic Nicholas Hall before some five thousand guests. "The intensity" of the service, recalled Cantacuzène, "was extreme."[4] Queen Olga's granddaughter Grand Duchess Marie surveyed the assembled crowd and noted that "in spite of the light-coloured dresses and festive array of the gathering, the faces were strained and grave. Hands in long white gloves nervously crumpled handkerchiefs, and under the large hats fashionable at that time many eyes were red with crying."[5]

Julia Cantacuzène was especially struck by the Tsarina Alexandra's demeanor that day. "I cannot forget," recalled the American princess, "the beautiful, touching Madonna of that day, stooping to console and encourage her people, drowning her own sorrows in her tears of sympathy for her subjects!" The gravity of the occasion also moved Grand Duchess Vladimir. She "wept copiously, but held herself as always with dignity and spoke here and there to friends in the crowd whom she knew to be unhappy, embracing them, or saying a kind word."[6]

Outside the Winter Palace, feverish excitement gripped the crowds. An impressive quarter of a million Russians gathered. They carried icons and waved banners, savoring the historic occasion. A great wave of patriotism swept through the crowds. When the tsar and tsarina appeared before them on the palace balcony, the crowds knelt and sang the imperial anthem, "God Save the Tsar." "I have rarely witnessed a sight more solemn and impressive," recalled Prince Nicholas of Greece.[7] A lady-in-waiting to the dowager empress recounted "that this loyal demonstration had no power to banish from the countenance of the Tzar and Tzarina the look of suffering which showed how profoundly they felt the solemnity of the moment."[8] These were disquieting but also heady days for Nicholas II, for "never during the twenty years of his reign had the Emperor been so beloved, so respected, so popular in the eyes of his subjects as at that moment . . . Portraits of the monarch were in all the principal shop windows, and the veneration was so deep that men lifted their hats and women—even well-dressed, elegant ladies—made the sign of the cross."[9]

V. V. Shulgin, a Duma member, recalled the wave of patriotism that swept the country. "All Russia was caught up in a patriotic fervor," wrote Shulgin. "Reservists from the provinces arrived in formed units and did not even mutiny when the sale of vodka throughout Russia was discontinued in [a] single drastic step. It was a miracle. Absolutely unbelievable."[10]

Desperate to return to Russia, the Dowager Empress Marie Feodorovna finally arrived home in a roundabout way via Denmark and Sweden, having detoured up to the Gulf of Bothnia after her harrowing delay in Berlin. Moved by the plight of "a large number of destitute countrymen," during her journey home, the dowager empress insisted they travel with her. At the Russian frontier, she "refused to leave [for St. Petersburg] without having arranged for the transportation of the poor people she had befriended."[11] In gratitude for her kindness, those she helped gave Marie Feodorovna a bouquet of wild flowers.

The outbreak of war allowed the dowager empress to state her feelings openly. "I have hated Germany for 50 years," declared Marie Feodorovna, "but now I hate it more than ever."[12] The dowager empress, whom an English nurse called a "a very charming but very slangy old lady," said the kaiser was "vulgar and detestable" as well as "a silly ass!"[13] Tsarina Alexandra was no less sympathetic toward the kaiser, as she told her children's French tutor: "I have never liked the Emperor William, if only because he is not sincere. He is vain and has always played the comedian. He was always reproaching me with doing nothing for Germany, and has always done his best to separate Russia and France, though I never believed it was for the good of Russia. He will never forgive me this war!"[14]

Tsar Nicholas II was also highly displeased with Kaiser Wilhelm. In conversation with Nicholas of Greece, the tsar expressed his sentiments: "He could have stopped the war had he wanted to." The tsar continued: "As for ourselves, it is impossible to sit quietly and see Serbia being strangled like a kitten by a huge dog. Now, alas, we are in for it, and God help us! But I can tell you one thing: now that we have been led into this abominable business against our will, I am determined to stick to my French Ally to the bitter end. We cannot afford to lose this war, as the triumph of Prussian militarism would mean the end of all liberty and civilization."[15]

Tsar Nicholas II and Tsarina Alexandra were not alone in their disdain for Kaiser Wilhelm. The Grand Duchess Vladimir was even more withering in her description of the kaiser. A few days after Russia went to war, Marie Pavlovna hosted a dinner at her home. Present were Kyril and Ducky, as well as Prince and Princess Nicholas of Greece. Maurice Paléologue, now France's ambassador to Russia, also attended and later described that evening. Despite the tranquil surroundings and convivial company, conversation centered on war. After dinner, the Grand Duchess Vladimir invited the French ambassador to join her at one end of the garden, telling him, "Now we can talk without restraint." And so she did. "I have a feeling that the Emperor and Russia are playing for a supreme stake," explained Miechen. She went on to add:

> This is not a political war as so many others have been. It is a duel between Slavism and Germanism. One of the two *must* succumb. I have seen many people these last few days; my ambulances and hospital trains have brought me into contact with folk of all social circles and classes. I can assure you that no one has any illusions about the serious nature of the struggle on which we have embarked. From the Tsar down to the humblest *moujik* all are determined to do their duty unflinchingly. We shall not shrink from any sacrifice. If our beginning is unfortunate—which God forbid!— you'll see the miracles of 1812 again.
>
> It is certainly probable that we shall have great difficulties at the outset. We must expect anything, even a disaster. All I ask of Russia is to hold fast.
>
> She will hold. Don't doubt it!

Miechen confided further to her French guest: "Many a time in the last few days have I turned the searchlight on my conscience. I have seen into the very depths of my soul. But neither in my heart nor my mind have I found anything which is not utterly devoted to my Russian fatherland. And I have thanked God for that! . . . it is my forty years' residence in Russia—all the happiness I have known here, all the dreams that have come to me, all the affection and kindness I have received—which has given me a wholly Russian soul." After declaring her allegiance to Russia, Miechen expressed contempt for Kaiser Wilhelm. "I am only a Mecklenburger on one point: in my hatred for the Emperor William. *He* represents what I have been taught from my childhood to detest the most—the tyranny of the Hohenzollerns. Yes, it is the Hohenzollerns who have perverted, demoralized, degraded and humiliated Germany and gradually destroyed in her all elements of idealism and generosity, refinement and charity."

Paléologue was impressed by what he described as Miechen's "long diatribe which made me feel all the sentiments of inveterate hatred, of mute and tenacious detestation which the small and once independent states of Germany have for the despotic house of Prussia."[16] Miechen's loathing of Wilhelm II was one of the few things she had in common with Tsarina Alexandra.

Signs that the war might not bode well for Tsarina Alexandra were already clear and unequivocal. Never popular among her subjects, the German-born Alexandra had to tread even more carefully with anti-German sentiments now sweeping Russia, lest she be perceived as being more loyal to Germany than to her adopted homeland. Alexandra was suspect, this despite the fact that she was highly influenced by her grandmother, Queen Victoria, and felt more sympathy toward Britain than Germany.

Anti-German feelings in the Russian capital were so strong in August 1914 that the name St. Petersburg was discarded as too German sounding and renamed Petrograd. The Dowager Empress Marie Feodorovna was fortunate in respect to the anti-German sentiment sweeping Russia. Her subjects had no doubt as to where the Danish-born Marie Feodorovna's loyalties lay. She was known to have harbored strong disdain for Germany all her life. In a letter to Grand Duke Michael, the dowager empress confided her livid opprobrium against Russia's official enemy, Germany: "For fifty years I have detested the Prussians, but now I feel towards them an implacable hatred."[17]

The one positive development for Marie Feodorovna during these worrying times was the return of her second son. Since his banishment, Grand Duke Michael had been living a comfortable life of exile near London with Natasha, their son, George, and Tata. Soon after World War I broke out, Tsar Nicholas granted his brother's request to return home. Grand Duke Michael returned to Russia with his family to serve as a general. The couple lived in a house at Gatchina and while there, Natasha became reacquainted with her old admirer, Dmitri Abrikossov. As a welcome guest in the couple's home, Abrikossov came to know Marie Feodorovna's younger son. Abrikossov observed that Michael was "uncorrupted and noble in nature." Michael "trusted everybody. Had his wife not watched over him constantly," concluded Abrikossov, "he would have been deceived at every step."[18]

Dmitri Abrikossov met a number of grand dukes during Sunday gatherings at Michael and Natasha's home. Abrikossov was surprised to find that "they felt Russia existed for the Romanovs, not the Romanovs for Russia." As bad news from the war front arrived, and concerns about a German invasion of Russia grew, Abrikossov was astounded at Grand Duke Boris's reaction. Abrikossov found Boris at his house at Tsarskoe Selo, pulling Natasha in a rickshaw in the garden. The grand duke then showed Abrikossov his collection of wines and "looking with sadness" at his collection, "Boris bemoaned the possibility of its loss to the Germans, as if there were no greater tragedy that could befall Russia."[19]

Boris's dismissive attitude was not shared by other Romanovs, whose priorities were more in sympathy with the fate of their fellow Russians. With war raging, the women of the imperial family hastened to serve their people. Marie Feodorovna's daughter Grand Duchess Olga labored as a nurse in the Ukraine. Tsarina Alexandra, with her eldest daughters, Olga and Tatiana, enrolled in an intensive two-month-long training course to become certified wartime Red Cross nurses. They dutifully carried out their roles, ministering to wounded soldiers. The tsarina did not shirk from the more gruesome tasks. Anna Viroubova saw Alexandra "assisting in the most difficult operations, taking from the hands of the busy surgeons amputated legs and arms, removing bloody and even vermin-infected dressings, enduring all the sights and smells and agonies of that most dreadful of all places, a military hospital in the midst of war." Alexandra "was spared nothing, nor did she wish to be."[20] The tsarina also supervised the running of dozens of hospitals around Petrograd. Even the impressive Catherine Palace at Tsarskoe Selo was turned into a military hospital. The war energized Tsarina Alexandra as never before. Whereas before she would spend hours on end at rest in the mauve boudoir at the Alexander Palace, she now spent much of her time on her feet, ministering to her wounded subjects. In her desire to help her countrymen, she was invigorated "with a renewed sense of purpose." In no time, "the tsarina plunged into war work, and for a while—at least while Alexei enjoyed good health—her thoughts were rarely consumed by the need to have Rasputin at her disposal."[21]

The tsarina kept busy with hospital work but was soon overworked. Her heart gave her trouble and weakened her—"I utterly overtire myself," Alexandra admitted to her old governess. Being unable at times to work at a hospital "is a great grief to me," wrote the tsarina, "as I love the work and find consolation in nursing the sick and binding up their wounds however terrible they may be."[22]

Grand Duchess Vladimir too threw herself into helping Russia's soldiers. Yet even in her altruism during the very early days of the war, Miechen's "two unpleasing traits: contempt and jealousy," reared their ugly heads. The grand duchess was angry at being excluded from early family meetings to organize aid "and she is supposed to have said that 'dearest Ella surely had her hands full already what with her convent and all the paupers in Moscow' and that 'poor Alicky's health could never make it possible for her to do much in any field.' The peevish remarks duly reached the Alexander Palace . . . Alexandra was indignant. Elisabeth [Ella] remained indifferent."[23]

Despite Miechen's jealousy for Ella and contempt for Alexandra, she did more than her fair share for Russia's war effort. Grand Duchess Vladimir easily shifted gears, directing her energy to new pursuits. Now sixty years old, the indefatigable Miechen immersed herself in support of her adopted land, not hesitating to minister to the wounded and dying. Wielding immense wealth and influence, the grand duchess supervised several projects, among which the oversight of hospital trains for the troops stood out. Her superb organization of her hospital trains, which ran with great efficiency, is documented by the Englishman Bertie Stopford. Stopford, "ostensibly a courier for the Foreign Office, though clearly in intelligence,"[24] recorded his dealings, impressions of personalities and goings-on in Petrograd during the war. As a frequent guest at Miechen's home at Tsarskoe Selo, Stopford wrote in October 1915: "The Grand Duchess Vladimir leaves tonight for ten days in her ambulance train for Minsk to visit her flying hospitals and food dépôts. She has ten concerns all along the Fronts."[25] After traveling with Miechen in one of her hospital trains, Stopford admitted: "It was the most divine time being with her. We ate with the Sisters, the priest, and the doctor, but had tea in her compartment. We talked of everybody and everything in the world. She is a marvellous woman, and always at her best where there is much to do—sparing herself no trouble, quite thorough, a woman after my heart!"[26]

Bertie Stopford's firsthand account captures what it was like in one of Miechen's hospital trains. Stopford traveled with her in one from St. Petersburg to Dvinsk in Latvia, a journey of 315 miles:

> We were within three miles of the trenches and saw and heard what I had not experienced for months—cannon and shrapnel all day and all night . . . we saw silhouetted against the snow, careering down a long straight avenue, a battery of artillery galloping up to the Front—[a] most dramatic effect!
>
> It was a weird sight as we went out of the station with torches to meet the wounded, who were being brought in by peasants in carts; there were only a few motor-ambulances as the roads are incredibly bad: many of the men were undressed, and the carts were dripping with blood. It must have been like this in Napoleon's time . . . But once the poor things were in the train there was every comfort and luxury . . .

All were splendidly fit, well fed, clothed, and booted. The arrangements are wonderful—perfect organization, and the wounded were admirably transferred to the train.

Her [the Grand Duchess Vladimir's] train is No. 1 out of 300; the next five belong to the Empress and her four daughters. Hers [Miechen], I am told, is the best organised of any. We started off with 492 wounded, but several died on the way; twelve of them were officers, of whom three were Mohammedans. The two trains were made up of twenty-nine carriages. After every man had been put in his cot, she [Miechen] went and visited each one . . .

Nearly a hundred received Communion from the train priest. Nobody murmured or complained, all most grateful. One boy who came in unconscious woke up and thought he was in Heaven! Those who died went out like watches run-down, without effort—just stopped breathing. It was intensely sad, though with so much to do I hadn't time to think until I went to bed; but one felt the very best had been done for them—each was a hero.

We were four nights away, the journey thirty hours each way: 12N Fahrenheit. The packing of the wounded into the train was done without hurry or fuss. The Russians are so kind; over all there was a feeling, from the highest to the humblest, of intense human sympathy for the suffering.

A man of 22, shot in the spine, was accompanied by his beautiful young wife . . . She nurses him, and the Grand Duchess has arranged that she live in his hospital.

When we got to Petrograd they were unpacked by volunteer students, who meet every train. The Grand Duchess waited till the last one had left for his hospital—no hitch, no flurry, all done like machinery. She was dead tired (so was I), but she never left till all had gone (9 p.m.). She looks very white—too white.[27]

Stopford also admired Miechen's leadership and generosity when aiding disabled Russian soldiers who were set to return to their homes, giving them a complete outfit and money upon their discharge. Granted permission by Tsar Nicholas, she took over and developed this charity. Under her patronage, the charity grew. Stopford noted that "she now runs it with State money, her own money, and money out of her own organisation fund . . . For the Siberians there are sheepskin coats; there are boots of every sort and size; socks, caps, shirts, fur caps, warm coats, thinner coats, crutches, sticks. It was very touching—so many blind, lame . . . Every day there passes through a stream of men up to the five hundred who can be accommodated . . . Automobiles drive them to their different stations, or else they go in tramcars free. One has to come to Russia to see how well things can be managed."[28]

Nevertheless, during those trying years very few Russian organizations ran as smoothly as Miechen's charity and hospital trains. The state of medical care in Russia during the Great War left much to be desired. Many soldiers arrived back from the front with badly dressed wounds, frequently hungry from days without food. Disorder prevailed, exacerbated by rivalry between the Red Cross and the War Ministry. At the front, an appalling lack of medical supplies and vehicles added to the soldiers' misery. M. Evdokimoff, the head of the army medical department, proved incompetent. Michael Rodzianko recalled that "it was necessary to place a dictator at the head of the whole medical and sanitary service, who could be entrusted with the task of bringing order out of chaos." When Rodzianko told the dowager empress of conditions, "she was horrified." "Tell me what you think ought to be done," she said to Rodzianko. The Duma's speaker advised the dowager empress to send a telegram to Grand Duke Nicholas Nikolaevich—Nikolasha—the Russian army's commander-in-chief, asking him to order Evdokimoff to permit Red Cross volunteers access to the front. Marie Feodorovna sent the telegram. Nikolasha replied that he agreed with Rodzianko. Nikolasha also told Rodzianko he had been longing to dismiss Evdokimoff but he was "in high favour" with the tsarina, who encouraged the tsar to keep him employed. The reason for this, according to Rodzianko, was Tsarina Alexandra's "desire to oppose the wishes of the Empress Marie [Feodorovna]."[29]

Besides helping Rodzianko sort out medical problems at the front, Marie Feodorovna oversaw hospital work. She accepted Countess Kleinmichel's generous offer for use of her villa on Elagin Island near the capital. Marie Feodorovna saw to it that the Kleinmichel villa housed two hundred wounded soldiers. The dowager empress's personal bodyguard, the Cossack Timofei Yaschik, who began serving her during the early war years, recalled that Marie Feodorovna "often visited many hospitals and lazarets [quarters for those ill with contagious diseases] and always found a friendly word for the wounded soldiers. She paid particular attention to helping invalids with prosthetic limbs find some job . . . Schools were organized for them, including for the blind, where they could study a certain craft."[30] The dowager empress turned the Anichkov Palace into a hospital too. She welcomed a steady stream of people requesting aid, be they soldiers or parents of soldiers who found little or no help through various charitable organizations. Marie Feodorovna became their last resort. She did what she could and "when unable to help materially, she at least never refused to instill new hope or to give consolation by a bright smile or a kind word."[31]

Hope and consolation were in short supply, for as the months passed, it became glaringly obvious that war against the German Empire was a formidable undertaking that was taking a punishing toll. Within a month of hostilities breaking out, Germans under the leadership of Paul von Hindenburg and Erich Ludendorff inflicted heavy losses on the Russian Second Army at the Battle of Tannenberg. It was a decisive victory. Of the 150,000 Russians who fought, only 10,000 escaped. The rest were killed or captured. Not long after the Battle of Tannenberg came another defeat for the Russians at the First Battle of the Masurian Lakes. In this battle, the Germans successfully ejected the Russians from Prussia, inflicting over 100,000 casualties in the process. There was good news in that the Russians repelled the Austrian attempt to invade Poland; nevertheless, staggering "casualties of 1,000,000 meant the loss of one-quarter of the army by the end of 1914."[32]

Heading the army was Grand Duke Nicholas Nikolaevich (Nikolasha), who stood an imposing six feet six inches tall. "Very thin with a short pointed beard over a slightly protruding jaw, and a ramrod military bearing,"[33] the grand duke delighted in wolf coursing, which involved hunting wolves with his magnificent pack of borzoi dogs, the finest in the empire. The hunting took place at Pershimo, his eleven-thousand-acre estate. When war came, Nikolasha diverted his attention from wolf coursing to commanding the millions of soldiers who comprised the Russian army.

Loyal to Russia and vehemently anti-German, Nikolasha remained popular with the troops. But the grand duke was soon in serious trouble thanks to his vocal opposition to Rasputin, which earned Nikolasha Tsarina Alexandra's enmity. Even though the general was married to Anastasia of Montenegro, who had introduced Rasputin to the tsarina, by the time World War I came, Nikolasha had developed a robust dislike of the *staretz*. In fact a rumor circulated that when Rasputin wanted to visit army headquarters, Nikolasha replied: "Come—and be hanged." When Michael Rodzianko asked the grand duke if this was true, he answered, "well, not exactly." "It was clear from his answer," however, "that something of the sort had actually taken place."[34] Nikolasha's unabashed and vigorous opposition to Rasputin did not go unnoticed. Alexandra complained bitterly to her husband. In August 1915, to Tsarina Alexandra's satisfaction, her husband dismissed Nikolasha from his post as head of the Russian forces, banishing him to the Caucasus as viceroy.

Bertie Stopford learned of the news from Miechen. He had been invited to the Vladimir Palace at six in the evening to drive with the grand duchess to Tsarskoe Selo. Stopford duly arrived at the appointed hour, but his hostess was nowhere to be seen. Stopford knew something was amiss because Miechen was always punctual. This time, however, she kept her guest waiting for forty-five minutes. At a quarter to seven, "full of apologies and looking very worried," Miechen arrived and explained that she had been with the dowager empress. During the hour's drive to Tsarskoe Selo with Stopford, the usually loquacious grand duchess was strangely silent.

At dinner—served an unheard of thirty-five minutes late—Miechen suddenly spoke to Stopford and blurted out, "the Emperor leaves to-morrow night to take over the Supreme Command at the Front . . . It is quite disastrous." Stopford recalled that "we both cried into our soup . . . Everybody during dinner was much depressed by this news."[35]

Miechen's son Grand Duke Andrei visited the dowager empress and found her "in a terribly worried state. She was especially excited over the question of Nicholas Nicholaevich," confided Andrei in his diary. "She thinks that his removal will be the ruin of N. [Nicholas II] because it will never be forgiven him. She exonerated Niki [Nicholas II] in all this and laid all the blame on Alix. When Niki came to see her before going off she [Marie Feodorovna] begged and begged him to think over everything carefully and not lead Russia to ruin. To her pleas he replied that everybody deceived him, that he must save Russia, that it was his duty. It was in vain that she pleaded with him that he was poorly prepared for this hard task and that State affairs required his presence at Petrograd. He remained unpersuaded and would not even promise to deal kindly with Nicholas Nicholaevich."[36]

Grand Duke Andrei confided in his diary that "Aunt Minny, as she related to me all this, was so excited, so stirred up, that I was frightened. She kept repeating the question: 'What are we coming to, what are we coming to? That is not at all like Niki—he is lovable, he is honest, he is good—it is all her work.'" When Andrei asked his aunt if there was hope that Nikolasha would remain at his post, she answered: "Not the least. It is all settled—Alix has just telegraphed me." The exasperated dowager empress told Andrei, "I can't understand anything anymore." Marie Feodorovna went on to recount to Andrei that a relative, Prince Alexander Petrovich of Oldenburg (whom Sergei Witte had found to be energetic and remarkable), begged her to stop Nicholas II from taking command. Predicting "terrible consequences, including popular uprisings" if the tsar became commander-in-chief, Oldenburg, according to the dowager empress, "rolled on the floor" in despair at what was happening.[37] Little wonder then that a stupefied Marie Feodorovna confessed in her diary: "All my words have been to no avail . . . There is no room in my brain for all this."[38]

For years Marie Feodorovna and Marie Pavlovna had had a frosty relationship, mirroring to some extent the friction between the dowager empress and tsarina, but with Nicholas II's decision to dismiss Nikolasha and take over his position, Marie Feodorovna showed no restraint in expressing her fears to Marie Pavlovna. The dowager empress told her that the times they were living in reminded her of the time of Tsar Paul I, "who began in the last year of his reign to drive away all his loyal subjects. She pictured to herself, in all its horrors," Grand Duke Andrei confided in his diary, "the tragic end of our ancestor."[39]

Marie Feodorovna and Miechen, as well as others, feared that should Russian forces continue to perform badly and suffer more huge losses, the blame would be placed squarely on the tsar's shoulders. "Many people were terrified by this act [of Nicholas assuming supreme command]," recalled Michael Rodzianko. "Princess Z. N. Yussopoff [Felix's mother] came to us in tears and said to my wife: 'This is dreadful. I feel it is the beginning of the end: it will bring us to revolution.' "[40] And so the die was cast. Replacing the seasoned Nikolasha, the tsar assumed control as commander-in-chief, despite vehement pleas to the contrary.

Once the tsar took over Nikolasha's role as commander-in-chief in the fall of 1915, Nicholas II was frequently at army headquarters (Stavka). First located in Baranovichi, in present-day Belarus, Stavka was later relocated to Mogilev on the Dnieper River, some five hundred miles south of Petrograd. With her son away, Marie Feodorovna wrote to him. In one letter, written at the end of 1915, the dowager empress expressed her hopes and wishes to the son on whose shoulders the burdens of ruling were weighing heavily: "My dear darling Nicky . . . God protect you and assist and help you in your difficult task . . . My thoughts are always with you and I am glad that little Alexei is with you, it must be a great joy . . . Tell him that his grandmother kisses him tenderly and loves him . . . God keep you and help you. Your loving Mama."[41]

Nicholas II's departure for Stavka opened a new and dangerous phase for Russia and the Romanovs. Because the tsar was often away from Petrograd, he delegated a deputy to man the helm of government. That deputy was none other than his wife. Once left to her own devices, Alexandra assumed a granitelike resolve to rule guided by her own baffling view of what was good for

Russia. This, above all, meant preserving autocracy. In a barrage of letters to her husband, the tsarina exhorted Nicholas II to exert his will, be firm, and to preserve autocracy. In one missive written in the spring of 1915 (some months even before Nicholes II took over as commander-in-chief), Alexandra wrote: "Forgive me, precious One, but you know you are too kind & gentle—sometimes a good loud voice can do wonders, & a severe look—do my love, be more decided & sure of yourself . . . You think me a medlesome [*sic*] bore, but a woman feels & sees things sometimes clearer than my too humble sweetheart . . . a Sovereign needs to show his will more often."[42]

Not all the Romanovs were as enamored of autocracy as Alexandra. Grand Duke Serge Mikhailovich (Sandro's brother), was one such doubter. As inspector-general of artillery, Serge saw firsthand the poor production capabilities of Russia's munitions factories. In April 1915, he remarked in exasperation: "French industry has reached an output of 100,000 rounds a day. We produce barely 20,000 here. What a scandal! When I think that this exhibition of impotence is all that our autocratic system has to show it makes me want to be a Republican!"[43] Furthermore, according to Robert Wilton who was the *Times* reporter during the war years in Petrograd, "it was said soon after the war began that the shortage of officers had reached an enormous figure—30,000 to 50,000."[44]

The war went from terrible to worse for Russia. Getting supplies to Russia was especially challenging, as Bulgarians and Turks had rendered routes from the south and west impassible. Added to this was the German blockade of the Baltic Sea. An inability to resupply Russia, plus enormous losses at the front demoralized citizens, soldiers, and leaders. In August 1915 a staggering 450,000 Russians died at the front. "This brought the total loss of life since the previous year to 1.5 million men. For the year 1915 alone, [an] astounding 2 million men were captured, wounded, or killed, and the whole Russian front had for all intents and purposes crumbled."[45] Russia could ill afford to continue hemorrhaging, but the war showed no signs of abating.

Anxieties over Russia's future greatly concerned everyone. Grand Duke Paul spoke for many when he exclaimed to Maurice Paléologue, "We're heading straight for revolution! The first steps have been taken! . . . Don't you feel that the Emperor and Empress are marked down already?"

"No, I don't think either the Emperor or Empress is actually menaced," replied Paléologue, "though the public is exasperated with the Empress. In fact I know some people who are talking of nothing less than shutting her up in a convent in the Urals or Siberia."

"What! Shut the Empress up in a convent!" exclaimed Grand Duke Paul.

"Do they think the Emperor will let anyone touch his wife? They can't! So the next thing is to kill the Emperor and overthrow the dynasty . . . And what will they put in its place?"

Then, after pacing up and down the room several times, the agitated grand duke stopped in front of Paléologue, his "eyes flashing [in] horror" and stated bluntly: "If revolution breaks out, its barbarity will exceed anything ever known . . . It will be hellish . . . Russia won't survive it!"[46]

Marie Feodorovna's younger son, Grand Duke Michael, was among those expressing this same anxiety. During a conversation with Dmitri Abrikossov, Michael laid a large part of the blame on his sister-in-law Alexandra. "Several times he [Michael] had tried to convey to Nicholas what people were saying about him and about the dangerous influence of the Empress," noted Abrikossov. "Nicholas would listen with great tenderness but would say nothing until Michael felt so upset that it was his brother who consoled him." Recalling the "intensity" of the grand duke's grief and how "tears choked his voice," Abrikossov recollected that "Michael was afraid of the future." This left Abrikossov in dismay. "I was shocked by the utter despair on the pale face before me," wrote Abrikossov, "and had the distinct feeling that we all stood on the threshold of great misfortune." With the empire in turmoil and suffering catastrophic defeats on the battlefront, little wonder, then, that Dmitri Abrikossov penned the following pessimistic sentiment: "Poor, doomed Russia!"[47]

24

NEARING IMPLOSION

When the Great War unfolded, the Duchess of Coburg surprisingly sided not with her native land, but with Germany. It was a remarkable revelation: Marie Alexandrovna's pride in the life she led in Germany now superseded her Russian fealty. The duchess sent letters to Missy and Ducky "fiercely defending the German empire and damning the Allies."[1]

Shortly after the war erupted, King Carol I of Romania died and Missy became Ferdinand's queen consort in October 1914. Then, after long prevarication and despite Ferdinand's pro-German inclinations, Romania finally entered the war on the Allies' side in August 1916, thanks to Queen Marie's influence. In contrast to her mother's antipathy toward England, Missy possessed strong Anglophile sympathies. She convinced King Ferdinand to throw Romania's lot with the Entente cause.

After Romania sided with the Allies and declared war on the Central Powers, the Duchess of Coburg wrote an impassioned letter to Missy: "Oh! why, why did you begin this war?" More painful words followed: "The worst of all is that they specially accuse 'you' of having been the chief element of bringing it about! . . . I can hardly believe in my old days, that a daughter of mine is at the head of such a movement, my former little beloved, peaceful, fair Missy, the sunshine in the house . . . But all Germany says it was you, you who pushed on towards the war from insane, blind confidence in the Entente."[2]

"Having entered the war, Romania found that the cost of siding with the Allies was dear."[3] In no time, the Germans attacked Bucharest, compelling the royal family and government to flee to the small town of Jassy, near the Russian border. French and Russian help was not forthcoming, essentially leaving

Romania to fend for itself. Only three months after entering the war on the Allied side, Romania already saw a staggering quarter of a million soldiers killed in the fighting.

Amidst the chaos and destruction of war, Marie Alexandrovna learned of the death in October 1916 of Missy's youngest child, three-year-old Prince Mircea. In December, Missy finally received a letter from her mother. Missy described it as "a terrible letter, full of overpowering grief about Mircea's death, full of irrevocable, unreconcilable [sic] bitterness because we have gone to war." "It seems," Missy recalled sadly of her mother's letter, "I am accused of having wanted the war . . . Mamma actually never meant to write to me, never to be in communication with me as long as the war lasts; it was only the death of Mircea which made her break through her silence to send me a word of sympathy, then to return to her silence!"

"Can she really believe that I am responsible for this war?" wrote Queen Marie. "And she, a Russian, minding so terribly that we should have turned to the side of her former *patrie*! . . . Her hard words are an added burden on my already oppressed heart, but above all I weep when I think of the bitterness which fills her. It must be a worse suffering than all I have to bear, because I feel no bitterness towards anybody!"[4] It was a painful revelation to Missy that her beloved mother's sympathy for the Central Powers would exact such opprobrium.

Though she was pro-German, the Duchess of Coburg could not fault her daughter's role as queen. Missy became indispensable to her husband, King Ferdinand, in buoying him during those trying years in which their country suffered unremittingly from war, for Romania was spared no brutality of violence, hunger, cold, devastation, and hopelessness. One contemporary chronicler of Romania, Winifred Gordon, described the hellish conditions that gripped the country, especially the small city of Jassy, whose population grew to four million, as endless streams of refugees from the war straggled into one of the few places in Romania that was not under German occupation: "Virtually the whole civil population was on the verge of starvation," wrote Winifred Gordon. "The hastily organized hospitals were lacking in everything— equipment, disinfectants, drugs, etc. . . . . Plague, pestilence, famine were rife." Yet through it all, Queen Marie was a beacon of hope for her countrymen as she went about encouraging her suffering people and sustaining them in their darkest hours. She worked "superbly with heroic devotion," recalled Gordon, "ceaselessly strove to alleviate the misery, and cope with the great streams of wounded pouring in."[5] In doing her duty as queen and serving her people, Missy had been taught well by her mother.

The Dowager Empress Marie Feodorovna became increasingly frustrated with her son's intransigence and her inability to guide him during the war years. With Nicholas II frequently away at Stavka and Alexandra ruling Russia in his stead, Marie Feodorovna felt there was little she could do to influence the course of events. Unable to convince the imperial couple to rid themselves of the notorious Rasputin, and always at loggerheads with her daughter-in-law, the dowager empress "declared that she could not remain a witness of the shame any longer."[6] Marie Feodorovna moved to the city of Kiev where her daughter Grand Duchess Olga was living. Marie Feodorovna's departure was much to Alexandra's liking. "Its [sic] much better Motherdear stays on at Kiev where the climate is milder & she can live more as she wishes & hears less gossip," wrote the tsarina to Nicholas II.[7]

Welcomed warmly by the inhabitants of Kiev, for "hers was [still] the most honored name in Russia," Marie Feodorovna was grateful to find that "everybody had a wave and a smile for her, including the groups of crippled soldiers who filled the streets."[8] The dowager empress welcomed those who managed to visit her in Kiev. These included Michael Rodzianko, who, during a two-hour talk with the dowager empress, commented on her long stay in Kiev. "Yes, it is so nice here," replied Marie Feodorovna, "I am going to stay as long as I like."[9]

While in Kiev, Marie Feodorovna saw her daughter Olga daily. The grand duchess spent much of her time working as a nurse, a task she found most rewarding. One day, while she was working, Grand Duchess Olga was called to meet an unshaven officer who had come to see her. To Olga's astonishment, the officer turned out to be Colonel Nikolai Kulikovsky. Olga was overjoyed to see Kulikovsky and threw her arms around him, to the surprise of those around her. Reunited with Kulikovsky, Olga was more determined than ever to marry the man she loved and informed her mother of her decision. Olga recalled that her mother "remained quite calm and said that she understood." "And that," added Olga, "was something of a shock in its own way."[10] In 1916, Olga was finally granted an annulment, and in November that year in Kiev, she married Colonel Kulikovsky in the presence of her sister Xenia and the dowager empress. Marie Feodorovna described her "great emotion" to Nicholas II regarding

Olga's wedding. "I am so very glad I was able to attend," added the dowager empress. "May God give her every happiness. She herself is more than happy."[11] To her mother, Grand Duchess Olga wrote: "I can't tell you how I thank you and how awfully happy and touched I am that you came to Church and to the wedding supper! Mama dear; I'll never forget how kind you were and how you put aside all your ideas and feelings for my sake. I can't imagine how you could change everything in yourself so quickly!"[12]

By this time, Marie Feodorovna had the satisfaction of seeing Olga reconciled with her brother Grand Duke Michael. For a time sister and brother had been estranged over Michael's marriage to Natasha. But in 1916, the dowager empress reported to Nicholas II that "at last he [Michael] has made it up with poor Olga. I am *so* happy and have shed tears of joy! Thank God all that is now settled and I can die in peace."[13]

Michael and Natasha's devotion remained relatively strong, though at times jealousy on Michael's part crept in. Early in the war, Grand Duke Michael fought the Austrians, while a thousand miles away, a worried Natasha awaited news of her husband's fate. During his absence Natasha struck up a friendship with Grand Duke Dmitri. In no time, Dmitri, eleven years Natasha's junior, fell in love with her. As fond as she was of Dmitri, Natasha had to tread carefully. In the end, she found a gentle way to "extricate both of them from a situation in which Dmitri might well have been humiliated, or Michael betrayed."[14] Before the "affair" ended, however, doubts, jealousies and reassurances of love were expressed by both husband and wife to each other. Michael was worried, even tormented about Dmitri—referred to by Natasha as "Lily-of-the-Valley," as the following letter shows: "What you are writing to me about Lily-of-the-Valley, i.e., how tenderly, tenderly you love him and also that he comes to see you because he likes you and totally succumbed to your charm and besides, you say that conquering such a heart *means much* to you—I believe that if you just stop to consider the meaning of these several sentences you have written, you will realise what pain you have given me by writing them." By way of assurance, Natasha replied: "My dearest Mishechka, it makes me very sad to know that you are so upset because of Lily-of-the-Valley. Believe me, my affection for him does not in the least interfere with my love for you."[15]

Even more devoted were Nicholas and Alexandra, whose marriage survived the long separation that the war brought. Blessed as they were with a supremely happy marriage of total fidelity, Miechen's suggestion that her son Grand Duke Boris marry their eldest daughter, Grand Duchess Olga Nicolaevna, horrified them. Alexandra would hear none of it. Mortified at the thought of sacrificing her daughter as a wife to the roué Boris, she wrote a disjointed and rambling letter to Nicholas:

> The oftener I think about Boris, the more I realise [*sic*] what an awful set his wife wld. be dragged into. His & Miechen's friends, rich french [*sic*] people, russian [*sic*] bankers, 'the society' . . . and all such types—intrigues without end—fast manners & conversations & Ducky not a suitable sister in-law at all—& then Boris'[s] mad past. Miechen gave into U.[ncle] Wladimir's ways so as to share all together, but she found pleasure in that life—with her nature that was easy. Well, why do I write about this, when you know it as well as I do. So give over a wee used half worn out, blase young man, to a pure, fresh young girl 18 years his junior & to live in a house in wh. many a woman has 'shared' his life. Only a 'woman' who knows the world & can judge & choose with eyes open, ought to be his wife & she wld. know how to hold him & make a good husband of him. But an inexperienced young girl would suffer terribly, to have her husband, 4, 5th hand or more.[16]

For this and many other reasons, the Grand Duchess Vladimir and Tsarina Alexandra's icy relations did not thaw. In her letters to the tsar, Alexandra could not resist criticizing Miechen:

> Miechen . . . She goes to see her hospital & train & motors [in Poland]. It's a great pitty [*sic*], as the Poles neither care for the way in wh. she invites herself to their houses to meals.[17]

> Miechen promenades with her decoration to all exhibitions[,] etc; you ought to find out really how she got it, & that such things don't happen again.[18]

> Miechen is playing a popular part in town & going about a lot & to musical evenings & acting her part as charmeuse [charmer].[19]

> Miechen was in a vile humour [—] she left last night for Minsk with her train & then to inspect her organisations in other towns.—for ever jealous with Ellas organisations [*sic*].[20]

> Really Miechen! She can drive one wild . . . as she really is very pretencious [*sic*]—only one does not wish needlessly to offend her, as she means

well, only spoils all by her jealous ambition.—Don't let her come bothering you & above all give her no promises.[21]

Tsar Nicholas had bitter words to say about his aunt to Alexandra too: "Miechen wrote me a cold letter asking me why I have not approved the *polozhenie* [regulation] . . . She is really insufferable—if I have time, I shall answer her sharply."[22] However, most of the complaints about Miechen came from the tsarina.

In the midst of one especially testy exchange between Miechen and Alexandra, both women sounded out others about what had taken place. Alexandra complained to Nicholas II about Marie Pavlovna, saying that, "Miechen arrives at Livadia . . . for 3 days!! (what confounded cheek) & we are to send linen, 2 servants & silver—I strongly protested & said first to find out whether she asked you—we have no Hotel there—beastly impertinence, needs sitting upon [i.e., to be disciplined]—[she] can live at Yalta."[23]

Once she was in the Crimea, Miechen then vented her frustration to A. A. Mossolov. Miechen handed to Mossolov a telegram in English she had received from the tsarina with a trembling hand: "Am astonished that you should be at Livadia without having asked the lady of the house [meaning her, the tsarina]. As for my hospitals, I know that they are in good order. Alexandra."

"Flushed with anger," Miechen then blurted out to Mossolov, "What impertinence!" She then added, "Anyhow, here is the answer I am sending." Mossolov then read what he described as "an endless message. Heavens! There was no mincing of words in it."

"I hope your Highness has not yet sent off this telegram," said Mossolov.

"No," answered Miechen, "I wanted to see what you think."

Mossolov then proceeded to discuss the telegram with Marie Pavlovna, "word by word." He admitted to having "heaved a great sigh of relief when at last" Miechen said: "You are right—I will leave it unanswered. It would be beneath my dignity, at my age, to take any notice of a piece of tactlessness on the part of a woman, and a princess at that, who had to come to me to learn how to behave in society."[24]

Miechen and Tsarina Alexandra were not the only ones not seeing eye to eye. Marie Feodorovna and Alexandra were more than ever poles apart in their views about the tsarina's unquestioning faith in Rasputin. Stolypin's successor, Vladimir Kokovtsov, met Gregory Rasputin, took an instant dislike to the *staretz*, and afterward produced a negative report for Nicholas II. Tsarina Alexandra interpreted this as an affront and saw Kokovtsov as hostile toward the throne.

Kokovtsov admitted that "she considered me, therefore, not a servant of the Tsar but a tool of the enemies of the state and as such deserving dismissal."[25] Nicholas II dismissed Kokovtsov and, in so doing, rid himself of another able servant.

The Dowager Empress Marie Feodorovna was again aghast. When she confronted Nicholas, he replied: "Do you think I feel happy about it? Some other time I shall tell you everything, but in the meantime I have come to understand that it is an easy thing to discharge a minister but very difficult to admit that it should not have been done." When Kokovtsov explained the details behind his dismissal to the dowager empress, Marie Feodorovna stayed silent and then wept. "I know you are an honorable man," she told Kokovtsov, "and I know that you bear no ill will toward my son. You must also understand my fears for the future. My daughter-in-law does not like me; she thinks that I am jealous of her power. She does not perceive that my one aspiration is to see my son happy. Yet I see that we are nearing some catastrophe, and the Tsar listens to no one but flatterers, not perceiving or even suspecting what goes on all around him. Why do you not decide to tell the Tsar finally all you think and know, now that you are at liberty to do so, warning him, if it is not already too late?"[26] But all Kokovtsov could say was that no one would listen or believe him. Vladimir Kokovtsov summed up what so greatly perturbed the dowager empress: that "in her [Alexandra's] mind, Rasputin was closely associated with the health of her son and the welfare of the Monarchy. To attack him was to attack the protector of what she held most dear."[27]

An incident in January 1915 further strengthened Rasputin's hold on the tsarina. In a railway accident, Anna Viroubova sustained horrific injuries to her head and legs, which were crushed. A doctor who looked her over, declared, "Do not disturb her. She is dying."[28] Rasputin went to the dying patient's bedside the day after the accident and cried out, "Annushka! Look at me!" At that, Anna opened her eyes and said, "Grigory. Thank God. It's you." Rasputin then "staggered from the room and fell into a faint."[29] Confounding the doctors' predictions, Anna survived. "She will live, but will always be a cripple" predicted Rasputin.[30] And that is precisely what happened.

Rasputin had performed yet another "miracle." Already sacrosanct in Alexandra's eyes, he became not just a miracle worker but her political counselor. Alexandra continuously exhorted Nicholas to heed "our Friend's" advice. In June 1915, the tsarina told Nicholas, "No, hearken unto our Friend, beleive [sic] him. He has yr. interest & Russia's at heart . . . we must pay more attention to what he says. His words are not lightly spoken and the gravity of having not only His prayers, but His advice is great." The next day Alexandra followed this with a similar message: "I am haunted by our Friend's wish and *know* it will be fatal for us and the country if it is not fulfilled. He means what He says when He speaks so seriously."[31]

Six months after she penned these words, almost as if by clockwork, Rasputin again demonstrated his indispensability to Marie Feodorovna's daughter-in-law. While Alexei was staying with his father at Stavka, the eleven-year-old had a severe nosebleed, which can be fatal in a hemophiliac. As Anna Viroubova recounted, "the doctors tried every known remedy, but the hemorrhage became steadily worse until death by exhaustion and loss of blood was threatened." When Alexei returned to Tsarskoe Selo, Anna remembered the sad sight before her: "Above the blood-soaked bandages his large blue eyes gazed at us with pathos unspeakable, and it seemed to all around the bed that the last hour of the unhappy child was at hand." In despair, Tsarina Alexandra sent for Rasputin. "He came into the room," Anna recalled, "made the sign of the cross over the bed and, looking intently at the almost moribund child, said quietly to the kneeling parents: 'Don't be alarmed. Nothing will happen.' " Alexei fell asleep and as was usual after all Rasputin's interventions, the child was well almost immediately. Anna Viroubova remembered that the tsarevich's doctors were so baffled by Alexei's instantaneous improvement that they told her "afterwards that they did not even attempt to explain the cure."[32]

Anxieties over Alexei, the war, the fate of Russia, and her family were greatly wearying the tsarina. In 1916, the Russian minister to Bulgaria, Anatoli Neklyudov, met Alexandra at Tsarskoe Selo. He had last seen her five years before when the tsarina, in his words, was "beautiful, charming and good tempered." But a noticeable change had taken place. Now Alexandra "had a deep vertical wrinkle between her eyebrows which gave her an expression of morbid tension. Her eyes were intensely sad."[33]

Two days after meeting with Tsarina Alexandra, Neklyudov spoke with the dowager empress. The topic of conversation inevitably fell on the war. During the audience, Marie Feodorovna spoke of the "unprecedented sufferings inflicted by Germany" on Russian prisoners of war, and of "the insults to which she had been subjected in Berlin when she passed through Germany the day before the declaration of war." "The dear good Empress," recalled Neklyudov, "did not conceal the feeling of profound disgust inspired in her by German cruelty and the duplicity of William II." "The terms she used," in describing the Germans and the kaiser, noted Neklyudov, "were as frank as they were cutting."[34]

As the war progressed, Tsarina Alexandra's loyalties were increasingly questioned. She was never able to shake off suspicions that she was pro-German.

Only those who knew her well could vouch for the tsarina's loyalty to Russia. Her friend, Lili Dehn, admitted that Alexandra had "no love for Germany."[35] Anatoli Neklyudov declared that "the Empress had never been an agent of the Berlin Court."[36] Maurice Paléologue was emphatic that Alexandra was German "neither in mind nor spirit and has never been so."[37] Even Britain's King George V said of his cousin Alexandra: "I have known her all my life, and pro-German that she is not."[38] Nevertheless, in her countrymen's eyes, Tsarina Alexandra's loyalties were more suspect than ever. Moreover, her unwavering support of Rasputin was destroying what little popularity she and Nicholas had with their subjects.

Alexandra was perceived as a pernicious influence upon Nicholas II, and her staunch championing of Rasputin redoubled the criticism. "Everyone spoke of Rasputin with the greatest apprehension,"[39] noted Michael Rodzianko, but people felt powerless to do anything about the *staretz*. Tsar Nicholas could not bring himself to be rid of the man on whom his beloved wife had placed so much faith. It was evident to all that Tsarina Alexandra dominated Marie Feodorovna's mild-mannered son. Alexandra's brother Ernie, the Grand Duke of Hesse, even dared to mention this during a visit to Russia. He was visiting Livadia, when Elizabeth Narishkin asked him about the tsarina. Ernie replied: "My sister? She is splendid. Only you people here don't know how to treat her. The Tsar is an angel, but he doesn't know how to deal with her. What she needs is a superior will which can dominate her, and which can, so to speak, bridle her."[40] Sergei Sazonov, Russia's foreign minister from 1910 to 1916, repeated what Ernie said, and reiterated that the grand duke had commented that the tsar "does not know how to deal with that woman."[41] Even Rasputin was not shy in expressing his thoughts about the imperial couple, once boasting to Prince Felix Yussoupov: "I'll tell you this much: the Czarina has a wise, strong mind and I can get anything and everything from her. As for *him*, he's a simple soul. He was not cut out to be a sovereign; he is made for family life, to admire nature and flowers, but not to reign. That's beyond his strength. So, with God's blessing we come to his rescue."[42]

By 1916, Russia and Nicholas II's misfortunes of war seemed insurmountable. An English nurse, Florence Farmborough, serving with the Russian troops, recorded the dismal state of Russia's fighting men: "Lately, ammunition had been sent in large quantities to our Front, but little of it had been of any use. Out of one consignment of 30,000 shells, fewer than 200 were found to be serviceable. Cartridges were sent in their hundreds of thousands and distributed amongst the men in the trenches, but they were of a foreign cast and would not fit the Russian rifle. Large stores of Japanese rifles had been despatched to neighbouring divisions, but the Russian cartridge failed to fit them. Later, we learnt that Japanese cartridges had been supplied to our Armies on other Fronts, with the same disastrous results. So once again our Russian soldiers raised the butt of their rifles against the advancing enemy, many of them hewed themselves clubs from the forest."[43]

Russia bled heavily. Besides the frightening casualty figures from the front, with over 12 million men mobilized, Russia's economy came to a near standstill as production decreased, resulting in shortages of basic necessities. Peter Durnovo, who had been a minister of the interior, composed a memorandum and presented it to Nicholas II. Durnovo expressed his conviction that social revolution would engulf whichever country lost. It was in Russia, however, "as he stated, [that] the danger of social upheaval was especially great given the instinctive socialism of the masses." Moreover, in Durnovo's view, "the masses cared nothing for the political rights and civil liberties demanded by the educated, but were intent on a full-scale social revolution aimed above all at the destruction of private property and economic inequality."[44]

The fact that the tsarist government was run by third-rate individuals was disturbing to many. The public, government officials, and almost all the Romanovs blamed the tsarina for the incompetent and floundering government. A dizzying change in ministerial posts took place between 1915 to 1917, thanks in part to the tsarina and Gregory Rasputin, who either influenced Alexandra in her decisions or confirmed them. In this political merry-go-round, seven senior ministerial positions changed hands twenty-seven times and were held by twenty-six men. Moreover, a number of these individuals proved unequal to the task. Those whom the tsarina championed were especially ineffectual or downright atrocious choices. The two most notorious and hated were Boris Stürmer and Alexander Protopopov, both appointed in 1916, prime minister and minister of the interior, respectively. Stürmer was a reactionary of whom the Russian diplomat Roman Rosen noted, "the best that could be said is that he was merely a very ordinary functionary of even less than average capacity."[45] Paléologue, who spent three days gathering information on Stürmer, was even more devastating in his critique, describing Stürmer as "worse than a mediocrity—third-rate intellect, mean spirit, low character, doubtful honesty, no experience, and no idea of State business. The most that can be said is that he has a rather pretty talent for cunning and flattery."[46] That Stürmer was pro-German fanned doubts about Alexandra's patriotism.

Alexander Protopopov was even less qualified for his position as interior minister, and Rasputin was instrumental in securing this appointment. Nicholas II was hesitant about appointing Protopopov, but Rasputin went to Tsarskoe Selo to convince him. When he met with Anna Viroubova, she whimpered and repeated to him: "We have failed, Gregory Efimovitch, you are our only hope. Thank Heaven you've come!" The tsar and tsarina then met Rasputin. "*She* [Alexandra] was in a bad temper," Rasputin recounted later in front of Felix Yussoupov, "*He* [Nicholas II] strode up and down the room. I raised my voice and they calmed down at once, particularly when I threatened to go away and leave them to their fate; they then agreed to everything," claimed the *staretz*.[47]

Protopopov, when asked about his proposed program for Russia, replied that "to talk of programmes in these days is to indulge in phraseology."[48] Most disconcerting was Protopopov's state of mind. Suffering from syphilis, the minister was well on his way to becoming insane. As one chronicler put it: "The appointment of this broken-down, half-crazed adventurer was flaunted by the agents of the autocracy as a gracious concession to the Duma, of which he had been vice-president in his sane and prosperous days."[49] Sir George Buchanan found Protopopov to be "mentally deranged."[50] A. A. Mossolov was more to the point when he described Protopopov as "a lunatic."[51]

As Russia's troubles deepened, Miechen was unsparing in her expression of concerns to Maurice Paléologue. During a dinner he hosted in February 1916, Paléologue eagerly listened to what Miechen had to say. She told him of her pro-French sentiments: "I'm glad to be in the French Embassy, on real French territory. It's a long time since I was first taught to love France, and since then I've always believed in her . . . And now it's not merely a feeling of friendship I have for your country, but still more of admiration and reverence."

Politics dominated the evening. Paléologue observed that another guest, the Russian foreign minister, Sergei Sazonov, monopolized the grand duchess's attention. Paléologue noted that Sazonov "has a high regard for her [Miechen]; he thinks her capable of courage, nobility of mind and judgment; he says she has never had the chance to show what she can do; he ascribes her failing—levity—to the minor parts she has always been given." In fact, Sazonov once admitted to Paléologue of Miechen: "*She's* the woman we ought to have had as empress! Possibly she'd have made a poor start, but she'd soon have taken to her task, thoroughly realized its obligations and gradually become perfect at it."

Noticing Sazonov's animated manner, the French ambassador guessed "that he was pouring out all the bitterness of his heart to the Grand Duchess." Later in the evening, in front of the embassy's magnificent Gobelin tapestries, Miechen related what had happened.

"What Sazonov has just been telling me is deplorable; the Empress is mad, and the Emperor blind; they don't see where they are going, and they don't want to."

"Is there no means of opening their eyes?"

"None."

"What about the Dowager Empress?"

"I spent two hours with Marie Feodorovna the other day. All we could do was grieve together."

"Why doesn't she speak to the Emperor?"

"It's not want of courage or inclination that keeps her back. But it's better that she shouldn't. She's too outspoken and impetuous. The moment she begins to lecture her son, her feelings run away with her; she sometimes says the exact opposite of what she should; she annoys and humiliates him. Then he stands on his dignity and reminds his mother that he is the Emperor. They leave each other in a rage."

"So Rasputin is still triumphant?"

"More than ever."

"Do you think the Alliance is in danger, Madame?"

"On no! The Emperor will always be faithful to the Alliance, I'll promise you that; but I'm afraid we have great internal difficulties ahead of us, and our military activities will necessarily feel the effect."

As Miechen descended the embassy staircase to say goodbye to her host, she said: "We're obviously approaching a stage which will be unpleasant, and even dangerous; I've seen it coming for a long time. I haven't much influence, and for several reasons I have to be extremely discreet. But I see many people who know and some others who occasionally are in a position to find out. Within those limits I'll give you all the help in my power. Make use of mine."

"I'm extremely grateful to Your Imperial Highness."[52]

Paléologue's observations on Miechen were in stark contrast to his impressions of her niece the Tsarina Alexandra, whom the ambassador met a month later. At the time, he found that Alexandra tried to be pleasant but "said little, as usual." Their talk, centering on "the war, its horrors, our inevitable victory, etc." was, however, nothing like his discussion with the Grand Duchess Vladimir, and amounted to "an interminable *tête-à-tête!*" The tsarina struck Paléologue as a kind of "automaton. The fixed and distant gaze made me wonder whether she was listening to me, or indeed heard me at all. I was horrified to think of the omnipotent influence this poor neurotic woman exercised on the conduct of affairs of State!"[53]

Russia's impending catastrophe was on many minds. Florence Farmborough recalled one colleague's prediction: "Mark my words! There will have to be a great *perevorot* [upheaval] in Russia, before Russia can recover her sanity and equilibrium again."[54] An official of the Russian foreign ministry declared: "We live in abnormal times and are gliding down a precipice."[55]

25

IGNOMINY

*T*he first half of 1914 appeared to bode well for Greece. That period was "the most carefree, the most prosperous Greece had ever known." Optimistic after his successes, King Constantine was eager to set his kingdom on a course of progress. And as his brother Christopher said, Constantine "thankfully laid aside his sword and began to make plans for reconstruction."[1] The outbreak of World War I thwarted these plans.

From the start, King Constantine insisted on neutrality, over objections from Eleutherios Venizelos, the country's prime minister. Venizelos called for Greece to join the Allied side, anticipating a brief war and the Allies' victory. Venizelos was tantalized by the prospect that the Ottoman Empire might enter the war and Greece could then defeat it, bringing the *Megali Idea* to fruition. To Venizelos, taking over Constantinople and freeing Greeks from Ottoman rule seemed a real possibility, if only Greece would throw in her lot with the Allies. Unlike Venizelos, Constantine I preferred caution above all else. As a military commander, he had learned from the immediate past. Defeat at the hands of the Turks in 1897 was still fresh in his mind, and Greece's armies were exhausted by two Balkan wars. If Greece sided with the Allies and the Ottoman Empire fell, the king thought it unlikely that the Russians would allow Greece to occupy Constantinople. On the other hand, siding with the Germans would likely lead to bombardment by the French and British navies. For these reasons, the king saw neutrality as Greece's only option. Yet, the impetuous, ambitious Venizelos could not accept Constantine's stand. A breach between the king and his prime minister had opened and would widen precipitously as the war raged. The explosive nature of Greek politics was set to spread like wildfire, with devastating consequences for Queen Olga's family.

Though Constantine I and Venizelos's relationship had been cordial at the beginning of the king's reign, the Cretan politician's earlier clashes with the Greek royal family still bothered the king. Constantine had not forgotten that in 1906 Venizelos had been instrumental in forcing Constantine's brother George from his post as high commissioner for Crete. Nor did the king forget the prime minister's role during the Military League's tenure in power when he acted as their political adviser.

Antagonism between King Constantine and Eleutherios Venizelos over Greece's role in the war played into the hands of the crown's opponents. It represented a golden opportunity to widen the breach, and what better way of doing so than by branding King Constantine as a traitorous pro-German, intent on delivering his country into Germany's hands.

King Constantine "was neither pro-German nor pro-Allied, he insisted to friends and detractors alike, merely pro-Greek."[2] Nevertheless, rumors about the king's loyalties and his supposed pro-German sympathies had been a topic since he visited Germany in the autumn of 1913. There, the kaiser invested Queen Olga's eldest son with the Order of the Black Eagle and made him a colonel of the Second Nassau Infantry Regiment. Constantine also politely accepted a German field marshal's baton from Kaiser Wilhelm II. Inevitably, Constantine's German visit subsequently left the Entente distrusting the king. In fact, "the seed of suspicion had already been sown, especially among the French, whose attitude from now on was to be dominated by the obsession that a Germanophil [*sic*] King sat on the throne of Greece."[3]

The kaiser tried to persuade his brother-in-law Constantine to side with Germany in the war, but to no avail. Prince Nicholas of Greece noted how indignant his brother had been with Kaiser Wilhelm's request. "It is extraordinary," said Constantine to Nicholas. "Does he take me for a German? And, because he has given me a German Field-Marshal's *bâton*, does he imagine that I am under any obligation towards him? If that is so, I am ready to return the *bâton* at any time. Besides, he seems to forget his geography and that Greece, twenty-four hours after she had declared herself Germany's ally, would be reduced to cinders by the Allied fleets. What folly! . . . We are Greeks, and the interests of Greece must come first. For the present, at any rate, it is imperative that we should remain neutral. But as to joining Germany, such an eventuality *is and always will be an impossibility*."[4]

Since Greece was still neutral and her prime minister openly pro-Entente, pressure for Greece to join the Entente increased, particularly when the Allies attacked the Dardanelles in February 1915. The Allies' plan was to capture the Dardanelle Straits, which separate the Gallipoli peninsula (part of present-day European Turkey) from Asiatic Turkey, thereby gaining navigable access from the Aegean Sea through the Sea of Marmara to Constantinople. Such a victory would introduce the very real possibility of capturing Constantinople, at the same time convincing additional neutral countries to side with the Allies. Moreover, the fall of the Dardanelles and Constantinople would open access to Russia via the Black Sea, which would help that beleaguered ally receive much needed supplies. Getting Greece to throw in her lot with this plan was thus an objective of the Entente—an objective the Central Powers were intent on thwarting.

Though initially prepared to consent to the Allies' plan, King Constantine ultimately opposed it, much to Venizelos's consternation. The king calculated that for the plan to succeed tens of thousands of Greek troops were needed to help the Allies. This, Constantine thought, might lead to the destruction of the Greek army. In this, Constantine was influenced by the chief of the Greek general staff, Colonel John Metaxas, who considered the Dardanelles campaign "a very dubious military proposition from which Greece should steer clear."[5] In the ensuing dispute with the king over the matter, the furious prime minister, left with little choice, resigned in March 1915. The Dardanelles campaign collapsed after the British Empire troops incurred heavy casualties and evacuated Gallipoli. The campaign did little to improve the Allied cause.

In the midst of all this, King Constantine fell seriously ill with pneumonia. Blood poisoning set in after two ribs were removed. So ill was the king that a miraculous icon of the Virgin Mary and Child was dispatched by warship from its shrine and placed by Constantine's bedside in the hopes that the Madonna's intercession on the king's behalf might help. When Constantine showed signs of recovering, Queen Sophie was so grateful that she donated a precious sapphire for the icon.

Sophie devotedly nursed the king through his illness, but anti-dynastic sentiment was so strong that Queen Sophie was rumored to have caused her husband to fall sick. Gossip suggested that she had stabbed him during an attempt at getting the king to side with the Germans. Like her cousin Tsarina Alexandra of Russia, Queen Sophie had been born a German princess. Both granddaughters of Queen Victoria were profoundly sympathetic toward England; nevertheless segments of the population in their adopted countries vilified the cousins as being in league with the Germans.

Even though Queen Olga had experienced some bouts of unpopularity in Greece, Olga never experienced the "flood of vituperation" that Queen Sophie suffered. In "the eyes of her critics—the French and British press and those Greek newspapers sympathetic to Venizelos—she was presented as a fanatically pro-German, hard-hearted virago, determined to force her weak-willed husband into fighting for the Kaiser."[6] One of the more outrageous stories had it that Queen Sophie went to the Phalerum (Athens's harbor) to watch an operation, involving "a diabolical subterranean and sub-aqueous contrivance by which submarines could arrive in full daylight and, while submerged, attach themselves, 500 metres from the shore, to a pipe which yielded them huge quantities of oil." Another rumor suggested that the kaiser's villa in Corfu, the Achilleion, was "no better than a formidable submarine base, which had been laid out in time of peace."[7] This particular outlandish story was reported by a French newspaper. As it turned out, "of the Entente Powers, France was the ringleader in the campaign to bring Constantine and his dynasty to its knees"[8]—a position France exercised to the hilt, beginning in October 1915.

Just two months before, with King Constantine still recuperating from his brush with death, Venizelos returned to power and became prime minister. Then, in the following month, Bulgaria, which had sided with the Central Powers, attacked Serbia. Venizelos insisted that Greek troops come to Serbia's aid. The king reluctantly agreed, but wanted this done purely as a defensive act. Nonetheless, his prime minister invited the French and British to land troops in Salonika as a gesture of support to Serbia. This unauthorized act reopened the breach between Constantine and Venizelos, and the king dismissed Venizelos from his prime ministerial post. As expected, Greece's Royalists and the Venizelists now clashed severely. Taking advantage of this grave rupture in Greek society gave the Allies the opportunity to ratchet up pressure on Constantine. French and British troops landed in Salonika and effectively took over the city in the autumn of 1915.

All this time, accusations of King Constantine and Queen Sophie's German sympathies continued to stick, making them vulnerable to danger. The French general M. P. E. Sarrail, who headed the Allied forces in Salonika, was advised to have Constantine "made away with by assassins." The French minister in Athens also "outlined a scheme for twenty men to abduct him [Constantine], and confine him aboard a French warship."[9]

The King of the Hellenes was "beside himself over French policy in Greece, warning the British to watch out for them in this part of Europe."[10] London heard from its military attaché in Athens of Constantine I's "fluent tirade against the French notably against the French Minister" and that the king complained that "they were leading us [the British] by the nose."[11] Attempting to make his position clear to the French minister of state, M. Denys Chochin, King Constantine declared: "I am not a German . . . I am Greek and nothing but Greek; I have no other care but for the interests of my people, and I wish to spare them, as far as possible, the evils of war. That is the whole secret of my policy."[12] King Constantine was well aware of his personal and political peril, confiding to his intimate confidante, Paola Princess of Saxe-Weimar: "I am playing a very dangerous game, but I am convinced that I am right, otherwise I would not act as I am doing."[13]

Constantine's mother, Queen Olga, was away from Greece while these conflicts raged. Olga had been in England a few months before the Great War erupted and there expressed her yearning for her native land: "Oh, how I am drawn to Russia . . . God willing, I am going to be there soon."[14] In the most unexpected way, Olga got her wish thanks to the war and had been living in Russia since 1914. Unable to return to Greece during this time of great crisis, the queen did not stay idle, and instead turned her attentions to Russians afflicted by the war. She helped nurse the wounded in a field hospital for maimed soldiers set up near Pavlovsk. "I spend every day in the hospital," the queen explained, "[I] apply the dressing and enjoy all those little talks with my dearest soldiers; we are big friends." Olga also described how exhausting her hospital work could be: "I returned home from the hospital at 9pm only . . . Around 11pm I fell asleep, and around one in the morning went back to the hospital where the soldiers were transported. All of them were in a bad condition, all were on stretchers, frozen to the bone and tired of all the shaking during their trip. I returned home at 4am; slept less than five hours and feel like I am in a fog." The queen was in her mid-sixties when she carried out these exhausting duties. But she did not begrudge the wounded for her work. On the contrary, said Olga: "the time that I spend in the hospital with the wounded soldiers is my true solace and comfort."[15]

While in Russia during these harrowing times, Queen Olga took solace in the company of her brother K.R. and his wife, Mavra, who lived in her childhood homes, Pavlovsk and the Marble Palace. The intellectual K.R. had distinguished himself as a man of letters and was proud of his translation of Shakespeare's *Hamlet* into Russian verse. Queen Olga was well aware of the difficulties K.R. faced during these years, leading up to and including the war. In 1911, her niece Princess Tatiana—K.R. and Mavra's daughter—had become engaged to the Georgian-born Prince Constantine Bagration-Mukhransky.

Opposition to the marriage sent Tatiana into a nervous breakdown. Tsar Nicholas II eventually sanctioned the marriage as the Bagrations were a former ruling dynasty. A number of Romanovs, including the Duchess of Coburg, considered Princess Tatiana's marriage morganatic, however. In a letter to her daughter Missy, Marie Alexandrovna wrote: "did you hear that Uncle Kostia's [K.R's] daughter Tatiana is engaged to a Caucasian Prince Bagration? The first morganatic female marriage in our family. She was simply dying and dwindling away on account of this morganatic love and now it has been sanctioned. A dangerous beginning in our family and the opening of a new social era."[16]

The other major event to affect K.R.'s family was a fatality at the front. Four of K.R.'s sons saw active military service for Russia during World War I. His middle son, Prince Oleg, was killed in 1914. As the dowager empress recorded: "Poor small Oleg died last night. He had a chance to see his poor parents and to confess to the priest. What an awful tragedy!"[17] Oleg's death greatly affected K.R. Within months, he fell seriously ill, much to Queen Olga's anxiety. In January 1915, Marie Feodorovna confided in her diary that "Olga wanted to stay longer [during a family dinner], but was too desperate about Kostia's condition."[18] In March 1915 his son-in-law Prince Constantine Bagration-Mukhransky died fighting on the Caucasian front, leaving the emotionally fragile Princess Tatiana a widow with two small children. Six months later, K.R. was dead.

Queen Olga sincerely mourned her brother's death. To her friend Ioulia Karolou, Olga wrote: "I still can't believe that he is no longer with us, and that I will not see him again in this world . . . I never thought that he would depart first . . . But such was our Lord's wish, and I can do nothing but bow my head and bless His Holy Name."[19] Olga's son Nicholas noted that "to no one" had the death of his uncle K.R. "been more cruel than to my mother, who worshipped him." During his visit to Russia in 1917, Prince Nicholas recalled how he used to read to his mother and Aunt Mavra while they knitted for the soldiers in the very room where K.R. died in Pavlovsk. Prince Nicholas remembered that his mother spent much of the day at the military hospital near Pavlovsk, "where she performed the duties of an ordinary nurse, returning to the palace only for meals. In this labour of love and charity," recalled Nicholas, "my mother found her true vocation, and she gave herself up to it with all her heart and soul, either by assisting the doctors or by cheering up the sick and wounded with the sweetness of her presence. Nothing would give her greater pleasure than when, after dressing some poor fellow's wounds, the doctor declared himself satisfied with her work."[20]

When the time came to leave Russia and his mother, Prince Nicholas did so "with a painful feeling of anxiety, as it was impossible to foretell under what circumstances I should see her again. My mother also felt this separation deeply, as she had been away from all her children since the spring of 1914, and there was no saying when and where we would be united again." Nicholas's only consolation was that "in spite of the harassing worries caused by the war, she was at least in her own home and in the country she loved with all her heart and soul. Her charitable work besides offered her ample occupation, and she was surrounded by many relations whose love and devotion would help her to bear the separation from her family."[21]

The fact that Queen Olga lived in Russia allowed Marie Feodorovna the pleasure of seeing her sister-in-law, particularly during the tumultuous years of the Great War. In July 1916, the dowager empress confided in her diary: "To my great happiness I met dear Olga at the station at 9.15, then took her to the hospital to Baby [Grand Duchess Olga Alexandrovna]."

Soon thereafter a horrendous fire broke out at Queen Olga's favorite residence of Tatoi, where the royal family was staying. That summer had been particularly hot and dry in and around Athens, leaving the region prone to fire. On the morning of July 14, 1916, Queen Olga's youngest son, Prince Christopher, who was staying in Kiphisisa, halfway between Athens and Tatoi, awakened to the smell of burning. Queen Sophie soon telephoned Miechen's daughter Elena to tell her that a fire had broken out at Tatoi and that King Constantine had gone to investigate. By afternoon, Tatoi's forest was ablaze. Prince Christopher rushed to Tatoi where "the smoke grew thicker" and near the estate "a red glow had spread over the whole horizon."[22] When Christopher arrived at Tatoi, he learned that King Constantine had been injured. The king, as it turned out, narrowly escaped death from the flames, as did Queen Sophie and her youngest child, three-year-old Princess Katherine. Trapped by the fire, Sophie had clutched Katherine and run for a mile and half, fleeing the flames. Meanwhile, the king led his son Paul and others to safety through clouds of thick, acrid smoke. Others were less fortune. The massive fire killed eighteen. Evidence pointed to arson. Empty petrol cans were found, suspicious individuals had been seen loitering; and a French airplane had flown low over Tatoi before the fire broke out. It was assumed that the plane was on some kind of reconnaissance mission.

The Dowager Empress Marie Feodorovna was shocked by the event. "Wonderful Tatoi burnt down, only the big house was saved," she recorded in her diary. Then in reference to her beleaguered nephew, the King of the Hellenes:

"Pure Tino is in great trouble. Troubles and disasters are following him."[23] This was followed some six weeks later by more sad entries in the dowager empress's diary: "Bad news from Athens. Their situation looks morbid. Poor Olga—all of it on her birthday."[24]

Marie Feodorovna was not the only member of the Romanov dynasty anxious about Greece. Tsarina Alexandra and Tsar Nicholas II followed events in Greece with concern. Alexandra wrote to Nicholas in the summer of 1916: "Why on earth this ultimatum to Greece, for sure England & France are at the bottom of it—to my simple mind, it seems unjust & hard—cannot imagine how Tino will get out of it & it may harm his popularity."[25]

In an effort to come to some kind of understanding with the Allied powers, King Constantine dispatched his brothers Andrew and Nicholas to France, England, and Russia to speak with those nations' leaders. But these attempts failed. Tsar Nicholas was one of the few who expressed sympathy over the predicament Queen Olga's family found themselves in, admitting that "the diplomats of the allies have blundered very often, as usual; in upholding that Veniselos [sic] we may come to grief. Tino thinks that perservering [sic] in this way the allies may force the dynastical question to rise & that might be playing with fire—for no reason."[26]

Two months after the tsar expressed those thoughts, Maurice Paléologue concluded that, "the situation in Athens is getting worse: the duel between the King and Venizelos has reached the critical phase."[27] The French ambassador was correct. Events rapidly deteriorated in Greece, and in October 1916, Venizelos, General Panagiotis Danglis, and Admiral P. Codouriotis set up a provisional government in Salonika, publicly supporting the Allies in defiance of their king. In a crass attempt to curry favor with Queen Olga, the triumvirate sent a telegram from Salonika to Pavlovsk on the fourth anniversary of the liberation of Salonika from the Turks, saying that, "we are anxious to dedicate a wreath as a just tribute of pious gratitude to the revered memory of our lamented King George . . . and we beg Your Majesty to graciously join her prayers with ours for the salvation of the country; and we offer her the respectful homage of our deep and unchanging devotion." Not wishing to answer the triumvirate directly, Queen Olga instead replied to the Metropolitan of Salonika: "I beg Your Holiness to inform Messrs. Venizelos, Codouriotis, and Danglis that I will gladly believe their sentiments expressed on the occasion of the anniversary of the glorious taking of Salonica by my son, when they remember their oath of allegiance to the Successor of him who sacrificed his life to a Greece made powerful by union, and not torn asunder by anarchy caused by the forgetfulness of their duty to their King, so disgracefully slandered. (Signed) Olga."[28]

Queen Olga's nephew, Britain's King George V, was perturbed with the deteriorating events in Greece, and wrote to the British prime minister:

> I am anxious at the way matters appear to be drifting in Greece, where, at the instigation of France, the Allies have agreed upon certain action which seems to me harsh and even open to question whether it is in accordance with International law . . . I cannot help feeling that in this Greek question we have allowed France too much to dictate a policy, and that as a Republic she may be some-what intolerant of, if not anxious to abolish, the monarchy in Greece. But this I am sure is *not* the policy of my Government. Nor is it that of the Emperor of Russia, who, writing to me a few days ago said:
>
> "I feel rather anxious about the internal affairs in Greece. It seems to me the protecting Powers, in trying to safeguard our in-terests concerning Greece's neutrality, are gradually immersing themselves too much in her internal home affairs to the detriment of the King [Constantine]" . . .
>
> Public opinion in Greece, as well as the opinion of the King [Constantine], is evidently changing and if the Allies would treat her kindly and not, if I may say so, in a bullying spirit, she will in all probability join them.[29]

However, the Allies did not treat Greece kindly. In December 1916, the French and British sent troops to the Piraeus. From there they marched on to Athens. Troops loyal to King Constantine forced them back. In retaliation, the Allies bombarded the Greek capital. They did not spare the royal family, who were at home at the Royal Palace. Shrapnel tore through the palace garden, prompting Queen Sophie to send the female servants to run for shelter. For several hours she and her daughters, Helen and Katherine, and the servants hid in the palace shelter in fear of their lives. "Can Belgium have suffered more at German hands?" asked an exasperated Queen Sophie.[30] The bombardment was followed by a brutal blockade on Greece implemented by the Allies. Hun-ger and disease set in. Even fishermen were stopped from trying to set off to catch something. When Greece protested this especially cruel tactic, the French commanders replied that if they wanted to be left alone, "you have only to drive out your King."[31] Little wonder then that Constantine wrote: "How weary I am of these dirty politics!"[32]

Despite the punishing blockade that brought extensive suffering, many Greeks still continued to support Queen Olga's son. Much of the people's anger was directed at Venizelos. The extent of the Greeks' disgust at Venizelos was marked. On Christmas Day 1916, the Greeks voiced their disgust with Venizelos by carrying out an anathema against him. Some sixty thousand Greeks gathered, headed by the Archbishop of Athens, who pronounced: "Accursed be Eleftherios [*sic*] Venizelos, who has imprisoned priests, who has plotted against his king and country!" Eight bishops of every district of Greece followed the archbishop by proclaiming more anathemas. The most poignant anathema was declared by an old woman "bent under a huge, rough rock brought from the stony land of her farm in Attica." In "a strident voice," reported one witness, the old lady cried out against Venizelos: "We made him premier; but he was not content. He would make himself king. Anathema!"[33]

During a good part of the war years, the Dowager Empress Marie Feodorovna continued to live away from her capital, at Kiev. At sixty-eight years of age, she was still full of energy, visiting the sick and wounded and staying involved with the Red Cross. Her visitors included Queen Olga of the Hellenes, who was as anxious as ever over the fate of her family and Greece, a concern Marie Feodorovna shared as a friend and sister-in-law. The dowager empress met with the Greek minister to Petrograd, Demetrius Caclamanos, in support of Greece and the Greek royal family. Marie Feodorovna, who had always been close to her brother King George I, asked Caclamanos when he last saw the late king. Caclamanos told the dowager empress that he had last seen King George before the Balkan Wars. The Greek minister added that, "the memory of the King was not separated in Greek hearts from the gratitude felt to his two sisters, Her Majesty the Empress, and Queen Alexandra. We knew well all that these two exalted ladies did to aid the King in promoting the Greek Cause. I even reminded the Empress," recalled Caclamanos, "of the salutary intervention of her son, Tsar Nicholas, to prevent the invading Turkish Army from advancing to Athens in 1897, when, as I knew, Queen Olga had addressed to him this eloquent, pathetic and hitherto unpublished telegram:—'I dip my pen into an inkstand of tears to solicit your intervention without delay in order to check the march of the enemy army, which is coming to camp beneath the shadow of the Acropolis.' The [Dowager] Empress was deeply moved by such memories" during the audience, wrote Caclamanos. "She burst into tears and among her sobs she said to me: 'You cannot imagine how right you are in speaking as you do about your late King. My beloved brother was a Greek, integrally Greek. He wrote to me and Queen Alexandra innumerable letters, and in each of them was pleading the cause of Greece, imploring our influence with our husbands to promote it, and to help him to be useful to the people to whom he devoted his whole life. This correspondence, if published, will some day prove to you how great has been your loss through this atrocious murder, in the city which he was trying to preserve for your nation by the shield of his own body.' In seeing this great lady, in the mourning she had never abandoned since the death of her husband, sobbing and speaking to me in such tones of sympathy about Greece, I was so deeply moved that I almost lost my composure," recalled Caclamanos.[34]

Much as Greece and the royal family's troubles preoccupied the dowager empress, first and foremost in her thoughts were those that beset Russia. Toward the end of 1916, Marie Feodorovna welcomed her son, the embattled Tsar Nicholas, and her grandson, Alexei, to Kiev. The anxious mother felt uneasy about the tsar. Nicholas II looked careworn and thinner, often appearing nervous. He was also extraordinarily quiet. Despite his worried appearance, the dowager empress did not hesitate to confront her son about the urgent need to get rid of the highly unpopular Stürmer and Rasputin.

Although it was good to see her son and grandson again, her pleas were in vain. After he left Kiev, Tsar Nicholas continued to allow his wife to run the empire from Tsarskoe Selo while he was away at Stavka. A showdown over the *staretz* was inevitable, and within weeks of the tsar's meeting with his mother things finally came to a head.

26

THE MOST DIRE

CATASTROPHES

oward the end of 1916, the Duma was in near open revolt. Its accusations rang loud and clear in attacking Boris Stürmer and, by implication, Tsarina Alexandra. "With his mother's pleas ringing in his ears," Nicholas II, upon his return from Kiev, could not disregard the Duma's outcry and finally dismissed the hated Stürmer in November 1916.[1] The tsarina disagreed with her husband's dismissal of Stürmer, and managed to convince Nicholas to retain the despised Protopopov in office. Alexandra tried, as she put it, to pour her will into the tsar's veins. She urged her vacillating husband to be strong: "Play the Emperor! Remember you are the Autocrat . . . Be like Peter the Great . . . Crush them all."[2]

By this stage, the rest of the Romanovs were united as never before. The tragedy was that it had taken their deepening concern over Tsarina Alexandra's harmful influence over Nicholas II to unite them. Her blind faith in Rasputin and its devastating effect on the monarchy had many in the family up in arms. Marie Feodorovna's brother-in-law Paul urged Nicholas and Alexandra to be rid of Rasputin. Alexandra spoke in defense of him, believing that Rasputin was "merely a victim of the calumny and envy of those who wished to be in his place."[3] Marie Feodorovna's son-in-law Sandro also tried to bring some sense to the tsar, but to no avail. Sandro visited Nicholas five times at Stavka, but each time Nicholas grew even less willing to listen. So exasperated had Sandro become that he half-jokingly said to the tsar: "You do not seem to trust your friends any more, Nicky." The tsar gave his brother-in-law an icy reply, saying simply: "I believe no one but my wife."[4]

Marie Feodorovna's sister-in-law Ella also tried to enlighten her sister,

Alexandra. In what may have been the most poignant of warnings, Ella, in her nun's habit, left Moscow and met Alexandra at Tsarskoe Selo in December 1916. Ella pleaded with her sister to send Rasputin away, saying; "Rasputin is exasperating society. He is compromising the imperial family and will lead the dynasty to ruin." The tsarina replied, "Rasputin is a great man of prayer. All these rumors are slander."[5] She then asked Ella to leave. The sisters were never to meet again. Ella promptly reported her audience with the tsarina to Felix Yussoupov. Felix recalled Ella "trembling and in tears" when she recounted her encounter with her sister. "She drove me away like a dog!" exclaimed Ella, who then cried, "Poor Nicky, poor Russia!"[6]

Hearing of Tsarina Alexandra's stubborn refusals to discuss Rasputin was nothing new to the dowager empress. Marie Feodorovna had once ended an audience she gave to the Russian historian and politician Paul Miliukov with an ominous prediction: "My unhappy daughter-in-law does not understand that she is ruining both the dynasty and herself. She sincerely believes in the holiness of some rogue and we are all helpless to avert misfortune."[7]

By late 1916, the people's obsession and anxiety over Rasputin reached new heights. Queen Olga's granddaughter the Grand Duchess Marie heard people "speaking of the Emperor and Empress with open animosity and contempt. The word 'revolution' was uttered more openly and more often; soon it could be heard everywhere. The war seemed to recede to the background. All attention was riveted on interior events. Rasputin, Rasputin, Rasputin—it was like a refrain; his mistakes, his shocking personal conduct, his mysterious power. This power was tremendous; it was like dusk, enveloping all our world, eclipsing the sun. How could so pitiful a wretch throw so vast a shadow? It was inexplicable, maddening, baffling, almost incredible."[8]

Soon stories of plots to usurp the throne from Nicholas and Alexandra circulated freely and caught the attention of numerous individuals, including Vladimir Purishkevich. A Duma member renowned for his fiery oratory, Purishkevich recorded his impressions of the Vladimir family in his diary in December 1916. Considering that Purishkevich was an ardent monarchist, his scathing remarks about the Vladimir clan were startling. Kyril and his brothers Boris and Andrei "have always filled me with disgust," penned Purishkevich. He was no less forgiving of Miechen.

> I feel no more kindly toward their mother, the Grand Duchess
> Maria Pavlovna, whose name has been hateful to me at the front
> from the very first day of the war. I feel that these dukes and their

mother have remained German and are at heart Germanophil [*sic*], that they do much harm to our troops at the front, that they set traps for the Emperor while proclaiming their devotion to Russia.

They have not given up the hope that some day the crown would pass to their line. I shall never forget the story of Ivan Grigorevich Scheglovitov, former Minister of Justice. He said that one day Grand Duke Boris Vladimirovich asked him whether the descendants of the Vladimir line have any legal rights to the throne and if not, why not?

Scheglovitov . . . told him that the Grand Dukes had no rights whatsoever because their mother continued in the Lutheran faith even after marriage.

Boris left him but came back sometime later with a paper showing that the Grand Duchess had given up her Protestant religion and had embraced the Orthodox.

Purishkevich also met with Kyril, whom Purishkevich highly suspected was disloyal to Nicholas II. "I carried an impression," recorded Purishkevich, "that he, together with [Alexander] Guchkov [Duma chairman] and Rodzianko, schemed something against the Emperor."[9]

The American-born Countess Nostitz recounted a similar story about Miechen's sons. In early December 1916, the countess dined with the Duke of Leuchtenberg, a cousin of the tsar, who told her quite frankly: "I have been sounded by the Vladimirs [the three grand dukes] to know whether I would lead my Cossack regiments in a planned revolt against the Government." In reply, the Duke of Leuchtenberg said: "I would take no sides in all this mess, so I resigned my command."[10]

Miechen, in the meantime, continued to speak openly of her disdain for Tsarina Alexandra. Maurice Paléologue asked the grand duchess if there was "anyone in his [the tsar's] household who can open his eyes?"

"No one. You know the crowd around him . . . In any case, you must not think that the Emperor's eyes need opening all that much. He knows quite well what he's doing; he fully realizes his mistakes and faults. His judgment is almost always sound. I'm sure that at the present moment he's extremely sorry he ever got rid of Sazonov [Russia's foreign minister from 1910 to 1916]."

"Then why does he go on making all these mistakes? After all, the consequences fall directly on his own head."

"Because he's weak. He hasn't the energy to face the Empress's brow-beating, much less the scenes she makes! And there's another reason which is far more serious: he's a fatalist. When things are going badly he tells himself it is God's will and he must bow to it! I've seen him in this state of mind before, after the disasters in Manchuria and during the 1905 troubles."[11]

"But is he in that frame of mind at the present moment?'

"I'm afraid he's not far from it; I know he's dejected, and worried to find the war going on so long without any result."

"Do you think he's capable of abandoning the struggle and making peace?"

"No, never; at any rate, not so long as there's an enemy soldier on Russian soil. He took that oath in the sight of God and he knows that if he broke it his eternal salvation would be jeopardized. And then he has a lofty conception of honour and will not betray his allies; he will be unshakable on that point. I believe I told you before that he would go to his death rather than sign a shameful or treacherous peace."[12]

In December 1916, Paléologue heard that in Moscow "the rage of the Muscovites against the imperial family" had reached fever pitch. "Everywhere one hears the same indignant outcry," recounted a countess who had recently returned from Moscow. "If the Emperor appeared on the Red Square to-day, he would be booed. The Empress would be torn to pieces. The kind, warm-hearted and pure-minded Grand Duchess Elisabeth dare not leave her convent now. The workmen accuse her of starving the people. There seems to be a stir of revolution among all the classes."[13]

Many Russians were frantic about what was happening to their country. Michael Rodzianko's wife, Anna, wrote to her good friend Princess Zenaida Yussoupov of her anxieties: "Never has Russia lived through such dark days, or seen such unworthy representatives of the monarchy. Let us pray and hope that God will save the long-suffering country, and that the blood of our martyrs at the front will cry out for vengeance to the throne of the Almighty."[14]

In a letter to her son Felix, Princess Zenaida Yussoupov summed up what was in the minds of many: "Tell Uncle Misha [Rodzianko] that *nothing can be done* unless the book [Rasputin] be destroyed and Valide [Tsarina Alexandra] tamed."[15] Zenaida followed this up with another letter, informing Felix that she wrote to Rodzianko, "telling him that *nothing can be done* while the manager [Rasputin] is left at large, and Valide [Tsarina Alexandra] is allowed to do harm, when she could easily be made innocuous by being declared unwell. This measure is *imperative*, and most *urgent*."[16] Felix decided to act. The dowager empress's granddaughter Irina wrote to her husband, telling him: "Many thanks for your mad letter. I could not understand half of it, but I can see that you are preparing for some wild action. Please, be careful, and don't mix yourself up in any bad business."[17]

R. H. Bruce Lockhart, a British agent and consular official in Moscow, wrote of the feelings that engrossed many: "Amongst the patriots depression assumed the proportions of hopelessness."[18] And that these months amounted to "a chronicle of almost unrelieved pessimism . . . In St. Petersburg and even in Moscow the war had become of secondary importance. The approaching cataclysm was already in every mind, and on everybody's lips."[19]

Something clearly had to be done to save Russia and the monarchy; and in the minds of three individuals, that something was the elimination of Gregory Rasputin. Vladimir Purishkevich, Prince Felix Yussoupov, and Grand Duke Dmitri Pavlovich undertook the task of Rasputin's removal as a necessary mission, an act of patriotism. Thus, the husband of the Dowager Empress Marie Feodorovna's granddaughter and Queen Olga's grandson colluded in one of history's most infamous events. The trio planned to murder Rasputin in December 1916 in Petrograd.

Felix lured Rasputin to the Yussoupov Palace, using a meeting with Irina as an enticement, since he knew the *staretz* was eager to know his lovely wife. Unbeknownst to Rasputin, Felix's wife was not in Petrograd, but in the Crimea. Once Rasputin arrived at the Yussoupov Palace, Felix plied him with poisoned cakes and poisoned wine. Unbelievably, these seemed to have had little effect. In desperation, Felix finally shot Rasputin. Later, believing the *staretz* was dead, and feeling no pulse, Felix shook the corpse violently. Then, in an appalling scene worthy of any horror film, the indestructible Rasputin rose to his feet and, roaring wildly, attacked his assassin. "Rasputin, the miracle man, had done it again. This time, instead of snatching the Tsarevitch Alexei from death, it was the *staretz* himself who seemed to be rising from the dead."[20]

With bulging eyes and blood oozing from his lips, Rasputin cried, "Felix! Felix! I will tell the Tsarina everything!" A frantic and terrified Felix screamed at his accomplice: "Purishkevich, shoot! Shoot! He's alive! He's escaping!"[21] As Rasputin staggered across the courtyard, Purishkevich shot him in the back and head. Joined by Grand Duke Dmitri, the conspirators then threw Rasputin's body in the river Neva.

Edward T. Heald, who was the secretary for the YMCA in Russia, remembered what it was like walking the streets of Petrograd just after the deed had been committed. In his diary, Heald recorded: "Rasputin killed. One of the imperial family involved. Walking home . . . near midnight, the atmosphere of the streets full of terror; people seemed to whisper of terrifying events and to be looking behind for the hand of doom from which they were preparing to rush for safety. A four mile walk of alarm and uneasiness."[22]

Soon, however, elation overtook doom as news of Rasputin's murder spread like wildfire. "I clearly remember," wrote Queen Olga's granddaughter Grand Duchess Marie, "the unprecedented excitement at the hospital" where she worked as a nurse, when news of Rasputin's death reached them. The news, noted the grand duchess, "was met everywhere with a joy bordering on hysteria; people in the streets embraced each other as they did at Easter, and women cried."[23] A Petrograd resident noted that the city "was electrified by the news of Rasputin's murder."[24] Countess Nostitz, who was attending a play, recalled that "the excitement in the theater was intense" when news of the murder broke. Upon hearing it whispered that Prince Felix Yussoupov was involved, Countess Nostitz's "mind flashed back to Rasputin's own words," repeated to her by Anna Viroubova: "The Holy Man told me that Felix Youssoupoff has the strangest destiny, but he sees blood on his hands."[25] According to Anatoli Neklyudov, "there was loud jubilation" in Petrograd, "in the theatres the National Anthem was played and sung; if it had been possible thanksgiving-services would have been held in the churches. The names of the principal authors of the deed were on every one's lips."[26] According to Felix, some urged him to have himself proclaimed emperor. Thus, as Felix put it, "the very man who had killed Rasputin in order to save the dynasty was himself requested to play the part of usurper!"[27] But Felix would have none of it.

Back at Stavka, word that Rasputin was dead was received with jubilation. "There was a general feeling," according to General A. S. Loukomsky who was there, that "we have got rid of him at last!"[28] When the tsar heard the news, Count Alexander Grabbe, a general in the Russian army, noted that Nicholas II "was in especially high spirits."[29] Count Grabbe concluded that the tsar's "good humor" stemmed from his belief that "he now felt free from a terrible burden."[30] The same reaction could not be said of Alexandra. The tsarina summoned Dr. Eugene Botkin as soon as she heard of the killing. She told him: "I am all alone. His Majesty is at the front, and, here, I have no one I can trust . . . I cannot get over it. Dimitriy [sic], whom I loved as my own son, conspiring against my life! And Yousoupoff—a nobody who owes all he has solely to the mercy of the Emperor! It is terrible."[31]

The tsarina was inconsolable. Pierre Gilliard remembered "how terribly she was suffering. Her idol had been shattered. He who alone could save her son had been slain. Now that he had gone, any misfortune, any catastrophe, was possible."[32] This was, after all, the man who insisted "with great urgency that he had some special significance for the dynasty" that "when I perish, they will perish."[33] In fact, Rasputin who had a premonition that he would meet an untimely death warned: "If I am killed by common assassins . . . you, Tsar of Russia, have nothing to fear . . . if it was your relations who have wrought my death then . . . none of your children or relations, will remain alive for more than two years . . . I shall be killed . . ."[34]

Bertie Stopford recorded his impressions of the Grand Duchess Vladimir around the time rumors were flying about Rasputin's murder. Greeting Miechen after Mass, Stopford said, "to-day even the sun is shining," to which she replied, "we are not yet sure of the fact." The grand duchess later told Stopford that "I telephoned Dmitri Pavlovich, and a strange voice first answered me in English; then he himself spoke to me. He swore that he knew nothing about the Rasputin affair."[35] When Stopford and Miechen met again soon afterward, the grand duchess informed him that Dmitri had been arrested. Bertie Stopford noted that "all the Imperial family are off their heads at the Grand Duke Dmitri's arrest."[36]

The Dowager Empress Marie Feodorovna received the sensational news in Kiev, where, according to Sandro, "people were congratulating each other in the streets and were praising the patriotic courage of Felix." Felix's father-in-law broke the news to Marie Feodorovna. When she heard what Sandro had to say, she exclaimed, "No! No!" Sandro noted that "the idea of her granddaughter's husband Felix and her nephew Dmitry [sic] stooping to murder caused her [the dowager empress] pain. As an Empress she was horrified; as a Christian she was opposed to the shedding of blood, no matter what noble considerations had prompted the culprits."[37]

Punishment meted out to the culprits varied. The popular Duma member, Purishkevich, who had fled to the front, was permitted to go free. For Felix and Dmitri, their proximity to the Crown meant that they had to be punished, as the tsar and tsarina regarded "the murder as a crime against the monarchy itself."[38] The tsar banished Prince Felix Yussoupov to one of his numerous estates; in this case, he was sent to central Russia. The tsar ordered his twenty-five-year-old nephew, Dmitri, to the Persian front.

Some two weeks after Rasputin's murder, Maurice Paléologue, accompanied by his first secretary, Charles de Chambrun, visited the Grand Duchess Vladimir at her Petrograd palace. A sense of dreadful foreboding permeated the place. The ambassador found Miechen looking "pale and emaciated." Miechen wanted to talk to the ambassador in detail, but a servant came and announced that the Grand Duke Nicholas Mikhailovich had arrived. Paléologue noticed that "his eyes were burning and grave" and he seemed to be in a "fighting attitude." Miechen left her guests to talk with the grand duke. When she returned, she did so trying to "appear self-possessed." The grand duchess then "fired questions" at Paléologue regarding his recent audience with Tsar Nicholas II. "So you weren't able to discuss the internal situation with him?" she asked the ambassador.

"No," Paléologue replied. "He obstinately shuts his ears to that subject. After beating about the bush time and time again, I thought at one moment that I was going to force him to hear me. But he cut me short."

"It's deplorable!" exclaimed Miechen, who dropped her arms in despair.

Then, after pausing, she added: "What can we do? With the exception of her [sic] who is the source of all the trouble, no one has any influence with the Emperor. During the last fortnight we have all worn ourselves out with trying to prove to him that he is ruining the dynasty and ruining Russia, and that his reign, which might have been so glorious, is going to end in a catastrophe. He won't hear a word. It's simply tragic! However, we are going to try joint action by the whole imperial family. That's what the Grand Duke Nicholas came to see me about."

"Will it be confined to a *platonic* action?" asked Paléologue.

Miechen and the ambassador then looked at each other in silence. "She guessed," according to Paléologue, "that what was in my mind was the tragedy of Paul I [of Russia, who was murdered by Russian officers], as she replied with a horrified state: 'Oh God! Whatever will happen?'"

"She sat dumb for a moment, fear staring in her eyes," recalled Paléologue. "Then she continued timidly.

'I could count on you, in case of need, couldn't I?' asked Miechen.

'Yes, Madame.'

"'Thank you,' she gravely murmured."

A servant interrupted them again. Miechen explained to Paléologue that "the whole of the imperial family had assembled in the next room and were only waiting for her to join them to start the discussion."

"And now pray to God to protect us!" exclaimed Miechen. She held her hand out to Paléologue. "It was trembling violently."[39]

After taking leave of the Grand Duchess Vladimir that night, Paléologue turned to Charles de Chambrun, and told him: "The Russian revolution has begun."[40]

At the Vladimir Palace that day, the Romanovs planned a dramatic action akin to a coup. Not until four months later, in April 1917, did Charles de Chambrun ask the Grand Duke Nicholas Mikhailovich what became of this initiative. The grand duke confirmed that it had been planned, "but our courage failed us at the last minute."[41]

Instead of a palace coup instigated by the Romanovs, the creation of a petition imploring the tsar to be lenient toward Grand Duke Dmitri materialized at Miechen's palace that day. The joint petition, composed by Miechen, was signed by numerous Romanovs. Queen Olga, Dmitri's grandmother, was the first to sign. The petition read:

> *Your Majesty,*
> *We all, whose names you will find at the end of this letter, implore you to reconsider your harsh decision concerning the fate of the Grand Duke Dmitri Pavlovich.*
> *We know that he is ill and quite unnerved by all he has gone through. You, who were his Guardian and his Supreme Protector in infancy and boyhood, well know how deeply he loved You and Our Country.*
> *Most heartily do we implore Your Majesty, in consideration of his weak health and his youth, to allow the Grand Duke to go and live on his own estates, either at Oncova or Illinskoe.*
> *Your Majesty must know the very hard conditions under which our troops live in Persia—without shelter and in constant peril to health and life.*
> *To have to live there would be for the Grand Duke almost certain death, and in the heart of Your Majesty surely a feeling of pity will be awakened towards this young man who from childhood had the joy of living in your house, and whom you loved and to whom you used to be like a father.*
> *May God inspire you and guide you to turn wrath into mercy!*
> *Your Majesty's most loving and devoted,*
> > *Olga, Queen of Greece:*
> > *Marie, Grand Duchess Vladimir . . .* [42]

Queen Olga handed the petition to Tsar Nicholas. He handed it back to her, refusing the family's pleas, having written his reply on the petition: "I do not permit anyone to give me advice. Murder is murder. Moreover I know that several among those who have signed this letter have not got a clean conscience either."[43] This was an allusion to alleged plans to overthrow Nicholas II, which had been discussed among some of the Romanovs. In fact, ten days after the Romanovs met at the Vladimir Palace, the tsar told his aunt Miechen that her sons, Kyril, Boris, and Andrei, should leave Petrograd, a move that would be "in their own interests."[44] Kyril was sent to the distant north "to thank the sailors for their service," while Andrei was sent to the Caucasus for "medical treatment." Boris was branded as being "interested only in getting drunk," and was consequently "dismissed as a person," but he too ended up exiled in the Caucasus.[45]

Talk of insurrection from the Vladimir clan undoubtedly spurred Nicholas to action. His aunt Miechen had at one point hoped that Nikolasha would "take *everything* into his hands," meaning that the grand duke should overthrow the tsar in order to save Russia. Even though Miechen would have preferred Kyril to take over the throne, she knew that "only a soldier, Nikolasha, the most popular Romanov, could curb the revolution."[46] The tsar's rejection of the family petition infuriated Miechen. The grand duchess was so incensed by the tsar's reaction, that "instead of keeping silent about the annotation of the Emperor, angrily showed it to everyone. Very soon the entire town knew by heart the short sentence that stood at the top of that page."[47]

In writing about the incident to her daughter Xenia, the dowager empress expressed her dismay: "I'm trying to keep a hold on myself, but it is too difficult. I think everybody is raving mad. The poor family wrote a stupid letter that was sent back to M.P. [Marie Pavlovna] with a dreadful inscription . . . Poor A. Olga [Queen Olga] having signed it too. They ought never to have done it, ridiculous style and why the whole family en bloc? . . . A. Miechen sent me the copy accompanied by a few words terribly offended and furious asking me to come back and help. As if there was a possibility for me to do it. Of course if I could help him out of it, I'd certainly go and try at once . . . I feel very low and horrified, one does not know what is coming next. Where will it lead us! to the devil, I think, if God won't stop it."[48]

Despite efforts by Miechen, Queen Olga, and other Romanovs to save Dmitri from being banished, the grand duke was summarily sent away. When Dmitri left for the Persian front, Bertie Stopford dined with the Vladimirs. He found "all the family looking disturbed." Stopford described Miechen as being "very much upset."[49]

Dmitri's fate continued to worry his aunt, the dowager empress. She wrote her own letter to her son Nicholas asking him to be lenient on Dmitri:

> So much has happened since we last met, but my thoughts never
> leave you and I can well understand that these last few months

have weighed heavily on you. This worries and distresses me terribly. You know how dear you are to me and how hard it is for me not to be able to help you. I can only pray to God for you, that He support you and inspire you to do all you can for the good of our dear Russia.

As we are now preparing for Holy Communion, and trying to purify our souls, one should search in oneself and forgive, and in turn beg the forgiveness of those one may have hurt in any way. I am sure you are aware yourself how deeply you have offended all the family by your brusque reply, throwing at their heads a dreadful and entirely unjustified accusation. I hope also with all my heart that you will alleviate the fate of Dmitri Pavlovich by not leaving him in Persia where the climate is so dreadful that with his poor health he will never be able to stand it. Poor Uncle Paul [Dmitri's father] wrote to me in despair that he had not even been given a chance to say good-bye to him or bless him, as he was whisked away so unexpectedly in the middle of the night. It is not like you with your kind heart to behave this way; it upsets me very much.[50]

Like Miechen and Queen Olga's pleas for Dmitri, Marie Feodorovna's also failed. Marie Feodorovna was deeply worried and wrote to Xenia, telling her: "All the bad passions seem to have taken possession of the capital. The hatred augments daily for her [Alexandra] that is disastrous, but doesn't open eyes yet. One continues quietly to play with the fire . . . What my poor dear Nicky must suffer makes me mad to think! Just everything might have been so excellent after the <u>man's</u> [Rasputin's] disappearance and now it was all spoiled by her rage and fury, hatred and feeling of revenge! . . . so sad."[51] Marie Feodorovna also made a startling comment: "Alexandra Feodorovna must be banished. I don't know how but it must be done. Otherwise she might go completely mad. Let her enter a convent or just disappear."[52]

Miechen sounded just as desperate. In January 1917, she summoned Michael Rodzianko at 1:00 A.M. by telephone: "Mikhail Vladimirovitch, could you come and see me at once?" Rodzianko replied that it was late and he was about to go to bed. "I must see you on an urgent matter. I will send my car to fetch you. Do come, please," replied the grand duchess. Rodzianko asked for some minutes to think it over. Miechen phoned back and asked: "Well, are you coming?" Rodzianko said no. The grand duchess insisted he arrive the next day for lunch to which Rodzianko agreed.

The next day at the Vladimir Palace, Rodzianko was startled by what Miechen had to say. Miechen spoke to him of the incompetent government and Tsarina Alexandra. Rodzianko recalled that when Miechen mentioned Alexandra's name, "she became more and more excited, dwelt on her nefarious influence and interference in everything, and said she was driving the country to destruction; that she was the cause of the danger which threatened the Emperor and the rest of the Imperial Family; that such conditions could no longer be tolerated; that things must be changed, something done, removed, destroyed . . ."

Rodzianko then inquired, "What do you mean by 'removed'?"

"Well, I don't know," replied the Grand Duchess Vladimir. "Some attempt must be made . . . The Duma must do something . . . She must be annihilated."

"Who?" asked Rodzianko

"The Empress," Miechen stated emphatically.

"Your Highness," said Rodzianko, "allow me to treat this conversation as if it had never taken place, because if you address me as the President of the Duma, my oath of allegiance compels me to wait at once on his Imperial Majesty and report to him that the Grand Duchess Marie Pavlovna has declared to me that the Empress must be annihilated."[53]

Not too long after this, Miechen left Petrograd. "I badly need sun and a rest," Miechen told Paléologue during a dinner he gave her in February 1917. "The emotions of recent times have worn me out," confessed the grand duchess. "I'm leaving with my heart heavy with apprehension. What will have happened by the time I see you again? Things can't go on like this!"

"So affairs are not improving?" asked the French ambassador.

"No," replied Miechen. "How could they? The Empress has the Emperor entirely under her thumb; her only adviser is Protopopov who consults the ghost of Rasputin every night! I can't tell you how downhearted I feel. Everything seems black, wherever I look. I'm expecting the most dire catastrophes. And yet God can't mean Russia to perish!"

"God only helps those who help themselves . . . what the Emperor is now doing is simply suicide, suicide for himself, his dynasty and his people."

"But what can we do?" asked a dejected Miechen.

"Fight on . . . But there is no time to lose! The danger is pressing; every hour counts. If salvation does not come from above, there will be revolution from below. And that will mean catastrophe!"[54]

In the hopes of helping Russia, Count Frederickz, a court intimate, suggested to the tsarina that she and Miechen should reconcile. Surprisingly, Alexandra agreed. Count Frederickz then asked A. A. Mossolov to broach the subject with the Grand Duchess Vladimir. Mossolov and the grand duchess proceeded to have a serious discussion over the matter. According to Mossolov, Miechen "recognized at the outset that a reconciliation was indispensable in the interests of the dynasty and of the whole country."

Mossolov then added: "But it would be necessary, Madame, for you to take the first step."

"If that is so I am not ready even to discuss the subject with you. It is impossible," declared the grand duchess.

Mossolov then insisted, prompting Miechen to agree to a compromise: "I will go to Tsarskoe Selo, if Count Freedericksz [sic] comes to invite me in Her Majesty's name."

That, recalled Mossolov, "was her last word." Count Frederickz agreed to extend the invitation personally to Miechen as soon as he was well and had hoped to tell her that the tsarina would be asking her to tea shortly. "I learned later that it had been impossible for this invitation to be conveyed to the Grand Duchess," recalled Mossolov.[55] Just three weeks after this, revolution plunged Russia into anarchy.

In March 1917, all hell broke lose in Petrograd. The revolution had arrived. Queen Olga's son-in-law Grand Duke George Mikhailovich wrote of it to his wife, Marie: "We are in the midst of a revolution and all the horrors that accompany it . . . the last news from Petersburg was very bad and the mob is murdering, firing and sacking on all sides . . . if things are allowed to go in this way, it will end in a formidable revolution."[56]

Shortages in food and fuel left people cold and hungry. Once the Petrograd factories and army barracks fell to Socialist propaganda, the revolution could not be stopped. One of the more shocking incidents involved the elite Preobrazhenski Guard Regiment. When ordered to fire on the people in the streets, the troops instead fired on their own officers. Seeing where the tide of revolution was turning, Grand Duke Kyril, in a move tantamount to treason, sided openly with the revolutionaries. Maurice Paléologue was appalled by Kyril, who, "in his naval captain's uniform," had been "seen leading the marines of the Guard, whose commander he is, and placing their services at the disposal of the rebels!"[57] The Countess Nostitz was equally horrified at seeing Kyril march "at the head of his Marines, leading them to the Douma [sic] to swear allegiance to the new Ministers, flying the red flag and with a red band on his arm."[58]

In no time, twenty-five thousand soldiers had revolted and joined the mobs. Once military discipline collapsed, repression was impossible. Crowds shouted, "bread, bread." Mobs marched on the Nevsky Prospekt "waving the black flag of anarchy and the red flag of revolution, singing the French Marseillaise"[59] and shouting "down with Alexandra!"[60]

In faraway Kiev, Marie Feodorovna expressed her anxieties: "No news from St. Petersburg. Not right at all . . . They say that my poor Nicky is in Pskov. Can only speak and think about this horror. Got a telegram from Xenia, who says no one knows where Nicky is; dreadful what they are going through! May the Lord help us."[61]

With Petrograd in chaos, Michael Rodzianko was compelled to send a message to the tsar: anarchy engulfed the capital. Various Russian generals, including Nikolai Ruzsky who commanded the Northern Front headquartered at Pskov, urged the tsar to abdicate. Fearing a civil war would erupt—and crucially, at a time while Russia was still fighting Germany, Tsar Nicholas II bowed to the inevitable and abdicated. "If it is necessary, for Russia's welfare, that I step aside," announced the tsar, "I am prepared to do so." It was not an easy decision. Abdication "was for him an immense sacrifice: not because he craved either the substance of power or its trappings—the one he thought a heavy burden, the other a tedious imposition—but because he felt by this action he was betraying his oath to God and country." In abdicating, Nicholas was animated utmost by "patriotic motives: the wish to spare Russia a humiliating defeat and to save her armed forces from disintegration, for if Nicholas's foremost concern had been with preserving his throne he would have quickly made peace with Germany and used front-line troops to crush the rebellion in Petrograd and Moscow. He chose instead, to give up the crown to save the front."[62]

Marie Feodorovna's son signed the instrument of abdication at Pskov, where his train had been sidelined. Nicholas, however, did more than abdicate for himself. Moved by Alexei's incurable hemophilia, Nicholas the father "could not bring himself to abandon his beloved child to strangers ignorant of all the ramifications of his disease."[63] Nicholas announced his decision to the Duma's two emissaries, M. Guchkov and V. V. Shulgin, who were astounded to hear from the tsar that he was abdicating in favor of Grand Duke Michael.

Nicholas himself wrote out the abdication manifesto to his people, part of which read: "I invite all the loyal sons of my country to fulfill their sacred duty which is to obey the Emperor in these difficult moments, and to help him, as well as the representatives of the nation, to lead Russia to victory, success, and glory. May God help Russia!"[64]

Alexander Kerensky, a member of the Duma, came to head the Provisional Government that took over power after Nicholas II's fall. Kerensky urged Michael to sign a document that amounted to a renunciation of the throne, which Michael did. V. V. Shulgin admitted that "the grand duke aroused my personal sympathy. He was frail and gentle, not born for such difficult times, but he was sincere and humane. He wore no masks. It occurred to me: 'What a good constitutional monarch he would have been.' "[65] But Michael did not seize the chance to be tsar. And so in the space of a few days, Marie Feodorovna's two sons and grandson saw the Russian throne slip from their hands.

Russia—Imperial and Orthodox Russia—was torn asunder. It was, in the words of Charles de Chambrun, "the end of a world."[66]

Sandro had the heavy burden of informing his mother-in-law of the tsar's abdication. Of that momentous moment, Sandro recalled how he dressed and "went to break the heart of a mother."[67] However shattered she must have been at learning of Nicholas's abdication, Marie Feodorovna would have been proud, had she watched him, of the dignified manner in which her son conducted himself in the final hours prior to, and after, abdicating. Nicolas de Basily, director of Nicholas II's Diplomatic Chancellery at Stavka, who had the unenviable task of composing the momentous document, met with the tsar on board the imperial train. It was a poignant and difficult meeting, punctuated by the "red light of the setting sun on the snowy landscape, lonely and desolate." De Basily, "deeply moved to encounter his sovereign under such circumstances," was able to "regain his own self-control," however, thanks in large part to Nicholas's "complete composure." De Basily was "amazed at the way this unfortunate ex-ruler of an immense Empire dominated himself with the greatest dignity. No apparent emotion, only the contraction of the throat muscles betrayed his anguish."[68] Within days, the former tsar of all the Russias was back at Mogilev, awaiting the arrival of his grief-stricken mother.

27

THE TRIUMPH OF MADNESS

*U*nbelievably, after nearly four centuries, tsarist Russia had crumbled. Having reigned for twenty-two tumultuous years, Marie Feodorovna's son Nicholas was no longer tsar. That the Russian Empire fell apart with "remarkable rapidity" was astonishing. "It was as if the greatest empire in the world, covering one-sixth of the earth's surface, were an artificial construction, without organic unity, held together by wires all of which converged in the person of the monarch. The instant the monarch withdrew, the wires snapped and the whole structure collapsed in a heap."[1]

At the Winter Palace, the day after the abdication, Bertie Stopford was amazed to encounter a menacing and highly charged symbolic spectacle—the palace had "the Red [revolutionary] Flag" prominently "flying and the eagles on the big gates are covered with red cloth."[2] Mathilde Kschessinska, the long-time mistress of Miechen's son Andrei, remarked that at the time of the tsar's abdication, Petrograd "was a nightmare world of arrests, the assassination of officers in the streets, arson, pillage . . . and I thought of the dangers which all the people I loved were undergoing—[Grand Dukes] André [*sic*], Serge, the Emperor and his Family."[3] Kschessinka was not the only one concerned about the tsar's fate. A Russian, Irina Skariätina, confided in her diary at the time of the abdication: "I cannot help thinking of the Emperor. Alone, hunted, frightened, humiliated, hurt. He certainly has drunk the cup of bitterness to its very dregs. What will happen to him now?"[4]

Alexandra learned the stunning news of her husband's abdication from Grand Duke Paul. She burst into tears and, still reeling from shock, Alexandra soon ran into her friend Lili Dehn. She clutched Lili's hands and cried out:

"Abdiqué!" At that moment Alexandra thought only of Nicholas and mumbled: "*le pauvre . . . tout seul là bas . . . oh, mon Dieu, par quoi il a passé! Et je ne puis pas être près de lui pour le consoler* [The poor one . . . all by himself . . . oh my God, why has it happened! And I was not there to console him]."[5]

Two days after Nicholas II took the momentous step, his sixty-nine-year-old mother arrived at Mogilev from Kiev with Sandro. Reunited at the army headquarters, Nicholas and Marie Feodorovna spent two hours together in the dowager empress's train. When Sandro joined them, he found his mother-in-law sitting in a chair, crying aloud while Nicholas stood quietly. At luncheon that day, through all the politeness and banalities expressed, Marie Feodorovna could not hide her dismay—her face was marred by tears. The American ambassador to Russia, David R. Francis, noted that the dowager empress had "endeavored to comfort him [Nicholas], but . . . she was more perturbed than he was."[6] In fact, "it was Nicholas, the son she had always lectured on behavior, who carefully steered his mother back toward courage and self-control."[7]

In reporting what had happened that day, Marie Feodorovna sent her daughter Grand Duchess Xenia a telegram: "We arrived in the morning. Happy to be together. He is wonderful. Everything too sad, not to be believed. My heart bleeds."[8]

Despite her inner turmoil, the dowager empress put on a brave face—a difficult task because as Grand Duchess Xenia described it, "the Empress was quite crushed by all she heard and saw."[9] Days after the abdication, Marie Feodorovna asked to speak to Major General Sir John Hanbury-Williams, who headed the British Military Mission at Stavka during the Great War. Hanbury-Williams spoke to the "Empress-Mother" as he described her, for half an hour, an audience which the general described as "a most sad and painful interview, in which she showed great courage."[10] During her conversation with Hanbury-Williams, Marie Feodorovna told him that "she thought it very distressing" that various generals with Nicholas at Pskov encouraged him to abdicate.[11]

Soon it was time to bid her son farewell. Nicholas "went quietly and calmly," while his mother "was overcome with emotion."[12] Nicholas covered his mother's face with kisses and embraced Sandro. The dowager empress's Cossack, Timofei Yaschik, recalled the moving goodbye between mother and son: "The Empress hugged, gently kissed and blessed him. She really cried—more than I have ever seen the strong Danish Princess cry at any time before and after this."[13] The former tsar entered his train carriage and waved goodbye, "his expression," recalled Sandro, "was infinitely sad." Sandro noted that "the old Empress" after bidding her son a final farewell, cried "unrestrainedly" once her son's train became "a stream of smoke on the horizon."[14] As she watched Nicholas's train disappear, Marie Feodorovna blessed him by making the sign of the cross. It was the last time the dowager empress would see her son.

Afterward, Marie Feodorovna described to Queen Alexandra the parting from her son as "heart-crushing."[15] To Queen Olga, with whom the dowager empress had always had a close relationship, Marie Feodorovna poured out her heartache in a letter:

> My heart is full with grief and despair. Just imagine the horrible indescribable times that we will have to go through. I don't even know how I am still alive after seeing how my poor dear son was treated. I thank God that I spent those terrible 5 days with him at Moghilev, when he was so lonely and abandoned by everyone. These were the most terrifying days of my life. God sends us too tough of a test, and we have to bear it with dignity, with all humility. But it is so difficult to endure when the people's animosity and rage are around. I cannot even describe to you the kind of humiliations and indifference that my poor Nicky went through. I would not believe it if I did not see it with my own eyes. He was like a true martyr.[16]

Not long after writing this, the dowager empress again wrote to Queen Olga of her anguish: "I would be happy to die—just not to live through all of this horror. However, there is God's will for everything! But it is still difficult to understand how God allows all these injustices and everything bad that is happening around."[17] This was followed by another letter to Queen Olga in which Marie Feodorovna wrote: "My little, dear, heavenly angel . . . My heart is overtaken with sorrow and despair . . . My dear [daughter] Olga and I are asking God to grant His blessing to you and help for all of us . . . Your loving miserable Minnie is hugging you."[18]

Once back in Kiev, Marie Feodorovna remained in shock. "My mother," recalled Grand Duchess Olga Alexandrovna decades later, "could not understand the reasons behind the abdication . . . she kept telling me that it was the greatest humiliation of her life." Upon their return to Kiev, Sandro rushed to the hospital where Olga was working and asked her to go to her mother's side to calm her. "I had never seen her in such a state," recounted Olga. "She kept pacing the floor, and I saw that she was more angry than miserable. She understood nothing of what had happened. She blamed poor Alicky for just everything. It was an afternoon to turn your hair grey," concluded Grand Duchess Olga.[19]

In relating what had happened, the dowager empress unburdened herself to Grand Duchess Xenia: "These times and conditions are so difficult and incomprehensible, that I don't understand <u>anything</u> anymore . . . poor Nicky, a true martyr! You can't imagine what happens to my soul and how I <u>suffer</u> to see him in this position! It's simply unbelievable!" Thirteen days later, the anguished mother again wrote to Xenia, still reeling from the shock of the abdication: "I still can't believe that this dreadful nightmare is real. I hear *nothing* from poor Nicky, for which I suffer *horribly*." Referring to Alexandra, Marie Feodorovna asked: "Will she ever understand what she did? I am sure not, she is too proud and obstinate, what hell it must be! I'm even frightened to think of it!"[20]

Alexandra greeted the former tsar on his return to Tsarskoe Selo. Though she had always harangued her husband about transmitting the throne to Alexei intact, when Nicholas abdicated for himself and his son, Alexandra did not begrudge him his actions, but offered him her solace and understanding. After maintaining his composure for days, when Nicholas at last met Alexandra after all he had been through, he fell into his wife's arms and "sobbed like a child."[21]

For the next five months, the imperial family was kept captive at the Alexander Palace. During this time, friends of the family such as Lili Dehn and Anna Viroubova were arrested. Alexander Kerensky himself, leader of the Provisional Government, went to Tsarskoe Selo to interrogate the former tsarina and try to discover the extent of her supposed pro-German sympathies. Kerensky was impressed by the clarity of her answers and admitted to Nicholas that his wife did not lie. Kerensky had even ventured to admit, "I had imagined her differently. She is very sympathetic. She is an admirable mother. What courage, what dignity, what intelligence and how beautiful she is!"[22]

The family's captivity at Tsarskoe Selo was not an easy one. One day at the end of March, Grand Duke Paul's wife, Olga, was overcome by pity as insolent soldiers loudly ridiculed the former tsar, telling him: "Well, well, Nicoloucka [Little Nicholas], so you are breaking the ice now, are you? Perhaps you've drunk enough of our blood?" Nicholas looked sadly at the soldiers and then seeing Olga, gave a "mournful gaze" in her direction. She saw "in his dear eyes a misery so deep, a hopeless resignation so great," that Princess Paley was moved to tears.[23] The family's captivity did not get easier. By the end of April, the tutor Pierre Gilliard, who shared the family's fate, confided in his diary that "it is apparent that the régime to which we are being subjected is becoming continually more severe."[24]

On Easter Sunday 1917, Queen Olga traveled to Tsarskoe Selo and left an Easter egg with the officer on duty to be given to the former tsarina. Unlike other Romanovs, Queen Olga, along with Marie Feodorovna's two daughters, had always tried to understand Alexandra. The former tsar appreciated Queen Olga's kindness. After months of captivity at Tsarskoe Selo, he wrote to the queen, telling her that, "if you write to my dear Mama, tell her that I am constantly with her in my prayers and my thoughts." In another letter, Nicholas wrote: "I congratulate you, dear Aunt Olga [on her name day] and wish you . . . [the] very best from the bottom of my loving heart."[25]

Not all the Romanovs showed such sympathy toward the former monarchs as Queen Olga. Bertie Stopford reported in March 1917 that, "the Kyrills are behaving tactlessly; he is attacked by all parties for his attempts to curry favour with the powers that be, at the expense of his family. Kyrill Égalité! A Radical newspaper said, 'Only rats leave a sinking ship!' "[26]

Stopford's great concern at this time was the Grand Duchess Vladimir. Miechen's exit from Petrograd occurred around the time the Vladimir clan were "cut down to size" by Tsar Nicholas in early 1917. Miechen left the capital, but haughtily pronounced that she would return "when everything is over."[27] She had established herself, temporarily she thought, at Kislovodsk in the northern Caucasus in "disguised exile."[28] Fashionable with the well-to-do as a resort town famed for its mineral waters, Kislovodsk was nearly three thousand feet above sea level.

In the newspapers, Stopford read that Miechen had been arrested "in her villa at Kislovodsk in the Caucasus. Their story is that she had given a letter for her son Boris to a general who was going to Stavka; that she had written to say the only hope for Russia was in Nicolai Nicolaievich. The general was arrested en route, and the letter was found . . . I feel quite sure that she has done nothing for which she can be attacked."[29]

In recording what had actually happened with Miechen, Charles de Chambrun of the French embassy wrote that "the grand duchess did not say a word, but waited for their [the soldiers'] departure before fainting . . . They searched . . . her cellar . . . They broke her [wine] bottles, piercing the casks . . . The neighborhood was rejoicing, the wines flowed in a stream, the breeze even had the breath of a drunkard. The journals announced in their headlines that 'Marie Holstein' was an accomplice of the treasons of 'Alix Rasputin.' " In recounting how far Miechen had fallen, de Chambrun added: "Poor Marie Pavlovna, whom fate, since her marriage to the grand duke Vladimir, was so envious!" De Chambrun recalled her as having been "affable, charming . . .

never will I forget her welcome in the house of Tsarskoe-Selo. She had the air of a Gervex portrait come out of its plush frame, vainly one searched behind her for a shape that generous nature had replaced. Her movements were short, alluring, her shoulders magnificent; a curled fringe softened her slightly heavy face like a joke animates. What a dignity without rigidity, she was so pleasant that a shy visitor smiled from ease."[30]

Echoing de Chambrun, Bertie Stopford also reported that "the grand duchess was so mortified [when the soldiers had threatened her with arrest] that she fainted and fell unconscious for hours." Stopford concluded that, "it is difficult for the daughter-in-law of Alexander II to imagine herself a prisoner! She told me she thought of the 'Ballad of Reading Gaol' all the time! She knew absolutely nothing of what has been going on in Russia."[31] The *Ballad of Reading Gaol*, to which Miechen referred is Oscar Wilde's long poem about condemned imprisoned men.

Bertie Stopford secretly visited Miechen at Kislovodsk on Easter. "Even if I don't see her," noted Stopford, "she will know that I have made the effort." Stopford was willing to endure the long journey—three nights in a train, a journey likely punctuated by lawlessness. "But," added Stopford, "I feel, after all her kindness to me, it is the least I can do . . . I fear I might do her harm; but I have heard she feels deserted, and also that she has had a bad heart attack."[32]

During his brief visit, Stopford advised Miechen to give up on the idea of going to the Crimea, where many members of the imperial family were already living. Instead, it was best to try to make her way to Finland and freedom. Taking his advice, Miechen asked to be allowed to go to a sanatorium for her health in Finland, but was refused permission. Once her lease expired on her villa, Miechen went on to stay with her son Andrei in his home in Kislovodsk. Miechen's other son, Boris, meanwhile, was under arrest in his home at Tsarskoe Selo.

In April 1917, Vladimir Lenin arrived in Russia in a sealed train from his life of exile. With the tsar's overthrow, the leader of the Bolsheviks returned to his native land in order to shape the direction of the revolution. The Germans facilitated Lenin's return, hoping that, by promoting anarchy in the country that was still at war with Germany, he would be a useful ally. Lenin ruthlessly pushed for a more radical direction, urging peasants to seize lands and Bolsheviks to deny support to the Provisional Government. It became increasingly obvious that a showdown would take place in the not too distant future. Queen Olga's son-in-law Grand Duke George Mikhailovich summed up what was in store when he wrote to his wife Marie, Queen Olga's daughter, who was still in

England, that Russia was heading toward "something between communism and anarchy," and that Lenin was inciting the mobs "to adopt communism." In another letter, George reported that "Lenin is continually exciting the mob and encouraging them to pillage . . . Lenin is making a present of all private houses to the mob. The people have gone crazy and this disease will go all through Russia."[33] In describing letters she was able to receive from her husband, Marie wrote how "utterly revolted" Grand Duke George was "over the indescribable vulgarity of everything, the tone of the papers, the expressions used and the venom poured on everyone's head, which, he said, were perfectly nauseating."[34] Grand Duke George had little hope for Russia's future, telling his wife: "The culture here is so low, that it is idiotic to imagine that the country will enjoy prosperity in the twinkling of an eye for the sole reason that the Tsar has been removed."[35]

Nicolas de Basily's wife, Lascelle Meserve de Basily, recalled what it was like in Petrograd at the time. She remembered how Vladimir Lenin "harangued the passersby" from the balcony of Mathilde Kschessinska's home. And "in the streets the epaulettes and insignia of former officers were often brutally torn off." Moreover, "socialist meetings were held in the city where anarchy and insubordination were preached." De Basily also added that it became evident "soon after the revolution," that in reality, "it was not the Provisional Government who ruled, but the Council [Soviet] of Workers' and Soldiers' Deputies, which had installed itself in the Duma."[36]

"As for the lower people and the peasantry, they understood nothing of all that had happened," concluded de Basily. There was, however, one thing that "impressed the peasantry deeply," added de Basily, "and that was the removal of the Emperor's name from the church services. The officiating priest had always prayed for the Tsar, the Tsarina and the Imperial family, and suddenly it was swept away, leaving them [the peasantry] like sheep without a shepherd, children without a father. 'Batiushka, batiushka, little father, do not forsake us,' they implored. Alas, only stony silence answered their cry, Nicholas II, Little Father of all the Russias, was a prisoner in his palace at Tsarskoe Selo, and the red flag waved in the land."[37]

Far from calming down, the atmosphere in Petrograd and other parts of Russia was infused with growing fear. The fate of Countess Kleinmichel and her nephew exemplified what was in store for many, including the Romanovs. The seventy-year-old countess, once the toast of the imperial capital, was left in the Duma for three days, with only a chair to sleep in. She was surrounded by other prisoners, some of whom died from their wounds right beside her. Then, under house arrest, the elderly countess endured a frightening incarceration. Insolent soldiers, sixty of them, left her home in shambles and stole her things. No one was allowed into her house, not even the countess's doctor. Left at the soldiers' mercy, the old woman was forced to stay in her bedroom as the soldiers smoked while describing the massacre of officers in gruesome detail. Moved by the countess's plight, Louis de Robien admitted that "she is as pitiful as a hunted animal." Even more wretched was the fate of Countess Kleinmichel's nephew, an officer: "After having been blinded, having seen two of his friends murdered, and having his hands cut off," his own men killed him. "His mother had the courage to go and ask the soldiers for his body, which was no more than a blood-stained bundle which they had rolled in the mud."[38] Such horrific stories were abundant and unceasing.

Russia was an extremely dangerous place in the wake of what became known as the February/March Revolution. To his wife, Grand Duke George Mikhailovich wrote of seeing everything "ruined . . . the streets are filthy, the soldiers' barracks, which used to be spick and span, have been turned into real pigsties. It is the reign of dirt, disorder . . . and the vulgarity surpasses anything imaginable. One is ashamed to think that a country could go to pieces like it has, in four short months."[39]

After the tsar's abdication, Queen Olga continued to spend her evenings at Pavlovsk, devoting the daytime to nursing. Like Countess Kleinmichel, she too had soldiers invade her home; some eighty of them armed with machine guns marched in demanding arms. They awakened the queen's elderly maid, who had served her for fifty years. She "pluckily told them not to make so much noise because the Queen was asleep, worn out from working for the wounded in her hospital."[40] The maid told them not to frighten "Her Majesty." "And who's Her Majesty?" the soldiers retorted. "The Queen of Greece," replied the maid. "We don't need any Greek Queen," the soldiers shouted back.[41] Fortunately, Queen Olga was left alone.

In Kiev, Sandro and Grand Duchess Olga struggled to convince the dowager empress to leave the city, which had become increasingly dangerous. Marie Feodorovna received a taste of what was in store should they stay, when she arrived at Kiev's main hospital to visit the ill and wounded. The head surgeon and his staff rudely told the dowager empress that she was no longer needed. After this shocking incident, Marie Feodorovna acquiesced to Sandro and Olga's pleas. Sandro was able to secure passage out of Kiev for the family for an exit without fanfare. The dowager empress, Sandro, Xenia, Olga, her husband, and a few retainers, including Timofei Yaschik, quietly boarded Marie

Feodorovna's carriage, which was attached to a train on a siding outside of Kiev. "And so began this strange journey into the unknown," recorded Yaschik. There was a chance that they would be apprehended along the way, but thanks to a small number of armed loyalists on board the train who ensured their safety, the family arrived in the Crimea after four nerve-racking days. Timofei Yaschik recounted that "in spite of the danger and the stress of the situation the Empress was always calm and maintained her courage, she handed out short and precise instructions, without the slightest shaking in her voice. She still remained Marie Feodorovna, the Russian Empress!"[42] Once the party arrived in the Crimea, they headed to Ai-Todor, Sandro and Xenia's villa near Yalta. It was the first time Marie Feodorovna had been back in the Crimea since her beloved husband had died there in 1894.

Situated close to the Black Sea and surrounded by lush scenery and vegetation, Ai-Todor would have been a veritable paradise had it not also been a prison for the dowager empress and her family. While in the Crimea, Marie Feodorovna was haunted by doubts about being in the south. She regretted not having gone north to Petrograd instead, in order to try to lend support to Nicholas and his beleaguered family. But much as she yearned to be with her imprisoned son, the dowager empress had no choice but to stay in the Crimea. Amidst all the doubts and uncertainty, one happy event took place; in the summer of 1917, Marie Feodorovna became a grandmother again when Grand Duchess Olga gave birth to her first son, Tikhon.

Soon enough, the troubles the family had been fearing erupted at Ai-Todor. One early morning, several hundred Bolshevik sailors, armed with hammers and axes, invaded the villa and made their way to the dowager empress's bedroom. A mortified Marie Feodorovna was helpless as she watched them ransack her room from top to bottom, tearing curtains, ripping carpets, emptying drawers viciously, and ripping apart her bed. Even the dowager empress's sacred icons were not immune as the sailors brutally smashed and split them apart in search for any incriminating evidence. They confiscated the icons, personal letters, photographs, other items, and even the dowager empress's treasured Danish Bible, which her mother, Queen Louise, had given her all those decades before when she left Denmark for Russia. In the meantime, Grand Duchess Olga and her husband were kept away from the dowager empress. Fearing for her mother's life, Olga finally dashed into her room to find the place in shambles and the dowager empress "in bed, her eyes blazing with anger." "The invective" Marie Feodorovna "poured on the marauders did not affect them in the least. They went on with their work until a particularly biting phrase" from the dowager empress "made one of them say that they might just as well take the old hag along with them."[43] Had it not been for Sandro's intervention, the dowager empress would have likely been dragged away by the Communists. The assault on Ai-Todor had been instigated by the Petrograd Soviet as a demonstration that they had the upper hand over the Provisional Government.

At one point, the Bolshevik sailors who ransacked the dowager empress's room demanded that she sign a piece of paper that claimed Marie Feodorovna was not involved in a counter-revolutionary plot. She signed it simply, "Marie." "That is not your proper name. Sign 'Marie Romanoff' or you will be made to pay dearly," a captor threatened.

Looking her captor in the eye, the dowager empress replied, "I know how to sign my name; and on that subject I take no instructions from you. For fifty years I have signed my name in this same way, and I do not mean to change. If you choose, you can kill me, of course; but you cannot alter the fact that I had my reign out and have not abdicated, so I am the Empress-Mother still, and that is my signature. Take it or leave it, as you please."[44]

Not long after the intruders left, Marie Feodorovna spoke to one of the guards assigned to watch over her. She asked him to show her the small cross that Russian soldiers tended to wear. Since the Bolsheviks forbade this display of Christianity, the soldier denied that he had a cross. But in no time, he sheepishly took his cross from a pocket and handed it to Marie Feodorovna. She then put the cross around the man's neck who then cried, ashamed that he had denied possessing this most tangible symbol of Christianity.

Life at Ai-Todor became more difficult once guards were posted to watch over the Romanovs. To Queen Olga, the dowager empress wrote that, "My sweet little angel, I want to try and send this letter to you with a reliable person, but this is still not easy . . . We are living in isolation from the rest of the world." "Here, we are looked at," Marie Feodorovna wrote mournfully, "as if we were real criminals and very dangerous people. It is difficult to believe in this . . . I am hugging you in my thoughts and asking God to bestow His blessing on you, my angel, my little sister. My best regards to everyone. Your always loving miserable sister."[45]

The strain of captivity at Ai-Todor took its toll on the family and servants alike. Some of the servants became impudent. Marie Feodorovna, who never really accepted Nikolai Kulikovsky—a commoner—as a son-in-law, found it difficult to include him in family gatherings. It was a bitter disappointment for the devoted Olga to see her husband being treated so, but she kept her frustrations to herself. Ironically, because Grand Duchess Olga was married to a commoner, she and Kulikovsky were allowed more liberty than the rest of the Romanovs. But there was no denying that life had changed for Olga and, most of all, her mother. Now seventy years old, Marie Feodorovna, the woman who had been so loved and so popular in Russia for decades, was now a prisoner with an uncertain future.

On Marie Feodorovna's seventieth birthday, a modest celebration took place. At the time, Prince Shervashidze, steward of the royal household, reflected on the dowager empress's demeanor during her captivity. The prince wrote to Grand Duke Michael of his admiration for Marie Feodorovna due to the "the dignity of her behaviour." Prince Shervashidze never heard "a single complaint" from the dowager empress about her "constrained situation." Moreover, because Marie Feodorovna was "quiet and cordial" such conduct "raises our spirit as well to some extent." It also helped her fellow captives "endure the burdens of imprisonment" more easily.[46]

One of the few consolations granted Marie Feodorovna during these harrowing times was the occasional letter from loved ones such as Queen Olga. In June 1917, Marie Feodorovna received such a letter, to which she replied: "I cannot express to you how happy I am to finally receive a cordial letter from you . . . For me it is an incredible delight to receive a message from my relatives and loved ones, a true celebration and a great consolation in my present life, because right now I feel absolutely lost . . . My thoughts are constantly with you, my dear, and I miss you a lot . . . It is terrible that there is no opportunity to write and hear each other. . . ."[47]

To her niece Xenia in the Crimea, Queen Olga sent a sympathetic letter from Pavlovsk: "I pray that this terrible time should pass, that we shall see better times in our beloved Motherland and that some happy experiences should blot the disgrace of recent days from all our minds . . . All kinds of vile acts are being committed in the name of liberty, national self-determination and justice and they are being substantiated by using pompous, meaningless words." Then, with a mixture of humor and sarcasm, the queen mockingly took the words out of the Communists' mouths and added: "Comrade Xenia, I hope that you have become self-determined and that you stand on a firm platform without any annexation and reparations for the good of the people and international love of your enemies and the world proletariat."[48]

Besides her concern about Russia, Queen Olga's abiding anxiety about the fate of Greece and her beleaguered family increased, because the overthrow of the Romanov dynasty had "emboldened the Greek royal family's enemies—the

Venizelists and their Allied partners—to seek the same outcome for Constantine and Sophie."[49] In June 1917, they succeeded.

The Allies were impatient with Greece's neutrality, and appointed the "overbearing" Charles Jonnart as the "High Commissioner" "in Athens to a nation both independent and neutral." This move by the French and British showed that they were more determined than ever to bring down Queen Olga's son. They "informed Constantine, with colossal arrogance, that they could no longer tolerate the exercise of his authority." Field Marshal Sir Henry Wilson, chief of the British imperial general staff, accurately summed up the British and French dealings when he said, "doubtless we have played fast and loose with Tino."[50] In a similar vein, the British ambassador in Athens, Sir Francis Elliot, related to his superiors in London that, "French members of [the] military mission openly advocate occupation of Greece and dethronement of king."[51] When Jonnart arrived in Greece, the French finally dethroned Queen Olga's son. Not wishing to ignite a civil war, the king succumbed. Like Marie Feodorovna's son Nicholas II, Queen Olga's son did not leave the throne to the rightful heir—in Constantine's case, his eldest son, Crown Prince George. George was considered "pro-German" by the Allies and so the throne passed to Queen Olga's other grandson, young Alexander, who became King Alexander of the Hellenes. On the morning that Constantine announced that he was vacating the throne, twenty-four-year-old Alexander had asked, "How are things today, Papa?" "They are as bad as can be" came the reply, "you are King."[52]

Unlike Nicholas II, Constantine I did not sign an instrument of abdication, but vacated the throne. The French threatened to bring Athens to ruins if Constantine and Sophie did not leave the country. Their departure, however, was far from smooth. Upon learning that Constantine and Sophie were set to leave Greece, Athenians by the thousands surrounded and besieged the palace in order to prevent the couple from departing. Emotions ran high. Distraught and weeping Greeks begged the couple to stay. Miechen's daughter Elena and son-in-law Nicholas were among the family members waiting with Constantine and Sophie to find the right moment to depart. Finally, the royal family tried to leave by car through a side entrance, but their guardsmen threw themselves on the ground in a vain attempt to keep the car from moving. When Nicholas, his brother Andrew, and Elena attempted again to leave, the crowds grew frantic. They cried out at them: "Go back, we shall not let you pass."[53] The royal family was finally able to leave the palace by using a ruse. The plan almost failed, when crowds congregated at one entrance espied the family exiting through another. Another chaotic scene ensued with the hysterical crowds. Prince Christopher recalled that they could "hear the wooden railing cracking in the general stampede" and that Constantine, Sophie, and their children "hurled themselves unceremoniously into the cars. The Crown Prince drove off lying on the floor of one, with his legs waving wildly out of the open door." The family finally reached Tatoi. Constantine, Sophie, and their children departed Greece the next day, into exile. Even at this farewell, crowds surrounded Constantine, begging on their knees for him to stay. Those members of the royal family who stayed behind, such as Christopher, "lived in an atmosphere of suspicion."[54] Soon enough, numerous royalists from all walks of life were arrested, tried, imprisoned, or denounced by Venizelists. In no time, Queen Olga's sons Nicholas and Andrew were also ordered to leave Greece. Christopher decided to join them in exile, leaving a lonely and worried King Alexander to deal with Venizelos, who had returned to Athens and power as prime minister.

Queen Olga relayed her feelings about the forcible departure of King Constantine and Queen Sophie to the Dowager Empress Marie Feodorovna by letter. Marie Feodorovna confided in her diary: "She [Queen Olga] is desperate—great powers forced poor Tino to abdicate the throne, but not in George's favor, but in favor of his second son, Alexander." It was, concluded Marie Feodorovna, a "frustrating story!"[55] From her nephew, the former tsar, Queen Olga received a message of sympathy: "We are living through all of this with you . . . we are praying, let our Lord grant solace and strength to you . . . [It is] so painful for you and your loved ones! There is so much suffering all around. Everywhere one looks, there is sorrow and sorrow. But God will be with us."[56]

One of the few happy events to take place for Queen Olga was the September 1917 wedding of her granddaughter Marie, who had divorced her previous husband in 1914. At Pavlovsk, she married her second husband, Prince Serge Putiatin. Of her wedding day, Marie recalled how "my dear grandmother, the Queen of Greece, met me that day with particular tenderness." And with "tears in her eyes," Queen Olga blessed Marie on her special day.[57]

By the time of Marie's wedding, the Provisional Government, under Kerensky's leadership, was in deep trouble. The government's decision to continue fighting in the Great War contributed to its unpopularity. More instability rocked Petrograd when General Lavr Kornilov attempted a coup that failed. But instead of coming out of the struggle stronger, the Provisional Government was weakened, paving the way for the Bolsheviks to position themselves as the ultimate masters of Russia. The situation in Russia had already prompted

Miechen's son Kyril and Marie Alexandrovna's daughter Ducky to flee the country in the summer of 1917. They fled to Finland, where Ducky gave birth in August to a son, Vladimir Kirillovich.

In Russia, food became scarce. Like so many other Russians, Queen Olga also suffered from food deprivation. Olga described what life was like: "We are living on what my brother Grand Duke Dmitri Constantinovich is getting when he sells his things . . . It is difficult to get potatoes; bread and everything else are scarce; we all have lost weight."[58] Queen Olga and Dmitri's own disgraced brother, Nicholas Constantinovich, who had been living in Tashkent, died in poverty. Queen Olga's sister-in-law Mavra "stole her own possessions" and sold them in the streets "in order to live."[59]

Mavra and Queen Olga were not the only ones facing difficulties. In June 1917, Miechen wrote to Bertie Stopford "a piteous letter" in which she wrote "most bitterly of her lot."[60] Miechen had not left her house for more than two months. At the end of July, Miechen was allowed some freedom of movement out of the house, but her three months' captivity had taken a toll, leaving the grand duchess complaining about her heart.

Stopford visited the grand duchess in the summer at Kislovodsk for her sixty-third birthday, and while he was there, he gave Miechen money brought secretly in his boots. It was the first time she had seen revolutionary notes, the new tender in Russia. In an act worthy of any thriller, Bertie Stopford had also daringly smuggled some of Miechen's jewels out of the Vladimir Palace. Stopford had sneaked into the Vladimir Palace disguised as a workman. In this cloak-and-dagger raid made with Miechen's approval, Stopford found his way to Miechen's Moorish-style boudoir to a secret safe that held her money and jewels. After placing the valuables in two Gladstone bags, Stopford left quickly.

While Stopford was in Kislovodsk for Miechen's name day on the feast of St. Mary Magdalen, he heard an old priest tell her: "As Mary Magdalen was the first to know of the Resurrection of Christ, so may you, after all your suffering, be the first to know that the order of former days has come back to Russia." "It was," concluded Stopford, "very brave of the old man to say so much. The Grand Duchess was much *émue* [moved]."[61]

By this time, Miechen's son Boris had made his way to Kislovodsk and was living with his brother Andrei. Always a stickler for propriety, Miechen refused to have Andrei's mistress, Mathilde, and her son, Vladimir ("Vova"), stay with her. Miechen was equally strict with Boris. Miechen also ordered that his mistress, Zenaida Rachevskaya, not live under the same roof as her, Andrei, and Boris. The two brothers had no choice but to follow their mother's dictates.

Miechen was terrified when Boris and Andrei were arrested and taken away after "a large detachment of Red forces" surrounded their home.[62] Both men were later freed and returned. But it was a close call. Boris and Andrei, recounted Mathilde Kschessinska, had been rescued by a sympathetic Bolshevik of some consequence who "had only been able to save them at the very last moment, and that they had almost been shot during the night."[63]

Miechen may have endured some difficulties in life, but some of her old indomitable spirit remained. All faith had not been extinguished in Miechen, for months later, some glimmer of hope had flickered in the grand duchess about the future. Vladimir Kokovtsov related what took place: "Nothing certain was known, and everybody made the most incredible conjectures, such as that the Germans were advancing to save Kislovodsk. The Grand Duchess Maria Pavlovna told me in all seriousness that she expected a train guarded by Germans to come and take her to Petrograd, where everything was ready for a restoration of the old order."[64] Unfortunately, no such scenario took place. Revolution had destroyed the old order. By October/November 1917, things looked even bleaker as the Bolsheviks overthrew the Provisional Government, seizing important places in Petrograd. The Provisional Government, holed up in the Winter Palace, capitulated after Russian warships, commandeered by mutinous sailors, bombarded the building. The Soviets seized power with Vladimir Lenin at the helm, ushering in a new, more violent era for the Russians.

Nicholas and Alexandra were no longer in Tsarskoe Selo when Lenin seized power. The family had hoped to join other members of their family in the Crimea, but in August, they had been ordered to leave for Tobolsk, in Siberia. The Duchess of Coburg wrote of the family's fate to her daughter Missy, explaining that they had been "bundled off in the middle of the night to some unknown destination! May God have mercy on them!" The duchess added a message to Missy, "I pray for you and love you!"[65] The dowager empress was in anguish about the imperial family's fate. When she heard the news of Nicholas and his family's departure for Siberia, Marie Feodorovna wrote to Queen Olga, saying that the news "was a shock for me—I was in such despair that I felt absolutely sick."[66]

More anxieties were in store for the imperial family. In recording the Bolshevik coup, Queen Olga wrote: "Such terrible horrors are happening in Petrograd ... There was an intense battle behind Tsarskoe Selo. Brothers fought against brothers ... Lord have mercy. This is what we have been reduced to. Here, in Pavlovsk, we could hear the strongest fire; my windows trembled ... Pavlovsk is completely under the Bolshevik control."[67]

At one point, a group of sailors barged into Pavlovsk, intent on wrecking havoc. Queen Olga bravely faced them, informing them of her high regard for Russia's sailors. Olga added that she might know some of them because they may have visited the Piraeus. This had the effect of disarming them and so "subdued by her gracious words, the sailors left peacefully without any acts of violence."[68] By November 1917, Olga could no longer stay at Pavlovsk, because it was to be turned into a "house of the people." Alexander Polovtsov, who had been named commissar curator of Pavlovsk, requested a meeting with Queen Olga. "I had to confess to Her Majesty," noted Polovtsov, "that I had only assumed the painful role of commissar in the hope of saving the palace and that my work would be easier if, in the eyes of the people, there were no more links with the Imperial family." The queen, according to Polovtsov, "deigned to agree," leaving Pavlovsk for the last time in November 1917.[69]

Queen Olga went to Petrograd. From there she wrote of her profound shock at the terrible anarchic conditions that prevailed: "Here, it is dangerous to walk down the streets because the break-ins into the wine cellars have been going on for several days. [They] started with the Winter Palace; there are many drunken people, and [there is] chaotic shooting on the streets, so that the bullets are flying around those who have the misfortune to find themselves amidst this drunken debauchery. This disgrace never stops." It was, concluded Olga, "the triumph of madness."[70]

Not long after the Bolsheviks seized power, the dowager empress wrote from Ai-Todor to her son Nicholas, who was in captivity with his family in Tobolsk.

My Dear Nicky

You know that my thoughts and prayers never leave you—I think of you day and night and sometimes feel so sick at heart that I believe I cannot bear it any longer. But God is merciful—He will give us strength for this terrible ordeal . . . A year has gone by already since you and darling Alexei came to see me at Kieff. Who could have thought then of all that was in store for us, and what we should have to go through. It is unbelievable. I live only in my memories of the happy past and try as much as possible to forget the present nightmare . . .

It is a blessing I am with Xenia, Olga and the grandchildren . . . My new grandson Tikhon is a source of joy to us all. He grows bigger and fatter every day and is such a darling, so charming and quiet. It is a pleasure to see how happy Olga is, and how delighted she is with her baby which she had hoped for such a long time.

. . . *She and Xenia come to see me every morning, and we have our cocoa together, as we are always hungry. It is so difficult to get provisions, white bread and butter are the things I miss most, but sometimes I get some sent by kind people . . .*

I am very glad to get those dear letters from Alix and my granddaughters who all write so nicely. I thank and kiss them all . . . I long for news . . .

On December 6th [day of the Tsar's patron saint] all my thoughts will be with you, my dear darling Nicky, and I send you my warmest wishes. God bless you, send you strength and peace of mind . . .

I kiss you tenderly. May Christ be with you.—Your fondly loving old

Mama[71]

28

ENDURE, ENDURE, AND ENDURE

*I*n December 1917, Nicholas wrote to his mother from Tobolsk:

> *My dear sweet Mama,*
> *I have just received your sweet, priceless letter. I can't find the words to express to You all my joy and gratitude for it . . .*
>
> *How I would like to see You, my dear Mama, live near You, and share the suffering with You! We also haven't lost the hope, for one moment, that when all's said and done, the Merciful Lord will arrange everything for the better, for the best! It can't be that all the woes, all the horrors and violence that have occurred in Russia have been for nothing . . .*
>
> *Christ be with You! Yours, limitless loving You.*
>
> *Nicky*[1]

And in another letter to his mother, Nicholas wrote: "In the next few days it will be a year since You came to me in Mogilev, dear Mama! On my knees I thank You for Your goodness and affection then. You gave me comfort and a lift in spirits in those first days—I will *never* forget that!"[2]

By the time the former tsar wrote these letters, life in Ai-Todor, where the royals were under house arrest, had become arduous. Xenia wrote to her brother Nicholas telling him that "soon we'll be quite destitute. We've begun to wonder how we'll go on living, and how we'll earn our bread . . . Everything's so sordid, cruel and painful."[3]

In February 1918, the Sebastopol Soviet moved the family from Ai-Todor to nearby Dülber—Grand Duke Peter Nikolaevich's oriental-style, fortresslike palace. Peter's wife, Militza, and sister-in-law Stana tried to make the dowager empress's stay at Dülber as easy as possible. But because they were captive, it was still uncomfortable and often humiliating. They were forbidden to leave the premises, and food became increasingly scarce and unpalatable. Mildewed potatoes were the staple. During roll call one day, a group of Bolsheviks called out "Citizenness Maria Feodorovona Romanovna," to which the dowager empress was expected to declare, "Here!" At one point, Marie Feodorovna held her small dog and proclaimed defiantly, "You have forgotten someone, put his name down too."[4] Marie Feodorovna wrote to Queen Alexandra about her family's predicament. The queen then conveyed to her son King George V what she read. "Aunt Minny's life is too awful; they [have] nearly starved & haven't got a penny left . . . I quite tremble to think of her future."[5]

In a letter to Nicholas, Xenia told him that their mother "doesn't write more often because the idea that the letters are read [before delivery] is so unpleasant for her." As for their life at Dülber, Xenia added, "here, we are more under lock and key than at Ai Todor . . . to understand anything of what is taking place is almost impossible." Xenia concluded: "You can see how the noose is being tightened but you don't know how to get out of it. Our poor Russia!"[6]

Xenia was right. Poor Russia, indeed. Starvation was rampant. Irina Skariä-tina described the pitiable starvation she saw in the once glorious imperial capital in January 1918:

> Oh hunger is a terrible thing! As I go down the streets and see that ghastly kaleidoscope of unnaturally thin or unnaturally bloated faces, I feel I'm living in a nightmare, impossible to describe. Many of the passers-by are so weak, that they creep alongside of the houses with hands outstretched towards the walls, so as to steady themselves as they go. Every now and then they fall down and remain lying or sitting on the sidewalk until they gain sufficient strength to get up again and continue their painful progress. No one helps them anymore, for such scenes occur so frequently as to be quite in the natural order of things. But no matter how hardened one has become, one cannot get accustomed to the pitiful crying of very old people and children. Everywhere one hears those starving wails. It is dreadful beyond description. Sometimes I wish I were blind and deaf so as not to see those faces or hear those unspeakable sounds of misery.[7]

"Watching and comprehending how our country is being thoughtlessly destroyed is unbearable," wrote Xenia to her brother, the former tsar. "What have they done with our unfortunate people? Will they ever come to their senses?" Xenia also added, "I don't know how we'll survive, everything's so incredibly expensive, and there's no money. We went several days without light, as there was no kerosene. But it's not important, as we'll get by, but it's such a pity for Mama. Why should she suffer and endure all these deprivations and insults at her age?" The Danish ambassador to Russia confirmed Xenia's grievances in March 1918, noting that "the Dowager Empress, her two daughters and son-in-law, are living under terrible conditions, without money, and experiencing terrible deprivations." When Carl Krebbs, a Danish Red Cross representative, petitioned Leon Trotsky, the commissar for foreign affairs, for permission for the dowager empress to leave Russia, Trotsky replied: "To us, Marie Feodorovna is an old reactionary woman, and her fate is of no interest to us."[8]

The fate of Marie Feodorovna and her family was in the minds of others, such as the Danish and British royals as well as the British government. The Provisional Government also grappled with the family's fate before ceding to the Bolsheviks. Several attempts to get the tsar and his family to England were aborted. George V had received protests "both anonymous and from friends, against the proposed arrival in London of the Tsar and his family."[9] Furthermore, there was concern that allowing the ex-tsar into England would be highly unpopular with the British and would ignite fierce opposition from the left. Prior to this time, there were rumors about King George V's true allegiance due to his German antecedents. To counteract these rumors, the king in June 1917 took the drastic step of proclaiming that his dynasty would henceforth be known by the more British-sounding name of Windsor. Thus, it was not surprising to find that George V and his advisers were susceptible to warnings about the negative implications that might arise should the tsar and his family be granted sanctuary in England. In the end, Nicholas and his family were denied asylum and so remained in Russia.

For eight months, while Nicholas, Alexandra, and their children lived in the governor's house in the town of Tobolsk, they kept busy with lessons for the children. Winter was especially difficult as the temperatures plunged. With her son and his family captive in Tobolsk, the dowager empress thought that a rescue attempt could be made. She accordingly "sent an officer to Bishop Hermogen of Tobolsk, proudly demanding his aid." "My Lord," wrote Marie Feodorovna, "you bear the name of St. Hermogen who fought for Russia. It is an omen. The hour has come for you to serve the motherland."[10] In the end, no one succeeded in rescuing the family.

Throughout the imperial family's ordeal, Alexandra's noble character came to the fore. During the family's Siberian exile, the former tsarina was able to send the occasional letter to friends, such as Princess Galitzine. According to the princess's granddaughter, these letters were "always full of hope and faith," and devoid of bitterness. In fact, Alexandra "never complained, seemed always contented and wished well to everyone."[11] It was also evident that Alexandra's faith sustained her and the family through their trials. To Baroness Buxhoeveden, she wrote: "My heart is troubled, but my soul remains tranquil, as I feel God always near . . . Life here is nothing—Eternity is everything, and what we are doing, is preparing our souls for the Kingdom of Heaven . . . and if they do take everything from us, they cannot take our souls . . . these days of suffering will end. We shall forget all anguish and thank God . . . All is in God's will . . . All sorrows are sent us to free us from our sins or as a test of our faith, an example to others.[12] Marie Feodorovna would have been proud of Alexandra's deportment during captivity had she learned its full extent.

In March 1918, Russia and the Central Powers signed the Treaty of Brest-Litovsk. In so doing, Lenin betrayed the Allies by making peace with Germany. The terms of the treaty were harsh, requiring Russia to deliver huge chunks of territory to the enemy. Nicholas was aghast when he learned what took place. "Had I known it would come to this," said the distressed former tsar to his physician, Dr. Eugene Botkin, "I would never have abdicated."[13] In the spring of 1918, Nicholas, Alexandra, and their family were sent to Ekaterinburg in the Urals. There, they were housed at the home of a local merchant, N. N. Ipatiev. A high wooden fence was hurriedly built around the Ipatiev house, named the "House of Special Purpose." For the next seventy-eight days the family, along with a few loyal retainers, were held captive in what would be their final prison. On the night of July 16/17, 1918, the family was awakened. Jacob Yurovsky of the Bolshevik secret police, the family's head jailer, ordered them to make their way to a cellar to await cars that were supposedly going to take them away from the advancing anti-Bolshevik White Army. Meekly, the family, along with their retainers, Dr. Botkin, and a valet and maid, waited in the cellar. Yurovsky later said that "there were no tears, no sobs, no questions" from the doomed prisoners. Yurovsky ordered the family to assemble as if to have their photograph taken. Without warning, five Russians and six Latvians joined Yurovsky, who then announced: "In view of the fact that your relatives are continuing their attack on Soviet Russia, the Ural Executive Committee has decided to execute you." Turning to his family, Nicholas then asked, "What? What?"[14] At which point Yurovsky repeated his announcement and pulled out a revolver, shooting the ex-tsar dead. The rest of the executioners then fired a hail of bullets at the prisoners. Alexandra and Olga, who had tried to make the sign of the cross, were killed immediately. Marie Feodorovna's other granddaughters suffered more because the girls' corsets had jewels sewn into them that sent the bullets ricocheting. To finish them off, the executioners used bayonets to stab them. The bodies were later taken to a nearby forest and buried.

According to Mathilde Kschessinska, rumors about the execution of the imperial family "spread through Kislovodsk." Children were running in the streets selling printed sheets and crying, "Murder of the Imperial Family!" "That was such terrible news," noted Kschessinska, "that we could not believe it. We all cherished the hope that it was merely a false rumour spread by the Bolsheviks, and that the Tsar and his family were really well. We kept this hope for a long time in our hearts."[15]

Just a day after the massacre, Marie Feodorovna met a man, a messenger sent by her son Nicholas. The messenger described the family's difficult captivity at Ekaterinburg, prompting the dowager empress to write in her diary: "And nobody can help or liberate them—only God! My Lord, save my poor, unlucky Nicky, help him in his hard ordeals!"[16] Of course, she did not yet know her son's fate.

Back at Ai-Todor, some German officers arrived and left an extraordinary message. They said that an announcement would soon appear in Russian newspapers declaring that the former tsar and his family were executed at Ekaterinburg, but the officers then added the encouraging news that the family was actually safe. When on the next day, Ai-Todor's residents saw the news in the papers about the murders, they found it hard to believe. They clung to what the German officers had told them. The dowager empress was certain that her son and his family were alive. Marie Feodorovna refused to accept that such a horrendous fate had befallen her son, daughter-in-law, grandchildren, and their servants. She requested that no one pray for their souls—to have done so would have meant acknowledgment that they had been killed. Timofei Yaschik, who saw much of the dowager empress in his capacity as her personal bodyguard, was convinced that Marie Feodorovna "constantly and fervently believed that she would see her son once again."[17]

Other surviving Romanovs were not as optimistic as Marie Feodorovna and her fellow captives at Ai-Todor. Within days of the executions, the Comte de Robien met with some of the grand dukes who were still alive. These included Sandro's brothers, Nicholas and George Mikhailovich (Queen Olga's son-in-law), and Queen Olga's brother, Dmitri Constantinovich. De Robien told them that the French ambassador would do what he could for them. However, the men knew they were doomed to die. Nicholas Mikhailovich, de Robien noted, had "few illusions" while George Mikhailovich asked de Robien to break the tragic news of their impending executions to Queen Olga's daughter Marie, who was still in England. De Robien found Olga's brother Grand Duke Dmitri "ill-shaven" and "dressed in a suit made of soldiers' cloth and wearing a shabby cap." He looked "impecunious but still had the grand air and the majestic bearing of this generation of Romanovs." To his credit, Grand Duke Dmitri did not forget his young widowed niece, Princess Tatiana Bagration, who was with them, and commended her to de Robien's care. The French diplomat felt sympathy for the princess, "poorly clad in an ugly worn-out dress and a wretched old hat." "We all had heavy hearts," wrote de Robien, not certain what the grand dukes' fates would be, but de Robien added, "the death of the Tsar" had given rise "to the gravest anxiety."[18]

Queen Olga was frantic and deeply worried about her relations, telling a friend: "My brother, the only one left, my son-in-law—my daughter Minny's [Marie's] husband—and two cousins have been imprisoned . . . Minny and I tremble for their lives; only the Lord can save them!!"[19]

In June 1918, Marie Feodorovna's son Grand Duke Michael met the same sinister fate as his brother Nicholas. The Bolsheviks had arrested Michael. Natasha fought for his release, even barging into Lenin's office to plead for her husband. But to no avail. The Bolsheviks sent Michael and his secretary, Nicholas Johnson, to Perm in Siberia. One evening, their jailers took them to the woods. While there, Michael accepted a cigarette offered by one of his jailers. As he smoked, Johnson was shot in the head. When Michael rushed to help his friend, his captors killed Michael by shooting him. However, there were rumors that he had escaped, leaving Michael's loved ones uncertain as to whether he was dead or alive.

Another town in Siberia, Alapayevsk, was the place of internment for other Romanovs. There, Sandro's brother, Sergei Mikhailovich; Prince Vladimir Paley (Grand Duke Paul's son from his second wife, and a gifted poet); the saintly Ella; and the Princes Ioann, Igor, and Constantine (Queen Olga's nephews—K.R. and Mavra's sons) were held prisoner. One night in July 1918, the group was taken to a nearby unused mine and blindfolded. Their captors ordered the Romanovs to make their way over a log that was positioned over the mine, which dropped sixty feet. As Sergei fought his guards, they killed him with a hail of bullets. The rest of the captives were brutally thrown down the mine. Their guards then threw grenades at them. Horribly, the captives did not die instantly. Instead, when their bodies were found, they were discovered to have suffered terribly. Among those who endured a gruesome fate was Prince Constantine. In a vain effort to fight off starvation, he had consumed some of the soil around him. Thus, in the space of one week, the Bolsheviks brutally murdered fourteen members of the Romanov dynasty.

Clearly, time was running out for the remaining Romanovs. Escape from Russia was their only chance at survival. The Romanovs in the Crimea had also come close to being massacred. Had it not been for the German troops who hurried to the region after the Treaty of Brest-Litovsk was signed, the Romanovs living there would likely have been killed by soldiers loyal to the Yalta Soviet, who having made it to the gates of Dülber came close to committing the deed. Gratitude toward the Germans did not come easily. Despite the terrors the imperial family suffered at the hands of their countrymen, the patriotic Romanovs felt a combination of shame, anger, and revulsion at having been rescued by the foreign enemy. The dowager empress "declared that she would not receive the German commander since she considered that Germany and Russia were still at war."[20]

In September 1918, after King George V confirmed that the Ekaterinburg massacres had taken place, his mother, Queen Alexandra, was filled with trepidation for her sister and relations: "I can hear *nothing* and they are quite cut off from the world and alone in their misery and despair. God help them all."[21] In the meantime, despite George V receiving confirmation of the Ekaterinburg killings, conflicting reports still circulated about the fate of Nicholas and Alexandra and their family. Attempts to help them were made, including offers from King Alfonso XIII of Spain and Pope Benedict XV. The pope also offered the Dowager Empress Marie Feodorovna "a life annuity to enable her to live in accordance with the dignity of her position."[22] However, after months of talks involving numerous countries, "during which the survival and whereabouts of the imperial family had been both assumed and discussed," everything "culminated in a dead-end."[23]

As for the surviving Romanovs, the danger they faced now reached a critical stage with the Bolsheviks more determined than ever to inflict harm on them and their fellow Russians. The Bolsheviks' ardent espousal of communism made them especially sinister. In reporting to Arthur Balfour, Britain's foreign secretary, about the state of affairs in Russia, R. Bruce Lockhart wrote from Russia in November 1918, that:

1. The Bolsheviks have established a rule of force and oppression unequalled in the history of any autocracy.
2. Themselves the fiercest upholders of the right of free speech, they have suppressed, since coming into power, every newspaper which does not approve their policy . . .
3. The right of holding public meeting has been abolished . . . those who dare to vote against the Bolsheviks are marked down by the Bolshevik secret police as counter-revolutionaries, and are fortunate if their worst fate is to be thrown into prison, of which in Russia to-day it may truly be said, 'many go in but few come out.' . . .
5. The Bolsheviks have abolished even the most primitive forms of justice. Thousands of men and women have been shot without even the mockery of a trial, and thousands more are left to rot in the prisons . . .
8. The Bolsheviks who destroyed the Russian army, and who have always been the avowed opponents of militarism, have forcibly mobilised officers who do not share their political views . . .
9. The avowed ambition of Lenin is to create civil warfare throughout Europe . . . he is destroying systematically both by executions and by deliberate starvation every form of opposition to Bolshevism.[24]

The extent of the brutality inflicted on the Russian people by the Bolsheviks was summarized by another British subject, who had been in Moscow: "The number of people who have been coldly done to death in Moscow is enormous. Many thousands have been shot, but lately those condemned to death were hung instead, and that in the most brutal manner. They were taken out in batches in the early hours of the morning to a place on the outskirts of the town, stripped to their shirts, and then hung one by one by being drawn up at the end of a rope until their feet were a few inches from the ground then left to die . . . [in another incident] 150 Russian officers who were taken prisoners at Pskoff by the Red Guards were . . . sawed in pieces."[25]

Even the cessation of the Great War, with the signing of an armistice between Germany and the Allied nations in November 1918, offered no respite for Russia, now convulsed in an orgy of violence. Thousands of lives continued to be destroyed in a bloody whirlpool of death and destruction.

On learning that her son Constantine, now in exile in Switzerland, had fallen dangerously ill, Queen Olga's plight gained new focus, as she tried desperately to be by his side. Prior to leaving, Olga contrived to get a splendid set of emeralds smuggled out of the country. A Greek student had taken them, disguised in a box, from the queen's secretary. He then deposited the emeralds with the Danish Legation and from there the jewels were sent to Denmark.

Thanks to the help of a Danish minister, the queen was finally able to leave Russia. Queen Olga left Russia by train. Her carriage was attached to a "military train filled with German prisoners of war." But her journey was not without incident. The Bolsheviks tried to "uncouple her carriage and leave it on the line to be overtaken by an express [train] which was due ten minutes later. Fortunately the vigilance of the officers had foiled the attempt!"[26] In this way, the queen was finally able to escape from Bolshevik Russia in mid-1918.

Queen Olga's son-in-law Grand Duke George Mikhailovich had written to his wife Marie not long after the tsar's abdication, predicting that Russia "in a very few years" would turn into "a country of savages."[27] His prediction came chillingly true. George was arrested in the summer of 1918, along with his brother Grand Duke Nicholas and Grand Duke Dmitri Constantinovich. In a letter to her nephew King George V dated November 19/December 2, 1918, Queen Olga pleaded for help:

> *My beloved Sunbeam!*
> *I write to you in the anguish of my heart! You know, that my brother—the last one I have . . . is in prison with Minny's [Queen Olga's daughter, Marie] husband George, his brother, Nicholas, and Paul, since this summer, they are kept as* hostages *. . . y[ou]r ships and troops are already at Odessa and as I hope, poor, darling Aunt Minny [Marie Feodorovna] under their protection . . . Do what you can, my darling Sunbeam, and God bless you and thank God peace has come at last; but* what *misery there is still all over the world.*
>
> Y[ou]r loving and devoted old Aunt Olga[28]

After various attempts to aid the grand dukes, no help came. Even a plea on behalf of the grand dukes from the writer Maxim Gorky to Vladimir Lenin fell on deaf ears. In January 1919, George Mikhailovich, his brother, the historian Nicholas Mikhailovich, and Dmitri Constantinovich, were taken to the

Fortress of Sts. Peter and Paul where the three grand dukes became the latest victims of the Bolsheviks' senseless cruelty. Upon passing the Sts. Peter and Paul Cathedral, the grand dukes crossed themselves. At the fortress, the three condemned men met their cousin Grand Duke Paul, whose gaunt frame made him difficult to recognize. George, Nicholas, and Dmitri were then lined up to face a ditch where over a dozen bodies already lay. Dmitri and George prayed. Shots were fired, killing the two along with Nicholas. Paul, who was too weak to stand up, was shot to death while still lying down in his stretcher. In that one brutal day, three of the four men the Bolsheviks killed were directly related to Queen Olga: her brother Dmitri, her son-in-law Paul (Marie Alexandrovna's brother and Miechen's brother-in-law), and Olga's other son-in-law, George.

With such terrors touching her life directly, Queen Olga of Greece was inconsolable and came close to abandoning hope, but she did not allow herself to collapse into despair. To have done so would have been out of character for a woman who was a deeply committed Christian. In a letter to a friend, the queen movingly explained what she was feeling: "Things get worse in my Motherland; and endless and nonsensical horror abound . . . Why did they kill my beloved brother? Why did they kill all others, whom I loved dearly . . . I am in deep mourning for my brother's death and the death of others . . . Now I am the last one remaining in our family . . . [I have] no brother, no home . . . but I need to endure, endure, and endure." An explanation of where Queen Olga drew her strength is found in another letter she wrote: "I am old, and my life is broken, but I do not despair because in my soul there is a firm faith in what was promised to us by our Savior."[29]

The situation in Russia became even more dire as civil war raged, pitting the Bolshevik forces, the Red Army, against their opponents, the White Army. Bolshevik forces grew increasingly stronger at the expense of the White Armies. The German troops, who had been in the Crimea, were evacuating the region, opening the way for the Bolsheviks to sweep through. It became imperative that the Romanovs in the Crimea flee Russia. Prince Felix Yussoupov aptly surmised that "when the Red Army approached the Crimea, we realized that as far as we were concerned the end had come."[30]

The dowager empress had moved to Harax, the Crimean home of Queen Olga's daughter Marie, who was still in England. Marie Feodorovna remained highly ambivalent about leaving the country that had meant so much to her. When her daughter Olga, pregnant for the second time, decided to go with her husband, Colonel Kulikovsky, to the Caucasus, Marie Feodorovna was sorely disappointed. She blamed her commoner son-in-law for this decision. Olga, in turn, wondered whether she would ever see her mother again.

Concerns over the plight of the dowager empress and her family haunted her relations abroad. The Duchess of Coburg's daughter, Queen Marie of Romania, while on a visit to England in early 1919, recalled a poignant meeting she had with her aunt, Queen Alexandra. "She clung to me," recalled Missy, "because I was a link with unfortunate Russia. Aunt Alix was suffering intensely because of the long and painful separation from her favourite sister, Empress Marie, still in a dangerously precarious situation in the Crimea, cut off from everything and surrounded by bolshevik danger. As I was harassed by the same sort of anxiety about Ducky, who was still in Finland, we understood each other perfectly." During Queen Marie's visit to the queen's home, Marlborough House, Queen Alexandra showed Missy "heaped up on her writing table, all her beloved sister's letters, and, her arm linked within mine, she led me through her different rooms, showing me all her Russian souvenirs and treasures, full of grief over all the terrible happenings which had swept away the old order of things. She spoke much of my mother and both our eyes were full of tears."[31]

Missy, who was immersed in her own set of challenging problems in Romania, nevertheless took the time to try to help her Romanov relations. Queen Marie wrote to her cousin Xenia urging her to leave Russia: "we are anxious for you all because there may be a very dangerous moment when the Germans leave and before the allies arrive."[32] Missy even sent her trusted confidant, the Canadian adventurer Colonel Joe Boyle, to try to rescue the Romanovs. Boyle made it to the Crimea and spoke to the dowager empress. Marie Feodorovna, though "deeply touched" by Boyle's mission, refused to leave. "I am an old woman now," said the dowager empress to Boyle, "my life is nearly over. Here I am able to help in organizing some resistance to the Bolsheviki. You cannot take with you all those who have sacrificed everything for me and my family. I cannot abandon them."[33]

Next to come to the family's rescue was the H.M.S. *Marlborough*, a battleship of Britain's Royal Navy, dispatched to the Black Sea. The ship arrived at Yalta on April 7, 1919, for the purpose of evacuating the dowager empress. Several British officers of high rank proceeded to plead with the dowager empress to leave for her own good, but Marie Feodorovna was adamant that she could not. While she was still in Russia there was some distant hope that she could act as a rallying symbol for anti-Bolshevik forces. Moreover, the dowager empress clung on because her departure would leave no one to help her sons,

Nicholas and Michael, for whom she still held out hope. She finally capitulated when Marie Feodorovna met the *Marlborough*'s captain, C. D. Johnson, who carried a letter from Queen Alexandra in which she beseeched her sister to leave. This, coupled with stories the captain related about atrocities taking place in nearby Sevastopol, finally convinced Marie Feodorovna that for the sake of those who were with her, she must leave. Her one stipulation was that all those who wanted to accompany her—relations and retainers—be allowed to flee with her. Captain Johnson agreed, even though it would mean the crew would have to take in more people on board than originally planned. According to Vice Admiral Sir Francis Pridham, who had been the H.M.S. *Marlborough*'s first lieutenant, Marie Feodorovna insisted that "she would not herself leave the country until arrangements were completed for the evacuation of all loyal people in the neighbourhood of Yalta who wished to leave."[34] And so several Allied warships were ordered to Yalta to evacuate countless refugees who were desperate to flee.

Pridham recalled the moment the dowager empress embarked on the battleship unexpectedly and unceremoniously, accompanied by her daughter Xenia. Pridham saw before him "an elderly little lady dressed in black" who resembled Queen Alexandra.[35] He knew instantly that she was none other than the Dowager Empress Marie Feodorovna. In no time, other Romanovs, retainers and their luggage made their way on board the *Marlborough*. It proved challenging trying to berth everyone. Pridham was impressed to discover the "kindly thoughtfulness shown by members of the Imperial family for those belonging to their households. Yet these were the people who had for years been accused of being pitiless tyrants, holding their people in bonds of cruel slavery."[36]

Altogether twenty members of the Romanov dynasty and their retainers accompanied the dowager empress on board the *Marlborough*. Included in the group were the Grand Dukes Nicholas Nikolaevich and Peter Nikolaevich and their wives, Militza and Stana. The closest relative who came with Marie Feodorovna was her daughter Xenia (Sandro and their eldest son had already left for France). Also on board were Xenia's daughter, Irina; her husband, Prince Felix Yussoupov; and his parents. Felix managed to take a long parcel with him on board. Inside it were two priceless Rembrandt paintings that had been rescued from the Yussoupov Palace where Rasputin had been murdered.

One of the most poignant moments took place when a group of about four hundred members of the Imperial Guard, sailing for Sevastopol on a British ship, rendered their empress aboard the *Marlborough* a final homage across the water. To Marie Feodorovna, they sang the Russian imperial anthem, their deep unaccompanied voices resounding over the water. She watched them in rapt attention. Silence ensued after the ship passed. "No one approached the Empress while she remained standing, gazing sadly for those who, leaving her to pass into exile, were bound for what seemed likely to be a forlorn mission," recalled Pridham.[37] Of the scene, Felix Yussoupov wrote that "tears streamed down her [Marie Feodorovna's] cheeks as these young men, going to certain death, saluted her."[38] The moving event "proved to be the last occasion on which the Russian Imperial Anthem was rendered to a member of the Imperial family within Russian territory."[39]

After Yalta had been evacuated as requested by the dowager empress, the *Marlborough* departed on April 11, 1919. As the ship cast off, the ever-faithful Timofei Yaschik watched the dowager empress on deck. It was an emotional moment for all the Russians on board, as "little by little, the slopes of the Crimean hills disappeared from the horizon." For Yaschik, the most moving sight of all was the seventy-one-year-old Marie Feodorovna. "I saw no tears in her eyes," recounted the dowager empress's Cossack. "But she stood there long and quiet and looked at the land, which had been her home for more than 50 years, and which kept the secret of what happened to her beloved son, his wife and their five children. I have never read anyone's thoughts, but I definitely felt that on that day the Empress Dagmar [*sic*] was completely convinced that she would see the Tsar once again."[40]

Vice Admiral Sir Francis Pridham was impressed by the Romanovs' demeanor, of the "extraordinary fortitude shown by these people on their day of severance from their country. For fifteen months many of them had been in constant danger of assassination, and even now none of them could have had a clear picture of their future. Though it seemed likely that the Empress Marie and those closest to her would go to England for a time, the destination of the remainder was not then known. Nevertheless, their chief concern was to cause us as little inconvenience as possible. They expressed repeatedly their gratitude for the little we were able to do in providing for their comfort."[41]

A fortnight after sailing away from Russia, the *Marlborough* approached Malta, the island that had many years before been the happy home of the dowager empress's sister-in-law Marie Alexandrovna. Before disembarking, the Russians on board the ship celebrated Easter. The dowager empress had insisted that they should all be together for this most precious of holy days for the Orthodox faithful. Marie Feodorovna had arranged that wine and biscuits, as well as the colored Easter eggs Russians were so accustomed to receiving, were handed out to her fellow travelers who, like her, were now refugees. Timofei Yaschik vividly remembered that "it was an Easter night which we, those on the ship, will never forget as long as live."[42] Before leaving the *Marlborough*, Marie Feodorovna thanked everyone on board who had helped her and others. The dowager empress also gave Francis Pridham a fabulous pair of ruby and diamond cuff links in gratitude.

Like her sister-in-law Marie Feodorovna, the Grand Duchess Vladimir had also steadfastly refused to leave Russia. The Communists' murderous rampage meant that Miechen, still at Kislovodsk, had to flee for her life. Guerilla warfare, pitting the Red Army against the Cossacks, wrecked havoc in the Caucasus, as terror and arbitrary arrests became widespread. At one point the Cossacks' Colonel Andrei Shkuro took Miechen to a village in the mountains for safety. Though the grand duchess was as adamant as her lifelong rival Marie Feodorovna about remaining in Russia, Miechen finally began to give in ever so gradually to the inevitable and prepared to take flight. She and her entourage made their way through southern Russia to the Black Sea coastal city of Anapa in the Caucasus, near the Crimea in October 1918. Andrei and Boris and their mistresses, Mathilde and Zenaida, as well as Miechen's grandson Vova were with her.

The final leg of the journey to Anapa took place on board a small trawler called the *Typhoon*. Many of their fellow refugees could not believe that the Grand Duchess Vladimir would agree to travel in such a rickety, old boat. Mathilde Kschessinska wondered how everybody was "to be accommodated in such a nutshell!" Indefatigable as ever, Miechen declared loudly to all, "what a wonderfully picturesque setting!" After that, the grand duchess, recalled Mathilde, "graciously acknowledging the Captain's welcome," proceeded to embark "without turning a hair. Sitting imperturbably in a deck-chair on the bridge, she began to look at the crestfallen refugees, who now hastened to follow her example."[43] Once the refugees arrived at Anapa, Miechen stayed at first at the Metropole Hotel. It was, in Mathilde's words, a "modest and fairly primitive" establishment where the lavatories "had been turned into skating rinks by the frost and were in a pitiful state."[44]

Miechen eventually lived in a house lent to her and her sons. The grand duchess still refused to have Zenaida and Mathilde live under the same roof with Boris and Andrei. Miechen's stay at Anapa was far from comfortable, with few basic comforts at hand. A few months after settling in Anapa, Miechen was visited by General Frederick Poole, who invited the grand duchess, on behalf of the British government, to seek refuge abroad, but she politely refused. Though his offer was rejected, Poole was nevertheless impressed by Miechen's resolve.

In March 1919, Boris and Zenaida left Russia. Boris had urged his mother to join them, and though she was, in Mathilde's words, "greatly distressed by her son's decision," Miechen again refused to leave.[45]

That same month, a British cruiser anchored off Anapa. A British officer, Commander Goldschmidt, disembarked and, accompanied by Admiral Seymour who commanded the British Black Sea Squadron, paid a visit to Miechen. Together, the officers offered her refuge on the cruiser, but she again declined politely, advising them that it was her duty to stay and that she would leave only if it was absolutely necessary. The grand duchess was invited to come on board the British cruiser for a visit but she could not go because her legs were too weak. It was evident that years of deprivation and worry had taken a toll on Miechen's health. In a letter to a friend, Miechen had confided that, "I am resigned to hardship . . . At my age it's hard to sleep in a bad bed, not to have enough linen, clothes, no baths, no dresses or furs for the winter and to eat badly."[46] Her health, already weakened by hunger and a diet of tainted meat, was worsening. Miechen's need to escape had new urgency.

In this corner of the Caucasus, amidst a life of deprivation, Miechen hoped against all odds that the White Armies would defeat the Red Army. But it was not to be. In January 1920, the civil war between the Whites and Reds had been settled. The Communists were victorious. Where others failed to convince Miechen to leave Russia, General Peter Wrangel, a prominent leader of the White Army in southern Russia, proved persuasive. Miechen bowed to fate and agreed to flee. She, Andrei, Mathilde, and Vova traveled to the nearby port city of Novorossiysk, also on the Black Sea. For her journey to Novorossiysk, Miechen traveled by train, even managing to sit in first class.

At Novorossiysk, Miechen met Marie Feodorovna's daughter Olga who was grateful to see her aunt. "I was amazed to learn that she had reached the town in her own train," recalled Olga years later, "manned by her own staff, and still had her ladies with her. For all the dangers and privations, she still appeared every inch a Grand Duchess. There had never been much love between Aunt Michen and my own family, but I felt rather proud of her. Disregarding peril and hardship, she stubbornly kept to all the trimmings of by-gone splendor and glory. And somehow she carried it off. When even generals found themselves lucky to find a horse cart and an old nag to bring them into safety, Aunt Michen made a long journey in her own train. It was battered all right—but it was hers. For the first time in my life I found it was pleasure to kiss her."[47]

For several weeks Miechen waited in Novorossiysk for a chance to leave. But it was not an easy wait. Far from living in splendor, let alone comfort, Miechen's home was a train carriage. The grand duchess, "racked with illness, frozen with cold, spent seven weeks on that train, living mainly on black bread and soup, cooped up in a tiny compartment with the most primitive sanitary arrangements. The whole place stank."[48]

Finally, in February 1920, Miechen, Andrei, Mathilde, and Vova boarded an Italian liner, the *Semiramisa,* and left Russia for good. Mathilde recounted their experience on board: "After so many hardships, a first-class cabin seemed a place of incredible luxury! But we really thought we were seeing a mirage at dinner: clean table-napkins, glasses, knives and forks! We uttered 'ohs' and 'ahs' of enchantment. We were rather embarrassed at having to sit in our shabby clothes; but when the impeccably dressed waiters began to serve us we felt as if we were in another world! Our state of mind can easily be imagined when it is realised that there was also the thought that we were at last safe, with nothing more to fear from the Bolsheviks!"[49] Because no one had money, including Miechen, she left an expensive brooch that covered the cost of all their fares. Once the ship went through the Bosporus days later, the passengers were ordered to undergo delousing, a process Miechen stubbornly refused to endure.

Miechen's next stop was Greece. She managed to spend a few hours visiting the Nicholas Palace, her daughter Elena's home. The place was eerily empty and stood as a reminder that Miechen's daughter and son-in-law had also been compelled to flee their country for a life of exile. Miechen managed to pick "five violets out of the garden—one of each of them—which she sent to [her granddaughter] Princess Marina and her family, together with a prayer that they would all see their homes again soon."[50] Miechen then boarded the *Semiramisa* again. After making its way through Greece, the *Semiramisa* arrived at Venice. Of the three Romanov women—Marie Pavlovna, Olga Constantinovna, and Marie Feodorovna—Miechen was the last to escape from Russia.

A regal looking Marie Alexandrovna,
Duchess of Edinburgh and of
Saxe-Coburg-Gotha.
(*Royal Russia Collection*)

The Duke and Duchess of Edinburgh with their family, and Prince Maximilian of Baden and Ernst
Louis, the Hereditary Grand Duke of Hesse. On the extreme right is Britain's future King George V,
who wished to marry Missy of Edinburgh, seated in front of him. (*The Royal Collection* © 2011 *H.M.
Queen Elizabeth II*)

TOP LEFT: Grand Duchess Olga Constantinovna with her mother, Grand Duchess Alexandra Iosifovna. Olga was only sixteen years old when she became queen of Greece upon her marriage to King George I.

TOP RIGHT: Queen Olga and King George I of Greece.

BOTTOM: The Edinburgh princesses. *From left to right*: Victoria Melita ("Ducky"), Marie ("Missy"), Alexandra ("Sandra"), and Beatrice ("Bea"). Ducky first married Ernst Louis, the Grand Duke of Hesse and by Rhine, and then Grand Duke Kyril of Russia. Sandra married Prince Ernst of Hohenlohe-Langenburg. Bea married the Infante Alfonso of Spain. Missy later became Queen Marie of Romania, consort of King Ferdinand I.

LEFT: King George I and Queen Olga of Greece with six of their eight children: Crown Prince Constantine, Prince George, Princess Alexandra, Prince Nicholas, Princess Marie, and Prince Andrew.

RIGHT: An impressive-looking Queen Olga of Greece in Russian court dress. Committed to helping her Greek subjects through her numerous charitable endeavors, Olga also remained deeply devoted to her native Russia.

LEFT: Queen Olga of Greece. The queen became briefly regent of Greece in 1920, after the tragic death of her grandson, King Alexander I. Olga died in exile in 1926.

RIGHT: Queen Olga in the last years of her life. She was widowed in 1913 when her husband, King George I, was assassinated. She lived in Russia during the First World War, where she nursed wounded soldiers. Many of her Romanov relatives, including her brother, Grand Duke Dmitri Constantinovich, and her son-in-law, Grand Duke George Mikhailovich, were killed by the Bolsheviks.

LEFT: Grand Duchess Marie Pavlovna ("Miechen"). Also referred to as the Grand Duchess Vladimir, Miechen became the preeminent hostess of St. Petersburg society during the reign of her nephew, Tsar Nicholas II, largely because his wife, Tsarina Alexandra, preferred to retreat from public life. (*Royal Russia Collection*)

RIGHT: The Grand Duchess Marie Pavlovna resplendent in a spectacular array of jewels. (*Royal Russia Collection*)

Grand Duchess Marie Pavlovna, her husband,
Grand Duke Vladimir, and their children:
Grand Dukes Kyril, Boris, Andrei, and
Grand Duchess Elena.

A formidable looking Miechen attired in Russian court dress.
She is wearing the magnificent Vladimir Tiara that was smuggled out of
Russia during the Russian Revolution.

Grand Duchess Marie Pavlovna with her daughter, Grand Duchess Elena (*second from left*), and Miechen's nephew and niece, Tsar Nicholas II and Tsarina Alexandra. Miechen and Alexandra's frosty relationship never improved. (*Royal Russia Collection*)

The Grand Duke Vladimir, Grand Duchess Marie Pavlovna, and their children in the late 1890s. *From left to right, back row*: Grand Duke Andrei, Grand Duchess Elena, Grand Duke Kyril, and Grand Duke Boris. Kyril became the son-in-law of Marie Alexandrovna, Duchess of Saxe-Coburg-Gotha, while Elena became Queen Olga's daughter-in-law when Elena married Prince Nicholas of Greece in 1902. (*Royal Russia Collection*)

Miechen in her later years. She escaped from the
Bolsheviks and died in exile in France in 1920.

The Hessian royal family in the 1890s with members of the Russian imperial
family. *Top row from left to right*: Nicholas; Alexandra; her sister,
Victoria; and her brother, Ernie. *Bottom row left to right*: Irene
and Ella; Ducky; and Ella's husband, Serge.

Queen Olga's son, Prince Nicholas of Greece, and his two eldest
daughters, Princesses Elizabeth (*left*) and Olga (*right*).

LEFT: Miechen's daughter, Grand Duchess Elena, who married Queen Olga's son, Prince Nicholas
of Greece.

RIGHT: Queen Elizabeth II wearing the Vladimir Tiara. Miechen's daughter, Elena, sold the tiara in
1921 to King George V's wife, Queen Mary. The Vladimir Tiara remains one of the most beautiful
pieces of jewelry in the collection of the British royal famil

29

VIA DOLOROSA

From Malta, the Dowager Empress Marie Feodorovna made her way to England, where her official welcome was subdued. The British royal family, mindful of the presence on English soil that a senior Romanov might have on public opinion, kept Marie Feodorovna's welcome private. When Marie Feodorovna arrived at Portsmouth, her sister Queen Alexandra eagerly greeted her, shouting welcome to her sister as her ship docked. They then took a train to London where Edward the Prince of Wales (the future King Edward VIII), awaited their arrival.

Observing that the prince wore a black armband, Marie Feodorovna asked whom he was mourning. When Edward answered that he was mourning for her son Nicholas and his family, the dowager empress became "extremely agitated," according to Timofei Yaschik who was with her. Reaching out, she furiously tore the black armband from the prince's arm. "It was clear," recalled Yaschik, that "the Empress wanted to underline the fact that she did not believe and did not want to believe the news about the murder of the Imperial family."[1] Word reached Buckingham Palace of the startling incident, prompting others in the palace to remove their black armbands lest the dowager empress take offense if she saw them.

Marie Feodorovna lived for some months with Queen Alexandra at the latter's London home, Marlborough House, and her country home, Sandringham, in Norfolk. As the dowager empress settled in, she met a number of visitors, including Grand Duke Dmitri, who had managed to leave Persia. Marie Feodorovna also received her son Michael's wife, Natasha, and grandson, George, both of whom had escaped from Russia. Though the dowager empress was polite, especially to young George, Natasha knew that an insuperable barrier still existed between her and Marie Feodorovna. "She was rather nice to me," disclosed Natasha to a friend, "but I feel she does not like me and will never forgive me that I married her son." The dowager empress, however, admitted of Natasha: "What a beautiful woman, she is so pretty, I had quite forgotten."[2]

The dowager empress met a few Russian officers as well, but none of these audiences ever took on political undertones or implications. Marie Feodorovna understood her place in London as a guest of the royal family and was careful not to overstep this boundary. In a letter to the former British prime minister, Andrew Bonar Law, Sir Arthur Davidson, a royal equerry, assured him that "it has been made quite clear to everyone Russian or English, Civil or Military, that the Empress Marie is staying here in England on a visit to her Sister, and that she [the dowager empress] wishes her visit to be as quiet and as private as it is possible for anything to be." Davidson added: "The last thing that the Empress Marie would wish is that any advantage should be taken of her presence here to advance any political or other claims in connection with Russia, as the Empress has far too high an idea of the hospitality afforded her by this Country to do anything that might offend those whose guest she is."[3]

After their initial happiness and relief at being reunited after several years— years that were marked by much tension and violence—Marie Feodorovna and Alexandra, now in their mid-seventies, began to chafe in each other's company. Queen Alexandra's deafness made communicating with her a challenge. The Dowager Empress Marie Feodorovna was so accustomed to being at the pinnacle of society and the center of attention amongst her family and friends that her staid, quiet existence in England made her feel left out. In addition, the dowager empress did not want to cause embarrassment to the British royal family because of her prolonged presence in England. Marie Feodorovna sensed that her life of exile might be better spent in her native Denmark and so wrote of her departure to her host, Queen Mary: "I am more than sorry that I might have caused involuntary trouble to you, but I hope & trust that my absence will help to calm everyone['s fears]. Everyone has only been kind to me & I have never even heard an unkind insinuation of any kind. With God's help things will blow over and I will return. I promise faithfully not to go near Buckingham Palace as long as my presence there might be misconstrued."[4]

Marie Fedorovna soon moved to her native Denmark. She stayed at Amalienborg Palace in Copenhagen, the Danish royal family's home. Unfortunately, she quickly clashed with her nephew King Christian X. Long accustomed to paying little attention to money and expenses, the dowager empress met her match in the parsimonious Christian X. The king did not hide his disdain for his exiled relative. He even accused his aged aunt of pawning some of the objets d'art found at Amalienborg, much to Marie Feodorovna's mortification. On one occasion Christian X sent his footman to tell the dowager empress to switch off the lights in her apartment because the electricity bill was too high. Marie Feodorovna replied by imperiously calling her servant and telling him, in front of the king's, to turn on the lights in the palace from top to bottom.

Fortunately, to help overcome the dowager empress's inability to economize, King George V assisted by granting her a yearly pension of £10,000. This, along with the appointment of a caretaker to watch over her expenditures, allowed for Marie Feodorovna's financial situation to stabilize. She continued to donate money generously to the countless Russian émigrés who besieged her for aid. A permanent move to Hvidovre helped ease the financial strain as well as the difficult relations with King Christian X.

In 1920, the dowager empress summoned her daughter, Olga, to come and live with her at Hvidovre. She dispatched Timofei Yaschik to Russia and with his help Olga escaped the country with her husband, Colonel Kulikovsky, and their sons, Tikhon, and Guri (who was born in 1919). With Xenia now separated from Sandro and living in England, Olga was left to be at Marie Feodorovna's beck and call. It was not an easy arrangement, as Marie Feodorovna often ignored her commoner son-in-law. Olga's presence was demanded to help entertain guests, but Kulikovsky was never invited. He accepted this graciously, to Olga's relief and gratitude, never complaining about his mother-in-law's unjust actions. Despite Marie Feodorovna's coolness toward him, Colonel Kulikovsky looked out for the dowager empress's interests.

He cautioned his wife, Olga, not to visit Berlin to see a woman who claimed to be the dowager empress's granddaughter, Anastasia Nikolaevna. Kulikovsky supported Marie Feodorovna, who tried to dissuade Olga from making the trip to Berlin. Olga admitted that "Mamma did not want me to [go]. She was so angry with me."[5] Olga, who had been close to Anastasia, made the trip to Berlin. Kulikovsky accompanied the grand duchess, and they were met by Pierre Gilliard and his wife, who had been Anastasia's nurse. The object of Olga's interest was a young woman who had been rescued from a Berlin canal in 1920 and was later known by the name of Anna Anderson. For several days, Olga spoke with the claimant. Eventually, Olga agreed with Gilliard that the woman was not Anastasia.

Marie Feodorovna steadfastly clung to the belief that her son and his family (as well as Grand Duke Michael) were still alive. The alternative was just too horrendous to contemplate. The dowager empress always spoke of the family as if they were alive. "Yet I am sure," admitted Grand Duchess Olga many years later, "that deep in her heart my mother had steeled herself to accept the truth some years before her death."[6]

A historian of Russia once described the country as "a tormented and tragic nation."[7] This description also aptly describes Greece in the early twentieth century. The country's internal crisis, which originated with the dispute between Eleutherios Venizelos and King Constantine I, continued. The turmoil had serious repercussions, both for Greece and for the royal family.

From revolutionary Russia, Queen Olga made her way to Switzerland, where the Greek royal family had taken refuge after being ejected from Greece. She was finally reunited with her family in 1918, in Zurich "where her son, King Constantine, was only just recovering from a dangerous attack of Spanish influenza, which nearly cost him his life a second time."[8] As Prince Nicholas put it, the reunion took place "under the saddest and most trying circumstances! . . . it was "one of joy mixed with untold pain. For us, poor exiles, to greet our dear mother, herself now deprived of her two homes, was like shipwrecked passengers meeting on a desert island. No one who has not trodden that Via Dolorosa can understand the bitterness of being deprived of one's home and, above all, one's native land."[9] Olga, a Romanov exiled from Russia and a Greek royal evicted from Greece, was "the ghost of her old self." Besides the anxieties over her Romanov and Greek relations, the elderly queen's deprivations left her "half starved," because she had lived for weeks at a time on "a diet of stale bread soaked in oil."[10]

In a letter to her nephew King George V written in the summer of 1918 from Lucerne, Queen Olga told him, "I just returned from the english [sic] church, where I prayed for you and sang 'God Save the King' from all my heart! . . . It is just 4 years now, since I saw you last & how much lies between . . . [sic] without God's help how could we ever carry our heavy cross . . . [sic] but with His help we do stand everything, as awful as it may be . . . It is such happiness to be with my chicks [children] again after so long—but the going away from my old home was terribly hard!"[11]

Queen Olga enjoyed being back in the bosom of her family, especially delighting in the company of her grandchildren. In Switzerland, she was away from danger, but the queen was still burdened with anxieties. "Living in exile is a great and bitter trial!" she wrote in September 1920 to her friend Ioulia Karolou. "There are moments that I am very pessimistic . . . because time is passing and things do not improve!" At nearly seventy years old, Queen Olga had moved an astonishing thirty times in the space of two years and four months, prompting her to confess, "I am becoming a true gypsy, and I am tired of it!" There continued to be a question of where she would live. Rome, where her sons, Andrew and Christopher, were at the time, seemed feasible because above all, it was less expensive than Switzerland. Olga, who had belonged to one of the wealthiest families on earth, in her old age admitted that "I must economize!"[12]

During their Swiss exile the Greek royals did economize. Queen Olga's youngest son, Christopher, called it a "hand-to-mouth existence with its daily worries over ways and means."[13] But despite being in economic straits, Queen Olga's generous spirit did not desert her. When she discovered that Countess Marguerite Cassini (who had sold dresses in Switzerland to help make ends meet) was desperate to reunite with her husband, Sacha, but needed to raise two thousand Swiss francs in order for him to leave Russia, the queen stepped in. The countess recalled, "I had to confess to Queen Olga that two thousand francs was more than I had. She offered the sum to me without hesitation. It was only when I talked to her lady-in-waiting that I discovered how truly royal a gesture she was making. The money came from a check that Ruth Hanna McCormick[14] gave the Queen to buy a winter coat and some new teeth. The lady-in-waiting was aghast at the sacrifice, but Sacha was already on his way to Switzerland and the Queen went without her new set of teeth."[15]

Queen Olga was not the only one working to reunite Oleg Cassini's mother, Countess Marguerite Cassini, with her husband. The Grand Duchess Vladimir, by then living in exile too, also helped. During a visit to Switzerland, Miechen, in Cassini's words, "really went into action. Telegrams and letters flew everywhere. All legations and consulates must find Sacha and help him get to Switzerland!"[16]

By this time, Miechen was highly mortified to learn that Boris had married his mistress, Zenaida Rachevskaya, in July 1919, in Genoa, Italy. Miechen had a low opinion of Zenaida, whom she described as a "monster of a woman" who was in the grand duchess's words, "noisy, common, ugly, stupid, bad, undesirable and unshowable in decent society."[17]

Miechen was not the only one who saw a highly unsuitable marriage foisted on the family. The Duchess of Coburg also had a similar situation take place within her family, though in a generation further away. Instead of having a son marrying an unsuitable wife, as Boris had done, Marie Alexandrovna learned of her grandson Crown Prince Carol of Romania's elopement with commoner Zizi Lambrino in 1918. Not only did Prince Carol marry without his parents' consent, he deserted his military regiment in the process, an act punishable by death. The scandal had the potential of destabilizing the Romanian dynasty at a critical time in the country's fortunes. In the end, Carol and Zizi's marriage was annulled.

Queen Olga was spared the matrimonial scandals among her children that had embarrassingly dogged her contemporaries, Miechen, Marie Feodorovna, and Marie Alexandrovna. Though Olga's youngest son, Christopher, married a divorced American commoner, Nancy Leeds, it was not until 1920, after a very lengthy engagement, due largely to the war, that the marriage could take place. The Greek royal family heartily embraced Nancy, who was created Princess Anastasia of Greece and Denmark.[18]

Meanwhile, Queen Olga's unmarried grandson, King Alexander, led a lonely life in Athens without his family, trying to stay politically afloat in Greece's treacherous political waters. Not groomed to be king, Alexander found himself thrust into a political maelstrom that would have been challenging even to a seasoned statesman or politician, but doubly difficult for an untrained youth like himself. His challenges were daunting, particularly as the young king was surrounded by Venizelist supporters who thwarted his contacts with his family. An especially vicious example of this took place in 1918 during Alexander's visit to Paris. While he was in the French capital Alexander's mother, Queen Sophie, tried to talk to her son by telephone, but was told that the king could not speak to her. The family later discovered that King Alexander had never even been informed that his mother had telephoned.

With such an unsympathetic group surrounding him, King Alexander turned to Aspasia Manos, the attractive daughter of one of his father's equerries. It was easy to see why the twenty-four-year-old King Alexander fell for the dark-haired Aspasia. The British novelist and secret agent Compton Mackenzie was also intrigued by Aspasia, whom he described as "beautiful" and having a profile fit "for a goddess." She also possessed a strong will; and Mackenzie recalled marveling at Aspasia as he watched her—"that glorious young woman, delivering" what amounted to a "glorious tirade against the oppressors of her country."[19] Thus did beauty and a fiery spirit combine to make Aspasia irresistible to Alexander. She offered the lonely king the companionship he deeply craved after seeing his family ejected from Greece. Alexander insisted on marrying Aspasia, the one person who supported and loved him.

Irene Noel-Baker, wife of a British diplomat, spoke in depth several times with the king and Aspasia, and wrote of the couple: "The best influence in his life at present is Miss Manos, <u>and the only thing he wants to do is to marry her</u>; he hates his present life, which he says over and over again is worse than a prisoner's, and he frequently talks of resigning. He naturally sees Venizelos often but he is afraid of him and does not talk openly with him." Irene Noel-Baker also noted that, "Athenians, including the members of Venizelos' party, slander Miss Manos in every possible way, but the impression she makes on unprejudiced minds is a good one; she seems sincere and sensible. Having seen her very often with the King, I am certain that her influence is a good one."[20]

King Alexander married Aspasia in secret in November 1919. The news did not remain secret for long. The Greeks did not like the idea of their king marrying a Greek commoner and were highly displeased. The marriage was to prove happy but brief.

Just as events for Queen Olga's descendants were tumultuous, so too were they for the family of Queen Olga's cousin and contemporary, the Duchess of Coburg. Though Marie Alexandrovna may not have seen the violence that was destroying Russia firsthand, she still suffered greatly from her Romanov relations' murders. A supporter of Germany, Marie Alexandrovna was first chagrined to see those she loved on opposing sides, then saddened to see Germany defeated in the Great War. Marie Alexandrovna could understand that her daughters Bee and Sandra's loyalties lay with neutral Spain, and with Germany, respectively. But the Duchess of Coburg found it more difficult to accept that Ducky and Missy sided with the Allies. Missy's strong championship of the Allied cause throughout the war was especially difficult to accept. When the Armistice was signed in November 1918, Missy's thoughts went out to her mother: "I keep thinking of Mamma, who must be at Coburg, and of how dreadful all this must be to her . . . the vision of my sad old Mamma, who lost everything in Russia, and must now assist at the collapse of her country of adoption."[21]

The lack of money, the war, the revolutions in Russia, the disintegration of the old order, and the brutal murders of thousands of Russians and of her Romanov relations—all had a profound impact on Marie Alexandrovna. Marie Alexandrovna also lost much of her Russian fortune in the upheavals in her native land. This meant that she had to live in reduced circumstances. It was hard to believe that Marie Alexandrovna, who had grown up amidst the incomparable splendor of the Russian court, now lived in a tattered annex of the Dolder Grand Hotel in Zurich, Switzerland. Her granddaughter Princess Ileana of Romania described the duchess's abode as being "an awful little pension" that was "very refugee-like."[22]

Missy, Queen Marie of Romania, eloquently summed up what her mother had gone through, when she received a letter from the duchess while attending the Paris Peace Conference, in March 1919:

> With trembling fingers I tore open the envelope and read . . . a letter, terrible in its grief. Every word was a fiery dart of pain, every sentence a cry of smothered anguish. Everything had fallen to pieces: first her beloved Russia, then Germany, the country of her adoption, [which had] become dear to her heart. Nearly her entire family had been murdered, she herself was ruined and had to live poorly in a country which had gone "red" and had upset the old order of things. She had lost everything at once: not only her fortune, but all her old beliefs, traditions, ideas and ideals had been shattered, desecrated. A new world had grown up around her in which she could find no footing, in which the grand old autocrat she was no longer had a place. She could not fit in; she would never be able to fit in. Wherever she turned, she saw nothing but change and destruction, and everything she heard augmented her pain. She dared not even look back and remember, for in remembering lay the greatest agony of all.[23]

When Missy visited her mother in 1919, the Duchess of Coburg was a shell of her former self. Marie Alexandrovna was no longer the "autocratic, domineering . . . awe-inspiring" woman of before.[24] Instead, Missy saw a much thinner, bent woman, whose once plump fingers were now "thin and trembling." It was an exceedingly difficult meeting for Missy who was shocked by the change in her mother. "The dominant look in her eyes," wrote Missy of the duchess, "formerly one of her great characteristics, had been tarnished; today they were anxious eyes, almost haunted."[25]

And yet, there was still something of the Russian grand duchess left in Marie Alexandrovna. "Beneath her changed exterior," wrote Missy of her mother, "burned the same proud spirit, unbending, refusing to admit defeat." Sadly, the chasm that divided Missy and her mother during the war was hard to bridge. "We had been in different camps; and our [Romania's] entering on the side of the Allies had helped to overthrow Germany. This thought was with us both, all the time, underlying our every conversation." And so "there was a feeling as of treading on thin ice," wrote Missy of their meeting, "knowing that dangerous depths gaped below." The strained reunion was made easier by the presence of Bee and her Spanish husband, Ali. But the tension between Missy and her mother was never far from the surface: "Mama still stuck to her old tradition of separating the generations," claimed Missy. But mother and daughter tried in their own way to reach out to each other; and the Duchess of Coburg allowed Queen Marie to take her to one of Marie Alexandrovna's favorite places, Florence.

Two weeks amidst the soothing and beautiful surroundings of that old city must have helped the duchess because Missy admitted that as she was leaving, "Mama's defences broke down and in hurried words she confessed to me something of her grief; she suddenly became soft and motherly, allowing, for once, her oppressed heart to speak. Not many words, as we both feared our emotion, but all the same she said some of those things I longed to hear and for which my soul had been hungering . . . She seemed so frail as I took her, for a last time, in my arms . . . Mama's tear-stained face, with its sunken cheeks and with those eyes out of which all fire had died, kept rising up before me, haunting every hour of my days. It was unbearable to know that I could do nothing for her, and that Fate had so irrevocably parted our ways."[26]

A year later, the Duchess of Coburg received another visit from Missy. This time, Marie Alexandrovna could not help unleashing her frustrations at Missy for "God knows what far-off lapses" as well as "certain half hours in my life when I did wrong," recalled Queen Marie. She "continues to bicker, bicker about quite forgotten things I did or left undone . . . poor dear, stormy old Mama!"[27]

The Duchess of Coburg also received another visitor in 1920, none other than her sister-in-law Miechen. Both women, tired and ill, had lived to see their old world brutally destroyed and their country convulsed in chaos and violence. Miechen had been in Montreux visiting her daughter Elena and son-in-law Nicholas, both still living in exile like the rest of the Greek royals. From Montreux the trio left for Zurich to see the Duchess of Coburg. Prince Nicholas noted both women "suffered so deeply" during the last years.[28] It must have been a somewhat difficult reunion for Miechen and Marie Alexandrovna, for "war had forced the two women to take opposing sides, abandoning the countries of their birth, and its aftermath had made exiles of them both."[29]

Miechen remained in touch with her dear friend Bertie Stopford, who had helped her spirit her jewels out of Russia. Early in 1920 he visited her to discuss how best to deal with the precious items. But then in July, Miechen was stricken ill. Miechen went to one of her favorite places, Contrexéville, France, in the hopes of improving her health. Her sister-in-law, the Dowager Empress Marie Feodorovna, wrote in her diary that, "poor Miechen is still very sick in Contrexéville—she suffers from terrible kidney pain."[30] Miechen's health worsened, and Grand Duke Andrei was called to her bedside. Andrei dutifully stayed with his mother. After a month, with Miechen finally showing signs of rallying, Andrei decided that it was all right to leave her. However, no sooner had Andrei departed than he was summoned again, along with Miechen's other children. Mathilde Kschessinska accompanied Andrei this time. Elena's husband, Nicholas, could not come because the Greek minister to France denied his request for a visa. The family found the grand duchess "in a desperate state: her death was only a question of days," recalled Mathilde, "and she was in great pain." But seeing Andrei lifted Miechen's spirits. He was, after all, the child who stayed by her side throughout much of the war. Miechen kept repeating Andrei's name in her final days. She even "tried to say some words about Vova."[31] Miechen died peacefully on September 6, 1920, surrounded by her children. She was sixty-six years old.

In recording the final chapter of Miechen's life, Marie Feodorovna wrote in her diary: "At 10 we had a funeral service here for Miechen. I received a response from Kyril and Elena. Their mother is to be buried in a small chapel, which Miechen herself ordered to be built in Contrexéville."[32]

Miechen was undoubtedly one of the most colorful members of the Romanov dynasty. She had her share of detractors, but she also had her share of admirers. One of them was the Russian diplomat A. N. Savinsky. In his memoirs, Savinsky dedicated his work to "the Memory of H.I.H. The Grand Duchess Vladimir." Savinsky eloquently wrote of his admiration for the grand duchess and her husband, stating that: "All those who had the privilege of meeting Their Imperial Highnesses remember the culture of the Grand Duke, the interest he devoted to all historical, political, and diplomatic questions, as well as the charm and intelligence of the Grand Duchess. I always recall with emotion and gratitude the kindness with which Their Imperial Highnesses received me, and which has never failed me since." In singling out his dedication to Marie Pavlovna, Savinsky wrote that:

> at the outbreak of the [Great] war [she] devoted herself entirely to the organization of helping the wounded. Tired and overworked, she decided in February, 1917, to rest for a few weeks in the Cauca-

sus, and it was there that she first experienced the Revolution. She was arrested and kept in her villa by armed and undisciplined soldiers. I hastened to join her there, and did not leave her until the moment of her death.

During our exile she constantly encouraged me to write down all I had heard and seen during my eventful career. To her influence, to her gracious and kind encouragement, this book owes its appearance.

Piously I evoke the image of this Great Lady (in the true sense of the word), and to her memory I respectfully dedicate my volume.[33]

With Miechen now dead, her son Andrei was finally at liberty to marry Mathilde Kschessinska, which he did in 1921. Also, after the Grand Duchess Vladimir's death, what was left of her impressive jewelry needed to be dispersed. Queen Mary acquired her legendary loop diamond and pearl tiara, which later became a favorite with her granddaughter Queen Elizabeth II. The 1909 sapphire and diamond *kokoshnik* Cartier tiara went to Miechen's niece Queen Marie of Romania, who wore it in 1922 to her own coronation. Other jewelry was divided among her children. The pearls went to Kyril, the emeralds to Boris, the rubies to Andrei, and the diamonds to Elena. The princess used the proceeds from the sale of some of her mother's jewels to rent a château at St. Germain-en-Laye, a suburb of Paris. Elena used the château to house numerous children of needy Russian refugees who had fled to Paris. She did this as "a memorial to her mother, who died as a result of the hardships she had endured in the country she loved and for which she worked unceasingly."[34]

Within weeks of Elena's mother's death in September 1920, an unexpected misfortune befell the Greek royals. While in Tatoi, King Alexander I was walking his dog when suddenly, the vineyard keeper's pet monkey attacked the dog. As Alexander attempted to separate the dog and the monkey, another monkey bit him. Within days, blood poisoning set in. For three weeks, King Alexander, often in agony, fought to stay alive. His distraught mother, Queen Sophie, desperately tried to get permission to see her very ill son, but Venizelos denied it. Sophie was heartbroken by this and implored her mother-in-law to go in her stead, believing that the Greek government would not deny Queen Olga entry to Greece. "She [Sophie] begged me to go!" wrote Olga of the heart-wrenching incident, and of course she rushed to Greece "because I consider it my duty, since it is a consolation to the parents."[35] It was a race against time. Marie Feodorovna recorded the event in her diary: "They say our dear Olga left for Athens to take care of her poor grandson Alexander, I hope it won't be too late. Messages that come [about his state] are very bad."[36] Queen Olga, though, was too late, delayed by bad weather in the Adriatic Sea during her trip. Sadly, wracked by pain and suffering from delirium, King Alexander died on October 25, 1920, some twelve hours before his grandmother arrived. He was only twenty-seven.

In reporting the tragic story, the *New York Times* recorded that "during his lucid moments," King Alexander's morale "seemed good. He only realized the gravity of his condition the last two days and all his thoughts were for his wife. At the very last Alexander attempted to embrace her but breathed his last before he could do so." When Queen Olga finally arrived at Tatoi, "there was a pathetic scene between the aged Dowager Queen and her morganatic grand-daughter, and the two remained alone in the death chamber half an hour."[37]

On the day of King Alexander's funeral, his coffin, draped in the royal flag, was taken from Tatoi to the cathedral in Athens in an "improvised hearse." The late king's body was driven in his own motor car to the Greek capital by a close friend. The funeral car was followed by several motor cars, the first of which carried Queen Olga and a lady-in-waiting. King Alexander's young pregnant widow and the grand marshal of the court followed in a separate vehicle. After the coffin was taken into the cathedral, the public was allowed to enter. "The crowd was so dense," according to the *New York Times*, "that it was extremely difficult to maintain order."[38] Queen Olga, the only other family representative present at the funeral, buried her grandson at Tatoi near his grandfather's grave.

In no time, Queen Olga had to absorb another shock. She received news that sixty-seven-year-old Marie Alexandrovna, the Duchess of Coburg, had died in her sleep of a heart attack in the annex of the Dolder Grand Hotel. Though thinner and weaker, the duchess still exhibited vitality; and thus her sudden death surprised some, coming as it did a mere six weeks after Miechen died. It was rumored that the duchess was mortified upon receiving a letter addressed simply as "Frau Coburg" and that the shock may have contributed to her death; though for the formidable woman that the duchess was, this seems very unlikely. Missy's description of her mother's life and death to King George V encapsulated eloquently what had taken place:

> Her death was a terrible, cruel shock to us all, we were in no wise prepared for it, I had been with her hardly two months before. She was certainly, thin weak & very changed, but nothing made us imagine that her end could be so near.

Her life had become too sad and all about her too had changed. She was breaking her heart over it, she could bear no more. The death of Uncle Paul [her brother, Grand Duke Paul] after all those other dreadful deaths was what was just too much for her—after all that news, according to those with her, she was never the same again, she became suddenly old and broke down—her usual splendid health forsaking her all at once.

She had seen everything crumble, Russia with all her family and her fortune, then Germany—everything she had believed in, it was too much; mourn her as we do, none of us are cruel enough to wish her back into this sad world where she has suffered over much.[39]

"She was profoundly religious," added Queen Marie of Romania in reflecting upon her mother. "I hope God will not disappoint her as most things & beings did in this life."[40]

Missy also noted that despite "feeling herself obliged to champion the cause of Germany and the central powers," Marie Alexandrovna was "eternally grateful for the moral support and financial assistance King George and Queen Mary had given her in her last days." In deep gratitude and even despite having sold most of her splendid jewelry, she nevertheless wanted Queen Mary to have "a chain with sapphires and a brooch to match." The Duchess of Coburg had insisted that it should be "a Russian jewel." "Bee will bring it to dear May," wrote Missy to King George, "and ask her to think of my sad old Mama sometimes when she wears it."[41]

Marie Alexandrovna and Miechen's deaths in such quick succession meant that of the four imperial matriarchs, only the Dowager Empress Marie Feodorovna and Queen Olga were still alive. The least political of the four matriarchs, Queen Olga, was suddenly asked to become regent after King Alexander's death. Alexander's brother Prince Paul had been invited to succeed Alexander as king, but Paul refused. His loyalty to his family meant that Paul could not accept the throne ahead of his father, Constantine, and older brother, George.

Venizelos then decided to call an election, set for November 14, 1920, confident that he would be elected. But the unthinkable took place. Earl Granville, the British ambassador to Greece, reported from Athens to the British foreign secretary Earl Curzon that Venizelos "is hopelessly beaten."[42] An eighty-year-old statesman, George Rallis, became prime minister and sought an audience with the sixty-nine-year-old Queen Olga. When the aged Rallis, who had served the late King George I, met the queen, he was so moved by the moment that he knelt before Olga and kissed her hand. Queen Olga was equally moved and begged the prime minister to rise. When he refused, the queen, in an act of, graciousness, then went down on her knees and told Rallis that she would get up only when he did. Rallis asked Queen Olga to become regent for the time being. With Venizelos defeated and Queen Olga acting as regent, the path was clear for Constantine's return to Greece. Constantine insisted on having a plebiscite on the issue. It was held on November 14, 1920. Only 10,800 votes were cast against, while 1,010,000 were cast for Constantine's return. Earl Granville reported to London that "nobody outside Greece can realise [the] complete change of popular opinion which has taken place . . . and almost insane enthusiasm at this moment for Constantine."[43]

Despite the Greek people's overwhelming desire to see their king return, the British, still displeased with Constantine's wartime neutrality, turned a deaf ear. Earl Granville, as the British representative in Athens, was instructed by Earl Curzon to "enter into no official or ceremonial relations with King Constantine or his court and attend no official functions of the present Greek Government."[44] Despite the muted reaction of the British and other Allied parties in Greece, the Greek people were overjoyed by Constantine's arrival.

Queen Olga could not but rejoice in her son's triumphant return. His subjects shouted *"Erchetai! Erchetai!"* ("He is coming! He is coming!") on the king's arrival in Greece. Greeks mobbed Constantine's train as it made its way to Athens. Queen Olga greeted her son upon his arrival at Athens. When Queen Olga and Queen Sophie were reunited, emotions overcame them, so much so that neither woman could utter a word to each other.

As King Constantine and Queen Sophie walked from the train to their carriage, they were nearly crushed by the enthusiastic crowd, who were almost delirious with joy. From the palace balcony Queen Olga, King Constantine, and Queen Sophie greeted the crowds below who shouted their approval and happiness at the return of their king and royal family.

The big question, of course, was would this wild enthusiasm for Queen Olga's son last? The British diplomat Harold Nicolson, in his report of the latest stunning events to take place in Greece, reflected on the future: "The return of King Constantine to Athens closes the first chapter of the Greek crisis. What is to be the next stage?"[45]

30

A MISERABLE FRAGMENT

OF THE PAST

he question over Tsar Nicholas II's fate prompted the opportunistic Kyril to make a bid for the throne, by declaring himself "guardian of the throne," in 1922.[1] That Miechen's son should make this move infuriated the dowager empress. Two years later, the *New York Times* reported that "she declared if a protector of the throne was [*sic*] needed it would be her husband's cousin, the universally respected and admired Grand Duke Nicholas Nicholaevitch" and not Kyril.[2]

In 1924, Kyril proclaimed himself emperor of Russia. Again, Marie Feodorovna condemned the move, writing to Nikolasha:

> *My heart was painfully depressed by reading the manifesto of the Grand Duke Cyril Wladimirovitch [sic], who declared himself Emperor of all the Russias.*
>
> *There is no definite news up to now about the fate of my beloved sons and grandson. I, therefore, consider the act of Grand Duke Cyril's proclamation as premature. Nobody is in a position to deprive me of the last gleam of hope.*
>
> *I am afraid that this manifesto may create division and instead of improving will render still worse the state of tortured Russia.*
>
> *If it would please the Almighty, in His unknown ways, to take unto Himself my beloved sons and grandson, I believe, without any forecast of the future and with firm hope in Divine Grace, that the future Emperor will be designated by our fundamental laws in unison with the Orthodox Church and together with the Russian people.*

I pray thee Almighty to spare us His anger and to save us by those ways known only to Him.

I am sure that you, as the oldest member of the House of Romanoff share my views.

Marie[3]

The dowager empress was correct. Kyril's action divided the Romanovs and the Russian monarchists in exile. Among the Romanovs: Nikolasha, Michael Mikhailovich, Dmitri, and Peter sided with Marie Feodorovna, while Boris, Andrei, and Sandro acknowledged Kyril as emperor.

Despite her advanced years and the unbearable tragedies that had befallen her, Marie Feodorovna had not lost the charm for which she had been renowned. When Miechen's godson Prince Serge Obolensky met with the dowager empress, he was struck by her demeanor. Marie Feodorovna had granted Obolensky and Paul Rodzianko an audience. Both men represented the Chevalier Guards, whose colonel-in-chief was none other than the aged dowager empress. When Obolensky and Rodzianko met her, they presented Marie Feodorovna with a bouquet in the guards' traditional colors of red and white. "She accepted them [the flowers] graciously," recalled Obolensky, "with a smile, and acted as if the whole regiment were drawn up before her, instead of two of its surviving officers."[4]

The Dowager Empress Marie Feodorovna was much respected by the thousands of Russian émigrés who fled Russia. Many were in contact with her during these years of exile, asking her help and advice. The dowager empress diligently wrote letters to numerous émigrés and relatives, often from the garden of her beloved Hvidovre. Marie Feodorovna's court in exile was modest, consisting mainly of close friends such as Prince Serge Dolgoruky and her lady-in-waiting, Countess Zenaida Mengen. Two chamber Cossacks, including the faithful Timofei Yaschik, attended the dowager empress frequently. These two fantastically bearded Cossacks provided much color as they were armed, while in attendance, with sabers and revolvers.

In spite of living through great tragedies, Marie Feodorovna at seventy-two, was unbowed and agile and still had the figure of a young woman. Her mind was as sharp as ever. The dowager empress was also imbued with an unshakeable spirit. When she discovered that the Soviets had overtaken Copenhagen's Orthodox church, making it an annex of their consulate, Marie Feodorovna hired a top Danish lawyer and won her case against the Soviets, ensuring that the building became a place of worship again. When the church reopened, the dowager empress attended the service despite the pains she had to endure from her arthritis and lumbago.

Queen Olga and the Greek royal family's fortunes fluctuated wildly in the early 1920s. King Constantine I's triumphant return to Athens in December 1920 appeared to presage a new and glorious future for the country and the Greek royal family. But it was not to be. Almost from the start of his second reign, Constantine's challenges were virtually insurmountable. The Allies' continued hostility toward him and tacit support for Venizelos made Constantine's task as king extremely difficult.

With the Ottoman Empire rapidly disintegrating after World War I, Venizelos, still in pursuit of the ever tantalizing *Megali Idea*, ordered the occupation of Smyrna (present-day Izmir in Turkey) and northern Epirus. The British prime minister David Lloyd George supported this action, as did the United States and France. The Greek landings in Smyrna, however, precipitated the revival of Turkish nationalism, which inevitably led to war. Constantine had cautioned Venizelos as early as 1915 about what an adventure in Asia Minor might mean: He predicted "the destruction of Greece would follow the invasion of Asia Minor, because Greece was not strong enough, rich enough, or numerous enough to hold a country overseas with their hereditary enemy the Turk sitting on the frontier." Constantine I bluntly told Venizelos: "It will bleed Greece to death."[5]

Queen Olga's son was soon proven correct. In October 1920, Venizelos, encouraged by Lloyd George, ordered Greek troops in Smyrna to move against the Turks. Already, the Turkish troops were under the leadership of a dynamic officer by the name of Mustafa Kemal, who would go down in history as Atatürk, the founder of modern-day Turkey.

Constantine was unable to extricate his country from the ill-advised campaign that Venizelos had started before falling from power. To leave Smyrna summarily would have exposed the city's large Greek population to the mercy of Turkish troops, "whose enmity," as Prince Nicholas pointed out, "had been thoroughly roused by Mr. Venizelos's Asiatic policy!"[6] Moreover, Constantine would also be open to the accusation of cheating Greece of the chance to fulfill her destiny by defeating the Turks decisively. Anti-royalists could accuse Queen Olga's son of going against the British and French, who had promoted the conflict. Thus, with a heavy heart, Constantine chose to continue fighting Kemal's forces. However, the Greek forces with newly drafted soldiers were badly equipped. Moreover, they were "often only barely trained."[7] And so, Greece's army, hampered by numerous shortcomings, "marched on to its destruction."[8]

While Queen Olga watched nervously as Greece enmeshed herself ever deeper in the Asia Minor campaign, major changes took place within her family. Marriages united the Greek and Romanian royal families when King Constantine's son Crown Prince George married Elisabetha, Queen Marie and King Ferdinand of Romania's daughter, in 1921. Also, Constantine's daughter Helen and Crown Prince Carol of Romania, whose marriage to Zizi Lambrino had by then been annulled, married. Though Helen's mother, Queen Sophie, was against the marriage, King Constantine granted his permission, as this was what Helen wanted. Thus did two of Queen Olga's grandchildren marry two of the Duchess of Coburg's grandchildren.

In 1920 Queen Olga once again became a great-grandmother when Aspasia, widow of King Alexander, gave birth to his posthumous daughter, Princess Alexandra. Queen Olga's daughter Marie who had been widowed in 1919 when the Bolsheviks murdered her husband, Grand Duke George, married again, in 1922 to Admiral Pericles Ioannides of the Greek navy. The last of Queen Olga's grandchildren was born in 1921, when Prince Andrew and Princess Alice became the parents of a boy, Prince Philip, born in Corfu. That same year, Queen Olga's granddaughter Princess Helen gave birth to a son, Prince Michael of Romania.

Soon after Prince Michael's birth, Princess Helen went to visit her family in Greece. She found her father "more harassed and careworn" than ever before, for he had been anxious about the war in Asia Minor and the confounding fact that the British and French "were still making his continued occupation of the throne a justification for withholding now even the political support on which the [military] campaign had been initiated." Constantine bitterly told his worried daughter that "they have arranged it to seem that it is only me who holds back Greece from recovery."[9] In fact, what had taken place was that, "since King Constantine's return, the Allies had begun to turn the screws on the Greeks . . . The British cut off the supply of war materials to Greece, the French and Italians concurring." Moreover, the French and Italians supplied war material to Kemal's forces. Greece was further hampered when the "Allies took steps to deny Greece . . . the right of visit and search of allied merchant ships." This had the effect of damaging the Greeks "by preventing them from stopping up the illicit trade with the Kemalists."[10]

Already, at this time, cracks were appearing in Helen and Carol's marriage, but her father and Greece's fate was upmost in Helen's mind. In June 1921, a decisive battle took place—the Battle of Sakaria. The river Sakaria turned out to be "the last obstacle between the Greeks and Ankara [Mustafa Kemal's new capital], and the line on which Kemal had chosen to fight."[11] His counter-attack proved victorious and sealed the Greeks' fate. King Constantine's forces failed to wrest Ankara from Mustafa Kemal and in the process, signaled the effective end of the Asia Minor campaign. Greece's hopes for defeating the Turks and fulfilling their grand dream of the *Megali Idea* were dashed. After the Battle of Sakaria, Greek forces retreated, heading to Smyrna.

Greece's fate prompted Queen Alexandra to write to her son King George V "to do all you can for Greece & poor excellent *honest* Tino who has been so infamously treated by the world & France."[12] But France and Britain gave no succor to Greece. King George V turned down another plea from Queen Olga, telling her, that he could not act against the Allies' policies. "The only way to help Tino in his difficult position would be to recognise him, but that at the present moment is impossible," wrote George V to Queen Alexandra. "Under the circumstances there is nothing to be done but to wait & see what happens" added the king. George V ended his letter by saying of Constantine I: "I am sorry for him, very sorry."[13]

An emboldened Mustafa Kemal demanded that Greece evacuate Asia Minor, even knowing that such a move was politically impossible. In August 1922, Kemal attacked the Greeks and won. Then, "in an orgy of violence lasting nearly a week, the Turks exacted their revenge on Greeks in Smyrna, plundering and burning the city." So many were killed that "conservative estimates place the Greek death toll at 30,000 people; some have placed it as high as 300,000."[14] Thus, ninety years after Greece gained independence, "the irredentist project of the *Megali Idea* was consumed in the ashes of Smyrna in 1922."[15]

After Greece's humiliating defeat in Asia Minor, the country had to deal with an unprecedented influx of refugees. Bearing "her cross bravely," Greece "gathered in her children . . . by receiving them—a million or more—within the existing Greek homeland. No nation has achieved so much as Greece on this occasion."[16]

Greece's defeat in the Greco-Turkish War of 1919–1922 and the massacres at Smyrna were catastrophic for the Greek royal family. The army and navy revolted; and at the end of September 1922, thousands of soldiers demanded that Queen Olga's son Constantine abdicate. Not wishing to inflict a civil war on his people, the king acquiesced to what had effectively been a coup d'état. Queen Olga's grandson George ascended the throne as King George II.

The royal family was in real jeopardy. F. O. Lindley, the British ambassador to Greece, reported to London on October 1, 1922, that, "Prince Nicholas had requested, on behalf of the King, that a British man-of-war be sent for since the lives of the Royal Family were in danger."[17] Lindley followed up this report a few days later by stating bluntly: "it became abundantly clear that there were a number of people at Athens who thought that the best thing to do was to murder King Constantine and his family as well as Nicholas, at once."[18] With the tragic fates of Marie Feodorovna's sons, Nicholas and Michael, as well as Alexandra and the children still fresh in mind, Queen Olga feared for her family's lives. She had left Greece reluctantly in the summer of 1922 to seek treatment for her failing eyesight. She regretted leaving: "I am being tortured by the idea that it was selfish of me to leave . . . but what could I do for my sick eyes?" wrote the queen to her friend Ioulia Karolou.[19] In September, Queen Olga wrote to Karolou from Hvidovre of her sorrow over Greece: "I wanted to be down there [in Greece], but it was impossible, I had to come here, to my so tried sister-in-law [Marie Feodorovna]."[20]

Queen Olga was saddened to see that Constantine and Sophie had to flee Greece again. The farewell this time was much more subdued than their frenzied exit five years before when their subjects were begging them to stay. This time, the couple fled to Palermo, Italy. Then, in the fall of 1922, Olga feared for the life of her fourth son, Prince Andrew, who was in grave danger, due to his involvement in the ill-fated Asia Minor campaign. Looking for scapegoats, the new government accused Andrew of military incompetence and placed him on trial. Six senior ministers and a general had already been tried for treason and executed by the new junta. Queen Olga frantically appealed to the French president and King Alfonso XIII of Spain for help. From Paris, where she was staying at the time, Queen Olga also sent a frantic telegram about Prince Andrew's plight to King George V: "Knowing your warm interest [I] implore you to save him. Aunt Olga."[21] In the end, Andrew was spared only a few hours before his scheduled execution. His anxious mother had gone to the Russian church in Paris to pray for her son. Prince Christopher, also in Paris, heard the verdict from a reporter: Andrew's life was spared; he was to be exiled. Christopher and his sister Marie then quickly drove to the church. They found their mother leaving the church. The color had "drained from her face when she saw us and her hand flew to her heart," recalled Christopher. "He's safe, he's safe. It's all right," came the news from Olga's two children. At that, "she turned back towards the church, made the sign of the cross and burst into tears."[22] A grateful Queen Olga wrote to King George V: "Words fail me to express all my gratitude to you for all you did to save my beloved Andrea! I can only say 'God bless you.'"[23] Andrew and his family, including his youngest child, eighteen-month-old Prince Philip, were banished from Greece.[24]

In describing the ordeal to Ioulia Karolou, Queen Olga wrote: "the massacre of the Ministers . . . this barbaric massacre has made the most horrific impression to the world—they now see us as some kind of cannibals! You can imagine my suffering, when my child was going to be sacrificed as a scapegoat . . . if the King of England hadn't intervened, they would have slaughtered him!"[25]

On the heels of Andrew's near brush with death, fifty-four-year-old Constantine died suddenly from a cerebral hemorrhage in Palermo. His widow, Sophie, tried to have Constantine buried in Greece, but was refused. She then brought her husband's remains to Florence to rest in the crypt of the city's Russian church. The sudden death of her eldest son, after he had been so sorely tried as king, was a bitter blow to his grieving, elderly mother, who wrote to a friend: "I live through a horrible new trial."[26]

Tragedy struck again when Prince Christopher's wife, Nancy, died in 1923. In thanking King George V for his message of sympathy regarding Nancy's death, Queen Olga wrote how his letter "touched me deeply and I thank you from all my heart! I can not tell you I suffer and how my head is torn to pieces for my own darling boy!! He was <u>so</u> happy with darling Nancy."[27]

During the closing years of Queen Olga's life, one of her great joys was the time she spent in England with the royal family. The queen especially liked visiting Windsor Castle. Queen Olga met with King George V and Queen Mary as well as Queen Alexandra and the Dowager Empress Marie Feodorovna during a visit. Prince Nicholas described the reunion between Olga and Marie Feodorovna as being "one of those joys that amount to the most acute suffering,"[28] as both had endured much pain during the past decade. One day, while she was being wheeled around the castle and grounds by a servant, the near-sighted Olga noticed a statue of a lady on horseback. She then exclaimed with great certainty: "that, of course, must be Queen Victoria on horseback." "Oh, no, Your Majesty!" came the reply. "That is Lady Godiva!"[29] King George V roared with laughter when he heard his aunt Olga recount the story.

In 1925, King George V's mother, Queen Alexandra died, aged eighty. The death of her beloved sister was a blow to Marie Feodorovna. The close sisterly bond that had linked the two women through eight decades was severed. After her sister's death, the years quickly caught up with the dowager empress. Timofei Yaschik recounted that Marie Feodorovna had said that "she loved her daughters and grandchildren, but she always said that they would get on fine without her, but the loss of her sister for her would be unendurable." And so, noted Yaschik, "in spite of the fact that" Olga lived nearby with her family and Xenia visited often from England, Marie Feodorovna "felt emptiness and loneliness. She stopped going out."[30]

Queen Olga too sincerely mourned her sister-in-law Queen Alexandra. In her letter of sympathy to King George V, the queen wrote: "My heart aches for you and I only wish words could express all one feels . . . y[ou]r darling, beloved motherdear, how terribly you must be missing her! I loved her so!" Queen Olga went on to add that she was the "dearest, loving, kindest sister to me all these many years since I was 15, and never changed for a moment."[31]

Other sad events clouding Queen Olga's last years included the expropriation of the Russian Hospital in Athens. The queen had purchased the land on which the hospital was built out of her own funds and erected the hospital in memory of her daughter Alexandra. Queen Olga also used her personal funds to furnish and maintain the hospital. More political turmoil also engulfed Greece. This time, her grandson King George II was effectively deposed and fled into exile in 1923. He lived for a while in Bucharest and later made his home in London. The Greek government stripped George of his nationality and confiscated his property, making this latest chapter in the history of the Greek monarchy all the more painful. Thus, Queen Olga lived to see the Greek monarchy abolished in 1924 and replaced by a republic.

To comfort his mother in her final years, Prince Christopher invited her to his home in the eternal city, Rome. Sharing the Villa Anastasia, where she was surrounded by her own things, was Christopher's way of compensating for his mother's nomadic life when she largely lived in hotels and friends' houses after fleeing Russia. "She accepted it all," recalled Christopher of his mother's fate, "with her usual profound and unswerving faith in God, with never one word of protest or complaint."[32] The queen's close friend Ioulia Karolou oversaw the shipment of many of the royal family's personal items from Greece to Rome. During the move, Karolou overheard a porter saying, of one of the trunks: "Come on guys, it is the holy old Queen's." After loading the trunk, the same porter touched the trunk tenderly and said: "Bring her the regards of the people who love her and never forget her . . . ah! How can I ever forget her, who came to the hospital daily when I had typhoid!!"[33]

At one point, Queen Olga left Italy to visit her sister-in-law Marie Feodorovna and her goddaughter Grand Duchess Olga at Hvidovre. Accompanying Queen Olga was Philip of Greece, her youngest grandchild. Grand Duchess

Olga recalled the golden-haired prince as being full of "humor and mischief." Young Philip "possessed a mind of his own, though he seemed rather subdued in the presence of mother," observed the grand duchess.³⁴ No doubt, the most touching sight during that visit was the reunion of Queen Olga and her sister-in-law, the Dowager Empress Marie Feodorovna. Queen Olga's son Nicholas summed up the two ageing matriarchs' trials: "Surely the cross that each had to bear was heavier than that given to most women and few sovereigns."³⁵

In one of her last letters to King George V, Queen Olga sent her "warmest, most loving wishes" for her nephew's sixty-first birthday, telling him: "God bless, my darling, beloved sunbeam and let us meet soon again—what joy *that* would be. XXX Give my best love to darling may [*sic*] [Queen Mary] & y[ou]r children. Ever y[ou]r devoted, faithful old owl, A[unt] Olga."³⁶ The letter was a touching reminder of the kind, selfless, down-to-earth woman who had been a Romanov grand duchess, Queen of the Hellenes, and the mother and grandmother of Greece's kings. Those words betrayed nothing of the terrible anguish Olga had endured in her lifetime: the murder of her husband, the vicious vilification of her sons, the premature deaths of two children and a grandson, the cruel murders of her Romanov relatives. Added to this was the destruction of Russia under the Communists and the turmoil that engulfed Greece, all of which resulted in the violent deaths of countless Russians and Greeks. Yet through all the torments, Olga never wavered in her faith. She bowed to the inscrutable ways of Providence; in fact, she cleaved to her faith, knowing that she could not endure the pain without God's help. Such was the message she wrote to a friend in 1923: "[There is] the holy God's will for everything. Amidst the countless trials I have the unwavering belief that everything that God grants us is for the best. You can only believe in this, it is [otherwise] impossible to comprehend rationally."³⁷

To the end of her days, Olga always remembered her native land and its tragic fate. These sentiments were encapsulated in one of Queen Olga's letters: "My heart aches . . . Everything, everything is gone with no return . . . My brothers are gone, I am the only one remaining in my family like a miserable fragment of the past."³⁸

It might have been for the best that Queen Olga fled Russia and that her brothers did not live to see what became of their country. Vera Pykhacheva, who had once been lady-in-waiting to the Dowager Empress Marie Feodorovna, described what became of St. Petersburg (renamed Leningrad in 1924) under the Communists during the years 1923 to 1926:

I was first struck by the terrible changes in the outward appearance of the once splendid and opulent capital city . . . It had been transformed into the huge, devastated, neglected and sordid village called "Leningrad" over which hung constantly an ominous black cloud creating a permanent atmosphere of fear.

The streets were unpaved, unrepaired, never swept, never watered and disgustingly dirty . . . In wet weather they became flowing rivers of mud and filth . . . In the great squares . . . red placards were erected bearing inflammatory Bolshevik inscriptions.

Many of the handsome houses and splendid places of former days had become lamentable . . . [and were] mere empty shells, retaining only their windowless facades, behind which everything was crumbling away. Often the empty rooms gave shelter to beggers [sic], thieves and evildoers . . .

When I saw it [Leningrad] after the Revolution one would have said that it had dropped back into the semi-barbarous past of two centuries ago . . .

One . . . met drunken men, women and, alas, even children, and theirs was a silent and sinister drunkenness . . .

A spirit of sadness pervaded the whole town . . . In the absence of all elegance the crowd gave the general impression of monotonus [sic] greyness. Gone were all the brilliant uniforms and elegant toilets, the splendid carriages and luxurious motor cars—all melted away like the snows of autumn. The poor horses that remained were half starved, the carriages shabby and neglected and the motor-cars a jingle of ironwork . . .

Little boys and girls, all alike insolent and impertinent, invaded the pavements, chasing each other round the pedestrians, hanging on to the tramway cars, or thrusting at the passers-by their "Red" news-papers. Alas, how sad a thing was childhood under the Soviet regime! Thousands and thousands of unfortunate little ones were taken from their parents to be educated by the State, which, when it found itself unable to maintain them, set them loose to fend for themselves. These orphans of the Revolution, victims of debauchery and or of famine, might be seen in their hundreds wandering along the great highways of Russia and across the wide steppes, or swarming in the streets of the towns, living from rapine and theft, or dying from sickness, hunger or cold . . . It was plainly seen that many of them had not long to live, and soon they would creep away like dogs to some dark corner to die. This is the greatest and most horrible crime committed by Bolshevism . . . [39]

"I went all over St. Petersburg looking for my former friends," recounted Vera Pykhacheva. Some were "employed by the Soviets, relegated to the position of slaves, paying dearly in humiliations and perpetual fear of death for the miserable pittance they were able to earn." But in her sad search for her old friends, Pykhacheva "almost always got the same sad answers to my enquiries. They had been killed, shot, or deported, had disappeared, died of inanition [exhaustion from lack of food], of cold, or in prison."[40] Clearly, life under the Communists in Russia had deteriorated into an existence punctuated by cruelty, vulgarity, and starvation.

In recalling what life had been before the Communists took over, Queen Olga wrote: "It was so good! . . . our dear beloved Russia!" Of Russia, she added: "I love her more . . . She is my everything; my compassion for her suffering and for her terrible trials only strengthens my love. Will I ever see my Motherland, my earthly paradise again?"[41] Queen Olga never did. The seventy-five-year-old queen died after a brief illness at the Villa Anastasia on June 18, 1926.

Prince Nicholas wrote of his mother's death to her old friend and correspondent Ioulia Karolou. He said a priest was called. When he asked Olga if she wished to receive Holy Communion, she whispered in Russian, "I do." Then, added Nicholas, "after she received Holy Communion, she followed attentively, and with great devoutness, the priest's prayers and supplications. Once he got to the Lord's Prayer, she wanted to cross herself, but such was her weakness that Christopher was forced to hold her hand and help her. After that, her strength declined rapidly. Christopher had put his arm around her shoulders, and was supporting her. And thus . . . she was extinguished, like a beautiful Icon candle! And thus she finished sweetly, with her beloved head resting on Christopher's shoulder . . . One could not have wished for her a more beautiful and sweeter death! . . . How merciful and beneficent the good God showed himself to be!! She died as a saint, as she had been all her life! . . . Now she is happy! . . . much happier than us! This thought must console you and strengthen you, as it consoles and strengthens us!" Echoing the sentiments of Queen Olga's family, Prince Nicholas wrote: "My Mother's departure has left a void, which will never be filled."[42]

Her son Christopher recounted that he had seen a bright light in her room the night Queen Olga died, the same luminous light in her room that he had seen from afar several days before. When Christopher had asked her about the mysterious light, Queen Olga was emphatic that there had been none and that she had slept soundly. But on the night she died, that same "golden glow was there again," recalled Christopher, "a glorious golden light, full of promise of the reward to come."[43]

After a funeral service in Rome, which was attended by the Russian and Greek communities as well as numerous foreign ambassadors, Queen Olga's remains were transported to Florence. She was laid to rest there in the crypt of the Russian church, next to the body of her son, King Constantine. Queen Sophie, who lived in Florence at the time, lovingly looked after the crypt, where a large Greek flag, icons, and red damask were hung. Greek, Russian, and Danish flags covered the biers, adding a profusion of colors to Queen Olga's temporary resting place.

Queen Olga's death meant that of the four imperial matriarchs, only the dowager empress was still alive. In Hvidovre, the aged Marie Feodorovna insisted that her daughter, the ever dutiful Olga, stay increasingly by her side. Pitifully, Grand Duchess Olga watched her mother stare for hours at photographs of Tsar Nicholas II, Alexandra, and their children. When the dowager empress gazed longingly at the faces of her beloved family, she seemed to be no longer a part of the present, but of the past. It was as if Marie Feodorovna retreated to a long lost world, one that was never to return.

The dowager empress also became obsessed with her jewel box, which contained numerous valuable items. She ordered that the box be kept under her bed so that she could look at its contents whenever she wanted. Though several family members insisted that Marie Feodorovna part with the items in the box, she steadfastly refused, insisting that they would have the chance to dispose of the items once she was gone. By September 1928, Marie Feodorovna knew her health was giving way to old age, and "she calmly prepared herself for death. Having been administered Extreme Unction, she said goodbye to her relatives and devoted servants. On the eve of her death the pain that had been torturing her left her, and she told her nearest, that she was dying without suffering."[44]

In October, Marie Feodorovna fell ill and slipped into a coma from which she never regained consciousness. Her ever devoted daughter, Olga, kept vigil by her mother's side, as did Xenia. The Dowager Empress Marie Feodorovna died on October 13, six weeks shy of her eighty-first birthday. A chapter in Russian history closed.

The dowager empress's coffin was sent for and Marie Feodorovna's two Cossacks placed her remains in it. Timofei Yaschik was struck by how thin, small, and light Marie Feodorovna's body was. The dowager empress's funeral took place in the Russian Orthodox Cathedral of Copenhagen that was built in 1883, thanks to Marie Feodorovna. In attendance were the dowager empress's daughters, Xenia and Olga, and their husbands. Also present at the cathedral were representatives of Europe's royal houses, as well as numerous relatives, including Prince Felix Yussoupov, his wife, Irina, and Grand Dukes Dmitri and Kyril.

Timofei Yaschik recalled the intense Russian flavor of the funeral service: "the Metropolitan with his gray hair, his tall crowned tiara with a cross; the Orthodox choir; the Byzantine vestments of the priests, which shone in the autumn sunshine; and the Russian speech gave the funeral a special unearthly distinctive feeling. Hundreds of former compatriots gathered from all the corners of the world to say goodbye to the Empress. Marie Feodorovna belonged to their Homeland, and for this reason the pain of loss weaved itself with sadness about the past and what had been lost in Russia."[45]

After the solemn and moving service, the funeral cortège made its way to the railway station. Thousands lined the streets of the city to bid farewell to the Danish princess who had become a beloved Russian empress. During the procession, soldiers escorted the hearse, and the funeral march played while cannons fired in salute. From the station, Marie Feodorovna's coffin traveled by train to the town of Roskilde. The dowager empress's remains were laid to rest in the town's cathedral, the burial place of the Danish royal family.

In a letter to Queen Mary, Xenia expressed what she and her sister Olga had felt: "You know how much we loved our mother & how we clung to her always & how in these cruel years of exile more than ever. She was *all* that was left to us—everything was centered in her—our home, our country, all the dear past . . . The light of our life is gone."[46]

In his memoirs, Alexander Izvolsky, Russia's foreign minister from 1906 to 1910, gave "tribute of an unreserved admiration to the mother of Nicholas II." Izvolsky wrote of "her charm, her goodness and her gracious demeanour." However, added Izvolsky, "can one imagine a more poignant tragedy than that of this superior soul, stricken in every fibre of her being by the martyrdom of her son and by the downfall of an Empire, of which she had been the good genius in other days? Having had the privilege of knowing the Empress Maria Feodorovna under particularly favourable conditions, and of receiving from her the most precious marks of confidence, I fulfil an imperious duty in laying at her feet the deep-felt homage of my devotion and of the pity that fills my heart when I evoke the image of her Calvary."[47]

Alexander Izvolsky's moving words were of the remarkable woman who had left her native Denmark as Princess Dagmar. She then spent "15 years as wife of the Heir Apparent, 13 years as Empress, 23 years as the Dowager Empress, and two years as citizeness Romanova. She left for Russia when she was an 18-year-old princess, and returned to her native Denmark when she was 71 years old, as a dethroned but not defeated empress."[48]

A highly successful empress, Marie Feodorovna had embraced her role and truly became a matriarch to her subjects, a fitting consort to Emperor Alexander III. And so it was with Marie Feodorovna's contemporaries—Marie Alexandrovna, Olga Constantinovna, and Marie Pavlovna, who each in her own way, had assumed in varying degrees the mantle of matriarch to subordinates and subjects: Marie Alexandrovna as wife of an Admiral of the Fleet and consort to Prince Alfred, the reigning Duke of Saxe-Coburg-Gotha; Olga Constantinovna as queen consort to King George I of the Hellenes; and Marie Pavlovna as wife of Grand Duke Vladimir. These four Romanov matriarchs were no less loving mothers to their own children and, for the most part, were mainstays in their offspring's lives.

And yet, Marie Feodorovna, Marie Alexandrovna, Olga Constantinovna, and Marie Pavlovna were far from perfect. Like lesser mortals, the women too had their share of shortcomings. Nonetheless, these Romanovs—an empress, a duchess, a queen, and a grand duchess—possessed an inordinate amount of strength that allowed them to overcome tremendous difficulties and hardships. A measure of the women's strength of character is evidenced by the manner in which they faced adversity. In times of crises and great misfortune, Marie Feodorovna, Marie Alexandrovna, Olga Constantinovna, and Marie Pavlovna never allowed tragedies, oftentimes unfathomable ones, to lead them to despair. Digging deep into their reserves of faith and hope, these matriarchs of imperial Russia, who had lived through splendor and revolution, and witnessed the destruction of their world and the murders of countless countrymen, left not only an indelible mark in the lives of those they touched, but also a legacy of grace under fire.

Epilogue

After the Dowager Empress Marie Feodorovna's death, her descendants sold Hvidovre. Grand Duchess Olga and her family lived on a farm near Copenhagen until 1948, when they were compelled to move away from Denmark. The Soviet Union had accused Olga of protecting Russians who had fought for the German army then defected in Denmark. After receiving threats, Olga and Nikolai Kulikovsky decided to leave with their family for Canada, which was in need of farmers. The family settled on a farm in Ontario, not far from Toronto. Olga continued to be a beacon for Russian émigrés and helped them as much as she could. As age and ill health plagued Olga and Nikolai, they sold the farm and moved to a small house in Cooksville, Ontario. Nikolai Kulikovsky died in 1958. Two years later, Grand Duchess Olga died in Toronto, in a modest apartment above a barbershop. She had gone to live her final days there in the home of Russian émigré friends. For the only child of the Empress Marie Feodorovna who had been "born in the purple," Olga Alexandrovna's death in the humblest of circumstances was a poignant ending to a life that had begun under such great splendor.

Empress Marie Feodorovna's other daughter, Xenia, faced similar circumstances to her sister. Xenia lived for some time in a house on the grounds of Windsor Great Park, thanks to her cousin King George V. Unlike Olga and Nikolai Kulikovsky, who remained devoted to each other to their dying days, Xenia and Sandro eventually separated. Sandro died in 1933 in France, having lived modestly in a small apartment. His daughter, Irina, and her husband, Felix Yussoupov, were with Sandro when he died. Xenia later moved to another modest home on the grounds of Hampton Court in England. She died in 1960, seven months before her sister Olga.

Irina and Felix Yussoupov lived largely in Paris. They started a couture business, which did not last long. The couple successfully sued MGM claiming that the 1932 film *Rasputin and the Empress* was an invasion of privacy. Years later, Irina and Felix sued CBS for a play the network televised on Rasputin's assassination. This time, the couple lost their case. Felix, who wrote his memoirs, died in 1967 and Irina in 1970.

Marie Feodorovna's daughter-in-law Natasha, Countess Brasova, lived in exile for a time in England with her daughter, Tata, and her son, George. Tragically, George was killed in a car accident in 1931. A penniless Natasha died in 1952 in a charity hospital in Paris.

Princess Paley, who was the widow of Grand Duke Paul and sister-in-law of Marie Feodorovna, Marie Alexandrovna and Miechen, managed to leave Russia and died in exile.

Queen Olga's Russian grandchildren Grand Duke Dmitri and Grand Duchess Marie also lived in exile. Grand Duke Dmitri married an American, Audrey Emery, in 1927. The marriage ended after ten years. Their only child, Paul Ilyinsky, served as mayor of Palm Beach, Florida, from 1993 until 2000. Grand Duke Dmitri died in 1942. Grand Duchess Marie lived in Europe, America, and Argentina and died in 1958.

Queen Olga's sister-in-law Mavra, widow of K.R., escaped Russia with her four surviving children. Of Mavra's nine children, three were murdered by the Bolsheviks. Mavra died in exile in 1927. Her daughter and Queen Olga's niece, the widowed Princess Tatiana, remarried in 1921 and was widowed three months later. Tatiana later became a nun and lived in Jerusalem, where she oversaw the Russian convent located on the Mount of Olives.

The Duchess of Coburg's daughter Queen Marie of Romania—Missy—became a widow in 1927 when King Ferdinand I died. He was succeeded by his five-year-old grandson, Prince Michael. Michael's father, Carol, had previously renounced the throne as heir in 1925. Queen Marie and her son, Carol, had a contentious relationship that lasted until the queen's death in 1938. Carol and his wife, Helen, Queen Olga's granddaughter, were divorced in 1928. Carol had by then begun his notorious liaison with Magda Lupescu, whom he eventually married. In 1930, Carol returned to Romania and effectively usurped the throne from his son, Michael. In 1940, Marie Alexandrovna's great-grandson Michael was reinstalled as king. He was forced to abdicate by the Communists in 1947 and has largely lived in exile.

Marie Alexandrovna's second daughter, Ducky, and Miechen's son, Kyril, lived in exile in Saint-Briac, France. Ducky supported Kyril who had hoped for some kind of restoration of the monarchy with himself as head. Ducky died in 1936 and Kyril in 1938. Their son, Vladimir, born in exile in 1917, continued to be the claimant to the imperial crown. The Duchess of Coburg's third daughter, Sandra, lived a relatively obscure life in Germany. She died in 1942, having joined the Nazi party. Marie Alexandrovna's fourth daughter, Bee, settled with her husband, Ali, in Spain. Their second son, Alonso, was killed during the Spanish Civil War. Bee died in 1966 and Ali in 1975.

Miechen's other sons, Boris and Andrei, stayed married to their respective wives, Zenaida Rachevskaya and Mathilde Kschessinska. Boris and Zenaida lived in France, where he died in 1943. Andrei and Mathilde lived in Paris along with Vova. Mathilde opened a ballet school in the city and published her autobiography. Boris died in 1943, Andrei in 1956, and Mathilde in 1971, aged ninety-nine.

Miechen's daughter, Elena, and Queen Olga's son, Prince Nicholas, also lived for a time in France, where Elena helped Russian émigrés. Their youngest daughter, Marina, became King George V's daughter-in-law when she married George, Duke of Kent, in 1934. Elena died in 1957 and Nicholas in 1938. Queen Olga's daughter Marie died in Greece in 1940. Her brother Andrew and his wife, Alice, eventually separated. Their only son, Prince Philip, married King George V's granddaughter Elizabeth in 1947. In 1952, she succeeded her father, King George VI, and became Queen Elizabeth II.

Queen Olga's youngest son, Christopher, died in 1940, having married as his second wife Princess Françoise of Orléans in 1929. Queen Olga's daughter-in-law Queen Sophie died in 1932. Her body was taken to the crypt of the Russian church in Florence to rest alongside those of King Constantine I and Queen Olga. In 1936, the bodies were returned to Greece. After a funeral service in Athens, Queen Olga's remains and those of her son and daughter-in-law were laid in their final resting place at Tatoi.

Throughout the twentieth century, the Greek monarchy's fortunes continued to fluctuate. In 1935, the monarchy was restored and Queen Olga's grandson King George II reigned again until his death in 1947. He and his wife, Elisabetha, the Duchess of Coburg's granddaughter, divorced in 1935. George II's brother, Paul I, succeeded him in 1947 and reigned until he died in 1964. His son and successor, Constantine II (Queen Olga's great-grandson), was forced into exile in 1967 after a failed attempt at a counter coup. Greece was officially declared a republic in 1974.

In Russia, renewed interest in the Romanovs after the fall of the Soviet Union has been growing. The bones of Tsar Nicholas II, Tsarina Alexandra, and their children were exhumed in 1991. A state funeral was held for the family in 1998 and their remains are now buried in the Cathedral of Sts. Peter and Paul. On the site of the murders in Ekaterinburg, the Cathedral on the Blood was built and consecrated in 2003 in memory of Nicholas and Alexandra and their children, who have been canonized as saints by the Russian Orthodox Church. One of the most dramatic events to take place was the reburial in the Cathedral of Sts. Peter and Paul of the remains of the Empress Marie Feodorovna in 2006. It was the latest astonishing event to take place in Russia in the ongoing rehabilitation of the Romanov dynasty.

The Grand Duchess Marie Pavlovna also made news around the world with the surprising revelation in January 2009 that a number of valuable items belonging to her had recently been found in the government archives of Sweden's foreign ministry in Stockholm. The stunning find—in two old pillowcases belonging to Miechen—consisted of sixty exquisite jeweled cuff links and cigarette cases made by the Swedish court jeweler Bolin and the famed Russian imperial jeweler Fabergé. It is believed that Bertie Stopford had spirited the items from the Vladimir Palace. The items were deposited at the Swedish Legation in Petrograd in November 1918 and then made their way to Sweden. It was only in 2008 that they were discovered when the Swedish foreign ministry moved its archives. The items were returned to Miechen's descendants and placed on auction on November 30, 2009, by Sotheby's. The sale, entitled, "Romanov Heirlooms: The Lost Inheritance of the Grand Duchess Maria Pavlovna," elicited much excitement. The items brought in £7.1 million (or $11.8 million), seven times above the estimate. Every lot sold and all but one sold for more than their presale high estimates.

An exquisite sapphire and diamond brooch and earrings set brought in $478,215, over three times its highest estimate. The Sotheby's auction also broke records. A record was set when a jeweled Fabergé cigarette case in four-color gold sold for £612,000, or $1 million, including the premium. This amounted to six times its presale estimate. The tenth wedding anniversary pair of Fabergé gold cuff links from Miechen's collection estimated to sell for £3,000 to £5,000, sold for an astonishing £103,250, nearly double the previous record sold at auction for a pair of cuff links. The top-selling item was the twenty-fifth wedding anniversary Fabergé jeweled cigarette case created for the Grand Duchess Marie Pavlovna, which sold for £612,250, twelve times its presale value. This shattered the previous record for a Fabergé cigarette case sold at auction by nearly £180,000. Even one of the pillow cases in which the objects were smuggled out of Russia sold for nearly $10,000 (its estimate was in the $330 range).

Much as the frenzied bidding from all corners of the globe was attached to the exquisite craftsmanship found in the works of the jewelers Bolin and Fabergé, it was the provenance of these items and the history of their journey from the Vladimir Palace in revolutionary Russia to the London premises of Sotheby's via Sweden, where the items lay forgotten for nine decades, that added incalculable luster to the already impressive objects and sent prices skyrocketing.

The fierce competition to acquire these items that once belonged to Grand Duchess Marie Pavlovna illustrates the enduring fascination with the Romanovs and their lost world—a world that Marie Pavlovna and her contemporaries, Marie Feodorovna, Olga Constantinovna, and Marie Alexandrovna, were very much a part of. Countess Marguerite Cassini had been correct in her assertion that there was much in that world that was fast becoming legend. The Sotheby's auction, "Romanov Heirlooms: The Lost Inheritance of the Grand Duchess Maria Pavlovna," held in November 2009, has underscored in a spectacular manner the extent that legend has come to be.

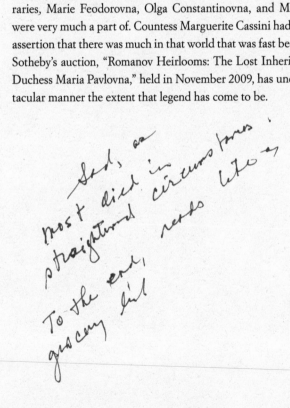

Notes

INTRODUCTION

1. Countess Marguerite Cassini, *Never a Dull Moment: A Toast to the Past by One Who Knew the Best and Worst of It* (New York: Harper & Brothers Publishers, 1956), p. 3.

I. A SPLENDID IMPERIAL COURT

1. Robert K. Massie, *Peter the Great: His Life and World* (New York: Alfred A. Knopf, 1980), p. 9.
2. Charles Lowe, *Alexander III of Russia* (New York: Macmillan and Co., 1895), p. 65.
3. George Augustus Sala, *The Life and Adventures of George Augustus Sala, Volume II* (New York: Charles Scribner's Sons, 1896), p. 329.
4. Mary King Waddington, "At the Coronation of the Czar Alexander III: Letters of the French Ambassadress," in *Scribner's Magazine*, Vol. XXXIII, March 1903, No. 3, p. 305.
5. Mrs. Frederic Chevenix Trench, "Moscow and the Coronation of the Czar," in Charlotte Yonge, ed., *The Monthly Packet of Readings for Members of the English Church*, Third Series, Volume VI, Parts XXXI to XXXVI (July–December, 1883), p. 563.
6. *Ibid.*
7. *Ibid.*
8. Waddington, "At the Coronation of the Czar Alexander III," pp. 302, 306.
9. *Ibid.*, p. 300.
10. Trench, "Moscow and the Coronation of the Czar," in *The Monthly Packet*, p. 564.
11. Vladimir Poliakoff, *Mother Dear: The Empress Marie of Russia and Her Times* (New York: D. Appleton and Company, 1926), pp. 169–170.
12. Trench, "Moscow and the Coronation of the Czar," in *The Monthly Packet*, p. 567.
13. Mary Grace Thornton, "The Crowning of a Czar: Journal of an Eye-Witness of the Coronation of Alexander III," in *The Century Magazine*, Vol. LII, May 1896, No. 1, p. 20.
14. Richard S. Wortman, *Scenarios of Power: Myth and Ceremony in Russian Monarchy: From Alexander II to the Abdication of Nicholas II, Volume Two*. Princeton, NJ: Princeton University Press, 2000), p. 220.

15. A. D. Barkhatova and T. V. Burkova, eds., *The Danish Princess Marie Sophie Friederike Dagmar—the Russian Empress Maria Fiodorovna.*, transl. by V. A. Fateyev (St. Petersburg: Alibris Publishers, 2006), p. 77.

16. Queen Marie of Roumania, *The Story of My Life, Volume I* (London: Cassell and Company, Ltd., 1934), p. 98.

17. *Ibid.*, p. 99.

18. Grand Duke Alexander, *Once a Grand Duke* (Garden City, NY: Garden City Publishing Company, Inc., 1932), p. 77.

19. Wortman, *Scenarios of Power, Volume Two*, p. 231.

20. Barkhatova and Burkova, *The Danish Princess—the Russian Empress*, p. 28.

21. Anna Feodorovna Tiutcheva, *Pri Dvore Dvukh Imperatorov. Vospominaniya, Dnevnik, 1853–1882* (Cambridge, UK: Oriental Research Printer, 1975), p. 126.

22. Marie, *The Story of My Life, Volume I*, pp. 99–100.

2. THE EARLY YEARS

1. W. Bruce Lincoln, *The Romanovs: Autocrats of All the Russias* (New York: The Dial Press, 1981), p. 17.

2. E. M. Almedingen, *The Emperor Alexander II* (London: The Bodley Head, 1962), p. 65.

3. Christopher Hibbert, *Queen Victoria: A Personal History* (New York: Basic Books, 2000), p. 103.

4. Edward Dicey, *A Month in Russia During the Marriage of the Czarevitch* (London: Macmillan and Co., 1867), p. 216.

5. E. A. Brayley Hodgetts, *The Court of Russia in the Nineteenth Century, Volume II* (London: Methuen & Co., 1908), pp. 57–58.

6. Tiutcheva, *Pri Dvore Dvukh Imperatorov*, p. 124.

7. *Ibid.*, p. 191.

8. Marquis de Custine, *Empire of the Czar: A Journey Through Eternal Russia* (New York: Doubleday, 1989), p. 121.

9. Nellie Ryan, *My Years at the Austrian Court* (London: John Lane, 1915), pp. 181–182.

10. Maturin M. Ballou, *Due North, or Glimpses of Scandinavia and Russia* (Boston: Houghton, Mifflin and Co., 1886), pp. 206–207.

11. James H. Bater, "Between Old and New: St. Petersburg in the Late Imperial Era," in Micheal Hamm, ed., *The City in Late Imperial Russia* (Bloomington, IN: Indiana University Press, 1986), p. 44.

12. Tiutcheva, *Pri Dvore Dvukh Imperatorov*, p. 110.

13. John van der Kiste and Bee Jordaan, *Dearest Affie: Alfred, Duke of Edinburgh, Queen Victoria's Second Son* (Stroud, Gloucestershire: Alan Sutton Publishing Ltd., 1995), p. 82.

14. Tiutcheva, *Pri Dvore Dvukh Imperatorov*, p. 171.

15. *Ibid.*

16. *Ibid.*, p. 41

17. A. N. Wilson, *Tolstoy: A Biography* (New York: W. W. Norton & Company, Inc., 1988), p. 148.

18. *Ibid.*

19. Count Paul Vassili pseudonym of Princess Catherine Radziwill, *Behind the Veil at the Russian Court* (New York: John Lane Company, 1914), p. 129.

20. Tiutcheva, *Pri Dvore Dvukh Imperatorov*, p. 161.

21. *Ibid.*, p. 156.

22. *Ibid.*, p. 157.

23. *Ibid.*, p. 171.

24. *Ibid.*, p. 192.

25. Princess Marie zu Erbach-Schönberg, *Reminiscences* (London: George Allen & Unwin, Ltd., 1925), p. 43.

26. Wortman, *Scenarios of Power, Volume Two,* p. 115.

27. "The Grand Duchess Marie," in *The Illustrated Review: Literature, the Drama, Music, Art, Current Events,* January 21, 1874.

28. Vassili, *Behind the Veil at the Russian Court,* p. 30.

29. *Ibid.*, p. 23

30. Countess Marie Kleinmichel, *Memories of a Shipwrecked World: Being the Memoirs of Countess Kleinmichel,* transl. by Vivian Le Grand (New York: Brentano's, 1923), p. 49.

31. Crown Princess Cecilie, *The Memoirs of Crown Princess Cecilie,* transl. by Emile Burns (London: Victor Gollancz, Ltd., 1931), p. 152.

32. Suzanne Massie, *Pavlovsk: The Life of a Russian Palace* (London: Hodder & Stoughton, 1990), pp. 3–4.

33. Ioulia N. Karolou, *Olga, Queen of the Greeks, August 22, 1851–June 19, 1926* (Athens: Hestia, 1934), chapter 1.

34. Kleinmichel, *Memories of a Shipwrecked World,* p. 19.

35. Lord Augustus Loftus, *Diplomatic Reminiscences of Lord Augustus Loftus 1837–1862, Volume II* (London: Cassell & Company, Ltd., 1892), p. 172.

36. *Ibid.*

37. *Ibid.*

38. Cecilie, *Memoirs,* p. 31.

39. *Ibid.*, p. 25.

40. Alexander Polunov, *Russia in the Nineteenth Century: Autocracy, Reform, and Social Change, 1814–1914,* ed. by Thomas C. Owen and Larissa G. Zakharova, transl. by Marshall S. Shatz (Armonk, NY: M. E. Sharpe, 2005), p. 90.

41. Larissa Zakharova, "Autocracy and the Reforms of 1861–1874 in Russia: Choosing Paths of Development," transl. by Daniel Field, in Ben Eklof, John Bushnell and Larissa Zakharova, eds., *Russia's Great Reforms, 1855–1881* (Bloomington, IN: Indiana University Press, 1994), p. 20.

42. Polunov, *Russia in the Nineteenth Century,* p. 92.

43. E. M. Almedingen, *The Romanovs: Three Centuries of an Ill-Fated Dynasty* (New York: Holt, Rinehart and Winston, 1966), p. 256.

44. *Ibid.*, p. 257.

45. W. Bruce Lincoln, *The Great Reforms: Autocracy, Bureaucracy, and the Politics of Change in Imperial Russia* (Dekalb, IL: Northern Illinois University Press, 1990), p. 62.

46. *Ibid.*, p. 143.

47. Mark Twain, *The Innocents Abroad, or The New Pilgrim's Progress: Being Some Account of the Steamship "Quaker City's" Pleasure Excursion to Europe and the Holy Land, Volume II* (New York: Harper & Brothers Publishers, 1903), p. 124.

48. *Ibid.*, p. 125.

49. *Ibid.*, p. 126.

50. "Some Account of the City of Copenhagen," *The Saturday Magazine,* 10: 298 (1837: February), no. 299 supplement, p. 77.

51. Walburga, Lady Paget, *Scenes and Memories* (New York: Charles Scribner's Sons, 1912), p. 85.

52. E. E. P. Tisdall, *Marie Fedorovna, Empress of Russia* (New York: The John Day Company, 1957), p. 23.

53. Queen Victoria, *Regina v. Palmerston: The Correspondence Between Queen Victoria and Her Foreign and Prime Minister, 1837–1865*. Edited by Brian Connell (London: Evans Bros., 1962), p. 333. In actuality, Prince Alfred was not yet the reigning Duke of Saxe-Coburg-Gotha, but Palmerston's point here was to emphasize a potential conflict of interest that could arise should Alfred be King of Greece and later also succeed to the dukedom of Saxe-Coburg-Gotha.

54. "The Past Week," in *The London Review of Politics, Society, Literature, Art, and Science*, 6: 136 (1863: February), p. 145.

55. "The Past Week," in *The London Review of Politics, Society, Literature, Art, and Science*, 6: 144 (1863: April), p. 359.

56. Queen Victoria to Victoria, the Crown Princess of Prussia, March 25, 1863, in Roger Fulford, ed., *Dearest Mama: Letters Between Queen Victoria and the Crown Princess of Prussia 1861–1864* (London: Evans Brothers Ltd., 1968), pp. 186–187.

57. Hans Roger Madol, *Christian IX: Compiled from Unpublished Documents and Memoirs*, transl. from the German and Danish by E. O. Lorimer (London: Collins Publishers, 1939), p. 140.

58. *Ibid.*, p. 144.

59. *Ibid.*, p. 143.

60. From the Mountain, "Prince Alfred's Romance," in *Once a Week*, 8: 187 (1863: January), p. 120.

3. BRIDAL TRAVAILS

1. Zoya Belyakova, *Grand Duke Alexei Alexandrovich, Pros and Cons* (St. Petersburg: Logos Publishing House, 2004), p. 64.

2. Queen Victoria to Victoria, the Crown Princess of Prussia, April 15, 1862, in Fulford, *Dearest Mama*, p. 54.

3. Queen Victoria to Victoria, the Crown Princess of Prussia, April 19, 1862, in *Ibid.*, p. 55.

4. Queen Victoria to Victoria, the Crown Princess of Prussia, April 19, 1862, in *Ibid.*, p. 56.

5. Queen Victoria to Victoria, the Crown Princess of Prussia, March 25, 1863, in *Ibid.*, p. 186.

6. Princess Mary Adelaide of Cambridge, letter to a friend, September 1861, in C. Kinloch Cooke, *A Memoir of Her Royal Highness Princess Mary Adelaide, Duchess of Teck: Based on Her Private Diaries and Letters, Volume I* (New York: Charles Scribner's Sons, 1900), p. 369.

7. Paget, *Scenes and Memories*, p. 85.

8. Tsarevich Nicholas to Tsarina Marie, August 24/September 5, 1864, in Alia Barkovetz, "Nixa, Minny, and Sacha," in *Maria Feodorovna, Empress of Russia: An Exhibition About the Danish Princess Who Became Empress of Russia* (Copenhagen: Christiansborg Palace,1997), p. 74.

9. Edvard Radzinsky, *Alexander II: The Last Great Tsar*, transl. by Antonina W. Bouis (New York: Free Press, 2005), p. 166.

10. John van der Kiste, *The Romanovs 1818–1959: Alexander II of Russia and His Family* (Stroud, UK: Sutton Publishing, 1999), p. 41.

11. Coryne Hall, *Little Mother of Russia: A Biography of Empress Marie Feodorovna* (London: Shepheard-Walwyn Publishers, Ltd., 1999).

12. Belyakova, *Grand Duke Alexei Alexandrovitch*, pp. 64–65.

13. Princess Alice to Queen Victoria, April 18, 1865, in Alice, Grand Duchess of Hesse and Helena Victoria, Princess Christian of Schleswig-Holstein, *Alice, Grand Duchess of Hesse, Princess of Great Britain and Ireland: Biographical Sketch and Letters* (New York: G. P. Putnam's Sons, 1885), p. 101.

14. Diary entry of N. P. Litvinov, April 10, 1865, in "Diary" chapter, in B. V. Ananich, R. S. Ganelin, M. A. Gordin, V. G. Chernuha, eds., *Alexander III: Memoirs, Diaries and Letters* from the series *Statesmen of Russia in the Eyes of Their Contemporaries* (St. Petersburg: Pushkinsky Fund, 2001), p. 54.

15. *Ibid.*, p. 55.

16. *Ibid.*, pp. 55–56.

17. D. S. Arsenyev notes in *Ibid.*, p. 60.

18. *Ibid.*, p. 57.

19. Princess Mary Adelaide of Cambridge to Mrs. Bridges Taylor, April 27, 1865, in Kinloch Cooke, *A Memoir of Her Royal Highness Princess Mary Adelaide,* p. 412.

20. Queen Victoria to Victoria, Crown Princess of Prussia, April 26, 1865, in Roger Fulford, ed., *Your Dear Letter: Private Correspondence of Queen Victoria and the Crown Princess of Prussia 1865–1871* (New York: Charles Scribner's Sons, 1971), p. 23.

21. Princess Dagmar of Denmark to King Christian IX of Denmark, April 26, 1865, in Preben Ulstrup, "Maria Feodorovna Through Diaries and Personal Letters" in *Maria Feodorovna, Empress of Russia.*

22. Lowe, *Alexander III*, p. 20.

23. *Ibid.*, p. 19.

24. Wortman, *Scenarios of Power, Volume Two*, p. 109.

25. Queen Louise of Denmark to Tsarina Marie of Russia, July 10, 1865, in Barkovetz, "Nixa, Minny, and Sacha," in *Maria Feodorovna, Empress of Russia*, p. 79.

26. Kleinmichel, *Memories of a Shipwrecked World*, p. 49.

27. Diary entry of Tsarevich Alexander Alexandrovich, May 15/27, 1865, in Barkovetz, "Nixa, Minny, and Sacha," in *Maria Feodorovna, Empress of Russia*, p. 84

28. Princess Marie of Battenberg, diary entry of May 4, 1865, in Erbach-Schönberg, *Reminiscences*, p. 57.

29. Diary entry of Tsarevich Alexander Alexandrovich, June 25/July 7, 1865, in *Ibid.*, p. 82.

30. Diary entry of Tsarevich Alexander Alexandrovich, May 19/31, 1866, in *Ibid.*, p. 86.

31. Barkhatova and Burkova, *The Danish Princess—the Russian Empress Maria Fiodorovna*, p. 12.

32. Hans Christian Andersen, *The Story of My Life* (New York: Hurd and Houghton, 1871), p. 542.

33. Diary entry of S. D. Sheremetyev, in Ananich, Ganelin, Gordin, Chernuha, *Alexander III*, pp. 314–315.

34. H. C. Romanoff, *Sketches of the Rites and Customs of the Greco-Russian Church* (London: Rivingtons, 1869), p. 305.

35. *Ibid.*, p. 306.

36. *Ibid.*, p. 310.

37. *Ibid.*, p. 314.
38. Tisdall, *Marie Feodorovna*, p. 46.
39. *Ibid.*, p. 46.
40. Barkhatova and Burkova, *The Danish Princess—the Russian Empress*, p. 22.
41. Diary entry of Tsarevich Alexander, November 26/December 8, 1866, in *Maria Feodorovna, the Danish Princess*, p. 86.
42. Dicey, *A Month in Russia*, p. 177.
43. *Ibid.*, p. 178.
44. *Ibid.*, p. 218.
45. *Ibid.*, p. 219.
46. *Ibid.*, p. 220.
47. Karoulou, *Olga, Queen of the Greeks*, chapter 1.
48. D. B. Grishin, *The Grand Duke's Tragic Destiny* (Moscow: Veche, 2006), p. 37.
49. E.E.P. Tisdall, *Royal Destiny: The Royal Hellenic Cousins* (London: Stanley Paul and Co., Ltd., 1955), p. 31.
50. Yulia V. Kudrina, "Our Beloved Empress," in *Maria Feodorovna, Empress of Russia: An Exhibition About the Danish Princess Who Became Empress of Russia* (Copenhagen: Christiansborg Palace, 1997), p. 44.
51. John van der Kiste, *Kings of the Hellenes: The Greek Kings 1863–1974* (Stroud, UK: Sutton Publishing, 1999), p. 25.
52. Grand Duchess George of Russia, *A Romanov Diary: The Autobiography of H. I. & R. H. Grand Duchess George* (New York: Atlantic International Publications, 1988), p.1.
53. Lord Charles Beresford, *The Memoirs of Lord Charles Beresford, Volume I* (Boston: Little, Brown & Company, 1914), p. 74.
54. Queen Victoria to Victoria, Crown Princess of Prussia, September 4, 1866, in Fulford, *Your Dear Letter*, p. 94.
55. Victoria, Crown Princess of Prussia to Queen Victoria, April 28, 1866 in Fulford, *Ibid.*, p. 71.
56. Queen Victoria to Victoria, Crown Princess of Prussia, August 7, 1867, in Fulford, *Ibid.*, p. 147.
57. John van der Kiste, *Princess Victoria Melita: Grand Duchess Cyril of Russia 1876–1936* (Stroud, UK: Alan Sutton Publishing, Ltd., 1991), p. 8.
58. Queen Sophie of the Netherlands to Mary, Countess of Derby, July 12, 1873, in Mary Catherine, Countess of Derby, *A Great Lady's Friendships: Letters to Mary, Marchioness of Salisbury, Countess of Derby, 1862–1890* (London: Macmillan and Co., Ltd, 1933), p. 376.
59. Sir Horace Rumbold, *Recollections of a Diplomatist, Volume II* (London: Edward Arnold, 1903), p. 290.
60. Eugene Schuyler, *Eugene Schuyler: Selected Essays* (New York: Charles Scribner's Sons, 1901), pp. 36–37.
61. Merritt Abrash, "A Curious Royal Romance: The Queen's Son and the Tsar's Daughter," in *The Slavonic and East European Review*, No. 109 (July 1969), p. 390.
62. *Ibid.*, p. 391.
63. Queen Victoria to Victoria, Crown Princess of Prussia, August 10, 1872, in Roger Fulford, ed., *Darling Child: Private Correspondence of Queen Victoria and the Crown Princess of Prussia 1871–1878* (London: Evans Brothers, Ltd., 1976), p. 57.
64. Abrash, "A Curious Royal Romance," p. 392.
65. *Ibid.*, p. 391.

66. van der Kiste and Jordaan, *Dearest Affie*, p. 86.

67. Count Egon Corti, *The Downfall of Three Dynasties*, transl. from the German by L. Marie Sieveking and Ian F. D. Morrow (Freeport, NY: Books for Libraries Press, 1970), p. 212.

68. Queen Victoria to Victoria, Crown Princess of Prussia, April 12, 1873, in Fulford, *Darling Child*, p. 85.

4. MARIE ALEXANDROVNA AND MIECHEN

1. Millicent Garrett Fawcett, *Life of Her Majesty Queen Victoria* (Boston: Roberts Brothers, 1895), p. 233.

2. Princess Alice to Queen Victoria, April 19, 1873, in *Alice, Princess of Great Britain, Grand Duchess of Hesse: Letters to Her Majesty the Queen* (London: John Murray, 1897), p. 223.

3. van der Kiste and Jordaan, *Dearest Affie*, p. 88.

4. Georgina Battiscombe, *Queen Alexandra* (Boston: Houghton Mifflin, Company, 1969), p. 128.

5. Barkhatova and Burkova, *The Danish Princess—the Russian Empress*, p. 69.

6. Victoria, Crown Princess of Prussia to Queen Victoria, October 2, 1867, in Fulford, *Your Dear Letter*, p. 153.

7. Victoria, Crown Princess of Prussia, to Queen Victoria, April 1, 1868, in *Ibid.*, p. 182.

8. Alia Barkovetz, "The Documentary Legacy of the Empress Maria Feodorovna," in *Maria Feodorovna, Empress of Russia*, p. 102.

9. Baroness Rahden to I. U. Samarin, in I. U. Samarin, August 10/22, 1869, in Terence Scully, Helen Swediuk-Cheyne and Loren Calder, eds. *The Corespondence of IU Samarin and Baroness Rahden (1861–1876)*. (Waterloo, Ontario: Wilfrid Laurier University Press, 1974), p. 125.

10. Jorma and Paivi Tuomi-Nikula, *Emperors on Vacation in Finland* (St. Petersburg: Kolo Publishing House, 2003), p. 63.

11. Sir Horace Rumbold, *Recollections of a Diplomatist, Volume I* (London: Edward Arnold, 1903), p. 220.

12. M.E.W. Sherwood, *Royal Girls and Royal Courts* (Boston: D. Lothrop Company, 1887), p. 158.

13. Corti, *Downfall of Three Dynasties*, p. 214.

14. Grand Duke Serge, *Grand Duke Serge Alexandrovich Romanov, Book 1, 1857–1877* (Moscow: Novospassky Monastery, 2006), p. 233.

15. *Ibid.*, p. 234.

16. Queen Victoria, *The Letters of Queen Victoria. Second Series: A Selection from Her Majesty's Correspondence and Journal Between the Years 1862 and 1878. Published by Authority of His Majesty the King. Volume II: 1870–1878,* ed. by Earle Buckle (London: John Murray, 1926), p. 261.

17. *Ibid.*, p. 262.

18. Abrash, "A Curious Romance," p. 398.

19. Queen Victoria to Victoria, Crown Princess of Prussia, July 12, 1873, in Fulford, *Darling Child*, pp. 101–102.

20. Queen Victoria to Victoria, Crown Princess of Prussia, July 16, 1873, in *Ibid.*, p. 102.

21. Queen Victoria to Empress Augusta, July 16, 1873, in Hector Bolitho, ed. *Further Letters of Queen Victoria: From the Archives of the House of Brandenburg-Prussia*, transl. from the German by Mrs. J. Pudney and Lord Sudney (London: Thornton Butterworth, Ltd., 1938), p. 198.

22. E. V. Khorvatova, *Marie Feodorovna: The Fate of the Empress* (Moscow: Ast-Press, 2006), p. 55.

23. Elizabeth Longford, *Queen Victoria: Born to Succeed* (New York: Harper & Row, Publishers, 1964), pp. 394–395.

24. Queen Sophie of the Netherlands to Mary, Countess of Derby, April 14, 1873, in Derby, *A Great Lady's Friendship*, p. 371.

25. Queen Sophie of the Netherlands to Mary, Countess of Derby, December 22, 1873 in *Ibid.*, p. 383.

26. Extract from Queen Victoria's Journal, 23rd January 1874 in Buckle, *The Letters of Queen Victoria, Second Series, Volume II*, p. 310.

27. *The Graphic*, January 24, 1874.

28. The "*l.*" symbol here represents pounds sterling.

29. "The Duke of Edinburgh's Marriage Treaty," in *The London Reader: of Literature, Science, Art and General Information*, 22: 571 (1874: April), p. 556.

30. Queen Victoria to Victoria, Crown Princess of Prussia, December 24, 1873, in Fulford, *Darling Child*, pp. 120–121.

31. Queen Victoria to Victoria, Crown Princess of Prussia, December 27, 1873, in *Ibid.*, p. 121.

32. Dean of Windsor and Hector Bolitho, eds., *Later Letters of Lady Augusta Stanley 1864–1876* (London: Jonathan Cape, 1929), pp. 204–205.

33. *Ibid.*, p. 215.

34. *Ibid.*, p. 205.

35. Lord Augustus Loftus, *Diplomatic Reminiscences of Lord Augustus Loftus 1862–1879, Volume II* (London: Cassell & Company, Ltd.), 1894.

36. *Ibid.*, pp. 87–88.

37. Serge, *Grand Duke Sergei Alexandrovich Romanov, Book 1*, p. 237.

38. F. R. Grahame, *Life of Alexander II: Emperor of All the Russias* (London: W. H. Allen, 1883), p. 225.

39. Extract from Queen Victoria's Journal, in Buckle, *The Letters of Queen Victoria, Second Series, volume II*, pp. 328–329.

40. Hope Dyson and Charles Tennyson, eds., *Dear and Honoured Lady: The Correspondence Between Queen Victoria and Alfred Tennyson* (Rutherford, NJ: Fairleigh Dickinson University Press, 1969), pp. 93–94.

41. Frederick Townsend Martin, *Things I Remember* (New York: John Lane and Co., 1913), p. 101.

42. "State Entry into London of Her Majesty the Queen and Their Royal Highnesses the Duke and Duchess of Edinburgh," in *The Graphic: An Illustrated Weekly Newspaper*, Vol. IX, No. 225, March 21, 1874.

43. David Chavchavadze, *The Grand Dukes* (New York: Atlantic International Publications, 1990), p. 113.

44. M. N. Velichenko and G. A. Mirolyubova, *The Palace of Grand Duke Vladimir Alexandrovich* (St. Petersburg: Almaz Publishing House, 1997), pp. 74–75.

45. Charlotte Zeepvat, *Romanov Autumn: Stories from the Last Century of Imperial Russia* (Stroud, UK: Sutton Publishing, 2001), p. 94.

46. *Ibid.*, p. 95.

47. Hodgetts, *The Court of Russia of Russia in the Nineteenth Century, Volume II*, p. 149.

48. Velichenko, Mirolyubova, *The Palace of Grand Duke Vladimir*, p. 71.

49. *Ibid.*, p. 76.

50. Charlotte Zeepvat, *The Camera and the Tsars: A Romanov Family Album* (Stroud, UK: Sutton Publishing, 2004), p. 45.

51. *New York Times*, October 11, 1874.

52. John Curtis Perry and Constantine Pleshakov, *The Flight of the Romanovs: A Family Saga* (New York: Basic Books, 1999), p. 38.

53. Princess Alice to Queen Victoria, May 4, 1874, in Princess Alice, *Alice—Letters to Her Majesty the Queen*, p. 328.

54. *New York Times*, October 11, 1874.

55. Lord Augustus Loftus to Queen Victoria, September 16, 1874, in Queen Victoria, *The Papers of Queen Victoria on Foreign Affairs: Files from the Royal Archives, Windsor Castle. Part 1. Russia and Eastern Europe, 1846–1900*. Edited by Kenneth Bourne (Bethesda, MD: University Publications of America, 1990).

56. Eugene Schuyler to U.S. Secretary of State, Hamilton Fish, August 29, 1874, No. 534, in United States, Department of State, *Papers Relating to the Foreign Relations of the United States, Transmitted to Congress, with the Annual Message of the President, December 7, 1874* (Washington: Government Printing Office, 1874), p. 843.

57. Thomas W. Knox, "A Gala Night in Russia" in *Harper's New Monthly Magazine*, No. CCXCVI, January 1875, Vol. L, p. 266.

58. *Ibid.*, p. 267.

59. *Ibid.*, p. 269.

60. *Ibid.*, p. 270.

5. ROSSIISKAIA IMPERIIA

1. Meriel Buchanan, *Recollections of Imperial Russia* (New York: George H. Doran Company, 1924), p. 9.

2. Dicey, *A Month in Russia*, p. 104.

3. Perry and Pleshakov, *The Flight of the Romanovs*, p. 11.

4. Dicey, *A Month in Russia*, pp. 174–175.

5. Cecilie, *Memoirs of Crown Princess Cecilie*, p. 158.

6. Hodgetts, *The Court of Russia in the Nineteenth Century, Volume II*, pp. 81–82.

7. W. Bruce Lincoln, *Between Heaven and Hell: The Story of a Thousand Years of Artistic Life in Russia* (New York: Viking, 1998), p. 109.

8. Dominic Lieven, "Russia as Empire," in Dominic Lieven, ed., *The Cambridge History of Russia, Vol. II, Imperial Russia, 1689–1917* (Cambridge: Cambridge University Press, 2006), p. 11.

9. Samuel Schmucker, *The Life and Reign of Nicholas the First, Emperor of Russia* (Philadelphia: John E. Potter and Company, 1856), p. 407.

10. Sacheverell Sitwell, *Valse des Fleurs: A Day in St. Petersburg and a Ball at the Winter Palace in 1868* (London: Faber and Faber, Ltd., n.d.), p. 63.

11. W. Bruce Lincoln, *Nicholes I: Emperor and Autocrat of All the Russias* (Bloomington, IN: Indiana University Press, 1978).

12. K. P. Pobyedonostseff, *Reflections of a Russian Statesman,* transl. from the Russian by Robert Crozier Long (London: Grant Richards, 1898), p. 62.

13. *Ibid.*, pp. 94–95.

14. Tisdall, *Marie Feodorovna*, p. 53.

15. Robert F. Byrnes, *Pobedonostsev: His Life and Thought* (Bloomington, IN: Indiana Unviersity Press, 1968), p. 75.

16. *Ibid.*, p. 75.
17. *Ibid.*, p. 75.
18. *Ibid.*, p. 76.
19. Theodore R. Weeks, "Managing Empire: Tsarist Nationalities Policy," in Lieven, *Cambridge History of Russia, Vol. II*, p. 27.
20. Dominic Lieven, *Empire: The Russian Empire and Its Rivals* (New Haven: Yale University Press, 2000), p. 237.
21. Ryan, *My Years at the Austrian Court*, p. 182.
22. Pobyedonostseff, *Reflections of a Russian Statesman*, p. 19.
23. John Bergamini, *The Tragic Dynasty: A History of the Romanovs* (New York: G. P. Putnam's Sons, 1969), p. 345.
24. Madol, *Christian IX*, pp. 205–206.
25. Abrash, "A Curious Romance," p. 400.
26. Tsarevna Marie Feodorovna to King Christian IX of Denmark, March 27/April 8, 1878, in Ulstrup, "Maria Feodorovna Through Diaries and Person Letters," in *Maria Feodorovna, Empress of Russia*, p. 132.
27. Bergamini, *The Tragic Dynasty*, p. 320.
28. Ivan Turgénieff, *Fathers and Sons: A Novel*, transl. from the Russian by Eugene Schuyler (London: Ward, Lock and Co., n.d.), p. 26.
29. Geoffrey Hosking, *Russia: People and Empire 1552–1917* (Cambridge, MA: Harvard University Press, 1997), p. 164.
30. *Ibid.*, p. 277.
31. *Ibid.*, p. 279.
32. Bergamini, *The Tragic Dynasty*, p. 320.
33. Lincoln, *The Romanovs*, p. 513.
34. *Ibid.*, p. 513.
35. Fyodor Dostoyevsky, *Crime and Punishment*, transl. by David McDuff (London: Penguin Books, 2003), p. 656.
36. Bergamini, *The Tragic Dynasty*, p. 339.
37. Hosking, *Russia: People and Empire 1552–1917*, p. 306
38. Serge Tomkeieff, "Russian Literature from Leo Tolstóy to the Present Date," in I. K. Shaknovski, *A Short History of Russian Literature* (London: Kegan Paul, Trench, Trubner & Co., Ltd., 1921), p. 138.
39. Lincoln, *The Romanovs*, p. 519.
40. *Ibid.*, p. 519.
41. Hosking, *Russia: People and Empire 1552–1917*, p. 308.
42. Robin Milner-Gulland, *The Russians* (Oxford: Blackwell Publishers, 1997), p. 133.
43. Dominic Lieven, "Russia as Empire," in Dominic Lieven, ed., *The Cambridge History of Russia,* p. 9.
44. Alexander Chubarov, *The Fragile Empire: A History of Imperial Russia* (New York: Continuum, 1999), p. 82.
45. *Ibid.*, p. 83.
46. van der Kiste, *The Romanovs*, p. 78.
47. Michael Karpovich, *Imperial Russia, 1801–1917* (New York: Henry Holt and Co., 1932), p. 47.
48. Virginia Cowles, *The Russian Dagger: Cold War in the Days of the Czars* (New York: Harper & Row, Publishers, 1969), p. 73.

49. Margaret Maxwell, *Narodniki Women: Russian Women Who Sacrificed Themselves for the Dream of Freedom* (Elmsford, NY: Pergamon Press, Inc., 1990), p. 31.

50. Richard Pipes, *The Russian Revolution* (New York: Alfred A. Knopf, 1991), p. 143.

51. Elizabeth Narishkin-Kurakin, *Under Three Tsars: The Memoirs of the Lady-in-Waiting, Elizabeth Narishkin-Kurakin*, ed. by René Fülöp-Miller, transl. from the German by Julia E. Loesser (New York: E.. Dutton & Co., Inc., 1931), p. 59.

52. Radzinsky, *Alexander II*, p. 179.

53. Almedingen, *Emperor Alexander II*, pp. 136–137.

54. Hodgetts, *The Court of Russia in the Nineteenth Century, Volume II*, p. 71.

55. *Ibid.*, p. 71.

56. *Ibid.*, p. 76.

57. Narishkin-Kurakin, *Under Three Tsars*, p. 57.

58. Cowles, *The Russian Dagger*, p. 72.

59. *Ibid.*, p. 22.

60. Victoria, Crown Princess of Prussia, to Queen Victoria, February 10, 1874, in Fulford, *Darling Child*, pp. 128–129.

6. A RUSSIAN IN QUEEN VICTORIA'S COURT

1. Victoria (b. 1819), was queen of the United Kingdom of Great Britain and Ireland from 1837 to 1901, and was proclaimed empress of India in 1876.

2. Diary entry of 7 May 1884, in Norman Rich and M. H. Fisher, eds., *The Holstein Papers: The Memoirs, Diaries and Correspondence of Friedrich von Holstein, 1837–1909*. Vol. II: *Diaries* (Cambridge: Cambridge University Press, 1957), p. 139.

3. Earl of Warwick and Brooke, *Memories of Sixty Years* (London: Cassell and Company, Ltd., 1917), pp. 45–46.

4. Lord Howard of Penrith, *Theatre of Life: Life Seen from the Pit 1863–1905* (London: Hodder and Stoughton, Ltd., 1935), p. 81.

5. William Boyd Carpenter, *Some Pages of My Life* (New York: Charles Scribner's Sons, 1911), p. 281.

6. Lytton Strachey, *Queen Victoria* (New York: Harcourt, Brace and Company, 1921), p. 389

7. Marie, *The Story of My Life, Volume I*, p. 75.

8. Hermann Eckardstein, *Ten Years at the Court of St. James's 1895–1905* (New York: E. P. Dutton & Co., 1922), p. 76.

9. Lord Frederic Hamilton, *The Vanished Pomps of Yesterday* (New York: George H. Doran Company, 1921), p. 116.

10. Michael John Sullivan, *A Fatal Passion: The Story of Victoria Melita, the Uncrowned Last Empress of Russia* (New York: Random House, 1997), pp. 15–16.

11. Corti, *Downfall of Three Dynasties*, p. 222.

12. *Ibid.*, pp. 243–244.

13. Queen Victoria to the Earl of Beaconsfield, December 13, 1877, in Buckle, *The Letters of Queen Victoria. Second Series: vol. II*.

14. Queen Victoria to Victoria, Crown Princess of Prussia, October 26, 1876, in Fulford, *Darling Child*, p. 229.

15. Queen Victoria to Victoria, Crown Princess of Prussia, July 11, 1877, in *Ibid.*, pp. 255–256.

16. Queen Victoria to Victoria, Crown Princess of Prussia, October 9, 1877, in *Ibid.*, p. 266.

17. Queen Victoria to Victoria, Crown Princess of Prussia, October 30, 1877, in *Ibid.*, pp. 268–269.

18. Queen Victoria to Victoria, Crown Princess of Prussia, March 9, 1874, in *Ibid.*, p. 132.

19. Queen Victoria to Victoria, Crown Princess of Prussia, March 12, 1874, in *Ibid.*

20. Lord Augustus Loftus to Queen Victoria, September 16, 1874, in Queen Victoria, *Papers of Queen Victoria on Foreign Affairs.*

21. Longford, *Queen Victoria,* p. 404.

22. *Ibid.,* p. 394.

23. Queen Sophie of the Netherlands to the Countess of Derby, May 6, 1874, in Derby, *A Great Lady's Friendships,* p. 394.

24. van der Kiste and Jordaan, *Dearest Affie,* p. 99.

25. Meriel Buchanan, *Queen Victoria's Relations* (London: Cassell & Co., Ltd., 1954), p. 115.

26. Extract from Queen Victoria's journal, May 13, 1874, in Buckle, *The Letters of Queen Victoria, Second Series, vol. II,* p. 337.

27. Extract from Queen Victoria's journal, May 14, 1874, in *Ibid.*

28. Extract from Queen Victoria's journal, May 14, 1874, in *Ibid.,* p. 338.

29. Anne Beale, "Three Glimpses at Royalty," in *Argosy: A Magazine of Tales, Travels, Essays, and Poems* 18 (1874: July), p. 60.

30. *Ibid.,* p. 60.

31. *Ibid.,* p. 61.

32. *The London Reader,* 23: (1874: May), p. 113.

33. Benjamin Disraeli to Anne, Lady Chesterfield, March 17, 1874, in William Flavelle Monypenny and George Earle Buckle, *The Life of Benjamin Disraeli, Earl of Beaconsfield, Volume II, 1860–1881* (London: John Murray, 1929), p. 643.

34. *Ibid.,* p. 684.

35. John Cornforth, *Queen Elizabeth the Queen Mother at Clarence House* (London: Michael Joseph, 1996), p. 12.

36. Marie, *The Story of My Life, Volume I,* p. 17.

37. *Ibid.,* p. 16.

38. *Ibid.,* p. 17.

39. Rumbold, *Recollections of Diplomatist, Volume I,* p. 220.

40. Queen Sophie of the Netherlands to the Countess of Derby, March 2, 1874, in Derby, *A Great Lady's Friendships,* p. 391.

41. Queen Sophie of the Netherlands to the Countess of Derby, November 1, 1874, in *Ibid.,* p. 411.

42. Marie, Duchess of Edinburgh to Countess Alexandrine Tolstoy, undated, 1879, Mountbatten Papers, MB1/U24, Hartley Library, University of Southampton.

43. Warwick and Brooke, *Memories of Sixty Years,* p. 90.

44. *Ibid.,* p. 89–90.

45. Queen Victoria to Victoria, Crown Princess of Prussia, September 23, 1874, in Fulford, *Darling Child,* pp. 153–154.

46. Queen Victoria to Victoria, Crown Princess of Prussia, January 27, 1875, in *Ibid.,* p. 159.

47. Queen Victoria to the Empress Augusta, November 25, 1874, in Bolitho, *Further Letters of Queen Victoria,* p. 202.

48. Sullivan, *A Fatal Passion,* p. 28.

49. Hannah Pakula, *The Last Romantic: A Biography of Queen Marie of Roumania* (New York: Touchstone, 1986), p. 33.

50. Queen Victoria to Victoria, Crown Princess of Prussia, January 4, 1874, in Fulford, *Darling Child*, pp. 123–124.

51. Giles St. Aubyn, *Edward VII: Prince and King* (London: Collins, 1979), p. 291.

52. Alfred, Duke of Edinburgh to Countess Alexandrine Tolstoy, November 9, 1875, Mountbatten Papers, MB1/U24, Hartley Library, University of Southampton.

53. Corti, *Downfall of Three Dynasties*, p. 216.

54. Mary Ponsonby to Henry Ponsonby, January 10, 1875, in Magdalen Ponsonby, ed., *A Lady in Waiting to Queen Victoria: Being Some Letters, and a Journal of Lady Ponsonby* (New York: J. H. Sears & Company, Inc., 1927), p. 80.

55. Corti, *Downfall of Three Dynasties*, p. 216.

56. *Ibid.*, p. 216.

57. Marie, *The Story of My Life, Volume I*, p. 15.

58. Corti, *Downfall of Three Dynasties*, p. 220.

59. Marie, *The Story of My Life, Volume I*, p. 3.

60. van der Kiste and Jordaan, *Dearest Affie*, p. 102.

7. HELLAS

1. "King of the Hellenes" (king of the Greeks) was George I's official title, as opposed to King of Hellas (king of Greece). George and his successors were also often referred to as "kings of Greece."

2. Rumbold, *Recollections of a Diplomatist, Volume II*, p. 103.

3. *Ibid.*, p. 104.

4. *Ibid.*, p. 110.

5. *Ibid.*, p. 103.

6. *Ibid.*, p. 125.

7. *Ibid.*

8. George M. Towle, *Modern Greece* (Boston: James R. Osgood and Company, 1877), p. 37.

9. Rumbold, *Recollections of a Diplomatist, Volume II*, p. 137.

10. *Ibid.*, p. 138.

11. Sophia Watson, *Marina: The Story of a Princess* (London: Weidenfeld & Nicolson, 1994), p. 11.

12. Isabel F. Hapgood, "An Imperial Pleasure Palace," in *The Cosmopolitan: A Monthly Illustrated Magazine*, Vol. XX (November, 1895–April, 1896), p. 648.

13. Prince Nicholas of Greece, *My Fifty Years* (London: Hutchinson & Co., Ltd., n.d,) p. 14.

14. *Ibid.*

15. *Ibid.*, p. 13.

16. *Ibid.*, p. 17.

17. George, *A Romanov Diary*, p. 5.

18. Prince Christopher of Greece, *Memoirs of H.R.H. Prince Christopher of Greece* (London: The Right Book Club, 1938), p. 17.

19. *Ibid.*, p. 18.

20. Nicholas, *My Fifty Years*, p. 21.

21. Charles K. Tuckerman, *Personal Recollections of Notable People at Home and Abroad, Volume II* (London: Richard Bentley and Son, 1895), p. 169.

22. Nicholas, *My Fifty Years*, p. 23.

23. Christopher, *Memoirs*, p. 37.
24. Chavchavadze, *The Grand Dukes*, p. 62.
25. Christopher, *Memoirs*, p. 23.
26. Richard Clogg, *A Concise History of Greece* (Cambridge: Cambridge University Press, 1992), p. 48.
27. *Ibid.*, p. 60.
28. Sherwood, *Royal Girls and Royal Courts*, p. 151.
29. Lowe, *Alexander III*, p. 313.
30. Velichenko and Mirolyubova, *The Palace of Grand Duke Vladimir Aleksandrovich*, pp. 90, 93.
31. Narishkin-Kurakin, *Under Three Tsars*, p. 41.
32. Cassini, *Never a Dull Moment*, p. 8.
33. *Ibid.*, pp. 7–8.
34. Alexander Tarsaïdze, *Katia: Wife Before God* (New York: The Macmillan Company, 1970), p. 90
35. *Ibid.*, p. 79.
36. Almedingen, *Emperor Alexander II*, p. 257.
37. van der Kiste, *The Romanovs*, p. 55.
38. Belyakova, *Grand Duke Alexei Alexandrovich*, p. 72.
39. Khorvatova, *Marie Feodorovna*, p. 61.
40. Narishkin-Kurakin, *Under Three Tsars*, p. 59.
41. Michael Knox Beran, *Forge of Empires, 1861–1871: Three Revolutionary Statesmen and the World They Made* (New York: Free Press, 2007), p. 27.

8. HOUNDED TO DEATH

1. Cowles, *Russian Dagger*, p. 129.
2. W. E. Mosse, *Alexander II and the Modernization of Russia* (London: I. B. Tauris & Co., Ltd., 1992), p. 137.
3. Radzinsky, *Alexander II*, p. 283.
4. Cowles, *Russian Dagger*, p. 127.
5. Maxwell, *Narodniki Women*, p. 25.
6. Cowles, *Russian Dagger*, p. 126.
7. Stephen Graham, *Tsar of Freedom: The Life and Reign of Alexander II* (New Haven, CT: Yale University Press, 1935), p. 275.
8. Alexander, *Once a Grand Duke*, pp. 38–39.
9. *Ibid.*, p. 30.
10. Wortman, *Scenarios of Power, Volume Two*, p. 129.
11. Letter of September 27, 1874, in Mary Cunliffe, *Letters from Abroad* (London: The Army and Navy Co-Operative Society, Inc., 1875. Printed for Private Circulation), p. 179.
12. Mosse, *Alexander II*, p. 165.
13. Maxwell, *Narodniki Women*, p.68.
14. Almedingen, *Alexander II*, p. 327.
15. Lincoln, *The Romanovs*, p. 442.
16. Radzinsky, *Alexander II*, p. 335.
17. Sidney Harcave, *Years of the Golden Cockerel: The Last Romanov Tsars 1814–1917* (New York: The Macmillan Company, 1968), p. 232.

18. Lord Dufferin to Queen Victoria, February 17/18, 1880, in Queen Victoria, *The Papers of Queen Victoria on Foreign Affairs. Part 1.*

19. Lord Dufferin to Queen Victoria, February 18, 1880, in *Ibid.*

20. Narishkin-Kurakin, *Under Three Tsars*, p. 62.

21. Henry Jones Thaddeus, *Recollections of a Court Painter* (London: John Lane Company, 1912), p. 113.

22. Albert Stopford (published anonymously), *The Russian Diary of an Englishman, Petrograd, 1915–1917* (New York: Robert M. McBride and Company, 1919), p. 96.

23. Thaddeus, *Recollections of a Court Painter*, pp. 114–117.

24. Narishkin-Kurakin, *Under Three Tsars*, p. 61.

25. Diary entry of Tsarevna Marie Feodorovna, February 5/17, 1880, in Ulstrup, "Maria Feodorovna Through Diaries and Person Letters," in *Maria Feodorovna, Empress of Russia*, p. 136

26. Queen Victoria to Victoria, the Crown Princess of Prussia, February 18, 1880, in Roger Fulford, ed., *Beloved Mama: Private Correspondence of Queen Victoria and the German Crown Princess 1878–1885* (London: Evans Brothers, Ltd., 1981), p. 65.

27. Alexandra, Princess of Wales to the Tsarevna Marie Feodorovna, February 24, 1880, in Ulstrup, "Maria Feodorovna Through Diaries and Person Letters," in *Maria Feodorovna, Empress of Russia*, p. 136

28. Lincoln, *The Romanovs*, p. 443.

29. van der Kiste, *The Romanovs*, p. 81.

30. Journal entry of February 18, 1881, in The Dowager Marchioness of Dufferin and Ava, *My Russian and Turkish Journals* (New York: Charles Scribner's Sons, 1916), p. 67.

31. *The Graphic*, February 28, 1880.

32. Harcave, *Years of the Golden Cockerel*, p. 233.

33. *Ibid.*, p. 232.

34. Ulstrup, "Maria Feodorovna Through Diaries and Person Letters," in *Maria Feodorovna, Empress of Russia*, p. 134.

35. Marie, *The Story of My Life, Volume I*, p. 3.

36. A memorandum recounting Lord Torrington's journey and visit to St. Petersburg to represent the Queen at the funeral of the Empress of Russia, which took place on Wednesday, June 9, 1880, in Queen Victoria, *Papers of Queen Victoria on Foreign Affairs, Part 1.*

37. Narishkin-Kurakin, *Under Three Tsars*, p. 68.

38. Barkhatova and Burkova, *The Danish Princess–the Russian Empress*, pp. 72–73.

39. *Ibid.*, p. 50.

40. Corti, *Downfall of Three Dynasties*, p. 271.

41. *Ibid.*, pp. 271–272.

42. *Ibid.*, p. 272.

43. Narishkin-Kurakin, *Under Three Tsars*, p. 70.

44. Barkhatova and Burkova, *The Danish Princess—the Russian Empress*, p. 73.

45. Harcave, *Years of the Golden Cockerel*, p. 242.

46. Almedingen, *Alexander II*, p. 344.

47. Adam B. Ulam, *In the Name of the People: Prophets and Conspirators in Prerevolutionary Russia* (New York: The Viking Press, 1977), p. 356.

48. Almedingen, *Alexander II*, p. 344.

49. Anonymous Stopford, *Russian Diary of an Englishman*, p. 96.

50. Alexander, *Once a Grand Duke*, p. 59.

51. Empress Marie Feodorovna of Russia to Queen Louise of Denmark, March 4/16, 1881, in Ulstrup, "Maria Feodorovna Through Diaries and Person Letters," in *Maria Feodorovna, Empress of Russia*, p. 140.

52. Alexander, *Once a Grand Duke*, p. 59.

53. Victor Laferté, *Alexandre II: Détails Inédits Sur Sa Vie Intime et Sa Mort* (Basel, Switzerland: H. Georg, 1882), p. 45.

54. Alexander, *Once a Grand Duke*, p. 60.

55. Meriel Buchanan, *Victorian Gallery* (London: Cassell & Co., Ltd., 1956), p. 51.

56. Tisdall, *Marie Fedorovna*, p. 105.

57. Alexander, *Once a Grand Duke*, p. 63.

58. Empress Marie Feodorovna of Russia to Queen Louise of Denmark, March 4/16, 1881, in Ulstrup, "Maria Feodorovna Through Diaries and Person Letters," in *Maria Feodorovna, Empress of Russia*, p. 142.

9. THE IDOL OF HER PEOPLE

1. Marie, *The Story of My Life, Volume I*, p. 87.

2. Extract from Queen Victoria's Journal, March 13, 1881, in George Earle Buckle, ed., *The Letters of Queen Victoria. Second Series: A Selection from Her Majesty's Correspondence and Journal Between the Years 1862 and 1885. Published by Authority of His Majesty the King. Volume III: 1879–1885* (London: John Murray, 1928.)

3. Queen Victoria to the Empress Augusta, March 14, 1881, in Bolitho, *Further Letters of Queen Victoria*, pp. 243–244.

4. Victoria, Crown Princess of Prussia, to Queen Victoria, March 14, 1881, in Sir Frederick Ponsonby ed., *Letters of the Empress Frederick*, (London: Macmillan and Co., Ltd., 1929), pp. 184–186.

5. Queen Victoria to Victoria, Crown Princess of Prussia, March 16, 1881, in Fulford, *Beloved Mama*, p. 97.

6. *The Graphic*, April 2, 1881.

7. Lowe, *Alexander III*, p. 51.

8. John W. Foster, *Diplomatic Memoirs, Volume I* (Boston: Hougton Mifflin Company, 1909), p. 185.

9. *Ibid.*, p. 186.

10. Journal entry of March 16, 1881, in Dowager Marchioness of Dufferin and Ava, *My Russian and Turkish Journals*, p. 111.

11. Foster, *Diplomatic Memoirs, Volume I*, p. 190.

12. *Ibid.*, p. 204.

13. Empress Marie Feodorovna of Russia to Queen Louise of Denmark, March 4/16, 1881, in Ulstrup, "Maria Feodorovna Through Diaries and Person Letters," in *Maria Feodorovna, Empress of Russia*, pp. 140, 142.

14. Sherwood, *Royal Girls and Royal Courts*, p. 149.

15. Letter of January 23, 1887, in William Prall, ed., *The Court of Alexander III: Letters of Mrs. Lothrop, Wife of the Late Honorable George Van Ness Lothrop* (Philadelphia: The John C. Winston Company, 1910), pp. 156–157.

16. Princess Catherine Radziwill, *Memories of Forty Years*, (New York: Funk and Wagnell Company, 1915), p. 277.

17. Cecilie, *Memoirs*, pp. 167–168.
18. Radziwill, *Memories of Forty Years*, pp. 271–272.
19. Narishkin-Kurakin, *Under Three Tsars*, p. 96.
20. Victoria, Crown Princess of Prussia, to Queen Victoria, May 10, 1874, The Royal Archives, RA/VIC/MAIN/Z/28/24.
21. Letter of February 6, 1886, in Prall, *Court of Alexander III*, p. 69.
22. Letter of January 10, 1886, in *Ibid.*, p. 58.
23. Buchanan, *Victorian Gallery*, p. 52.
24. Poliakoff, *Mother Dear*, p. 139.
25. *Ibid.*, p. 140.
26. Tisdall, *Marie Feodorovna*, p. 112.
27. Geoffrey Hosking, *Russia and the Russians: A History* (Cambridge, MA: The Belknap Press of Harvard University Press, 2001), p. 318.
28. Hans Heilbronner, "Alexander III and the Reform Plan of Loris-Melikov," *Journal of Modern History*, Vol. 33, No. 4 (December 1961), p. 387.
29. *Ibid.*, p. 396.
30. Pulonov, *Russia in the Nineteenth Century*, p. 177.
31. *New York Times*, March 16, 1881.
32. *"Moujik"* refers to a Russian peasant.
33. Lincoln, *The Romanovs*, p. 413.
34. Poliakoff, *Mother Dear*, p. 147.
35. Hamilton, *Vanished Pomps of Yesterday*, p. 208.
36. *Ibid.*, p. 209.
37. Greg King and Penny Wilson, *Gilded Prism: The Konstantinovichi Grand Dukes & the Last Years of the Romanov Dynasty* (East Richmond Heights, CA: Eurohistory.com, 2006), p. 81.
38. Ludmila Kuzmina, *August Poet* (Saint Petersburg: Aurora, 2004), p. 44.
39. Queen Victoria to Princess Victoria of Hesse, March 7, 1883, in Richard Hough, *Advice to My Grand-daughter: Letters from Queen Victoria to Princess Victoria of Hesse.* (New York: Simon and Schuster, 1975), pp. 44–45.
40. Christopher Warwick, *Ella: Princess, Saint & Martyr* (Chichester, UK: John Wiley & Sons, Ltd., 2006), pp. 82–83.
41. Mrs. George Cornwallis-West, *The Reminiscences of Lady Randolph Churchill.* (New York: The Century Co., 1908), p. 185.
42. Grand Duchess Elizabeth Feodorovna to Queen Victoria, November 21, 1884, in Lubov Millar, *Grand Duchess Elizabeth of Russia: New Martyr of the Communist Yoke* (Redding, CA: Nikodemos Orthodox Publication Soceity, 1991), p. 40.
43. Prince Nicholas, *My Fifty Years*, p. 64.
44. Ian Vorres, *The Last Grand Duchess: Her Imperial Highness Grand Duchess Olga Alexandrovna June 1882–24 November 1960* (New York: Charles Scribner's sons, 1964, p. 37.
45. Theo Aronson, *A Family of Kings: The Descendants of Christian IX of Denmark* (London: Cassell, 1976), p. 82.
46. Empress Marie Feodorovna of Russia to King Christian IX of Denmark, October 29/November 10, 1888, in Ulstrup, "Maria Feodorovna Through Diaries and Person Letters," in *Maria Feodorovna, Empress of Russia*, p. 158.
47. Narishkin-Kurakin, *Under Three Tsars*, p. 117.

10. THE MATERNAL INSTINCT

1. Princess Catherine Radziwill, *Nicholas II: The Last of the Tsars* (London: Cassell and Company, Ltd., 1931), p. 18.

2. The *London Reader*, 51 (September 29, 1888), p. 551.

3. Vassili, *Behind the Veil of the Russian Court*, p. 120.

4. *Report of the Commissioner of Education for the Year 1893–94*, Volume 1 (Washington, DC: Government Printing Office, 1896), p. 407.

5. Nadine Wonlar-Larsky, *The Russia That I Loved* (London: Elsie MacSwinney, 1937), p. 61.

6. Vorres, *The Last Grand Duchess*, p.25.

7. Mark D. Steinberg and Vladimir M. Khrustalëv, *The Fall of the Romanovs: Political Dreams and Personal Struggles in a Time of Revolution* (New Haven: Yale University Press, 1995), p. 12.

8. Marie, *The Story of My Life, Volume I*, pp. 29–30.

9. *Ibid.*, p. 29.

10. *Ibid.*, p. 71.

11. *Ibid.*, p. 72.

12. Vassili, *Behind the Veil at the Russian Court*, p. 128.

13. Captain the Hon. Sir Seymour Fortescue, *Looking Back* (London: Longmans, Green and Co., 1920), pp. 156–157.

14. Marquise de Fontenoy, *The Marquise de Fontenoy's Revelations of High Life Within Royal Palaces* (Philadelphia: Edgewood Publishing Co., 1892), pp. 98–99.

15. Mary Howard McClintock, *The Queen Thanks Sir Howard: The Life of Major-General Sir Howard Elphinstone, V.C., K.C.B., C.M.G.* (London: John Murray, 1945), p. 157.

16. Marie, *The Story of My Life, Volume I*, p. 16.

17. Arthur H. Beavan, *Popular Royalty* (London: Sampson Low, Marston and Company, 1904), p. 181.

18. Marie, *The Story of My Life, Volume I*, pp. 126–127.

19. Diary entry of Prince George of Wales, October 28, 1887, The Royal Archives, RA GV/PRIV/GVD/1887.

20. Diary entry of Prince George of Wales, October 29, 1887, The Royal Archives, RA GV/PRIV/GVD/1887.

21. Diary entry of Prince George of Wales, October 28, 1887, The Royal Archives, RA GV/PRIV/GVD/1887.

22. Queen Olga to Prince George of Wales, November 7/19, 1888, The Royal Archives, RA/PRIV/AA46/20.

23. Diary entry of Prince George of Wales, October 30, 1887, The Royal Archives, RA GV/PRIV/GVD/1887.

24. Card from Queen Olga to Prince George of Wales, included in diary entry of Prince George of Wales, November 2, 1887, The Royal Archives, RA GV/PRIV/GVD/1887.

25. James Pope-Hennessy, *Queen Mary 1867–1953* (New York: Alfred A. Knopf, 1960), pp. 141–142.

26. Vorres, *The Last Grand Duchess*, p. 35.

27. Marie, Duchess of Edinburgh to Lady Randolph Churchill, August 2, 1886, in Cornwallis-West, *Reminiscences of Lady Randolph Churchill*, p. 242.

28. Marie, Duchess of Edinburgh to Lady Randolph Churchill, June 16, 1886, in *Ibid.*, p. 241.

29. Marie, Duchess of Edinburgh to Lady Randolph Churchill, August 2, 1886, in *Ibid.*, p. 242.

30. *Ibid.*, p. 243.

31. Virginia Tatnall Peacock, *Famous American Belles of the Nineteenth Century* (Philadelphia: J. B. Lippincott Company, 1901), p. 240.

32. Marie, Duchess of Edinburgh, to Lord Randolph Churchill, February 1, 1886, Churchill Archives Centre, The Papers of Lord Randolph Churchill, RCHL 1/12/1357, University Library.

33. "You do not play so badly for a Princess."

34. Cornwallis-West, *Reminiscences of Lady Randolph Churchill*, p. 238.

35. Ralph G. Martin, *Jennie: The Life of Lady Randolph Churchill, Volume I: The Romantic Years 1854–1895* (Englewood Cliffs, NJ: Prentice-Hall, Inc., 1969), p. 51.

36. Marie, Duchess of Edinburgh, to Lady Randolph Churchill, January 13, 1888, in Cornwallis-West, *Reminiscences of Lady Randolph Churchill*, p. 244.

37. Anita Leslie, *Jennie: The Life of Lady Randolph Churchill* (London: Arrow Books, 1969), p. 127.

38. Marie, Duchess of Edinburgh, to Lady Randolph Churchill, January 13, 1888, in Cornwallis-West, *Reminiscences of Lady Randolph Churchill*, p. 244.

39. Marie, Duchess of Edinburgh, to Lord Randolph Churchill, January 9, 1886, Churchill Archives Centre, The Papers of Lord Randolph Churchill, RCHL 1/11/1263.

40. Marie, Duchess of Edinburgh, to Lady Randolph Churchill, January 13, 1888, in Cornwallis-West, *Reminiscences of Lady Randolph Churchill*, p. 244.

41. Elizabeth Longford, ed., *Darling Loosy: Letters to Princess Louise 1856–1939* (London: Weidenfeld & Nicolson, 1991), p. 59.

42. Sir Arthur Sullivan to Princess Louise, in *Ibid.*, pp. 242–243.

43. Marie, *The Story of My Life, Volume I*, p. 16.

44. Prince Nicholas, *My Fifty Years*, p. 55.

45. Sir Horace Rumbold, *Final Recollections of a Diplomatist,* (London: Edward Arnold, 1905), p. 27.

46. *Ibid.*, p. 27.

47. Karolou, Olga, *Queen of the Greeks*, chapter 3.

48. Rumbold, *Final Recollections*, p. 27.

49. "A Queen's Charity: The Evangelismos of Athens," in W. T. Stead, *The Review of Reviews*, Vol. VIII, July–December, 1893, p. 275.

50. Cecilie, *Memoirs*, p. 151.

51. M. U. Garshin, *The Hellenes' Queen Olga Constantinovna* (Prague, 1937), chapter 2.

52. Queen Olga to Prince George of Wales, December 5/17, 1888, The Royal Archives, RA/PRIV/AA46/29.

53. Nicholas, *My Fifty Years*, p. 87.

54. Radziwill, *Memories of Forty Years*, pp. 230–231.

55. Count Egon Corti, *The English Empress: A Study in the Relations Between Queen Victoria and Her Eldest Daughter, Empress Frederick of Germany* (London: Cassell and Company Ltd., 1957), p. 338.

56. Queen Olga to Prince George of Wales, 25 April/7 May 1888, The Royal Archives, RA/PRIV/AA46/43.

57. Marie, *The Story of My Life, Volume I*, p. 212.

58. Hugo Mager, *Elizabeth: Grand Duchess of Russia* (New York: Carroll & Graf Publishers, Inc., 1998), p. 143.

59. Grand Duchess Marie, *Education of a Princess: A Memoir* (New York: The Viking Press, 1931), p. 9.

60. Nicholas, *My Fifty Years*, p. 91.
61. Queen Olga to Prince George of Wales, October 7/19, 1891, The Royal Archives, RA/ PRIV/AA46/49.
62. *Ibid.*

II. LOVE IN THE AIR

1. Ballou, *Due North*, pp. 225–227.
2. Lowe, *Alexander III*, pp. 252–253.
3. *Ibid.*, p. 256.
4. Theodore Child, "Palatial Petersburg," in *Harper's New Monthly Magazine*, July 1889, p. 207.
5. Nicolas Notovitch, *L'Empereur Alexandre III et Son Entourage* (Paris: Paul Ollendorff, 1893), p. 92.
6. Baroness Souiny (Leonie Ida Philipovna Souiny-Seydlitz), *Russia of Yesterday and Tomorrow* (New York: The Century Co., 1917), p. 149.
7. *Ibid.*, p. 150.
8. Millar, *Grand Duchess Elizabeth*, p. 59.
9. John C. G. Röhl, *Wilhelm II: The Kaiser's Personal Monarchy 1888–1900* (Cambridge: Cambridge University Press, 2004), pp. 649–650.
10. van der Kiste, *The Romanovs*, p. 158.
11. Vassili, *Behind the Veil of the Russian Court*, pp. 164–165.
12. Zeepvat, *Romanov Autumn*, p. 97.
13. Marie, *The Story of My Life, Volume I*, p. 91.
14. Princess Antoine Radziwill to General de Robilant, November 26, 1891, in Princess Marie Radziwill, *Lettres de la Princesse Radziwill au Général de Robilant 1889–1914, Vol. I: 1889–1895* (Bologna, Italy: Nicola Zanichelli, 1923), p. 92.
15. Khorvatova, *Marie Feodorovna*, pp. 115–117.
16. *Ibid.*, p. 136.
17. Perry and Pleshakov, *Flight of the Romanovs*, p. 38.
18. *Ibid.*, p. 33.
19. Narishkin-Kurakin, *Under Three Tsars*, p. 129.
20. Sergei Witte, *The Memoirs of Count Witte*, transl. and ed. by Abraham Yarmolinsky (Garden City, NY: Doublday, Page & Co., 1921), p. 40.
21. *Ibid.*, p. 39.
22. Mikhail P. Iroshnikov, Yury B. Shelayev, Liudmila A. Prostai, *Before the Revolution—St. Petersburg in Photographs: 1890–1914* (New York: Harry N. Abrams, Inc., Publishers; Leningrad: Nauka Publishers, JV Smart, 1991), p. 122.
23. The calculation is based upon www.measuringworth.com/ppowerus/?redirurl=calculators/ ppowerus/ (viewed on February 9, 2009) and www.pmeasuringworth.com/exchange/ (also viewed on the same date).
24. Toby Faber, *Fabergé's Eggs: The Extraordinary Story of the Masterpieces That Outlived an Empire* (New York: Random House, 2008), p. 8. The calculation is based upon Faber's, Fabergé's Eggs, p. 8 and www.measuringworth.com/ppowerus/?redirurl=calculators/ ppowerus/ (viewed on February 9, 2009) and www.pmeasuringworth.com/exchange/ (also viewed on the same date).
25. John A. Logan, *In Joyful Russia* (New York: D. Appleton and Company, 1897), p. 27.
26. *Ibid.*

27. Cornwallis-West, *Reminiscences of Lady Randolph Churchill*, p. 173.

28. N. A. Epanchin, "Serving Three Tsars," in Ananich, Ganelin, Gordin, Chernuha, *Alexander III: Memoirs, Diaries and Letters*, pp. 208–209.

29. Empress Marie Feodorovna to Tsarevtich Nicholas, October 24, 1890, in Edward Bing, ed., *The Letters of Tsar Nicholas and Empress Marie: Being the Confidential Correspondence Between Nicholas II, Last of the Tsars, and His Mother, Dowager Empress Maria Feodorovna* (London: Ivor Nicholson and Watson, Ltd., 1937), p. 42.

30. Alexander, *Once a Grand Duke*, pp. 121–122.

31. Empress Marie Feodorovna to Tsarevich Nicholas, June 27, 1894, in Bing, *Letters of Tsar Nicholas and Empress Marie*, p. 87.

32. John van der Kiste and Coryne Hall, *Once a Grand Duchess: Xenia, Sister of Nicholas II* (Stroud, UK: Sutton Publishing, 2002), p. 33.

33. Terence Elsberry, *Marie of Romania: The Intimate Life of a Twentieth Century Queen* (New York: St. Martin's Press, 1972), p. 22.

34. Pakula, *The Last Romantic*, p. 47.

35. Marie, *The Story of My Life, Volume I*, p. 256.

36. Pope-Hennessy, *Queen Mary*, p. 240.

37. Pakula, *The Last Romantic*, p. 57.

38. Queen Victoria to Princess Victoria of Hesse, June 2, 1892, in Hough, *Advice to My Grand-daughter*, p. 117.

39. Pope-Hennessy, *Queen Mary*, pp. 241–242.

40. *Ibid.*, p. 231.

41. *Ibid.*, p. 232.

42. Marie, *The Story of My Life, Volume I*, p. 242.

43. *Ibid.*, p. 285.

44. *Ibid.*, p. 290.

45. Diary entry of the Tsarevich Nicholas, December 21, 1891, in Andrei Maylunas and Sergei Mironenko, *A Lifelong Passion: Nicolas and Alexandra, Their Own Story* (London: Weidenfeld & Nicolson, 1996), p. 20.

46. Diary entry of the Tsarevich Nicholas, January 29, 1892, in *Ibid.*, p. 22.

12. THE BEGINNING OF THE END

1. General Sir Richard Harrison, *Recollections of a Life in the British Army During the Latter Half of the 19th Century* (London: Smith, Elder, & Co., 1908), p. 321.

2. van der Kiste, *Princess Victoria Melita*, pp. 31–32.

3. Marie Alexandrovna and Alfred will be referred to from now on as the Duke and Duchess of Coburg.

4. Sullivan, *A Fatal Passion*, p. 74.

5. Arthur Gould Lee, ed., *The Empress Frederick Writes to Sophie, Crown Princess and Queen of the Hellenes* (London: Faber and Faber, Ltd., 1955), p. 150.

6. Sullivan, *A Fatal Passion*, p. 34.

7. van der Kiste and Jordaan, *Dearest Affie*, p. 148.

8. Fontenoy, *Within Royal Palaces*, p. 99.

9. Pakula, *The Last Romantic*, p. 96.

10. Queen Marie, *The Story of My Life, Volume II* (London: Cassell and Company, Ltd., 1934) p. 48.

11. *Ibid.*, p. 49.

12. Queen Victoria to Princess Victoria of Hesse, July 15, 1890, in Hough, *Advice to My Grand-daughter*, p. 106.

13. Princess Alix of Hesse to Grand Duchess Xenia of Russia, November 8, 1893, in Maylunas and Mironenko, *A Lifelong Passion*, p. 32.

14. Diary entry of the Tsarevich Nicholas, November 18, 1893, in *Ibid.*, p. 33.

15. Pope-Hennessy, *Queen Mary*, p. 142.

16. Queen Victoria to Princess Victoria of Hesse, September 24, 1893, in Hough, *Advice to My Grand-daughter*, p. 120.

17. Pakula, *The Last Romantic*, p. 100.

18. E. M. Almedingen, *The Empress Alexandra 1872–1918* (London: Hutchinson, 1961), p. 21.

19. Diary of the Tsarevich Nicholas, April 8, 1894, in Maylunas and Mironenko, *A Lifelong Passion*, p. 47.

20. David Duff, *Hessian Tapestry* (London: Frederick Muller, 1967), p. 233.

21. Almedingen, *The Empress Alexandra*, p. 24.

22. Julia P. Gelardi, *Born to Rule: Five Reigning Consorts, Granddaughters of Queen Victoria* (New York: St. Martin's Press, 2005), p. 51.

23. Empress Marie Feodorovna of Russia to Tsarevich Nicholas, April 10, 1894, in Bing, *Letters of Tsar Nicholas and Empress Marie*, p. 73.

24. Empress Marie Feodorovna of Russia to Tsarevich Nicholas, April 14, 1894, in *Ibid.*, p. 77.

25. Empress Marie Feodorovna of Russia to Tsarevich Nicholas, June 27, 1894, in *Ibid.*, p. 87.

26. Nicholas, *My Fifty Years*, p. 116.

27. St. Aubyn, *Edward VII*, p. 296.

28. Queen Victoria to Princess Victoria of Hesse, October 21, 1894, in Hough, *Advice to My Grand-daughter*, p. 126.

29. Aronson, *A Family of Kings*, p. 117.

30. Diary entry of Princess Alix in Tsarevich Nicholas's diary, October 15, 1894, in Maylunas and Mironenko, *A Lifelong Passion*, p. 98.

31. *New York Times*, October 21, 1894.

32. Frederick Wycollar, "A Secret Chapter of Russian History" in *Munsey's Magazine*, May 1904, vol. XXXI, no. 2, p. 176.

33. *Ibid.*, p. 175.

34. Empress Marie Feodorovna to Queen Louise, October 25/November 6, 1894, in Ulstrup, "Maria Feodorovna Through Diaries and Person Letters," in *Maria Feodorovna, Empress of Russia*, p. 162.

35. Vassili, *Behind the Veil*, p. 198.

36. Lowe, *Alexander III*, p. 288

37. Perry and Pleshakov, *Flight of the Romanovs*, p. 63.

38. Diary entry of Tsar Nicholas II, October 20, 1894, in Maylunas and Mironenko, *A Lifelong Passion*, p. 99.

39. Alexander, *Once a Grand Duke*, pp. 168–169.

40. Yulia Kudrina, *Mother and Son: Empress and Emperor* (Togliatti: Glagol, 2004), p. 35.

41. Grishin, *Grand Duke's Tragic Destiny*, p. 120.

42. Empress Marie Feodorovna to Queen Louise, October 25/November 6, 1894, in Ulstrup,

"Maria Feodorovna Through Diaries and Person Letters," in *Maria Feodorovna, Empress of Russia*, p. 164.

43. Empress Marie Feodorovna to Queen Louise, October 29/November 10, 1894, in *Ibid.*, pp. 164, 166.

44. Empress Marie Feodorovna to Queen Louise, October 25/November 6, 1894, in *Ibid.*, p. 162.

45. Empress Marie Feodorovna to Queen Louise, October 29/November 10, 1894, in *Ibid.*, p. 164.

46. *The Graphic*, November 24, 1894.

47. Pope-Hennessy, *Queen Mary*, p. 302.

48. Witte, *Memoirs*, p. 47.

49. Charlotte Knollys to Mrs. Archibald Knollys, November 25, 1894, MSS21M69/25/2, Knollys Papers, Hampshire Record Office.

50. Tsarina Alexandra to Queen Victoria, November 16, 1894, in Maylunas and Mironenko, *A Lifelong Passion*, p. 112.

51. Empress Marie Feodorovna to Queen Louise, October 29/November 10, 1894, in Ulstrup, "Maria Feodorovna Through Diaries and Person Letters," in *Maria Feodorovna, Empress of Russia*, p. 166.

52. Empress Marie Feodorovna to Queen Louise, November 5/November 17, 1894, in *Ibid.*, p. 166.

53. Diary entry of K.R., November 16, 1894, in Maylunas and Mironenko, *A Lifelong Passion*, p. 114.

54. Queen Victoria to Tsar Nicholas II, November 10, 1894, in *Ibid.*, p. 107.

55. Baroness Sophie Buxhoeveden, *The Life and Tragedy of Alexandra Feodorovna, Empress of Russia* (London: Longmans, Green and Co., 1930), p. 44.

56. Tsarina Alexandra to the Reverend William Boyd Carpenter, Bishop of Ripon, February 13, 1895, Add. MSS. 46721/99, The British Library.

57. Wycollar, "A Secret Chapter of Russian History," in *Munsey's Magazine*, p. 175.

58. *Ibid.*, p. 176.

59. Corti, *The English Empress*, p. 349.

13. A FAILURE TO UNDERSTAND

1. The *zemstvo* was a form of local government, representing various levels of society. These were instituted by Alexander II.

2. van der Kiste, *The Romanovs*, p. 155.

3. Vorres, *The Last Grand Duchess*, p. 61.

4. Virginia Cowles, *The Last Tsar and Tsarina* (London: Weidenfeld & Nicolson, 1977), p. 52.

5. Maria Petrovna von Bok, *Reminiscences of My Father, Peter A. Stolypin*, transl. and ed. by Margaret Patoski (Metuchen, NJ: The Scarecrow Press, Inc., 1970), pp. 183–184.

6. Buchanan, *Victorian Gallery*, pp. 159–160.

7. Grand Duke Nicholas Mikhailovich to Frédéric Masson, April 10, 1902, in Nadine Vogel and William Smith, *Correspondance Entre le Grand-Duc Nicolas Mikhaïlovitch de Russie et Frédéric Masson, 1897–1914: Au Temps de l'Alliance Franco-Russe* (Paris: Bernard Giovanangeli, Association des amis de Frédéric Masson, 2005), p. 163.

8. Vorres, *The Last Grand Duchess*, p. 60.

9. Buxhoeveden, *The Life and Tragedy of Alexandra Feodorovna*, p. 49.

10. F. S. Olferev, "Remembrances of the Imperial Family," in Thomas E. Berry, ed. and transl., *Memoirs of the Pages to the Tsars* (Mississauga, Ontario: Gilbert's Royal Books, 2001), pp. 274–275.

11. Andrew Dickson White, *Autobiography of Andrew D. White*, Volume II (New York: The Century Co., 1906), p. 9.

12. Buxhoeveden, *Life and Tragedy of Alexandra Feodorovna*, p. 58.

13. Kleinmichel, *Memories of a Shipwrecked World*, p. 206.

14. Vladimir Poliakoff, *The Tragic Bride: The Story of the Empress Alexandra of Russia* (New York: D. Appleton and Company, 1928), p. 87.

15. Buxhoeveden, *Life and Tragedy of Alexandra Feodorovna*, p. 59.

16. Tor Bomann-Larsen, *Kongstanken: Haakon and Maud—I* (Oslo: J. W. Cappelen, 2002), p. 336.

17. Dowager Empress Marie Feodorovan to Tsar Nicholas II, August 8, 1895, in Bing, *The Letters of Tsar Nicholas and Empress Marie*, pp. 96–97.

18. Diary entry of K.R., February 4, 1897, in Maylunas and Mironenko, *A Lifelong Passion*, p. 161.

19. van der Kiste, *The Romanovs*, p. 158.

20. Kleinmichel, *Memories of a Shipwrecked World*, p. 207.

21. A. A. Mossolov, *At the Court of the Last Tsar: Being the Memoirs of A. A. Mossolov, Head of the Court Chancellery, 1900–1916*, ed. by A. A. Pilenco and transl. by E. W. Dickes (London: Methuen & Co. Ltd., 1935), p. 78.

22. Count Paul Vassili [pseudonym of Princess Catherine Radziwill], *Confessions of the Czarina* (New York; Harper and Brothers Publishers, 1918), pp. 70–73.

23. van der Kiste, *The Romanovs*, p. 158.

24. "Remembrances of Kamer-page B. A. Engelgardt Class of 1896," in Thomas E. Berry, ed. and transl., *Memoirs of the Pages to the Tsars* (Mississauga, Ontario: Gilbert's Royal Books, 2001), p. 173.

25. Princess Catherine Radziwill, *My Recollections* (London: Isbister & Company, 1904), p. 318.

26. Richard Harding Davis, *A Year from a Reporter's Note-Book* (New York: Harper & Brothers, 1903), p. 32.

27. Letter of May 24, 1896, in Kate Koon Bovey, *Russian Coronation 1896: The Letters of Kate Koon Bovey* (Minneapolis: Privately Printed, 1942), p. 16.

28. Logan, *In Joyful Russia*, p. 117.

29. *Ibid.*, p. 122.

30. The Bishop of Peterborough, "The Imperial Coronation at Moscow," *The Cornhill Magazine*, Vol. I, July to December 1896 (London: Smith, Elder & Co., 1896), p. 319.

31. Empress Marie Feodorovna to Queen Louise, May 16/28, 1896, in Ulstrup, "Maria Feodorovna Through Diaries and Person Letters," in *Maria Feodorovna, Empress of Russia*, p. 168.

32. Letter of May 28, 1896, in Bovey, *Russian Coronation*, p. 27.

33. N. I. Burmeiester, "Fifty Years Ago," in Thomas E. Berry, ed. and transl., *Memoirs of the Pages to the Tsars* (Mississauga, Ontario: Gilbert's Royal Books, 2001), p. 228.

34. B. A. Engelgardt, "Remembrances of Kamer-page," in *Ibid.*, p. 194.

35. Empress Marie Feodorovna to Queen Louise, undated letter of 1896 in Ulstrup, "Maria Feodorovna Through Diaries and Person Letters," in *Maria Feodorovna, Empress of Russia*, p. 172.

36. Pakula, *The Last Romantic*, p. 103.
37. Charlotte Zeepvat, *From Cradle to Crown: British Nannies and Governesses at the World's Royal Courts* (Stroud, UK: Sutton Publishing, 2006), p. 125.
38. Thaddeus, *Recollections of a Court Painter*, pp. 111–112.
39. *Ibid.*, p. 111.
40. *Ibid.*, pp. 111–113.
41. "Gifts at a Royal Silver Wedding," in *The Jewelers' Circular* (October 11, 1899).

14. IN MOURNING

1. Pakula, *The Last Romantic*, p. 120.
2. *Ibid.*, pp. 107–108.
3. Paul D. Quinlan, *The Playboy King: Carol II of Romania* (Westport, CT: Greenwood Press, 1995), pp. 15–16.
4. *Ibid.*, p. 17.
5. Pakula, *The Last Romantic*, p. 123.
6. *Ibid.*, p. 124.
7. Quinlan, *Playboy King*, p. 17.
8. Letter of March 20, 1899, in Victor Mallet, *Life with Queen Victoria: Marie Mallet's Letters from Court 1887–1901* (Boston: Houghton Mifflin Company, 1968), p. 158.
9. Marlene A. Eilers, *Queen Victoria's Descendants* (Falköping, Sweden: Rosvall Royal Books, 1997), p. 62.
10. John Wimbles, "Grand Duchess Marie Alexandrovna—Duchess of Edinburgh and Saxe-Coburg & Gotha," in Arturo E. Beéche, ed., *The Grand Duchesses: Daughters and Grand-daughters of Russia's Tsars* (Oakland: Eurohistory.com, 2004), pp. 49–50.
11. Pakula, *The Last Romantic*, p. 121.
12. Letter of March 20, 1899, in Mallet, *Life with Queen Victoria*, p. 158.
13. Prince Alfred to Princess Louise, February 21, 1899, in Longford, *Darling Loosy*, p. 250.
14. Marie, *The Story of My Life, Volume II*, p. 145.
15. Diary entry of February 7, 1899, in Edgar Sheppard, ed., *George, Duke of Cambridge: A Memoir of His Life Based on the Journals and Correspondence of His Royal Highness, Vol. II, 1871–1904* (London: Longmans, Green, and Co., 1906), p. 272.
16. Queen Victoria to the Duke of Cambridge, February 21, 1899, in *Ibid.*
17. Longford, *Queen Victoria*, p. 552.
18. Xavier Paoli, *Their Majesties as I Knew Them*, transl. by A. Teixeira de Mattos (New York: Sturgis & Walton Company, 1911), pp. 131–132.
19. Hall, *Little Mother*, p. 186.
20. Tsar Nicholas II to Queen Victoria, July 8, 1899, in Maylunas and Mironenko, *A Lifelong Passion*, p. 187.
21. Diary entry of Grand Duchess Xenia, July 14, 1899, in *Ibid.*, pp. 188–189.
22. Empress Marie Feodorovna to Tsar Nicholas II, October 27, 1899, in Bing, *Letters of Tsar Nicholas and Empress Marie*, p. 140.
23. Wycollar, "A Secret Chapter of Russian History," in *Munsey's Magazine*, May 1904, vol. XXXI, no. 2, p. 177.
24. Grand Duke Nicholas Mikhailovich to Frédéric Masson, November 11/24, 1900, in Vogel and Smith, *Correspondance Entre le Grand-Duc Nicolas Mikhaïlovitch de Russie et Frédéric Masson*, p. 101.

25. Diary entry of K.R., June 6, 1901, in Maylunas and Mironenko, *A Lifelong Passion*, p. 206.

26. Diary entry of Grand Duchess Xenia, June 5, 1901, in *Ibid.*

27. Pope-Hennessy, *Queen Mary*, p. 247.

28. E.C.F. Collier, ed., *A Victorian Diarist: Later Extracts from the Journals of Mary, Lady Monkswell, 1895–1909* (London: John Murray, 1946), p. 136.

29. *The Times*, April 8, 1897.

30. R. W. Stallman and E. R. Hagemann, eds., *The War Dispatches of Stephen Crane* (New York: New York University Press, 1964), p. 22.

31. Röhl, *Wilhelm II, 1888–1900*, p. 941.

32. Lee, *The Empress Frederick Writes to Sophie*, p. 243.

33. Theodore George Tatsios, *The Megali Idea and the Greek-Turkish War of 1897: The Impact of the Cretan Problem on Greek Irredentism, 1866–1897* (New York: Columbia University Press, 1984), p. 119.

34. Gelardi, *Born to Rule*, p. 79.

35. Tatsios, *The Megali Idea*, p. 215, note 56.

36. Empress Frederick to the Reverend William Boyd Carpenter, Bishop of Ripon, December 28, 1897, Add. MSS. 46721/99, The British Library.

37. Queen Olga to Harriet Boyd Hawes, December 22/January 2, 1898/99, in Mary Allsebrook, *Born to Rebel: The Life of Harriet Boyd Hawes* (Oxford: Oxbow Books, 1992), p. 79.

38. Karolou, *Olga, Queen of the Greeks*, chapter 7.

39. *Ibid.*

40. Philip Carabott, "Politics, Orthodoxy and the Language Question in Greece: The Gospel Riots in Greece, 1901," in *Journal of Mediterranean Studies*, Vol. 3, No. 1, 1993, p. 125.

41. Baron Roman Rosen, *Forty Years of Diplomacy, Volume I* (New York: Alfred A. Knopf, 1922), pp. 183–184.

42. *Ibid.*, p. 184.

43. Charles S. Francis to John Hay, November 22, 1901, in United States, Department of State, *Papers Relating to the Foreign Relations of the United States, Transmitted to Congress, with the Annual Message of the President, December 3, 1901* (Washington, D.C.: Government Printing Office, 1902), no. 39, p. 250.

44. Diary entry of K.R., May 21, 1898, in Maylunas and Mironenko, *A Lifelong Passion*, p. 172.

45. Wonlar-Larsky, *The Russia That I Loved*, pp. 60–61.

46. *"Elle se fait vieille . . . elle voit aussi très mal,"* Marie, Duchess of Edinburgh to Countess Alexandrine Tolstoy, November 20 (2 December), 1896, Mountbatten Papers, MB1/U24, Hartley Library, University of Southampton.

47. van der Kiste, *Dearest Affie*, p. 170.

48. Princess Beatrice to the Reverend William Boyd Carpenter, Bishop of Ripon, August 8, 1900, Add. MSS. 46721/99, The British Library.

49. *The Times*, August 1, 1900.

50. Extract from Queen Victoria's Journal, July 31, 1900, in Queen Victoria, *The Letters of Queen Victoria. Third series. A Selection from Her Majesty's Correspondence and Journal Between the Years 1886 and 1901, Published by Authority of His Majesty the King, Volume III, 1896–1901*, edited by George Earle Buckle (New York: Longmans and Green, 1930–32), p. 579.

51. The Empress Frederick to Queen Victoria, July 31, 1900, in Agatha Ramm, ed., *Beloved and Darling Child: Last Letters Between Queen Victoria and Her Eldest Daughter 1886–1901* (Stroud: Gloucestershire, Alan Sutton, 1990), pp. 254–255.

52. Queen Victoria to the Empress Frederick, June 24, 1900, in *Ibid.*, p. 252.

53. Duchess of Saxe-Coburg-Gotha to Crown Princess Marie of Romania, January 26, 1901, Romanian National Archives V/1898.

15. LOVE AND WAR

1. Sullivan, *A Fatal Passion*, p. 207.

2. Tsar Nicholas II to Empress Marie Feodorovna, October 27, 1901, in Bing, *Letters of Tsar Nicholas and Empress Marie*, p. 158.

3. Empress Marie Feodorovna to Tsar Nicholas II, November 5, 1901, in *Ibid.*, p. 159.

4. Princess Antoine Radziwill to General de Robilant, November 20–21, 1901, in Princess Marie Radziwill, *Lettres de la Princesse Radziwill an Général de Robilant 1889–1914, Vol. II: 1896–1901* (Bologna, Italy: Nicola Zanichelli, 1923), pp. 324–325.

5. *Ibid.*, p. 325.

6. Princess Antoine Radziwill to General de Robilant, December 2–3, 1901, in *Ibid.*, p. 320.

7. Princess Antoine Radziwill to General de Robilant, December 6–7, 1901, in *Ibid.*, p. 330.

8. Sullivan, *A Fatal Passion*, p. 181.

9. Cowles, *The Last Tsar and Tsarina*, p. 84.

10. Mossolov, *At the Court of the Last Tsar*, p. 79.

11. *Ibid.*, p. 199.

12. Diary entry of K.R., May 24, 1900, in Maylunas and Mironenko, *A Lifelong Passion*, p. 198.

13. Zeepvat, *Romanov Autumn*, p. 161.

14. Prince Nicholas, *My Fifty Years*, p. 194.

15. Diary entry of K.R., June 19, 1902, in Maylunas and Mironenko, *A Lifelong Passion*, p. 198.

16. Diary entry of Grand Duchess Xenia, December 21, 1903, in *Ibid.*, p. 233.

17. Rosemary and Donald Crawford, *Michael and Natasha: The Life and Love of the Last Tsar of Russia* (Vancouver: Douglas & McIntyre, 1997), pp. 9–10.

18. Sometimes referred to as Marie Pavlovna "the Younger" to differentiate her from Miechen, who was sometimes referred to as Marie Pavlovna "the Elder."

19. Marie, *Education of a Princess*, p. 52.

20. Tsar Nicholas II to Empress Marie Feodorovna, October 20, 1902, in Bing, *Letters of Tsar Nicholas and Empress Marie*, pp. 169–170.

21. Empress Marie Feodorovna to Tsar Nicholas II, October 23, 1902, in *Ibid.*, p. 171.

22. Marie, *Education of a Princess*, p. 50.

23. *Ibid.*, p. 56.

24. Harrison E. Salisbury, *Black Night, White Snow: Russia's Revolutions 1905–1917* (New York: Doubleday & Company, Inc., 1977), p. 209.

25. Prince Bernhard von Bülow, *Memoirs of Prince von Bülow, Volume II, From the Morocco Crisis to Resignation, 1903–1909*, transl. by Geoffrey Dunlop (Boston: Little, Brown, and Company, 1931), p. 6.

26. Wycollar, "A Secret Chapter of Russian History," in *Munsey's Magazine*, May 1904, vol. XXXI, no. 2, p. 178.

27. Diary entry of March 16, 1904 in Maurice Paléologue, *The Turning Point Vol. I, July 20, 1914–June 2, 1915*, transl. by F. A. Holt (New York: George H. Doran Company, n.d.), p. 44.

28. Narishkin-Kurakin, *Under Three Tsars*, p. 177.

29. Perry and Pleshakov, *Flight of the Romanovs*, p. 85.

30. Diary entry of Tsar Nicholas II, July 30, 1904, in Maylunas and Mironenko, *A Lifelong Passion*, p. 243.

31. Olferev, "Remembrances of the Imperial Family" in Berry, *Memoirs of the Pages to the Tsars*, pp. 265–266.

32. Diary entry of Tsar Nicholas II, September 8, 1904, in Maylunas and Mironenko, *A Lifelong Passion*, p. 247.

16. THE YEAR OF NIGHTMARES

1. Diary entry of November 21, 1904, in Paléologue, *The Turning Point*, p. 152.

2. Diary entry of January 2, 1905, in *Ibid.*, p. 171.

3. Edward Crankshaw, *The Shadow of the Winter Palace: Russia's Drift to Revolution 1825–1917* (New York: The Viking Press, 1976), p. 336.

4. Diary entry of January 19, 1905 in Paléologue, *The Turning Point*, p. 178.

5. Lincoln, *The Romanovs*, p. 646.

6. "Resolution of the Russian Democratic Party, January 23," in R. W. Postgate, ed., *Revolution from 1789 to 1906* (Boston: Houghton Mifflin Co., 1921), Document 145, p. 366.

7. Leon Trotsky, "The Events in St. Petersburg," February 2, 1905, in *Ibid.*, p. 369.

8. Sir Charles Hardinge to the Marquess of Lansdowne, January 23, 1905, in D. C. B. Lieven, Kenneth Bourne, and D. C. Watt, eds., *British Documents on Foreign Affairs: Reports and Papers from the Foreign Office Confidential Print, Part I, from the Mid-Nineteenth Century to the First World War. Series A, Russia 1859–1914. Vol. 3: 1905–1906*, ed. Dominic Lieven (Frederick, MD: University Publications of America, 1983), Document 18.

9. Diary entry of Tsar Nicholas II, January 9, 1905, in Maylunas and Mironenko, *A Lifelong Passion*, p. 256.

10. Diary entry of January 22, 1905, in Paléologue, *The Turning Point*, p. 180.

11. Diary entry of February 17, 1905, in *Ibid.*, p. 190.

12. H. Montgomery to Sir Charles Hardinge, February 21, 1905, in Lieven, Bourne, and Watt, *BDFA, Part I, Series A, Russia 1859–1914, Vol. 3*, Document 38.

13. Grand Duke Nicholas Mikhailovich to Frédéric Masson, February 9/22, 1905, in Vogel and Smith, *Correspondance Entre le Grand-Duc Nicolas Mikhaïlovitch de Russie et Frédéric Masson*, p. 302.

14. Grand Duke Nicholas Mikhailovich to Frédéric Masson, February 16/March 1, 1905, *Ibid.*, p. 305.

15. Marie, *Education of a Princess*, p. 71.

16. Diary entry of February 17, 1905, in Paléologue, *The Turning Point*, p. 190.

17. Diary entry of March 5, 1905 in *Ibid.*, p. 197.

18. Théophile Delcassé, Foreign Minister of France, a strong adherer to the Franco-Russian Alliance and staunchly anti-German in pursuing French foreign policy.

19. Diary entry of March 5, 1905, in Paléologue, *The Turning Point*, p. 198.

20. Diary entry of March 16, 1905, in *Ibid.*, p. 204

21. Raymond A. Esthus, "Nicholas II and the Russo-Japanese War," in *The Russian Review*, 1981–40 (4), p. 400.

22. Narishkin-Kurakin, *Under Three Tsars*, p. 178.

23. *Ibid.*, p. 179.

24. Mossolov, *At the Court of the Last*, p. 36.

25. W. Bruce Lincoln, *In War's Dark Shadow: The Russians Before the Great War* (New York: The Dial Press, 1983), p. 266.

26. Vorres, *The Last Grand Duchess*, p. 113.

27. Esthus, "Nicholas II and the Russo-Japanese War," in *The Russian Review*, p. 403.

28. *Ibid.*, p. 404.

29. D. Chapman-Huston, ed., *The Private Diaries of Daisy, Princess of Pless 1873–1914* (London: John Murray, 1950), p. 133.

30. Lincoln, *In War's Dark Shadows*, p. 270.

31. *Ibid.*, p. 294.

32. *Ibid.*, p. 295.

33. Crankshaw, *Shadow of the Winter Palace*, p. 346.

34. Diary entry of K.R., June 20, 1905, in Maylunas and Mironenko, *A Lifelong Passion*, p. 278.

35. Diary entry of Grand Duchess Xenia, June 25, 1905, in *Ibid.*, p. 278.

36. Diary entry of Tsar Nicholas II, November 3, 1905, in *Ibid.*, p. 284.

37. Lincoln, *In War's Dark Shadows*, p. 297.

38. *Ibid.*, p. 296.

39. Empress Marie Feodorovna to Tsar Nicholas II, undated, 1905 in Bing, *Letters of Tsar Nicholas and Empress Marie*, p. 184.

40. Abraham Ascher, *The Revolution of 1905: Russia in Disarray* (Stanford: Stanford University Press, 1988), pp. 18–19.

41. Salisbury, *Black Night, White Snow*, p. 160.

42. Robert K. Massie, *Nicholas and Alexandra.* (New York: Atheneum, 1967), pp. 109–110.

43. Prince Gavril Constantinovich, *In the Marble Palace: Memoirs* (Moscow: Zakharov, 2005), pp. 54–55.

44. Alexander, *Once a Grand Duke*, p. 225.

45. Salisbury, *Black Night, White Snow*, p. 162.

46. Tsar Nicholas II to Empress Marie Feodorovna, October 19, 1905, in Bing, *Letters of Tsar Nicholas and Empress Marie*, pp. 185–189.

47. Empress Marie Feodorovna to Tsar Nicholas II, November 1, 1905, in *Ibid.*, pp. 192–193.

48. Tsar Nicholas II to Empress Marie Feodorovna, November 17, 1905, in *Ibid.*, p. 195.

49. Massie, *Nicholas and Alexandra*, p. 110.

50. *New York Times*, December 2, 1905.

51. *New York Times*, December 4, 1905.

52. Hosking, *Russia*, p. 378.

53. *The Times*, November 2, 1905.

54. von Bülow, *Memoirs of Prince von Bülow, Volume II*, p. 144.

55. Wycollar, "A Secret Chapter of Russian History," in *Munsey's Magazine*, May 1904, vol. XXXI, no. 2, p. 178.

56. *New York Times*, December 25, 1905.

57. *New York Times*, December 26, 1905.

58. Mager, *Elizabeth*, p. 220.

59. Tsar Nicholas II to Empress Marie Feodorovna, December 15, 1905, in Bing, *Letters of Tsar Nicholas and Empress Marie*, pp. 204–205.

60. Empress Marie Feodorovna to Tsar Nicholas II, December 2, 1905, in *Ibid.*, pp. 198–199.

61. Empress Marie Feodorovna to Tsar Nicholas II, December 29, 1905, in *Ibid.*, pp. 208–209.

17. SCANDAL

1. Madol, *King Christian IX*, p. 207.

2. Infanta Eulalia, *Court Life from Within* (London: Cassell and Company, Ltd., 1915), pp. 209–211.

3. Constance Battersea, *Reminiscences* (London: Macmillan and Co., Ltd., 1922), pp. 321–322.

4. *New York Times*, January 4, 1906.

5. Cecil Spring Rice to Sir Edward Grey, May 9, 1906, in D.C.B. Lieven, Kenneth Bourne, and D. C. Watt, eds., *British Documents on Foreign Affairs: Reports and Papers from the Foreign Office Confidential Print, Part I, from the Mid-Nineteenth Century to the First World War. Series A, Russia 1859–1914. Vol. 4: 1906–1907*, ed. by Dominic Lieven (Frederick, MD: University Publications of America, 1983), Document 38.

6. Marie, *Education of a Princess*, p. 84.

7. Crankshaw, *Shadow of the Winter Palace*, p. 362.

8. Vladimir Kokovtsov, *Out of My Past: The Memoirs of Count Kokovtsov*, ed. by H. H. Fisher, transl. by Laura Matveev (Stanford: Stanford University Press, 1935), pp. 129–130.

9. Ascher, *The Revolution of 1905*, pp. 85, 132.

10. Marie, *Education of a Princess*, p. 84.

11. Cecil Spring Rice to Sir Edward Grey, May 9, 1906, in Lieven, Bourne and Watt, *BDFA, Part I, Series A, Russia 1859–1914, Vol. 4*, Document 38.

12. Ascher, *The Revolution of 1905*, p. 83.

13. Cecil Spring Rice to Sir Edward Grey, May 23, 1906, in Lieven, Bourne and Watt, *BDFA, Part I, Series A, Russia 1859–1914, Vol. 4*, Document 43.

14. Diary entry of Grand Duchess Xenia, April 30, 1906, in Maylunas and Mironenko, *A Lifelong Passion*, p. 293.

15. Kokovtsov, *Out of My Past*, pp. 130–131.

16. Princess Catherine Radziwill, *Secrets of Dethroned Royalty* (New York: John Lane Company, 1920), p. 87.

17. *Ibid.*, p. 88.

18. Diary entry of Grand Duchess Xenia, May 12, 1905, in Maylunas and Mironenko, *A Lifelong Passion*, p. 276.

19. Sullivan, *A Fatal Passion*, p. 214.

20. *Ibid.*

21. van der Kiste, *Princess Victoria Melita*, p. 80.

22. Tsar Nicholas II to Empress Marie Feodorovna, October 5, 1905, in Maylunas and Mironenko, *A Lifelong Passion*, p. 282.

23. Sullivan, *A Fatal Passion*, p. 232

24. *Ibid.*, p. 238.

25. *New York Times*, December 3, 1905.

26. *Public Opinion: A Comprehensive Summary of the Press Throughout the World on All Important Current Topics*, Vol. XXXIX, No. 19, November 4, 1905.

27. Zeepvat, *Romanov Autumn*, p. 163.

28. van der Kiste, *Princess Victoria Melita*, p. 90.

29. Virginia Cowles, *1913: An End and a Beginning* (New York: Harper & Row, Publishers, 1967), p. 122.

30. Tsar Nicholas II to Empress Marie Feodorovna, October 5, 1905, in Maylunas and Mironenko, *A Lifelong Passion*, p. 282.

31. von Bülow, *Memoirs of Prince von Bülow, Volume II*, pp. 194–195.

32. *Ibid.*, p. 195.

33. Tsar Nicholas II to Empress Marie Feodorovna, October 5, 1905, in Maylunas and Mironenko, *A Lifelong Passion*, p. 282.

34. Sullivan, *A Fatal Passion*, p. 241.

35. *Ibid.*, p. 247.

36. Massie, *Nicholas and Alexandra*, p. 218.

37. *New York Times*, August 26, 1906.

38. Empress Marie Feodorovna to Tsar Nicholas II, undated, 1906, in Bing, *Letters of Tsar Nicholas and Empress Marie*, p. 216.

39. Erbach-Schönberg, *Reminiscences*, p. 315.

40. Perry and Pleshakov, *Flight of the Romanovs*, p. 70.

41. Chavchavadze, *The Grand Dukes*, p. 235.

42. Crawford, *Michael and Natasha*, p. 30.

43. Hermann Hagedorn, *The Roosevelt Family of Sagamore Hill* (New York: The Macmillan Company, 1954), p. 164.

44. *New York Times*, August 29, 1902.

45. Theodore Roosevelt, "Personal Account of His Trip From Khartoum to London, Written to Sir George Otto Trevelyan" Seventh Paper in "Theodore Roosevelt and His Time— Shown in His Letters," ed. by Joseph Bucklin Bishop, in *Scribner's Magazine*, vol. LXVII, January–June, no. 3, March, 1920 (New York: Charles Scribner's Sons, 1920), p. 275.

46. Perceval Gibbon, "What Ails Russia: Glimpses of the Inefficiency and Dissoluteness of the Royal Family," in *McClure's Magazine*, vol. XXIV, April 1905, no. 6, p. 613.

47. Vorres, *The Last Grand Duchess*, p. 109.

48. Diary entry of Grand Duchess Xenia, April 30, 1907, in Maylunas and Mironenko, *A Lifelong Passion*, p. 301.

49. Tsar Nicholas II to Empress Marie Feodorovna, July 25, 1906, in Bing, *Letters of Tsar Nicholas and Empress Marie*, p. 214.

50. Empress Marie Feodorovna to Tsar Nicholas II, undated, 1906, in *Ibid.*, pp. 214–215.

18. A DELUSORY WORLD

1. Viscount Crawley on the Internal Situation in Russia During the Fortnight from June 20 to July 4, 1906, in Lieven, Bourne, and Watt, *BDFA, Part I, Series A, Russia 1859–1914, Vol. 4*, Document 76.

2. Memorandum by Viscount Crawley, Political Survey, June 19, 1906, in *Ibid.*, Document 60.

3. Cecil Spring Rice to Sir Edward Grey, May 9, 1906, in *Ibid.*, Document 38.

4. Ascher, *The Revolution of 1905*, p. 242.

5. Hans Rogger, *Russia in the Age of Modernisation and Revolution 1881–1917* (London: Longman, 1983), p. 223.

6. Sir Arthur Nicolson to Sir Edward Grey, August 18, 1906, in Lieven, Bourne, and Watt, *BDFA, Part I, Series A, Russia 1859–1914, Vol. 4*, Document 121.

7. Cecil Spring Rice to Sir Edward Grey, May 9, 1906, in *Ibid.*, Document 38.

8. Rogger, *Russia in the Age of Modernisation*, p. 208.

9. George, *A Romanov Diary*, p. 81.

10. Gelardi, *Born to Rule*, pp. 96–97.

11. George, *A Romanov Diary*, p. 82.

12. *Ibid.*, p. 81.

13. Massie, *Nicholas and Alexandra*, p. 117.

14. Buxhoeveden, *Alexandra Feodorovna*, p. 103.

15. Pierre Gilliard, *Thirteen Years at the Russian Court*, transl. by F. Appleby Holt (Bath: Cedric Chivers, Ltd., 1921), p. 26.

16. Massie, *Nicholas and Alexandra*, p. 137.

17. Renée Elton Maud, *One Year at the Russian Court: 1904–1905* (London: John Lane, The Bodley Head, 1918), p. 73.

18. Gilliard, *Thirteen Years at the Russian Court*, p. 72.

19. *Ibid.*, p. 26.

20. *Ibid.*, p. 73.

21. Buxhoeveden, *Life and Tragedy of Alexandra Feodorovna*, p. 154.

22. Gilliard, *Thirteen Years at the Russian Court*, p. 75.

23. Buxhoeveden, *Life and Tragedy of Alexandra Feodorovna*, p. 156.

24. Gleb Botkin, *The Real Romanovs: As Revealed by the Late Czar's Physician and His Son.* (New York: Fleming H. Revell Company, 1931), p. 28.

25. Empress Marie Feodorovna to Tsar Nicholas II, February 28, 1907, in Bing, *Letters of Tsar Nicholas and Empress Marie*, p. 222.

26. Tisdall, *Marie Fedorovna*, p. 246.

27. Alexander, *Once a Grand Duke*, p. 234.

28. Perry and Pleshakov, *Flight of the Romanovs*, p. 71.

29. Alexander, *Once a Grand Duke*, p. 137.

30. Lynn Garafola, *Diaghilev's Ballets Russes* (New York: Oxford University Press, 1989), p. 168.

19. DISCORD

1. Crawford, *Michael and Natasha*, p. 42.

2. *Ibid.*, p. 33.

3. *Ibid.*, p. 37.

4. *Ibid.*, p. 16.

5. Nathalie Majolier, *Step-Daughter of Imperial Russia* (London: Stanley Paul & Co., Ltd., 1940), p. 16.

6. *Ibid.*, pp. 19–20.

7. Crawford, *Michael and Natasha*, p. 64.

8. *New York Times*, December, 17, 1911.

9. Ana de Sagrera, *Ena y Bee: En Defensa de Una Amistad* (Madrid: Velecio Editores, 2006), p. 142.

10. *Ibid.*, p. 145.

11. *Ibid.*, p. 155.

12. *Ibid.*, p. 156.

13. *Ibid.*, pp. 161–162.

14. *Ibid.*, p. 167.

15. *Ibid.*, p. 169–170.

16. *Ibid.*, p. 183.

17. Massie, *Nicholas and Alexandra*, p. 194.

18. Count Bohdan D. de Castellane, *One Crowded Hour: An Autobiography* (London: George Allen & Unwin, Ltd., 1934), pp. 189–190.

19. M. V. Rodzianko, *The Reign of Rasputin: An Empire's Collapse, Memoirs of M. V. Rodzianko*, transl. by Catherine Zvegintzoff (London: A. M. Philpot, Ltd., 1927), p. 24.

20. de Castellane, *One Crowded Hour*, pp. 203–104.

21. Lilli Dehn, *The Real Tsaritsa* (London: Thornton Butterworth, Ltd., 1922), pp. 100, 103.

22. Alex de Jonge, *The Life and Times of Grigorii Rasputin* (New York: Coward, McCann and Geoghegan, 1982), p. 152.

23. Buchanan, *Victorian Gallery*, p. 53.

24. A Russian, *Russian Court Memoirs, 1914–16: With Some Accounts of Court, Social and Political Life in Petrograd Before and Since the War* (London: Herbert Jenkins Ltd., 1917), pp. 111–112.

25. Velichenko and Mirolyubova, *Palace of Grand Duke Vladimir*, p. 154.

26. Sullivan, *A Fatal Passion*, p. 249.

27. *Ibid.*, p. 250.

28. Empress Marie Feodorovna to Tsar Nicholas II, May 7, 1910, in Bing, *Letters of Tsar Nicholas and Empress Marie*, p. 254.

29. Crawford, *Michael and Natasha*, p. 104.

30. A. Nekludoff, *Diplomatic Reminiscences Before and During the World War, 1911–1917*, transl. by Alexandra Paget (New York: E. P. Dutton and Company, 1920), p. 79.

31. Edvard Radzinsky, *The Rasputin File*, transl. from the Russian by Judson Rosengrant (New York: Nan A. Talese, 2000), p. 137.

32. Harold Nicolson, *Portrait of a Diplomatist: Being the Life of Sir Arthur Nicolson First Lord Carnock, and a Study of the Origins of the Great War* (Boston: Houghton Mifflin Company, 1930), p. 165.

33. Sir George Buchanan, *My Mission to Russia and Other Diplomatic Memories, Volume I* (Boston: Little, Brown and Company, 1923), p. 160.

34. Lincoln, *In War's Dark Shadow*, pp. 341–343.

35. von Bock, *Reminiscences of My Father*, p. 263.

36. Ascher, *P. A. Stolypin*, p. 348.

37. Empress Marie Feodorovna to Tsar Nicholas II, September 9, 1911, in Bing, *Letters of Tsar Nicholas and Empress Marie*, pp. 263–264.

38. Rodzianko, *Reign of Rasputin*, pp. 36–38.

39. Radzinsky, *The Rasputin File*, p. 139.

40. Nekludoff, *Diplomatic Reminiscences*, p. 79.

41. Rodzianko, *Reign of Rasputin*, p. 38.

42. Kokovtsov, *Out of My Past*, pp. 295–296.

20. GRANDEUR AND PAIN

1. Paoli, *Their Majesties as I Knew Them*, pp. 209–210.

2. Hugo Vickers, *Alice: Princess Andrew of Greece* (London: Hamish Hamilton, 2000), p. 79.

3. *Ibid.*, pp. 69–70.

4. Stella King, *Princess Marina: Her Life and Times* (London: Casell, 1969), pp. 39–40.

5. Buchanan, *Victorian Gallery*, p. 56.

6. King, *Princess Marina*, p. 41.

7. *Ibid.*, p. 42.

8. Buchanan, *Victorian Gallery*, pp. 56–57.

9. James H. Cockfield, *White Crow: The Life and Times of Grand Duke Nicholas Mikhailovich Romanov, 1859–1919* (Westport, CT: Praeger, 2002), p. 26.

10. Mossolov, *At the Court of the Last Tsar*, pp. 78–79.

11. Aronson, *A Family of Kings*, p. 207.

12. Elinor Glyn, *Romantic Adventure: Being the Autobiography of Elinor Glyn* (New York: E. P. Dutton & Co., Inc., 1937), p. 82.

13. *Ibid.*, p. 83.

14. *Ibid.*, p. 179.

15. *Ibid.*, p. 182.

16. *Ibid.*, p. 194.

17. Elinor Glyn, *His Hour* (New York: D. Appleton and Company, 1910), dedication page.

18. Hans Nadelhoffer, *Cartier: Jewelers Extraordinary* (New York: Harry N. Abrams, Inc., Publishers, 1984), p. 82.

19. Buchanan, *Victorian Gallery*, p. 58.

20. *Ibid.*, pp. 119–120.

21. Prince Nicholas, *My Fifty Years*, pp. 42–43.

22. Sir Vincent Corbett, *Reminiscences: Autobiographical and Diplomatic of Sir Vincent Corbett, K.C.V.O., Late a Minsiter in H.M. Diplomatic Service* (London: Hodder and Stoughton, n.d.), p. 288.

23. Rosen, *Forty Years of Diplomacy*, 183.

24. Charles Edward Lloyd, "Modern Greece," in *The Cosmopolitan*, vol. XXII, April 1897, no. 6, p. 589.

25. *The Christian Life*, January 26, 1884, p. 38.

26. King, *Princess Marina*, p. 12.

27. Corbett, *Reminiscences*, pp. 288–289.

28. E. F. Benson, *Our Family Affairs 1867–1896* (New York: George H. Doran Company, 1921), p. 283.

29. Battersea, *Reminiscences*, p. 295.

30. Sir Francis Elliot and A. Young to Sir Edward Grey, Annual Report on Greece for 1909, February 14, 1910, in Kenneth Bourne, D. Cameron Watt, and John F.V. Keiger, eds., *British Document on Foreign Affairs, Part I, Series F: Europe, 1848–1914, Vol. 14: Greece, 1847–1914*, ed. David Stevenson and John F. V. Keiger (Frederick, MD: University Publications of America, 1987), Document 55.

31. van der Kiste, *Kings of the Hellenes*, p. 68.

32. Gelardi, *Born to Rule*, p. 157.

33. Thanos Veremis, *The Military in Greek Politics: From Independence to Democracy* (Montreal: Black Rose Books, Ltd., 1997), p. 46.

34. van der Kiste, *Kings of the Hellenes*, pp. 68–69.

35. Nicholas, *My Fifty Years*, p. 223.

36. Minute to a confidential despatch by Sir Francis Elliot, British Ambassador to Greece, to Sir Edward Grey, British Foreign Secretary, December 21, 1909, The National Archives, P.R.O., F.O. 371/679/No. 98.

37. Sir Francis Elliot and A. Young to Sir Edward Grey, Annual Report on Greece for 1909, February 14, 1910, in Bourne, Watt, and Keiger, eds., *BDFA, Part I, Series F: Europe, 1848–1914, Vol. 14: Greece, 1847–1914*, Document 55.
38. Vickers, *Princess Alice*, p. 87.
39. Karolou, *Olga, Queen of the Greeks*, chapter 11.
40. Anna Viroubova, *Memories of the Russian Court* (New York: The Macmillan Company, 1923), p. 94.
41. Gilliard, *Thirteen Years at the Russian Court*, p. 29.
42. Mossolov, *At the Court of the Last Tsar*, p. 150.
43. Buxhoeveden, *Alexandra Feodorovna*, p. 131.
44. *Ibid.*, p. 132.
45. Viroubova, *Memories of the Russian Court*, p. 94.
46. Mossolov, *At the Court of the Last Tsar*, p. 152.
47. Tsar Nicholas II to Empress Marie Feodorovna, October 20, 1912, in Bing, *The Letters of Tsar Nicholas and Empress Marie*, pp. 276–277.

21. A TERRIBLE BLOW!

1. Dmitrii I. Abrikossow, *Revelations of a Russian Diplomat: The Memoirs of Dmitrii I. Abrikossow*, ed. by George Alexander Lensen (Seattle: University of Washington Press, 1994), p. 213.
2. Crawford, *Michael & Natasha*, pp. 129–130.
3. *Ibid.*, p. 131.
4. Empress Marie Feodorovna to Tsar Nicholas II, November 4, 1912, in Bing, *The Letters of Tsar Nicholas and Empress Marie*, p. 283.
5. Tsar Nicholas II to Empress Marie Feodorovna, November 7, 1912, in *Ibid.*, p. 284.
6. Crawford, *Michael and Natasha*, p. 136.
7. *Ibid.*
8. *Ibid.*, p. 144.
9. *Ibid.*, p. 146.
10. Empress Marie Feodorovna to Tsar Nicholas II, July 27, 1913, in Bing, *The Letters of Tsar Nicholas and Empress Marie*, pp. 287–288.
11. de Sagrera, *Ena y Bee*, p. 192.
12. *Ibid.*, p. 198.
13. *The Independent*, Volume LXXIV, January–June 1913, p. 720.
14. Karolou, *Olga, Queen of the Greeks*, chapter 12.
15. van der Kiste, *Kings of the Hellenes*, p. 73.
16. Theo Aronson, *Crowns in Conflict: The Triumph and Tragedy of European Monarchy 1910–1918* (London: John Murray, 1986), p. 86.
17. *The Times*, March 7, 1913.
18. *The Times*, March 10, 1913.
19. King, *Princess Marina*, p. 40.
20. Zeepvat, *From Cradle to Crown*, p. 152.
21. King, *Princess Marina*, p. 44.
22. Zeepvat, *From Cradle to Crown*, p. 155.
23. *Ibid.*, p. 156.
24. King, *Princess Marina*, p. 47.

25. Zeepvat, *From Cradle to Crown*, p. 158.

26. *Ibid.*, p. 159.

27. Nicholas, *My Fifty Years*, p. 238.

28. Arthur Gould Lee, *Helen, Queen Mother of Rumania: Princess of Greece and Denmark* (London: Faber and Faber, 1956), p. 28.

29. Karolou, *Olga, Queen of the Greeks*, chapter 13.

30. *Ibid.*

31. Vickers, *Alice*, p. 106.

32. George, *A Romanov Diary*, p. 146.

33. Karolou, *Olga, Queen of the Greeks*, chapter 13.

34. *The Times*, March 20, 1913.

22. ON THE EVE

1. Sir Francis Elliot, et. al., to Sir Edward Grey, May 20, 1914, Annual Report on Greece for 1913, *BDFA, Series F, vol. 14*, Document 64.

2. Hellenic Army General Staff, Army History Directorate, *A Concise History of the Balkan Wars 1912–1913* (Athens: An Army History Directorate Publication, 1998), p. 269.

3. Christopher, *Memoirs*, p. 120.

4. Queen Olga to King George V, December 26, 1913/January 8, 1914, The Royal Archives, RA GV/PRIV/AA 46/93.

5. Diary entry of Empress Marie Feodorovna, June 8/21, 1914, in U. V. Kudrin, ed., *Diaries of the Empress Marie Feodorovna: Years 1914–1920, 1923* (Moscow: Vagrius Publishing House, 2005), p. 38.

6. *Ibid.*

7. Rodzianko, *The Reign of Rasputin*, pp. 76–77.

8. Viroubova, *Memories of the Russian Court*, p. 100.

9. Irina Galitzine, *Spirit to Survive: The Memoirs of Princess Nicholas Galitzine* (London: William Kimber, 1976), p. 36.

10. Kokovtsov, *Out of My Past*, p. 361.

11. Viroubova, *Memories of the Russian Court*, p. 99.

12. The surname is variously spelled as Yussoupov, Yusupov, Youssoupov, Youssopoff, Yossopov, Iossopov, etc.

13. Greg King, *The Man Who Killed Rasputin: Prince Felix Youssoupov and the Murder That Helped Bring Down the Russian Empire* (Toronto: Citadel Press Book, 1995), pp. 63–64.

14. Marie, *Education of a Princess*, p. 154.

15. Prince Felix Youssoupoff, *Lost Splendor: The Amazing Memoirs of the Man Who Killed Rasputin*, transl. from the French by Ann Green and Nicholas Katkoff (New York: Helen Marx Books, 2003), p. 94.

16. Anonymous (Stopford), *The Russian Diary of an Englishman*, p. 93.

17. Radzinsky, *The Rasputin File*, p. 196.

18. A Russian, *Russian Court Memoirs* p. 35–36.

19. Youssoupoff, *Lost Splendor*, p. 182.

20. Gilliard, *Thirteen Years*, p. 94.

21. Marie, *The Story of My Life, Volume II*, p. 272.

22. *Ibid.*, pp. 277–278.

23. Gordon Brook-Shepherd, *Archduke of Sarajevo: The Romance and Tragedy of Franz Ferdinand of Austria* (Boston: Little, Brown and Company, 1984), p. 251.

24. *New York Times*, June 28, 1914.

25. Lee, *Helen, Queen Mother of Rumania*, p. 34.

26. Buxhoeveden, *Alexandra Feodorovna*, p. 184.

27. Marie, *Education of a Princess*, p. 159.

28. *Ibid.*, p. 161.

29. Barkhatova and Burkova, *The Danish Princess—the Russian Empress*, p. 121.

30. Massie, *Nicholas and Alexandra*, p. 256.

31. Marie, *A Romanov Diary*, p. 158.

32. Charles Louis Seeger, ed. and transl., *The Memoirs of Alexander Iswolsky: Formerly Russian Minister of Foreign Affairs and Ambassador to France* (Gulf Breeze, FL: Academic International Press, 1974), p. 72.

33. Tisdall, *Marie Fedorovna*, pp. 265–267.

23. POOR, DOOMED RUSSIA!

1. Bernard Pares, *My Russian Memoirs* (New York: AMS Press, 1969), p. 355.

2. *Ibid.*, p. 275.

3. Massie, *Nicholas and Alexandra*, p. 277.

4. Princess Julia Cantacuzène, *Revolutionary Days: Recollections of Romanoffs and Bolsheviki 1914–1917* (Boston: Small, Maynard & Company, 1919), pp. 13–14.

5. Marie, *Education of a Princess*, p. 162.

6. Cantacuzène, *Revolutionary Days*, p. 16.

7. Nicholas, *Political Memoirs*, p. 21.

8. Vera D. Pykhacheva, *Memoirs by Vera Pihatcheff née Nabokoff, Demoiselle d'Honneur to H.I H. the Empress Marie Feodorovna*, transl. by Janet Crawford (Rowsley, UK: "Bibliophilia" Library, 1936), p. 84.

9. A Russian, *Russian Court Memoirs, 1914–16*, p. 73.

10. V. V. Shulgin, *The Years: Memoirs of a Member of the Russian Duma, 1906–1917*, transl. by Tanya Davis (New York: Hippocrene Books, 1984), p. 133.

11. Poliakoff, *Mother Dear*, pp. 309–310.

12. Roderick R. Mclean, *Royalty and Diplomacy in Europe 1890–1914* (Cambridge: Cambridge University Press, 2001), p. 20.

13. Hall, *Little Mother of Russia*, p. 261.

14. Gilliard, *Thirteen Years at the Russian Court*, pp. 107–108.

15. Prince Nicholas of Greece, *Political Memoirs, 1914–1917: Pages from My Diary* (Freeport, NY: Books for Libraries Press, 1972), p. 20.

16. Maurice Paléologue, *An Ambassador's Memoirs, Vol. I: July 20, 1914–June 2, 1915*, transl. by F. A. Holt (New York: George H. Doran Company, n.d.), pp. 71–72.

17. Barkhatova and Burkova, *The Danish Princess—the Russian Empress*, p. 121.

18. Abrikossow, *Revelations of a Russian Diplomat*, p. 233.

19. *Ibid.*, pp. 234–235.

20. Viroubova, *Memories of the Russian Court*, p. 109.

21. Gelardi, *Born to Rule*, p. 221.

22. Buxhoeveden, *Alexandra Feodorovna*, p. 194.

23. E. M. Almedingen, *An Unbroken Unity: A Memoir of Grand-Duchess Serge of Russia, 1864–1918* (London: The Bodley Head, 1964), p. 84.

24. William Clarke, *The Lost Fortune of the Tsars* (New York: St. Martin's Press, 1994), p. 160.

25. Anonymous (Stopford), *Russian Diary*, p. 31.

26. *Ibid.*, p. 33.

27. *Ibid.*, pp. 34–36.

28. *Ibid.*, p. 38.

29. Rodzianko, *Reign of Rasputin*, pp. 113–114.

30. Tomofei Ksenofonotovich Yaschik, *Beside the Empress: Memoirs of a Life-Cossack* (St. Petersburg: Nestor-Historia, 2004), p. 68.

31. Poliakoff, *Mother Dear*, p. 311.

32. Bergamini, *The Tragic Dynasty*, p. 435.

33. Chavchavadze, *The Grand Dukes*, p. 161.

34. Rodzianko, *Reign of Rasputin*, p. 118.

35. Anonymous (Stopford), *Russian Diary*, pp. 21–22.

36. Diary entry of Grand Duke Andrei Vladimirovich, September 6, 1915, in Frank Alfred Golder, ed., *Documents of Russian History 1914–1917* (Gloucester, MA: Peter Smith, 1964), pp. 239–240.

37. *Ibid.*, p. 240.

38. Radzinsky, *The Rasputin File*, p. 334.

39. Diary entry of Grand Duke Andrei Vladimirovich, September 6, 1915, in Golder, *Documents of Russian History*, pp 241.

40. Rodzianko, *Reign of Rasputin*, p. 151.

41. Empress Marie Feodorovna to Tsar Nicholas II, December 3, 1915, in Bing, *The Letters of Tsar Nicholas and Empress Marie*, pp. 294–295.

42. Tsarina Alexandra to Tsar Nicholas II, April 4, 1915, in Joseph T. Fuhrmann, ed., *Complete Wartime Correspondence of Tsar Nicholas II and the Empress Alexandra, April 1914–March 1917* (Wesport, CT: Greenwood Press, 1999), No. 218/Her No. 287, p. 100.

43. Paléologue, *An Ambassador's Memoirs, Vol. I*, p. 323.

44. Robert Wilton, *Russia's Agony* (New York: E. P. Dutton & Company, 1919), p. 237.

45. Gelardi, *Born to Rule*, p. 217.

46. Maurice Paléologue, *An Ambassador's Memoirs, Vol. II: June 3, 1915–August 18, 1916*, transl. by F. A. Holt (New York: George H. Doran Company, n.d.), p. 52.

47. Abríkossow, *Revelations of a Russian Diplomat*, pp. 236, 238.

24. NEARING IMPLOSION

1. Sullivan, *A Fatal Passion*, p. 290.

2. *Ibid.*

3. Gelardi, *Born to Rule*, p. 218.

4. Queen Marie, *The Story of My Life, Volume III* (London: Cassell and Company, Ltd., 1934), p. 107.

5. Mrs. Will Gordon, *Roumania: Yesterday and To-day* (London: John Lane The Bodley Head, 1918), p. 221.

6. Poliakoff, *Mother Dear*, p. 314.

7. Tsarina Alexandra to Tsar Nicholas II, November 1, 1916, in Fuhrmann, *Complete Wartime Correspondence*, No. 1542/Her No. 619, p. 635.

8. Tisdall, *Marie Fedorovna*, pp. 273–274.

9. Rodzianko, *Reign of Rasputin*, p. 201.

10. Vorres, *The Last Grand Duchess*, p. 146.

11. Empress Marie Feodorovna to Tsar Nicholas II, November 16, 1916, in Bing, *Letters of Tsar Nicholas and Empress Marie*, p. 298.

12. Perry and Pleshakov, *Flight of the Romanovs*, p. 130.

13. Empress Marie Feodorovna to Tsar Nicholas II, May 22, 1916, in Bing, *Letters of Tsar Nicholas and Empress Marie*, p. 297.

14. Crawford, *Michael and Natasha*, p. 174.

15. *Ibid.*, pp. 192–193.

16. Tsarina Alexandra to Tsar Nicholas II, February 13, 1916, in Fuhrmann, *Complete Wartime Correspondence*, No. 823/Her No. 445, p. 388.

17. Tsarina Alexandra to Tsar Nicholas II, January 26, 1915, in *Ibid.*, No. 151/Her No. 270, p. 73.

18. Tsarina Alexandra to Tsar Nicholas II, March 8, 1915, in *Ibid.*, No. 207/Her No. 285, p. 96.

19. Tsarina Alexandra to Tsar Nicholas II, March 10, 1916, in *Ibid.*, No. 867/Her No. 457, p. 407.

20. Tsarina Alexandra to Tsar Nicholas II, May 26, 1916, in *Ibid.*, No. 1055/Her No. 500, p. 477.

21. Tsarina Alexandra to Tsar Nicholas II, June 2, 1916, in *Ibid.*, No. 1085/Her No. 507, p. 486.

22. Tsar Nicholas II to Tsarina Alexandra, June 16, 1916, in *Ibid.*, No. 1147, p. 506. The "regulations" refers to Miechen trying to get approval for her charitable institutions.

23. Tsarina Alexandra to Tsar Nicholas II, September 12, 1916, in *Ibid.*, No. 1398/Her No. 587, p. 580.

24. Mossolov, *At the Court of the Last Tsar*, p. 47.

25. Kokovtsov, *Out of My Past*, p. 454.

26. *Ibid.*, pp. 470–471.

27. *Ibid.*, p. 454.

28. Viroubova, *Memories of the Russian Court*, p. 119.

29. Salisbury, *Black Night, White Snow*, p. 269.

30. Viroubova, *Memories of the Russian Court*, p. 121.

31. de Jonge, *Rasputin*, p. 254.

32. Viroubova, *Memories of the Russian Court*, pp. 169–170.

33. Nekludoff, *Diplomatic Reminiscences*, pp. 402–403.

34. *Ibid.*, p. 404.

35. Dehn, *The Real Tsaritsa*, p. 74.

36. Nekludoff, *Diplomatic Reminiscences*, p. 435.

37. Paléologue, *An Ambassador's Memoirs, Vol. I*, p. 238.

38. W.H-H. Waters, *Secret and Confidential: The Experiences of a Military Attaché* (New York: Frederick A. Stokes Co., 1926), p. 360.

39. Rodzianko, *Reign of Rasputin*, p. 101.

40. Narishkin-Kurakin, *Under Three Tsars*, pp. 203–204.

41. Pares, *My Russian Memoirs*, p. 439.

42. Youssoupoff, *Lost Splendor*, p. 224.

43. Florence Farmborough, *With the Armies of the Tsar: A Nurse at the Russian Front 1914–18* (New York: Stein and Day, 1975), p. 92.

44. Dominic Lieven, "Pro-Germans and Russian Foreign Policy 1890–1914, in *The International History Review*, vol. II., no. 1, January 1980, p. 49.

45. Roman Romanovich Rosen, *Forty Years of Diplomacy, Volume II* (New York: Alfred A. Knopf, 1922), p. 205.

46. Paléologue, *An Ambassador's Memoirs, Vol. II*, p. 166.

47. Youssoupoff, *Lost Splendor*, p. 220.

48. Arthur Judson Brown, *Russia in Transformation* (New York: Fleming H. Revell Company, 1917), p. 62.

49. Wilton, *Russia's Agony*, p. 39.

50. Buchanan, *My Mission to Russia, Vol. II*, p. 51.

51. Mossolov, *At the Court of the Last Tsar*, p. 174.

52. Paléologue, *An Ambassador's Memoirs, Vol. II*, pp. 174–177.

53. *Ibid.*, p. 204.

54. Farmborough, *With the Armies of the Tsar*, p. 246.

55. Abrikossow, *Revelations of a Russian Diplomat*, p. 239.

25. IGNOMINY

1. Christopher, *Memoirs*, p. 120.

2. van der Kiste, *Kings of the Hellenes*, p. 89.

3. Stelio Hourmouzios, *No Ordinary Crown: A Biography of King Paul of the Hellenes* (London: Weidenfeld and Nicolson, 1972), pp. 28–29.

4. Nicholas, *My Fifty Years*, pp. 259–260.

5. Hourmouzios, *No Ordinary Crown*, p. 29.

6. Aronson, *Crowns in Conflict*, p. 135.

7. S. P. P. Cosmetatos, *The Tragedy of Greece* (London: Kegan Paul, Trench, Trubner & Co., 1928), pp. 118–119.

8. Gelardi, *Born to Rule*, p. 212.

9. van der Kiste, *Kings of the Hellenes*, p. 96.

10. Gelardi, *Born to Rule*, p. 212.

11. Christos Theodoulou, *Greece and the Entente: August 1, 1914–September 25, 1916* (Thessaloniki: Institute for Balkan Studies, 1971), p. 218.

12. Cosmetatos, *Tragedy of Greece*, p. 108.

13. King Constantine II to Paola, Princess of Saxe Weimar, February 17, 1916, in Paola, Princess of Saxe-Weimar, *A King's Private Letters: Being Letters Written by King Constantine of Greece to Paola, Princess of Saxe-Weimar During the Years 1912–1923* (London: Eveleigh Nash & Grayson, 1925), p. 173.

14. Garshin, *The Hellenes' Queen Olga Constantinovna*, chapter 1.

15. *Ibid.*

16. Zeepvat, *The Camera and the Tsars*, p. 102.

17. Diary entry of Empress Marie Feodorovna, September 29/October 12, 1914, in Kudrin, *Diaries of the Empress Marie Feodorovna*, p. 62.

18. Diary entry of Empress Marie Feodorovna, January 1/14, 1915, in *Ibid.*, p. 85.

19. Karolou, *Olga, Queen of the Greeks*, chapter 14.

20. Nicholas, *Political Memoirs*, p. 167.

21. *Ibid.*, p. 180.

22. Christopher, *Memoirs*, p. 133.

23. Diary entry of Empress Marie Feodorovna, July 1/17, 1916, in Kudrin, *Diaries of the Empress Marie Feodorovna*, p. 128.

24. Diary entry of Empress Marie Feodorovna, August 22/September 4, 1916, in *Ibid.*, p. 138.

25. Tsarina Alexandra to Tsar Nicholas II, June 9, 1916, in Fuhrmann, *Complete Wartime Correspondence*, No. 1119/Her No. 515, p. 498.

26. Tsar Nicholas II to Tsarina Alexandra, July 15, 1916, in *Ibid.*, No. 1242, p. 535.

27. Maurice Paléologue, *An Ambassador's Memoirs, Vol. III: August 19, 1916–May 17, 1917*, transl. by F. A. Holt (New York: George H. Doran Company, n.d.), p. 39.

28. Nicholas, *Political Memoirs*, pp. 178–179.

29. Harold Nicolson, *King George the Fifth: His Life and Reign* (London: Constable & Co. Ltd., 1952), pp. 281–282.

30. Aronson, *Crowns in Conflict*, p. 136.

31. G. F. Abbott, *Greece and the Allies, 1914–1922* (London: Methuen & Co., 1922), p. 174.

32. Aronson, *Crowns in Conflict*, p. 136.

33. Paxton Hibben, *Constantine I and the Greek People* (New York: The Century Co., 1920), p. 521.

34. Demetrius Caclamanos, "Reminiscences of the Balkan Wars," in *The Slavonic and East European Review*, Vol. 16, No. 46 (July 1937), p. 124.

26: THE MOST DIRE CASTASTROPHES

1. Massie, *Nicholas and Alexandra*, p. 361.

2. Edmund A. Walsh, *The Fall of the Russian Empire: The Story of the Last of the Romanovs and the Coming of the Bolsheviki* (Boston: Little, Brown and Company, 1928), p. 117.

3. Princess Paley, *Memories of Russia 1916–1919* (London: Herbert Jenkins, Ltd., 1924), pp. 26–27.

4. Alexander, *Once a Grand Duke*, p. 275.

5. Mager, *Elizabeth*, pp. 302–303.

6. Yousoupoff, *Lost Splendor*, p. 202.

7. Paul Miliukov, *Political Memoirs 1905–1917*, ed. by Arthur P. Mendel, transl. by Carl Goldberg (Ann Arbor: The University of Michigan Press, 1967), p. 235.

8. Marie, *Education of a Princess*, pp. 248–249.

9. "The Vladimir Line" from Vladimir Purishkevich's Diary, December 9, 1916, in Golder, *Documents of Russian History 1914–1917*, pp. 246–247.

10. Countess Nostitz (Lilie de Fernandez-Azabal), *The Countess from Iowa* (New York: G. P. Putnam's Sons, 1936), p. 184.

11. Nicholas II was fully cognizant of being born on the Feast of the Prophet Job and thus always considered that he would undergo many trials in his life.

12. Paléolgue, *An Ambassador's Memoirs, Vol. III*, pp. 23–24.

13. *Ibid.*, p. 131.

14. Anna Rodzianko to Princess Zenaida Yussoupov, December 1, 1916, in C. E. Vulliamy, ed., *The Red Archives: Russian State Papers and Other Documents Relating to the Years 1915–1918*, transl. by A. L. Hynes (London: Geoffrey Bles, 1929), pp. 118–119.

15. Princess Zenaida Yussoupov to Prince Felix Yussoupov, November 18, 1916, in *Ibid.*, p. 110.

16. Princess Zenaida Yussoupov to Prince Felix Yussoupov, December 3, 1916, in *Ibid.*, pp. 113–114.

17. Princess Irina Youssoupov to Prince Felix Yussoupov, November 25, 1916, in *Ibid.*, p. 115.
18. R. H. Bruce Lockhart, *British Agent* (New York: G. P. Putnam's Sons, 1933), p. 153.
19. *Ibid.*, p. 155.
20. Gelardi, *Born to Rule*, p. 250.
21. King, *The Man Who Killed Rasputin*, p. 158.
22. Edward T. Heald, *Witness to Revolution: Letters from Russia 1916–1919*, edited by James B. Gidney (Kent, OH: Kent State University Press, 1972), p. 36.
23. Marie, *Education of a Princess*, p. 250.
24. Lascelle Meserve de Basily, *Memoirs of a Lost World* (Stanford: Hoover Institution Press, 1975), p. 77.
25. Nostitz, *Countess from Iowa*, p. 184.
26. Nekludoff, *Diplomatic Reminiscences*, p. 457.
27. Yousoupoff, *Lost Splendor*, p. 277.
28. General A. S. Loukomsky, *Memoirs of the Russian Revolution* (Westport, CT: Hyperion Press, Inc., 1975), p. 57.
29. Paul and Beatrice Grabbe, *Private World of the Last Tsar: In the Photographs and Notes of General Count Alexander Grabbe* (Boston: Little, Brown and Co., 1984), p. 167.
30. *Ibid.*, p. 168.
31. Botkin, *The Real Romanovs*, pp. 127–128.
32. Gilliard, *Thirteen Years at the Russian Court*, p. 183.
33. de Jonge, *Grigorii Rasputin*, p. 138.
34. Sir Bernard Pares, *Fall of the Russian Monarchy: A Study of the Evidence* (New York: Random House, 1961), p. 399.
35. Anonymous (Stopford), *Russian Diary*, pp. 75, 77–78.
36. *Ibid.*, p. 87.
37. Alexander, *Once a Grand Duke*, pp. 277–278.
38. King, *The Man Who Killed Rasputin*, p. 188.
39. Paléolgue, *An Ambassador's Memoirs, Vol. III*, pp. 160–162.
40. Charles de Chambrun, *Lettres à Marie: Pétersbourg-Pétrograd 1914–1917* (Paris: Librairie Plon, 1941), p. 40.
41. Louis de Robien, *The Diary of a Diplomat in Russia, 1917–1918*, transl. by Camilla Sykes (New York: Praeger Publishers, 1970), p. 37.
42. Anonymous (Stopford), *Russian Diary*, pp. 213–214.
43. Bing, *Letters of Tsar Nicholas and Empress Marie*, p. 299.
44. Paléolgue, *An Ambassador's Memoirs, Vol. III*, p. 170.
45. Perry and Pleshakov, *Flight of the Romanovs*, p. 141.
46. *Ibid.*, p. 149.
47. Marie, *Education of a Princess*, p. 279.
48. Zoya Belyakova, *The Romanovs: The Way It Was* (St. Petersburg: Ego Publishers, 2000), pp. 113–114.
49. Anonymous (Stopford), *Russian Diary*, p. 89.
50. Empress Marie Feodorovna to Tsar Nicholas II, February 17, 1917, in Bing, *Letters of Tsar Nicholas and Empress Marie*, p. 300.
51. Belyakova, *The Romanovs*, p. 114.
52. Hall, *Little Mother of Russia*, p. 279.
53. Rodzianko, *Reign of Rasputin*, pp. 245–247.
54. Paléolgue, *An Ambassador's Memoirs, Vol. III*, pp. 202–203.

55. Mossolov, *At the Court of the Last Tsar*, p. 100.

56. George, *A Romanov Diary*, pp. 177–178.

57. Paléolgue, *An Ambassador's Memoirs, Vol. III*, p. 232.

58. Nostitz, *Countess from Iowa*, p. 196.

59. de Basily, *Memoirs of a Lost World*, p. 82.

60. Major-General Alfred W.F. Knox, *With the Russian Army 1914–1917* (New York: Arno Press, Inc., 1971), p. 558.

61. Hall, *Little Mother of Russia*, pp. 281–282.

62. Pipes, *The Russian Revolution*, pp. 312–313.

63. Massie, *Nicholas and Alexandra*, p. 416.

64. Dimitri von Mohrenschildt, *The Russian Revolution of 1917: Contemporary Accounts* (New York: Oxford University Press, 1971), pp. 80–81.

65. V. V. Shulgin, *Days of the Revolution: Memoirs from the Right 1905–1917*, ed. and transl. by Bruce F. Adams (Gulf Breeze, FL: Academic International Press, 1990), p. 209.

66. de Chambrun, *Lettres à Marie*, p. 67.

67. Alexander, *Once a Grand Duke*, p. 288.

68. de Basily, *Memoirs of a Lost World*, pp. 137–138.

27. THE TRIUMPH OF MADNESS

1. Pipes, *The Russian Revolution*, p. 336.

2. Anonymous (Stopford), *Russian Diary*, p. 121.

3. Princess Romanovsky-Krassinky, *Dancing in Petersburg: The Memoirs of Kschessinka*, transl. by Arnold Haskell (Garden City, NY: Doubleday & Company, Inc., 1961), p. 166.

4. Irina Skariätiina, *A World Can End* (New York: Jonathan Cape & Harrison Smith, 1931), p. 107.

5. Dehn, *Real Tsaritsa*, p. 165.

6. David R. Francis, *Russia from the American Embassy: April, 1916-November, 1918* (New York: Charles Scribner's Sons, 1921), p. 80.

7. Massie, *Nicholas and Alexandra*, p. 426.

8. Barkhatova and Burkova, *The Danish Princess—the Russian Empress*, p. 130.

9. George, *A Romanov Diary*, p. 181.

10. Major-General Sir John Hanbury-Williams, *The Emperor Nicholas II As I Knew Him* (London: Arthur L. Humphreys, 1922), p. 165.

11. Note of the conversation of General [Hanbury] Williams with the Dowager Empress Maria Feodorovna and the Grand Duke Alexander Miklailovitch in Vulliamy, *The Red Archives*, p. 277.

12. Francis, *Russia from the American Embassy*, p. 80.

13. Yaschik, *Beside the Empress*, p. 67.

14. Alexander, *Once a Grand Duke*, p. 292.

15. Battiscombe, *Queen Alexandra*, p. 291.

16. Kudrina, *Mother and Son*, p. 104.

17. *Ibid.*, p. 110.

18. *Ibid.*, p. 256.

19. Vorres, *Last Grand Duchess*, pp. 149–150.

20. Belyakova, *The Romanovs*, p. 116.

21. Massie, *Nicholas and Alexandra*, p. 440.

22. de Chambrun, *Lettres à Marie*, p. 233.

23. Paley, *Memories of Russia*, p. 87.

24. Gilliard, *Thirteen Years at the Russian Court*, p. 228.

25. Kudrina, *Mother and Son*, p. 115.

26. Anonymous (Stopford), *Russian Diary*, p. 135.

27. Perry and Pleshakov, *Flight of the Romanovs*, p. 141.

28. *Ibid.*, p. 148.

29. Anonymous (Stopford), *Russian Diary*, p. 139.

30. de Chambrun, *Lettres à Marie*, p. 80.

31. Anonymous (Stopford), *Russian Diary*, p. 53.

32. *Ibid.*, pp. 149–150.

33. George, *A Romanov Diary*, pp. 184–185.

34. *Ibid.*, p. 183.

35. *Ibid.*, p. 185.

36. de Basily, *Memoirs of a Lost World*, pp. 84–85.

37. *Ibid.*, p. 85.

38. de Robien, *Diary of a Diplomat in Russia*, pp. 54–55.

39. George, *A Romanov Diary*, p. 215.

40. *Ibid.*, p. 180.

41. Belyakova, *The Romanovs*, p. 116.

42. Yaschik, *Beside the Empress*, p. 70.

43. Vorres, *The Last Grand Duchess*, pp. 153–154.

44. Princess Julia Cantacuzène, *Russian People: Revolutionary Recollections* (New York: Charles Scribner's Sons, 1920), pp. 158–159.

45. Kudrina, *Mother and Son*, p. 258.

46. Barkhatova and Burkova, *The Danish Princess—the Russian Empress*, p. 137.

47. Kudrina, *Mother and Son*, p. 263.

48. van der Kiste and Hall, *Once a Grand Duchess: Xenia*, p. 116.

49. Gelardi, *Born to Rule*, p. 261.

50. David Walder, *The Chanak Affair* (London: The Macmillan Company, 1969), p. 51.

51. Sir Francis Elliot to Mr. Balfour, May 7, 1917, The National Archives, P.R.O., F.O. 286/602/No. 1013.

52. Walder, *The Chanak Affair*, p. 51.

53. Nicholas, *My Fifty Years*, p. 272.

54. Christopher, *Memoirs*, pp. 144–145.

55. Diary entry of Empress Marie Feodorovna, June 15, 1917, in Kudrin, *Diaries of the Empress Marie Feodorovna*, p. 193.

56. Kudrina, *Mother and Son*, p. 115.

57. Marie, *Education of a Princess*, p. 331.

58. Garshin, *Queen Olga Constantinovna*, chapter 1.

59. Chavchavadze, *The Grand Dukes*, p. 150.

60. Anonymous (Stopford), *Russian Diary*, p. 162.

61. *Ibid.*, pp. 188–189.

62. Romanovsky-Krassinsky, *Dancing in Petersburg*, p. 184.

63. *Ibid.*, p. 185.

64. Kokovtsov, *Out of My Past*, p. 496.

65. Pakula, *The Last Romantic*, p. 223.

66. Kudrina, *Mother and Son*, p. 122.
67. Garshin, *Queen Olga Constantinova*, chapter 1.
68. Massie, *Pavlovsk*, p. 139.
69. *Ibid.*, pp. 139–140.
70. Garshin, *Queen Olga Constantinova*, chapter 1.
71. Empress Marie Feodorovna to Tsar Nicholas II, December 21, 1917, in Bing, *Letters of Tsar Nicholas and Empress Marie*, pp. 301–304.

28. ENDURE, ENDURE, AND ENDURE

1. Belyakova, *The Romanovs*, pp. 146–147.
2. *Ibid.*, p. 154.
3. *Ibid.*, p. 148.
4. Perry and Pleshakov, *Flight of the Romanovs*, p. 197.
5. *Ibid.*, p. 196.
6. Belyakova, *The Romanovs*, p. 150.
7. Skariätina, *A World Can End*, pp. 259–260.
8. Belyakova, *The Romanovs*, pp. 152–153.
9. Kenneth Rose, *King George V* (New York: Alfred A. Knopf, 1984), p. 213.
10. Massie, *Nicholas and Alexandra*, p. 488.
11. Galitzine, *Spirit to Survive*, p. 67.
12. Buxhoeveden, *Life and Tragedy of Alexandra Feodorovna*, pp. 319–320.
13. Botkin, *The Real Romanovs*, p. 165.
14. Robert K. Massie, *The Romanovs: The Final Chapter* (Toronto: Random House of Canada Ltd., 1995), pp.4–5.
15. Romanovsky-Krassinky, *Dancing in Petersburg*, p. 184.
16. Barkhatova and Burkova, *The Danish Princess—the Russian Empress*, p. 140.
17. Yaschik, *Beside the Empress*, p. 70.
18. de Robien, *Diary of a Diplomat*, pp. 280–281.
19. Karolou, *Olga, Queen of the Greeks*, chapter 15.
20. Perry and Pleshakov, *Flight of the Romanovs*, p. 198.
21. Battiscombe, *Queen Alexandra*, p. 291.
22. Clarke, *Lost Fortune of the Tsars*, p. 89.
23. *Ibid.*, p. 91.
24. R. H. B. Lockhart to Sir G. Clerk, November 10, 1918, in Tim Coates, series ed., *Uncovered Editions: The Russian Revolution, 1917* (London: The Stationery Office, 2000), p. 60–62.
25. Memorandum on Conditions in Moscow by a British Subject, Who Left Moscow on December 1 in *Ibid.*, p. 95.
26. Christopher, *Memoirs*, pp. 149–150.
27. George, *A Romanov Diary*, p. 185.
28. Queen Olga to King George V, November 19/December 2, 1918, The Royal Archives, RA GV/PRIV/AA 46/95.
29. Garshin, *The Hellenes' Queen Olga Constantinovna*, chapter 1.
30. Youssoupoff, *Lost Splendor*, p. 302.
31. Diana Mandache, *Later Chapters of My Life: The Lost Memoir of Queen Marie of Romania* (Stroud, Gloucestershire: Sutton Publishing, 2004), p. 53.
32. Hall, *Once a Grand Duchess*, p. 139.

33. Ethel Greening Pantazzi, *Roumania in Light and Shadow* (Toronto: The Ryerson Press, n.d.), p. 270.

34. Vice-Admiral Sir Francis Pridham, *Close of a Dynasty* (London: Allan Wingate, 1956), p. 58.

35. *Ibid.*, p. 62.

36. *Ibid.*, p. 65.

37. *Ibid.,* p. 74.

38. Youssoupoff, *Lost Splendor*, p. 303.

39. Pridham, *Close of a Dynasty*, p. 74.

40. Yaschik, *Beside the Empress*, p. 82.

41. Pridham, *Close of a Dynasty*, p. 69.

42. Yaschik, *Beside the Empress*, p. 85.

43. Romanovsky-Krassinsky, *Dancing in Petersburg*, p. 190.

44. *Ibid.*, p. 192.

45. *Ibid.*, p. 194.

46. William Clarke, *Hidden Treasures of the Romanovs: Saving the Royal Jewels* (Edinburgh: NMS Enterprises, Ltd., 2009), p. 115.

47. Vorres, *The Last Grand Duchess*, p. 165.

48. J. Wentworth Day, *H.R.H. Princess Marina, Duchess of Kent: The First Authentic Life Story* (London: Robert Hale, Ltd., 1962), p. 54.

49. Romanovsky-Krassinsky, *Dancing in Petersburg*, p. 200.

50. King, *Princess Marina*, p. 76.

29. *VIA DOLOROSA*

1. Yaschik, *Beside the Empress*, p. 88.

2. Crawford, *Michael and Natasha*, p. 383.

3. Sir Arthur Davidson to Andrew Bonar Law, June 5, 1919, The National Archives, PREM 1/4.

4. Perry and Pleshakov, *Flight of the Romanovs*, p. 241.

5. Massie, *The Romanovs*, p. 173.

6. Vorres, *Last Grand Duchess*, p. 171.

7. W. Bruce Lincoln, *Sunlight at Midnight: St. Petersburg and the Rise of Modern Russia* (New York: Basic Books, 2000), p. 6.

8. Nicholas, *Political Memoirs*, p. 180.

9. *Ibid.*, p. 285.

10. Christopher, *Memoirs*, p. 150.

11. Queen Olga to King George V, June 24/July 7, 1918, The Royal Archives, RA/GV/PRIV/AA 46/94.

12. Karolou, *Olga, Queen of the Greeks*, chapter 15.

13. Christopher, *Memoirs*, p. 147.

14. She was the wife of U.S. Senator Joseph McCormick and she later became a U.S. representative.

15. Cassini, *Never a Dull Moment*, pp. 300–301.

16. *Ibid.*, p. 300.

17. Clarke, *Hidden Treasures of the Romanovs*, p. 116.

18. Princes and princesses of the Greek royal house are styled as princes and princesses of Greece and Denmark.

19. Compton Mackenzie, *First Athenian Memories* (London: Cassell & Co., Ltd., 1931), p. 50.

20. Letter of Irene Noel-Baker, April 6, 1918, LG/F/94/3/41 Lloyd George Papers, Parliamentary Archives.

21. Marie, *The Story of My Life, volume III*, pp. 435–436.

22. Pakula, *The Last Romantic*, p. 304.

23. Mandache, *Later Chapters of My Life*, pp. 76–77.

24. Buchanan, *Queen Victoria's Relations*, p. 119.

25. Mandache, *Later Chapters of My Life*, p. 116.

26. *Ibid.*, pp. 116–117.

27. Pakula, *The Last Romantic*, pp. 301–302.

28. Nicholas, *My Fifty Years*, p. 280.

29. Zeepvat, *Romanov Autumn*, p. 172.

30. Diary entry of Empress Marie Feodorovna, August 21/September 3, 1920, in Kudrin, *Diaries of the Empress Marie Feodorovna*, p. 460.

31. Romanovsky-Krassinsky, *Dancing in Petersburg*, p. 207.

32. Diary entry of Empress Marie Feodorovna, August 26/September 8, 1920, in Kudrin, *Diaries of the Empress Marie Feodorovna*, p. 461

33. Alexander Savinsky, *Recollections of a Russian Diplomat* (London: Hutchinson & Co., Ltd., n.d), dedication page.

34. Meriel Buchanan, *Ladies of the Russian Court* (Calgary, Alberta: Gilbert's Royal Books, 2005), p. 19.

35. Karolou, *Olga, Queen of the Greeks*, chapter 16.

36. Diary entry of Empress Marie Feodorovna, October 13/26, 1920, in Kudrin, *Diaries of the Empress Marie Feodorovna*, p. 477.

37. *New York Times*, October 29, 1920.

38. *Ibid.*

39. John van der Kiste, *Crowns in a Changing World: The British and European Monarchies 1901–36* (Stroud, UK: Alan Sutton, 1993), p. 150.

40. Pakula, *The Last Romantic*, p. 305.

41. van der Kiste, *Crowns in a Changing World*, pp. 149–150.

42. Earl Granville to Earl Curzon, November 15, 1920, in Rohan Butler, J.P.T. Bury, M. E. Lambert, eds., Great Britain Foreign Office, *Documents on British Foreign Policy 1919–1939, First Series, Vol. XII* (London: Her Majesty's Stationery Office, 1962), No. 428, p. 503.

43. Earl Granville to Earl Curzon, November 19, 1920, in *Ibid.*, No. 436, p. 508

44. Earl Curzon to Earl Granville, December 15, 1920, in *Ibid.*, No. 230, p. 544.

45. Memorandum by Harold Nicolson on Future Policy Towards King Constantine, December 20, 1920 in *Ibid.*, No. 488, p. 550.

30. A MISERABLE FRAGMENT OF THE PAST

1. *Washington Post*, August 13, 1922.

2. *New York Times*, November 2, 1924.

3. *New York Times*, December 13, 1924.

4. Serge Obolensky, *One Man in His Time: The Memoirs of Serge Obolensky* (New York: McDowell, Obolensky Inc., 1958), p. 282.

5. Mark Kerr, *Land, Sea, and Air: Reminiscences of Mark Kerr* (London: Longmans, Green and Co., Ltd., 1927), p. 196.

6. Nicholas, *My Fifty Years*, p. 295.

7. Michael Llewellyn Smith, *Ionian Vision: Greece in Asia Minor 1919–1922* (London: Allen Lane, 1973), p. 212.

8. C. M. Woodhouse, *A Short History of Greece* (New York: Frederick A. Praeger, 1968), p. 206.

9. Lee, *Helen, Queen Mother of Rumania*, pp. 92–93.

10. Smith, *Ionian Vision*, p. 215.

11. Woodhouse, *A Short History of Greece*, p. 206.

12. van der Kiste, *Crowns in a Changing World*, p. 151.

13. *Ibid.*, pp. 151–152.

14. Gelardi, *Born to Rule*, pp. 302–303.

15. Clogg, *A Concise History of Greece*, p. 47.

16. Douglas Dakin, *The Unification of Greece 1770–1923* (New York: St. Martin's Press, 1972), pp. 268–269.

17. F. O. Lindley to the Marquess Curzon of Kedleston, October 1, 1922, in W. N. Medlicott, Douglas Dakin and M.E. Lambert, eds., Great Britain Foreign Office, *Documents on British Foreign Policy 1919–1939, First Series, Vol. XVIII* (London: Her Majesty's Stationery Office, 1972), No. 85, p. 127.

18. F. O. Lindley to the Marquess Curzon of Kedleston, October 6, 1922, in *Ibid.*, No. 105, p. 153.

19. Karolou, *Olga, Queen of the Greeks*, chapter 17.

20. *Ibid.*

21. Vickers, *Alice: Princess Andrew of Greece*, p. 170.

22. Christopher, *Memoirs*, p. 181.

23. Queen Olga to King George V, November 23/December 6, 1922, The Royal Archives, RA GV/PRIV/AA 46/99.

24. Years later, King George V's granddaughter, the future Queen Elizabeth II, would marry Queen Olga's grandson, Prince Philip.

25. Karolou, *Olga, Queen of the Greeks*, chapter 17.

26. Garshin, *Queen Olga Constantinovna*, chapter 2.

27. Queen Olga to King George V, August 31/September 13, 1923, The Royal Archives, RA GV/PRIV/AA 46/104.

28. Nicholas, *My Fifty Years*, p. 315.

29. *Ibid.*, p. 316.

30. Yaschik, *Beside the Empress*, p. 183.

31. Queen Olga to King George V, December 8/21, 1925, The Royal Archives, RA GV/PRIV/AA 46/112.

32. Christopher, *Memoirs*, p. 229.

33. Karolou, *Olga, Queen of the Greeks*, chapter 17.

34. Vorres, *The Last Grand Duchess*, p. 171.

35. Nicholas, *My Fifty Years*, p. 315.

36. Queen Olga to King George V, May 17/30, 1926, The Royal Archives, RA GV/PRIV/AA 46/113.

37. Garshin, *Queen Olga Constantinovna*, chapter 2.

38. *Ibid.*

39. Pykhacheva, *Memoirs*, pp. 232–233, 236–238.

40. *Ibid.*, p. 247.

41. Garshin, *Queen Olga Constantinovna*, chapter 2.
42. Karolou, *Olga, Queen of the Greeks*, chapter 20.
43. Christopher, *Memoirs*, p. 237.
44. Yaschik, *Beside the Empress*, p. 183.
45. *Ibid.*, p. 187.
46. Perry and Pleshakov, *Flight of the Romanovs*, p. 247.
47. Seeger, *Memoirs of Alexander Izvolsky*, pp. 281–282.
48. Alia Barkovetz, "The Documentary Legacy of the Empress Maria Feodorovna," in *Maria Feodorovna, Empress of Russia*, p. 96.

Bibliography

PRIMARY SOURCES

Unpublished Archival Material

United Kingdom
The Royal Archives, Windsor Castle
Diary Entries of King George V (as Prince of Wales)
Correspondence of Queen Olga of Greece to King George V
Correspondence of Victoria, Crown Princess of Prussia, to Queen Victoria

The British Library
William Boyd Carpenter Papers

Cambridge University
Churchill Archives Centre
Lord Randolph Churchill Papers

Hampshire Record Office
Knollys Papers

Parliamentary Archives
David Lloyd George Papers

The National Archives
Foreign Office Files: F.O. 371
Prime Minister's Office: PREM 1

The University of Southampton
Correspondence of Marie, Duchess of Edinburgh, and Alfred, Duke of Edinburgh, to Countess Alexandrine Tolstoy, Mountbatten Papers, Hartley Library

Romania
Romanian National Archives
Correspondence of Duchess of Saxe-Coburg-Gotha to Crown Princess Marie of Romania

Published Material

Books

Abrikossow, Dmitrii I. *Revelations of a Russian Diplomat: The Memoirs of Dmitrii I. Abrikossow*, Edited by George Alexander Lensen. Seattle: University of Washington Press, 1994.

Alexander, Grand Duke. *Once a Grand Duke*. Garden City, NY: Garden City Publishing Company, Inc., 1932.

Alice, Princess. *Alice, Princess of Great Britain, Grand Duchess of Hesse: Letters to Her Majesty the Queen.* London: John Murray, 1897.

Alice, Grand Duchess of Hesse and Helena Victoria, Princess Christian of Schleswig-Holstein. *Alice, Grand Duchess of Hesse, Princess of Great Britain and Ireland: Biographical Sketch and Letters.* New York: G. P. Putnam's Sons, 1885.

Almedingen, E. M. *An Unbroken Unity: A Memoir of Grand-Duchess Serge of Russia, 1864–1918.* London: The Bodley Head, 1964.

Ananich, B. V., R. S. Ganelin, M. A. Gordin, V. G. Chernuha, eds. *Alexander III: Memoirs, Diaries and Letters* from the series *Statesmen of Russia in the Eyes of Their Contemporaries.* St. Petersburg: Pushkinsky Fund, 2001.

Andersen, Hans Christian. *The Story of My Life.* New York: Hurd and Houghton, 1871.

Ballou, Maturin M., *Due North or Glimpses of Scandinavia and Russia.* Boston: Houghton, Mifflin and Co., 1886.

Battersea, Constance. *Reminiscences.* London: Macmillan and Co., Ltd., 1922.

Benson, E. F. *Our Family Affairs 1867–1896.* New York: George H. Doran Company, 1921.

Beresford, Lord Charles. *The Memoirs of Lord Charles Beresford, Volume I.* Boston: Little, Brown & Company, 1914.

Bing, Edward, ed. *The Letters of Tsar Nicholas and Empress Marie: Being the Confidential Correspondence Between Nicholas II, Last of the Tsars, and His Mother, Dowager Empress Maria Feodorovna.* London: Ivor Nicholson and Watson, Ltd., 1937.

Bolitho, Hector, ed. *Further Letters of Queen Victoria: From the Archives of the House of Brandenburg-Prussia,* translated from the German by Mrs. J. Pudney and Lord Sudney. London: Thornton Butterworth Ltd., 1938.

Botkin, Gleb. *The Real Romanovs: As Revealed by the Late Czar's Physician and His Son.* New York: Fleming H. Revell Company, 1931.

Bourne, Kenneth, D. Cameron Watt, and John F. V. Keiger, eds. *British Document on Foreign Affairs, Part I, Series F: Europe, 1848–1914, Vol. 14: Greece, 1847–1914,* eds. David Stevenson and John F. V. Keiger. Frederick, MD: University Publications of America, 1987.

Bovey, Kate Koon. *Russian Coronation 1896: The Letters of Kate Koon Bovey.* Minneapolis: Privately Printed, 1942.

Buchanan, Sir George. *My Mission to Russia and Other Diplomatic Memories, Volume I.* Boston: Little, Brown and Company, 1923.

Buchanan, Meriel. *Recollections of Imperial Russia.* New York: George H. Doran Company, 1924.

Buckle, George Earle, ed. *The Letters of Queen Victoria. Second Series: A Selection from Her Majesty's Correspondence and Journal Between the Years 1862 and 1878. Published by Authority of His Majesty the King. Volume II: 1870–1878.* London: John Murray, 1926.

———. *The Letters of Queen Victoria. Second Series: A Selection from Her Majesty's Correspondence and Journal Between the Years 1862 and 1885. Published by Authority of His Majesty the King. Volume III: 1879–1885.* London: John Murray, 1928.

―――. *The Letters of Queen Victoria, Third Series: A Selection from Her Majesty's Correspondence and Journal Between the Years 1886 and 1901. Published by Authority of His Majesty the King. Volume II: 1891–1895.* London: John Murray, 1931.

Burmeiester, N. I. "Fifty Years Ago," in Thomas E. Berry, ed. and transl., *Memoirs of the Pages to the Tsars.* Mississauga, Ontario: Gilbert's Royal Books, 2001.

Butler, Rohan, J. P. T. Bury, M. E. Lambert, eds. Great Britain Foreign Office. *Documents on British Foreign Policy 1919–1939, First Series, Vol. XII.* London: Her Majesty's Stationery Office, 1962.

Buxhoeveden, Baroness Sophie. *The Life and Tragedy of Alexandra Feodorovna, Empress of Russia.* London: Longmans, Green and Co., 1930.

Cantacuzène, Princess Julia. *Revolutionary Days: Recollections of Romanoffs and Bolsheviki 1914–1917.* Boston: Small, Maynard & Company, 1919.

―――. *Russian People: Revolutionary Recollections.* New York: Charles Scribner's Sons, 1920.

Carpenter, William Boyd. *Some Pages of My Life.* New York: Charles Scribner's Sons, 1911.

Cassini, Countess Marguerite. *Never a Dull Moment: A Toast to the Past by One Who Knew the Best and Worst of It.* New York: Harper & Brothers Publishers, 1956.

Cecilie, Crown Princess. *The Memoirs of Crown Princess Cecilie.* Translated by Emile Burns. London: Victor Gollancz, Ltd., 1931.

Chapman-Huston, D., ed. *The Private Diaries of Daisy, Princess of Pless, 1873–1914.* London: John Murray, 1950.

Christopher, Prince of Greece. *Memoirs of H.R.H. Prince Christopher of Greece.* London: The Right Book Club, 1938.

Coates, Tim, series ed. *Uncovered Editions: The Russian Revolution, 1917.* London: The Stationery Office, 2000.

Collier, E. C. F., ed. *A Victorian Diarist: Later Extracts from the Journals of Mary, Lady Monkswell, 1895–1909.* London: John Murray, 1946.

Cooke, C. Kinloch. *A Memoir of Her Royal Highness Princess Mary Adelaide, Duchess of Teck: Based on Her Private Diaries and Letters. Volume I.* New York: Charles Scribner's Sons, 1900.

Corbett, Sir Vincent. *Reminiscences: Autobiographical and Diplomatic of Sir Vincent Corbett, K.C.V.O., Late a Minister in H.M. Diplomatic Service.* London: Hodder and Stoughton, n.d.

Cornwallis-West, Mrs. George. *The Reminiscences of Lady Randolph Churchill.* New York: The Century Co., 1908.

Cunliffe, Mary. *Letters from Abroad.* Printed for Private Circulation. London: The Army and Navy Co-Operative Society, Inc., 1875.

de Basily, Lascelle Meserve. *Memoirs of a Lost World.* Stanford: Hoover Institution Press, 1975.

de Castellane, Count Bohdan D. *One Crowded Hour: An Autobiography.* London: George Allen & Unwin Ltd., 1934.

de Chambrun, Charles. *Lettres à Marie: Pétersbourg-Pétrograd 1914–1917.* Paris: Librairie Plon, 1941.

de Custine, Marquis. *Empire of the Czar: A Journey Through Eternal Russia.* New York: Doubleday, 1989.

Davis, Richard Harding. *A Year from a Reporter's Note-Book.* New York: Harper & Brothers, 1903.

Dehn, Lili. *The Real Tsaritsa.* London: Thornton Butterworth, Ltd., 1922.

Derby, Mary Catherine, Countess of. *A Great Lady's Friendships: Letters to Mary, Marchioness of Salisbury, Countess of Derby, 1862–1890.* London: Macmillan and Co., Ltd., 1933.

Dicey, Edward. *A Month in Russia During the Marriage of the Czarevitch.* London: Macmillan and Co., 1867.

Dufferin and Ava, The Dowager Marchioness of. *My Russian and Turkish Journals.* New York: Charles Scribner's Sons, 1916.

Dyson, Hope, and Charles Tennyson, eds. *Dear and Honoured Lady: The Correspondence Between Queen Victoria and Alfred Tennyson.* Rutherford, NJ: Fairleigh Dickinson University Press, 1969.

Eckardstein, Hermann. *Ten Years at the Court of St. James's 1895–1905.* New York: E. P. Dutton & Co., 1922.

Engelgardt, B. A. "Remembrances of Kamer-page B.A. Engelgardt Class of 1896," in Thomas E. Berry, ed. and transl. *Memoirs of the Pages to the Tsars.* Mississauga, Ontario: Gilbert's Royal Books, 2001.

Epanchin, N. A. "Serving Three Tsars," chapter in B. V. Ananich, R. S. Ganelin, M. A. Gordin and V. G. Chernuha, eds. *Alexander III: Memoirs, Diaries and Letters* from the series *Statesmen of Russia in the Eyes of Their Contemporaries.* St. Petersburg: Pushkinsky Fund, 2001.

Erbach-Schönberg, Princess Marie zu. *Reminiscences.* London: George Allen & Unwin, Ltd., 1925.

Eulalia, Infanta. *Court Life from Within.* London: Cassell and Company, Ltd., 1915.

Farmborough, Florence. *With the Armies of the Tsar: A Nurse at the Russian Front 1914–18.* New York: Stein and Day, 1975.

Fortescue, Captain the Hon. Sir Seymour. *Looking Back.* London: Longmans, Green and Co., 1920.

Foster, John W. *Diplomatic Memoirs, Volume I.* Boston: Houghton Mifflin Company, 1909.

Francis, David R. *Russia from the American Embassy: April, 1916–November, 1918.* New York: Charles Scribner's Sons, 1921.

Fuhrmann, Joseph T., ed. *The Complete Wartime Correspondence of Tsar Nicholas II and the Empress Alexandra, April 1914–March 1917.* Wesport, CT: Greenwood Press, 1999.

Fulford, Roger, ed. *Beloved Mama: Private Correspondence of Queen Victoria and the German Crown Princess 1878–1885.* London: Evans Brothers, Ltd., 1981.

———. *Darling Child: Private Correspondence of Queen Victoria and the Crown Princess of Prussia 1871–1878.* London: Evans Brothers, Ltd., 1976.

———. *Dearest Mama: Letters Between Queen Victoria and the Crown Princess of Prussia 1861–1864.* London: Evans Brothers, Ltd., 1968.

———. *Your Dear Letter: Private Correspondence of Queen Victoria and the Crown Princess of Prussia 1865–1871.* New York: Charles Scribner's Sons, 1971.

Galitzine, Irina. *Spirit to Survive: The Memoirs of Princess Nicholas Galitzine.* London: William Kimber, 1976.

Gavril Constantinovich. *In the Marble Palace: Memoirs.* Moscow: Zakharov, 2005.

George, Grand Duchess of Russia. *A Romanov Diary: The Autobiography of H.I. & R.H. Grand Duchess George.* New York: Atlantic International Publications, 1988.

Gilliard, Pierre. *Thirteen Years at the Russian Court.* Translated by F. Appleby Holt. Bath: Cedric Chivers, Ltd., 1921.

Glyn, Elinor. *His Hour.* New York: D. Appleton and Company, 1910.

———. *Romantic Adventure: Being the Autobiography of Elinor Glyn.* New York: E. P. Dutton & Co., Inc., 1937.

Golder, Frank Alfred, ed. *Documents of Russian History 1914–1917.* Gloucester, MA: Peter Smith, 1964.

Gordon, Mrs. Will. *Roumania: Yesterday and To-day.* London: John Lane, The Bodley Head, 1918.

Grabbe, Paul and Beatrice. *The Private World of the Last Tsar: In the Photographs and Notes of General Count Alexander Grabbe.* Boston: Little, Brown & Co., 1984.

Hamilton, Lord Frederic. *The Vanished Pomps of Yesterday.* New York: George H. Doran Company, 1921.

Hanbury-Williams, Major-General Sir John. *The Emperor Nicholas II As I Knew Him.* London: Arthur L. Humphreys, 1922.

Harrison, General Sir Richard. *Recollections of a Life in the British Army During the Latter Half of the 19th Century.* London: Smith, Elder, & Co., 1908.

Heald, Edward T. *Witness to Revolution: Letters from Russia 1916–1919.* Edited by James B. Gidney. Kent, OH: The Kent State University Press, 1972.

Hough, Richard. *Advice to My Grand-daughter: Letters from Queen Victoria to Princess Victoria of Hesse.* New York: Simon and Schuster, 1975.

Howard of Penrith, Lord. *Theatre of Life: Life Seen from the Pit 1863–1905.* London: Hodder and Stoughton, Ltd., 1935.

Kerr, Mark. *Land, Sea, and Air: Reminiscences of Mark Kerr.* London: Longmans, Green and Co., Ltd., 1927.

Kleinmichel, Countess Marie. *Memories of a Shipwrecked World: Being the Memoirs of Countess Kleinmichel.* Translated by Vivian Le Grand. New York: Brentano's, 1923.

Knox, Major-General Alfred W. F. *With the Russian Army 1914–1917.* New York: Arno Press Inc., 1971.

Kokovtsov, Vladimir. *Out of My Past: The Memoirs of Count Kokovtsov.* Edited by H. H. Fisher. Translated by Laura Matveev. Stanford: Stanford University Press, 1935.

Kudrin, U. V., ed. *Diaries of the Empress Marie Feodorovna: Years 1914–1920, 1923.* Moscow: Vagrius Publishing House, 2005.

Lee, Arthur Gould, ed. *The Empress Frederick Writes to Sophie, Crown Princess and Queen of the Hellenes.* London: Faber and Faber, Ltd., 1955.

Lieven, D. C. B., Kenneth Bourne, and D. C. Watt, eds. *British Documents on Foreign Affairs: Reports and Papers from the Foreign Office Confidential Print, Part I, from the Mid-Nineteenth Century to the First World War. Series A, Russia 1859–1914. Vol. 3: 1905–1906; Vol. 4: 1906– 1907,* ed. Dominic Lieven. Frederick, MD: University Publications of America, 1983.

Litvinov, N. P. "Diary" chapter, in B. V. Ananich, R. S. Ganelin, M. A. Gordin, and V. G. Chernuha, eds., *Alexander III: Memoirs, Diaries and Letters* from the series *Statesmen of Russia in the Eyes of Their Contemporaries.* St. Petersburg: Pushkinsky Fund, 2001.

Lockhart, R. H. Bruce. *British Agent.* New York: G. P. Putnam's Sons, 1933.

Loftus, Lord Augustus. *Diplomatic Reminiscences of Lord Augustus Loftus 1837–1862, Volume II.* London: Cassell & Company, Ltd., 1892.

———. *Diplomatic Reminiscences of Lord Augustus Loftus 1862–1879, Volume II.* London: Cassell & Company, Ltd., 1894.

Logan, John A. *In Joyful Russia.* New York: D. Appleton and Company, 1897.

Longford, Elizabeth ed. *Darling Loosy: Letters to Princess Louise 1856–1939.* London: Weidenfeld & Nicolson, 1991.

Loukomsky, General A. S. *Memoirs of the Russian Revolution.* Westport, CT: Hyperion Press, Inc., 1975.

Mackenzie, Compton. *First Athenian Memories.* London: Cassell & Co., Ltd., 1931.

Majolier, Nathalie. *Step-Daughter of Imperial Russia.* London: Stanley Paul & Co., Ltd., 1940.

Mallet, Victor. *Life with Queen Victoria: Marie Mallet's Letters from Court 1887–1901.* Boston: Houghton Mifflin Company, 1968.

Mandache, Diana. *Later Chapters of My Life: The Lost Memoir of Queen Marie of Romania.* Stroud, UK: Sutton Publishing, 2004.

Marie, Grand Duchess of Russia. *Education of a Princess: A Memoir.* New York: The Viking Press, 1931.

Marie, Queen of Roumania, *The Story of My Life, Volumes I, II, III.* London: Cassell and Company, Ltd., 1934.

Martin, Frederick Townsend. *Things I Remember.* New York: John Lane and Co., 1913.

Maud, Renée Elton. *One Year at the Russian Court: 1904–1905.* London: John Lane, The Bodley Head, 1918.

Maylunas, Andrei, and Sergei Mironenko. *A Lifelong Passion: Nicolas and Alexandra, Their Own Story.* London: Weidenfeld & Nicolson, 1996.

Medlicott, W. N., Douglas Dakin, and M. E. Lambert, eds. Great Britain Foreign Office, *Documents on British Foreign Policy 1919-1939, First Series, Vol. XVIII.* London: Her Majesty's Stationery Office, 1972.

Miliukov, Paul. *Political Memoirs 1905–1917.* Edited by Arthur P. Mendel, translated by Carl Goldberg. Ann Arbor: The University of Michigan Press, 1967.

Mohrenschildt, Dimitri von. *The Russian Revolution of 1917: Contemporary Accounts.* New York: Oxford University Press, 1971.

Monypenny, William Flavelle, and George Earle Buckle. *The Life of Benjamin Disraeli, Earl of Beaconsfield, Volume II, 1860–1881.* London: John Murray, 1929.

Mossolov, A. A. *At the Court of the Last Tsar: Being the Memoirs of A. A. Mossolov, Head of the Court Chancellery, 1900–1916.* Edited by A. A. Pilenco and translated by E. W. Dickes. London: Methuen & Co., Ltd., 1935.

Narishkin-Kurakin, Elizabeth. *Under Three Tsars: The Memoirs of the Lady-in-Waiting, Elizabeth Narishkin-Kurakin,* edited by René Fülöp-Miller. Translated from the German by Julia E. Loesser. New York: E. Dutton & Co., Inc., 1931.

Nekludoff, A. *Diplomatic Reminiscences Before and During the World War, 1911–1917.* Translated by Alexandra Paget. New York: E. P. Dutton and Company, 1920.

Nicholas, Prince of Greece. *My Fifty Years.* London: Hutchinson & Co., Ltd., n.d.

———. *Political Memoirs, 1914–1917: Pages from My Diary.* Freeport, NY: Books for Libraries Press, 1972.

Nostitz, Countess (Lilie de Fernandez-Azabal). *The Countess from Iowa.* New York: G. P. Putnam's Sons, 1936.

Obolenksy, Serge. *One Man in His Time: The Memoirs of Serge Obolensky.* New York: McDowell, Obolensky Inc., 1958.

Olferev, F. S. "Remembrances of the Imperial Family," in Thomas E. Berry, editor and translator, *Memoirs of the Pages to the Tsars.* Mississauga, Ontario: Gilbert's Royal Books, 2001.

Paléologue, Maurice. *An Ambassador's Memoirs, Vol. I, July 20, 1914–June 2, 1915.* Translated by F. A. Holt. New York: George H. Doran Company, n.d.

———. *An Ambassador's Memoirs, Vol. II, June 3, 1915–August 18, 1916.* Translated by F. A. Holt. New York: George H. Doran Company, n.d.

———. *An Ambassador's Memoirs, Vol. III, August 19, 1916–May 17, 1917.* Translated by F. A. Holt. New York: George H. Doran Company, n.d.

———. *The Turning Point: Three Critical Years, 1904–1906.* Translated by F. Apppleby Holt. London: Hutchinson & Co., Ltd., 1935.

Paley, Princess. *Memories of Russia, 1916–1919.* London: Herbert Jenkins, Ltd., 1924.

Pantazzi, Ethel Greening. *Roumania in Light & Shadow.* Toronto: The Ryerson Press, n.d.

Paola, Princess of Saxe-Weimar. *A King's Private Letters: Being Letters Written by King Constantine of Greece to Paola, Princess of Saxe-Weimar During the Years 1912–1923.* London: Eveleigh Nash & Grayson, 1925.

Paoli, Xavier. *Their Majesties As I Knew Them.* Translated by A. Teixeira de Mattos. New York: Sturgis & Walton Company, 1911.

Pares, Bernard. *Fall of the Russian Monarchy: A Study of the Evidence.* New York: Random House, 1961.

———. *My Russian Memoirs.* New York: AMS Press, 1969.

Pobyedonostseff, K. P. *Reflections of a Russian Statesman.* Translated from the Russian by Robert Crozier Long. London: Grant Richards, 1898.

Ponsonby, Sir Frederick, ed. *Letters of the Empress Frederick.* London: Macmillan and Co., Ltd., 1929.

Ponsonby, Magdalen, ed. *A Lady in Waiting to Queen Victoria: Being Some Letters, and a Journal of Lady Ponsonby.* New York: J. H. Sears & Company, Inc., 1927.

Postgate, R. W., ed. *Revolution from 1789 to 1906.* Boston: Houghton Mifflin Co., 1921.

Prall, William, ed. *The Court of Alexander III: Letters of Mrs. Lothrop, Wife of the Late Honorable George Van Ness Lothrop.* Philadelphia: The John C. Winston Company, 1910.

Pridham, Vice-Admiral Sir Francis. *Close of a Dynasty.* London: Allan Wingate, 1956.

Pykhacheva, Vera D. *Memoirs by Vera Pihatcheff née Nabokoff, Demoiselle d'Honneur to H. I H. the Empress Marie Feodorovna.* Translated by Janet Crawford. Rowsley, UK: "Bibliophilia" Library, 1936.

Radziwill, Princess Catherine. *Memories of Forty Years.* New York: Funk and Wagnalls Company, 1915.

———. *My Recollections.* London: Isbister & Company, 1904.

Radziwill, Princess Marie. *Lettres de la Princesse Radziwill au Général de Robilant, 1889–1914, Vol. I: 1889–1895.* Bologna, Italy: Nicola Zanichelli, 1923.

———, *Lettres de la Princesse Radziwill au Général de Robilant, 1889–1914, Vol. I: 1889–1895, Vol. II: 1896–1901.* Bologna, Italy: Nicola Zanichelli, 1923.

Ramm, Agatha, ed. *Beloved and Darling Child: Last Letters Between Queen Victoria and Her Eldest Daughter, 1886–1901.* Stroud, UK: Sutton Publishing, 1990.

Report of the Commissioner of Education for the Year, 1893–94, Volume 1. Washington, DC: Government Printing Office, 1896.

Rich, Norman, and M. H. Fisher, eds. *The Holstein Papers: The Memoirs, Diaries and Correspondence of Friedrich von Holstein, 1837–1909.* Vol. II: *Diaries.* Cambridge: Cambridge University Press, 1957.

Romanovsky-Krassinsky, Princess. *Dancing in Petersburg: The Memoirs of Kschessinka.* Translated by Arnold Haskell. Garden City, NY: Doubleday & Company, Inc., 1961.

Robien, Louis de. *The Diary of a Diplomat in Russia, 1917–1918.* Translated by Camilla Sykes. New York: Praeger Publishers, 1970.

Rodzianko, M. V. *The Reign of Rasputin: An Empire's Collapse, Memoirs of M.V. Rodzianko.* Translated by Catherine Zvegintzoff. London: A. M. Philpot, Ltd., 1927.

Rosen, Baron Roman. *Forty Years of Diplomacy, Volumes I and II.* New York: Alfred A. Knopf, 1922.

Rumbold, Sir Horace. *Final Recollections of a Diplomatist.* London: Edward Arnold, 1905.

———. *Recollections of a Diplomatist, Volumes I, II.* London: Edward Arnold, 1903.

A Russian. *Russian Court Memoirs, 1914–16: With Some Accounts of Court, Social and Political Life in Petrograd Before and Since the War.* London: Herbert Jenkins Ltd., 1917.

Ryan, Nellie. *My Years at the Austrian Court.* London: John Lane, 1915.

Sala, George Augustus. *The Life and Adventures of George Augustus Sala, Volume II.* New York: Charles Scribner's Sons, 1896.

Savinsky, Alexander. *Recollections of a Russian Diplomat.* London: Hutchinson & Co., Ltd., n.d.

Schuyler, Eugene. *Eugene Schuyler: Selected Essays.* New York: Charles Scribner's Sons, 1901.

Scully, Terence, Helen Swediuk-Cheyne, and Loren Calder, eds. *The Correspondence of I. U. Samarin and Baroness Rahden (1861–1876).* Waterloo, Ontario: Wilfrid Laurier University Press, 1974.

Seeger, Charles Louis, ed. and transl. *The Memoirs of Alexander Iswolsky: Formerly Russian Minister of Foreign Affairs and Ambassador to France.* Gulf Breeze, FL: Academic International Press, 1974.

Serge, Grand Duke. *Grand Duke Serge Alexandrovich Romanov, Book 1, 1857–1877.* Moscow: Novospassky Monastery, 2006.

Sheppard, Edgar, ed. *George, Duke of Cambridge: A Memoir of His Life Based on the Journals and Correspondence of His Royal Highness, Volume II, 1871–1904.* London: Longmans, Green, and Co., 1906.

Shulgin, V. V. *Days of the Revolution: Memoirs from the Right, 1905–1917.* Edited and translated by Bruce F. Adams. Gulf Breeze, FL: Academic International Press, 1990.

———. *The Years: Memoirs of a Member of the Russian Duma, 1906–1917.* Translated by Tanya Davis. New York: Hippocrene Books, 1984.

Skariätiina, Irina. *A World Can End.* New York: Jonathan Cape & Harrison Smith, 1931.

Souiny, Baroness (Leonie Ida Philipovna Souiny-Seydlitz). *Russia of Yesterday and To-morrow.* New York: The Century Co., 1917.

Stallman, R. W. and E. R. Hagemann, eds. *The War Dispatches of Stephen Crane.* New York: New York University Press, 1964.

Steinberg, Mark D., and Vladimir M. Khrustalëv. *The Fall of the Romanovs: Political Dreams and Personal Struggles in a Time of Revolution.* New Haven: Yale University Press, 1995.

Stopford, Albert (published anonymously). *The Russian Diary of an Englishman, Petrograd, 1915–1917.* New York: Robert M. McBride and Company, 1919.

Thaddeus, Henry Jones. *Recollections of a Court Painter.* London: John Lane Company, 1912.

Tiutcheva, Anna Feodorovna. *Pri Dvore Dvukh Imperatorov. Vospominaniya, Dnevnik, 1853–1882.* Cambridge, UK: Oriental Research Printer, 1975.

Tuckerman, Charles K. *Personal Recollections of Notable People at Home and Abroad, Volume II.* London: Richard Bentley and Son, 1895.

Twain, Mark. *The Innocents Abroad, or The New Pilgrim's Progress: Being Some Account of the Steamship "Quaker City's" Pleasure Excursion to Europe and the Holy Land, Volume II.* New York: Harper & Brothers Publishers, 1903.

U.S. Department of State. *Papers Relating to the Foreign Relations of the United States, Transmitted to Congress, With the Annual Message of the President, December 7, 1874.* Washington, DC: Government Printing Office, 1874.

———. *Papers Relating to the Foreign Relations of the United States, Transmitted to Congress, With the Annual Message of the President, December 3, 1901.* Washington. DC: Government Printing Office, 1902.

Victoria, Queen. *The Papers of Queen Victoria on Foreign Affairs: Files from the Royal Archives, Windsor Castle. Part 1. Russia and Eastern Europe, 1846–1900.* Edited by Kenneth Bourne. Bethesda, MD: University Publications of America, 1990.

———. *Regina v. Palmerston: The Correspondence Between Queen Victoria and Her Foreign and Prime Minister, 1837–1865.* Edited by Brian Connell. London: Evans Bros., 1962.

Viroubova, Anna. *Memories of the Russian Court.* New York: The Macmillan Company, 1923.

Vogel, Nadine, and William Smith. *Correspondance Entre le Grand-Duc Nicolas Mikhaïlovitch de Russie et Frédéric Masson, 1897–1914: Au Temps de l'Alliance Franco-Russe.* Paris: Bernard Giovanangeli Association des amis de Frédéric Masson, 2005.

von Bock, Maria Petrovna. *Reminiscences of My Father, Peter A. Stolypin.* Translated and edited by Margaret Patoski. Metuchen, NJ: The Scarecrow Press, Inc., 1970.

von Bülow, Prince Bernhard. *Memoirs of Prince von Bülow, Volume II, From the Morocco Crisis to Resignation, 1903–1909.* Translated by Geoffrey Dunlop. Boston: Little, Brown, and Company, 1931.

Vulliamy, C. E., ed. *The Red Archives: Russian State Papers and Other Documents Relating to the Years 1915–1918.* Translated by A. L. Hynes. London: Geoffrey Bles, 1929.

Walburga, Lady Paget. *Scenes and Memories.* New York: Charles Scribner's Sons, 1912.

Warwick and Brooke, Earl of. *Memories of Sixty Years.* London: Cassell and Company, Ltd., 1917.

Waters, W.H-H. *Secret and Confidential: The Experiences of a Military Attaché.* New York: Frederick A. Stokes Co., 1926.

White, Andrew Dickson. *Autobiography of Andrew D. White,* Volume II. New York: The Century Co., 1906.

Windsor, Dean of, and Hector Bolitho, eds. *Later Letters of Lady Augusta Stanley, 1864–1876.* London: Jonathan Cape, 1929.

Witte, Sergei. *The Memoirs of Count Witte.* Translated and edited by Abraham Yarmolinsky. Garden City, NY: Doubleday, Page & Co., 1921.

Wonlar-Larsky, Nadine. *The Russia That I Loved.* London: Elsie MacSwinney, 1937.

Yaschik, Tomofei Ksenofonotovich. *Beside the Empress: Memoirs of a Life-Cossack.* St. Petersburg: Nestor-Historia, 2004.

Youssoupoff, Prince Felix. *Lost Splendor: The Amazing Memoirs of the Man Who Killed Rasputin.* Translated from the French by Ann Green and Nicholas Katkoff. New York: Helen Marx Books, 2003.

Articles

Beale, Anne. "Three Glimpses at Royalty," in *Argosy: A Magazine of Tales, Travels, Essays, and Poems* 18 (July 1874), pp. 56–63.

Caclamanos, Demetrius. "Reminiscences of the Balkan Wars," in *The Slavonic and East European Review*, vol. 16, no. 46 (July 1937), pp. 113–128.

Child, Theodore. "Palatial Petersburg," in *Harper's New Monthly Magazine* (July 1889), pp. 187–207.

From the Mountain. "Prince Alfred's Romance," in *Once a Week*, 8: 187 (January 1863), p. 120.

Gibbon, Perceval. "What Ails Russia: Glimpses of the Inefficiency and Dissoluteness of the Royal Family," in *McClure's Magazine*, vol. XXIV, April 1905, no. 6, pp. 609–615.

"Gifts at a Royal Silver Wedding," in *The Jewelers' Circular* (October 11, 1899).

Hapgood, Isabel F. "An Imperial Pleasure Palace," in *The Cosmopolitan: A Monthly Illustrated Magazine*, vol. XX (November 1895–April 1896), pp. 641–648.

Knox, Thomas W. "A Gala Night in Russia," in *Harper's New Monthly Magazine*, no. CCXCVI, vol. L (January 1875), pp. 266–272.

Lloyd, Charles Edward. "Modern Greece," in *The Cosmopolitan*, vol. XXII, no. 6, (April 189), pp. 587–598.

The Christian Wife, January 26, 1884.

"The Duke of Edinburgh's Marriage Treaty," in *The London Reader: of Literature, Science, Art and General Information*, 22: 571 (April 1874).

"The Grand Duchess Marie," in *The Illustrated Review: Literature, the Drama, Music, Art, Current Events* (January 21, 1874).

The Independent, Volume LXXIV, January–June 1913.

The London Reader, 23: (1874: May).

The London Reader, 51: (September 29, 1888).

"The Past Week," in *The London Review of Politics, Society, Literature, Art, and Science*, 6: 136 (February 1863).

"The Past Week," in *The London Review of Politics, Society, Literature, Art, and Science*, 6: 144 (April 1863).

Peterborough, The Bishop of. "The Imperial Coronation at Moscow," in *The Cornhill Magazine*, vol. I, July to December 1896 (London: Smith, Elder & Co., 1896), pp. 305–325.

Public Opinion: A Comprehensive Summary of the Press Throughout the World on All Important Current Topics, vol. XXXIX, no. 19 (November 4, 1905).

Roosevelt, Theodore. "Personal Account of His Trip From Khartoum to London, Written to Sir George Otto Trevelyan." Seventh Paper in "Theodore Roosevelt and His Time—Shown in His Letters," edited by Joseph Bucklin Bishop, in *Scribner's Magazine*, vol. LXVII, January–June, no. 3 (March 1920), pp. 266–282.

"Some Account of the City of Copenhagen," in *The Saturday Magazine*, 10: 298 (no. 299 supplement, February1837).

"State Entry into London of Her Majesty the Queen and Their Royal Highnesses the Duke and Duchess of Edinburgh," in *The Graphic: An Illustrated Weekly Newspaper*, vol. IX, no. 225 (March 21, 1874).

Stead, W. T. "A Queen's Charity: The Evangelismos of Athens," in *The Review of Reviews*, Vol. VIII (July–December, 1893), p. 275.

Thornton, Mary Grace. "The Crowning of a Czar: Journal of an Eye-Witness of the Coronation of Alexander III," in *The Century Magazine*, vol. LII, no. 1 (May 1896), pp. 8–27.

Waddington, Mary King. "At the Coronation of the Czar Alexander III: Letters of the French Ambassadress," in *Scribner's Magazine*, vol. XXXIII, no. 3 (March 1903), pp. 293–316.

Wycollar, Frederick. "A Secret Chapter of Russian History," in *Munsey's Magazine*, vol. XXXI, no. 2 (May 1904), pp. 170–178.

Yonge, Charlotte, ed. "Moscow and the Coronation of the Czar" by Mrs. Frederic Chevenix Trench, in *The Monthly Packet of Readings for Members of the English Church*, Third Series, volume VI, Parts XXXI to XXXVI (July–December 1883), pp. 560–576.

Microfilm

Victoria, Queen of Great Britain. *The Papers of Queen Victoria on Foreign Affairs: Files from the Royal Archives, Windsor Castle*. Edited by Kenneth Bourne (Bethesda, MD: University Publications of America, 1990).

Newspapers
The New York Times
The Times
The Washington Post

SECONDARY SOURCES

Books

Abbott, G. F. *Greece and the Allies, 1914–1922*. London: Methuen & Co., 1922.

Alice, Grand Duchess of Hesse and Helena Victoria, Princess Christian of Schlewig-Holstein. *Alice, Grand Duchess of Hesse, Princess of Great Britain and Ireland: Biographical Sketch and Letters*. New York: G. P. Putnam's Sons, 1885.

Allsebrook, Mary. *Born to Rebel: The Life of Harriet Boyd Hawes*. Oxford: Oxbow Books, 1992.

Almedingen, E. M. *The Emperor Alexander II*. London: The Bodley Head, 1962.

———. *The Empress Alexandra 1872–1918*. London: Hutchinson, 1961.

———. *The Romanovs: Three Centuries of an Ill-Fated Dynasty*. New York: Holt, Rinehart and Winston, 1966.

Aronson, Theo. *Crowns in Conflict: The Triumph and Tragedy of European Monarchy, 1910–1918*. London: John Murray, 1986.

———. *A Family of Kings: The Descendants of Christian IX of Denmark*. London: Cassell, 1976.

Ascher, Abraham. *P. A. Stolypin: The Search for Stability in Late Imperial Russia*. Stanford: Stanford University Press, 2001.

———. *The Revolution of 1905: Russia in Disarray*. Stanford: Stanford University Press, 1988.

Barkhatova, A. D., and T. V. Burkova, eds. *The Danish Princess Marie Sophie Friederike Dagmar—the Russian Empress Maria Fiodorovna*. Translated by V. A. Fateyev. St. Petersburg: Alibris Publishers, 2006.

Barkovetz, Alia. "The Documentary Legacy of the Empress Maria Feodorovna," in *Maria Feodorovna, Empress of Russia: An Exhibition About the Danish Princess Who Became Empress of Russia*, pp. 90–107. Copenhagen: Christiansborg Palace,1997.

———. "Nixa, Minny, and Sacha" in *Maria Feodorovna, Empress of Russia: An Exhibition About the Danish Princess Who Became Empress of Russia*, pp. 90–107. Copenhagen: Chrstiansborg Palace, 1997.

Bater, James H. "Between Old and New: St. Petersburg in the Late Imperial Era," in Michael Hamm, ed., *The City in Late Imperial Russia*. Bloomington, IN: Indiana University Press, 1986.

Battiscombe, Georgina. *Queen Alexandra*. Boston: Houghton Mifflin, Company, 1969.

Beavan, Arthur H. *Popular Royalty*. London: Sampson Low, Marston and Company, 1904.

Belyakova, Zoya. *Grand Duke Alexei Alexandrovitch: Pros and Cons*. St. Petersburg: Logos Publishing House, 2004.

———. *The Romanovs: The Way It Was*. St. Petersburg: Ego Publishers, 2000.

Beran, Michael Knox. *Forge of Empires, 1861–1871: Three Revolutionary Statesmen and the World They Made*. New York: Free Press, 2007.

Bergamini, John. *The Tragic Dynasty: A History of the Romanovs*. New York: G. P. Putnam's Sons, 1969.

Bomann-Larsen, Tor. *Kongstanken: Haakon and Maud—I*. Oslo: J. W. Cappelen, 2002.

Brook-Shepherd, Gordon. *Archduke of Sarajevo: The Romance and Tragedy of Franz Ferdinand of Austria*. Boston: Little, Brown and Company, 1984.

Brown, Arthur Judson. *Russia in Transformation*. New York: Fleming H. Revell Company, 1917.

Buchanan, Meriel. *Ladies of the Russian Court*. Calgary, Aberta: Gilbert's Royal Books, 2005.

———. *Queen Victoria's Relations*. London: Cassell & Co., Ltd., 1954.

———. *Victorian Gallery*. London: Cassell & Co., Ltd., 1956.

Byrnes, Robert F. *Pobedonostsev: His Life and Thought*. Bloomington, IN: Indiana University Press, 1968.

Chavchavadze, David. *The Grand Dukes*. New York: Atlantic International Publications, 1990.

Chubarov, Alexander. *The Fragile Empire: A History of Imperial Russia*. New York: Continuum, 1999.

Clarke, William. *Hidden Treasures of the Romanovs: Saving the Royal Jewels*. Edinburgh: NMS Enterprises Ltd., 2009.

———. *The Lost Fortune of the Tsars*. New York: St. Martin's Press, 1994.

Clogg, Richard. *A Concise History of Greece*. Cambridge: Cambridge University Press, 1992.

Cockfield, James. *White Crow: The Life and Times of Grand Duke Nicholas Mikhailovich Romanov, 1859–1919*. Westport, CT: Praeger, 2002.

Cornforth, John. *Queen Elizabeth the Queen Mother at Clarence House*. London: Michael Joseph, 1996.

Corti, Count Egon. *The Downfall of Three Dynasties*. Translated from the German by L. Marie Sieveking and Ian F. D. Morrow. Freeport, NY: Books for Libraries Press, 1970.

———. *The English Empress: A Study in the Relations Between Queen Victoria and Her Eldest Daughter, Empress Frederick of Germany*. London: Cassell and Company, Ltd., 1957.

Cosmetatos, S. P. P. *The Tragedy of Greece*. London: Kegan Paul, Trench, Trubner & Co., 1928.

Cowles, Virginia. *1913: An End and a Beginning*. New York: Harper & Row, Publishers, 1967.

———. *The Last Tsar and Tsarina*. London: Weidenfeld & Nicolson, 1977.

———. *The Russian Dagger: Cold War in the Days of the Czars*. New York: Harper & Row, Publishers, 1969.

Crankshaw, Edward. *The Shadow of the Winter Palace: Russia's Drift to Revolution, 1825–1917*. New York: The Viking Press, 1976.

Crawford, Rosemary and Donald. *Michael and Natasha: The Life and Love of the Last Tsar of Russia*. Vancouver: Douglas & McIntyre, 1997.

Dakin, Douglas. *The Unification of Greece 1770–1923*. New York: St. Martin's Press, 1972.

Day, J. Wentworth. *H.R.H. Princess Marina, Duchess of Kent: The First Authentic Life Story*. London: Robert Hale, Ltd., 1962.

de Jonge, Alex. *The Life and Times of Grigorii Rasputin*. New York: Coward, McCann and Geoghegan, 1982.

de Sagrera, Ana. *Ena y Bee: En Defensa de Una Amistad*. Madrid: Velecio Editores, 2006.

Dostoyevsky, Fyodor. *Crime and Punishment*. Translated by David McDuff. London: Penguin Books, 2003.

Duff, David. *Hessian Tapestry*. London: Frederick Muller, 1967.

Eilers, Marlene A. *Queen Victoria's Descendants*. Falköping, Sweden: Rosvall Royal Books, 1997.

Eklof, Ben. "Introduction," in Ben Eklof, John Bushnell, and Larissa Zakharova, eds., *Russia's Great Reforms, 1855–1881*. Bloomington, IN: Indiana University Press, 1994.

Elsberry, Terence. *Marie of Romania: The Intimate Life of a Twentieth Century Queen*. New York: St. Martin's Press, 1972.

Faber, Toby. *Fabergé's Eggs: The Extraordinary Story of the Masterpieces That Outlived an Empire*. New York: Random House, 2008.

Fawcett, Millicent Garrett. *Life of Her Majesty Queen Victoria*. Boston: Roberts Brothers, 1895.

Fontenoy, Marquise de. *The Marquise de Fontenoy's Revelations of High Life Within Royal Palaces*. Philadelphia: Edgewood Publishing Co., 1892.

Garafola, Lynn. *Diaghilev's Ballets Russes*. New York: Oxford University Press, 1989.

Garshin, M. U. *The Hellenes' Queen Olga Constantinovna*. Prague: Para, 1937.

Gelardi, Julia P. *Born to Rule: Five Reigning Consorts, Granddaughters of Queen Victoria*. New York: St. Martin's Press, 2005.

Glyn, Elinor. *His Hour*. New York: D. Appleton and Company, 1910.

Graham, Stephen. *Tsar of Freedom: The Life and Reign of Alexander II*. New Haven, CT: Yale University Press, 1935.

Grahame, F. R. *Life of Alexander II: Emperor of All the Russias*. London: W. H. Allen, 1883.

Grishin, D. B. *The Grand Duke's Tragic Destiny*. Moscow: Veche, 2006.

Hagedorn, Hermann. *The Roosevelt Family of Sagamore Hill*. New York: The Macmillan Company, 1954.

Hall, Coryne. *Little Mother of Russia: A Biography of Empress Marie Feodorovna*. London: Shepheard-Walwyn Publishers, Ltd., 1999.

Hamm, Michael, ed. *The City in Late Imperial Russia*. Bloomington, IN: Indiana University Press, 1986.

Harcave, Sidney. *Years of the Golden Cockerel: The Last Romanov Tsars, 1814–1917*. New York: The Macmillan Company, 1968.

Hellenic Army General Staff, Army History Directorate. *A Concise History of the Balkan Wars 1912–1913*. Athens: An Army History Directorate Publication, 1998.

Hibben, Paxton. *Constantine I and the Greek People*. New York: The Century Co., 1920.

Hibbert, Christopher. *Queen Victoria: A Personal History*. New York: Basic Books, 2000.

Hodgetts, E. A. Brayley. *The Court of Russia in the Nineteenth Century, Volume II*. London: Methuen & Co., 1908.

Hosking, Geoffrey. *Russia and the Russians: A History*. Cambridge, MA: The Belknap Press of Harvard University Press, 2001.

———. *Russia: People and Empire 1552–1917*. Cambridge, MA: Harvard University Press, 1997.

Hourmouzios, Stelio. *No Ordinary Crown: A Biography of King Paul of the Hellenes*. London: Weidenfeld and Nicolson, 1972.

Iroshnikov, Mikhail P., Yury B. Shelayev, and Liudmila A. Prostai, *Before the Revolution— St. Petersburg in Photographs: 1890–1914*. New York: Harry N. Abrams, Inc., Publishers; Leningrad: Nauka Publishers, JV Smart, 1991.

Karolou, Ioulia N. *Olga, Queen of the Greeks, August 22, 1851–June 19, 1926*. Athens: Hestia, 1934.

Karpovich, Michael. *Imperial Russia, 1801–1917*. New York: Henry Holt and Co., 1932.

Khorvatova, E. V. *Marie Feodorovna: The Fate of the Empress*. Moscow: Ast-Press, 2006.

King, Greg. *The Man Who Killed Rasputin: Prince Felix Youssoupov and the Murder That Helped Bring Down the Russian Empire*. Toronto: Citadel Press Book, 1995.

King, Greg, and Penny Wilson, *Gilded Prism: The Konstantinovichi Grand Dukes & the Last Years of the Romanov Dynasty*. East Richmond Heights, CA: Eurohistory.com, 2006.

King, Stella. *Princess Marina: Her Life and Times*. London: Casell, 1969.

Kudrina, Yulia V. "Our Beloved Empress," in *Maria Feodorovna, Empress of Russia: An Exhibition About the Danish Princess who Became Empress of Russia*. Copenhagen: Christiansborg Palace, 1997, pp. 34–53.

———. *Mother and Son: Empress and Emperor*. Togliatti: Glagol, 2004.

Kuzmina, Ludmila. *August Poet*. Saint Petersburg: Aurora, 2004.

Laferté, Victor. *Alexandre II: Détails Inédits Sur Sa Vie Intime et Sa Mort.* Basel, Switzerland: H. Georg, 1882.

Lee, Arthur Gould. *Helen, Queen Mother of Rumania: Princess of Greece and Denmark.* London: Faber and Faber, 1956.

Leslie, Anita. *Jennie: The Life of Lady Randolph Churchill.* London: Arrow Books, 1969.

Lieven, Dominic. "Russia as Empire," in Dominic Lieven, ed., *The Cambridge History of Russia, Vol. II, Imperial Russia, 1689–1917.* Cambridge: Cambridge University Press, 2006, pp. 9–26.

———. *Empire: The Russian Empire and Its Rivals.* New Haven: Yale University Press, 2000.

Lincoln, W. Bruce. *Between Heaven and Hell: The Story of a Thousand Years of Artistic Life in Russia.* New York: Viking, 1998.

———. *The Great Reforms: Autocracy, Bureaucracy, and the Politics of Change in Imperial Russia.* Dekalb, IL: Norhtern Illinois University Press, 1990.

———. *In War's Dark Shadow: The Russians Before the Great War.* New York: The Dial Press, 1983.

———. *Nicholas I: Emperor and Autocrat of All the Russias.* Bloomington, IN: Indiana University Press, 1978.

———. *The Romanovs: Autocrats of All the Russias.* New York: The Dial Press, 1981.

———. *Sunlight at Midnight: St. Petersburg and the Rise of Modern Russia.* New York: Basic Books, 2000.

Longford, Elizabeth. *Queen Victoria: Born to Succeed.* New York: Harper & Row, Publishers, 1964.

Lowe, Charles. *Alexander III of Russia.* New York: Macmillan and Co., 1895.

Madol, Hans Roger. *Christian IX: Compiled from Unpublished Documents and Memoirs.* Translated from the German and Danish by E. O. Lorimer. London: Collins Publishers, 1939.

Mager, Hugo. *Elizabeth: Grand Duchess of Russia.* New York: Carroll & Graf Publishers, Inc., 1998.

Martin, Ralph G. *Jennie: The Life of Lady Randolph Churchill, Volume I: The Romantic Years 1854–1895.* Englewood Cliffs, NJ: Prentice-Hall, Inc., 1969.

Massie, Robert K. *Nicholas and Alexandra.* New York: Atheneum, 1967.

———. *Peter the Great: His Life and World.* New York: Alfred A. Knopf, 1980.

———. *The Romanovs: The Final Chapter.* Toronto: Random House of Canada Ltd., 1995.

Massie, Suzanne. *Pavlovsk: The Life of a Russian Palace.* London: Hodder & Stoughton, 1990.

Maxwell, Margaret. *Narodniki Women: Russian Women Who Sacrificed Themselves for the Dream of Freedom.* Elmsford, NY: Pergamon Press, Inc., 1990.

Mclean, Roderick R. *Royalty and Diplomacy in Europe 1890–1914.* Cambridge: Cambridge University Press, 2001.

McClintock, Mary Howard. *The Queen Thanks Sir Howard: The Life of Major-General Sir Howard Elphinstone, V.C., K.C.B. C.M.G.* London: John Murray, 1945.

Millar, Lubov. *Grand Duchess Elizabeth of Russia: New Martyr of the Communist Yoke.* Redding, CA: Nikodemos Orthodox Publication Soceity, 1991.

Milner-Gulland, Robin. *The Russians.* Oxford: Blackwell Publishers, 1997.

Mosse, W. E. *Alexander II and the Modernization of Russia.* London: I. B. Tauris & Co., Ltd., 1992.

Nadelhoffer, Hans. *Cartier: Jewelers Extraordinary.* New York: Harry N. Abrams, Inc., Publishers, 1984.

Nicolson, Harold. *King George the Fifth: His Life and Reign.* London: Constable & Co., Ltd., 1952.

————. *Portrait of a Diplomatist: Being the Life of Sir Arthur Nicolson First Lord Carnock, and a Study of the Origins of the Great War.* Boston: Houghton Mifflin Company, 1930.

Notovitch, Nicolas. *L'Empereur Alexandre III et Son Entourage.* Paris: Paul Ollendorff, 1893.

Pakula, Hannah. *The Last Romantic: A Biography of Queen Marie of Roumania.* New York: Touchstone, 1986.

Peacock, Virginia Tatnall. *Famous American Belles of the Nineteenth Century.* Philadelphia: J. B. Lippincott Company, 1901.

Perry, John Curtis and Constantine Pleshakov. *The Flight of the Romanovs: A Family Saga.* New York: Basic Books, 1999.

Pipes, Richard. *The Russian Revolution.* New York: Alfred A. Knopf, 1991.

Poliakoff, Vladimir. *Mother Dear: The Empress Marie of Russia and Her Times.* New York: D. Appleton and Company, 1926.

————. *The Tragic Bride: The Story of the Empress Alexandra of Russia.* New York: D. Appleton and Company, 1928.

Polunov, Alexander. *Russia in the Nineteenth Century: Autocracy, Reform, and Social Changes, 1814–1914.* Edited by Thomas C. Owen and Larissa G. Zakharova. Translated by Marshall S. Shatz. Armonk, NY: M. E. Sharpe, 2005.

Pope-Hennessy, James. *Queen Mary, 1867–1953.* New York: Alfred A. Knopf, 1960.

Quinlan, Paul D. *The Playboy King: Carol II of Romania.* Westport, CT: Greenwood Press, 1995.

Radzinsky, Edvard. *Alexander II: The Last Great Tsar,* Translated by Antonina W. Bouis. New York: Free Press, 2005.

————. *The Rasputin File.* Translated from the Russian by Judson Rosengrant. New York: Nan A. Talese, 2000.

Radziwill, Princess Catherine. *Nicholas II: The Last of the Tsars.* London: Cassell and Company, Ltd., 1931.

————. *Secrets of Dethroned Royalty.* New York: John Lane Company, 1920.

Rogger, Hans. *Russia in the Age of Modernisation and Revolution 1881–1917.* London: Longman, 1983.

Röhl, John C. G. *Wilhelm II: The Kaiser's Personal Monarchy 1888–1900.* Cambridge: Cambridge University Press, 2004.

Romanoff, H. C. *Sketches of the Rites and Customs of the Greco-Russian Church.* London: Rivingtons, 1869.

Rose, Kenneth. *King George V.* New York: Alfred A. Knopf, 1984.

Salisbury, Harrison E. *Black Night, White Snow: Russia's Revolutions 1905–1917.* New York: Doubleday & Company, Inc., 1977.

Schmucker, Samuel. *The Life and Reign of Nicholas the First, Emperor of Russia.* Philadelphia: John E. Potter and Company, 1856.

Sherwood, M.E.W. *Royal Girls and Royal Courts.* Boston: D. Lothrop Company, 1887.

Sitwell, Sacheverell. *Valse des Fleurs: A Day in St. Petersburg and a Ball at the Winter Palace in 1868.* London: Faber and Faber Ltd., n.d.

Smith, Michael Llewellyn. *Ionian Vision: Greece in Asia Minor, 1919–1922.* London: Allen Lane, 1973.

St. Aubyn, Giles. *Edward VII: Prince and King.* London: Collins, 1979.

Strachey, Lytton. *Queen Victoria.* New York: Harcourt, Brace and Company, 1921.

Sullivan, Michael John. *A Fatal Passion: The Story of Victoria Melita, the Uncrowned Last Empress of Russia.* New York: Random House, 1997.

Tarsaïdze, Alexander. *Katia: Wife Before God.* New York: The Macmillan Company, 1970.

Tatsios, Theodore George. *The Megali Idea and the Greek-Turkish War of 1897: The Impact of the Cretan Problem on Greek Irredentism, 1866–1897.* New York: Columbia University Press, 1984.

Theodoulou, Christos. *Greece and the Entente: August 1, 1914–September 25, 1916.* Thessaloniki: Institute for Balkan Studies, 1971.

Tisdall, E. E. P. *Marie Fedorovna, Empress of Russia.* New York: The John Day Company, 1957.

———. *Royal Destiny: The Royal Hellenic Cousins.* London: Stanley Paul and Co. Ltd., 1955.

Tomkeieff, Serge. "Russian Literature from Leo Tolstóy to the Present Date," in I.K. Shaknovski, *A Short History of Russian Literature.* London: Kegan Paul, Trench, Trubner & Co., Ltd., 1921.

Towle, George M. *Modern Greece.* Boston: James R. Osgood and Company, 1877.

Tuomi-Nikula, Jorma and Paivi. *Emperors on Vacation in Finland.* St. Petersburg: Kolo Publishing House, 2003.

Turgenieff, Ivan. *Fathers and Sons: A Novel.* Translated from the Russian by Eugene Schuyler. London: Ward, Lock and Co., n.d.

Ulam, Adam B. *In the Name of the People: Prophets and Conspirators in Prerevolutionary Russia.* New York: The Viking Press, 1977.

Ulstrup, Preben. "Maria Feodorovna Through Diaries and Personal Letters," in *Maria Feodorovna, Empress of Russia: An Exhibition About the Danish Princess who Became Empress of Russia.* Copenhagen: Christiansborg Palace, 1997, pp. 110–207.

van der Kiste, John, and Bee Jordaan. *Dearest Affie: Alfred, Duke of Edinburgh, Queen Victoria's Second Son.* Stroud, UK: Sutton Publishing, 1995.

van der Kiste, John, and Coryne Hall, *Once a Grand Duchess: Xenia, Sister of Nicholas II.* Stroud, UK: Sutton Publishing, 2002.

van der Kiste, John. *Crowns in a Changing World: The British and European Monarchies 1901–36.* Stroud, UK: Sutton Publishing, 1993.

———. *Kings of the Hellenes: The Greek Kings 1863–1974.* Stroud, UK: Sutton Publishing, 1999.

———. *Princess Victoria Melita: Grand Duchess Cyril of Russia 1876–1936.* Stroud, UK: Sutton Publishing, 1991.

———. *The Romanovs 1818–1959: Alexander II of Russia and His Family.* Stroud, UK: Sutton Publishing, 1999.

Vassili, Count Paul (pseudonym of Princess Catherine Radziwill). *Behind the Veil at the Russian Court.* New York: John Lane Company, 1914.

———. *Confessions of the Czarina.* New York: Harper and Brothers Publishers, 1918.

Velichenko, M. N., and G. A. Mirolyubova. *The Palace of Grand Duke Vladimir Aleksandrovich.* St. Petersburgh: Almaz Publishing House, 1997.

Veremis, Thanos. *The Military in Greek Politics: From Independence to Democracy.* Montreal: Black Rose Books, Ltd., 1997.

Vickers, Hugo. *Alice: Princess Andrew of Greece.* London: Hamish Hamilton, 2000.

Vorres, Ian. *The Last Grand Duchess: Her Imperial Highness Grand Duchess Olga Alexandrovna 1 June 1882–24 November 1960.* New York: Charles Scribner's Sons, 1964.

Walder, David. *The Chanak Affair.* London: The Macmillan Company, 1969.

Walsh, Edmund A. *The Fall of the Russian Empire: The Story of the Last of the Romanovs and the Coming of the Bolsheviki.* Boston: Little, Brown and Company, 1928.

Warwick, Christopher. *Ella: Princess, Saint & Martyr.* Chichester, UK: John Wiley & Sons, Ltd., 2006.

Watson, Sophia. *Marina: The Story of a Princess.* London: Weidenfeld & Nicolson, 1994.

Weeks, Theodore R. "Managing Empire: Tsarist Nationalities Policy," in Dominic Lieven, Dominic Lieven, ed. *The Cambridge History of Russia, Vol. II, Imperial Russia, 1689–1917*. Cambridge: Cambridge University Press, 2006, pp. 27–44.

Wilson, A. N. *Tolstoy: A Biography*. New York: W. W. Norton & Company, Inc., 1988.

Wilton, Robert. *Russia's Agony*. New York: E. P. Dutton & Company, 1919.

Wimbles, John. "Grand Duchess Marie Alexandrovna—Duchess of Edinburgh and Saxe-Coburg & Gotha," in Arturo E. Beéche, ed., *The Grand Duchesses: Daughters and Granddaughters of Russia's Tsars*. Oakland: Eurohistory.com, 2004.

Woodhouse, C. M. *A Short History of Greece*. New York: Frederick A. Praeger, 1968.

Wortman, Richard S. *Scenarios of Power: Myth and Ceremony in Russian Monarchy: From Alexander II to the Abdication of Nicholas II, Volume Two*. Princeton: Princeton University Press, 2000.

Zakharova, Larissa. "Autocracy and the Reforms of 1861–1874 in Russia: Choosing Paths of Development," in Ben Eklof, John Bushnell, and Larissa Zakharova, eds. *Russia's Great Reforms, 1855–1881*. Bloomington, IN: Indiana University Press, 1994.

Zeepvat, Charlotte. *The Camera and the Tsars: A Romanov Family Album*. Stroud, UK: Sutton Publishing, 2004.

———. *From Cradle to Crown: British Nannies and Governesses at the World's Royal Courts*. Stroud, UK: Sutton Publishing, 2006.

———. *Romanov Autumn: Stories from the Last Century of Imperial Russia*. Stroud, UK: Sutton Publishing, 2001.

Articles

Abrash, Merritt. "A Curious Royal Romance: the Queen's Son and the Tsar's Daughter," in *The Slavonic and East European Review*, No. 109 (July 1969), pp. 389–400.

Carabott, Philip. "Politics, Orthodoxy and the Language Question in Greece: The Gospel Riots in Greece, 1901," in *Journal of Mediterranean Studies*, vol. 3, no. 1 (1993), pp. 117–138.

Esthus, Raymond A. "Nicholas II and the Russo-Japanese War," in *The Russian Review*, 40 (4) (1981), pp. 396–411.

Heilbronner, Hans. "Alexander III and the Reform Plan of Loris-Melikov," in *Journal of Modern History*, vol. 33, no. 4 (December 1961), pp. 384–397.

Lieven, Dominic. "Pro-Germans and Russian Foreign Policy, 1890–1914," in *The International History Review*, vol. II., no. 1 (January 1980), pp. 34–54.

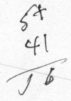

Acknowledgments

I wish to thank the numerous individuals who helped me bring to life the stories of Marie Feodorovna, Marie Alexandrovna, Olga Constantinovna, and Marie Pavlovna.

It was a privilege to conduct research at the Royal Archives, Windsor Castle, to examine letters, diaries, and photographs in search of material for the book. I am grateful to H.M. Queen Elizabeth II for granting permission to quote from material deposited in the Royal Archives. Special thanks are due to the registrar, Pamela Clark, and her staff, most especially Jill Kelsey, the deputy registrar, for their assistance and hospitality during my visit to Windsor Castle. Thanks are due as well to Sophie Gordon, curator of the Royal Photograph Collection. Her colleague, Lisa Heighway, the assistant curator of the Royal Photograph Collection, was also very helpful in setting aside a number of superb photographs for me to examine.

I am indebted to my Russian translator, Tamara von Schmidt-Pauli, who was always prompt in getting the job done. Tamara not only translated plenty of material in a timely and professional manner, she was also very helpful with ideas when it came to pursuing various leads. I wish to thank as well my Greek translator, Melina Papadimitriou, who did an excellent job of translating some challenging Greek material into English.

Many thanks are due to Tershia d'Elgin, for her suggestions in helping to tighten the manuscript. I also want to thank my literary agent, Julie Castiglia, of the Castiglia Literary Agency, for her sage advice. I owe a great debt of gratitude to my editor at St. Martin's Press, Charles Spicer, for his indefatigable enthusiasm and support for the project. This is the third book I have had the privilege of having published by St. Martin's and it has always been a pleasure to work with Charles Spicer and his staff, including his first-rate assistant, Allison Strobel.

Others who have also encouraged me and have been of assistance include Della L. Marcus, Marlene Koenig, Bela Sheyavich, as well as Diane Svoboda. Special thanks go to Diana Mandache and Paul Gilbert for their support and generosity in sharing research material, and to Arturo Beéche for his excellent suggestions in helping to improve the book. Thank you as well to Fr. Curtis Lybarger for his generosity in lending some excellent books from his collection. I am grateful to the many librarians and archivists in the United States and Europe who have helped in a variety of ways, especially Patrycja Barczyska of the School of Slavonic and East European Studies, University College, London; Richard Davies of the Leeds Russian Archive, University of Leeds; C. M. Woolgar of the Hartley Library, University of Southampton; Carol Leadenham and Ronald Bulatoff of the Hoover Institution, Stanford University; Horst Gehringer of the Staatsarchiv Coburg; Sarah Lewin of the Hampshire Record Office; Mari Takayanagi of the Parliamentary Archives, London; and Madelin Terrazas of the Churchill Archives Centre, Churchill College, Cambridge University. To all the others who encouraged and helped me, a big thank-you.

Finally, many thanks go to my family, including my daughters, Victoria and Gabriella. I owe special thanks—as always—to my husband, Alec, for his never-ending support and help in reading and critiquing numerous drafts of the manuscript.

Index

forced to leave Greece, 334–36
marriage alliances, 374
popularity of, 167–68, 373
succession, 165, 387
threats to, 244, 301, 376
Greek War of Independence (1821-1829), 20
Gregorian calendar, xxvi
Grey, Sir Edward, 203, 215, 216
Grinevitsky, Ignatius, 96–97
Guchkov, Alexander, 311, 322
Guildhall, 68
Gurko, Vladimir, 203

Habsburg dynasty, 267
Halla (an American court lady of Miechen), 239
Hall of Nobles, 241
Hamilton, Lord Frederic, 64, 105
Hampton Court, 386
Hanbury-Williams, Major General Sir John, 325
Harax, 257, 350
Hardinge, Sir Charles, 188, 189, 192
Harrison, Sir Richard, 136
Heald, Edward T., 313
Helen, Duchess of Albany, 172
Helena of England, Princess (1846-1923), 65
Hélène, Princess (d. of Comte de Paris), 134–35
Helen of Greece, Princess (1896-1982), 165, 256, 267, 306, 374, 386
Helsinki, 38
hemophilia, 65, 217–19
Henry VII of Reuss, Prince, 180
Henry of Battenberg, Prince, 56
Hermogen, Bishop of Tobolsk, 343
Herzen, Alexander, 57
Hesse, 13
Hindenburg, Paul von, 280
His Hour (novel by Elinor Glyn), 241
Hohenzollern, House of, 16, 132, 274
"House of Special Purpose," 344–45
Howard of Penrith, Lord, 64
Hvidovre, 201–2, 359, 372, 382, 385

Igor Constantinovich of Russia (d. 1918), 346
ikon, 54

Ileana of Romania, Princess, 364
Ilinskoe, 121
Ilyinsky, Paul, 386
Imperial Academy of Art, 125, 221
Imperial Guard, 352–53
India, 65
intelligentsia, Nihilist views of, 57
Ioann Constantinovich of Russia (d. 1918), 346
Ioannides, Pericles, 374
Ipatiev, N. N., house of, 344–45
Irene of Greece, Princess (1904-1974), 165
Irina Alexandrovna of Russia, Princess (1895-1970), 155, 262–65, 269–70, 312, 313, 352, 383, 385–86
irredentism, 81
Italy, pressure on Greece, 374
Izvolsky, Alexander, 269, 383–84

Janina, 253, 259
Japan, 181–83
Jassy, 285–87
Jerome, Jennie. *See* Churchill, Lady Randolph
Jerusalem, 386
jewels, 7, 47, 70–71, 101, 203, 241, 337, 349, 367, 388–89
Jews, 11
discrimination against, 104
John of Kronstadt, Father, 145
Johnson, Nicholas, 346
Johnson, Captain C. D., 352
Johnson, Mrs., 72
Jonnart, Charles, 335
Josephine de Beauharnais, 242
Julian calendar, xxvi

Kaliaev, Ivan, 189
Karakozov, Dmitri, 61
Karl of Württemberg, King, 80
Karolou, Ioulia N., 168, 252, 256–57, 258, 303, 361, 376, 377, 378, 381
Katherine of Greece, Princess (1913-2007), 304, 306
Katya. *See* Dolgorukaya, Princess Ekaterina
Kavala, 259
Kazan Cathedral (Cathedral of Our Lady of Kazan), 46, 261–62

Delve deeper into history with
ও Julia P. Gelardi ও

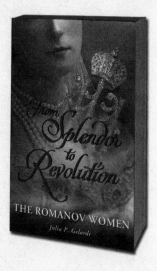

"A complex story well told . . .
an absorbing account."
—*Richmond Times-Dispatch*

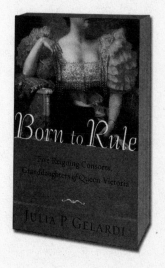

"Engaging and lively . . .
highly recommended."
—*Library Journal*

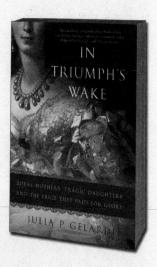

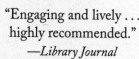

"An excellent, comprehensive
study of six fascinating
women and the troubled times
that shaped their lives."
—*Publishers Weekly*